Gija Dictionary

Gija Dictionary

Frances Kofod, Eileen Bray, Rusty Peters†, Joe Blythe and Anna Crane

Gija contributors:
Hector Jandany†, Mabel Juli, Doris Fletcher†, Phyllis Thomas†, Peggy Patrick†, Shirley Purdie, Queenie McKenzie†, Paddy Williams†, Left Hand George†, George Mung Mung†, Shirley Drill, Nancy Nodea†, Mary Thomas and many other Gija people

Other contributors:
Patrick McConvell, Glenn Wightmann, Francesco Possemato, Thomas Saunders, Tony Redmond, Caroline de Dear

ABORIGINAL STUDIES PRESS

First published in 2022
by Aboriginal Studies Press
Reprinted 2023

© Gija Dictionary: Gija people, c/- Warmun Art Centre LMB 24 Warmun, via Kununurra WA 6743, Australia

© Dictionary Compilation: Frances Kofod, PO Box 1918, Kununurra WA 6743; Eileen Bray, c/- Warmun Art Centre, LMB 24 Warmun, via Kununurra WA 6743; Estate of Rusty Peters c/- Warmun Art Centre, LMB 24 Warmun, via Kununurra WA 6743; Joe Blythe, Macquarie University, 12 Second Way, North Ryde NSW 2109; Anna Crane, 259 Skimmings Gap Road, Main Creek NSW 2420.

The Gija knowledge in this book is the intellectual property of the Gija people. This knowledge should only be used with written consent of the intellectual property owners and with proper attribution.

All rights reserved. No part of this book may be reproduced or transmitted in any form or by any means, electronic or mechanical, including photocopying, recording or by any information storage and retrieval system, without prior permission in writing from the publisher. The Australian *Copyright Act 1968* (the Act) allows a maximum of one chapter or 10 per cent of this book, whichever is the greater, to be photocopied by any educational institution for its education purposes provided that the educational institution (or body that administers it) has given a remuneration notice to Copyright Agency Limited (CAL) under the Act.

The opinions expressed in this book are the authors' own and do not necessarily reflect the view of AIATSIS or ASP.

Aboriginal and Torres Strait Islander people are respectfully advised that this publication contains names and images of deceased persons and culturally sensitive information.

Aboriginal Studies Press is the publishing arm of the Australian Institute of Aboriginal and Torres Strait Islander Studies.

GPO Box 553, Canberra, ACT 2601
Phone: (61 2) 6246 1183
Email: asp@aiatsis.gov.au
Web: www.aiatsis.gov.au/asp/about.html

National Library of Australia Cataloguing-in-publication data:

Gija Dictionary / Compiled by Frances Kofod and Eileen Bray
ISBNs: (pb) 978-1-922752-10-9
(ePub) 978-1-922752-11-6
(eBook) 978-1-922752-12-3
(Kindle) 978-1-922752-13-0
Gija language – Dictionaries – English – English language – Dictionaries – Gija
Other Authors/Contributors:

    Kofod, Frances, 1948–
    Bray, Eileen, 1950–
    Peters, Rusty, 1935–2020
    Blythe, Joe, 1968–
    Crane, Anna, 1983–

© Photographs: used with permission of Frances Kofod, Rusty Peters, Dominic Kavanagh, Ted Beard, Vina Goulden, Bill Genat, Joe Blythe, Jan van der Kam, Josua Dahmen, Cath Rouse, Sylvia Page. Photographs are by Frances Kofod unless marked otherwise. Readers are advised that these photographs include images of people who have died. All photographs have been viewed and discussed by many Gija people who have approved their inclusion.

© Cover painting: Hector Jandany 1999. *Rawooliliny doo Warnambany*, Mt Buchanan and Glass Hill, two mountains east of Warrmarn that were Gija and Miriwoong speaking men in dreamtime. They became part of the country and stayed forever. The mountains are still said to be speakers of the two languages today. Used with permission of the Estate of Hector Jandany.

© Map: Brenda Thornley, based on original map and research by Francesco Possemato, Macquarie University

Design: Christine Bruderlin
Typesetting: Brenda Thornley & Christine Bruderlin

Proudly funded by the Australian Government and Ground Up Community Support Network

Australian Indigenous Languages Dictionary Project, an initiative of the Australian Institute of Aboriginal and Torres Strait Islander Studies. Proudly funded by the Australian Government.

Contents

Gija speakers vii
Preface and acknowledgements viii

1. The Gija language and Gija country 1
   1.1. Varieties of Gija 2
   1.2. Bibliography 3

2. Gija spelling and pronunciation 5
   2.1. Consonant sounds 5
      2.1.1. Notes about pronunciation of consonants 6
      2.1.2. Consonant sound contrasts in Gija words 9
   2.2 Vowel sounds 11
      2.2.1. Notes about pronunciation of vowels 11

3. Gija skin names and relationship terms 12
   3.1. Gija skin 12
      3.1.1. Fathers and their children 16
   3.2. Gija relationship terms 16
      3.2.1. Other relationship words 20
      3.2.2. Talking about relations 20
   3.3. Saying names 23
      3.3.1. Ways of avoiding restricted names 23
      3.3.2. Avoidance, respect and familiarity 24
   3.4. The skins of Gija dreamtime animals 28

4. Gija word classes and grammar 32
   4.1. Gender and number 32
   4.2. Nouns and adjectives 34
      4.2.1. Suffixes that express place and time 35
      4.2.2. Other nominal suffixes 38
      4.2.3. Making new nouns 40
   4.3. Numerals, quantifiers and number suffixes 41
   4.4. Time and place in Gija – locatives, temporals and directionals 43
      4.4.1. Locatives and temporals 44
      4.4.2. Directionals 44
   4.5. Asking questions in Gija 45
      4.5.1. Polar questions 45
      4.5.2. Content questions 46
      4.5.3. Word search words 49
      4.5.4. Indeterminate interrogatives using -*anyji* 50
   4.6. Demonstratives 51
   4.7. Personal pronouns 52
      4.7.1. Cardinal pronouns 52
      4.7.2. Possessive pronouns 53
      4.7.3. Enclitic pronouns 54
   4.8. Gija verbs 56
      4.8.1. Inflecting verbs 56
      4.8.2. Coverbs 68
      4.8.3. Gerunds – 'for doing …' 70
      4.8.4. Verbs in subordinate clauses 70
   4.9. Adverbs, particles and interjections 71

5. About the entries in this dictionary 72
      5.1. Layout of entries 72

6. Gija to English Dictionary 75

7. English to Gija word finder 323

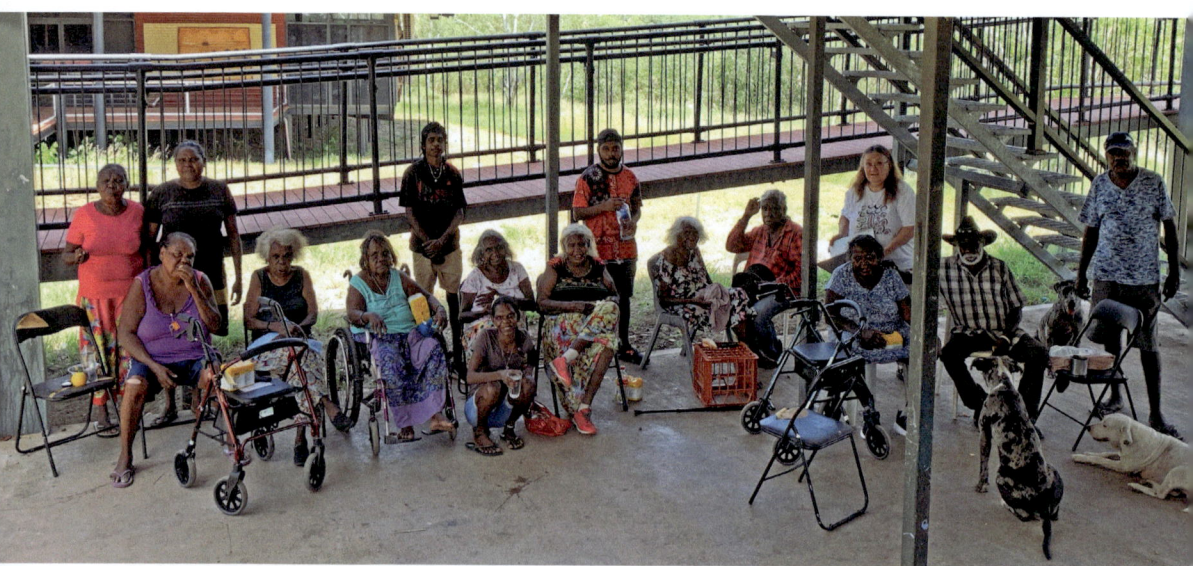

Figure 1. Gija meeting at Warmun Art Centre, March 2020, checking photos the day before commencement of the community lockdown to protect people from Covid-19. Left to right, standing: Jane Yalangga, Serena Pinday, Leonardo Nodea, Eddie Nulgit, Frances Kofod and Mark Nodea. Sitting: Sylvia Thomas, Mabel Juli, Mary Thomas, Eileen Bray with Kalenisha Peters in front, Nancy Nodea, Betty Carrington, Patrick Mung Mung, Shirley Purdie and Gordon Barney. (Photo: Dominic Kavanagh)

Gija speakers

This dictionary includes contributions from many Gija language speakers over many years. Their European names followed by their Gija name(s) are listed here.

Ben Duncan – Garlgarrangarnany
Berylene Mung Mung – Manyjoorrbal
Betty Carrington – Marayal
Bob Nyalcas – Joonbany
Buttercup Mung Mung – Gawoornel
Chocolate Thomas
Churchill Cann – Yoonany
Daisy Chatanalgie – Moordangali
Daisy Walkabier – Walgbiya
Doris Fletcher – Boolmarriya, Binayi
Dottie Watbi – Wadbi
Doug Macale – Jibilyiwoony
Eileen Bray – Joomena
Gabriel Nodea – Janggardi
George Mung Mung – Lirrmayirriny, Magany
Goody Barrett – Lilwayi
Gordon Barney – Loogngayirriny, Lawoony
Hector Jandany – Jandany
Helen Clifton – Garnanil
Henry Wambiny – Wambiny
Jack Britten – Yalarrji, Warnngayirriny
Jacko Dawalngoo – Dawalngoo
Joe Thomas – Gilmarriyi
John Patrick – Moodji
Josie Farrer – Nangala
Judy Turner – Darrngarri
Larry Thomas – Jadarrji
Left Hand George – Dingmayirriny
Lena Nyadbi – Nyadbi
Linda Timms – Milgbarriyal
Lulu Trancolino – Yooroojil
Mabel Juli – Wirringgoon, Bardngarri
Madigan Thomas – Jawoodjil
Martin Joogoord – Joogoord

Mary Thomas – Yarangalil
Mavis Wallaby
Mick Jawalji – Jawalji
Mona Ramsey – Wirrid
Nancy Nodea – Warlambal
Nora Nocketta – Bardngarri
Paddy Bedford – Nyoon'goony, Goowoomji
Paddy Springvale – Yangganji
Paddy Williams – Jaroonggarrawoony
Patrick Mung Mung – Gajoowoodany, Nhirrmayirriny
Paul Butters – Warramba
Peggy Patrick-Barradjil, Dirrmingali
Phyllis Thomas – Boorljoonngali
Pilot Henry – Jawooji
Polly Widalji
Queenie McKenzie – Garagarag
Rammel Peters – Warlagarriny
Rammey Ramsey – Warlawoon
Roberta Daylight – Barrala
Rosie Malgil – Goobooji
Rusty Peters – Dirrji Wandarrany
Sandy Thomas – Nayany, Goolawoony
Shirley Bray – Dimbali
Shirley Drill – Dardayal
Shirley Purdie – Birrmarriya
Simon Drill – Wirrindiny
Sophia Mung Warlambal
Tiger Henry – Wawoorany
Timmy Timms – Gamaliny, Balmendarri
Tommy Babajiny
Topsy Springvale – Joordjoordel
Winnie Badbarriya – Yinamayil

Preface and acknowledgements

This dictionary has been many years in the making. It incorporates an original 900-word list recorded by Patrick McConvell in the years before 1987 while he was working at the Ngalangangpum School. This was expanded in the two subsequent years when Frances Kofod also worked at the school. Some of the vocabulary recorded during a project for the Kimberley Language Resource Centre during 1995 and 1996 and vocabulary recorded by Joe Blythe for *Yuwurriyangem Kijam: a phrasebook of the Kija language* (Blythe 2001) is also included.

During 2009 to 2012 the Toolbox database was completely revised and substantially extended by Kofod as part of a Major Documentation Project funded by a grant from the Hans Rausing Endangered Languages Project (SOAS in London) to the University of Manchester with the support of Professor Eva Schultze-Berndt. This database includes vocabulary from Purdie et al., 'Gija plants and animals' (2018), produced by Joe Blythe and Glenn Wightman and some vocabulary from Gija conversations recorded by Joe Blythe as part of the research project *Conversational interaction in Aboriginal and remote Australia*.

The dictionary includes much vocabulary recorded by Frances Kofod while working to document paintings with many famous Gija artists who worked with Waringarri Aboriginal Arts, Jirrawun Arts and the Warmun Art Centre. Gija artists have long been committed to Gija language maintenance and have been using painting as a means of passing on their linguistic knowledge for many years. Several Gija publications at the Warmun Art Centre resulting in additions to the database were supported by the Government of Western Australia Department of Culture and the Arts, the Australian Government Indigenous Visual Arts Industry Support, Gerlganyem Limited, Savannah Nickel Mines, the University of Melbourne, the National Climate Change Adaptation Research Facility (NCCARF), the Estate of Paddy Bedford and Ground Up Community Support Network. It also includes vocabulary from Peggy Patrick's autobiography project supported by AIATSIS, the Scully Foundation and Maria Manning.

A weekly Gija language session at Warmun Art Centre led by linguist Anna Crane was supported by Ground Up Community Support Network between 2014 and June 2016. In 2016 one hundred copies of a draft of the dictionary were printed with a dual orthography for distribution to stakeholders and benefactors. This was funded by the Friends of Warmun for the University of Melbourne with the help of Professor Robyn Sloggett, Director of the Grimwade Centre for Cultural Materials Conservation, on behalf of the Warmun Art Centre.

In 2019 and 2020 further revision was undertaken with a grant from AIATSIS managed by Ground Up, which also provided help with additional funding. Uncertain entries in the 2016 draft were checked with senior speakers and updated. After discussion with stakeholders including the staff of the Purnululu Aboriginal Independent Community School it was decided that, to avoid confusion, only one orthography — that being used in the schools — would be used for this AIATSIS–funded edition.

Thank you to Francesco Possemato, Macquarie University, for the lovely map; to Amanda Lissarrague, Doug Marmion and Rhonda Smith from AIATSIS; and also to Christine Mason and Ground Up Community Support Network. Special thanks are due to Stephanie Rajalingam, Manager of Warmun Arts for three years to June 2020, for ongoing support in many ways including organising Gija speaker interviews.

In revising the dictionary since the draft printing in 2016, most of the consultation was undertaken with Joomena Eileen Bray and Dirrji Rusty Peters. Mr Peters sadly passed away on 31 July 2020 —

PREFACE AND ACKNOWLEDGEMENTS

Figure 2. Gija mob at Bottom Camp, 1970s. Left to right, standing: Phyllis Cann, Violet Winnie Merewal, Harriet, Mona Ramsey Wirrid, John Toby, Hector Barrett, Joowoonji holding baby, George Mung Mung, Simon Drill, Jacko Dawalngoo, Rover Thomas, Paddy Jambinji and Paddy Williams. Seated: Goody Barrett, Liddy Mooloonggool, Lena Nyadbi, Topsy Manyjoorrool, Bandy, Mary Gagayil, Jilibiriny, Paddy Bedford, Ted Beard, Birrbi and Henry Wambiny. (The photograph was given to Rammel Peters by Ted Beard; photographer unknown.)

a huge loss to the Gija community. Most checking sessions saw the addition of new vocabulary that he wanted to include. This document represents a great part of his life's work and his very long-term dedication to Gija language maintenance.

Gija consultants Wirringgoon Mabel Juli, Birrmarriya Shirley Purdie, Dardayal Shirley Drill, Warlambal Nancy Nodea and Warlambal Sophia Mung were also involved in recent checking sessions. Anna Crane did much of the work to update and edit the English to Gija finder list and of overall proofreading. The introductory sections were written by Frances Kofod and Joe Blythe.

Particularly inspirational teachers and collaborators in the past include Hector Jandany, Magany George Mung Mung, Garagarag Queenie McKenzie, Jaroonggarawoony Paddy Williams, Dingmayirriny Left Hand George, Boolmarriya Doris Fletcher, Boorljoonngali Phyllis Thomas and Dirrmingali Barradjil Peggy Patrick.

This version of the Gija Dictionary includes all entries in the Toolbox database maintained by Frances Kofod as at 3 May 2021.

Figure 3. Map of Gija country (based on original map and research by Francesco Possemato, Macquarie University, 2020)

1. The Gija language and Gija country

Gija is a member of the Jarragan language family, a non-Pama-Nyungan language family from the East Kimberley in northwestern Australia. It has been spelled in a number of ways over the years including Kija, Kitja, Kidja and Gidja. The names Kuluwarrang, Guluwarin, Goorloowarrin, Lungga, Lungka, Lunga and Jarrag are alternative names for Gija or have been used to refer to different dialects of Gija.

The traditional country in which the Gija language was spoken extends from an area north of Warrmarn (Warmun – Turkey Creek) in the upper reaches of the Ord and Dunham Rivers, south to Halls Creek and west to Lansdowne and Tableland stations. The Purnululu (Bungle Bungles – Boornoolooloo) National Park is mainly in Gija country. The Argyle Diamond Mine is in country near the borders of Miriwoong and Gija country. Europeans first arrived in the East Kimberley in 1879 when 'explorer' Alexander Forrest came and reported 'the sighting of a vast tract of well-watered pastoral country' (Bolton 1981). The first cattle arrived soon after with tragic results for the Gija (Kofod 2013:10–11).

From the early 1880s invading pastoralists brought large numbers of cattle to Gija people's country, damaging the waterholes and devastating the ecosystems. Gold was discovered in Halls Creek and huge numbers of fortune hunters arrived. Life in the old way changed forever and the Gija people were rounded up and forced onto the government owned stations, Moola Bulla and Violet Valley, or to work on other cattle stations that were established in Gija country. The Gija names for these stations are Thildoowan (Lissadell), Gawoornben (Texas Downs), Joowoorlinji (Bow River), Diringin (Greenvale), Gilban (Mabel Downs), Barangen (Bedford Downs), Balinyin (Springvale), Baloowa (Violet Valley), Binoowoo (Alice Downs), Gawarre (Bungle Bungle Outcamp), Ngarraarnji (Moola Bulla), Garlgarran (Mt Amherst), Garragin (Lansdowne) and Yooloomboo (Tableland).

In the late 1960s Aboriginal stockmen were granted wages equal to non-Aboriginal workers along with citizenship of Australia. Gija people who had been living and working on stations in their own country were mostly thrown off the land. This second dispossession saw Gija people move initially to Wyndham and Halls Creek. In the 1970s the community that is now usually spelled Warmun (Warrmarn, in the Gija orthography) was established at the site of the old telegraph station at what was then called Turkey Creek by Europeans. Many Gija people went to live there.

Gija people today mostly live at Warrmarn (Warmun), Yarliyil (Halls Creek), Woorreranginy (Frog Hollow), Joowoorlinji (Bow River) and Roogoon (Crocodile Hole). Some Gija people from the western part of the country live at Imintji on the Gibb River Road. There are also Gija people living at community outstations at Dirralinji (Tirralintji), Warlawoon and Yooloomboo (Yulumbu).

1. THE GIJA LANGUAGE AND GIJA COUNTRY

1.1. Varieties of Gija

These days Gija can be said to have three dialects. The Northern dialect is spoken in and around Warrmarn (Warmun – Turkey Creek). The Southern dialect is spoken at Halls Creek and surrounds. A Western dialect is spoken by Gija people living at Imintji. Some Gija speakers describe this western variety as 'high Gija'. This dictionary includes vocabulary from each of these varieties. When entries are distinctive of these various dialects they are marked as **Southern**, **Western** or **Northern**.

Gija, like other languages, has many different words used by different people in various situations. For example, there are three words for 'emu' used by Gija people. The word **wiyarrel** is generally used to mean 'emu' by people who come from the northern part of Gija country such as Ngarrgooroon on Texas Downs. The other two words, **garnanganyjel** and **ngarabarrel**, are more likely to be found when speaking to people from the southern and western parts of Gija country. There are two words for water, **goorloom** and **goorrngam**, and two words for 'tree/plant/stick', **goowooleny** and **goonyjany**. Occasionally, there are cultural reasons why a Gija person might choose to use a particular word instead of its alternative. This can happen when one word sounds similar to the name of a relation that they are unable to pronounce.

As well as the completely different words for some things there are variations in pronunciation. Some people pronounce the word for 'small, little boy, child' as **wanyageny**. Some people say

Figure 4. Gija people at Woorreranginy (Frog Hollow) 1990. Left to right: Boorljoonngali Phyllis Thomas, Dora Ramsey carrying Reynella Nocketta, Philip Wiffen (Balanggarri co-ordinator) standing behind, Yoonany Churchill Cann with his son, Mosha Patrick, Sam Butters, Goowoomji Paddy Bedford with an unidentified child, Dooloo Tracy Ramsey, an unidentified person (partly obscured), Gardany David Turner, Darrngarri Judy Turner, Polly Nijay, Malgbarriya Dolly, Doreen Mosquito, Angelina Sampi and Jawoodjil Madigan Thomas. (Photo: Vina Goulden)

wanyanggeny. Others say ***winyangginy***. Some people say ***minyjiwarrany*** for 'black plum' and some say ***minyjaarrany***. People from the southern part of Gija country tend to elide words with intervocalic ***w*** or ***y***, making the words a bit shorter, e.g. ***yarriyangem*** 'ours' becomes ***yarrangem*** and ***berroowardbe*** 'they went down/fell' becomes ***berraardbe*** the closer you get to Halls Creek. There is a lot of speaker variation in the pronunciation of some verb forms. All of these words and their alternate forms, where recorded, have been included in this dictionary.

1.2. Bibliography

Barney, G, C Cann, B Carrington, M Juli, N Nodea, L Nyadbi et al. 2013, *Jadagen – warnkan – barnden (Wet time – cold time – hot time): Changing climate in Gija country*. F Kofod & S Leonard (eds). Warmun Art Centre, Warmun, WA.

Binayi, H A, S Brumby, S Butters, E Button, R Button, E Cox et al. 1996, *Moola Bulla: in the shadow of the mountain*. M Wrigley (ed.), Kimberley Language Resource Centre, Magabala Books, Broome, WA.

Blythe, J 2001, *Yuwurriyangem Kijam: a phrasebook of the Kija language*. Kimberley Language Resource Centre, Halls Creek, WA.

Bolton, G C 1981, Forrest, Alexander (1849–1901) in *Australian Dictionary of Biography* (vol. 8), Melbourne University Press, Carlton, Vic. https://adb.anu.edu.au/biography/forrest-alexander-6208

Clement, C 1989, *Historical notes relevant to impact stories of the East Kimberley*, East Kimberley Working Paper No 29, Centre for Resource and Environmental Studies, Australian National University, Canberra.

de Dear, C 2019, Place reference and pointing in Gija conversation, unpublished Master of Research Thesis, Macquarie University, Ryde, NSW.

de Dear, C, F Possemato & J Blythe 2020, 'Gija (East Kimberley, Western Australia) – language snapshot'. *Language Documentation and Description* 17:134–41. www.elpublishing.org/PID/189

Dillon, M & R Dixon 1990, *Aborigines and diamond mining: the politics of resource development in the East Kimberley, Western Australia*. University of Western Australia Press, Nedlands, WA.

Doohan, K 2008, *Making things come good: relations between Aborigines and miners at Argyle*. Backroom Press, Broome, WA.

Jandany, H 1986, *Warrarnany tu Jalariny*, transcribed and translated by Patrick McConvell, illustrated by Rossi Widalji. Ngalangangpum School, Warrmarn, Jawa Curriculum Support, Broome, WA.

—— 1987, *Jampalngarri-warriny du Juwarriny*, transcribed and translated by Frances Kofod, illustrated by Hector Jandany. Ngalangangpum School, Warrmarn, Jawa Curriculum Support, Broome, WA.

—— 2014, *Thambarlum-ngirri nyinge-nyinge ngenarn girli-girrim: my feet are itchy for walking*. F Kofod & A Crane (eds). Warmun Art Centre, Warmun, WA.

Juli, M 2014, 'Garnkiny' in A Crane & A Hunt (eds), *Garnkiny: constellations of meaning*. Warmun Art Centre Exhibition Catalogue, Warmun WA, pp 30–41.

—— 2015, *Jiregewoorrarrem: all kinds of birds*, transcribed and translated by Frances Kofod. Exhibition Catalogue curated and edited by Alana Hunt. Warmun Art Centre, Warmun WA.

Kaberry, P 1937a, 'Notes on the languages of the east Kimberley, north-west Australia', *Oceania* 8(1):90–103.

—— 1937b, 'Subsections in the east and south Kimberley tribes of north-west Australia', *Oceania* 7(4):436–58.

—— 1939, *Aboriginal women: sacred and profane*. Routledge & Sons, London.

Kofod, F 1996, *Kija learner's grammar*, Unpublished manuscript produced for the Kimberley Language Resource Centre, Halls Creek, WA.

—— 2013, 'Traversing Borders'. Catalogue essay for exhibition of Kimberley Art at QUT Art Museum, The William Robinson Gallery. Queensland University of Technology, Brisbane.

Kofod, F & A Crane 2020. 'The body and the verb: emotion in Gija'. *Pragmatics and Cognition* 27(1). Special Issue *Emotion, Body and Mind across a Continent*, M Ponsonnet, D Hoffmann & I O'Keefe: 209–239.

Kofod, F with the Gija people. 2016, *Gija-Kija-English dictionary: edition 1*. Printed for Warmun Arts and the Gija Community. Friends of Warmun, University of Melbourne, Melbourne.

Leonard, S, J Mackenzie, F Kofod, M Parsons, M Langton, P Russ et al. 2013, *Indigenous climate change adaptation in the Kimberley region of north-western Australia. Learning from the past, adapting in the future: identifying pathways to successful adaptation in Indigenous communities.* National Climate Change Adaptation Research Facility, Gold Coast, Qld.

McAdam, C & family, as told to E Tregenza 1995, *Boundary lines: a family's story of winning against the odds.* McPhee Gribble. Ringwood, Vic.

McConvell, P 1986, *Kija sounds and spelling.* Kimberley Educational Printing Service, Derby, WA.

—— 2003, 'Headward migration: a Kimberley counter-example' in N Evans (ed.), *The non-Pama-Nyungan languages of northern Australia: comparative studies of the continent's most linguistically complex region.* Pacific Linguistic, Canberra, pp 75–92.

Michael, L (ed.) 2006, *Paddy Bedford.* Museum of Contemporary Art, Sydney.

Nyalcas, B (Junpany) as told to P McConvell 1985, *Warrkam yirramante mayarunka*, transcribed, translated and illustrated by P McConvell. Ngalangangpum School, Turkey Creek, WA.

Oliver, T, M Langton & F Kofod 2002, *Blood on the spinifex.* Ian Potter Museum of Art, University of Melbourne, Melbourne.

Owen, C 2016, *Every mother's son is guilty: policing the Kimberley frontier of Western Australia 1882–1905.* UWA Publishing, Crawley, WA.

Peters, R 2002, *Waterbrain.* Grantpirrie Gallery, Redfern, NSW. https://www.artgallery.nsw.gov.au/collection/works/97.2002.a-h/

—— 2004, *Two laws: one big spirit.* S Grant & B Pirie (eds). Grantpirie Gallery, Redfern, NSW.

—— 2014, 'Gooroorroonggoony: the nail-tailed wallaby' in A Crane & A Hunt (eds), *Garnkiny: constellations of meanin.* Warmun Art Centre Exhibition Catalogue, Warmun, WA, pp 50–5.

Purdie, S, P Patrick, L Nyadbi, P Thomas, D Fletcher, G Barrett et al. 2018, 'Gija plants and animals: Aboriginal flora and fauna knowledge from the east Kimberley, north Australia', *Northern Territory Botanical Bulletin* 47. Dept of Environment and Natural Resources (NT), Batchelor Institute of Indigenous Tertiary Education & Warmun Arts Centre, Batchelor, NT and Warmun, WA.

Ramsey, R 2004, *Deeper than paint on canvas.* Jirrawun Arts, William Mora Galleries, Melbourne.

Ray, S H 1897, 'Note on the languages of north-west Australia: with Aboriginal vocabularies collected by E B Rigby', *Journal of the Royal Anthropological Institute* 27(2):346–60.

Ride, W D L 1970, *A guide to the native mammals of Australia.* Oxford University Press, London.

Rose, D B 1984, *Preliminary report: ethnobotany in the Bungles.* East Kimberley Working Paper No. 5, Centre for Resource and Environmental Studies, Canberra.

Ross, H (ed.) 1989, *Impact stories of the East Kimberley*, translated by E Bray. East Kimberley Working Paper No. 28. Centre for Resource and Environmental Studies, Australian National University, Canberra.

Scarlett, N 1984, *A preliminary account of the ethnobotany of the Gija people of Bungle Bungle outcamp.* East Kimberley Working Paper No. 6. Centre for Resource and Environmental Studies, Australian National University, Canberra.

Shelley, J J, D L Morgan, M P Hammer, M C Le Feuvre, G I Moore, M F Gomon et al. 2018, *A field guide to the freshwater fishes of the Kimberley.* Murdoch University Print Production Team, Perth.

Taylor, P & J Hudson 1976a, 'Metamorphosis and process in Kitja', *Talanya* 3:25–36.

—— 1976b, 'A tentative statement of Kitja phonology' in B Blake et al. (eds), *Papers on the languages of Australian Aboriginals.* Australian Institute of Aboriginal and Torres Strait Islander Studies, Canberra, pp 100–119.

Thomas, P, P Mung Mung, S Purdie, M Juli, R Peters, H Jandany et al. 2014, *Garnkiny: constellations of meaning.* A Crane & A Hunt (eds). Warmun Art Centre Exhibition Catalogue, Warmun, WA.

2. Gija spelling and pronunciation

Gija has nineteen consonant sounds and seven vowel sounds that make a difference to meaning. English letters or combinations of letters are used to represent these sounds even though some are not the same as in English. Because there is a clear match between the sounds and the letters, Gija is easy to read once you get used to it.

2.1. Consonant sounds

The sixteen consonant sounds and three semi-consonants or glides that make a difference to meaning in Gija are shown with examples in Table 1.

Table 1. Gija consonants

	Beginning of word	Middle of word	End of word
b	**b**aga**b**al 'prickly one, echidna'	nga**b**oony 'father' nga**b**ayi 'dad'	boora**b** 'appear, come out'
th	**th**alalam 'tongue' **th**ambarlam 'foot' **th**oowerndem 'mouth'	boo**th**al 'have a bad feeling' we**th**ed 'throw/fall to ground' yiloowoog**th**a 'ready'	–
d	**d**abaroony 'pelican'	ja**d**any 'rain' goo**d**am 'hair belt'	ba**d** 'to put foot on, step on' tha**d** 'to stand'
rd	–	wa**rd**al 'star' be**rd**ij 'to climb'	roo**rd** 'sit down' da**rd** 'to be hanging', da**rd**a**rd** 'to be all hanging'
j	**j**alijgel 'freshwater prawn', 'cherabin'	nga**j**iny 'brother' bena**j**tha 'you (one) PUT them/it'*	ma**j** 'to touch' joolo**j** 'to carry under arm'
g	**g**anggayi 'maternal grandmother, woman's daughter's child'	Na**g**arra 'a skin name' mela**g**awoom 'many' ma**g**ardal 'hat'	joodoo**g** 'to straighten' bal**g** 'stay in one place'
m	**m**arranyji 'dingo'	ma**m**ag 'pour water on someone/something'	ma**m** 'put hands on someone, feel someone'
nh	**nh**embad 'to be/get stuck' **nh**oonbam 'mud'	me**nh**ang 'to lick' biya**nh**a 'you (one) COME'	–
n	**N**agarra 'a skin name'	bana**n**be 'road, track, path'	nawa**n** 'cave'
rn	–	ma**rn**em 'fire' bi**rn**'girrbal 'bush turkey, bustard' wa**rn**'gam 'cold ones'	marra**rn** 'go away'

* Translations of the generic meanings of the verbs are written in capital letters showing that they have a general meaning when combined with coverbs. See section 4.8.

2. GIJA SPELLING AND PRONUNCIATION

Table 1 continued

	Beginning of word	Middle of word	End of word
ny	*nyaganyji* 'uncle'	*manyanyiny* 'wild tea'	*nyagoornany* 'rock cod'
ng	*ngaboony* 'father' *ngenengga* 'here'	*wangalam* 'mad ones' *wanggarnal* 'crow'	*lang* 'to stare' *doowoorrng* 'to turn over'
l	*lalanggarrany* 'crocodile'	*moowoolem* 'forehead' *thalg* 'hook up a spear in woomera' *dilg-dilg* 'put dots on painting'	*gool* 'to try' *loomoogool* 'blue-tongue lizard'
rl	–	*moorloo* 'eye' *lerlb* 'peel' *loorlg* 'wash something away (flood)'	*garl-garl* 'to laugh' *goorl* 'to stretch arms out'
ly	–	*jibilyiwool* 'duck' *dalyalya* 'hit the ground (lightning)' *goolyoolyool* 'budgerigar'	*jily-jily* 'burn with the end of a stick, brand cattle'
rr	–	*loorroob* 'to chase' *lirrgarn* 'to instruct' *warrg* 'to dance' *therrb-therrb* 'to scrape'	*ngerr* 'to throw'
r	*ragim* 'ants'	*ngarag* 'to make'	*ger* 'wind blow'
w	*wawooleny* 'frillneck lizard'	*nawarrany, nawarral, nawarram* 'big' *werlwe* 'become part of country in dreamtime'	–
y	*yalarrngarnany* 'jabiru' *yingajalil* 'Livistona palm'	*mayim* 'non-meat food' *jirrayam* 'alright, OK'	–

2.1.1. Notes about pronunciation of consonants

b Similar to 'b' or 'p' in English, as in '**b**ee**p**', '**p**i**p**' or '**b**i**b**'. It can be at the beginning, middle or end of words. It sounds more like 'b' at the beginning and in the middle of words. At the end of a word it sounds a bit more like 'p' but there is no little puff of air as in English so it can also sound like 'b'. It can sometimes be hard to hear in final position.

th, nh The two-letter combinations **th** and **nh** represent sounds not found in English. These two sounds do not occur at the end of words or syllables. It is important to be able to hear these sounds as they are very frequently heard at the beginning of the last syllable in verbs that include 'you'; for example, *bamberrajtha* 'you all PUT them!', *yindiyinnha* 'you should give (it) to me', *biyanynha* 'you (one) come'.

The **th** sound is not a breathy sound as in English. It is a stop sound made by putting the tongue behind the teeth and trying to make a 'd' or 't' sound.

The **nh** sound is made by putting the tongue behind the teeth and trying to make an 'n' sound.

d Similar to 'd' or 't' in English, as in '**d**ot'. It sounds more like 'd' at the beginning and in the middle of words. It can sound a bit more like a 't' at the end of a word.

g Used for sounds similar to 'g' or 'k' in English, as in '**g**iggle' or '**k**ick'. At the beginning of words, it sounds more like the 'g' in '**g**iggle'. At the end of words *g* sometimes sounds more like an English 'k', or somewhere between a 'g' and a 'k'.

Note that the combination **ng** represents a different sound. See below.

2. GIJA SPELLING AND PRONUNCIATION

rd, rn, rl These letter combinations represent sounds not found in English. They are called 'retroflex' sounds because they are made by turning the tip of the tongue towards the roof of the mouth. These sounds are not heard at the beginning of Gija words, only in the middle or at the end of words.

j Similar to the 'ch' in '**ch**ance' or the 'j' in '**j**am'. It can be hard to hear at the end of a word (e.g. *jalij* 'to be raining') and at the end of a syllable within a word (e.g. *birlirrijgel* 'peewee, magpie lark'). This is because *j* is unreleased in these environments (there is no puff of air at the end of the sound).

l Similar to English as in '**l**o**ll**y'.

ly A two-letter combination similar to the '**ll**i' in 'mi**lli**on'. This sound is not heard at the beginning of Gija words.

m Similar to English as in '**m**u**m**'.

n Similar to English as in '**n**u**n**'.

ng A two-letter combination similar to the 'ng' at the end of 'si**ng**' or in the middle of 'si**ng**er'. It is not like the 'ng' in 'fi**ng**er' or 'li**ng**er'. 'Linger' would be spelled '*lingge*' in Gija orthography. It is also not like the 'ng' in 'gi**ng**er'. In Gija this **ng** sound is very common at the beginning of words.

ngg A letter sequence that combines **ng** with **g** in the middle of words. It sounds like 'ng' in English 'fi**ng**er' and 'li**ng**er'.

n'g, rn'g The two-letter combination **n'g** is similar to the 'ng' in English 'o**ng**oing' or the 'nc' in 'e**nc**ounter'. The combination **rn'g** is not like any sound in Australian English. These combinations only occur in the middle of words. Examples include *wan'gil* 'rifle', *warn'gam* 'cold', *men'gawoom* 'good', *birn'girrbal* 'bush turkey'.

Note: Prior to March 2020, these sounds were written in Gija using **nk** and **rnk**. This was to distinguish between the velar nasal **ng** [ŋ] and the sequences **ng-g** [ŋ.g] and **n-g** [n.g] or **rn-g** [ɳ.g]. Gija teachers asked that instead of **nk** and **rnk**, the spelling system should use **n'g** and **rn'g**.

These contrast with Gija words with **ng** between vowels. Examples are *wangalany*, *wangalal*, *wangalam* 'mad ones', *wanga-wanga* 'to be lonely'.

ny Similar to the 'ny' in the name So**ny**a or the 'ni' in o**ni**on. Unlike in English, it occurs at the beginning and the end of Gija words. It is very confusing for readers of English when they see **ny** at the end of a Gija word and discover that it is not like the 'ny' in English ma**ny**. To make this sound at the end of a word practise saying 'Sonya' but stop halfway and leave out the 'a' sound.

It is important to be able to hear the difference between **ny** and **n** at the end of Gija words. This is because **ny** marks masculine nouns and **n** can replace the final **ny** giving the meaning 'in, at, on or the place of'; for example, *garn'giny* 'moon', *garn'gin* 'in, at, on the place of the moon'.

r Similar to the English sound in '**r**un' or the sound in 'ca**r**' when pronounced with a North American accent. This sound is heard at beginning and in the middle of words; for example, *ragim* 'ants', *gerewoole* 'eggs'. It is also heard at the end of a very small number of Gija words as in *ger* 'to be wind blowing'.

2. GIJA SPELLING AND PRONUNCIATION

rr   Similar to the rolled 'r' sound in Scottish English. Sometimes it sounds a bit like the 'tt' in bu**tt**er when said quickly. This sound is not heard at the beginning of Gija words.

Note that there are some words in Gija that use both **r** and **rr** in the same words, making it hard for English speakers to hear and pronounce. Examples: *waringarrim*, *waringarriny*, *waringarril* 'many, plentiful', *gooroorroonggoony* 'nail-tailed wallaby', *Goorirr-goorirr* 'name of a song and dance cycle'.

w   Similar to the English sound in '**w**in'. It is heard at the beginning and in the middle but not at the end of Gija words. At the beginning of words **w** is sometimes not heard before the vowel **oo**; for example, **w**oomberrama 'they did, they said' may sound like **oomberrama**.

y   Similar to that in English '**y**es'. It occurs at the beginning and in the middle of Gija words. Sometimes **y** is not heard before the vowel **i**; for example, **y**ijiya 'true' is often heard as **ijiya**. In words that are written with **ayi**, it is sometimes hard to hear the **y** with some speakers, for example, in *ra**y**iny* 'little spirit man', *da**y**iwool* 'barramundi', *jarramba**y**iny* 'type of goanna'. When found following 'l' or 'n' the letter 'y' is helping to represent the **ly** or **ny** sound. In these cases, it is not pronounced separately as we would in English 'dai**ly**' or 'a**ny**'.

rrg, lg, rlg   These sound combinations can be heard at the end of Gija syllables, usually in coverbs or words that have been derived from coverbs. Examples include *warrg* 'to dance', *mirnilg-mirnilg* 'to blink, to flicker (stars)', *loorlg* 'flood water rush down'. These sound combinations do not occur in English.

rrng   This sound combination is heard at the end of syllables in a small number of words. Examples: *nyirrng* 'to grab someone from two sides', *dooboorrngbeny*, *dooboorrngbel*, *dooboorrngbem* 'very hot'. This sound combination does not occur in English.

rrb, rlb   These sound combinations can be heard on rare occasions at the end of Gija coverbs. Examples: *therr-therrb* 'to scrape', *lerlb* 'to peel'. These sound combinations do not occur in English.

Figure 5. George Mung Mung; Ngalangangpum School, 1987. *Magany lirrgarn benamanyji wanyanyagem.*

2. GIJA SPELLING AND PRONUNCIATION

Figure 6. Garagarag Queenie McKenzie; Ngalangangpum School, 1987. *Nagarral giwaji benamenya ngoorrwany wanyanyagem.*

2.1.2. Consonant sound contrasts in Gija words

The following contrasting Gija words show why we need the different letters **d** and **r** or the two-letter combinations **th**, **rd** and **rr** in the middle of words.

*joo**d**oom*	'straight ones'
*joo**rd**oom*	'dust'
*joo**rr**oo*	'put down'
*joo**r**oony*	type of tree
*goo**th**oongoony*	'short one (male)'
*goo**d**oo-goo**d**oo*	'to grind'
*goo**rd**ooroom*	'fighting stick, nulla-nulla'
*goo**rr**oobardool*	type of boomerang
*goo**r**oongoony*	type of small medicinal plant
*gooroomoo**rr**oo*	'mist, heat haze'
*ba**rr**em*	'you (plural) get him/her/it (singular)'
*ba**d**em*	'red ochre'
*ba**rd**oon*	'behind'

2. GIJA SPELLING AND PRONUNCIATION

Figure 7. Garagarag Queenie McKenzie, Dingmayirriny Left Hand George and Jaroonggarawoony Paddy Williams; Ngalangangpum School 1987. *Ngalany boorroorn-birri wanyanyagem.*

Figure 8. Standing: Yooroojil Lulu Trancolino, Garlgarrangarnany Ben Duncan, Felicity Smith, Goobooji Rosie Malgil, Mavis Wallaby. Sitting: Wawoorany Tiger Henry, Boolmarriya Doris Fletcher and Joe Blythe, Halls Creek 2001. *Deg bemberremenbe boorriyangem mirli-mirlim.* (Photo: Cath Rouse courtesy of Joe Blythe)

2.2 Vowel sounds

Vowel sounds are made without the tongue blocking the air anywhere in the mouth. There are seven different vowel sounds that make a difference to the meaning of words in Gija. They are four short sounds represented by *a*, *i*, *e* and *oo* and three long sounds *aa*, *iyi* and *oowoo*. Gija vowels are shown in Table 2.

Table 2. Gija vowels

a	*ma**r**la**m* 'hand' *da**r**nda**l* 'turtle' *da**m* 'those, that (non-singular)'*	e	*de**r**re**b* 'to camp' *ge**m**e**rre* 'tribal scars'
aa	*daa**m* 'country, camp, home' *baa**r**nji* 'spider'	oo	*moo**lo**o**nggoo**m* 'fat' *doo**m**boo**ny* 'owl'
i	*l**ili**n**yil* 'bony bream' *b**i**r**lbi**rl**ji**m* 'grasshoppers' *j**i**r**r**i* 'to show'	oowoo	*goo**woo**lem* 'trees, plants, sticks' *th**oowoo* 'what thing (non-singular)?'
iyi	*j**iyi**liny* 'man' *ng**iyi* 'yes'		

2.2.1. Notes about pronunciation of vowels

a   similar to the 'u' in 'but' or 'mum'

aa similar to the 'a' in 'father' but more drawn out

e   similar to the 'er' in 'butter'

i   similar to 'i' in 'bit'

iyi similar to the 'ee' in 'seen', often sounds like two syllables

oo similar to the 'u' in 'put'

oowoo   like the 'oo' in 'pool' but more drawn out, often sounds like two syllables.

The vowel sounds *iyi* and *oowoo* frequently sound as though they include the glides *y* and *w* and are really two syllables. This is more likely to be heard in the speech of speakers from the northern part of Gija country.

The long *aa* sound does not include a glide as part of the sound. Gija words occur with *awa* and *aya* as part of the word (e.g. *th**awa**lam* 'flowers', *m**aya**room* 'house').

Some words that include a vowel-glide-vowel sequence in the speech of people from Warrmarn are elided in the speech of people from around Halls Creek.

	'they are FALLING/GOING DOWN'	'ours (inclusive)'
Northern dialect	*berroowardbe*	*yoowoorriyangem*
Southern dialect	*berraardbe*	*yoorrangem*

---

* Gija nouns have three genders: masculine, feminine, and non-singular that includes plural animates, mass nouns, parts of entities and many objects and parts of the landscape. All adjectives, demonstratives, pronouns and interrogatives asking about nouns must agree in gender with the noun referred to. See section 4.1.

3. Gija skin names and relationship terms

3.1. Gija skin

In the East Kimberley and in much of the Northern Territory Aboriginal people divide their society into eight 'skin' groups. In the anthropological literature these are known as 'subsections'. The Gija skin names are shown in Figure 9. The names shown in brackets are really the Miriwoong names but they are in common usage among many Gija. Male names in each subsection begin with *J* and female names begin with either *N* or *Ny*. Every person is in the same skin group as their siblings. In fact, people in the same skin group can call each *ngaji* ('brother'/'sister') even if they are not closely related.

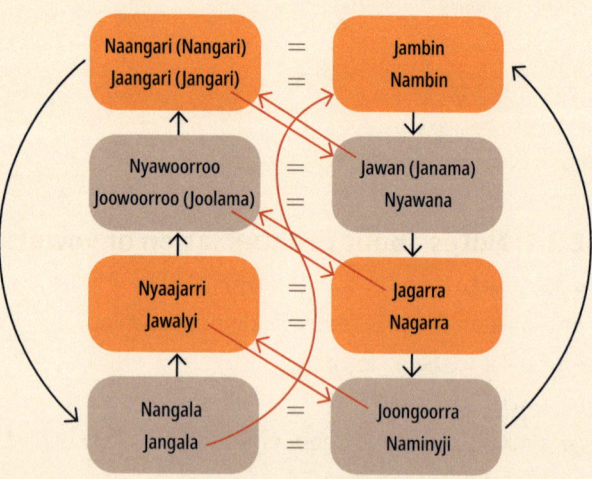

Figure 9. Gija skin names

Everyone is born into a skin group that is determined by the skin of the mother. The black arrows in Figure 9 show matrilineal descent (from mother to child). These make two 'matricycles'. On the left side **Naangari** is the mother of **Nangala** and **Jangala**; **Nangala** is the mother of **Nyaajarri** and **Jawalyi**; **Nyaajarri** is the mother of **Nyawoorroo** and **Joowoorroo**; **Nyawoorroo** is the mother of **Naangari** and **Jaangari**, completing one of the matricycles. On the right side **Nambin** is the mother of **Nyawana** and **Jawan**; **Nyawana** is the mother of **Nagarra** and **Jagarra**; **Nagarra** is the mother of **Naminyji** and **Joongoorra** and **Naminyji** is the mother of **Nambin** and **Jambin**, completing the other matricycle. Straight marriages (the ideal partners for marriage) are indicated with the 'equals' sign (=); for example, **Naangari** is straight for **Jambin** and **Nambin** is straight for **Jaangari**.

The Gija forms given in Figure 9 are the basic skin names. The forms in this chart are used when directly addressing someone. People are often addressed by their skin name, as this is a useful a way of avoiding the use of personal names (see section 3.3.1). When people are referred to in Gija sentences the skin names usually take masculine (masc) or feminine (fem) gender suffixes (see section 4.1), as in examples (1) and (2). The reference forms with their gender suffixes, used when speaking about people in full Gija sentences, are compared to the address forms in Table 3. The

3. GIJA SKIN NAMES AND RELATIONSHIP TERMS

different brown versus orange boxes show the two generational moieties discussed below (this section, under example 14). The orange lines show the father/son pairs (see section 3.1.1).

Table 3. Address and reference forms of the Gija skin names

Address forms	Reference forms	Address forms	Reference forms
Naangari (Nangari)	Naangaril (Nangaril)	Nambin	Nambinel
Jaangari (Jangari)	Jaangariny (Jangariny)	Jambin	Jambinji
Nyawoorroo	Nyawoorrool	Nyawana	Nyawanal
Joowoorroo (Joolama)	Joowoorroony (Joolamany)	Jawan (Janama)	Jawanji (Janamany)
Nyaajarri	Nyaajarril	Nagarra	Nagarral
Jawalyi	Jawalyiny	Jagarra	Jagarrany
Nangala	Nangalal	Naminyji (Naminyjili)	Naminyjili (Naminyjilel)
Jangala	Jangalany	Joongoorra	Joongoorrany

(1) **Dala** **Nangalal** roord nyinya marnen.
    that-fem-TOP skin name-fem sit she STAYS fire-LOC*
    There is Nangala sitting near the fire.

(2) **Danya** **Jangalany** roord nginji goowoolen.
    that-masc-TOP skin name-masc sit he STAYS tree-LOC
    There is Jangala sitting near the tree.

When people tell you their skin they add a locative suffix **-n** (following a vowel) or **-e** (following a consonant, see section 4.2.1). In this situation it means something like 'am' or 'are'. It is then followed by an enclitic pronoun** **-nga** meaning 'I'.

(3) **Ngayin-ga** **Nangala-n-nga.**
    I/me skin name-LOC-I/me
    I am Nangala skin.

(4) **Ngayin-ga** **Jawalyi-n-nga.**
    I/me skin name-LOC-I/me
    I am Jawalyi skin.

If you want to tell someone what skin they are you can use a similar sentence with the enclitic pronoun **-ngoo**, as in (5) and (6).

(5) **Nyengen-ga** **Nangala-n-ngoo.**
    you (one) skin name-LOC-you (one)
    You are Nangala.

(6) **Nyengen-ga** **Jawalyi-n-ngoo.**
    you (one) skin name-LOC-you (one)
    You are Jawalyi skin.

---

* For a description of the uses of the locative suffix (LOC) see section 4.2.1.
** An enclitic pronoun is one that follows the word it is attached to without becoming part of the word, but cannot stand alone as can the free-form pronouns. See section 4.7.3 for further discussion.

3. GIJA SKIN NAMES AND RELATIONSHIP TERMS

To ask someone about their skin, a different suffix *-nha* 'are you' is used before the enclitic pronoun.

(7) **Thiwinge-nha-ngoo.**
what thing-are you-you (one)
What is your skin? What kind are you?

The questions used to ask about other people's skin are shown in (8) to (10). You can use (8) to ask about a male and (9) to ask about a female. You can use (10) to ask about any people, whether male or female. You can also use (10) when asking about a person whose gender you don't know.

(8) **Thiniwa   nginyjinyi?**
what thing masc   this masc
What is his skin? What kind is he?

(9) **Thengela   ngeli?**
what thing fem   this fem
What is her skin? What kind is she?

(10) **Thoowoorra   berrembi?**
what thing plural these
What skin are these people? What kind are they? What is this person's skin?

These questions are a little different in the Southern dialect, as examples (11) to (14) demonstrate.

(11) **Thoowoonginya   nginyjiny?**
what thing-masc   this masc
What is his skin? What kind is he?

(12) **Thoowoongela   ngelel?**
what thing-fem   this fem
What is her skin? What kind is she?

(13) **Thoowoongooma   berrem?**
what thing-plural these
What skin are these people? What kind are they?

(14) **Thoowoonge-nha-ngoo?**
what thing-are you-you (one)
What skin are you (one)? What kind are you?

In Figure 9 there are four skin groups that are brown and four that are orange. These are the generational moieties, or ***jarlinybaroom*** in Gija (also known as 'companies' in Kimberley Kriol). People in the skin groups Joowoorroo/Nyawoorroo, Jawan/Nyawana, Joongoorra/Naminyji and Jangala/Nangala belong to the same ***jarlinybaroom*** (alternatively pronounced as ***jarlinyjaroom***). The other ***jarlinybaroom*** / ***jarlinyjaroom*** consists of the skin groups Naangari/Jaangari, Jambin/Nambin, Jagarra/Nagarra and Nyaajarri/Jawalyi. A person belongs in the same generational moiety as their siblings and fathers' brothers' and fathers' sisters' children, their grandparents and their grandchildren — even generations. A person should marry someone in their own generational moiety (***jarlinybaroom***), as long as that person is not their own sibling. They shouldn't marry into the opposite ***jarlinybaroom***. These are the odd generations: your parents, uncles and aunts, children, nephews and nieces, great grandparents and great grandchildren. In early days people used to group together into ***jarlinybaroom*** for ceremonies (Kaberry 1939:175, 196, 260).

3. GIJA SKIN NAMES AND RELATIONSHIP TERMS

(15) **Nginyjiny** **Jagarrany,** **Jaangariny,** **Jawalyiny,** **Jambinji,**
this masc-masc skin name-masc skin name-masc skin name-masc skin name-masc
wayiningerreg jarlinybaroo-warriny.
this many generational moiety-together
The 'skins' Jagarra, Jaangari, Jawalyi and Jambin, this many are 'company' together (they form a group together at ceremony times).

People in opposite ***jarlinybaroom / jarlinyjaroom*** (generational moieties) are said to be in a relationship called ***yinara***. In late 2019 Frances Kofod, who is Nambin skin, offered a new colourful shirt to Eileen Bray, who is Naangari. This happened while they were in the presence of Nancy Nodea, who is Nyawoorroo. Nancy claimed the shirt on the grounds that Nambin and Naangari are ***yinara*** to Nyawoorroo, so Frances and Eileen had obligations toward her as their ***yinara***. Nancy explained the ***yinara*** relationship by saying, 'We play against you two fellas.'

(16) **Yinara-noonggoorroo-yoo-ngageny**
opposite generational moiety-you-two-my/mine
You two are in the other group from me.
You two are 'yinara' to me.

Sometimes the skin names are heard with the suffix ***-ngeny/-nginy/-ngoony*** (masculine) or ***-ngel/-ngil/-ngool*** (feminine) meaning 'that kind of a one'. These forms are listed in Table 4.

Table 4. Gija skin names with the 'that kind' suffix

Naangaringel	Nambinngel
Jaangaringiny	Jambinnginy
Nyawoorroongool	Nyawanangel
Joowoorroongoony	Jawannginy
Nyaajarringel	Nagarrangel
Jawalyinginy	Jagarranginy
Nangalangel	Naminyjilingel
Jangalanginy	Joongoorrangeny

As mentioned above, the first choice for marriage are the 'straight' skin partners marked by the equals sign in Figure 9. So, the first choice of husband for **Nangala** would be **Joongoorra** and for **Naminyji** it would be **Jangala.** It must be remembered that these 'straight' marriages represent an idealized situation. If the first choice of spouse is not available someone else should be chosen from their own ***jarlinybaroom***. The second choice is from the skin group that the person calls ***thamany*** (the group that includes their mother's father and his siblings and their fathers' brothers' and sisters' children, see Figure 9). So, if **Nangala** cannot find a **Joongoorra**, the next choice would be **Jawan**. The third choice would be the skin group which the person calls **ganggayi** (the group that includes their maternal grandmother and her siblings). So, if **Nangala** cannot find a **Joongoorra** or a **Jawan,** the next choice would be **Joowoorroo**. Older people say that marriage outside the generational moiety, the ***jarlinyjaroom***, is not acceptable so people should not marry a person from the skin groups they call 'mother' or 'father', 'aunt' or 'uncle', 'son' or 'daughter', 'mother-in-law' or 'son-in-law'.

Figure 10. Back: Erica Nodea and April Nulgit. Middle: Warlambal Nancy Nodea and Savanah Nulgit. Front: Cassius Nulgit and Wayne Nulgit Junior Dooboo–li. *Nyawoorrool thad benoomoorloonya ngaliyangem wanyanyagem, ganggagam doo thamanygam.*

3.1.1. Fathers and their children

As well as the two divisions already mentioned, the matricycles and the generational moieties, we can look at the skins from the point of view of fathers and their children. There are four sets of father/son pairs which divide the eight groups in yet another way. If marriages are straight, the skins of fathers and sons alternate every two generations (see the orange arrows in Figure 9). Thus, while **Joongoorra** is father of **Jawalyi** and **Nyaajarri**, the children of **Jawalyi** are **Joongoorra** and **Naminyji**. Everyone gets their skin from their mother. However, there are people whose parents were not married straight. Some of these people say they have 'two skins', one determined by their mother and one determined by their father.

3.2. Gija relationship terms

Gija people use family words not only for their close family but also for people who are not their immediate relatives. Relationship terms (kinterms) intersect with the skin system. So, a term like **goorayi**, which is usually translated as 'mother', is really a category term that includes not only your actual mother, but also your mother's sisters and many other people your mother calls 'sister'. In fact, **goorayi** can be extended to any female in the same subsection or skin as your actual mother.

Although many kinterms are used in the same way by men and women, there are some for which the meanings differ.

Table 5 shows some frequently used kinterms that take a woman's point of view while Table 6 shows frequently used kinterms that take a man's point of view. The definitions in the fourth column list only the most immediate relatives; however, all of these kinterms can be extended to include more distant relatives in the same skin groups as the immediate relatives.

3. GIJA SKIN NAMES AND RELATIONSHIP TERMS

Table 5. Relationship terms that take a woman's point of view

Generation	Address forms (when spoken to)	Reference forms (when spoken about)	Relationship
grandparents	gelagi	gelaginy	father's father, father's father's brother
		gelagil	father's father's sister
	ngawooji	ngawoojiny	father's mother's brother
		ngawoojil	father's mother
	thamany	thamanyji	mother's father, mother's father's brothers
		thamanyel	mother's father's sister
	ganggayi	ganggany	mother's mother's brother
		ganggal	mother's mother
parents	ngabayi	ngaboony	father, father's brother
		ngabool	father's sister
	gawayi	gawangel	father's sister
	goorayi	gooral	mother, mother's sister
	gamelany	gamelanyel	mother's sister (Southern dialect)
	thamboorroo	thamboorroony	husband's mother's brother
		thamboorrool	husband's mother
	goorriji	goorrijil	husband's mother
	nyagayi	nyaganyji	mother's brother
	lambarra	lambarrany	husband's father
your own	ngaji	ngajiny	brother (of any age), cousin (mother's father's son, father's sister's son)
		ngajil	sister (of any age), cousin (mother's father's daughter, father's sister's daughter)
	booloongoo	booloongoony	elder brother
		booloongool	elder sister
	goorabeny	goorabeny	elder brother
	goorabel	goorabel	elder sister
	bariyi	bariyiny	younger brother
		bariyil	younger sister
	thamany	thamanyji	mother's father's son, father's sister's son
		thamanyel	mother's father's daughter, father's sister's daughter
	ngoolnga	ngoolngany	husband, husband's brother
	mandirri	mandirril	sister-in-law of woman (husband's sister, brother's wife)
	wardoo	wardool	sister-in-law of woman (husband's sister, brother's wife)

Table 5 continued

Generation	Address forms (when spoken to)	Reference forms (when spoken about)	Relationship
children	ngalanga, ngalayi	ngalangal, ngalangangal	daughter
		ngalangany ngalangangeny	son
		wigil	daughter
		wiginy	son
	ngabayi	ngaboony	brother's son
		ngabool	niece of aunt, (woman's brother's daughter)
	thamboorroo	thamboorroony	son-in-law (daughter's husband)
	goorriji	goorrijil	daughter-in-law (son's wife)
grandchildren	gelagi	gelaginy	brother's son's son
		gelagil	brother's son's daughter
	ngawooji	ngawoojiny	daughter's son
		ngawoojil	daughter's daughter
	thamany	thamanyji	brother's daughter's son
		thamanyel	brother's daughter's daughter
	ngawooji	ngawoojiny	son's son
		ngawoojil	son's daughter

Table 6. Relationship terms that take a man's point of view

Generation	Address forms (when spoken to)	Reference forms (when spoken about)	Relationship
grandparents	gelagi	gelaginy	father's father, father's father's brother
		gelagil	father's father's sister
	ngawooji	ngawoojiny	father's mother's brother
		ngawoojil	father's mother
	thamany	thamanyji	mother's father, mother's father's brothers
		thamanyel	mother's father's sister
	ganggayi	ganggany	mother's mother's brother
		ganggal	mother's mother
parents	ngabayi	ngaboony	father, father's brother
		ngabool	father's sister
	gawayi	gawangel	father's sister
	goorayi	gooral	mother, mother's sister
	gamelany	gamelanyel	mother's sister (Southern dialect)
	thamboorroo	thamboorroony	wife's mother's brother
		thamboorrool	wife's mother
	goorriji	goorrijil	wife's mother
	nyagayi	nyaganyji	mother's brother
	lambarra	lambarrany	wife's father

3. GIJA SKIN NAMES AND RELATIONSHIP TERMS

Table 6 continued

Generation	Address forms (when spoken to)	Reference forms (when spoken about)	Relationship
your own	ngaji	ngajiny	brother (of any age), mother's father's son, father's sister's son
		ngajil	sister (of any age), mother's father's daughter, father's sister's daughter
	booloongoo	booloongoony	elder brother
		booloongool	elder sister
	goorabeny	goorabeny	elder brother
	goorabel	goorabel	elder sister
	bariyi	bariyiny	younger brother
		bariyil	younger sister
	thamany	thamanyji	mother's father's son, father's sister's son
		thamanyel	mother's father's daughter, father's sister's daughter
	langgoornoo	langgoornool	wife
	ngoolnga	ngoolngal	wife
		ngoolngany	brother-in-law of man (wife's brother, sister's husband)
	wardoo	wardoony	brother-in-law of man (wife's brother, sister's husband)
children	ngabayi	wigil	daughter
		wiginy	son
		ngaboony	son
		ngabool	daughter
	garli	garlil	sister's daughter
		garliny	sister's son
	thamboorroo	thamboorroony	sister's daughter's husband
		goorrijil	daughter-in-law (son's wife)
grandchildren	gelagi	gelaginy	son's son
		gelagil	son's daughter
	gangga	ganggany	sister's daughter's son
		ganggal	sister's daughter's daughter
	thamany	thamanyji	daughter's son
		thamanyel	daughter's daughter
	ngawooji	ngawoojiny	sister's son's son
		ngawoojil	sister's son's daughter

Like the skin names, Gija relationship terms have both address forms and forms used when speaking about the relation that include the gender suffixes (reference forms). Note that the words **wiginy** 'son' and **wigil** 'daughter' used by both men and women have not been recorded as forms of address. Eileen Bray says she has not heard **wigi** as an address form at Warrmarn. When addressing a brother or a sister as **goorabeny** or **goorabel** the gender suffixes are retained. This is a way of talking 'sideways' that reflects avoidance between brothers and sisters (see section 3.3.2).

19

3. GIJA SKIN NAMES AND RELATIONSHIP TERMS

3.2.1. Other relationship words

Some other relationship words are listed in Table 7. Only the first four have address forms.

Table 7. Other Gija relationship terms

Address (when spoken to)	Reference (when spoken about)	Relationship
goorndooga	goorndoogal, goorndoogany, goorndoogam	child, little one; these words are used to mean 'daughter, niece, son, nephew' by both men and women
jangada	jangadany, jangadal, jangadam, REDUP* jangangangadam	child, little one; these words are used to mean 'daughter, niece, son, nephew' (Southern dialect)
ben'gali	ben'galiny, ben'galil	spouse of someone a person calls *ganggayi* 'granny', man's wife's mother's mother, husband's mother's mother, daughter's son's wife, husband's mother's mother's brother, daughter's daughter's husband
gimili	gimiliny, gimilil, gimilim	child of man's brother or sister (Southern dialect only)
	barnalnginy, barnalngel	brother's child. LIT. 'one who is carried on shoulders'
	doomoorrngarnany, doomoorrngarnal, doomoorrngarnam	cousins from one family (mother's brother's children, father's sister's children), blood relations from one family
	manaroony, manarool, REDUP mana-manaroom	parents and their siblings, relationship term used to refer to the active middle-aged adult generation (i.e. mothers and mothers' brothers, fathers and fathers' sisters, the parent generation)
	melgabawoorroony, melgabawoorrool, melgabawoorroom	person whose name someone can't say who is married to son or daughter or in-law of speaker, also used to refer to 'mother-in-law' or 'father-in-law' by a son-in-law
	nyingginy, nyinggil, nyinggim	people in avoidance or restricted relationship
	garloomboo-bawoorrool	sister. LIT. 'she who has no spear' (man speaking)
	garloomboo-bany	brother. LIT. 'he who has a spear' (woman speaking)

3.2.2. Talking about relations

There are a number of kinterm suffixes that adjust the kinterm's meaning. One of these, meaning 'his/her/their relation', has forms **-gany, -gal, -gam** that inflect for gender (masculine, feminine and plural, see section 4.1). The suffix agrees in gender with the relation possessed, not with the possessor. Examples are seen in (17): **thamany-gany** 'his maternal grandfather', (18): **goora-gal** 'his mother', and (19): **goora-gam doo ngaboo-gam** 'their mothers and their fathers'.

(17) **Nginya   ngagenyji   ngaboony   thamany-gany-noongoo   daam.**
this-masc my-masc father mother's father-his/her/their relation-masc-his country
This (image) is my father's maternal grandfather's country.

---

* For reduplicated forms, marked REDUP, the word is doubled or partially doubled to show that more than one person or thing was involved, or the action went on for some time or in more than one place. See section 5.

3. GIJA SKIN NAMES AND RELATIONSHIP TERMS

Figure 11. Birrmarriya Shirley Purdie and Lawoony Gordon Barney. *Ngoolngabem roord boorroonboo-yoo.*

(18) **Doorroon   nginiyanya   goora-ga-l.**
put down   she PUT him   mother-his/her/their relation-fem
His mother put him down.

(19) **Berrngerl   berrayin   dambi**
have a funny feeling   they WENT   those

goora-ga-m   doo   ngaboo-ga-m.
mother-his/her/their relation-plural   and   father-his/her/their relation-plural
All those mothers and fathers of theirs had a funny feeling.

The suffix set **-goorroony, -goorrool, -goorroom** that attaches to relationship terms means 'your relation'. Again, the suffix agrees in gender with the relation possessed, not the possessor. The examples **goora-goorrool** 'your mother' and **ngaboo-goorroony** 'your father' are seen in (20).

(20) **Goora-goorroo-l   joo   ngaboo-goorroo-ny,   ngoowan**
mother-your relation-fem   and   father-your relation-masc   not

boorroordboo-yoo   boorroowany   ngarem-boorroo?
they GO/COME-two   they themselves   sugarbag-for
Your mother and your father couldn't go for sugarbag by themselves?

The suffix **-bem/-boom** can be attached to a relationship term meaning 'two together', as in the name of the **Ngalangangpum School** (*Ngalangangboom* 'mother and child') in Warrmarn. In the captions to Figure 11 and Figure 12 **ngoolngabem** means 'husband and wife'.

If someone wants to say 'me and my husband', they usually use the expression **Ngayin yirranji-ngarri-yoo**, 'I when we two stay'.

Another way of speaking about two related people is the use of the suffix **-lang** 'two people who call each other . . .' as in **ngaboo-lang** 'two people who call each other father and son' (see Figure 13). Further examples are **thamany-lang** 'two people who call each other **thamany**' and **ngaji-lang** 'two people who call each other brother/sister'.

3. GIJA SKIN NAMES AND RELATIONSHIP TERMS

Figure 12. Nyoon'goony Paddy Bedford Goowoomji and Dardayal Topsy Bedford. *Berrem-doo thad boorroonboo-yoo ngoolngabem.*

Figure 13. Warlawoon Rammy Ramsey and Goowoomji Paddy Bedford. *Ngaboo-lang roord boorroonbi-yoo.*

3.3. Saying names

Gija people often talk about others by using their skin names or by using relationship terms. Personal names are also used but there are many restrictions on personal names in Gija. The names of the deceased are not spoken for a long time after the person's death. Men may not say the names of their sisters and women may not say the names of their brothers. The personal names of in-laws, especially in-laws of the opposite sex, are strongly avoided. Taboos on names extend to the namesakes of the person whose name should not be pronounced. It is therefore very important to know what other people's names are, even if you are not able to pronounce everybody's name. To ask about someone's name you can say:

> *Gaboo-ninggi yinginybe?*
> What is your name?

To answer you would say:

> *Yinginybe-ngirri . . .*
> My name is . . .

For Gija people there is a lot of importance attached to saying people's names aloud. They talk about this using the coverb ***garij*** 'to say a name', which is usually combined with the transitive verb GET (see section 4.8.1.1). They ask questions about names using the interrogative word ***gaboo*** 'what action' (instead of 'what thing', as with the skin names), because ***garij*** (saying a name) is an action. Skin is seen as an integral part of the quality of the person. The saying of names is spoken about in a different way, treating it as an action.

(21) Ngoowana   garij   jimbimnhande   thamboorroombi.
     not   say name   you will be GETTING them son-in-law (of woman) mother-in-law-plural
     Don't go saying the names of people you call 'mother-in-law', 'mother-in-law's brother' (speaking to a man), or son-in-law (speaking to a woman).

(22) Ngaji-goorroom   ngoowan   garij   joowimnhande.
     sibling-your relations not   say name   you will be GETTING him/her
     Your siblings, don't say the name.

3.3.1. Ways of avoiding restricted names

In Gija there is no specific 'no-name' word (like the Central Australian ***kumuntjayi***) that is used in place of the name of a person who has died. Nevertheless, there are a number of ways that Gija people avoid producing names that they shouldn't say. These include using skin names and relationship terms. If the person with the tabooed name is married then a speaker might use the name of the spouse to invoke the married couple. So, if someone called George is married to Mary, and Mary is related to the speaker (who is male) as a sister, sister-in-law or mother-in-law, he can use the Kriol expression 'George doobala' to mean either 'George and his wife' or just 'George's wife'. In Gija he would refer to Mary by saying ***George ngidji-ngarri-berroowa***, 'George when he goes after them'. In Kimberley Kriol, a woman whose daughter is called Sylvia would talk about her daughter's husband, i.e. her son-in-law, as 'Sylvia doobala'. In Gija she could say ***Sylvia nyidja-ngarri-berroowa***, 'Sylvia when she goes after them' meaning 'Sylvia's husband' or 'Sylvia and her husband'.

3. GIJA SKIN NAMES AND RELATIONSHIP TERMS

If the person who is to be avoided is single the words **merlgabawoorrool** or **merlgabawoorroony** can be used to refer to that person. The context will tell the listener the person's identity.

The English words 'widow' and 'widower' are used to refer to people whose spouse has passed away. In Gija there are four words that are used to refer to people who have lost relations. These are listed in Table 8.

Table 8. Gija bereavement kinterms: terms used for people who have lost a relation

thoombawoony, thoombawool	person whose husband or wife has died (widower, widow)
ngamanyiny, ngamanyil	person whose parent, uncle or aunt has died
thalebany, thalebal	person whose child has died
yawoorroony, yawoorrool	person whose brother or sister has died

A more indirect way of referring to a person who has died is to use a verbal expression. Each of the terms in Table 8 have a corresponding coverb in Table 9. When the deceased person is known to both the speaker and the addressee one of these coverbs can be used. They are normally combined with the GO/COME verb (see section 4.8.1.2).

Table 9. Gija coverbs used to describe the state of being bereaved of a particular relative

thoombawoogboo	being a person whose husband or wife has died, widower/widow *coverb+GO/COME*
ngamanyigboo	being a person whose parent, uncle or aunt has died *coverb+GO/COME*
thalebagboo	being a person whose child has died *coverb+GO/COME*
yawoorroogboo	being a person whose brother or sister has died *coverb+GO/COME*

An example of the use of one of these coverbs can be seen in (23). The speaker is talking about a location on a steep road where a man had been killed many years previously in a car accident. One of the women in this conversation used to call the man who died 'brother'. In (23) the speaker addresses the woman in question, identifying the person spoken about as the brother who died.

(23) **Ngenengga yawoorroogboo-ngarriya nirda**
here   being a person whose sibling died   you (one) GO/COME

gendang   jambab-jen   Mabel Down   jambab.
from up there   jump-up-LOC   Mabel Downs   jump-up

This brother of yours who died coming down on the Mabel Downs Jump-up (an ascending track, part of the road that rises to a high point). LIT: 'here, where you go as a person with no brother, on the way down on the Mabel Downs Jump-up'.

3.3.2. Avoidance, respect and familiarity

There are four interjections in Table 10 that are produced as responses when someone hears the name of a deceased person. They are also produced by the listener when a speaker produces the name of a person in the context of swearing or obscenity. Gija people describe this as 'being sworn'. The hearer selects the relevant interjection based on the relationship the speaker has to the person who is sworn, or on the basis of the speaker's relationship to the person who has passed away. As well as being an interjection, **warri-warri** is also used in sentences as a euphemism for things that are indecent.

Table 10. Interjections produced upon hearing the names of people who have died, or upon hearing someone swear about their own relatives

warri-warri	when someone swears about their father, mother, uncle or aunt
yigelany	when someone swears about their brother, sister or grandparent (*thamany, ganggayi, gelagi, ngawooji*)
ngagoony	when someone swears about their brother-in-law or sister-in-law
a kissing noise, or two clicks	made when someone swears about their mother-in-law or son-in-law

Three of the interjections: **warri-warri**, **yigelany** and **ngagoony**, sound like regular Gija words. The fourth interjection, used when the speaker's **thamboorroo**, mother-in-law or son-in-law, has been sworn, is the least word-like. The person who hears this makes a kind of kissing noise with the lips, or goes 'tsk-tsk' with the tongue. They should also look away, make a hand sign to stop the speaker swearing and then move their hand up to block their ear, showing that the swearing should not be heard. The coverb **melera** means 'to speak using respect forms of language'. An example of the 'mother-in-law' respect style is the word the moon says when he is asked which woman he wants and he answers '*Dawiyan, dawiyan*', as in (24). This was a 'sideways' reference to **Dawool**, the 'black-headed python' who is his 'mother-in-law', according to the Gija skin system.

(24) **Melera** wanemayinde, '*Dawiyan dawiyan*'.
      speak respectfully   he was SAYING   black-headed python   black-headed python
      He was speaking sideways, saying, '*Dawiyan dawiyan*'.

Another respectful use of language is when a man addresses or speaks about his brother-in-law using the third person plural ('they') verb forms, even though he is talking about a single person, as in extract (25). This extract is from Hector Jandany's story of **Jalariny**, the 'white crane' or 'egret' and **Warrarnany**, the 'eaglehawk' or 'wedge-tailed eagle', which was recorded by Patrick McConvell. These two are the dreamings for the patrilineal moieties in some parts of the East Kimberley. They are 'brothers-in-law'. Another example of this respectful **melera** speech style can be found in Rusty Peters' story about **Gooroorroonggoony**, the nail-tailed wallaby, who is the brother-in-law of the moon (Peters 2014).

(25) '**Ngenengga-gili**   birriyanybeyi!   Roord   berrenbe   ngenengga
      here-towards   let them COME   sit   let them STAY   here

      berlag-ngarri   ngelama,   berarr-ngarri   noonayid,'   nginini   yagoorn.
      clean   I DID   sweep-where   I HIT them   he SAID   lie
      'Would they (you) be so kind as to come over and sit down here, where I have cleared an area for them (you)?' he said deceitfully.

Another example of euphemism to speak indirectly about a relation to be avoided is seen in the exchange from Rusty Peters' *Two laws: one big spirit* (2004) where his father refers to his future daughter-in-law as **merndam** 'paperbark'. The possible daughter-in-law is referred to as the third person plural, 'them' as respect language in **lamba-lambarra birrirn-ngirri,** 'she will be my daughter-in-law'.

3. GIJA SKIN NAMES AND RELATIONSHIP TERMS

Figure 14. Yalarrji Jack Britten and Patrick McConvell; Woorreranginy 1986. *Deg ngoorremenbe-yoo ngoorrngoorroo goorloom-boorroo.*

(26) **Ngaginyji ngaboony,   'Nawarran-ngoo na,   marra   biyarra**
mine-masc father-masc   big-LOC-you   then   go away you (one) should GO

gara   mernda-ba   joowijtha.'
later   paperbark-having you (one) will BECOME

My father said, 'Now you are grown up you should go somewhere and find something, you will become someone who has paperbark.'

Ngayindi   ngenani,   'Thoowoorra   merndambi?'
I/me   I SAID   what   paperbark-plural

I said, 'What do you mean by paperbark?'

'Wayina   ngoolngambi,'   wanemayinde.
like that spouse-plural   he was SAYING

'I'm talking about a wife,' he said.

Ngenani   ngayin,   'Thoowooba   merndambi?'
I SAID   I/me   what-having   paperbark-plural

I said, 'What's in the paperbark?'

'Dam ngenanyji   lamba-lambarra   birrirn-ngirri.'
that I do to him/her-bring/take-I   father-in-law/daughter-in-law   they will say/do-to me

'If you have a wife she will be my daughter-in-law.'

The opposite type of speech is the joking-swearing register which is appropriate for people who call each other **ganggayi**. A typical teasing exchange for two men in a **ganggayi** relationship is given in (27) where A says **goolyam ngardben-ngoo** to B, to which B replies by saying **ngarndam gajoowoom-birri**.

(27) A: **Goolyam   ngardbe-n-ngoo.**
testicles   smelly-LOC-you (one)
You have smelly balls.

B: **Ngarndam   gajoowoom-birri.**
semen   soft-to them
Soft semen.

3. GIJA SKIN NAMES AND RELATIONSHIP TERMS

If a person hearing this exchange happens to call one of the men **ngaboony** 'father', they should respond with something like the example in (28).

(28) **Warri-warri,**   **ngidiyi**   **ngaginyji**   **ngaboony**
response to swearing   let him STAY   my-masc   father-masc

goorlanggeny.
poor thing-masc
Warri-warri, leave my poor dad be.

Figure 15. Magany George Mung Mung, Gawoornel Buttercup Mung Mung and Rebecca Ramsey; Warrmarn 1988.

Figure 16. Yangganji Paddy Springvale, Dirrji Rusty Peters, Jaroonggarawoony Paddy Williams and Neil Carter; at Neil Carter's house in Halls Creek with the stone carving he had just completed, 1988.

3.4. The skins of Gija dreamtime animals

In the dreamtime the animals had human forms. The skin groups of these are shown in Table 11. This list was created a long time ago with the help of Hector Jandany, George Dingmayire, Paddy Williams Jaroonggarrawoony and Rusty Peters. Rusty Peters, Phyllis Thomas and Mabel Juli added to it in recent times. Many more skin names for plants and animals can be found in Purdie et al. (2018). Some of those are different from these listed here as the information came from many Gija people from all over Gija country.

Table 11. Skins of dreamtime animals

Jawan (Janama)	Nyawana	Joowoorroo (Joolama)	Nyawoorroo
gooroorroonggoony 'nail-tailed wallaby'	*gawoorrngarndil* 'female plains kangaroo' (mother of *jarlangarnany*)	*lalanggarrany* 'freshwater crocodile'	*wiyarrel*, *ngarabarral* or *garnanganyjel* 'emu'
yiroowoonji 'marsupial mouse'	*goonjal* 'kapok bush'	*garn'giny* 'moon'	*gernanyjel* 'echidna (porcupine)'
ngamarriny or *ngayirr-ngayirrji* 'sulphur-crested cockatoo (top-knot cocky)'	*Nyidbarriya* 'hill in Purnululu National Park'	*jigirridji* 'willie wagtail'	*barawool* 'female hill kangaroo' (mother of *jirrgany*)
binggoo-binggoony 'white-necked heron'		*dabaroony* 'pelican'	*birlirrijgel* 'peewee, magpie lark'
Jagarra	**Nagarra**	**Jawalyi**	**Nyaajarri**
jarlangarnany 'plains kangaroo'	*derranel* 'black cockatoo'	*marranyji* 'dingo'	*birn'girrbal* 'turkey'
garrang-garranginy 'diver jack, snake bird, darter'	*jigerrel* 'kingfisher'	*bayirrany* or *jalgirrigirriny* 'long tom or freshwater garfish'	*woorlemerewal* or *lawarrbal* 'long-necked turtle'
barnanggarny 'nightjar'	*jirliwoorril, mawoorroony thawalam-ni* 'flowers of bloodwood tree'	*gilbany* 'rasp-tailed goanna'	*goolyoolyool* 'budgerigar'
Joongoorra	**Naminyji**	**Jangala**	**Nangala**
wawooleny 'frillneck lizard'	*dayiwool* or *nyilibal* 'barramundi'	*wirrindiny* 'butcher bird'	*goorrarndal* 'brolga'
doomboony 'owl'	*gerliny-gerlinyel* 'galah'	*jangalangalany* type of ant	*nangala-nangalal* 'small sand frog'
warlenggenany 'water python'	*bijil* 'tree goanna'	*ginyany* 'white-necked heron, blue crane'	*loomoogool* 'blue-tongue lizard'
Jambin	**Nambin**	**Jaangari**	**Naangari**
jalariny 'egret (white crane)'	*wirndoowool* 'curlew'	*warrarnany* 'wedge-tailed eagle'	*wanggarnal* 'crow'
garnjalji 'fork-tailed kite (black kite)'	*dawool* 'black-headed python'	*jirrgany* 'hill kangaroo'	*booloogool* 'whistling kite (chicken hawk)'

3. GIJA SKIN NAMES AND RELATIONSHIP TERMS

Table 11 continued

Jambin	Nambin	Jaangari	Naangari
binyjirrminy 'insect-eating bat'	*wandawandal* 'whip snake'		
jambinbaroony or *garriyiny* 'bream'	*garriyil* 'black bream'		
joowijgarneny 'bowerbird'	*joogoorrool* 'bush orange'		
thirringgenji 'owlet nightjar'			
loonboorroony or *lan'gerrji* 'king brown snake'			

Figure 17. Jawan: *Jawanji dany ngamarriny deg ngerne.*

Figure 18. Nyawana: *Nyawanal dal ngarrgalel Nyidbarriya.*

Figure 19. Joowoorroo: *Garn'giny laarne nginji birrinyen dany Joowoorroony.*

Figure 20. Nyawoorroo: *Nyawoorrool dal garnanganyjel wiji nyerne.* (Photo: Sylvia Page)

3. GIJA SKIN NAMES AND RELATIONSHIP TERMS

Figure 21. Nyawana doo Jagarra: *Nyawanal dal gawoorrngarndil doo Jagarrany dany jarlangarnany.*

Figure 22. Nagarra: *Nagarral dal jirliwoorril thawalam-ni mawoorroony.*

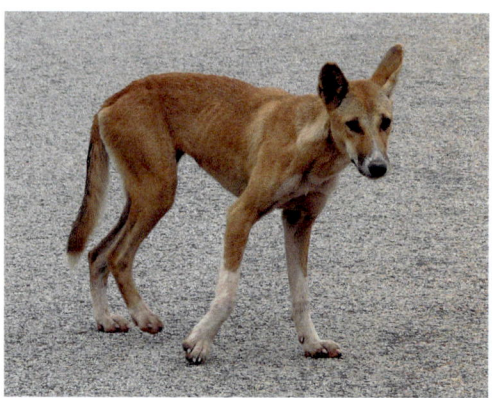

Figure 23. Jawalyi: *Jawalyiny dany marranyji joogboo ngidji miyale-boorroo.*

Figure 24. Nyaajarri. *Dal nyaajarril birn'girrbal girli wiyinya banane.*

Figure 25. Joongoorra: *Joongoorrany dany warlenggernany men'gawoony daa-wany ngininiyinde.*

Figure 26. Naminyji: *Naminyjilii-woorrarrem gerliny-gerlinybe laarne goowoolen.*

3. GIJA SKIN NAMES AND RELATIONSHIP TERMS

Figure 27. Jangala: *Jangalany dany wirrindiny ngalanygaleny.*

Figure 28. Nangala: *Nangala-warriny goorrarnda-warriny.*

Figure 29. Jambin: *Jambinji jalareny deg ngerne goorndarrim-boorroo.*

Figure 30. Nambin: *Nambinel dal dawool nyaloonggooj nyinya.*

Figure 31. Naangari doo Jaangari: *Jaangariny dany warrarnany jang ngerne miyale, dal wanggarnal ngaji-gal Naangaril mernji woomenyande boorrale-boorroo.* (Photo: Joe Blythe)

4. Gija word classes and grammar

The entries in the dictionary show Gija words belonging to the word classes listed here.

noun	adjective
pronoun	demonstrative
verb	coverb
adverb	temporal
locative	directional
interrogative	particle
interjection	

4.1. Gender and number

One of the notable things about Gija is the system of grammatical gender. This is an agreement system whereby adjectives, demonstratives, pronouns and interrogative words must agree in terms of gender with the nouns they specify (if there are nouns in the sentence), or must agree with the gender of the person or thing being spoken about when there are no nouns. Person marking on the verb is also on the basis of gender agreement.

Table 12. The three gender classes in Gija

Gender classes	What the categories include	Examples
masculine	singular masculine persons and things	*jiyiliny* 'man', *lalanggarrany* 'crocodile'
feminine	singular feminine persons and things	*ngalil* 'woman', *bindirijgel* 'water scorpion'
plural/non-singular	non-singular persons and things (masculine plural things, feminine plural things, neuter things, body parts, mass nouns)	*jiyilem* 'men', *lalanggarram* 'crocodiles', *ngalim* 'women', *bindirijgem* 'water scorpions', *goorloom* 'water', *joordoom* 'dust' *daam* 'country', *jaam* 'stomach'

There are three genders which we will call 'masculine', 'feminine' and 'plural/non-singular' (see Table 12). It is important to understand that these are really just labels for the three categories listed in Table 12. What we are calling 'masculine' and 'feminine' should really be understood as 'masculine singular' and 'feminine singular'. What could be called 'plural' is better understood as 'non-singular' because this category includes not only plural things (like men, women, crocodiles and water scorpions) but also things like water and dust that can't easily be counted. Body parts when attached to a body are always 'non-singular'. There is gender agreement with prefixes and suffixes to verbs and also with demonstratives, pronouns and interrogatives asking about nouns. In the dictionary these are translated as this/that (masculine/feminine/non-singular), it (masculine/feminine/non-singular) and what (masculine/feminine/non-singular).

4. GIJA WORD CLASSES AND GRAMMAR

All nouns in the language belong to one of these three gender classes. Suffixes indicate the gender. There are different gender suffixes depending on the final sound of the noun stem, as shown in Table 13. The variant vowels in the feminine forms (*-il, -el, -ool*) and plural forms (*-be, -boo, -e* and *-oo*) tend to harmonise with the preceding vowel of the stem.

Table 13. Gija gender suffixes

Stem ending	Masculine	Feminine	Plural/Non-singular
vowel	*-ny*	*-l*	*-m*
stop or nasal	*-ji*	*-il, -el, -ool*	*-be, -boo*
l, rl or *rr*	*-ji*	*-il, -el, -ool*	*-e, -oo*

Some examples of the different genders of Gija nouns are shown in Table 14. All living things are either masculine or feminine. Male persons always take masculine gender and female persons always take feminine gender, provided they are singular. Animals and plants are regarded as having been men and women in the dreamtime and their genders reflect their dreaming status as either men or women. A crocodile is masculine because **lalanggarrany** was a man and the black-headed python is feminine because **dawool** was a woman. Many kinterms can be either masculine or feminine, depending on whether they are referring to a male or female person.

Table 14. Gija nouns of different genders

Masculine	Feminine	Plural/Non-singular
jiyili-ny 'man'		*jiyile-m* 'men',
	ngali-l 'woman'	*ngali-m* 'women', *ngali-ngali-m* 'many women'
lalanggarra-ny 'freshwater crocodile'		*lalanggarra-m* 'freshwater crocodiles'
	dawool 'black-headed python'	*dawoo-m* 'black-headed pythons'
thamany-ji 'mother's father', 'a man's daughter's son', 'a woman's brother's daughter's son'	*thamany-el* 'mother's father's sister', 'a man's daughter's daughter', 'a woman's brother's daughter's daughter'	*thamany-be* 'mother's father and his siblings', 'a man's daughter's children', 'a woman's brother's daughter's children'
gangga-ny 'mother's mother's brother', 'a woman's daughter's son', 'a man's sister's daughter's son'	*gangga-l* 'mother's mother', 'mother's mother's sister', 'a woman's daughter's daughter', 'a man's sister's daughter's daughter'	*gangga-m* 'mother's mother and her siblings', 'a woman's daughter's children', 'a man's sister's daughter's children'
		moorl-oo 'eye', 'eyes'
		yambarra-m 'hair', 'hairs'
miyal-ji 'a masculine animal that can be eaten'	*miyal-el* 'a feminine animal that can be eaten'	*miyal-e* 'meat'
mayi-ny 'a masculine plant bearing an edible part', 'the edible part of a masculine plant'	*mayi-l* 'a feminine plant bearing an edible part', 'the edible part of a feminine plant'	*mayi-m* 'non-meat food', 'vegetable food', 'bread'
waloorr-ji 'a specific hot wind'		*waloorr-oo* 'hot wind', 'hot winds'
	warda-l 'star'	*warda-m* 'stars'
ngoomool-ji 'a specific cloud'		*ngoomool-oo* 'cloud', 'clouds'

Plural number of living things is shown through the use of the plural gender suffixes. A larger number can be indicated by reduplicating (REDUP) the stem (e.g. 'women' **ngali-m**, 'lots of women' **ngali-ngali-m**). Body parts of living things always take the 'plural' suffixes, even when a single body part is spoken about (e.g. **moorloo** is both 'eye' and 'eyes'). Mass nouns such as 'water', **goorloom** or **goorrngam**, 'fire and firewood', **marnem** and 'dust', **joordoom** are really neither singular nor plural, but they take the 'plural' gender suffixes. Many natural phenomena like the 'sky' **birrinybe,** and 'cloud' **ngoomooloo** are also technically 'non-singular' so they take the 'plural' gender. Similarly, 'bush honey' **ngarem**, 'meat' **miyale** and 'non-meat food' **mayim** are generic mass nouns taking the 'plural' gender suffixes. However, most of the above items have also been recorded as singular masculine or feminine nouns in particular circumstances. The general words for water, **goorloom** or **goorrngam**, change to the masculine singular **goorloony** or **goorrngany** if someone is talking about a particular water place. Specific foods from particular species can be gendered masculine or feminine depending on the gender of the species. Body parts that are removed from the body usually take the gender of the entity from which they were removed.

New words that speak about things that have been introduced since the arrival of white people often take feminine gender. For example, the usual citation form for the word for 'fire' or 'firewood' is **marnem**. A particular fire can be masculine singular **marneny**. However, 'dynamite', which is recently introduced, takes the feminine form **marnel**. Similarly, 'a flat coolamon' **larndoorrji** is masculine. However, the feminine form **larndoorrool** has been adapted to mean 'boat' or 'truck with a tray back', both of which are somewhat similar to the shape of a coolamon.

The mother tongue of many younger Gija people is Kimberley Kriol. When Gija people use Gija nouns in Kriol these sounds usually use only the bare stems, leaving off the gender markers. For example, they might say **goorloo** or **goorrnga** for 'water', instead of **goorloom** or **goorngam**, or they might say **goowoole** or **goonyja** for 'tree/plant/stick' instead of **goowoolem** or **goonyjam**. Fluent Gija speakers frequently codeswitch between Gija and Kriol. In Kriol sentences they tend to drop the gender markers from Gija words but in Gija sentences they are always retained. They also tend to leave off the gender markers when using Kriol to translate or explain Gija words and sentences.

When nouns end with an **l** or **ny** it can be difficult to determine whether they are part of the stem or whether they are the feminine or masculine gender suffixes. In these cases, it is useful to know the plural forms of these nouns. Noun stems ending in **l** take the plural suffixes **-e** or **-oo** and noun stems ending in **-ny** take the plural suffixes **-be** or **-boo**, whereas stems ending in vowels take the plural suffix **-m**. Where the plural or non-singular form has been recorded, these are listed as part of the dictionary entry.

4.2. Nouns and adjectives

Nouns are words that name people, places and things. Adjectives describe the properties or qualities of people, places and things. In some Australian Aboriginal languages, there is no grammatical difference between nouns and adjectives but in Gija the gender system makes it necessary to establish these as separate word classes. Adjectives have no inherent gender. Adjectives must agree with the gender of the entities they describe, taking the same suffixes as the noun stems and following the same sound rules described above in Table 13. In the dictionary, the three different gender forms are shown for each adjective (masculine, feminine and plural).

jarlboorrji, jarlboorrel, jarlboorroo	*adjective* 'blind'
merlarnji, merlarnel, merlarnbe	*adjective* 'mad'
nawarrany, nawarral, nawarram redup: *nawarrarram*	*adjective* 'big', 'many', 'important'

In English adjectives cannot stand alone without a noun. Gija adjectives can occur without a corresponding noun. If the above adjectives were to stand alone, they could be translated as 'the male blind one', 'the female blind one', 'the blind ones'; 'the mad man', 'the mad woman', 'the mad people; 'the big male one', the big female one', 'the big ones'.

Typically, a referent is introduced with a noun (or a noun phrase) and from there on a gender-marked adjective is sufficient for subsequent references. In the first line of (29) two dogs are introduced. The stem ***joola-*** 'dog' only appears once. The following adjectives ***nawarrany*** and ***wanyageny*** are understood to be referring to the dogs.

(29) **Joola-warriny   loorroob   ngoorrayidbi-yoo,   nawarra-ny,   wanyage-ny.**
dog-two   chase   they HIT him-two   big-masc   little-masc
Two dogs were chasing him, a big male one, a little male one.

Nawarra-ny   werd   nginiyidji,
big-masc   bite   he HIT him
The big male one bit him.

wanyage-ny   menhang   nginimanyji.
little-masc   lick   he GOT him
The little male one licked him.

If a dog is female it could be referred to as ***nawarral*** 'the big female one'.

(30) **Joola-warriny   loorroob   ngoorrayidbi-yoo,   nawarra-l,   wanyage-ny.**
dog-two   chase   they HIT him-two   big-fem   little-masc
Two dogs were chasing him, a big female one, a little male one.

Nawarra-l   werd   nginiyidja,
big-fem   bite   she HIT him
The big female one bit him.

wanyage-ny   menhang   nginimanyji.
little-masc   lick   he GOT him
The little male one licked him.

4.2.1. Suffixes that express place and time

As discussed later in section 4.4, the same suffixes are used to express both position in space and position in time and these are referred to as the **locative** (LOC). The **locative** suffix attaches to nouns, adjectives, demonstratives and possessive pronouns. It indicates the location of a person or thing. It can be translated as 'in', 'at', 'on', 'near' or 'the place of'. It can also indicate a point or period of time ('in the time of'). The locative replaces any gender suffixes. The form of the locative changes according to the last sound of the stem, as shown in Table 15. The forms in the last two rows (*-jin*, *-jen*; *-nyin*, *-nyen*) mostly attach to introduced words from English.

4. GIJA WORD CLASSES AND GRAMMAR

Table 15. Gija locative suffixes

Stem ending	Locative	Examples
vowels	-n	*goowoole-n* 'in, on, at the tree/stick/branch' *warn'ga-n* 'in a cold place', 'in the cold time'
n, rn	-e	*nawane* 'in the cave/hole' *bilirn-e* 'in, on, at the river red gum'
l, rl, rr	-e, -oo	*werrgal-e* 'on the grass'
b, d, g, j	-jen, -jin	*Walgrig-jin* 'in Halls Creek'
m, ng	-nyen, -nyin	*Broom-nyen* 'in Broome'

The locative is used to form place names from common nouns and adjectives, e.g. **barnanggany** 'nightjar', **Barnanggan** 'the place of the night jar'; **garn'geny** 'moon', **Garn'gen** 'the place of the moon'. Most place names in the dictionary include this suffix. There are also a number of locative words that use this suffix, such as **banbinan** 'a clear way through' and **garn'girrayijirran** 'in the moonlight'.

There are also other functions of the locative. As we saw in section 3.1, the locative suffix can be used, in combination with the benefactive pronominal enclitics (see section 4.7.3), to mean 'am' or 'are' in verbless statements. These are especially attached to adjective stems, as in (31) and (32).

(31) **Babinyi-n-ngoo.**
fighter-LOC-you (one)
You (one) are a fighter.

(32) **Goorninya-n-nga.**
hungry-LOC-I/me
I am hungry.

The same suffix can also indicate that someone or something is being spoken to directly, as in *joolan* 'you dogs!', as in (33).

(33) **Nag   barriyi   joola-n!**
be quiet   you all GO   dog-LOC
You dogs be quiet!

Figure 32. Jandany Hector: *Jandany roord nginji. Danya doomboony nyoon nginimanyji gooma nhawoon.*

4. GIJA WORD CLASSES AND GRAMMAR

Figure 33. Joomena Eileen Bray and Frances Kofod holding Sonia Bray, Osmond Creek 1988: *Gooloongarri-minyin yirraniyin-ngarri-yoo*. (Photo: Rusty Peters)

There are other suffixes relating to place and time in Table 16. Like the locative, they occur in the same position as the gender suffixes, which they replace. One of these, **-wirrin**, attaches to both nouns and coverbs. The suffix **-gan** attaches to coverbs to form temporal adverbials.

Table 16. Nominal suffixes of place and time

-yoorroong	allative: 'towards', 'into', 'onto'	*Jarrg nginewardji goorloo-yoorroong.* 'He jumped down into the water.' *Jany benem gardag-yoorroong.* 'Squeeze it into the cup.'
-biny	ablative: 'from'	*Rerr nyanemanyji goorloo-biny.* 'He pulled it (feminine) from the water.'
-wirrin	'habitual location'	*daa-wirrin* 'habitual camping place, living area in country' *Ngarranggarniny goorloony yilag, goorndarri-wirrinji.* '(There is) a dreamtime waterhole down there, a frequent fishing place.' *boorooj-wirrin* 'playground'
-yirrin	'collective location' ('in all the . . .')	*jamernde-yirrin* 'in all the termite mounds (antbeds)' *garndi-yirrin* 'in all the roots'
-minyin	'period of time'	*warramba-minyin* 'at the time of the flood' *ngarranggarni-minyin* 'in dreamtime'
-joolan	'period of time'	*wanyage-joolan* 'when small', 'when a child'
-gen	'season'	*jada-gen* 'in the time of rain, wet season' *marli-gen* 'in the time of cane grass' (when the 'knock-em down' rains flatten the grasses but the cane grass grows)
-gan	'when verb-ing'	*wanda-wandajgan* 'when carrying' *bawoo-wawoo-gan* 'when calling out' *jang-gan* 'when eating/eaten'

4. GIJA WORD CLASSES AND GRAMMAR

Another suffix **-gili** 'towards' attaches only to the locative suffix or to spatial demonstratives like **ngoorroon** (34) or to temporal adverbials like **gerag** in (35).

(34) **Ngoorroon-gili   yindegbany-yarri-yoo   mayaroo-n-gili   mayim-boorroo.**
there-toward   you TAKE us two   house-LOC-towards food-for
You (one) take us two there to the shop for food.

(35) **Marrge,   gerag-gili   berrenbe-gala.**
wait   later-towards   let it STAY-imperative
Wait, let it stay for later.

4.2.2. Other nominal suffixes

There are many other suffixes to nouns and adjectives in Gija. Some of these follow the stem but precede the gender suffix. There are some that replace the gender suffix and there are others that are added after the gender suffix.

The intensifying suffixes **-jiya**, **-iya**, **-ya**, **-aya** follow the stem and precede the gender or locative suffix. These suffixes are based on the adjective **yijiyam** 'true'. Examples include **men'gawoo-ny** 'good (masculine)', **men'gawoo-jiya-ny** 'really good (masculine)'; **daa-n** 'in the country', 'at home', **daa-ya-n** 'really in the country', 'right at home'. It can also attach to coverbs where it means 'do the action properly', for example, **deg** 'to look', **deg-ijiya** 'to look properly'.

The suffixes in Table 17 are attached to the stem and are followed by gender or locative suffixes.

Table 17. Nominal suffixes that precede the gender suffix

-ba	'having'	A tree with fruit may be described as 'fruit/food having', *mayi-bany* or *mayi-bal*, depending on the gender of the tree. *goorloo-ban* 'a place having water'
-woorroo	'not', 'negative' (attaches mainly to adjectives)	*men'gawoo-woorroony*, *men'gawoo-woorrool* 'not good' *binarri-woorroony*, *binarri-woorrool* 'not knowing'
-ba-woorroo	'not having' (combines *-ba* 'having' with *-woorroo* 'negative')	*mayi-bawoorroony*, *mayi-bawoorrool* 'having no fruit/food' *goorloo-bawoorroon* 'a place having no water'
-moowa	'only'	*daliny-moowam* 'only catfish' *Marloogany Joola-moowany* 'only Old Dog (name of the dog)'
-gi	'large body part' (the gender agrees with the possessor of the body part; with certain body parts this can be swearing)	*yambarra-giny* 'a male with big hair' *yambarra-gil* 'a female with big hair'
-ja	'similar to'	*ngamarra-jany* 'thing like a snake', *goorrarnda-jal* 'thing like a brolga'
-ngoowi	'resembling', 'similar to'	*dany wajbaloo-ngoowiny banariny, ngoowan dany jiyile-ngoowiny* 'like that white people's potato, not like that Aboriginal people's bush potato'
-joorroo	'little ones', 'little bit'	*wanyagi-joorroony*, *wanyagi-joorrool* 'a bit smaller' *wanyagi-joorroom yindiyinnha* 'give me a little bit'

4. GIJA WORD CLASSES AND GRAMMAR

Table 17 continued

-bebe	'a bit' (when attached to adjectives the gender suffix follows; also attaches to coverbs — without a gender suffix)	*nawarra-bebeny, nawarra-bebel, nawarra-bebem* 'a bit bigger' *Nawarra-bebe benajtha-nga.* 'Put one bit bigger for me.' *Wethed-bebe benayidjende.* 'He kept throwing them down for a bit.'
-mili	'originating from' (attaches only to locative, demonstrative and directional words)	*Warlawoon-miliny, Warlawoon-milil* 'person from the place called Warlawoon' *ngenengga-miliny, ngenengga-milil* 'person from here'
-ngarna	'denizen of', 'dweller'	*goorloo-ngarnany, goorloo-ngarnal, goorloo-ngarnam* 'something that lives/belongs in the water'

The topic, focus and emphatic suffixes **-bi, -i, -a, -da, -di, -ga** and **-wa** follow the gender suffixes.

The suffixes in Table 18 replace the gender or locative suffixes. They are always in the last position after a nominal.

Table 18. Nominal suffixes that replace the gender suffix

-baya	'by means of', 'with' (combines *-ba* 'having' with the intensifier *-ya*)	*ngoorrngoorrgaji-baya* 'by car' *joola-baya* 'with a dog'
-jaya	'similar to' (attaches to noun stems and coverbs)	*ngamarra-jaya* 'acting like a snake' *ngare-jaya* 'tasting sweet like honey'
-geny	purposive: 'for' (attaches to noun stems)	*mayi-geny* 'for vegetable food, for bread' *miyal-geny* 'for meat' *goorndarri-geny* 'for fish'

The two suffixes in Table 19 only ever follow the plural gender suffix (**-m**, **-be**, **-e** or **-oo**).

Table 19. Nominal suffixes that follow the plural gender suffix

-boorroo	purposive: 'for'	*mayi-m-boorroo* 'for vegetable food, for bread' *miyal-e-boorroo* 'for meat' *goorndarri-m-boorroo* 'for fish' *ngawoony-be-boorroo* 'for pencil yams'
-birri	instrumental: 'with, using'	*nawoole-m-birri* 'with a nulla-nulla' *goorloo-m-birri* 'with water'

4. GIJA WORD CLASSES AND GRAMMAR

4.2.3. Making new nouns

There are a number of suffixes in Table 20 that are used to make new nouns from coverbs, some of which also attach to noun stems. The suffixes are always followed by the gender suffixes.

Table 20. Suffixes used to form new nouns

Form	Meaning	Examples
-gaji, -waji	'used for' (often used to create neologisms)	*ngoorrngoorr-gajil, ngoorrngoorr-gajim, ngoorr-ngoorrwajil* 'growl-used for' i.e. 'engines, cars' *gerrbij-gajiny* 'cut up-used for', 'knife'
-gale, -gali	'good at'	*ngalany-galeny, ngalany-galel, ngalany-galem* 'good singer' *mernmerd-galeny, mernmerd-galel, mernmerd-galem* 'good at tying up' (i.e. 'police') *mayi-galeny, mayi-galel, mayi-galem* 'someone good at cooking', 'a plant that bears lots of fruit/food'
-gale-woorroo	'not good at' (combines *-gale* 'good at' with *-woorroo* 'negative')	*ngalany-gale-woorroony, ngalany-gale-woorrool, ngalany-gale-woorroom* 'no good at singing'
-girri, -girre	purposive: 'for doing . . .' (most frequently used with coverbs with the non-singular *-m* suffix to form gerunds; occasionally used to form nominals)	*ngoorrngoorr-girrel* 'growl-purposive' (i.e. 'car') *bagoo-girrem* 'lie down-purposive' (i.e. 'couch')
-girri-woorroo	'someone who can't do something, something not used for/not useful for' (combines *-girri* 'for doing' with *-woorroo* 'negative')	*girli-girri-woorroony* 'a man who can't walk around' *rangga-girri-woorrool* 'a woman who can't listen'
-nge, -ngi, -ngoo	'that kind' (often added to skin names; see Table 4, section 3.1)	*deberrnginy, deberrngel, deberrngem* 'broken one'
-nhawoo, -thawoo	'habitual doer'	*jang-nhawoony, jang-nhawool, jang-nhawoom* 'someone who is always eating' *ngoorloorloog-thawoony, ngoorloorloog-thawool, ngoorloorloog-thawoom* 'someone who is always drinking'
-wanggoo	'belonging to a place, born at a place'	*ngenengga-wanggoom* 'the people from here'

4. GIJA WORD CLASSES AND GRAMMAR

4.3. Numerals, quantifiers and number suffixes

In Gija there are numerals that correspond to 'one', 'two' and 'three'. The numeral 'one' agrees with the gender of the referent, like an adjective. There are variant forms for 'one' in the corpus. The most frequently used are ***jirrawoony***, ***jirrawool*** and ***jirrawoom***. Alternate forms for 'one' include ***jirrawoogoony***, ***jirrawoogool*** and ***jirrawoogoom***, as well as ***jirrawoonginy***, ***jirrawoongil*** and ***jirrawoongim***. The reduplicated form ***jirra-jirrawoom*** is used to mean 'a few'.

The numeral word for 'two' is ***bangariny***. The final ***ny*** is part of the stem, not the masculine suffix. Gija sentences including the word ***bangariny*** 'two' nearly always bear the nominal dual suffix ***-warriny*** in addition to the numeral, as we can see in (36). The previous examples (29) and (30) demonstrate that the dual suffix ***-warriny*** is sufficient to give the meaning of 'two'. We don't really need the numeral ***bangariny***. Often, however, dual marking occurs in several places in a sentence, including on the verb. In (36) we see a form of the dual suffix ***-yoo/-joo/-doo*** attached to the verb, two tokens of the nominal dual suffix ***-warriny***, one which is attached to the numeral ***bangariny***.

(36) **Dam   bangariny-warriny   joomooloo-warriny   boorroonboo-yoo**
     those   two-two   boab tree-two   they stay-two

   ngoorroo-n   goorloowoorr.
   there-LOC   up
   Those two boab trees are up over there.

The numeral for 'three' has a number of variants, some of which incorporate plural gender suffixes: ***merrgern***, ***merrgernbe***, ***merrgernbem***, ***moorrgoorn***, ***moorrgoornboo***.

There are four different adjective stems, ***waringarri-***, ***melagawoo-***, ***garawirri-*** and ***yiwirrirri-*** that are used to mean 'many' or 'all'. The words ***waringarrim*** and ***melagawoom*** are the most frequently used. The reduplicated form ***melelagawoom*** means 'very many'. The stems ***waringarri-*** and ***melagawoo-*** occur with masculine or feminine singular suffixes to mean 'plentiful'. The masculine and feminine forms agree in gender with the entity to which they refer. For example, in (37) both ***melagawoony*** and ***thawalany*** (flower) agree with snappy gum (***thalngarrji***), which is masculine.

Figure 34. Rover Thomas and Joonbany Bob Nyalcas. *Bangariny ngalany-gale-warriny roord boorroonboo-yoo.* (Photo: Ted Beard)

4. GIJA WORD CLASSES AND GRAMMAR

(37) **Doorloorloog   ngiyinji   thawala-ny   melagawoo-ny**
come out   he HITS it   flower-masc   plentiful-masc
Many (snappy gum) flowers come out (at that time).

The intensified forms **waringarriya**, **melagawiya** and **melaya** are used meaning 'all, the whole lot' as in examples (38) and (39).

(38) **Yirrinji-ngarri   ngenengga,   waringarriya**
we are SITTING-when   here   all

jarrag   yirriyande   Gija-moowa-m.
speak   we will be COMING/GOING   Gija language-only-plural
When we sit here, we will all be speaking only Gija.

(39) **Nyirreg-gala   barrawoo-gili   melagawiya.**
dive in-imperative   you (plural) GO DOWN-plural   whole lot.
You all dive in the water, the whole lot of you!

There are a number of collective suffixes used to talk about different kinds of groups, as shown in Table 21.

Table 21. Collective suffixes for referring to groups

-ngarrim, -ngarrem	'all that kind' (used when giving a list of participants in an event)	*Dambi dabaroony-ngarrimbi dambi ginyany-ngarrimbi; galba-galbany-ngarrimbi* . . . 'Those pelicans and all that kind, those cranes and that kind, spoonbills and that kind . . .'
-wanem	'that kind together' (relations, group of humans)	*ngaji-wanem* 'all the brothers/sisters' *warnarre-wanem* 'all the people from long ago', 'all the old people'
-woorrarrem, redup: -woorrarrerrarrem.	'all, all kinds of'	*gangga-woorrarrem* 'all the maternal grandmothers/grandchildren and siblings' *thawala-woorrarrem* 'all kinds of flowers' *warda-woorrarrem* 'all the stars'
-balengem	'all who do' (attaches to coverbs)	*bawoo-balengem* 'people who call out' *joogboo-balengem* 'people who go hunting'
-ba-yilim, -ba-yiliny, -ba-yilil	'having all'	*wirnbel ngarnbe-ngiyi bagaba-yilil* 'the things belonging to pandanus (leaves) are all prickly' *merrji-ba-yilim goorndoorndoogam* 'the children all have boils'
-ba-woorroo-yilim	'all those not having'	*Yinggili-ba-woorroo-yilim* 'all the people without English' (people who don't speak English)
-ba-yilin	'at all those having'	*werlwe-ba-yilin* 'at all the places with dreaming sites'
-ga-yilim	'all his/her/their relations' (attaches to relationship terms)	*goora-ga-yilim* 'all his/her/their mothers' *jaliji-ga-yilim* 'all his/her/their friends'
-merrale, -merrarre	'in all that kind'	*nyiyirri-merrale* 'in all the spinifex' *wirnbe-merrale* 'in all the pandanus'

In verbless sentences a range of suffixes may combine with the locative, which is then followed by an enclitic pronoun, as in (40).

(40) Moojoongbi-yili-n-jaya-nonggoorroo   jarrag-ba-woorroo-n-noonggoo.
      shy-all-LOC-like that-for you all   speak/word-having-negative-LOC-for you all
      You lot are all the same, too shy, you can't talk.

4.4. Time and place in Gija – locatives, temporals and directionals

4.4.1. Locatives and temporals

Locative and temporal words tell us where or when an action takes place. Some Gija words refer to both time and place. For example, **welangen** or **woolangen** mean 'before' (in time), 'already' or 'previously'; but they also mean 'in front' or 'ahead' (of you, me, it, etc.). Similarly, **bardoon** means 'later', 'after' or 'afterward', but it also means 'behind' (you, me, it, etc.). Related to **bardoon**, the adjective **bardoongeny**, **bardoongel**, **bardoongem** means 'the person or thing that comes after/last'. So **bardoongeny** or **bardoongel** might be 'the youngest child', while **bardoongem** might be 'the new generation'.

Locative and temporal words can be derived from nouns and adjectives by the addition of a locative or temporal suffix. For example, **warn'gany**, **warn'gal**, **warn'gam** 'cold' becomes **warn'gan**

Figure 35. Gajoowoodany Patrick Mung Mung, Warrmarn 2010: *Yilangbiny girli wiyinji ngalany-ngarri ngerne wanggarnal-ngooyoo.*

'in the cold season' with the locative suffix **-n**. In the right context this could also mean 'in/at a cold place'.

4.4.2. Directionals

The four cardinal directions corresponding to 'north', 'south', 'east' or 'west' are listed in Table 22. The base direction names imply direction towards. There are additional forms for 'towards' as well as others indicating motion from or location at the cardinal directions. Gija country is rather hilly with lots of rivers and creeks. There are terms used for the sagittal directions 'up' and 'down', which are also used for 'uphill' or 'downhill', and there are also terms relating to directions of river flow. These terms can also be modified to indicate directions of motion or location, as in Table 23.

Table 22. Gija cardinal directions

Direction names	*boowoorr* 'north'	*ngela* 'east'	*nyoowool* 'south'	*gerliyirr* 'west'
allative (towards)	*boowoorroogoo, boowoorryoorroong* 'to the north'	*ngelamoogoo, ngelayoorroong* 'to the east'	*nyoowooloogoo, nyoowoolyoorroong* 'to the south'	*gerlirroogoo, gerliyirryoorroong* 'to the west'
further onwards	*boowoorrgoorloorr* 'further north'	*ngelagoorloorr* 'further east'	*nyoowoolgoorloorr* 'further south'	*gerliyirrgoorloorr* 'further west'
ablative (coming from)	*biyoorroong* 'from the north'	*ngelmang* 'from the east'	*ngerig* 'from the south'	*gerlirrang* 'from the west'
locative (in/at)	*biyirrin* 'in the north'	*ngelmin* 'in the east'	*ngerijin* 'in the south'	*gerlirrin* 'in the west'

Table 23. Gija topographical directions

Direction names	*gerloowoorr* 'up, uphill'	*yilag* 'down, downhill', 'down to water'	*gendoowa* 'upstream'	*yoorloo* 'downstream'
allative (towards)	*gerloowoorroogoo* 'upward'	*yilangoogoo* 'downward'	*gendoowagoo* 'to upstream'	*yoorloongoogoo* 'to downstream'
further onwards	*gerloowoorroojarriny* 'further up'	*yilagjarriny* 'further down'	*gendoowajarriny* 'further upstream'	*yoorloongoojarriny* 'further downstream'
ablative (from)	*gerloowoorrng* 'from up there'	*yilang, yilangbiny* 'from down there'	*gendang* 'from upstream'	*loonggoong* 'from downstream'
locative (in/at)	*laarne* 'on top'	*yiligin* 'under/ underneath', 'inside'	*gaande* 'there upstream'	*loowoongoo* 'there downstream'

4.5. Asking questions in Gija

The two main types of questions are polar questions and content questions. Polar questions are sometimes called 'yes/no' questions because the normal ways to respond to them are with the equivalents of 'yes' or 'no'. Content questions expect lexical responses such as names, phrases or sentences. They are built around content interrogative words such as 'where', 'who', 'what', 'why'.

4.5.1. Polar questions

4.5.1.1 The interrogative *'Garninya'*

The question word **garninya** is often translated into Kimberley Kriol as, 'What now?'. However, it is frequently used as a polar interrogative for requests. **Garninya** is more accurately translated as 'Are there any?' or 'Is there any?' As such, it expects a 'yes/no' answer, as the response from B to A's request in (41) demonstrates.

(41) A: Garninya   boorrale?
           is there any   substantial meal
           Is there anything to eat?
      B: Ngoowan.   Ngoowangarnan-yarre.
           no   nothing-for us
           No. We haven't got anything.

Garninya is also used as a greeting. The standard response to this greeting is **ngoowangarnan** 'nothing'. The content questions **gaboowa**, **gaba** and **thoowoorra** can also be used as greetings (see section 4.5.2).

4.5.1.2. The polar interrogative *-ma/-ba*

Polar questions can also be asked using the polar interrogative clitics **-ma** and **-ba**. These usually attach to the first word or first phrase in the sentence. They create questions that invite a 'yes' or a 'no' answer. They are frequently used in verbless questions that are built around adjectives. In example (42) the adjective **jirraya-** 'alright' is followed by the locative suffix **-n**, the polar interrogative **-ma**, and the benefactive pronominal **-ngoo** 'for you' (see section 4.7.3).

(42) Jirraya-n-ma-ngoo?
      alright-LOC-question-you (one)
      Are you alright?

A positive response is shown in example (43).

(43) Ngiyi.   Jirraya-n-nga.
      yes   alright-LOC-I/me
      Yes. I am alright.

The polar interrogative clitics can attach to inflecting verbs, as seen in examples (44) and (45).

(44) Joowangnha-ma   ngabayi?
      you (one) EAT it-question   dad
      Dad, do you want to eat?

4. GIJA WORD CLASSES AND GRAMMAR

(45) **Joonoomoorloonnha-ma   jarragbiyi?**
you (one) HAVE it-question   language/word/story
Do you have language? Do you have a story? Do you have something to say?

In coverb–inflecting verb compounds (see section 4.8), they generally attach to the coverb, as with **marrarn** 'go away' in (46), and with **rangga** 'hear, listen' in (47).

(46) **Marrarn-ma   nirda?**
go away-question   you (one) COME/GO
Are you going away?

(47) **Rangga-ma   yiniyinnha?**
hear/listen-question   you (one) bring me/TAKE me
Can you hear me?

Following a stop sound (**b, d, j, g**) the form **-ba** is sometimes used, as in (48).

(48) **Yalawoog-ba   jarrema?**
get a lot-question   you (plural) GOT
Did you all get a big lot?

The polar interrogative usually attaches to the first element of the sentence, regardless of the word class. In (49) it is attached to the directional word **gerlirroogoo** 'to the west'.

(49) **Gerlirroogoo-ma   berdij   yarrayan?**
to the west-question   climb   we all will COME/GO
Will we all climb up to the west?

It can also be attached to **ngiyi** 'yes' where it produces a question tag **Ngiyi-ma**? 'Is that right?'

4.5.2. Content questions

Gija has content question interrogatives (like 'who', 'where', 'what', etc.) that are normally the first word in the question. If the question enquires about a person or a thing, these interrogatives agree in terms of gender with the entity being asked about. However, if the gender is unknown the plural form is used. They also have forms for asking about you (one) or you (plural). Some of the interrogatives have different forms in the Southern dialect. In fact, a number of Gija speakers have their own personal variants of these words.

4.5.2.1. 'Who?'

Gender-specific question words for asking 'Who?' about people are shown in Table 24.

Table 24. Who?

Yangirni?	'Who is he?'
Yangela?	'Who is she?'
Yangoorra?	'Who are they?', 'Who is it?' (gender unknown)
Yangoo-nha-ngoo?	'Who are you (one)?'
Yangoo-nha-noonggerroo?	'Who are you (plural)?'

4.5.2.2. 'What (thing)?'

Words for asking 'what' about things are shown in Table 25. There are two dialectal versions of this interrogative. These question words are also used to ask people about their skin (see section 3.1).

Table 25. 'What thing?'

Northern dialect	Southern dialect	Meaning
Thini? Thiniwa?	Thoowoonginy?	'What masculine thing?'
Thengela?	Thoowoongela?	'What feminine thing?'
Thoowoo? Thoowi? Thoowoorra?	Thoowoongoom?	'What things?', 'What kind of thing/s (unknown gender)?'
Thininge-nha-ngoo? Thoowoo-nha-ngoo?	Thoowoonge-nha-ngoo?	'What are you?'
Thoowoo-nha-noonggerroo?	Thoowoonge-nha-noonggerroo?	'What are you (plural)?'

The plural forms for 'what', ***thoowoo*** and ***thoowoorra***, can be used to derive other questions using ***-boorroo*** 'purposive', ***-berra*** 'from them', ***-ba*** 'having', ***-girriny*** 'for' as in Table 26.

Table 26. Content question words derived from *thoowoo/thoowoorra* 'what'

Thoowoo-boorroo, thoowoorra-boorroo	'Why?', 'For what purpose?'
Thoowoo-berra, thoo-berra	'Why?', 'From what?', 'Because of what?'
Thoowoo-ba	'Having what?', 'With what?'
Thoowoo-girriny	'For doing what?'

4.5.2.3. 'What (action)?'

The question words ***gaboo*** and ***gaboowa*** are used with verbs to ask about actions, as in (50).

(50) Gaboowa   boorroorn?
      what   they say/do
      What are they doing? What are they saying?

The southern variant of this word is ***gaba***. ***Gaba*** and its equivalents combine with the purposive suffix ***-girri/-girre*** to ask about problems, as in (51) and (52).

(51) Gaba-girrema
      what-for/wrong
      What is wrong?

(52) Gaboowa-girri-nha-ngoo   gawayi?
      what-wrong- are you-you (one)   father's sister
      Auntie, what is wrong with you?

As seen in section 3.3, the interrogative ***gaboo*** and its variants combine with the indirect object enclitic pronouns (see section 4.7.3) to ask about people's names. Some examples are given in Table 27.

4. GIJA WORD CLASSES AND GRAMMAR

Table 27. 'What name?'

Gaboo-ninggi yinginybe?	'What is your (singular) name?', 'What are you (one) called?'
Gaboo-narri yinginybe?	'What are your (plural) names?', 'What are you (plural) called?'
Gaboo-ni yinginybe?, Gaboo-ningi yinginybe?	'What is his name?', 'What is he called?'
Gaboo-ngiyi yinginybe?, Gaboowa-ngiyi yinginybe?	'What is her name?', 'What is she called?'
Gaboo-birri yinginybe?	'What are their names?', 'What are they called?'

4.5.2.4. 'Where?'

For inquiring about locations and directions there are a range of different Gija interrogative words. Some of these are restrictive in that they must agree with the gender of the referent. There are also general 'where' question interrogatives that don't have to agree. These are **gawoo**, **gayi** and **gayiwa**. They are non-restrictive. They can be used to ask 'where' about anything. We see these words being used to ask 'where' about a party or a card game in (53), a person in (54), and about feelings in (55).

(53) **Gayiwa   boorooj-girrembi?**
     where   play-for.plural
     Where's the party? / Where is the card game?

(54) **Gawoo,   gawoo?   Deg-gala   yarrem-ngooyoo-gili.**
     where   where   look-IMP   let us GET-for her-plural
     Where, where? Let's all look for her.

(55) **Jigili   ganybel-bawoorroo-n-ga.   Gawoo-birri   nganyjoombi?**
     yuck   shame-not_having-LOC-FOC   where-to them   feelings
     Yuck, they have no shame! Where are their feelings?

Gayi also takes the ablative suffix **-biny**. **Gayibiny** is used for asking 'where from?'. There are also allative forms for asking 'where to?'. These are **gabi**, **gabiyi**, **gabiya**, and the form **gabinga**, which is particularly associated with the Southern dialect.

In Table 28 we see some of the place-based interrogatives that agree with the gender of the referent. These may be used to inquire about the locations or directions of persons, animals, plants, cars, trucks and houses – in fact most things that take gender suffixes.

4. GIJA WORD CLASSES AND GRAMMAR

Table 28. Gender-marked interrogatives for asking 'where' about people and things

Where?	masculine	*Garniwa?* *Garnang?* (Southern dialect)	'Where is he/it (masculine)?'
	feminine	*Gangala?, Gangela?* *Gangangel?* (Southern dialect)	'Where is she/it (feminine)?'
	plural	*Gawoorra?*	'Where are they/it (non-singular)?'
Comes from where?	masculine	*Gayi-miliny?*	'Where is he from?'
	feminine	*Gayi-milil?*	'Where is she from?'
	plural	*Gayi-milim?*	'Where are they from?'
	singular address	*Gayi-mili-nha-ngoo?*	'Where are you (one) from?'
	plural address	*Gayi-mili-nha-noonggoo?,* *Gayi-mili-nha-noonggoorroo?*	'Where are you (plural) from?'
Belongs where?, Lives where?	masculine	*Gayi-ngarnany?*	'Where does he/it belong/live?'
	feminine	*Gayi-ngarnal?*	'Where does she/it belong/live?'
	plural	*Gayi-ngarnam?*	'Where do they/does it belong/live?'
	singular address	*Gayi-ngarna-nha-ngoo?*	'Where do you (one) belong/live?'
	plural address	*Gayi-ngarnan-noonggoo?,* *Gayi-ngarnan-noonggoorroo?*	'Where do you (plural) belong/live?'

4.5.2.5. 'When?', 'How?' and 'How many?'

Gija interrogatives for 'when?', 'how?' and 'how many? are shown in Table 29.

Table 29. 'When?', 'How?' and 'How many?'

Gayigan?, Gayigana? *Gaboogan?* (Southern dialect)	'When?'
Gaboojana?	'How?'
Gaboongerreg?	'How many?' / 'How much?'

4.5.3. Word search words

When Gija people momentarily forget the name of a person, place or thing they often combine an interrogative meaning 'what' or 'who' with one of the special 'word search' interrogatives ***garniga***, ***garningga***, ***garnega***, ***garnengga*** (these are pronounced differently by different speakers). The combinations are similar to the questions 'What's his name?' or 'What's its name?' that speakers ask themselves. Listeners are not expected to provide answers. Examples can be seen in (56) and (57).

(56) **Yangoowoo   garnengga   berraniyin   ngenengga   wajbaloombi?**
who.plural   word search   they STAYED   here   white people
What were their names, the white people who used to live here?

(57) **Gaboo   garnengga   garij   bemberramangbende**
what   word search   say name   they were GETTING it

berrembi   daam-boorroo-gili?
this.plural   place/country-for-plural
What's the name that they used to call this place of theirs?

4.5.4. Indeterminate interrogatives using -*anyji*

Words expressing uncertainty are derived from interrogatives using the suffix **-anyji**. These have been classified as 'interrogatives' when noting the word class in the dictionary. They are used when the person who is asked a question does not know the answer.

For example, if someone asks **Yangirini danyi**? 'Who is that man?' and the other does not know, the answer could be **Yangirnanyji**. 'Some man, I don't know who.' Some other examples are shown in Table 30.

Table 30. Indeterminate interrogative examples

Yangirnanyji	'some man, I don't know who' / 'it is unknown who'
Yangalanyji	'some woman, I don't know who' / 'it is unknown who'
Yangoorranyji	'some people, I don't know who' / 'it is unknown who'
Thiwingenyanyji	'some kind of masculine one'
Thengangelanyji	'some kind of feminine one'
Thoowoorranyji, Thoowiyanyji, Thoorranyji	'something'
Gayi-ngarnanyanyji	'person belonging/living somewhere'
Gaboowanyji, *Gabaanyji* (Southern dialect)	'somehow, I don't know what/how'
Gabiyanyji, Gabinganyji	'to some place / to somewhere'
Gayiyanyji	'at some place' / 'somewhere'
Gayi-binyanyji	'from somewhere'

4.6. Demonstratives

Words used to point out a direction or a location (e.g. 'here', 'there'), or to indicate specific items within a range of possible items ('this' and 'that', 'these' and 'those') are called **demonstratives**. They are often combined with gestures so as to demonstrate how to do things or where things are located with respect to the speaker or the action. The first two rows in Table 31 are used to indicate items or locations that are close to the speaker or the action (here), or that are distant from the speaker or the action (there). The demonstratives in the third row are used when the speaker believes their addressee will recognise which person or thing they are talking about ('that one we both know about'). The three sets of demonstratives agree in terms of gender with the person or thing being spoken about.

Table 31. Gija demonstratives

	Masculine	Feminine	Plural/Non-singular	Locative
close by, here	*nginy, nginya, nginyi, nginyjiny, nginyjinya, nginyjinyi* 'this masculine (thing)'	*ngel, ngela, ngeli, ngelel, ngelela, ngeleli* 'this feminine (thing)'	*berrem, berrema, berrembi, berrewam* 'these, this stuff'	*ngenengga, ngenega* (Southern dialect) 'here'
distant, there	*ngoorroony, ngoorriny, ngoorroonya, ngoorrinya, ngoorroonyi, ngoorrinyi* 'that masculine (thing)'	*ngoorrool, ngoorroola, ngoorrooli* 'that feminine (thing)'	*ngoorroom, ngoorrooma, ngoorroombi* 'those, that stuff'	*ngoorroon* 'there' *ngoorroo-ngoorroon* 'everywhere'
'you know the one'	*dany, danya, danyi* 'that masculine (thing) you know about'	*dal, dala, dali* 'that feminine (thing) you know about'	*dam, dama, dambi* 'those/that stuff you know about'	*dan* 'that place you know about'

Emphatic forms of each demonstrative include the intensifying suffix **-jiya, -iya, -ya**.

Table 32. Gija emphatic demonstratives

	Masculine	Feminine	Plural/Non-singular	Locative
this, these	*nginyjiyanya, nginyjiyanyaya* 'this is the one masculine'	*ngeliyala, nginiyala* 'this is the one feminine'	*birriyama* 'these are the ones', 'this is the stuff'	*ngenenggayana, gayana* 'right here'
that, those (over there)	*ngoorriyanya* 'that is the masculine one over there'	*ngoorriyala* 'that is the feminine one over there'	*ngoorriyama* 'those are the ones over there', 'that is the stuff'	*ngoorriyana* 'right there'
that, those (you know about)	*diyanya, deyenya* 'that is the one (masculine) you know about'	*diyala, deyela* 'that is the one (feminine) you know about'	*diyama, deyema* 'those are the ones', 'that is the stuff'	*diyana, deyena* 'that is the place'

4. GIJA WORD CLASSES AND GRAMMAR

4.7. Personal pronouns

Personal pronouns are words like **I**, **me**, **you**, **he**, **she**, etc. that can refer to people without naming them. Gija has free-standing **cardinal pronouns** like *ngayin* 'I/me' and *nyengen* 'you (one)', as well as free-standing **possessive pronouns** like *nyengiyangeny* 'yours' and *ngagenyji* 'mine'. There are also **bound pronouns**. Pronominal prefixes and suffixes are bound to the verb. These will be discussed in section 4.8. There are also pronominal enclitics (see section 4.7.3). These enclitics follow other words (including verbs) without really becoming part of the word. They cannot stand alone.

4.7.1. Cardinal pronouns

The free-form cardinal pronouns are shown in Table 33.

Table 33. Gija free-form pronouns

ngayin	I/me
yayin, yayiben	we two/us two (you (one) and I/me)
yoowoorroon yoorroon (Southern dialect)	we/us including you
yarren, yarroon	we/us but not you
yarreben, yarreben-doo, yarreben-joo	we/us two but not you
nyengen, nyingin	you (one)
nenggerren	you mob
nenggerreben	you two
nhawoon	he/him
ngalen	she/her
boorroon	they/them
boorrooben	they/them two

The cardinal pronouns also have emphatic forms. These are shown in Table 34.

Table 34. Gija emphatic pronouns

ngayana	I'm the one
yayana	you (one) and I are the ones
yoowoorriyana yoorriyana (Southern dialect)	we (all of us) are the ones
yarriyana	we (not you) are the ones
nyingiyana	you are the one
nenggerriyana	you are the ones
nhawiyana	he is the one
ngaliyana	she is the one
boorriyana, boorriyama	they are the ones

4.7.2. Possessive pronouns

Possessive pronouns behave like adjectives. They agree with the gender or number of the person or thing possessed, as demonstrated in Table 35

Table 35. Gender agreement in possessive pronouns

Masculine	ngagenyji ngaboony	'my father'
	ngagenyji garloomboony	'my spear'
Feminine	ngagenyel gooral	'my mother'
	ngagenyel ngawalel	'my woomera'
Plural	ngagenybe ngaboom	'my fathers"
	ngagenybe gooram	'my mothers"
	ngagenybe goorloom	'my water'

Versions of the possessive pronouns heard in the Southern dialect are often shorter. For example: **yarriyangeny** 'ours (not including you)' is pronounced **yarrangeny** and **yoowoorriyangeny** 'ours (including all of you)' is pronounced **yoorrangeny**. The possessive pronouns are shown in Table 36.

Table 36. Gija possessive pronouns

English	Masculine	Feminine	Non-singular
my, mine	ngagenyji	ngagenyel	ngagenybe
our, ours (you one and me)	yayiyangeny	yayiyangel	yayiyangem
our, ours (all of us)	yoowoorriyangeny, yoorriyangeny, yoorrangeny (Southern dialect)	yoowoorriyangel, yoorrangel (Southern dialect)	yoowoorriyangem, yoorrangem (Southern dialect)
our, ours (but not yours)	yarriyangeny, yarriyanginy, yarrangeny (Southern dialect)	yarriyangel, yarriyangil, yarrangel (Southern dialect)	yarriyangem, yarriyangim, yarrangem (Southern dialect)
your, yours (one)	nyingiyangeny	nyingiyangel	nyingiyangem
your, yours (plural)	nenggerriyany, nenggerriyangeny, ninggerriyany (Southern dialect)	nenggerriyangel, nenggerriyal, ninggerriyal (Southern dialect)	nenggerriyangem, nenggerriyam, ninggerriyam (Southern dialect)
his	nhawiyangeny	nhawiyangel	nhawiyangem
her, hers	ngaliyangeny	ngaliyangel	ngaliyangem
their, theirs	boorriyany, boorriyangeny	boorriyangel	boorriyangem

Just as adjectives may stand alone (see section 4.2), Gija possessive pronouns can occur without a corresponding noun if the referent has already been introduced, for example, **berrembi nhawiyangem** 'these things are his', **berrembi ngaliyangem** 'these things are hers'.

4. GIJA WORD CLASSES AND GRAMMAR

4.7.3. Enclitic pronouns

Gija has four sets of enclitic pronouns that attach to verbs, nouns and adjectives. They have been named **indirect object**, **benefactive**, **ablative** and **comitative** enclitics, on the basis of their behaviour when attached to verbs. The four sets of enclitic pronouns are shown in Table 37. When attached to inflecting verbs they each add an extra participant to the action described by the verb. Enclitic pronouns follow the words they are attached to without becoming part of the word. They are different from pronoun prefixes and suffixes as seen in the verbs (see section 4.8) that become part of the word and cannot be separated. They cannot stand alone as can the free-form pronouns (see section 4.7.1).

Table 37. The four series of enclitic pronouns

	Indirect object 'to'	Benefactive 'for'	Ablative 'from, after, because of'	Comitative 'with'
me	-ngirri	-nga, -ngage, -ngageny	-ngerroowa, -ngerra (Southern dialect)	-ngerrab
you (one) and me	-yayi	-yoowoo	-yoowa	
us all (including you)	-yarri	-yoowoorroo -yoowoorr	-yoowoorroowa, -yoorroowa, -yoorra (Southern dialect), -yarrewa	-yarrab
us (three)	-yarri-yoo	-yoorroo-yoo		
us (not you)	-yirri	-yarre	-yirroowa, -yirrewa	-yirrab
us two (not you)	-yirri-yoo	-yarri-yoo		
you (one)	-ni, -ninggi	-ngoo, -ngoongoo	-nenggoowa	-nenggab
you (all)	-narri	-nooggoo, -noonggoorroo	-narroowa	-narrab
you (two)	-narri-yoo	-noonggoorroo-yoo		
him	-ni, -ningi	-noo, -noongoo	-noowa	-niyab
her	-ngiyi	-ngooyoo	-ngiyiwa	-ngiyab
them	-birri	-boorroo	-berroowa, -berra	-berrab
them (two)	-birri-yoo	-boorroo-yoo		

4.7.3.1. Indirect object enclitic pronouns

When an indirect object enclitic attaches to a SAY/DO verb, it normally indicates who is being addressed within reported speech, as in (58). When an indirect object enclitic attaches to a body part, it normally indicates who the body part belongs to. For instance, in (59) the enclitic **-ni** indicates that it was the kangaroo's fur that was singed (the kangaroo is masculine). The second person enclitic **-ninggi** ('to you (one)') is often used in an idiomatic fashion where the presence of a person or a thing is brought to the attention of the person or people being addressed, as in (60).

(58) **Wanema-yirri,**   'Joord   barroo.'
      he SAID-to us but not you   eat   you all DO it
      He said to us (but not you), 'You all eat.'

(59) **Gawal   ngoorrayid-doo   warloom-ni   dam.**
singe   they HIT it-two   fur-to him   that
The two of them singed its (the kangaroo's) fur.

(60) **Danya-ninggi!**
that-masc-to you (one)
There he is! / There it is! / There you go!

4.7.3.2. Benefactive enclitic pronouns
Benefactive enclitics often indicate that an action is performed for someone's benefit. Thus, in (61) the water is being requested for the benefit of the speaker. As mentioned previously, benefactive enclitics form verbless sentences by attaching to nouns or adjectives that already carry the locative suffix, as in (62) (see also (31), (32), (42) and (43)). Benefactive enclitics are also frequently used to express ownership of country, which is what **-noongoo** does in (63).

(61) **Goorloom   benanynha-ngage.**
water   you (one) BRING/TAKE it-**for me**
Bring water **for me.**

(62) **Jirraya-n-yarre.**
alright-LOC-we but not you
We are alright.

(63) **Berrema   Goorloongooroogayiny   daam   ngaginy-noongoo   ngaboonya-noongoo.**
this   place name   place   my-for him   father-**for him**
This place called Goorloongooroogayiny is my father**'s** country.

4.7.3.3. Ablative enclitic pronouns
Ablative enclitic pronouns can be used to indicate the source of an object, or the source of some information, as in (64). When attached to motion verbs, they also indicate which participant should be followed, as in (65). They may be translated as 'from', 'after (referring to both time and space)' or 'because of' the person or thing referred to.

(64) **Yardem   dam   noonamoorlardge-noowa.**
ear   those   I -KEEP it-**from him**
I keep those things (stories my grandfather told me) **from him** in my mind (my ears).

(65) **Biyarr-gala-noowa.**
You (one) GO!-do it!-**after him**
Go **after him**!

4.7.3.4. Comitative enclitic pronouns
The comitative enclitic pronouns have been found only with inflecting verbs. These add an extra participant to the action. The extra participant accompanies the persons participating in the action described by the verb.

(66) **Nyananyande,   joolooj   benanyande-ngiyab   ngalangangal.**
She was going   carry under arm   she took them-with her   woman's daughter
She used to go along with her daughter carrying things under her arm.

4.8. Gija verbs

There are two sorts of verbs in Gija. These are **coverbs** and **inflecting verbs**. Inflecting verbs have prefixes and suffixes that tell us who does the action and, in some cases, to whom the action is done. They also tell us when the action transpires (in the past, in the present or in the future). Inflecting verbs like ***berrani*** in (67), have quite general meanings ('say/DO', 'go/COME', 'BE/stay', 'hit', 'become', etc.). Coverbs like ***wiji*** ('run') in (68) have more specific meanings that modify the general meanings of inflecting verbs.

(67) **Berrani.**
 they SAID/DID
 They were saying. / They were doing.

(68) **Wiji berrani.**
 run they SAID/DID
 They were running.

We will refer to the combination of coverb plus inflecting verb as a **compound verb**. These are very common in Gija.

4.8.1. Inflecting verbs

There are four different kinds of inflecting verbs in Gija: transitive, intransitive, middle and reflexive/reciprocal.

4.8.1.1. Transitive verbs

Transitive verbs express active processes in which someone or something is affected by the process they describe. Inflecting verbs like ***ngenangaboordji*** in examples (69) and (70) are transitive verbs because they tell us both who is doing the action and who the action is done to. We call the person or thing that performs the action the **subject**. The subject is a male person in both (69) and (70). The person or thing to whom the action is performed is called the **object**. In these cases, the object is the speaker.

(69) **Ngena-ngaboord-ji.**
 he did it to me-SPEARED-he
 He speared me.

(70) **Derlbawoo ngena-ngaboord-ji.**
 shoot he did it to me-SPEARED-he
 He shot me.

The seventeen transitive verb stems inflect for tense. This is shown by changes in the forms of the stems, depending on whether events take place in the past, the present or the future; see Table 38.

4. GIJA WORD CLASSES AND GRAMMAR

Table 38. Gija transitive verb stems

	Past	Present	Future
GET	-ma, -mang, -many	-men	-m
PUT	-ya, -yan, -yany	-lin (Northern dialect) -loon (Southern dialect)	-yaj
BRING/TAKE	-any	-yin (Northern dialect) -aan (Southern dialect)	TAKE -g BRING -any
HIT	-yid	-yin	-ij
GIVE		-yin	-iyi
SPEAR	-ngaboord	-nganboorn, -ngambern	-ngany
HIT/CUT	-wooran, -woon, -wan	-waren	-wan
BITE/BURN	-woorran	-warren	-warri
EAT	-ngoon	-ngan	-ang
HAVE	-moorlooward (Northern dialect) -moorlaard (Southern dialect)	-moorlin -moorlen	-moorloo
LEAVE	-woorrood	-woorroon	-woorroob
SWEAR	-mooran	-moorin	-moord
WAIT for someone	-ngirriward		-ngirriyin
KICK	-ngarremang	-ngarremen	-ngarrem
FOLLOW	-mimang, -mimany		
GO and GET	-wamang, -wamany	-wamen	-wam
GET and HIT	-moowang	-moowoon	

Transitive verbs have prefixes which provide information about both subjects and objects, that also inflect for tense and mood. The suffixes usually provide information about the subject but sometimes they also provide information about objects. The most common inflection patterns are given in Table 39 and Table 40. In these tables the subjects are listed in rows and the objects are listed in columns. As well as the past, present and future forms we also list the forms for imperative ('Do it!') and hortative ('Let it happen!', 'Let them do it!') moods. You can build verbs by inserting verb stems from Table 38 into the relevant stem slots in Table 39 and Table 40, which we represent with square brackets. The results will provide a close approximation to how Gija people pronounce these verbs. However, due to various sound changes, fluent Gija speakers may pronounce these verbs slightly differently. For example, when the final vowel of the prefix before the stem is *e*, it will usually be pronounced similar to the first vowel in the stem. Gija people vary in how they pronounce inflecting verbs, especially with regard to how vowels are realised.

The underlined suffixes shown in Table 40, which provide information about subjects, are sometimes added but they are often missing. When they are missing, it usually means that the action has been completed or will be completed. When they are present it usually means that the action is ongoing. These suffixes also appear on middle verbs and reflexive/reciprocal verbs where they provide similar meanings.

4. GIJA WORD CLASSES AND GRAMMAR

Table 39. Prefixes and suffixes to transitive verbs with first person objects (me, us)

Subjects	Objects Tense / mood	Me	Us but not you	You (one) and me	Us including you
I		–	–	–	–
we but not you		–	–	–	–
you (one) and I		–	–	–	–
we incl. you		–	–	–	–
you (one)	past	yina-[ ]	yina-[ ]-yarre	–	–
	pres	yine-[ ]-nha	yina-[ ]-nha-yarre	–	–
	fut	yinbi-[ ]-nha	yinbi-[ ]-nha-yarre	–	–
	imp/hort	yinde-[ ]-nha	yinde-[ ]-nha-yarre	–	–
you mob	past	yimberra-[ ]	yimberra-[ ]-yarre	–	–
	pres	yimberra-[ ]-nha	yimberre-[ ]-nha-yarre	–	–
	fut	yimbirri-[ ]-nha	yimbirri-[ ]-nha-yarre	–	–
	imp/hort	yimberre-[ ]-<u>nha</u>	yimberre-[ ]-nha-yarre	–	–
he	past	ngena-[ ]	yine-[ ]-yarre	yina-[ ]-yayi	yina-[ ]-yoowoo
	pres	ngene-[ ]-ji	yina-[ ]-ji-yarre	yina-[ ]-ji-yayi	yina-[ ]-ji-yoowoo
	fut	nginbi-[ ]-ji	yinbi-[ ]-ji-yarre	yinbi-[ ]-ji-yayi	yinbi-[ ]-ji-yoowoo
	imp/hort	ngende-[ ]-ji	yinde-[ ]-ji-yarre	yinde-[ ]-ji-yayi	yinde-[ ]-ji-yoowoo
she	past	ngena-[ ]	yine-[ ]-yarre	yina-[ ]-yayi	yina-[ ]-yoowoo
	pres	ngene-[ ]-nya	yine-[ ]-nya-yarre	yine-[ ]-nya-yayi	yine-[ ]-nya-yoowoo
	fut	nginbi-[ ]-nya	yinbi-[ ]-nya-yarre	yinbi-[ ]-nya-yayi	yinbi-[ ]-nya-yoowoo
	imp/hort	ngende-[ ]-nya	yinde-[ ]-nya-yarre	yinde-[ ]-nya-yayi	yinde-[ ]-nya-yoowoo
they	past	ngemberra-[ ]	yimberra-[ ]-yarre	yimberra-[ ]-yayi	yimberra-[ ]-yoowoo
	pres	ngemberra-[ ]-be	yimberra-[ ]-be-yarre	yimberra-[ ]-bi-yayi	yimberra-[ ]-be-yoowoo
	fut	ngimbirri-[ ]-be	yimbirri-[ ]-bi-yarre	yimbirri-[ ]-bi-yayi	yimbirri-[ ]-bi-yoowoo
	imp/hort	ngemberre-[ ]	yimberre-[ ]-yarre	yimberre-[ ]-yayi	yimberre-[ ]-yoowoo

Table 40. Prefixes and suffixes to transitive verbs with second person objects (you) and third person objects (him, her, them)

Subjects	Objects Tense/mood	You (one)	You mob	Him	Her	Them
I	past	nane-[ ]-ngoo	nane-[ ]-noonggoo	nine-[ ]	nyile-[ ]	noona-[ ]
	pres	ne-[ ]-nha-ngoo	nane-[ ]-nha-noonggoo	ne-[ ]-ge	nyile-[ ]-ge	noona-[ ]-ge
	fut	nimbi-[ ]-nha-ngoo	nanbi-[ ]-nha-noonggoo	noowi-[ ]-ge / nhiyi-[ ]-ge	nyile-[ ]-ge	noonbe-[ ]-ge
	imp/hort	nhare-[ ]-ngoo	nande-[ ]-noonggoo	nhere-[ ]	nyile-[ ]	noonde-[ ]
we but not you	past	yirre-[ ]-ji-ngoo	yirre-[ ]-ji-noonggoo	yirra-[ ]	yirra-[ ]	yirra-[ ]
	pres	yirre-[ ]-ji-ngoo	yirri-[ ]-ji-noonggoo	yirra-[ ]-ji	yirra-[ ]-ji	yirra-[ ]-ji
	fut	yirri-[ ]-ji-ngoo	yirri-[ ]-ji-noonggoo	yirri-[ ]-ji / yirri-[ ]-ji	yirri-[ ]-nyi / yirri-[ ]-ji	yirri-[ ]-nyi / yirri-[ ]-ji
	imp/hort	yirri-[ ]-ngoo	—	yirre-[ ]	yirre-[ ]	yirre-[ ]
you (one) and I	past	–	–	yane-[ ]	yane-[ ]	yoone-[ ]
	pres	–	–	yi-[ ]-ya	yi-[ ]-ya	yoonbi-[ ]-nya
	fut	–	–	yoowe-[ ]-nya	yoowe-[ ]-nya	yoonbe-[ ]
	imp/hort	–	–	yare-[ ]	yare-[ ]	yamberra-[ ]
we including you	past	–	–	yarre-[ ]	yarre-[ ]	yamberra-[ ]-ya
	pres	–	–	yarre-[ ]-ya	yarre-[ ]-ya	yambirri-[ ]-**nya**
	fut	–	–	yarri-[ ]-nya	yarri-[ ]-nya	yamberre-[ ]
	imp/hort	–	–	yarre-[ ]	yarre-[ ]	joona-[ ]
you (one)	past	–	–	jane-[ ]	jane-[ ]	joona-[ ]-nha
	pres	–	–	je-[ ]-nha	je-[ ]-nha	jimbi-[ ]-nha / joonbi-[ ]-nha
	fut	–	–	jiwi-[ ]-nha / joowi-[ ]-nha	jiwi-[ ]-nha / joowi-[ ]-nha	bene-[ ]-**nha**
	imp/hort	–	–	biyi-[ ]-**nha**	biyi-[ ]-**nha**	jamberra-[ ]
you mob	past	–	–	jarra-[ ]	jarra-[ ]	jamberra-[ ]-nha
	pres	–	–	jarra-[ ]-nha	jarra-[ ]-nha	jambirri-[ ]-nha
	fut	–	–	jarre-[ ]-nha	jarre-[ ]-nha	bamberre-[ ]-**nha**
	imp/hort	–	–	barre-[ ]-**nha**	barre-[ ]-**nha**	

4. GIJA WORD CLASSES AND GRAMMAR

Table 40 continued

Subjects	Objects	Tense /mood	You (one)	You mob	Him	Her	Them
he		past	nane-[ ]-ni	nane-[ ]-ni	ngini-[ ]	nyane-[ ]	bena-[ ]
		pres	ne-[ ]-ji-ni	nane-[ ]-ji-ni	nge-[ ]-ji	nye-[ ]-ji	bena-[ ]-ji
		fut	nimbi-[ ]-ji-ni	nanbi-[ ]-ji-ni	ngiwi-[ ]-ji	nyiwi-[ ]-ji	binbi-[ ]-ji
		imp/hort	nende-[ ]-ji-ni	nande-[ ]-ji-ni	ngere-[ ]-ji	nyare-[ ]-ji	bende-[ ]-ji
she		past	nane-[ ]-ngal	nane-[ ]-ngal	ngini-[ ]	nyane-[ ]	bena-[ ]
		pres	ne-[ ]-nha-ngal	nane-[ ]-nha-ngal	nge-[ ]-nya	nye-[ ]-nya	bena-[ ]-nya
		fut	nimbi-[ ]-nha-ngal	nanbi-[ ]-nha-ngal	ngiwi-[ ]-nya	nyiwi-[ ]-nya	binbi-[ ]-nya
		imp/hort	nende-[ ]-nha-ngal	nande-[ ]-**nha**-ngal	ngere-[ ]-**nya**	nyare-[ ]-nya	bende-[ ]-nya
they		past	nemberre-[ ]-boorroo	namberre-[ ]-boorroo	ngoorre-[ ]	nyimberra-[ ]	bemberra-[ ]
		pres	nemberre-[ ]-nha-boorroo	namberre-[ ]-nha-boorroo	ngoorra-[ ]-be	nyimberra-[ ]-be	bemberra-[ ]-be
		fut	nimbirri-[ ]-nha-boorroo	nambirri-[ ]-nha-boorroo	ngoorri-[ ]-be	nyimbirri-[ ]-be	bimbirri-[ ]-be
		imp/hort	nimberre-[ ]-nha-boorroo	namberre-[ ]-nha-boorroo	ngoorroo-[ ]-boo	nyimberre-[ ]-be	bemberre-[ ]-be

4. GIJA WORD CLASSES AND GRAMMAR

4.8.1.2. Intransitive verbs

The verbs seen above in (67) and (68) are called **intransitive** verbs. Intransitive verbs have a subject but no object. In Gija there are four intransitive inflecting verbs: BE/STAY (Table 41), GO/COME (Table 42), FALL/GO DOWN (Table 43) and SAY/DO (Table 44). The forms of the verb inflect for tense (past, present or future). As with the intransitives, the underlined suffixes in the next 4 tables are also only added sometimes. When they are missing, generally it means that the action has been completed or will be completed; when present, it usually means that the action is ongoing. When they appear on middle verbs and reflexive/reciprocal verbs they provide similar meanings. Continuous or habitual actions are conveyed by the addition of a final suffix *-nde* to past, present or future forms (e.g., 'was verb-ing', 'is verb-ing', 'will be verb-ing'). The **Past irrealis** forms tell us about things that should have happened but didn't actually eventuate.

Table 41. Intransitive verb BE/STAY

Doer	Past	Past irrealis	Present	Future	Imperative/Hortative
I	ngenaniyin	ngoonbiniyin	ngenan'ge	nginbin-'ge	ngenden-'ge
we but not you	yirraniyin	yirrooniyin, yirriweniyin	yirranji	yirrinji	yirranyi
you (one) and I	yaniniyin, yaniniya	yoowiniyin	yinya	yiwinya	yadin, yadinya
we including you	yarraniyin, yarraniya, yarrooniya	yarrooniyin, yoorrooniyin	yarroonya	yarrinya	yarrenya
you (one)	naniniyin, nanininha	noombooniyin, noombininha	ninha	nimbinha	benenha
you plural	narraniyin, narraniyinha	narrooniyinha	narroonha	narrinha	barrenha
he	ngininiyin	ngoowooniyin, ngoowiniyin	nginji	ngiwinji	ngidiyi, ngidiyin
she	nyaniniyin, nyaniniyinya	nyoombiniyinya, nyoombooninya, nyoombininya	nyinya	nyimbinya	nyadinya
they	berraniyin	boorrooniyin	boorroonboo	birrinbe	berrenbe

Table 42. Intransitive verb GO/COME

Doer	Past	Past irrealis	Present	Future	Imperative/Hortative
I	ngenayi(n)	ngoonbiyin	ngenardge	nginbiyan	ngenda(n)
we but not you	yirrayi(n)-*ji*	yirriyin	yirradji	yirriyan	yirra
you (one) and I	yaniyi(n)	yoowiyin	yidja	yiwiya	yara
we including you	yarrayi(n)	yarriyin	yarroordja	yarriyan	yarra
you (one)	naniyi(n)-*nha*	noombiyin	nirda	nimbiyan-*nha*	biyarr-*a* 'go' biyany-*nha* 'come'
you plural	narrayi(n)-*nha*	narriyin	narroorda	narriyanha	barriyi-*nha* 'go' barriyany-*nha* 'come'
he	nginiyi(n)	ngoowiyin	ngidji	ngiwiyayi ngiwiyayin	ngira 'go' ngeriyanyji 'come'
she	nyaniyi(n) nyaniyinya	nyoombiyin	nyidja	nyimbiyanya	nyara 'go' nyaranya; nyariyanya 'come'
they	berrayi(n)	boorriyin	boorroordboo	birriyan	berra 'go' birriyanybe 'come'

4. GIJA WORD CLASSES AND GRAMMAR

Table 43. Intransitive verb FALL/GO DOWN

Doer	Past	Past irrealis	Present	Future	Imperative/ Hortative
I	ngenaward-**ge** ngenaard-**ge**	ngoonboowardge ngenboowardge	ngenawoon'ge	nginboowoon nginboowoon'**ge**	ngendoowoo
we but not you	yirraward-**ji**	yirroowardji	yirrawoonji	yirrewoon	
you (one) and I	yanooward-**ja**	yoowardja	yoowoonya	yiwoon	yarewoo
we including you	yarreward-**ja**	yarroowardja	yarroowoonya	yarroowoon	yarrewoo
you (one)	nanooward-**a**	nimboowarda	noowoonha	nimboowoonha noomboowoonha	boowoo
you plural	narrooward-**a**	narroowarda	narroowoonha	narriwoon	barrewoo barrewoo**nha**
he	nginiward-**ji** nginaard-**ji**	ngoowardji	ngoowoonji	ngiwoon	ngiroowoo
she	nyanooward-**ja**	nyimboowardja	nyoowoonya	nyimboowoonya	nyaroowoo
they	berraward-**be** berrooward-**be** berraard-**be**	boorrooward**boo**	berroowoonbe boorroowoonbe boorroowoonboo	birriwoon	berrewoo

Table 44. Intransitive verb SAY/DO

Doer	Past	Past irrealis	Present	Future	Imperative/ Hortative
I	ngenani	ngoonbini	ngenarn	nginbirn	ngendern
we but not you	yirrani	yoorrooni	yirrarn	yirrirn	yirrern
you (one) and I	yanini	yoowini	yerne	yiwirn	yarde
we including you	yarrani	yarrooni	yarroorn	yarrirn	yarrern
you (one)	nanini	noombooni	nerne, nirni	nimbirn	berne
you plural	narrani	narrooni	narroorn	narrirn	barrern
he	nginini	ngoowooni	ngerne, ngirni	ngiwirn	ngerde
she	nyanini	nyoombooni	nyerne	nyimbirn	nyarde
they	berrani	boorrooni	boorroorn	birrirn	berrern

The intransitive verb SAY/DO is a very general doing verb. On its own it usually reports prior speech, but it also occurs with coverbs in many compound verbs. It never takes the pronominal suffixes, nor the continuous/habitual suffix **-nde**. Although we describe the verb as intransitive, it can still combine with a coverb that is semantically transitive, like **jang** 'eat', to produce a transitive sentence. In (71) the nominal object, **mayim** 'food', is not expressed by prefixes to the verb. The sentence is transitive but the verb is not.

(71) **Jang   ngerne   mayi-m.**
      eat   he DOES   food-plural
      He eats/is eating food.

The event described in (71) is a general statement about an unremarkable event, or an unsurprising state of affairs. When talking about particular instances of eating, such as a significant moment within a story, Gija speakers are more likely to produce a genuinely transitive verb with a prefix expressing both the object and the subject of the verb, such as **benangoonjende-ni** in (72). For less noteworthy events, they are more likely to use the intransitive SAY/DO or a middle verb (see below).

(72) Mooloonggoombi   gerrij-boo   bena-ngoon-jende-ni.
     fat-plural   finish-then   he/she did to them-ATE-he was continuously-to him
     He (tata lizard) was finishing up all his (dead crocodile's) fat then.

4.8.1.3. Middle verbs

In Gija the transitive verbs have prefix/suffix combinations that provide information about both subjects and objects, whereas the intransitive verbs have prefix/suffix combinations that provide information about the subjects only. A third type, named **middle verbs**, is similar in some respects to the transitives and resembles the intransitives in other respects. Middle verbs have stems which are related in form and meaning to certain transitive verb stems. The five middle verb stems are shown in Table 45. The middle verbs have a different set of subject prefixes (see Table 46). The suffixes are the same subject suffixes discussed previously in 4.8.1.2, that also indicate that the action is potentially ongoing. Those that are underlined are sometimes absent in past and future tenses. When they are absent, this suggests that the action is already or will be complete.

Table 45. Gija middle verb stems

	Past	Present	Future
SAY/DO_M*	-ma, -mang, -many	-men	-m
TAKE a PLACE/POSITION	-yang, -yany	-yilen, -yooloon	-aj
GO ALONG	-any	-in, -an	-g
BECOME	-yid	-yin	-ij
GO THROUGH	-ngaboord	-ngamen	

---

* SAY/DO_M is used here to differentiate the middle SAY/DO verb from the intransitive SAY/DO verb shown in Table 44.

4. GIJA WORD CLASSES AND GRAMMAR

Table 46. Prefixes and suffixes to middle verbs

Doer	Past	Present	Future	Imperative/ Hortative
I	ngele-[ ]	ngele-[ ]-'ge	ngeli-[ ]-'ge	ngel-[ ]-'ge
we but not you	yirr-[ ]	yirre-[ ]-ji	yirri-[ ]-ji	
you (one) and I	yin-[ ]	ye-[ ]-nya ye-[ ]-ja	yi-[ ]-nya yi-[ ]-ja	
we including you	yarr-[ ]	yarr-[ ]-nya yarr-[ ]-ja	yarri-[ ]-nya yarri-[ ]-ja	
you (one)	joone-[ ]	je-[ ]-nha je-[ ]-tha	jeni-[ ]-nha jeni-[ ]-tha	be-[ ]-nha be-[ ]-tha
you plural	jarre-[ ]	jarre-[ ]-nha jarre-[ ]-tha	jarri-[ ]-nha jarri-[ ]-tha	barre-[ ]-nha barre-[ ]-tha
he	wane-[ ]	we-[ ]-ji	wimbi-[ ]-ji	
she	wane-[ ]	we-[ ]-nya we-[ ]-ja	wimbi-[ ]-nya wimbi-[ ]-ja	
they	woomberre-[ ]	woomberre-[ ]-be	wimbirri-[ ]-be	

Middle verbs, however, frequently combine with semantically transitive coverbs to produce transitive sentences with nominal objects. In (73) the middle verb **wananyji** 'he was going along' is combined with the semantically transitive coverb **woonboorr** 'to knock down' giving **woonboorr wananyji**, 'he/it (masculine) went along knocking things down'. The object of the sentence (houses) is not expressed on the verb.

(73)   Mawoongarriny   nginyga   woonboorr   wan-any-ji   mayaroo-m.
      murderer   this.masc   knock down   he/she-WENT ALONG-he   house-plural
      This destroyer (the flood) went along knocking down houses.

In (74) the person is eating a specific type of food, **gawarroony** 'emu berries'. The object of the sentence (emu berries) is not expressed on the verb. Unlike the eating of the crocodile's fat in (72) in which a significant, dramatic action within a narrative is being described using a transitive verb, the middle verb in (74) describes an ongoing, non-dramatic event within a narrative. It is not a high point within the story.

(74)   Ngarnji   dany   gawoorroo-ny   jang   wane-ma-nya-nde.
      that thing-masc   that.masc   emu berry-masc   eat   he/she did-SAID/DID-she-continuously
      She kept eating that thing, the fruit of the emu berry.

Gija is unusual in that it has two SAY/DO verbs, an intransitive verb (SAY/DO) and a middle verb (SAY/DO_M). Both are regularly used, without a coverb, to frame reported speech. The middle verbs tend to be used in more dramatic contexts. For example, in (75) the possum man makes a foreboding announcement using the middle form **wanemayi-ngiyi** 'he said to her'. This situation contrasts with the normal, everyday action of going to look for bush food described in (76).

(75)   'Ngayin-ngoongoo   ngoolnga-ga-n-nga,'   wanemayi-ngiyi.
      I-for you   spouse-relation-LOC-I   he SAID-to her
      'I am your husband now,' he said to her.

(76) 'Ngenda   gala   goonja-giny,'   nyanini-ningi.
    I want to go should   kapok bush roots-for   she SAID-to him
    'I want to go for kapok bush roots,' she said to him.

4.8.1.4. Reflexive and reciprocal verbs

Reflexive verbs express active processes in which the person affected by the action is the same person as the one who performs the action, as in (77). Plural forms of the verbs used for expressing reflexive actions are also used for expressing reciprocal actions (actions that are done to each other), as in (78). This is determined from the context.

(77) **Loogoorr**   **ngini-miyin.**
    wash   He did-DID TO SELF
    He washed himself.

(78) **Loogoorr**   **berra-miyin.**
    wash   they did-DID TO THEMSELVES/EACH OTHER
    They washed themselves. / They washed each other.

The reflexive/reciprocal verb stems are listed in Table 47. The prefixes and suffixes used in reflexive and reciprocal verbs are more or less the same as those used in intransitive verbs. They are listed here in Table 48.

Table 47. Gija reflexive/reciprocal verb stems

	Past	Present	Future
SAY/DO to self/each other	-ngirriyin	-ngirriyan	-ngirrij
DO to self/each other	-miyin	-miyan	-mij
SAY to self/each other	-iyilin	-iyiliyan	-lij
HIT self/each other	-ngirrid		-ngirrij
SPEAR self/each other		-ngaboon	-ngandij
CUT self/each other	-woon, -wayin	-wan	-wan
BURN/BITE self/each other	-woorran	-waren	
LEAVE EACH OTHER	-woorroomiyin		-woorroomij
SWEAR each other	-mooriyin	-moorriyan	-moorij

4. GIJA WORD CLASSES AND GRAMMAR

Table 48. Prefixes and suffixes used with reflexive and reciprocal stems

Doer	Past	Past irrealis	Present	Future	Imperative/ Hortative
I	ngena-[ ]-'ge	ngoonb-[ ]-'ge	ngena-[ ]-'ge	nginbi-[ ]-'ge	ngende-[ ]-'ge
we but not you	yirre-[ ]-ji	yirroo-[ ]-ji	yirre-[ ]-ji	yirri-[ ]-ji	yirre-[ ]-ji
you (one) and I	yin-[ ]-ya yin-[ ]-ja	yoowi-[ ]-ya yoowi-[ ]-ja	ye-[ ]-ya ye-[ ]-ja	yiwi-[ ]-ya yiwi-[ ]-ja	ya-[ ]-ya ya-[ ]-ja
we including you	yarre-[ ]-ya yarre-[ ]-ja	yoorroo-[ ]-ya yoorroo-[ ]-ja	yarre-[ ]-ya yarre-[ ]-ja	yarri-[ ]-ya yarri-[ ]-ja	yarre-[ ]-ya yarre-[ ]-ja
you (one)	nane-[ ]-nha nane-[ ]-tha	noombe-[ ]-nha noombe-[ ]-tha	ne-[ ]-nha ne-[ ]-tha	nimbi-[ ]-nha nimbi-[ ]-tha	be-[ ]-nha be-[ ]-tha
you plural	narre-[ ]-nha narre-[ ]-tha	noorre-[ ]-nha noorre-[ ]-tha	narre-[ ]-nha narre-[ ]-tha	narri-[ ]-nha narri-[ ]-tha	barre-[ ]-nha barre-[ ]-tha
he	ngini-[ ]-ji	ngoowi-[ ]-ji	nge-[ ]-ji	ngiwi-[ ]-ji	ngi-[ ]-ji
she	nyane-[ ]-ya nyimbi-[ ]-ja	nyoombe-[ ]-ya nyoombe-[ ]-ja	nye-[ ]-ya nye-[ ]-ja	nyimbi-[ ]-ya nyimbi-[ ]-ja	nya-[ ]-ya nya-[ ]-ja
they	berra-[ ]-be	boorre-[ ]-be	boorroo-[ ]-be	birri-[ ]-be	berre-[ ]-be

The suffixes provide information about subjects. Their meanings are discussed above in 4.8.1.2. Some cells of the table provide alternative forms for these suffixes. The forms **-ja** and **-tha** follow stems that end in either **d** or **j**. They may be followed by the suffix **-nde** which indicates continuous or habitual action.

4.8.1.5. Gija verb stems — summary

In the dictionary many verb forms found in the Toolbox corpus have been included as individual entries. This is for the convenience of readers of Gija who may not want to have to work out verb forms using the stem and prefix/suffix tables. It does not include every possible verb form that could exist. It is important to remember that in coverb–verb compounds the meaning of the inflecting verb contributes subject, object, tense and mood but only a subtle meaning to the compound. The literal meaning of each verb is only used when occurring as a simple verb without a coverb. This is why the decision was made to represent the translations of the stems in capitals to distinguish them from normal translations. A summary list of Gija verbs with their tense forms is shown in Table 49. In this table the abbreviations _M and _REFL refer to middle and reflexive verb forms.

Table 49. Gija verb stems

	Past	Present	Future
GET	-ma, -mang, -many	-men	-m
PUT	-ya, -yan, -yany	-lin (Northern dialect) -loon (Southern dialect)	-yaj
BRING/TAKE	-any	-yin (Northern dialect) -aan (Southern dialect)	TAKE -g BRING -any
HIT	-yid	-yin	-ij
GIVE		-yin	-iyi
SPEAR	-ngaboord	-nganboorn, -ngambern	-ngany
HIT/CUT	-wooran, -woon, -wan	-waren	-wan
BURN/BITE	-woorran	-warren	-warri
EAT	-ngoon	-ngan	-ang
HAVE	-moorlooward (Northern dialect) -moorlaard (Southern dialect)	-moorlin -moorlen	-moorloo
LEAVE	-woorrood	-woorroon	-woorroob
SWEAR	-mooran	-moorin	-moord
WAIT for someone	-ngirriward		-ngirriyin
KICK	-ngarremang	-ngarremen	-ngarrem
FOLLOW	-mimang, -mimany		
GO and GET	-wamang, -wamany	-wamen	-wam
GET_HIT	-moowang	-moowoon	
SAY/DO_M	-ma, -mang, -many	-men	-m
PLACE_M	-yang, -yany	-yilen, -yooloon	-aj
GO_ALONG	-any	-in, -an	-g
BECOME	-yid	-yin	-ij
GO THROUGH	-ngaboord	-ngamen	
SAY/DO_REFL	-ngirriyin	-ngirriyan	-ngirrij
DO_REFL	-miyin	-miyan	-mij
SAY/PUT_REFL	-iyilin	-iyiliyan	-lij
HIT_REFL	-ngirrid		-ngirrij
SPEAR_REFL		-ngaboon	-ngandij
CUT_REFL	-woon, -wayin	-wan	-wan
BURN/BITE_REFL	-woorran	-waren	
LEAVE_REFL	-woorroomiyin		-woorroomij
SWEAR_REFL	-mooriyin	-moorriyan	-moorij
BE/STAY	-n	-niyin	-in
GO/COME	-d, -rd	-iyi	-yan
FALL/GO_DOWN	-woon	-ward -aard	-woon
SAY/DO	-arn, -erne, -oorn	-ini	-irn

4.8.2. Coverbs

Coverbs are a word class that does not occur in English but is very common in Gija and in many languages in the north of Australia. In compound verbs they usually occur before the inflecting verb. While the lexical meanings of coverbs are more specific than the general meanings of inflecting verbs, the lexical meanings really lie in the ways coverbs combine with inflecting verbs to form compound verbs. A single coverb may occur with a range of different inflecting verbs in different compounds, each yielding slightly different meanings. For example, when the coverb **berdij** occurs with the intransitive inflecting verb SAY/DO, as in (79), the meaning is approximately 'to get up'. When it occurs with the intransitive inflecting verb GO/COME, as in (80), the meaning is 'climb up' or 'ascend'. When it occurs with the transitive verb BRING/TAKE, as in (81), the meaning is 'to take someone climbing'. When it occurs with the transitive verb PUT, as in (82), the meaning is 'to wake someone up'. In the dictionary, every coverb–verb combination that has been recorded is listed separately.

(79) **Berdij ngini-ni.**
get up   he did-SAY/DO
He got up

(80) **Gerloowoorra berdij nyi-d-ja.**
Up there   climb up   she-GOES/COMES-she
It (the road) climbs up there then.

(81) **Berdij nane-any-nha-ngoo.**
take climbing   I did to you-BRING/TAKE-you-you (one)
I took you climbing.

(82) **Berdij-berdij bena-yany-je-nde goorndoorndoogam.**
wake someone-wake someone   he did to them-PUT-he-used to   children
He used to wake the children.

Most coverbs can be reduplicated (doubled or partly doubled). Reduplicated coverbs usually indicate repeated or ongoing action, as in (82). Reduplicated forms are marked REDUP in the dictionary.

Many concepts that are expressed in English using adverbs or adjectives can be expressed in Gija using a coverb. In fact, many noun and adjective stems (without their gender suffixes) can be used as coverbs with the middle verb BECOME, as in (83) and (84).

(83) **Men'gawoo wani-yid-ji.**
good   he did-BECAME-he
He became good. / He was cured of illness.

(84) **Baga-ba wani-yid-ja.**
prickle-having   she did-BECAME-she
She became prickly. / She became an echidna (in the dreamtime).

In fast speech there is a sound change that affects certain compound verbs. When a coverb ending with a stop sound (**b**, **d**, **rd**, **j** or **g**) is followed by an inflecting verb beginning with a nasal sound (**n**, **nh**, **ng** or **ny**) the nasal changes to a stop (**n > d**, **nh > th**, **ng > g**, **ny > j**). For example, **roord nginji** 'he is sitting' sounds more like **roord ginji** and **gamboord nyimberramangbe** 'they grabbed her' sounds like **gamboord jimberramangbe**. This process usually doesn't happen in slow, careful speech. Only the careful speech versions are included in the dictionary.

4.8.2.1. Between the coverb and the inflecting verb

Coverbs generally occur immediately before the inflecting verb. However, the particles *nyaliny* 'again, also', and *wanyji* 'maybe, if' may occur in this position acting as temporal and modal adverbs, as in (85) and (86).

(85) **Biri   nyaliny   nginiyi.**
     return   again   he WENT
     He went back again.

(86) **Ngarayi   wanyji   nyaniyid.**
     find   maybe   he/she HIT her
     Maybe he found her.

The imperative/hortative suffix *-gela, -gala* 'do it!, want to!' follows coverbs before the verb in compound verbs, as in (87). If there is no coverb, the suffix will follow the inflecting verb, as in (88).

(87) **Gool-gala   biyil!**
     try-do it!   you (one) PUT it!
     You try it!

(88) **Biyany-gala!**
     you (one) COME-do it!
     Come here!

There are a small set of other suffixes that may attach to coverbs, thus preceding the inflecting verb. One of these is the causative suffix *-g, -ge*. Normally the causative derives a transitive verb from a verb that is ordinarily intransitive.

The causative suffix can also be added to coverbs to make new coverbs meaning 'to make someone do the action'; e.g. *garl-garl* 'to laugh', *garl-garlge* 'to make laugh'; *ngardawoo* 'to cry', *ngardawooge* 'to make cry'.

(89) **Garl-garlge   ngemberre-men-be   dam   jarragboo   dam   barlijbem.**
     laugh-make   they do to me-GET-they   that   story   that   joking thing
     That joking story is making me laugh.

The causative *-g, -ge* can be added to nominal stems like *yilgoowoorroo-* 'bad' and *men'gawoo-* 'good' to derive coverbs such as *yilgoowoorroog* ('make bad') and *men'gawoog* ('make good, cure'), as in (90).

(90) **Men'gawoog   nginimanyji   jaam.**
     good-cause   it did to him-GOT-it   belly
     It made him feel good.

There are a number of other suffixes to coverbs shown in Table 50.

4. GIJA WORD CLASSES AND GRAMMAR

Table 50. Suffixes to coverbs

-a, -aa, -wa	'and then'	*Goorninyany, jagijaa ngoowirn-ngooyoo, bib-garri nyimbimji boorrale nhawiyangem.* 'He (jabiru) is hungry, then he will stab for it (fish, with his beak) when he grabs it for his meal.'
-ji	'and then/and now'	*Gelengen, binarrigji noonemen'ge wanyanyanggem.* 'These days, I teach the children now.'
-boo, -woo	'and then'	*Berabboo nyimbiyanya gilyingen.* 'She (my child) will arrive today then (after I had a feeling indicating she would come).'
-bany, -wany	continuously	*Ngerr-ngerrji woomberrama, ngardawoo-ngardawoogoowany ngoorramangbe.* 'They were throwing things (at him) (and by doing this) they kept on making him cry.'
-bebe, -booboo	repeatedly	*Liwoojbebe nginingoonjende mooloonggoom.* 'He (lizard) kept on sucking bits of his (crocodile's) fat.' *Nyirreg-bebe nginiwardjende.* 'He used to keep getting in for a bit of a swim.'
-gayan	constantly	*Wela goonthoorr-gayan ngelemen'gende.* 'Goodness, I keep on coughing.'
-wayi, -ayi	'like that'	*Moondoorr-ayi benayanyji, goorriya, gendoowa deyena, Joorlboone.* 'He put them (his spears and things) down like that (and went) just further up there to Joorlboone.' *Ragim nyinge-nyingeg-ayi, berde-werdij woomberramande-birri ragi-baya, berdij-ayi berraniyin-gili.* 'Ants were annoying them like that, climbing all over them, then they all got up like that.'
-merrarre, -merrarriny	collectively (all of them/us)	*Ngardawoo-merrarriny, naw yirrarn-gili bardoon nhawoon gooroogoorany.* 'We all cry then after (because of) that old man (at his funeral).'
-bijal, -woojal, -bija, -wija	want to do	*Warnngemaj-bijal nginiwardji.* 'He wanted to go and get him.'

4.8.3. Gerunds – 'for doing . . .'

The suffix **-girrem** or **-girrim** may be attached to coverbs forming gerunds meaning 'for doing . . .', e.g. **jang** 'to eat', **jang-girrem** 'for eating'. *Ngoorramangbende dany ganyjinyi jang-girrem.* 'They used to get that seed for eating.'

4.8.4. Verbs in subordinate clauses

Verbs in subordinate clauses take the suffix **-ngarri, -garri**. If the verb phrase is a simple inflecting verb only, the suffix is attached to the verb, e.g. **nginji-ngarri** 'when he is, when he is staying'. If the verb phrase comprises a coverb together with an inflecting verb, the suffix is attached to the coverb, e.g. **roord-garri nginji** 'when he is sitting', **thad-garri nginji** 'when he is standing'.

4.9. Adverbs, particles and interjections

Adverbs are words that describe how an action is done. Only a very small number of words are classified as adverbs in this dictionary. Many of the words that we here call locative or temporal specifiers, directionals and particles would probably be classified as adverbs in English. Some common manner adverbs include **gaardaya** 'slow (speed), soft (hitting)', **waranggan** 'fast' and **garda-gardawoo** 'loud (of speech, singing), hard (of hitting), with all you've got (of dancing), the very best you can'.

Particle is a name given to a mixed bag of words with varying functions. It includes words used to introduce new sentences and ideas and words used to combine phrases and clauses like English 'and'. Gija particles usually have to be associated with another word, phrase or sentence to impart meaning. For example, **ngoowan** 'not' precedes verbs meaning that the action did not happen. Other particles are **gawayin** 'never mind/doesn't matter' and **googan** 'just for nothing, for no particular purpose'.

Interjections are usually short words that stand alone outside the sentence. They are mostly commands, calls, cries or words that make some kind of comment on a situation. For example, **warri-warri** is said when swearing is heard or the name of a dead person is uttered accidentally. Sometimes interjections use expressive sounds that are not found in other Gija word classes. Interjections are the only Gija words that can begin with a vowel sound. For example, **anyany** is an exclamation expressing affectionate feelings about someone being discussed, most often a child. *Anyany* is usually heard with a falling tone as well as the unusual initial vowel.

Suffixes to words belonging to all classes except for verbs have been included in the main body of the dictionary. Notes on the use of most suffixes have been included in this introduction.

5. About the entries in this dictionary

The Gija–English section shows the word, the class of the word, the gloss or translation, and the scientific name for plants and animals where these are known. Example sentences with free translations are included for many entries. In some cases, Kriol translations are also given.

5.1. Layout of entries

1. **Headword** – The main Gija word(s) are set out to the left of the rest of the entry in bold. Gija words separated by a comma are different gender forms (masculine, feminine, plural/non-singular) of nouns, adjectives or possessive pronouns; e.g.:

    babijgeny, babijgel, babijgem *adjective.* ripe, cooked. • Miyale babijgem. *Cooked meat.* • Babijgel-ma dali gernanyjel? *Is the echidna cooked?* SEE: **baberr**.

    Gija words separated by a semi-colon are alternatives that are pronounced slightly differently and therefore spelled slightly differently; e.g.:

    baalinyji; balinyji *noun masculine.* turpentine wattle. *Acacia lysiphloia.*

    The symbol '-' (a hyphen) at the beginning of a word indicates that it is a suffix or an enclitic that cannot stand alone but must follow another word; e.g.:

    -ba *suffix.* having. [NOTE: usually followed by gender suffixes **-ny**, **-l**, or **-m** or the locative suffix **-n**]

2. **Parts of speech** – The type of the word is shown next: noun, pronoun, verb, etc. These are discussed in section 4 of the Introduction.

    As discussed earlier in section 4.2, Gija nouns are marked by suffix as masculine singular, feminine singular or with a third non-singular suffix that indicates plural, neuter, mass noun or part of a whole. Nouns that have been confirmed as innately masculine or feminine are marked as such; e.g.:

    girliwirringiny *noun masculine.* wedge-tailed eagle, 'eaglehawk'. *Aquila audax.* LIT. 'one who is up high'. [NOTE: Southern dialect] SEE: **warrarnany, garnbarrany, garnbidany, wirliwirlingarnany**.

    gernanyjel *noun feminine.* echidna, 'porcupine'. *Tachyglossus aculeatus.* SEE: **bagabal**.

    Some nouns have been recorded as either masculine or feminine with both forms shown; e.g.:

    garriyil, garriyiny *noun.* black bream, sooty grunter. *Hephaestus jenkinsi.* SEE: **jambinbaroony**. [NOTE: word also used for long-nose or Butler's Grunter, *Syncomistes butleri*]

    Nouns that have been recorded only as plural/non-singular are not marked for gender.

    In some entries both singular and plural/non-singular forms are given where known. This is needed particularly to avoid confusion between a final **-ny** or **-l** as part of the noun stem,

5. ABOUT THE ENTRIES IN THIS DICTIONARY

and a final **-ny** or **-l** as gender suffixes. The stems **jirlany-** 'water leech' and **malnginy-** 'large grasshopper species' both end in **-ny** but **jirlany-** is feminine and **malnginy-** is masculine as shown here. The non-singular/plural suffix following a stem ending in **ny** is **-be**.

    jirlanyel, jirlanybe *noun feminine.* water leech.

    malnginyji, malnginybe *noun masculine.* very large grasshopper species.

The stems **dayimbal-** 'red-flowered kurrajong' and **werreral-** 'blow fly' both end in **l**. However, **dayimbal-** is masculine and **werreral-** is usually feminine but has also been recorded as masculine. The non-singular/plural suffix following a stem ending in **l** is **-e** (or **-oo** following **oo** sounds in the stem). This is also true following a stem ending in **-rr**.

    dayimbalji, dayimbale *noun masculine.* red-flowered kurrajong. *Brachychiton viscidulus.*

    werreralel, werreralji, werrerale *noun.* blowfly.

Adjectives include all three possible gender forms.

    nawarrany, nawarral, nawarram REDUP: **nawarrarram.** *adjective.* big, many, important.

Many coverbs have multiple entries because known coverb–verb combinations forming compound verbs are listed separately. The coverb entries show the separate coverb–verb combinations where they occur in the corpus. Many other possibilities can be expected.

    roord *coverb+BE/STAY.* be sitting. • *Danya woogoony roord nginji. That is a frog sitting there.* SEE: plural subject **roorrjib**.

    roord *coverb+FALL/GO_DOWN.* sit down. • *Nginiyin roord nginiwardji. He went and sat down.* • *Ngoorrool ngalil thad-gayan nyanininyande, ngoowan roord joowoonya? That woman has been standing up all day, why can't she sit down now?* • *Marrge! Roord-gala nginboowoon. Wait! I want to sit down.*

    roord *coverb + HAVE.* sit looking after someone (e.g. children). • *Naminyjili Janamany doo Nyawanel roord benemoorloonya-yoo. Naminyjili is sitting looking after Janama and Nyawana.* • *Gangga-gal roord benemoorloonya-yoo berremga. Their grandmother is sitting with these two looking after them.*

    roord *coverb + HIT.* put down. • *Bib barrem-joo nawarrany dany lalanggarrany, roord barrij-joo yilag. You two pick up that big crocodile and put him down there.*

    roord *coverb + PUT.* put down, bury person (put in ground at funeral). • *Dama wirlmerrem roord boomberrayangbe ganarran. They put this kidney on the leaves.* • *Marrarn roord yirrayanyji yilag jilan. We buried her (at the funeral). / We already put her down in the ground.* [NOTE: funeral example from Southern dialect]

    roord *coverb + PUT.* promise daughter to man. • *Dany yagenginy jiyiliny, roord nyilangge-ni ngelela boonthal, ngalilel ngaginyil. I promised my daughter to that other man (I put her to him).*

Linguists sometimes describe the kind of inflecting verb found in Gija as 'event classifiers'. In this dictionary the translations of the generic meanings of the verbs are written in capital letters showing that they have a general meaning when combined with coverbs. For example:

    ngerne *verb.* he/it (masculine) SAYS/DOES

    nginji *verb.* he/it (masculine) IS/IS STAYING

    ngemenji *verb.* he/it (masculine) is GETTING him/it (masculine)

    ngemenya *verb.* she/it (feminine) is GETTING him/it (masculine)

5. ABOUT THE ENTRIES IN THIS DICTIONARY

3. **Reduplicated words** – The abbreviation 'REDUP' is used to indicate forms of headwords that are reduplicated. See sections 4.1 and 4.8.2.
4. **Definition** – A brief definition is given, often followed by examples of the headword's use. When a verb or pronoun is singular, dual or plural, this is indicated in brackets.
5. **Examples** – These are introduced by the symbol '•' and are examples from Gija speakers recorded over the years. The majority are taken from fluent texts including painting descriptions, dreamtime stories, oral histories, descriptions of plants and conversation. A frequent storytelling device sees the lengthing of the vowel in the final syllable of a clause. This usually indicates ongoing action before a concluding action in the following clause. This vowel lengthening is indicated by three colons :::
6. **Translations** – These have been made to sound as much like fluent everyday English as possible, while still giving some clues to how Gija expresses that meaning.
7. **Scientific names** – These are given in *italics* after the common name of plants and animals, where available. Abbreviations used are sp. = species; spp. = more than one species; ssp. = subspecies.
8. **Dialect words** – Words from Southern, Northern and Western dialects are included. When entries are distinctive of these various dialects they are marked as Southern dialect, Western dialect or Northern dialect and shown in brackets. If a note referring to a dialect relates to only one meaning of the word, it goes at the end of the information on that meaning. If it relates to all meanings in the entry, it goes at the end of the entry, and if it refers to only some of the words, they will be included in the note. If there is no dialect mentioned, the word is used (by at least some of the people some of the time) in all areas. See the map (Figure 3) and explanation in the Introduction.
9. **Kriol words.** Some Kriol translations of head words or examples are given in brackets and marked as Kriol; e.g.:

    wawooleny *noun masculine.* frillneck lizard, (Kriol: 'blanket lizard'). *Chlamydosaurus kingii.* SEE: **gerdanji**.

    banbinan *locative noun.* clear way through. • Ngoorroo-binyga-moowam men'gawoon banbinan. *Coming from over there was the only clear way through.* (Kriol: 'From that jayid na thadan good wan road.')

10. **Other local languages** – A few words from languages surrounding Gija country (e.g. Jaru and Miriwoong) are included. The language names are shown in brackets after the word they refer to or are mentioned in the notes.
11. **SEE references** – These cross-references direct you to other words with the same or similar meanings elsewhere in the dictionary section. If the cross-reference (SEE) to another word relates to only one meaning of the word, it goes at the end of the information on that meaning. If it relates to all meanings in the entry, it goes at the end of the entry.
12. **NOTE** – Additional information (e.g. grammatical or cultural notes, the way a word is used) is included in notes in square brackets ([ ]) after the word they refer to, or at the end if they refer to the entire entry.
13. **LIT** – Where words have a different literal meaning, this is indicated by the abbreviation 'LIT' (literally) and might appear after the definition or in the notes, or 'lit.' that might appear in translations.

6 Gija to English Dictionary

Aa

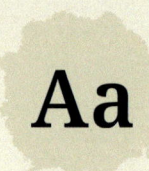

-a *suffix.* topic/focus marker on nominals. SEE: **-wa**.

-a, -aa *suffix.* sequential suffix to coverbs, then. SEE: **-wa**.

aa *interjection.* ah.

anyany *interjection.* exclamation expressing affectionate feelings about someone being discussed, usually a child. [NOTE: usually with falling tone onto stressed second syllable]

-anyji *suffix.* maybe. SEE: **-wanyji**. [NOTE: *-anyji* follows consonants, *-wanyji* follows vowels]

ayi *interjection.* what did you say?

-ayi, -wayi *suffix.* in this/that way, like that. SEE: **-wayi**. [NOTE: *-ayi* follows consonants, *-wayi* follows vowels]

Bb

-ba *suffix.* having. [NOTE: usually followed by gender suffixes *-ny, -l* or *-m* or the locative suffix *-n*]

-ba, -ma *suffix.* interrogative suffix. [NOTE: the usual form is *-ma; -ba* sometimes, but not always, follows stems ending in stops]

baagoo *coverb+BE/STAY.* be sleeping (plural). • *Baagoo boorroonboo. They are all sleeping.* SEE: **bawagoo, bagoo**.

baagoo *coverb+GO/COME.* go and sleep (plural). • *Baagoo boorroordboo. They all go to sleep.* SEE: **bawagoo**.

baalinyji; balinyji *noun masculine.* turpentine wattle. *Acacia lysiphloia.*

baam-baamboony, baam-baambool, baam-baamboom *adjective.* fat baby, cute baby. • *Dany wanyagoowarrany baam-baamboony. That little baby is fat and cute.*

baard *coverb+GO/COME.* climb plural. [NOTE: Southern dialect] SEE: **baward**.

baarnji *noun masculine.* spider. • *Ngayin-ga baarne-nga. I am a spider.* • *Baarne. Spiders.*

Baarran *noun.* place name.

baberr *coverb+BURN/BITE.* get burnt, get cooked. • *Baberr nginiwoorran. Something got burned.* • *Baberr benewarrenji. He is cooking them. / It is cooking. / They/those things are getting burnt.* • *Baberr ngenewarrenji. It is burning me. / I'm burning.*

babij *coverb+BURN/BITE.* get burnt, be cooked, be ripe. • *Babij benawoorranyji miyale. The meat got burned.* • *Loordbem jilam babij ngenawoorranji thambarlam. The hot ground is burning my feet.*

babij *coverb+PUT.* burn something. • *Babij-garri ngoorriyajbe, ngard gerne men'gawoony. When they burn it (conkerberry (konkerberry) wood), it smells good.*

babijgeny, babijgel, babijgem *adjective.* ripe, cooked. • *Miyale babijgem. Cooked meat.* • *Babijgel-ma dali gernanyjel? Is the echidna cooked?* SEE: **baberr**.

babinyiny, babinyil *noun.* fighter, aggressive person, one who sneaks up behind someone and attacks, a wild one. • *Ngayindi babinyin-nga. I'm a fighter. / I am a wild one.*

bad *coverb+SAY/DO_M.* step on, put foot on. • *Bad wanemanya-birri ragim. She put her foot on an ants' nest.*

bad REDUP: **bad-bad.** *coverb+GET.* tread on, put foot on something, step on something. • *Bad nginimanyji. He put his foot on him.* • *Bad yinama thambarlam. You trod on my foot.* • *Bad yinbimnha thambarlam. You are about to tread on my foot.* • *Thambarlam-birri, bad-bad-garri ngoorramangbende lamba-lambarnbe, googbeny-birri. It is forbidden for young men to step on it with their feet.*

badel, badem *noun feminine.* red ochre. SEE: **danggal**.

bag *coverb+GET.* cut up meat. • *Bag dinemangge. I cut it up.* • *Bagboo benamenyji. He's cutting it now.* SEE: **begerr**.

bag REDUP: **bag-bag.** *coverb+HIT.* cut up meat. • *Bag benayidji. He cut it.* • *Bag-bag niwijge danyga miyalji. I will cut up that meat.* [NOTE: used only for meat, e.g. cutting up kangaroo when people pull it out from a ground oven; not for cutting bread or other food]

bagaba *coverb+BECOME.* become prickly, become an echidna. • *Bagaba waniyidja. She turned into a real echidna.*

bagabal *noun feminine.* echidna. *Tachyglossus aculeatus.* LIT: 'having prickles'. • *'Bagabal' yarroorn-ngiyi, yinginybi yijimbi gernanyjel-ngiyi Gijamga-birri. We call her Prickly One, but her real Gija name is Gernanyjel.* SEE: **gernanyjel**.

bagany, bagam REDUP: **baga-bagam.** *noun.* prickle, sharp spine, bindi-eye. • *Baga-baga-ban-jaya-ngoongoo gelengenji. Now you are really spiky, you have lots of prickles like that now.* • *Thambarlam baga-ban-nga. I have a prickle in my foot.* SEE: **boorndalji**.

bagarr *coverb+GO_ALONG.* stick tight, fight for something in a strong way (e.g. country). • *Men'gawoony, daany, yoowoorriyangeny, wayinigana bagarr yarriyinya. It is our good country, that's why we are fighting hard for it (sticking to it).* • *Deyala deyala wariwool, manoombi bagarr wiyinyande. That woman, that one is a 'cheeky' one, she has hard/strong*

bagarrji

words (when arguing for her country).

bagarrji *coverb+HIT.* be hard with someone, refuse to listen to someone's advice.
- *Jirrawoony gardiyany bagarrji yinayidji-yarre.* One white man refused to listen to our advice.

bagarrji *coverb+BECOME.* become strong, become firm, become stuck. • *Bagarrjiwa ngilijge girli-girrimbi.* I'll be strong for walking then.
- *Bagarrji waniyid.* It was hard to push (i.e. it was stuck fast).

bagarrjig *coverb+GET.* make strong, tighten.
- *Bagarrjig yindemnha.* Make me strong.

bagarrjiny; bagarrjil; bagarrjim *adjective.* strong, tight (e.g. spearhead stuck in tight), hard. • *Nginyi ngarrgarliny bagarrjiny. Ngoowan belalg wanyji noowimge.* This rock is stuck too hard. I can't pull it out.

bagawagany *noun masculine.* prickly wattle species. *Vachellia farnesiana.* [NOTE: previously *Acacia farnesiana*; used to make boomerangs and fighting sticks. Word also used to refer to the prickle bush, *Dichrostachys spicata*.] SEE: **moorrooloomboony**.

bag-bag *coverb+SAY/DO.* be cutting something up.
- *Miyale bag-bag nginini.* He was cutting up meat. SEE: **bag**.

bagoo *coverb+FALL/GO_DOWN.* lie down, go to sleep. • *Bagoo berrawardbe-yoo.* Then both of them went to sleep. • *Bagoo-gala yarroowoo ngaaloon.* Let's go to sleep in the shade.
- *Girrij-ngarri waniyid, bagoo ngineward.* When he had finished he went to sleep.

bagoo *coverb+DO_REFL.* lie self down. • *Jang nginini, bagoo-wayi nginimiyinji.* He ate and he laid himself down to sleep like that.

bagoo *coverb+BE/STAY.* be sleeping, be lying down. • *Ngoolnga-gany nyanini-ningi, 'Diyana bagoo benennha.'* She told her husband, 'You stay here and have a sleep.'
- *Danya ngamarrany bagoo nginji yiligin ngarrgalen.* That snake is sleeping inside under the rock. SEE: **bawagoo**.

bagoo *coverb+GO_ALONG.* lie down.
- *Bagoo ngelanyge therlan wayini, an benayanyji-ngirri moorloo.* I lay down on my back like that and he put (eyedrops) in my eyes.

baja-baja *coverb+GO_ALONG.* go looking for a fight, go looking for trouble. • *Baja-baja jarriyinha-ngirri?* Why are you all looking for a fight with me? • *Ngoorrinya wanyaginy baja-baja wiyinji nawarrarram-birri.* That little one is looking for a fight with all the big ones.

bajalarriny *noun masculine.* billy can, bucket.
- *Bajalarriny rarrwayi nginji dana goowoolen.* The billy can is hanging there on the tree. • *Bajalarrim bijid-bijidbe-boorroo.* Jerry can. LIT: 'a bucket for petrol'. SEE: **balayarriny, gardag**.

bajoog *noun.* mother-in-law/son-in-law (address form). SEE: **thamboorroo**. [NOTE: refers to anyone of the possible mother-in-law/son-in-law relationship, maybe a borrowing from Miriwoong; traditionally people belonging to these relationships did not speak to each other]

bal *coverb+SAY/DO.* talk, tell, chat. • *Bal nginini-yirri.* He talked to us. He told us. SEE: **jarrag**.

bal *coverb+SAY/DO_REFL.* talk to each other; tell each other. • *Bal birringirriyin.* They told each other. • *Bal yarengerrij.* Let's talk (you (one) and me).

bal *coverb+BE/STAY.* talk, tell, chat. • *'Bala ngenden-ngiyi,' ngenani-ninggi.* 'I should talk to it then (to test the cassette recorder),' I said to you. SEE: **jarrag**.

bal *coverb+SAY/DO_M.* talk, tell, chat. • *Ngagenyji ganggany bal-ngarri wanemayinde-ngirri, Williamji.* My granny Williamji used to tell me. SEE: **jarrag**.

balalayingarnany *noun masculine.* Richard's pipit. *Anthus novaeseelandiae.* [NOTE: type of bird that hovers in the air making a constant whirring/twittering sound]

Balan'gerr *noun.* long hill on the way to Texas Downs.

balarayil *noun feminine.* crested pigeon. *Ocyphaps lophotes.*

balarnel *noun feminine.* turtle. SEE: **darndal, wayiwoorrool, bilidbal**. [NOTE: Southern dialect, except *darndal* which is Northern]

balarrji, balarre REDUP: **bala-balarre; balarr-balarre**. *noun masculine.* white mud, clay. • *Balarre bemberrayangbende-ngarri wayinigana jiyirrinyi ngoowan ngard benamanyjende yoorrwambi malngoonybe.* When they painted themselves with white mud, kangaroos were not able to smell them, their armpits or their body sweat. • *Jirriliny-ngarri benamanyjende, balarr-moowam ngard woomberramande.* When they sweat only the *white paint smells.*

balawam *noun.* flat ground. [NOTE: can be used to mean 'island' or 'flat ground in the river bed']

balayarriny *noun masculine.* bucket. [NOTE: Southern dialect] SEE: **bajalarriny**.

balbirrin; baljirrin REDUP: **balbi-balbirrin**. *coverb+BE/STAY.* sit cross-legged. • Balbirrin nginji. *He is sitting cross-legged.*

balem; baalem *noun.* bundle of things given out at ceremony (e.g. at young man ceremonies or smoking after someone has died); presents; something that is bundled together for later use. • Balemga boorroordboo-nga. *The things for the smoking are coming for me (being sent later on the bus).* SEE: **balwam, boolbam**.

-balengem *suffix.* people who do something. [NOTE: attached to coverbs forming nominals, e.g. *joogboo* 'go hunting', *joogboobalengem* 'people who go hunting']

balg REDUP: **balg-balg**. *coverb+BE/STAY.* stay in one place, grow flat on the ground. • Googanda balg jinya. *It just stays there in the one place (bush tobacco growing flat on the ground).*

balg *coverb+FALL/GO_DOWN.* grow down flat (e.g. bush tobacco plant). • Ngoowan thayarr nyinya, balg nyoowoonya yilag. *It (bush tobacco) does not stand up, it just grows down flat.*

balg *coverb+GO/COME.* sit and refuse to move, sit right down as if stuck there. [NOTE: see example under **nhembad**]

Balga *noun.* song and dance style. SEE: **Joonba**.

balgal *noun feminine.* barramundi. *Lates calcarifer.* SEE: **dayiwool, dawoogjil, nyllibal, wawoordjil**.

balgam *noun.* flat ground, open place.

balilmal SEE: **barlilmal**.

Balinyin *noun.* Springvale Station. [NOTE: name of the area around the homestead. LIT: 'place of the turpentine wattle'.]

balinyji; baalinyji *noun masculine.* turpentine wattle. *Acacia lysiphloia.* • Melagawoom balinybe. *Many turpentine wattles.*

baliyany *noun masculine.* man's sister's daughter's husband.

baliyarram; baliyarrem *noun.* thigh, upper leg.

baljarranggool *noun feminine.* boomerang. • Ngoorroonyga goonyjany men'gawoony ngarag-girremga baljarranggoom. *That tree is good for making boomerangs.* SEE: **gamanyjel,** garrabiril, goorroobardool, jinybal, jaranggarril.

baljanggarrji *noun masculine.* lily species. *Crinum angustifolium.* SEE: **lanboodany**. [NOTE: has white flowers in the wet season]

Baljarran'ga *noun.* Pelican Hole.

baljawoorroo *noun.* glands in groin.

baljawoorrool *noun feminine.* Burton's legless lizard. *Lialis burtonis.* [NOTE: said to make people swell up in the glands in the groin *baljawoorroo*]

balmarr *coverb+BE/STAY.* be kneeling. • Balmarr nginji. *He is kneeling.* SEE: **nadiling, yerderr**.

Balmendarri *noun.* place on Lissadell Station. [NOTE: place where person of this name was killed when he stole someone's wife very long ago, sung about in the Dayiwool Moonga-moonga, a song and dance cycle in the Moonga-moonga style that was created in response to and frequently performed at the Argyle Diamond Mine; Timmy Timms was reborn from and named for this person]

balmendeg *coverb+SAY/DO.* form a junction with another river. • Nginya nawarragawoony nginji, wayini gendoowa balmendeg ginini. *This is a river, it goes like this up to where it makes a junction (with the other river) (painting description).*

balmendoowoobany, balmendoowoobal, balmendoowoobam *adjective.* forked.

balmendoowoom *noun.* junction of two creeks.

Balngandim *noun.* place somewhere near Elgee Cliffs.

balngarnag *coverb+FALL/GO_DOWN.* come into the open, be born. • Danya jiyirriny balngarnag nginiward. *That kangaroo came into the open.* • Dany jangadany ngenenggayana balngarnag nginiwardji. *That little one was born here.* [NOTE: used to refer to birth in Southern dialect only]

balngarnam *noun.* plain country, open country.

balngarram REDUP: **balngarrangarram**. *noun.* dance artefacts. • Joonbam dam balngarrangarrabam. *That dance has all the dance artefacts.* SEE: **woorranggool**.

balngawoon, balngawoonji *noun masculine.* large sand frog with striped face, giant burrowing frog. *Litoria australis.* • Balngawoonbe melagawoom. *Many giant burrowing frogs.*

Baloobaloon *noun.* place north of road to

baloobanggoony

Purnululu National Park near Frank River.

baloobanggoony *noun masculine.* little male hill kangaroo. SEE: **jirrgany**.

Baloowa *noun.* Violet Valley.

balwam *noun.* bundle, something that is bundled together for later use (e.g. sugar leaf, ground fruit like black plum). SEE: **balem, boolbam**.

bambalam *noun.* shoulders.

bambarrangnha *verb.* you all EAT them/it (non-singular)!

bamberraj *verb.* you all PUT them/it (non-singular)!

bamberrajtha *verb.* you all PUT them/it (non-singular)!

bamberramoorloonnha *verb.* you all HAVE/KEEP them/it (non-singular)!

bamberranynha *verb.* you all BRING them/it (non-singular)!

bamberreda *verb.* you all TAKE them/it (non-singular)!

bamberrem *verb.* you all GET them/it (non-singular)!

bamberremnha *verb.* you all GET them/it (non-singular)!

bamberrij *verb.* you all HIT them/it (non-singular)!

bamberrooja *verb.* you all should PUT them/it (non-singular)!

bambilyiny *noun masculine.* fruit species, 'bush pawpaw'. *Capparis lasiantha.* [NOTE: very prickly creeper with edible fruit, does not look anything like a pawpaw despite the common name] SEE: **marranyil**.

bananbe *noun.* road, path, track. • Bananbe dam deg noonamangge-ngiyiwa, walig-garri nyanoowardja. *I looked at her tracks where she had gone in (under the spinifex).* • Danya roord nginji banane. *That one is sitting on the road.*

banariny *noun masculine.* bush potato, sweet round yam. *Brachystelma glabriflorum.* [NOTE: comes up in the wet season, 'round like a knee cap']

banbinan *locative noun.* clear way through.
• Ngoorroo-binyga-moowam men'gawoon banbinan. *Coming from over there was the only clear way through.* (Kriol: 'From that jayid na thadan good wan road.')

banbinag *coverb+GET.* clear the ground, make a clear way through. • Banbinag bemberramangbe Joonbam-boorroo. *They cleared the ground for a Joonba.*

bandaj *coverb+BRING/TAKE.* sneak up on.
• Ngoorroonya jiyirriny bandaj-gala biyigbany-noo, boonganynha. *You sneak up on that kangaroo and spear him.* SEE: **mari**.

bandaj *coverb+GO_ALONG.* sneak up on.
• Ngarranggarniny jiyiliny bandaj wiyinji-noo jiyirriny. *The dreamtime man is sneaking up on the kangaroo (speaking about painting).*

bandarram *noun.* tent. • Bandarram roorrji-girrem. *Canvas, tarp.*

banderanil *noun.* small paperbark tree with hard bark that cannot be peeled off. *Melaleuca nervosa.*

banderre *noun.* bank, edge of creek.
• Yagengerram bawoo-wawoo berrani banderr-biny girliwirring. *The others shouted out from up on the bank.*

Bandirrim *noun.* women's song and dance cycle. [NOTE: dance done in the Argyle Diamond mine area for the barramundi dreaming prior to mining, mentioned in the Dayiwool Moonga-moonga song for the mine area]

baneng SEE: **banheng**.

bang *coverb+FALL/GO_DOWN.* fall from top. • Bang nginiward. *He fell down from the top.*

bang *coverb+HIT.* open bank of river or creek so that someone falls. • Garlooroony bang benayidji-birri-yoo. *The rainbow snake opened the bank on the two of them.*

bangariny *adjective.* two.

bangganoongoony *adjective.* smart, fantastic one. [NOTE: Recorded in Halls Creek, possibly swearing a bit like *winggernanggoo*]

banggoonji; banggoornji *noun masculine.* rock fig. *Ficus platypoda, F. atricha, F. brachypoda.* SEE: **jimirlbiny**.

banheng *coverb+GET.* make smooth.
• Banheng-gala nherem dany larndoorrji ganarram-birri yingarrjiny-noowa. *I should make the coolamon smooth with leaves from the sandpaper fig.*

banjal; banjalgjel *noun feminine.* blanket, something that has been spread out.
• Yindiyinnha dal banjalgjel. *Give me that blanket.*

banjalg *coverb+PUT.* spread something out (e.g. blanket, leaves to put things on). • Bilirnji men'gawoony banjalg-garri ngoorrayangbe jaa-jaa-girrem thoowoo-thoowoom-boorroo. *The river red gum (leaves) are good* *when they spread them out to warm people for all kinds of things (ailments).*

banjaroony *noun masculine.* a kurrajong. *Brachychiton viscidulus, B. fitzgeraldianus.* SEE: **therrangkelji.**

banji REDUP: **banji-banji.**
coverb+GO_ALONG. create, cause to exist.
- *Ngaboonyi banji-ngarri wananyji-yoowoo ngarranggarninji.* When the father (God) made everything for us in the dreamtime. • *Googanja banji-banji wananyji Gawoothany J. Brave J is just a made-up story.*

banji *coverb+GET.* create, cause someone to find song. • *Joowarrim-birri banji-ngarri nyimberramangbe, warrgaa wananyande dali ngalil. When spirits made her find it (the song and dance cycle) then that woman danced.*

ban'galji *noun masculine.* insect-eating bat species, including the yellow-bellied sheathtail bat. *Saccolaimus flaviventris.* [NOTE: can be seen at night when driving]

ban'gerr *coverb+FALL/GO_DOWN.* smash into.
- *Barljarra nginewardji yijiyan, ban'gerr nginewardji mayaroo-yoorroong. He fell right down and smashed into the house.*

Ban'goorr *noun.* important place near Glenroy to the west of Mount House Station. [NOTE: Rusty Peters says that Gija language came from this big hill in the dreamtime and that it is the western boundary of Gija country]

-bany *coverb suffix.* continuous action. SEE: **-wany.**

bany *coverb+HIT.* disbelieve, ignore. • *Bany niniyidge. I didn't believe him.* • *Bany ngenayidji. He didn't believe me.*

banya *coverb+SAY/DO.* ask for. • *Banya nginini-ngirri. He asked me for something.*

banya-banya *coverb+GO_ALONG.* be asking for something (e.g. food). • *Banya-banya wiyinji. He is asking.*

-banyen *suffix.* from. (Miriwoong) SEE: **-biny.**

banyiny *noun masculine.* succulent plant with small edible tubers and yellow flowers. *Portulaca filifolia.* [NOTE: same name is also used for a small pink-flowered plant with a little edible tuber, *Calandrinia uniflora*]

banyji SEE: **banji.**

banynha *verb.* you (one) BRING him/her/it! [NOTE: BRING/TAKE has separate directional forms in future and imperative]

baralala *coverb+BECOME.* become clear (e.g. sky). • *Birrinyjiga baralala waniyid. The sky is clear now.*

Barangen *noun.* Bedford Downs Station.

bararril *noun feminine.* slippery lizard. *Glaphromorphus sp.* and others.

barawool *noun feminine.* female hill kangaroo. *Macropus robustus.* [NOTE: Nyawoorroo skin, mother of *jirrgany*; some people use this word to mean any female kangaroo]

barawoorroom *noun.* open place used for ceremony or fighting (Kriol: 'ring place'). SEE: **baroowoorroom.**

bard *coverb+FALL/GO_DOWN.* fall down. • *Bard nginiward. He fell down.* SEE: **bardal.**

bardal *coverb+HIT.* throw down. • *Bardal nyaniyidji nyiyirri-yoorroong. He threw her down into the spinifex.*

bardal *coverb+FALL/GO_DOWN.* fall down.
- *Biyoorroong yirrayin, bardal ngenaward belegan, yirrawardji. When we were coming from the north (Wyndham) I fell down halfway, we all fell.* • *Gerneg yimberrem-joo, bardal ngenboowoo. You two hold me, I might fall.* SEE: **bard.**

bardarramalbal *noun feminine.* buffalo, calf with horns. SEE: **barndalebany.**

barda-wardaj *coverb+SAY/DO_M.* go hunting.
- *Barda-wardaj wanemayinde ngarabarram-boorroo. He used to go hunting for emus.*

bardawoog *coverb+GO_ALONG.* just start walking (baby). • *Nginy wanyagaarriny bardawoog waanyji gilyingen. This little boy is just starting to walk along today.* [NOTE: Southern dialect]

bard-bard *coverb+SAY/DO.* jump about (e.g. fish after being caught). • *Goorndarrim bard-bard boorroorn. The fish are jumping about (on the bank).*

bardgi *coverb+HIT.* go hunting. • *Wayini bardgi yarija miyale-boorroo. You and me can go hunting like that for beef (meat).*

bardgiwany *coverb+GO/COME.* go hunting (e.g. with dog). • *Bardgiwany yarraya joolabaya. We will go hunting around with a dog.*

bardib *coverb+GO_ALONG.* walk along the edge of something. • *Danya bardib wiyinji thayin. That one is walking along the edge on the side.* [NOTE: single coverb recorded in Halls Creek previously listed as meaning 'crawl on stomach']

bardiginy, bardigel *noun.* nutwood, 'bush peanut'. *Terminalia arostrata.* SEE: **baregel (Jaru).** [NOTE: edible nuts; 'bush peanut' is also

bardil

used to refer to the seeds of *dayimbalji* 'red-flowered kurrajong']

bardil *noun feminine.* small spotted tree goanna. *Varanus scalaris.* SEE: **bijil**.

bardim *noun.* spindle.

bardoo-bardoo *adverb.* late.

bardoobiny; bardebiny *adverb.* behind (in place), after (in time).

bardoon REDUP: **bardoo-wardoo**. *temporal.* afterwards. *locative.* behind. • Welangen biyarra, bardoon nginbiyan-nenggoowa. *You go ahead, I will come along after you.* • Liwija wanamayinde-ni mooloonggoom bardoon-ngiyiwa. *He was sucking out his fat while she was away (behind her back).*

bardoongeny, bardoongel, bardoongem; bardoongoony, bardoongool, bardoongoom REDUP: **bardoo-bardoongem; bardoo-wardoongem**. *adjective.* person or thing that comes after or behind, new generation, baby due afterwards, youngest child. • Bardoo-bardoongoom boorarrgarr birrirn. *The new generation will come.* • Bala woomberramande-yirri, jimerrawoon, jimerrawoon nawarrarra-ngarri yirrayinde, bardoo-wardoongoom bal yirrani-birri. Wayinigana binarriya boorroonboo. *They always used to tell us when we were growing up, and we told the new generation. That is how they know.*

baregel *noun.* nutwood. *Terminalia arostrata.* SEE: **bardiginy**. [NOTE: edible nuts; Jaru but used by Gija]

baremanbeny, baremanbel *noun.* clever person, doctor, sorcerer, magic man. SEE: **baroomanbeny, mabarn, mooroonggoorroony, nyangoobany**.

baremanbege *coverb+GET.* make clever person. • Joonbam, ngalany-ngarri woomberramande, baremanbege benamanyjende. *When they (spirits) used to sing they made people clever like a doctor.*

bareng *coverb+GET.* kill by hitting against something. • Barengji bemberramangbe. *They killed them by banging them against (a tree) then.*

barij *coverb+BRING/TAKE.* follow someone's track. • 'Barij yimbirrigbende-yoowoorroo,' nyanini-waya-birri. *'They will be following our tracks,' she told them.* • Barijbe-gela biyigbany gayiwanyi merreb ginji. *Follow his track, he must be hidden somewhere.*

barij-barij; bari-warij *coverb+GET.* track someone. • 'Garnengga barij-barij yimbirrimbi-yarre,' berrani. *'Some of them might follow our tracks,' they said.* • Bari-warij wanyji ngemberramenbe thambarlam. *Someone must be tracking me.*

bariyil REDUP: **bariyi-bariyem**. *noun.* younger sister.

bariyiny REDUP: **bariyi-bariyem**. *noun.* younger brother.

barl REDUP: **barl-barl**. *coverb+GO_ALONG.* swim like a turtle (breast stroke), flap wings (bird). • Barl wiyinji. *He is swimming.* • Ngela derranel, barl-barl wiyinya wirli-wirlin. *This is a black cockatoo flapping her wings high in the sky.*

barlabil *noun feminine.* insect gall species found on the *Eucalyptus* spp. called *booniny* and *mawoorroony*, 'bush coconut'. Hemiptera, *Cystococcus* spp.

barlalim *noun.* flat rock. • Barlalijam jang-girrem. *Table.* LIT: 'thing like a flat rock for eating'. SEE: **barloom, barlwany**.

Barlarran *noun.* place in Rusty Peters' country.

barlanbe *coverb+GO/COME.* big floodwater coming, rising. • Barlanbe nginiyin gendangji warrambany. *The big floodwater came, rising from upstream.*

barlawam SEE: **balawam**.

barlwany *noun.* flat rock. • Barnda-warndeg bemberriyilinbe barlwanyen. *They spread them out on a flat rock to dry in the sun.* • Ngoorroo-ngoorrooma barlwanybe boorroonboo. *There are flat rocks everywhere.* [NOTE: *-ny* is part of the stem, not the masculine suffix] SEE: **barlalim, barloom**.

barlberr *coverb+DO_REFL.* separate, go different ways, split up. • Barlberr berramiyinbi-yoo. *The two of them split up (went different ways).* • Barlberra yoowimija. *You (one) and I will split up from each other then. / You and I are going different ways then.*

barlberr *coverb+LEAVE.* go away and leave. • Marra barlberr yarrewoorreb. *We have to go away and leave it.*

barlberr; barlberrwany *coverb+GO/COME.* separate, go different ways, split up. • Barlberr barriyi-gili! *You all split up!*

barle *coverb+HIT.* ride something, carry someone on shoulders. • Grisdobany ngoowan barle nyoomboojjiyi bajinggelel. *Christopher*

barle-warle

couldn't ride the bicycle properly. • **Barle ngiyinji goorndoodany barnale.** *He is carrying the kid on his shoulders. / The little boy is riding on his shoulders.*

barle *coverb+GO/COME.* ride, go carrying (child) on shoulders. • **Barle-gela ngenda-noo joonba-giny.** *I will carry her to the Joonba on my shoulders.* • **Jiyiliny barle ngidji dimanan.** *The man is riding the horse.* • **Barle ngenardge ngoorr-ngoorrgajin.** *I'm going on the motor bike.* • **Raymondji barle nginiyinde-ngiyi bajinggelel.** *Raymond used to ride his bike.*

barle *coverb+FALL/GO_DOWN.* get astride, get on shoulders (e.g. horse). • **Barle boowoo-ningi dany dimanany.** *You get on that horse.* • **Grisdobany barle nginewardji-ngiyi bajinggelel.** *Christopher got on the bike.*

barle *coverb+PUT.* put on shoulders to carry. • **Barle-bewoo nginiya.** *She put him on her shoulders to carry him then.*

barle *coverb+GET.* ride something. • **Dimanany barle ngemenji jiyiliny.** *The man is riding the horse.*

barle *coverb+BRING/TAKE.* carry along on shoulders. • **Barle-gala nharegbany.** *Let me carry you along on my shoulders.*

barleg-barleg *coverb+BE/STAY* be together. • **Bangariny berrem jangadam barleg-barleg, roord boorroonboo-yoo goornawoo-warriny nawarra-warriny.** *These two little ones sitting here together are fat little girls.*

barlegboo *coverb.* kill parent and child together. • **Barlegboo ngoorramiyidbe diyena.** *They killed the father and son together there.* • **. . . barlegboo ngoorramingaboordboo jiyilem . . .** *the men killed the father and son together* [NOTE: object is singular because two together are indicated by -mi- in the verbs and seen as a single unit]

barle-warle *coverb+SAY/DO.* ride (e.g. horses). • **Nawarrarra yirrani, yawardam barle-warle yirrani.** *We all grew up and rode horses.* SEE: barle.

barle-warle *coverb+FALL/GO_DOWN.* be riding. • **Barle-warle berraward dimanan.** *They all got*

Figure 36. *Barle: Ngalil barle ngiyinya goorndoogany.*

on the horses. • Waringarriyan nenggerren barle-warle barroowoo-birri dimanam waranggan. *All of you hurry up, get on the horses.* SEE: **barle**.

barlganyel; barn'ganyil *noun feminine.* witchetty grub. SEE: **lagarnel, lajel**. Lepidoptera, Cossidae larvae. [NOTE: not allowed to be eaten or touched by young people]

barlij *coverb+SAY/DO_REFL.* be joking together, be having fun together. • Barlijbe barlij berrangerriyan-doo. *They are joking, those two keeping each other happy.* SEE: **birriman, jawoorijbe, ngoolya-ngoolya**.

barlij-bawoorroony, barlij-bawoorrool, barlij-bawoorroom *adjective.* one who does not/cannot joke. • Jirrawoonyga binarri-woorroony boorooj-girrimbi jarliji-gam-birri. Barlij-bawoorroony. *This one doesn't know how to play with his friends. He can't make a joke.*

barlijbem *noun.* joking words, joking story.

barlij-barlij *coverb+GO_ALONG.* make jokes. • Nyengena barlij-barlij jananynhande. *You keep on making jokes all the time.*

barlijbeny, barlijbel, barlijbem *adjective.* funny, joking.

barlijgoowool *coverb+SAY/DO_REFL.* all make jokes with each other, have fun together. • Barlijgoowool birringirriyan. *They are all having fun together.*

barlilmal *noun.* land snail. Gastropoda, *Xanthomelon* spp.

Barlin'gin *noun.* very tall hill in the black soil near Old Texas.

barljarr *coverb+HIT.* throw down on ground. • Barljarr nyaniyidji gerlerne-yoorroong. *He threw her down hard in the spinifex.*

barljarr; barljarrwany *coverb+SAY/DO.* fall down. • Barljarra boorroorn-joo girliwirring goonyja-biny. *Those two fell down from up in the tree then.* • Barljarrwany berraward joowarrim doo jarrinyinbi. *All the ghosts and devil dogs fell on top of one another.*

barljarr *coverb+FALL/GO_DOWN.* fall down. • Barljarr nginewardji bajinggel-biny. *He fell off the bike.*

barlngel *noun.* banyan. *Ficus virens*.

Barlngen *noun.* Flat Rock, a place near Billy Mac Spring.

Barlooban *noun.* Motor Car Yard, a place on Bedford Downs. LIT: 'place having flat rock'.

barloom *noun.* flat rock. SEE: **barlalim, barlwany**.

barloongarnany *noun masculine.* kind of lizard said to be 'red on red'. LIT: 'flat rock dweller', probably 'earless dragon'. *Tympanocryptis lineata*.

barl-warl *coverb+GO_ALONG.* swim. • Deg benamanya-yoo bangariny-warriny, lalanggarra-warriny, barl-warl woomberranybi-yoo goorrngan. *She saw the two crocodiles swimming in the water.*

barnabeliny *noun masculine.* wild tea, bush tea-leaf. *Ocimum tenuiflorum*. SEE: **lamba-lambarrji, manyanyiny**.

barnale *noun.* back of shoulders (where child is carried).

barnalnginy, barnalngel *noun.* brother's child. LIT: 'one who is carried on shoulders'. [NOTE: Doris Fletcher (1995, Halls Creek) said this refers to a man's brother's child; Mabel Juli (2016, Warrmarn) said it refers to a woman's brother's child]

Barnanggan *noun.* place on Violet Valley. LIT: 'place of the nightjar'.

barnanggany *noun masculine.* nightjar. *Caprimulgus argus*. • Danyi barnanggany nyarlany lerndijgaleny warrarnany-wirrim. *That nightjar is very clever at making spearheads together with the wedge-tailed eagle.*

barndaj SEE: **bandaj**.

barndale *noun.* branches (e.g. on trees). SEE: **barndalebany**.

barndalebany REDUP: **barnda-barndaleba**. *noun.* forked branch, forked root. • Barndalebam noonamang-ngooyoo. *I got a forked stick to get her.* SEE: **barndale**.

barndalebany *noun masculine.* buffalo. *Bubalus bubalis*. SEE: **bardarramalbal**.

barndalgaa *coverb+GO_ALONG.* fall down. • Berdij giniyin barndalgaa wananyji goonyjambi dam yilag. *He climbed up on the tree and then he fell down.*

barndam *noun.* wing.

barndan'ge *coverb+HIT.* cause to stretch out by shooting. • Barndan'ge nyilayidge. *I made her stretch out. Made her go stiff (when I shot her).* [NOTE: talking about an echidna's body stretching out and going stiff at the moment of impact]

barndawarlawarla *coverb+BE/STAY.* be lonely, stay by oneself. • Barndawarlawarla, derrebbe ngenan'ge-narroowa. *By myself, I will make a camp away from all of you.*

barndiny, barndil, barndim

- Barndawarlawarla ngenan'ge ngenengga. *I am lonely here, I have nobody.* SEE: **wang-wang, menyawenya, wanganga.**

barndawooggalim *adjective.* good at making drum sound by hitting space between crossed legs.

barndawoom *noun.* drum, space between crossed legs hit with hands cupped together on top of one another to make an echoing drum sound as a singing accompaniment (instead of clapping on thighs).

barndeg REDUP: **barnde-warndeg**. *coverb+PUT.* put in sun. • Warl-ngarri barndeg bemberrayangbende barnden garloomboom-boorroo. *When they had wrapped them (the sinews) on the spear shaft they would put them in the sun to dry to be used for making spears.*
- Barnde-warndeg-garri ngoorrayangbende, yara-yaraj woomberramande ngarag woomberramande. *When they dried it out in the sun, they would straighten it and make spears.*

barndeg *coverb+BE/STAY.* be lying in the sun. • Danya wigamany barndeg nginji ngarrgalen. *That water goanna is lying on the rock in the sun.*

barndel *noun feminine.* type of small lizard like a blue-tongue. [NOTE: same name as the sun]

barndel *noun.* sun. SEE: **malalal, malwalal.**

barndel, barndem *noun feminine.* time of day (as indicated by sun), watch, clock, mobile phone showing the time. • Garninya, barndel? *Is there a clock (mobile phone showing the time)?*
- Barndem ngoowan noonanyge-nga. *I didn't bring my clock (i.e. mobile phone for time).*
- Barndem-boorroo yanggi biyil. *Ask him for the time.*

barnden *temporal.* hot season. SEE: **malwalan.**

barnderre SEE: **banderre.**

barndim *noun.* pillow. • Barndin nyimberranybende mendoowoon, ngarda woomberramande men'gawoom. *They used to put it (medicinal herb) under the pillow and it smelled good.* SEE: **dirdim, wanangem.**

barndiny, barndil, barndim *adjective.* flat arsed. • Manam-ayi barndin-ngoo! *You have a really flat arse!* • Danya manam barndiny. Dala manam barndil. Mana-bawoorroo-yilem, barndi-woorrarrem. *That man has a flat arse,*

Figure 37. *Barnanggany: Barnanggany roord nginji banane mendoowoon.*

barndiny

that woman has a flat arse, they all have no arse, all flat-arsed. [NOTE: swearing]

barndiny *coverb+BECOME.* become hot. • Barndinyboo winan wayinigana daambi ngoowoob boorroorn. *It is getting hot and because of that the country has a heat haze.*

barndi-warndim *noun.* traditional skirt made from spun hair or fur, worn by women before the arrival of Europeans.

barniny *coverb+SAY/DO.* pick up small objects one by one with fingers. • Barniny nyerne ganyjim. *She is picking up the seeds one by one.*

barn'ga *coverb+SAY/DO_M.* make tracks. • Biyaya wiyinyande berrema, barn'ga wanema thambarlam dam barn'ga. *She (emu chick) goes looking all along here, and makes all the tracks seen here.*

barn'galji SEE: **ban'galji**.

baroomanbeny, baroomanbel *noun.* clever person, doctor, sorcerer, magic man. SEE: **baremanbeny, mabarn, mooroonggoorroony, nyangoobany**.

baroowoorroom *noun.* ring place (for ceremony or fighting), open place. • Manam wanyage-woorroo-ma-nga, babinyen-nga, baroowoorroon-nga. Nenggerren-ma bad jarramanande baroowoorroon? Baja-baja jarriyinha-ngirri. *I'm not a little boy (lit. 'Do I have only a little bottom?'), I'm a proper murderer (I'm a wild one/one who sneaks up and attacks people), I've been in the ring place (i.e. I've been made a man). Can you put your feet in the ring. Can you push me out?* SEE: **barawoorroom**.

barr REDUP: **barre-warre**. *coverb+FALL/GO_DOWN.* land (e.g. bird, plane). • Barr nyaneward wirli-wirligajil. *The plane landed.*

barra *particle.* that (emphasised). • Dany barra mawoondebany ngenengga, binggoo-binggoony. *That one with white here is the bird called* binggoo-binggoony. • Nginyjinyji barra jiyiliny, gaboowa ngerne? *This man now, what is he doing?* [NOTE: usually immediately follows a demonstrative, locative or interrogative as the second element in an utterance giving extra emphasis to the whole]

barradan *noun.* dry camp (i.e. make camp at a place without water) in hot time. • Thoowoo-boorroo joondoo-joondoo nini, barradan goorrnga-bawoorroon. *Why are you making camp, this is a dry place without water.*

barragal *noun.* sesbania bean, type of annual plant that has tall stems used as spear shafts. *Sesbania cannabina, S. simpliciuscula.* SEE: **gilin'goowoony**. [NOTE: stem of the word probably *barragal* because Miriwoong is 'barragalng']

barrag-barrag *noun.* spur-winged plover. *Vanellus miles.* [NOTE: in most neighbouring languages this word is used to mean 'darter, diver jack, snake bird']

barraj *verb.* you all PUT him/her/it!

barraj *coverb+BURN/BITE_REFL.* cut self. • Barraj ngenawoorran. *I cut myself.* • Goorndoogany dany barraj giniwoorranji ngarnbe-birri jaabalem. *That little boy cut himself with that sharp knife.*

barraj *coverb+HIT.* cut, slice. • Barraj ngenayidji. *He cut me.* • Barraj benayidji miyale. *He cut the meat.* • Barraj-girrim yindiyi. Barraj-gala miyale! *Give me something to cut with. Cut the meat!* • Barraj-gala noondijge. *Let me cut it.*

barrajgajiny *noun masculine.* knife. SEE: **begerrgajiny, gerrbijgajiny**.

barranggan *temporal.* hot time when people depend on small permanent waterholes (Kriol: 'living water').

barranggany *noun masculine.* permanent water, 'living water'.

barrany *verb.* you all BRING him/her/it! • Goorloonyi biri barrany-ngirri-yoo ngoolnga-warriny! *Bring the water back to me, (you) two wives!*

barranynha *verb.* you all BRING him/her/it along! • 'Barranynha biri!' yirrani-birri. *'You all bring it back!' we told them.*

barrayi *coverb+SAY/DO_M.* speak to country. • Barrayi wanemayinde. *He used to talk to the country in a special way.* [NOTE: important senior community members (Kriol: 'law bosses') used to talk loudly to the country in this way to let people know things that were important but which they did not want to say directly]

barreda *verb.* you all GO!

barredande *verb.* you all keep GOING!

barrem *verb.* you all GET him/her/it!

barremijtha *verb.* you all DO TO yourselves!

barremnha *verb.* you all GET him/her/it!

barremnhande *verb.* you all keep on GETTING him/her/it!

barremoorloo *verb.* you all HAVE/HOLD

him/her/it!
barren-gili *verb.* you all STAY!
barrengirrijtha *verb.* you all keep SAYING/DOING TO EACH OTHER!
barrennha; barrenha *verb.* you all keep on STAYING!
barrern *verb.* you all SAY, you all DO!
barre-warre *coverb+SAY/DO.* be landing (e.g. birds, planes). • Deyena barre-warre-ngarri boorroorn yilag goorloon. *They land down there near the water.*
barrewoo, barroowoo *verb.* you all FALL/GO DOWN!
barrewoonnha; barrewoonha *verb.* you all keep FALLING/GOING DOWN! • Roorrji barrewoonha! *You all should be sitting down!*
barrewoorroobtha *verb.* you all LEAVE him/her/it!
barrg *coverb+CUT_REFL.* paint self. • Miya, gawayin, barrg geroowoo gawayin, berroowoon, thamboorrooganya. *Never mind, his mother-in-law's brother (the crocodile being there) let him get painted up.* • Ngoowan barrg ngooroowoon, thamboorroo-gam. *He should not get painted with his mother-in-law's brother there.*
barrg *coverb+DO_REFL.* paint self. • Barrg-gala yarremij yiloogtha warrg-girrem mendoowoon. *Let's paint ourselves to get ready to dance tonight.*
barrg-barrg *coverb+GO_ALONG.* paint someone, paint something. • Barrg-barrg-garri woomberranybende-birri joonbam. *They used to use it to paint up for Joonba.* SEE: **boonoo, nyoon, yoorr.**
barrgoorany *noun masculine.* magic ladder.
barrij *verb.* you all HIT him/her/it!
barrijtha *verb.* you all HIT him/her/it!
barringirrij *verb.* you all SAY to each other, you all DO TO EACH OTHER!
barrinnha; barrinha *verb.* you all keep GOING! SEE: **barriyinnha.**
barriyany *verb.* you all COME!
barriyanynha *verb.* you all keep COMING!
barriyi; barriyin *verb.* you all GO!
barriyinnha; barriyinha *verb.* you all keep GOING! SEE: **barrinnha.**
barroo *verb.* you all SAY! you all DO!
barroonande *verb.* you all keep on SAYING/DOING!
barroowoorroomij *verb.* you all LEAVE EACH OTHER!
bawagoo *coverb+BE/STAY.* be sleeping (plural). • Bawagoo yirranji. *We are all sleeping.*
bawagoo *coverb+GO/COME.* go and sleep (plural). • Baagoo boorroordboo. *They all go to sleep.*
bawagoo *coverb+FALL/GO_DOWN.* go to sleep (plural). • Bawagoo berrawardbe. *They went to sleep.* SEE: **bagoo.**
baward *coverb+LEAVE.* climb up and leave someone (plural/more than three). • Baward yarroowoorroob. *We'll climb up away from him (leaving him).* SEE: **berdij.**
baward *coverb+GO/COME.* climb (plural). • Baward-garri yirrayin. *When we climbed up.* • Bawardboo yirradji wayirran. *We'll all climb along the side of the hill then.* SEE: **baard.**
baward *coverb+SAY/DO.* get up/be reborn. *'Nyaajarriwanem baward boorroorn-noowa-gili,' nyanini. 'All the women of Nyaajarri skin are born from that place,' she said.*
bawardjangoorroom *noun.* line of spikes on crocodile's tail.
bawardngoorriny *adjective.* reborn from something or someone that previously existed. (Kriol: 'jumped up')
bawoo REDUP: **bawoo-wawoo.** *coverb+SAY/DO.* call out, shout. • Bawoo ngenani-birri. *I called out to them.* • Yagengerram bawoo-wawoo berrani banderr-biny girliwirring. *The others shouted out from up on the bank.*
bawoo REDUP: **bawoo-wawoo.** *coverb+SAY/DO_M.* call out. • Dirranden dan bawoo woomenjende wayiniya merdbenyge, merdbendi dan bawoo woomenjende wayinigana wanggarnembi ganggerre ngoorroowarrenbe. *He calls out in the day and he calls out in the night, that is why the crows do not like him (koel).* • Mana-binyaya bawoo-wawoo wanemayinde. *He was singing out himself from his anus.*
bawoo *coverb+GO_ALONG.* go along calling out.
bawoodany *noun.* lizard species, chameleon dragon. *Chelosania brunnea.* • Wariwoony danyga bawoodany, jarloongoorroony, dilg-dilgmawoony, ngalanygaleny. *That chameleon dragon is a cheeky one, he is good looking, spotted and a good singer.* [NOTE: the bearded dragon, *Pogona* spp. is also called *bawoodany*]
bawoogool *noun feminine.* fish species with three sharp spikes on back. [NOTE:

barramundi's mother]

bawoogoony *noun masculine.* quoll, native cat. *Dasyurus hallucatus.*

-baya *suffix.* by means of, with. • *Nginya garndoowoolany bilij diniyidge yirrayin-ngarri ngoorr-ngoorrgaji-baya.* This is the goanna I found when we were going with the car.

bayirrany *noun masculine.* long tom, freshwater garfish. *Strongylura krefftii.* [NOTE: name also given to the freshwater sawfish, *Pristis microdon*, found rarely in Gija country] SEE: **jalgirrigirriny**.

bayiwayiloob *coverb+BE/STAY.* be lying together facing different ways, sleep/lie down 'top to tail' i.e. one with their head at the top of the bed and the other with their head at the bottom. • *Bangariny-warriny bayiwayiloob boorroonboo-yoo bagoo-ngarri boorroonboo-yoo.* The two of them are top and tail when they are sleeping. [NOTE: also used to talk about two kangaroos placed in an earth oven in this way]

Bayoorloon; Bayooloon *noun.* place near Merrewoon (Fish Hole on Springvale Station).

-be, -bi, -boo *suffix.* non-singular suffix following nominal stems ending in stops or nasals. [NOTE: vowel harmony with stem]

-bebe *suffix.* a bit. [NOTE: attached to nominals and coverbs]

bed REDUP: **bed-bed**. *coverb+GO/COME.* peep over (just the top of the head to eyes). • *Bed nginiyi ngarrgale-biny.* He peeped over from behind the rock.

bed *coverb+SPEAR.* peep over at someone briefly. • *Bed nginingaboordji.* He peeped over at him.

bed *coverb+BE/STAY.* be peeping over. • *Beda nyinya thoogooli.* The female goanna is looking over now.

bed *coverb+SAY/DO_M.* grow, emerge (e.g. plants). • *Joomooloony bed woomenji melagawoom-birri daam.* The boab grows in lots of different country. SEE: **bood**.

bedada *coverb+SAY/DO_M.* grow, emerge (e.g. plants). • *Thoowoo berrembi weloowoom bedada woomberrama?* What is this long water grass that has come out here? • *Berrema bedada berrani-nga garrjam men'gawoom.* Here good waterlilies have grown for me. SEE: **boodada**.

bedagbeny, bedagbel, bedagbem *adjective.* lazy, slow. SEE: **bedawoony, yambirloowoony**.

bedajbayiny, bedajbayil, bedajbayim *adjective.* sticking up. • *Dala jarnangerrel bedajbayil.* That bush cockroach has its back bent and sticking up. [NOTE: like a bush cockroach's backside]

bedal *coverb+SAY/DO.* come out to top. SEE: **bedada**.

bedalg *coverb+SAY/DO.* grow, be born. • *Yoowoorroon ngoowan bedalg yarrani, ngoowangarnan.* We were not born then, we did not exist then (humans in dreamtime story), no. SEE: **bedada, bedawalg**.

bedarrel *noun.* lizard species, barking gecko. • *Bedarrel, roong-roong-nhawoola, deg-garri nimbimnha-ngal, roong-roonga nimbijtha-ngal.* A barking lizard, one who barks (was there when she was a woman in dreamtime). If she sees you she will bark at you. SEE: **booyooj-booyoojgel**. [NOTE: barks like a dog, *bedarrel* is listed as the 'ring-tailed dragon', *Ctenophorus caudicinctus*, in Purdie et al. (2018); *bawoodany*, the 'chameleon dragon', *Chelosannea brunnea*, is also called *bedarril* by some people as listed in Purdie et al. Shirley Purdie says *bawoodany* is like *bedarrel* but has a big head and is red or orange colour; *bedarrel* has a rough part around the neck like a mountain devil; *booyooj-booyoojgel* pumps itself up and has a short tail.]

bedawalg *coverb+GO/COME.* grow, come out of ground (new plants). • *Thawalam bedawalg berrayi.* The flowers came out. SEE: **bedada**.

bedawalge *coverb+GET.* grow, come out of ground (new plants). • *Bedawalge benamanyji werrgale jalij-ngarri nginini.* The grass is growing after (has been made to grow by) the rain. SEE: **bedada**.

bedawoony, bedawool, bedawoom *adjective.* someone who is very slow. SEE: **bedagbeny, yambirloowoony**.

begerr *coverb+HIT.* cut meat, cut off. • *Begerr ngoorrayid-doo nyawam-ni.* The two of them cut off its tail. • *Begerr-gela noondooj-noonggoorroo-gili.* Let me cut it up for all of you.

begerrgajiny *noun masculine.* knife. SEE: **barrajgajiny, gerrbijgajiny**.

bela *coverb+GET.* frighten an animal. • *Ngayin-ga birn'girrbal-nga. Bela-ngarri* ngemberramenbe, therrilaj nooniyin'ge manam-ngirri. *I am a bush turkey. When they frighten me I shit myself.*

bela *coverb+HIT.* frighten an animal. • *'Dama bela boomberrayid-yarri wajbaloom-anyji,' nyanini, 'mernmerdgalem-anyji.' 'Something frightened them (dogs) on us, maybe white people,' she said, 'maybe policemen.'*

belag *coverb+SAY/DO_M.* clean ground. • *'Roord berrenbe ngenengga, belag-ngarri ngelama, berarr-ngarri noonayid?' nginini yagoorn. 'Would you sit here, where I have cleared an area for you?' he (wedge-tailed eagle, 'eaglehawk') asked him (egret, 'white crane'), to trick him.* [NOTE: eaglehawk is talking in the old polite style used with a brother-in-law when you address him indirectly in the third person plural]

belag *coverb+GET.* take something off (covering or clothes), peel. • *Belag nginimanyji. He took it (masculine) off.* • *Belagboo benamanyji. He peeled it (non-singular) then.*

belag *coverb+HIT.* clean something. • *Belag-garri ngoorriyinbe wel ngara-ngaraga ngoorriyinbe besinjayany. When they clean it out (burl, lump from tree) then they make it like a real basin.*

-belala *suffix.* more/all. • *Marra yarra, warn'ganybe-belala. Come on let's go, it's getting colder.* • *Ngoowa-belala. Nothing more.*

belalg *coverb+GO/COME.* come off, unwrap. • *Belalg nginiyin nganyjoowarrji. The snake (that had been wrapped around an old woman) came off.* SEE: **beralg**.

belalg *coverb+GET.* pull out, take off, undress. • *Belalg benamanyji joorrooloonggoom. He took off his trousers.* • *Ngenardge-ni nyangoobany beralg ngirem-ngirri. I'm going to the doctor to let him pull it (loose tooth) out.* SEE: **beralg**.

belan; balan *coverb+GO/COME.* spread out something in a fan shape (e.g. frillneck lizard putting up frill, brolga spreading out tail feathers). • *Belan nginiyi yambarram. He (frillneck lizard) makes his hair stand on end.* • *Berrema balan nyaniyi dam-ngiyi, bardoobiny nyawam-ngiyi. Here she has spread out her tail behind (talking about a painting of a brolga with a tail spread out in a fan shape).*

belany-belany *coverb+SAY/DO.* be shining (like glass). • *Wayinindi belany-belany nyerne men'gawoom. It (white rock) shines like that there (on the side of the hill) and looks good.* SEE: **berleng-berlengeny**, **miliny-miliny**.

belayig REDUP: **belayig-belayig**. *coverb+SAY/DO_M.* follow. • *Gawayin, gawayin ngaboony bardoobiny belayig wanemayinde ganarra-baya goonyjam-birri. Never mind, my father just used to come along behind with leafy sticks (to hit me and make me keep walking when I didn't want to).*

belayig REDUP: **belayig-belayig**. *coverb+GET.* follow someone. • *Belayig nginimanyji ngenenggawa gendangbe waringarrim-birri berab. He followed him (white crane's track) from here upstream then until he came upon a lot of people.*

belayig *coverb+SAY/DO_REFL.* follow each other. • *Belayig yarrangirriyin, yilag goorrngan-gili nawarran-gili. We followed each other down to the big water place.*

belayiny *noun.* little spirit that lives in springs and caves. SEE: **rayiny**.

belegag *coverb+FALL/GO_DOWN.* go right into the middle of something. • *Nyaniyinya gerlerne-merrale, belegag nyanoowardja. She went into all the spinifex and fell right into the middle.*

belegan *locative.* in the middle, between.

belegany, belegal, belegam REDUP: **bele-welegam**. *adjective.* being in the middle, middle sized. • *Bele-welegam. All the middle-sized ones (said of the children in the middle classes at school).*

belegawirrin *temporal.* midnight.

belegawirrin *locative.* in the middle.

belewawirrin; belawirrin; belaawirrin *temporal.* midnight.

beleweny, belewel, belewem *adjective.* being in the middle, middle-sized, middle child. [NOTE: Southern dialect] SEE: **belegany**, **beloowany**.

beloowany, beloowal, beloowam *adjective.* being in the middle, middle-sized, middle child. SEE: **belegany**.

bembere *coverb+GO/COME.* swell up. • *Gamoomga bembere nyaniyi ngelga joolal ngagenyil. My dog's breasts are swollen.* • *Booloomanel bembere nyaniyi. The dead bullock is swollen up.* • *Thambarlam bembere ngenayin. My foot was swollen up.*

bemberramang *verb.* they GOT them/it (non-singular).

bemberramangbe *verb.* they were GETTING them/it (non-singular).

bemberramangbende *verb.* they used to GET them/it (non-singular). • Jiyilem warna-warnarram goorndarrim bemberramangbende. *Aboriginal people used to get fish there in olden times.*

bemberramenbe; bemberremenbe *verb.* they are GETTING them.

bemberramidboo *verb.* they DID SOMETHING to two or more together. • Goord bemberramidboo. *They killed them all together at the same time.* [NOTE: -mi- inserted before the verb stem denotes some things happening simultaneously]

bemberramimangbende *verb.* they used to FOLLOW them/it (non-singular).

bemberramoorlardbe *verb.* they HAD them/it (non-singular), they KEPT them/it (non-singular), they LOOKED AFTER them/it (non-singular). [NOTE: elided form of bemberramoorloowardbe]

bemberramoorlardbende *verb.* they used to HAVE them/it (non-singular), they used to KEEP them/it (non-singular), they used to LOOK AFTER them/it (non-singular).

bemberramoorloowardbe *verb.* they HAD them/it (non-singular), they KEPT them/it (non-singular), they LOOKED AFTER them/it (non-singular).

bemberrangbe *verb.* they PUT them/it (non-singular). [NOTE: Southern dialect] SEE: **bemberrayangbe**.

bemberrangbende *verb.* they used to PUT them/it (non-singular). [NOTE: Southern dialect] SEE: **bemberrayangbende**.

bemberrangoonbe *verb.* they ATE them/it (non-singular).

bemberranybe; boomberranybe *verb.* they were BRINGING/TAKING them/it (non-singular).

bemberranybende *verb.* they used to BRING/TAKE them/it (non-singular). • Binarriya berraniyande-noo warn'ganyga diyal bemberranybende-ngiyiwa lingambi. *They knew the cold weather was coming because she's the one (green grasshopper calling) who made them think about it.*

bemberrawoon *verb.* they HIT/WOUNDED them/it (non-singular).

Bemberrawoonany *noun.* Brumby Spring, a place in Paddy Bedford's country.

bemberrawoonbe *verb.* they were HITTING/WOUNDING them/it (non-singular).

bemberrayang; bemberraya *verb.* they PUT them/it (non-singular).

bemberrayangbe *verb.* they were PUTTING them/it (non-singular).

bemberrayangbende *verb.* they used to PUT them/it (non-singular).

bemberrayid; boomberrayid *verb.* they HIT them/it (non-singular).

bemberrayidbe; boomberrayidbe *verb.* they HIT them/it (non-singular).

bemberrayidbende; boomberrayidbende *verb.* they used to HIT them/it (non-singular).

bemberregbe *verb.* they should TAKE them/it (non-singular).

bemberregbende *verb.* they should keep on TAKING them/it (non-singular).

bemberrembe *verb.* they should GET them/it (non-singular).

bemberremoorlenbe *verb.* they HAVE them/it (non-singular).

bemberriyilinbe; bemberriyilinbe, boombirrilinbe *verb.* they are PUTTING them/it (non-singular). SEE: **bemberriyooloonboo**.

bemberriyinbe *verb.* they are HITTING them/it (non-singular).

bemberriyooloonboo *verb.* they are PUTTING them/it (non-singular). SEE: **bemberriyilinbe**.

bemberrooloonboo *verb.* they are PUTTING them/it (non-singular). [NOTE: Southern dialect] SEE: **bemberriyooloonboo**.

bemij *verb.* you (one) DO to yourself.

ben *coverb+PUT.* push. • Ben benayanyji. *He pushed them.*

benaj *verb.* you (one) PUT them/it (non-singular)!

benajtha *verb.* you (one) PUT them/it (non-singular)!

benama; benema *verb.* he/she GOT them/it (non-singular).

benamanya; benemanya *verb.* she was GETTING them/it (non-singular).

benamanyande *verb.* she used to GET them/it (non-singular).

benamanyjende; benemanyjende *verb.* he used to GET them/it (non-singular).

benamanyji; benemanyji *verb.* he was GETTING them/it (non-singular).

benamenjende *verb.* he keeps on GETTING them/it (non-singular).

benamenji *verb.* he is GETTING them/it (non-singular).

benamenya; benemenya *verb.* she is GETTING them/it (non-singular).

benamenyande; benemenyande *verb.* she keeps on GETTING them/it (non-singular).

benamoorlaardja *verb.* she HAD/KEPT them/it (non-singular). [NOTE: Southern dialect] SEE: **benamoorloowardja**.

benamoorlaardjande *verb.* she used to HAVE/KEEP them/it (non-singular). [NOTE: Southern dialect]

benamoorlaardjende *verb.* he used to HAVE/KEEP them/it (non-singular). [NOTE: Southern dialect]

benamoorlaardji *verb.* he HAD/KEPT them/it (non-singular). [NOTE: Southern dialect] SEE: **benamoorloowardji**.

benamoorloonya *verb.* she HAS/KEEPS them/it (non-singular).

benamoorloowardja; benemoorloowardja *verb.* she HAD/KEPT them/it (non-singular). SEE: **benamoorlaardja**.

benamoorloowardjende *verb.* he used to HAVE/KEEP them/it (non-singular).

benamoorloowardji; benemoorloowardji *verb.* he HAD/KEPT them/it (non-singular). [NOTE: Northern dialect] SEE: **benamoorlaardji**.

benang *verb.* you (one) EAT them.

benangaboordja *verb.* she SPEARED him/it (masculine).

benangarremanyjende *verb.* he used to KICK them/it (non-singular).

benangoonjende *verb.* he was EATING them/it (non-singular).

benangoonji *verb.* he was EATING them/it (non-singular).

benany *verb.* you (one) BRING them/it (non-singular).

benanya *verb.* she BROUGHT/TOOK them/it (non-singular).

benanyande *verb.* she used to BRING/TAKE them/it (non-singular).

benanyjende *verb.* he used to BRING/TAKE them/it (non-singular).

benanyji *verb.* he BROUGHT/TOOK them/it (non-singular).

benanynha *verb.* you (one) BRING them/it (non-singular)!

benawoon *verb.* he HIT/CUT them/it (non-singular).

benawoonjende *verb.* he used to HIT/CUT them/it (non-singular).

benawoonji *verb.* he was HITTING/CUTTING them/it (non-singular).

benawoorran *verb.* he/it (masculine) BURNED/BIT them/it (non-singular).

benawoorranyji *verb.* he/it (masculine) BURNED/BIT them/it (non-singular).

benawoorrood *verb.* he/it (masculine) LEFT them/it (non-singular).

benawoorroodja *verb.* she/it (feminine) LEFT them/it (non-singular).

benawoorroodji *verb.* he/it (masculine) LEFT them/it (non-singular).

benaya *verb.* he/she PUT them/it (non-singular).

benayanya *verb.* she PUT them/it (non-singular).

benayanyande *verb.* she used to PUT them/it (non-singular).

benayanyjende *verb.* he used to PUT them/it (non-singular).

benayanyji *verb.* he was PUTTING them/it (non-singular).

benayid *verb.* he/she HIT them/it (non-singular).

benayidjande *verb.* she used to keep HITTING them/it (non-singular).

benayidjende *verb.* he used to keep HITTING them/it (non-singular).

benayidji *verb.* he HIT them/it (non-singular).

benayinha *verb.* you (one) GIVE them/it (non-singular)! (the recipient, not the thing given, is the object).

bendegja *verb.* let her TAKE them/it (non-singular)!

bendereg *coverb+GET.* make sticky (e.g. cheeky yams with ashes). • Bendereg yarrimnya gawoornbe-birri garnawoonyga. *We make the cheeky yams sticky with ashes.*

bendija *verb.* she will HIT them/it (non-singular).

bendoowarre *verb.* let it BURN/BITE them/it (non-singular).

beneda *verb.* you (one) TAKE them/it (non-singular). • Beneda marra Pandanus Yard-yoorroong yawardamga. *You can take those horses down to Pandanus Yard.*

benegbany *verb.* you (one) TAKE them/it (non-singular) along.

beneg-doo *verb.* you (one) TAKE them (dual).

benem *verb.* you (one) GET them/it (non-singular).

benemanyande *verb.* she used to GET them/it (non-singular).

benemenji

benemenji *verb.* he is GETTING them/it (non-singular).
benemnha *verb.* you (one) GET them/it (non-singular).
benemoorlardja *verb.* she HAD them/it (non-singular). SEE: **benamoorloowardja**.
benemoorlenji *verb.* he HAS them/it (non-singular).
benemoorloonnha *verb.* you (one) should HAVE/KEEP them/it (non-singular).
benemoorloonya; benemoorlenya *verb.* she HAS them/it (non-singular).
benenande *verb.* you keep on STAYING!
benengoonya *verb.* she EATS them/it (non-singular).
benennha; benenha *verb.* you (one) STAY.
benewarre *verb.* you (one) BURN/BITE them/it (non-singular).
benewarrenji; benoowarrenji *verb.* he/it (masculine) is BURNING/BITING them/it (non-singular).
ben'galiny, ben'galil *noun.* spouse of someone a person calls *ganggayi* 'granny': man's wife's mother's mother, husband's mother's mother, daughter's son's wife, husband's mother's mother's brother, daughter's daughter's husband
benij *verb.* you (one) HIT them/it (non-singular)!
benijtha *verb.* you (one) HIT them/it (non-singular)!
beniyilinji; benilinji *verb.* he is PUTTING them/it (non-singular). SEE: **beniyooloonji**.
beniyilinya *verb.* she is PUTTING them/it (non-singular). SEE: **beniyooloonya**.
beniyinha *verb.* you GIVE them.
beniyinji *verb.* **1.** he is GIVING them. **2.** he is HITTING them/it (non-singular).
beniyinya *verb.* she is HITTING them/it (non-singular).
beniyooloonji *verb.* he is PUTTING them/it (non-singular). SEE: **beniyilinji, boonooyooloonyi**.
beniyooloonya *verb.* she is PUTTING them/it (non-singular). SEE: **beniyilinya, boonooyooloonya, biniyilinya, binilinya**.
benjilgoowany *coverb+GET.* make someone shake and stagger, make someone giddy or drunk. • Ngoorroo-ngoorroo-biny darroorl woomberrama-noo, benjilgoowany ngoorramangbe. *They belted him from all sides, made him shake and stagger around.*
benoowam; benewam *verb.* you (one) GO AND GET them/it (non-singular). • Benoowam-gala-ngage goorrngambi, reminy ngenayi. *Go and get me some water, I'm thirsty.*
benyeg *coverb+HIT.* slap, hit with hand (done to kid when naughty). • Benyeg nginiyid. *He hit him with his hand.* • Thoowoo-berra benyeg janiyida? *What did you hit him for?* SEE: **booboorrg**.
berabwarlen; berabwarloon; berabwarloojen *temporal, locative.* place where one is about to appear/arrive/emerge (Kriol: 'come out'), time when ready to appear/arrive/emerge.
berag *coverb+BRING/TAKE.* go and tell on someone, dob someone in. • Beraga noonanyge-yoo ngoorroom-birri Thildoowa-ngarnam wajbaloom. *I went and told the Lissadell whitemen about those two.*
berag *coverb+DO_REFL.* look for a fight, be spoiling for a fight. • Ngoorrinya berag nginimiyin-birri warim-boorroo. *He is looking for a fight with them.* • Beragbe birrimiyanbe-birri. *They have all gone for a fight.*
beraj REDUP: **beraj-beraj**. *coverb+GO/COME.* go past, slip past, just miss (e.g. spear past side of body).
beraj *coverb+BE/STAY.* be passing through. • Beraj berraniyinde. *They used to be passing through.*
beraj REDUP: **beraj-beraj**. *coverb+HIT.* go past something, slip past someone. • Beraj benayid dambi daambi na Ngarraarnjindi. *He went right past that place, Mt Barrett.* • Beraj-beraj nyimberrayidbe-yoo. *They two slipped past her (standing woman who took a large step, parting her legs to allow two dingoes to run between her legs).* • Ngoowan beraj-beraj jarrijtha, mayiny nginyga. *Don't go past, this (plant) is food.*
Berane *noun.* Rock Hole, a place in Rusty Peters' country.
beranggool *noun feminine.* tree-living bee species, tree 'sugar-bag' species that has a flat entrance hole. *Tetragonula* spp. [NOTE: Nagarra skin] SEE: **nhawiny, gayirriny**.
Beranggoolnginy *noun.* second mountain north of Mount King. LIT: 'place of a species of tree-living bush honey bee'.
beralg *coverb+DO_REFL.* undress. • Goorndoogal beralg nyanimiyinya jina-jinam. *The little girl took her dress off.*
beralg *coverb+GET.* pull out, take off, undress.

- Beralg nginimanyji. *He took it off.* • Magardal beralg nyilamangge. *I took off my hat.* • Beralgboowa nemen'ge marne-biny. *I pull it out of the fire then.* SEE: **belalg**.

berarr *coverb+HIT.* clean, sweep. • Berarr-girrem biriwoorr ngenardge. *I'm going home to clean up.* • Berarr noonayidge ngagenybe daam. *I cleaned up my place.*

berawoony, berawool, berawoom *adjective.* person who goes his/her own way, someone who doesn't interfere or talk about people, not interested. • Ngayin-ga baarne-nga. Googanda warr-warr ngilin'gende. Binarri-woorroon-ngage. Berawoon-nga. *I am a spider. I do nothing but make webs. I don't know anything, I am not interested, I do my own thing.*

berawooroony *noun.* ironwood tree. *Erythrophleum chlorostachys.* [NOTE: found only in the northern areas of Gija country]

berd *coverb+FALL/GO_DOWN.* kick something accidentally, get very sick. • Berd ngoowoonji-birri ngarrgalem. *He accidentally kicked the rock.* • Berd-garri ngoowoonji ngoowan-anyji men'gawoo ngiwirn. *When he gets really sick and might not get better.* [NOTE: word with two meanings given by Shirley Purdie] SEE: **nyalg**.

berd *coverb+HIT.* kick someone/something. • Berd nyaniyidji, thoowoorra-boorroo. *He kicked her, what for?* SEE: **nyalg**.

berdajbayiny SEE: **bedajbayiny**.

berdawarlg SEE: **bedawalg**.

berdbaj *coverb+FALL/GO_DOWN.* fall down. • Berdbaj nginiward. *He fell down.* SEE: **boodbaj**.

berde-werdij *coverb+GO_ALONG.* be climbing. • Berde-werdij woomberramande-birri. *They were climbing all over them.*

berdi-berdij *coverb+SAY/DO.* get up. • Berdi-berdij nginini lalanggarrany, yilag wiji nginini goorloo-yoorroong. *The crocodile got up and ran down to the water.*

berdij *coverb+SAY/DO_M.* climb, go up. • Dala bananel nyidja Garlmarnderr-biny. Gerloowoorr berdij woomenya. *That road comes from Elgee Cliff. It is climbing up here (talking about painting).* SEE: **baward**.

berdij *coverb+GO/COME.* to climb, get up, wake up (up to three people), take identity or 'jump up' from a dreaming place when born. • Berdijbe nyidja. *She is climbing up.* • Gerloowoorra berdij jidja. *It (road) climbs up there then.* • Ngoowan, ngoowan! Gerloowoorr berdijboo ngenardge. *Oh! I'm just climbing up here.* • Dama-yoo berdij berrayayi-yoo, barljarra boorroorn-joo girliwirring goonyja-biny. *Those two climbed up and fell down from the tree.* • Ngarranggarnim mooloonggoom berdij janiyinya-berroowa narroogoo. *This is the dreamtime fat that she was reborn from. / She jumped up from the dreamtime fat here.* SEE: **baward**.

berdij *coverb+SAY/DO.* get up. • Berdij ginini, marra biri nginiyi daa-yoorroong. *He got up and set off back to camp.* • Berdij-gala barrern wela. *Hey, can't you mob wake up?*

berdij *coverb+BRING/TAKE.* take climbing. • Daboonggool-yoorroong berdij-garri nananynha-ngoo diyamawa miyi-miyi ngenarn-noonggoowa. *I am thinking of the time I took you climbing to Horse Creek.*

berdij *coverb+BE/STAY.* get up. • Ngoowan berdij berraniyin-doo rangarrwayan. *Those two did not get up early.* • Berdij nyanininya. *She got up (from her bed in the night).*

berdij REDUP: **berdij-berdij**. *coverb+PUT.* wake someone up. • Nginiyin, berdij benayanyji goorndoorndoogam. *He came and woke up the children.* • Thoowoo-boorroo berdij-berdij yimberriyilinha? *What are you waking me up for?*

berdijge *coverb+HIT.* make climb. • Berdijge bemberrayid-doo. *They made the two of them climb up.*

berdi-werdij *coverb+GO_ALONG.* go along climbing. • Berdi-werdij wananyji mayaroon wirli-wirlin. *It (floodwater) went along climbing up high into the houses.*

bereg REDUP: **bereg-bereg**. *coverb+HIT.* tie up spears with sinew, tie spear parts together. • Gamanggerr wanyji jirlwam bereg ngoorrayidbende garloomboom. *They maybe used to tie the bamboo part of the spear on with sinews.* • Nyaarndem boomberrayangbende ngarnbe jirlwa-yoorroong bereg, merd ngoorramangbende bagarrjig. *They used to put gum on that thing, onto the sinews when they were tying them on, they tied them up very tight.*

beremerrel *noun feminine.* cumbungi, bullrush. *Typha domingensis.* • Beremerrel, ngoolnga-gany nginyjiny jarn'girriny. *The bullrush's*

berenggarrji

husband is this itchy grass. [NOTE: ends of stems can be pulled up, peeled and eaten]

berenggarrji noun. white currant. *Flueggea virosa*. SEE: **ngoorrwany, roonggoony, goowarroolji**. [NOTE: shrub bearing masses of small edible white fruit in the wet season; names *goowarroolji* and *berenggarrji* also given to the 'black currant', *Antidesma ghesaembilla*]

berewereny noun masculine. **1.** yellow jacket, tree species with edible gum. *Terminalia canescens*. [NOTE: resembles *Terminalia* species called *warraroony* but grows on ground away from the river; when it flowers it indicates that the big hill kangaroo is fat; grows near Argyle and has a smokey leaf] SEE: **yirriyarreny**. **2.** club-leaf wattle. *Acacia hemignosta*. [NOTE: there are two types of this plant, one has very glaucous (grey coloured) leaves and the other one has green leaves; both grow at Violet Valley] SEE: **boorroornji**.

berinyge coverb+GET. keep asking without stopping. • Dambi lambarnbe berinyge ngemberremenbe. *Those young men keep on asking me without letting up.* • Berinyge-berinyge yimberremenbe-yoowooo. *They keep on asking all of us.* SEE: **nyirle-nyirleg**.

berl coverb+SAY/DO. open something. • Berl gala berne waliga ngendoowoon. *Open it, I want to go in now.*

berl coverb+DO_REFL. open mouth. • Ngoowan berl ngimiyaji. *He can't open his mouth.*

berl coverb+GET. open. • Berl nginimanyji moorloo. *He opened his eyes.*

berl coverb+GO/COME. open. • Berl nginiyin-boorroo, walilig berroowardbe. *It opened for them and they went in (boab tree in dreamtime story).*

berlag SEE: **belag**.

berlalg; berlarlg SEE: **belalg**.

berlayiny noun. edible tuber species, type of bush potato. *Ipomoea costata*. SEE: **bigoordany, dawoonyil, larrwany, yalamarriny**.

berleb coverb+GET. miss. • Berleb nginemanyji ngenengga yilag, waniyid jilan. *It (lightning) missed (the tree) and struck the ground down here.*

berlengbeg coverb +GET. make slippery, make smooth. • Dama berlengbeg benama, dana boorr-boorr wanemayinde jimbirlam. *He made those things smooth, there (where) he was sharpening spearheads.*

berleng-berlengeny, berleng-berlengel, berleng-berlengem adjective. shiny.

berlengbeny, berlengbel, berlengbem adjective. slippery, smooth, nice looking.

berlentherrg coverb+FALL/GO_DOWN. slide down. • Wiji-ngarri boorroorn berlentherrga boorroowoonbe nhoonban. *When they run they slide down in the mud.*

berlgerren coverb+BECOME. become stuffed with food. [NOTE: see example under *therraj*]

berlgerren coverb+SAY/DO_M. grow thickly, grow together. • Berlgerren woomberrama mangoonybe. *The water weeds have all grown up together like a scrub.*

bernderre noun. tree burial platform, structure made of sticks placed high (e.g. eagle's nest).

berndoowaleb coverb+DO_REFL. put on a forehead band. • Berndoowaleb nginimiyinji-boorroo, jiyilinya boorab giniyin, joolany ngininiyin-ngarri. *He put a headband on for them and came out as a man, having been a dog before.*

berndoowalem noun. forehead band. • Ngayin-ga werrgal-ban-nga berndoowalemga. *I have a green headband.* • Jiyiliny berndewale-bany. *A man with a headband.*

berne verb. you (one) SAY/DO.

bernngam noun. bark.

bernngam noun. saddle.

Bernngawaren noun. place name. • Berre-binyga, Bernngaware-biny, jarrngarengaj-garri nginji nginya, boorrgoorloorr. *From here, from the place called Bernngawaren, is where the hills are standing close all around going further to the north.* [NOTE: mentioned in painting stories by Jack Britten]

beroowal coverb+HIT. miss, make a mistake. • Gelengiyana beroowal nyilayid. *This is the first time I made a mistake.*

berr coverb+GO/COME. look bright (e.g. trees growing together in a group), look light coloured. • Yingajalil berr nyaninya. *The Livistona palm trees (growing in one big mob together) look bright.* • Berrwany berrayi. *It was bright.*

berr coverb+PLACE_M. become bright. • Garrwaroon berr-ngarri wiyooloonya. *When it gets bright in the afternoon.*

- Malwalal therrij-garri nyanoowardja, berr woomberraya daam. *When the sun went down the sunset was bright.*

berra *coverb+HIT.* send. • Berra noonayidge-ngooyoo wilymoorre ngaginyel goorndoogal Wyndham-yoorroong. *I sent a telegram to Wyndham to my daughter.* • Berra nooniyin'ge-ngoo. *I am sending it (a letter) to you.* SEE: **berra-werra**.

-berra; -berroowa; -berrewa; -boorroowa *ablative enclitic pronoun.* from/because of/after them/it (non-singular).

berraard *verb.* they FELL/WENT DOWN. [NOTE: Southern dialect] SEE: **berrooward**.

berraardbe *verb.* they were FALLING/GOING DOWN. SEE: **berrawardbe, berroowardbe**.

berraardbende *verb.* they used to FALL/GO DOWN. SEE: **berrawardbe, berroowardbe**.

-berrab *commitative enclitic pronoun.* with them.

berralg *coverb+SAY/DO.* be born. SEE: **bedalg**.

berramawoonbende *verb.* they used to GO AND HIT.

berramengirriyin *verb.* they DID IT TOGETHER.

berramiyin *verb.* they did to themselves/each other.

berramiyinbe *verb.* they were DOING to themselves/each other. • Wari-wari nyaliny berramiyinbe-gili. *They had another argument.*

berramiyinbende *verb.* they used to DO to themselves/each other. • Wari-wari berramiyinbende thoowiya-berrewa. *They used to fight over various things.*

berramooriyinbe *verb.* they were SWEARING at each other.

berrangendinbe *verb.* they were SPEARING/POKING themselves/each other.

berrangerriyan; berrangirriyan; berrengirriyan *verb.* they are DOING to themselves/each other.

berrangirrij *verb.* they will DO/SAY themselves/each other.

berrangirriyin *verb.* they DID to themselves/each other.

berrangirriyinbe *verb.* they were SAYING/DOING to themselves/each other.

berrangirriyinbende *verb.* they used to DO to themselves/each other.

berrani *verb.* they SAID, they DID.

berraniyin; berranin *verb.* they were, they WERE STAYING.

berraniyinde *verb.* they USED TO BE/STAY.

berraward *verb.* they FELL/WENT DOWN. SEE: **berrooward, berraard**.

berrawardbe *verb.* they were FALLING/GOING DOWN. SEE: **berroowardbe, berraardbe**.

berrawardbende *verb.* they used to FALL/GO DOWN. SEE: **berroowardbende, berraardbende**.

berra-werra *coverb+HIT.* send. • Berra-werra binbija-yoowoo. *She will send them for us (Wanggarnal the crow, sending presents at Christmas time — dreaming for Warrmarn who comes instead of Santa Claus).* SEE: **berra**.

berrawoog *coverb+LEAVE.* go and leave someone (plural subject). • Berrawoog ngoorrawoorrood diyena ngininiyinde. *They left him there and he stayed there.*

berrawoog *coverb+GO/COME.* go and leave (plural subject), have hair or feathers stand on end on the head. • Marra berrawoog yarra. *Come on, let's leave now.* • Garnanganyjel Tableland-biny berrawoog berrayi gerlirrang. *The emu came travelling, setting off with people from the west, from Tableland Station country.* • Berdij-garri nginiyi belana nginiyi doomoombi dam, berrawoog nginiyi. *When he (frillneck lizard) climbed up, his hair stood on end on his head.* • Girli-ngarri yarroordja dam, birriyan-ngarri-yarre dam, gern'galem, wel doomoombi berrawoog yarroordja, gere-gere-ngarri nginiyi-yarri. *When we walk along, and the wind comes to us, well, our hair stands on end when it blows on us.* [NOTE: In the sentence about the frillneck lizard, the coverb is used with a singular verb but still refers to the head and, indirectly, the dreamtime hair, that is non-singular. When speaking about humans it usually means 'many' and goes with non-singular verbs. However, in the sentence about 'our hair' standing on end the owners of the hair are the subject, this time plural, but the coverb *berrawoog* applies to the hair.]

berrayi *verb.* they WENT, they CAME.

berrayilinbe *verb.* they were PUTTING themselves.

berrayilin-doo *verb.* they two were PUTTING themselves.

berrayiliyin *verb.* they PUT themselves.

berrayin *verb.* they went, they were going.

berrayinde *verb.* they kept on GOING/COMING.

berreb

berreb *coverb+PUT*. close something.
• *Yangoorranyji ngoowan berreb bemberrangbe dama.* Someone did not close that thing (the window). SEE: **theb**. [NOTE: *theb* is much more frequently heard than *berreb*]

berrebaarriny *demonstrative*. these two. [NOTE: Southern dialect]

berrebem *demonstrative*. these two.

berrebiny *demonstrative*. on this side, from here, this way.

berreg-berreg *coverb+SAY/DO*. have heart beating. • *Giningim berreg-berreg gerne.* His heart is beating.

berrem; berrewam REDUP: **berre-berrem**. *demonstrative*. these, here, this (non-singular).
• *Berrema googan ngarag doonamangge, bijam, deg-girrim, googan.* This one, this picture I just made for looking at. • *Diringen berremga.* • *Ngenengga yilag, berrema born ngenoowardge.* This (in painting) is Greenvale. Down here is where I was born. • *Ngenengga jidawoo-ngarri wananyande berre-berrembi.* Here she kept on going along, stabbing the ground to look for water, here, there and everywhere.

berremiyanbe *verb*. they are DOING TO THEMSELVES/EACH OTHER.

berremoowoonbe *verb*. they are GOING/BECOMING.

berrenbe *verb*. let them BE/STAY.

berren-doo *verb*. let the two of them BE/STAY.

berrern *verb*. let them DO/SAY.

berre-warriny *demonstrative*. these two. SEE: **berrebem**.

berrewoonbe; berrawoonbe *verb*. they are FALLING/GOING DOWN.

berrgen *coverb+PUT*. close in on someone (e.g. spiritually dangerous country on people travelling), jam someone up, become narrow and make someone stuck. • *Ngoowan doomboo nimbiyanha ngenengga, berrgen nimbiyaji-ni ngenengga.* You can't go through here, it will be too narrow for you here (it will jam you up). SEE: **nyimbe**.

berriliyanbe *verb*. they are PUTTING themselves/SAYING to each other.

berrimingirriyan *verb*. they are doing to themselves/each other.

berriyany-joo *verb*. let them (dual) COME, they two should COME!

berrjelji, berrjelel, berrjele *adjective*. dry leaves, sticks, tinder.

berrngerl *coverb+GO/COME*. get a fright, get a funny feeling. • *Ngela lawagbel deg-garri benamanya dam mirrngim-ngooyoo, berrngerla nyaninya ngenengga-milili.* When she saw that white woman's face, the one from here (the rainbow snake) got a fright.

berrngerl *coverb+SAY/DO*. have a funny feeling.
• *Ngoorriri-wanyji ngemberriyilinbe, wayinigana liyanbe dam berrngerl ngenarn.* Maybe they are talking about me behind my back, that is why I have a funny feeling in the guts.

berrewan *verb*. they WOUNDED themselves/each other.

berrewanbe *verb*. they WOUNDED themselves/each other.

berrooward *verb*. they FELL/WENT DOWN. SEE: **berraard, berraward**.

berroowardbe *verb*. they were FALLING/GOING DOWN. SEE: **berraardbe, berrawardbe**.

berroowardbende *verb*. they used to FALL/GO DOWN. SEE: **berraardbende, berrawardbende**.

berroowoonbe *verb*. they are FALLING/GOING DOWN.

berrthaba; bethaba *coverb+BECOME*. have friends. • *Ngiyi jirrayam melagawoo-ban-nga bethaba ngelayid.* It's alright, I've got lots of mates. • *Biyanynha-ngerroowa berrtha-bawoorroon-nga. Berrthaba ngelijge.* You come with me (follow me), I have no mate. Then I will have a mate.

berrthany, berrthal, berrtham; betham *noun*. friend, companion, mate.
• *Bawoo-wawoo nginini betham-boorroo.* He called out for help (for his friends).
• *Ngagenyel berrthal, goorndarri-geny yirrayin-doo.* My female friend and I went for fish. [NOTE: mate for doing something together]

-bi *suffix*. Topic/focus marker. SEE: **-i, -iyi, -ji**.

-bi; -be; -boo *suffix*. non-singular suffix following nominal stems ending in stops or nasals. [NOTE: vowel harmony with stem]

bib *coverb+GET*. pick up. • *Yagengerram bib ngoorramangbe goorloo-biny.* The others lifted him out of the water. • *Nginiyin-noongoo bib nginemanyji.* He went to him and took hold of him. • *Bib joowimnha balayarri-biny.* You will pick it up from out of the bucket.

bib *coverb+BRING/TAKE*. pick up and take.

- Nginbiyan-ngoo bib nimbiyinnha-ngoo. *I will come and pick you up.*

bigi-bigil noun. pig. *Sus scrofa*. SEE: **ngoorrg-ngoorrgjil**. [NOTE: a few feral pigs live in Gija country]

bigininy noun. bush yam, vine/creeper species with edible roots. *Cayratia trifolia*.

bigirrel noun feminine. desert woomera. [NOTE: wide flat woomera from the desert south of Gija country]

bigoordany noun. edible tuber species, bush potato. *Ipomoea costata*. SEE: **berlayiny, dawoonyil, larrwany, yalamarriny**.

-bija; -bijal; -wija; -woojal, coverb suffix. want to.

bijabany interjection. having a foreskin. [NOTE: swearing, said for example, when hitting a big bump when driving, or if you bump yourself]

bijaj coverb+FALL/GO_DOWN. fall and break. • Ngerr wanemayinde:::, ngoowan berrayinde, bijaj berraardbende belega-gayiny. *He used to throw (spears) but they didn't get there, they used to fall and come apart halfway there.* [NOTE: Southern dialect]

bijam noun. beaten stringy inner bark from coolibah trees. [NOTE: used for filtering or mopping up and sucking bush honey (sugarbag)]

bijam noun. foreskin.

biji coverb+SAY/DO. find. • Biji berrani-ngerra yangoorranyji. *Someone found them (the thing I had hidden) behind my back.* • Gayiyanyji biji nyimbirn damga jililem. *She might find some boab seeds somewhere.* [NOTE: Southern dialect] SEE: **bilij**.

biji coverb+GO_ALONG. go finding/looking for something. • Ngare-geny yirrayin, joorndam-boorroo yalamarrim-boorroo biji woomberranybende ngalimbi. *We went for sugarbag while the (other) women were looking for bush onions and bush potatoes.* [NOTE: Southern dialect] SEE: **bilij**.

bijid-bijidbe noun. petrol. • Yagengem bijid-bijidbe mooloonggoojam. *Diesel (other petrol-like fat).* [NOTE: old word used on Moola Bulla and Alice Downs stations when Rusty Peters was young]

bijil noun. spotted tree goanna. *Varanus tristus*. SEE: **bardil**.

bilg coverb+GO/COME. become unable to walk properly, become crippled. • Bilg nimbiyanha, maj-garri joowimnha dany wengariny. *You will swell up and be unable to walk if you touch a kangaroo joey.*

bilg coverb+FALL/GO_DOWN. be unable to walk properly. • Yagengerram bilg berroowoonbe. *The others cannot walk properly (they have become crippled).*

bilgbayi coverb+BECOME. be no good in the knee. • Bilgbayi woomberriyinbe. *They all have bad knees.*

bilgbayiny, bilgbayil, bilgbayim adjective. having a bad knee, having a 'bendy leg'.

bilidbal noun. turtle. SEE: **darndal, wayiwoorrool, balarnel**. [NOTE: Southern dialect, except for *darndal* which is Northern]

bilij coverb+HIT. find something, see something. • Gayiwa bilij janiyida goorayi nyaman? *Where did you find it, old woman, mummy?* • Nginya garndoowoolany bilij niniyidge. *This is the goanna I found.* SEE: **biji**.

bilij coverb+BURN/BITE. find place (conception spirit). • 'Bilij ngenawoorran jaan, gananybamanyji, garloomboobamanyji,' nyanini-ningi. *'I'm pregnant, we might have a boy or girl.* LIT: 'Something, a conception spirit, has got into my stomach, maybe one who has a digging stick or maybe someone with a spear,' she told him. [NOTE: this is the right way for a man to speak indirectly about pregnancy]

bilijig coverb+CUT_REFL. cut hair off. • Bilijig nginewooranji. *He cut off his hair (and then he had a bald head).*

bililib coverb+BRING/TAKE. drag concealed spear with toes. • Bililiba benanyjende thambarlan dambi, merd benema garloomboom. *He tied up his spear and was dragging it along hidden in his toes.*

bilim noun. knee-cap.

bilinyirrinyirril noun feminine. black-fronted dotterel (Kriol: 'red leg'). *Elseyornis melanops*. [NOTE: small bird that lives at the edge of water]

bilirnji, bilirnbe noun masculine. river red gum. *Eucalyptus camaldulensis*. [NOTE: good firewood; leaves used in earth oven when cooking lots of fish; *warrayiny*, 'type of sugar leaf', found on *bilirn*, 'leaves used in smoking ceremonies'; Jagarra skin]

Bilirnngarriny noun. a creek near the women's law ground on the Texas Downs road.

Bilirr noun. a hill on Old Texas.

bilyoog-bilyoog; biloog-biloog

bilyoog-bilyoog; biloog-biloog *coverb.* slice something to kill it/them. • 'Yangirni jarroongany? Yangirni bilyoog-bilyoog?' wanema bardoobiny. *'Who can spear me? Who can kill me?' he said from behind.* • Yangirni biloog-biloog? *Who can kill me?* [NOTE: from the bat and crocodile story, what the bat says when he peeps out from the cave.]

bimbinginy *noun masculine.* Children's python. *Liasis childreni.* [NOTE camps in trees; quiet one; a long pretty one that laughs, this small snake can whisper its own name]

bimbirrijbe *verb.* they will HIT them/it (non-singular).

bimbirrimbe *verb.* they will be GETTING them/it (non-singular).

bimbirrinbe; bimbirriyinbe *verb.* they will GIVE them (something).

bimbirriyaj *verb.* they will PUT them/it (non-singular).

bimbirriyajbe *verb.* they will be PUTTING them/it (non-singular).

bimbiyi *verb.* he/she/it will GIVE them. • Thoowiyanyji bimbiyi. *He will give them something. (Kriol: 'He gota give it la em something.')* [NOTE: recipient is direct object]

bina *coverb+BRING/TAKE.* teach, show someone something. • Ngagenyi ngaboony, ngenanyji, bina ngenanyji lambarne-nga. *My father took me (there) and taught me about it when I was a young man.* • Bina-gala nharayig-ngoo, men'gawoom bilij-garri noonayidge. *I want to show you something good I found.* • Bina nananyji-ni dam mawoondem-boorroo. *He showed you all where to find the white paint.*

bina *coverb+GO/COME.* go to find out, go to learn about. • Bina ngenayinde goorrngam. *I used to go and find out about the water.*

bina *coverb+PUT.* show something, teach something. • Bina-gala nandaj-noonggoorroo goorrngam. *I'll show you where the water is.*

binarri *coverb+BRING/TAKE.* learn something. • Ngoowan-anyji binarri nyilige. *Maybe I won't learn it.*

binarrig *coverb+GET.* teach. • 'Ngoowan, binarrig-gala nharem-ngoo,' nginini-ningi warrarnanyga. *'Wait there, I'm going to teach you a lesson first,' the wedge-tailed eagle said to him.*

binarrig *coverb+BE/STAY.* learn. • Gelengen binarrigbe ngenan'ge ngayin-ga. *I'm just learning today.* • Binarrig ngenden'ge ngenarn ngayin-gawa FK. *I, FK, am learning.*

binarrig *coverb+GIVE.* teach. • 'Binarrig-gala yirriyi-ngoongoo, derlmenji-nhawoon-ngoo,' berrani. *'We want to teach you a lesson because you are always staring,' they said (and so they beat him up).*

binarriny, binarril, binarrim *adjective.* knowing, understanding.

binarriwoo *coverb+GO_ALONG.* come to learn. • Marrarna binarriwoo ngilige Gijambi-boorroo. *I'm just about learning Gija.*

binarri-woorroony, binarri-woorrool, binarri-woorroom *adjective.* not knowing, not understanding. • Jirrawoonyga binarri-woorroony boorooj-girrimbi jarliji-gam-birri. Barlij-bawoorroony. *This one doesn't know how to play with his friends. He is a person who does not make jokes.*

binbarrji *noun.* fruit of *minyjaarrany*, the black plum, when it gets dry. • Woorrg nginiward binbarrji minyjaarrany. *The black plum fruit fell down dry now.*

binbija *verb.* 1. she will HIT them/it (non-singular), 2. she will GIVE them/it (non-singular. • Wanggarnali boolbambi binbija-yoowoo. *The crow will give us presents.*

binbiji *verb.* 1. he will HIT them/it (non-singular). • . . . ngarayi-ngarri binbiji . . . *when he finds it.* 2. he will GIVE them/it (non-singular).

binbimji *verb.* he will GET them/it (non-singular).

binbimnya *verb.* she will GET them/it (non-singular).

binbimoorlin *verb.* he/she will have/keep them/it (non-singular).

binbinajgel *noun feminine.* olive-backed oriole. *Oriolus sagittatus.*

binbininidgel *noun feminine.* spotted pardalote. *Pardalotus spp.* SEE: **joonjoonoonoojgel**. [NOTE: very small bird that nests in holes in the ground]

binbiwarri *verb.* he/she will burn/bite them/it (non-singular).

binbiyaja *verb.* she will PUT them/it (non-singular).

binbiyi *verb.* he/she will GIVE them/it (non-singular). • Binbiyi-yoowoo. *He/she will give it to us.*

binbiyinji *verb.* he will be GIVING them.

binbiyinya *verb.* she will HIT them/it (non-singular). SEE: **binbija**.

bindid *coverb+PUT.* block hole. • *Bindid-gala benaj! Goorndarrim thoorrboorl birriyan.* Block off the holes! The fish will go through.

bindid-bindid *coverb+SAY/DO.* block holes. • *Ngarrgalem bindid-bindid boorroorn gelengawoony mayaroony wanyanyagem-boorroo.* They are blocking up the holes between the stones (with concrete) for the new schoolhouse.

bindirijgel *noun feminine.* water-scorpion, toe-cutter. *Lethocerus* sp.

binggoo *coverb+GET.* take lover away leading by arm. • *Binggoo nyanemanyji.* He took her away, leading her by the arm.

binggoo-binggoo *coverb+SAY/DO_M.* take lover or loved one away leading by the arm. • *Binggoo-binggoo wanemayinde.* He used to take them away, leading them by the arm. [NOTE: in early 1990s Henry Wambiny and Rusty Peters watched the film *Jedda* many times at the home of Frances Kofod; they always spoke about the man who seduces the woman and takes her away as the *binggoo-binggoo-nhawoony*]

binggoo-binggool *noun feminine.* cricket species SEE: **birrird-birrirdel**.

binggoo-binggoony *noun masculine.* white-necked heron. *Egretta pacifica.* • *Ngoolnga-ngoolnga-nhawoony danya binggoo-binggoonyi.* He likes loving up to women, that binggoo-binggoony bird. [NOTE: this is a larger heron than *ginyany*, the white-faced heron that is also known as the blue crane]

binggoom *noun.* person who leads lover away by the wrist.

binggoonyel, binggoonyji *noun.* bush tobacco. *Lobelia quadrangularis.*

binginy *noun.* black smelly ant species. SEE: **thengawiny**.

biniyilinya; binilinya *verb.* she is PUTTING them/it (non-singular). SEE: **beniyooloonya, boonooyooloonya**.

biniyinha *verb.* you should GIVE them/it (non-singular). • *Ngirribawoorroon ngerr biniyinha waranggan.* You should throw it (fishing line) a long way quickly.

biniyinji; bininji *verb.* 1. he is HITTING them/it (non-singular). 2. he is BRINGING/TAKING them/it (non-singular). • *Wagon-baya boorroordboo, jiyilemga bininji jirrawoony gardiyany.* They went there with a wagon, one white man, the Aboriginal men. He took them there.

bin'gany *noun.* type of sugar leaf, edible lerp species found on coolibah and bloodwood trees.

Binoowoo *noun.* Alice Downs.

binoowoonggool *noun.* mushroom that grows on trees in the mangroves near Derby. SEE: **moorrji**. [NOTE: word given when Peggy Patrick and Paddy Bedford were eating mushrooms for breakfast and discussing Gija words for different types]

-biny *nominal suffix.* from (location or direction), along.

biny *coverb+BURN/BITE.* suck something from someone. • *Biny-gala boowarre goongoorloom-ni.* Suck blood from him.

biny *coverb+SAY/DO.* suck. • *Biny nginini-ni goongoorloom warnarra-bebeyan.* He sucked out his blood a long time ago.

biny-biny *coverb+SAY/DO.* make a kissing movement with lips on hearing someone swearing mothers-in-law or sons-in-law. • *Roorraj-ngarri bemberremenbe goorrijim-yoowoo, biny-biny yarroorn.* If people swear our mothers-in-law we should make a kissing movement with our lips. [NOTE: often while clicking with the tongue and putting the hand to the ear to indicate that the swearing should not be heard]

binyjawinyjal, binyjawinyjam *noun.* small white shells carried in the ears or nose by clever men, small shells on string. • *Ngaginyji ngaboony berrembi, binyjawinyjam-birri gardij genayidji, berrema wayininanga ngenayinde na. 'Yayi! Yayi! Yayi!'* My father cut out my voice with the little shells in his ears (and refused to listen me) when I was going along calling, 'Yayi! Yayi! Yayi!' (when speaker was still a child spirit trying to get his father to take him to his mother so he could be born). [NOTE: used to be traded on *wirnan* together with *jagoorlim* and other goods]

binyinyiny *noun masculine.* 1. ant species. 2. resin from spinifex gathered by ants. [NOTE: ants gather it from a short spinifex]

binyji-binyjil *noun.* kerosene wood, tree with small edible red fruit. *Erythroxylum ellipticum.* [NOTE: Southern dialect] SEE: **mindi-mindil**.

binyjirliny *noun.* wild prune, tree species

binyjirrminy

growing in rocky areas bearing edible fruit. *Sersalisia sericea*.

binyjirrminy *noun masculine.* little insect-eating bat found in caves and hollow logs.

binyjiwinyjiny; binyjiwoonyjiny *noun masculine.* small fork-tailed catfish. *Neorius graeffei, N. midgleyi*. [NOTE: same species as *dalinyji* but is used to talk about little ones]

binyjirrmiyanma *noun masculine.* rufous songlark. *Cincloramphus mathewsi*. SEE: **gawarnngarnany**.

Birdibany *noun.* Donkey Spring, also called Joowarringayin; a place in Paddy Bedford's mother's country.

biri *coverb+GET_HIT.* bring back.
• Ngooloo-ngooloona biri nginbimoowoon miyalega-nonggoorroo-gili ngenengga. *I will bring back meat for all of you here this afternoon.*

biri *coverb+GIVE.* give back. • Jarrag woomberramenbende Geyelsiyem dam, birima boomboorriyin berrem daam. *They keep talking to the land council asking them can they (the pastoralists) give this country back to them.*

biri *coverb+FALL/GO_DOWN.* return, come back, go back. • Ngaboo-gany dany biri nginiwardji daan-gili. *Their father came back to the camp.*

biri *coverb+BRING/TAKE.* take back, carry back. • Biri ninbige melagawoom-anyji. *I might bring back a big mob.* • Marrarn biri nanbida-yoo daa-giny. *I'll take you two back to camp.*

biri REDUP: **biri-biri**. *coverb+GO/COME.* return, come back, go back. • Biri nyaniyinya-ningi ngoolngagany. *She went home to her husband.* • Biri-biri nginiyi, garloomboo benema. *He went back and got his spear.* SEE: **biriwoorrg**.

biri *coverb+SAY/DO_M.* return, come back.
• Gendang biri woomberrama. *They all came back from upstream.*

birinyboorrool *noun feminine.* type of small crustacean with a long thin tail.

biriwoorrg *coverb+BRING/TAKE.* bring back, take back. • Biriwoorrg benanyji. *He brought them back.*

biriwoorrg *coverb+GIVE.* give back. • Ngoowan daam biriwoorrg yimberrayin-yarre ngoowangarnan. *They are not giving us back the country, no.*

biriwoorrg; biriwoorr *coverb+GO/COME.* return (plural), all go/come back. • Biriwoorrg

Figure 38. *Binyjirrminy: Jangardi Gabriel Nodea: Binyjirrminy boorab ngidji boolmi-biny.*

berrayin. *They all came back.*

Biriyalji *noun.* Fish Hole, a place on Bedford Downs.

biriyalji, biriyale *noun masculine.* conkerberry (konkerberry). *Carissa lanceolata*. • Biriyale denggij nyerne mayim. *She is picking the conkerberry (konkerberry) fruit.* SEE: **maboorany**.

birlbirljil, birlbirljim *noun feminine.* grasshopper species similar to *malnginyji* and *girndilji* but smaller and softer. [NOTE: people used to chase swarms into a hole, set the grass on fire to cook them and then eat them]

birlijig *coverb+BURN/BITE.* cut hair off self. • Birlijig nginewooranji. *He cut off his own hair.*

birlijig *coverb+HIT.* cut hair off someone.
• Ngenayin-ningi dany birlijiga ngenayidji yambarram. *I went to that man (the barber) and he cut my hair off.*

birlinyil *noun feminine.* small tick. • Birliny-ban-nga. *I have a tick.* • Birlinyil doo wekerlel, diyama-boorroo biya ngilin'ge. Birliny dam boorralega-nga. *Little ticks and big ticks; those are what I look round for. Those ticks are my*

food. SEE: **loorrma-loorrma, wegerlel.**
birlirre *noun.* spirit of person. SEE: **joowany.**
birlirrijgel *noun feminine.* peewee, magpie lark. *Grallina cyanoleuca.* SEE: **goorliyirrel.**
birn'girre *noun.* feather. SEE: **darrgam, ganalam.**
birn'girrbal *noun feminine.* bush turkey, bustard. *Ardeotis australis.* • Birn'girrbal miyale men'gawool. *The bush turkey is good meat.* SEE: **galamoordal.** [NOTE: Nyaajarri skin]
birn'goolji, birn'goolool, birn'gooloo *adjective.* deaf. • Nginyjiny birn'goolji. *This one (man) is deaf.* • Nyengen-ga birn'gooloo-ngoongoo. *You are deaf.* SEE: **yardewoorriny.**
birraroob *coverb+GO/COME.* go right away (e.g. eagle flying).
birr-birr *coverb+SAY/DO.* clap with boomerangs (while singing). • Birr-birr ngerne Magany, joonbam-anyji ngalany ngerne. *Magany is playing boomerangs, he must be singing Joonba (said of photo).*
birrga-wirrga *coverb+GET.* tease. • Birrga-wirrga nemenji-ningi. *He is winding you up.* SEE: **birriman**, **jing**, **goonyjiri.**

birrga-wirrga *coverb+SPEAR.* tease. • Birrga-wirrga yinangabennha. *You are teasing me.* • Birrga-wirrga yinangaboorda. *You were teasing me.*
birrgoolany *noun masculine.* centipede. *Myriapoda, Chilopoda.*
-birri *indirect object enclitic pronoun.* to them, to it (non-singular). [NOTE: homophonous with instrumental suffix]
-birri *suffix.* instrumental suffix. [NOTE: homophonous with 3rd person non-singular indirect object enclitic pronoun]
birrid-birridel *noun feminine.* rainbow bird. *Merops ornatus.* [NOTE: the rainbow birds make a call rather like a cricket]
birrid-birridel *noun feminine.* cricket. SEE: **binggoo-binggool.**
birriman 1. *coverb+GET.* tease, make fun of someone. • Jimerrawoog yilgoowoorroo woomenji birriman-ngarri ngimenya. *He always gets wild when she teases him.*
2. *coverb+HIT.* tease. • Jimerrawoon yilgoowoorri nyimbirn birriman-ngarri nyiyinji. *She always gets wild when he teases her.*

Figure 39. *Biriyalji, Biriyale: Kalenisha Peters: Biriyale denggij nyerne mayim Binoowoon.*

birriman

3. *coverb+PUT.* tease. • *Nyingan birriman nooloonha-ngal. She's teasing you.* SEE: **birrgawirrga, jing, goonyjiri.**

birriman *coverb+SAY/PUT_REFL.* make fun of each other. • *Birriman birriliyanbi-yoo. They were making fun together.*

birriman *coverb+SAY/DO_REFL.* make jokes together. • *Ngaga! Birriman birringirriyan-joo:::, magarniyam, wayina ngooloo-ngooloonybe boorroonboo. Well! They were making jokes to one another from early in the morning until late afternoon.* SEE: **barlij.**

birrimiyanbe *verb.* they are doing to themselves/each other.

birrinbe *verb.* they will BE/BE STAYING.

birrinbende *verb.* they will all BE/BE STAYING.

birrindilinyji *noun masculine.* skinny-leaf wattle. *Acacia plectocarpa.* [NOTE: wattle tree species used to make hard spear points; bigger plant than *jiwiny*]

birringanybi *verb.* they will SPEAR/POKE THEMSELVES/EACH OTHER.

birringirriyan *verb.* they are DOING TO THEMSELVES/EACH OTHER.

birringirriyin *verb.* they DID TO THEMSELVES/EACH OTHER.

birrinyji, birrinybe *noun.* sky.

birrinyoorlji *noun masculine.* wasp species.

birrinyoowoorlji *noun masculine.* dragonfly. • *Ngayin-ga birrinyoowoorle-nga. I am a dragonfly.*

birrinyoowoorlel *noun feminine.* helicopter. SEE: **galayigajil.**

birrirn *verb.* they will SAY/DO.

birriwoon *verb.* they will FALL/GO DOWN.

birriyama; birriyam *demonstrative.* these are the ones, this (non-singular) is the one, these/this here. • *'Jarrag barremnhande nenggerriyangiyam birriyama Gijayam,' wanemayinde-yirri. 'You should all keep on talking your own real language, this real Gija,' he used to tell us.* • *Birriyam-nga daambi. This is my home.* • *Birriyama-nga gamerrem doorloog-garri ngelayid. This is my birth country, where I was born.*

birriyan *verb.* they will be GOING/COMING.

birriyanbe *verb.* they will be GOING/COMING.

birriyanybe *verb.* let them keep COMING, they should be COMING.

birrmale *noun.* lap. SEE: **jamoorr.**

biwoorre *noun.* eyebrow.

biya *coverb.* look for something on self. • *Bagama-boorroo biya nyingiyarrayen jina-jinany. She is looking for prickles in her dress.*

biya *coverb+SAY/DO.* look around. • *Biya nginini. He looked around.*

biya *coverb+GO_ALONG.* go looking around for something. • *Biya jarranynha-yoo, ngoowanganarn. You two were looking for it, but there was none (you couldn't find any).* • *Biya-gela ngelegbany. I should go looking around.*

biya *coverb+HIT/CUT.* look for something. • *Wentha, biya-ngarri yirroowanji-yoo, ngoorlan'gayiny bilij-anyji yirroowiji nawanega dan. Well, if we go looking around again we might find that cave there.*

biya *coverb+HIT.* look for something. • *Biya yirrijende-ngooyoo ngelga. We will keep looking for this thing (painting in cave).*

biya REDUP: **biyaya.** *coverb+GET.* look for. • *Biyaya yirramenjendi-yoo yarreben-doo. We two are still looking for it.*

biya *coverb+GO/COME.* go looking for.

biyajtha *verb.* you (one) PUT him/her/it!

biyanga *coverb+GO_ALONG.* look for. • *Berremboowa Gabamendji biyanga wananyjende wanyagem-boorroo, wanyagem-boorroo . . . ngayindi bib ngemberramang. These Government people were looking for children . . . they picked me up (from the bush and took me to Moola Bulla).*

biyany *verb.* you (one) COME here! SEE: **biyanynha!**

biyanynha *verb.* you (one) should COME here! SEE: **biyany.**

biyarr *verb.* you (one) GO!

biyarra *verb.* you (one) must be GOING!

biyarrande *verb.* you (one) keep GOING!

biyawany *coverb+GO/COME.* go looking for. • *Biyawany ngenardge boorrale-boorroo goorndarrimga. I go looking around for a feed of fish.*

biya-wiya *coverb+SAY/DO.* look for. • *Girli wananyji, biya-wiya nginini, boorrale-bawoorroo-jiyan. He walked along, he was looking around, there was really nothing to eat.* • *Biya-wiya-ma narroorn? Are you all looking around?*

biya-wiya *coverb+GO_ALONG.* go looking for someone/something. • *Marrarn nginiyin,* biya-wiya wananyji-boorroo-yoo lambarn-warrinyji nhawiyange-warriny. *He went away looking for his two young sons.* • **Danya warlenggenany biya-wiya wiyinji-boorroo miyale.** *This water snake is looking for meat.* • **Dala wiyarrel biya-wiya wiyinya mayim-boorroo.** *This emu is looking for food.*

biyi *verb.* you DO it.

biyida *verb.* you (one) TAKE him/her/it.

biyigbany *verb.* you (one) TAKE him/her/it along. [NOTE: BRING/TAKE has directional forms in future and imperative]

biyig-biyiggel *noun feminine.* yellow-faced miner. *Manorina flavigula.* [NOTE: warns kangaroos when hunters are coming]

biyij *verb.* you (one) HIT him/her/it.

biyijtha *verb.* you (one) HIT him/her/it.

biyil; booyool; biyool *verb.* you (one) PUT him/her/it.

biyilij *verb.* you (one) SAY/PLACE YOURSELF. • **Wara gool nyaliny biyilij!** *OK you try again! You try too!*

biyim *verb.* you (one) GET him/her/it!

biyimnha *verb.* you (one) should GET him/her/it!

biyird-biyird *coverb+SAY/DO.* make fire by friction, make fire with fire sticks. • **Biyird-biyird nginini jirrawoony.** *One man made fire.*

biyird-biyird *coverb+HIT.* make fire by friction, make fire with fire sticks. • **Goonggalam-birri biyird-biyird boomberrayidbe-yoo.** *The two of them made fire with a fire drill.*

biyirr *coverb+GET.* rub hands down a stick using a movement similar to making fire to get lots of small fruit off. • **Biyirr-gala biyim nawarrany berenggarrji.** *Rub the branches to get the big amount of white currant fruit off. / Get this big lot of fruit off the white currant bushes.*

biyirr-biyirrbe *coverb+PUT.* rub hands down a stick to get something off. • **Ngoorrwany biyirr-biyirrbe niniyangge jina-jinan.** *I was rubbing the white currants off the bushes between my hands into my dress.* [NOTE: using a movement similar to making fire but not for making fire]

biyirri-biny *directional.* from the north. SEE: **biyoorroong**.

biyirrin *directional.* in the north.

biyoorroong; booyoorroong REDUP: **bibiyoorroong**. *directional.* from the north. • **Biyoorroong ngenad noonanygende gardagbi-yoorroong.** *I came back from the north carrying it (honey and pollen lumps) in a billy can.* • **Booyoorroong-milin-nga.** *I come from the north.*

-boo; -be; -bi *suffix.* non-singular suffix following nominal stems ending in stops or nasals. [NOTE: vowel harmony with stem]

-boo; -woo *coverb suffix.* sequential suffix to coverbs, 'and then'. SEE: **-woo**.

boobayi *coverb+SAY/DO.* sool up a dog. • **Boobayi nginini-birri jarrinyinbi.** *He sooled up his devil dogs.*

booboogarral *noun.* caterpillar. SEE: **joombayiny**. [NOTE: meaning used at Halls Creek; in Warrmarn means round seed pods of kapok bush and *joombayiny* is the word for 'caterpillar']

booboogarral *noun.* round fluffy seed pods of kapok bush, balloon. [NOTE: meaning used at Turkey Creek; also used for 'balloon' at Turkey Creek; in Halls Creek this means 'caterpillar' (Josie Farrer); at Warrmarn *joombayiny* is the word for 'caterpillar' (Hector Jandany and Left Hand George)]

booboorrg *coverb+HIT.* slap. • **Booboorrg-gala biyi!** *Slap him/her (that kid)!* • **Thoowoo-boorroo booboorrg janiyida?** *Why did you slap them?* SEE: **benyeg, boorrg**.

bood *coverb+SAY/DO_M.* grow. • **Beremerrel bood wanema goorloon.** *The reeds are growing up in the water. / The bullrushes are growing out of the water.* SEE: **bed**.

boodada *coverb+SAY/DO_M.* grow, emerge (e.g. plants). • **Dama rard-garri nyanande, berrembe boodada berrani-ngiyi na.** *When she fell down hard like that they (prickles that had been spinifex) grew all over her (echidna) then.* [NOTE: Southern dialect] SEE: **bedada**.

boodbaj *coverb+FALL/GO_DOWN.* fall (e.g. from tree or when wounded). • **Boodbaj nginiward.** *He fell.* SEE: **berdbaj**.

boodooj *coverb+PUT.* set fire to something (plural subject). • **Boodooj bemberriyilinbe.** *They set fire to it (grass, for grasshoppers).* SEE: **booj, booj-booj**.

boodooj *coverb+BURN/BITE* burn something • **Boodooj-gala noondoowarren.** *I'll burn this lot up.*

boodoom *noun.* ankle. [NOTE: Southern dialect] SEE: **lenggale**

boodoonggili; boodoonggooloo *noun.* sweat. [NOTE: *boodoonggili* (Doris Fletcher),

boog

boodoonggooloo (Rusty Peters)]
boog *coverb+GET.* pull out of fire, get something out of earth oven. • *Boog benama.* He got it out of the oven. • *Boogboo nemen'ge marne-biny.* I am just getting it out of the fire.

booj *coverb+PUT.* set fire to something.
• *Goonggalam benama biyird-biyird-ngarri, booj benayanyji-noowa.* He (egret) got two special sticks and set fire (to the spinifex) behind his (eagle's) back. SEE: **boodooj, booj-booj**.

booj *coverb+BURN/BITE_REFL.* get burnt.
• *Ngoowana booj nginiwoorranji.* He did not get burnt up. SEE: **boodooj, booj-booj**.

booj *coverb+BURN/BITE.* burn something. • *Booj benawoorran!* Burn it! • *Booj benawoorranyji.* He set fire to things. SEE: **boodooj, booj-booj**.

booj *coverb+PLACE_M.* set on fire. • *Booj woomberrayangbe berrembi, deyema yoorloo, Ngiwoowayan.* They set fire here (shows place in painting), down over there, right at Ngiwoowan. SEE: **boodooj, booj-booj**.

booj-booj *coverb+PUT.* burn something.
• *Booj-booj-gala yamberraj. Men'gawoog-gala yamberraj daam.* We'll burn all around to clear the place. SEE: **booj, boodooj**.

booj-booj *coverb+SAY/DO.* set fire to something (e.g. bush or grass). • *Ngoorroonyayi booj-booj wiyinjende.* He's over there setting fire to something. SEE: **booj, boodooj**.

boojigadji *noun masculine.* cat. *Felis catus.* SEE: **dijarrji, ngirrngiliny, ngirrngiliwoony, goordoony.** [NOTE: from English 'pussy-cat']

bool *coverb+HIT.* cover. • *Merndam-birri bool yarrija.* We cover it (cooking food) with paperbark. • *Bool yamberrija merndam-birri.* We will cover them with paperbark.

bool *coverb+GO/COME.* make nest (bird).
• *Bernderre dan laarne, boolmin, bool-ngarri nginiyi laarne ngarrgalen.* At that nest up high, where he (eagle) makes a nest of sticks high up on the rocky hill.

bool REDUP: **bool-bool**. *coverb+SAY/PLACE_REFL.* cover self. • *Bool nginbiyilijge merndam-birri.* I'll cover myself with a blanket (of paperbark).
• *Bool-bool nginiyiliyin.* He covered himself up.

Boolanji *noun.* small gorge on Frank River west of Purnululu with painting of upside-down woman.

boolbam *noun.* present, gift, thing.

bool-bool *coverb+BE/STAY.* be covered.
• *Bool-bool nginji.* He is covered.

bool-bool *coverb+DO_REFL.* cover self. • *Bool-bool nyanimiyinya.* She covered herself up.

bool-boole *noun.* blanket. • *Garninya, bool-boole yindiyinnha bool-bool-girrem.* Is there one, give me a blanket (something to cover myself up). • *Bool-bool-gajim bagoo-girrem gibin.* Swag (lit. thing for covering up for sleeping in the bush). SEE: **banjal, banjalgjel**.

boolgam REDUP: **boolga-boolgagem**. *noun.* grey hair.

boolganybany *coverb+GET.* get grey hair.
• *Berrema boolganybany-ngarri yarremenya.* Here when we get grey hair.

booliyi *coverb+GO_ALONG.* come and talk to people who have had a death in the family as if nothing had happened. • *Booliyi wiyinji-yarri. Ngoowan thayad wananyji-yarri goonyingarr-boorroowa.* He bin come in blind. He didn't talk to us about the dead man and how the accident happen.

booliyirrg SEE: **boorliyirrg**.

boolmim *noun.* bough shed; bird nest; leafy shelter where dancers paint up, emerge from and return to during performances; bowerbird's bower.

Boolmiwoony *noun.* place near Gawoorrngarndiny in Ngarrgooroon country.

boolngan-boolngan *noun.* light-coloured soil type.

boolngarrbany, boolngarrbal, boolngarrbam *adjective.* rough, having lumps.

boolngayirriny *noun masculine.* bull. *Bos taurus, B. indicus.* SEE: **boorroonany, booloomanji**.

booloogool *noun.* whistling kite. *Haliastur sphenurus.* [NOTE: same word also recorded meaning bar-shouldered kite, *Elanus axillaris*]

booloomanel, booloomanbe *noun feminine.* cow, cattle. *Bos taurus, B. indicus.*

booloomanji, booloomanbe *noun masculine.* bullock, cattle, small bull, steer. *Bos taurus, B. indicus.* SEE: **boolngayirriny, boorroonany**.

Booloongoo *noun.* a place on Mabel Downs where two of Shirley Purdie's maternal grandmother's uncles are buried.

booloongool REDUP: **booloo-booloongoom**. *noun.* older sister.

booloongoony REDUP: **booloo-booloongoom**. *noun.* older brother.

booloorrji *noun masculine.* king brown snake. *Pseudechis australis.* SEE: **lankerrji, loonboorroony**.

booloorroony *noun masculine.* fine, smooth, slippery stone.
boolyam *noun.* calf muscle. [NOTE: Southern dialect] SEE: **dimboom**.
booma *verb.* you (one) SAY/DO!
boomanha *verb.* you (one) GET him/her/it!
boomanhande *verb.* you (one) keep on SAYING/DOING!
boomberrama; boomberramang *verb.* they GOT them/it (non-singular).
boomberramangbe; boomberramangboo *verb.* they were GETTING them/it (non-singular).
boomberramenbe *verb.* they are GETTING them/it (non-singular).
boomberramenbende *verb.* they keep on GETTING them/it (non-singular).
boomberramoorloowardbe; boomberramoorlaardbe *verb.* they HAD them/it (non-singular)..
boomberramoorloowardbende *verb.* they used to HAVE them/it (non-singular).
boomberrangaboord *verb.* they SPEARED them/it (non-singular).
boomberrangaboordbe *verb.* they were SPEARING them/it (non-singular).
boomberrangoonbe *verb.* they were EATING them/it (non-singular).
boomberrawoorroodboo *verb.* they LEFT them/it (non-singular).
boomberraya *verb.* they PUT them/it (non-singular).
boomberrayangbe *verb.* they were PUTTING them/it (non-singular).
boomberrayangbende *verb.* they used to PUT them/it (non-singular).
boomboongel *noun feminine.* pupa of *joombayil*. [NOTE: eaten by old women]
boomboorriyin *verb.* they will GIVE them. [NOTE: recipicent is direct object]
boomi REDUP: **boomi-boomi**. *coverb+PUT.* blow something, play didjeridoo. • *Boomi-gala benaj marnem.* Blow on the fire. • *Gooloomboo boomi nyiyooloonji.* He is blowing the didjeridoo. • *Boomi biniyilinya nyamanil.* Old woman is blowing them/it (non-singular). • *Boomi-boomi bembirriyilinbe yangoorranyji.* Some people are playing the didjeridoo.
boomoo-girrem *noun.* air compressor. LIT: 'thing for blowing'.
boomoorloonnha; boomoorloonha *verb.* you (one) keep him/her/it!
boonany REDUP: **boonany-boonany**. *coverb+SAY/DO.* be bubbling up. • *Boonany ngerne giliwirring-biny winyjinyji, nginyjiny na goorloonyi.* This water bubbles up from up at the spring. • *Goorrngam boonany-boonany ngerne balawa-biny.* The water is bubbling up from the ground (hot spring).
boonany-boonany *coverb+BURN/BITE.* be boiling. • *Boonany-boonany benoowarrenji.* It's boiling now.
boonarram *noun.* carved groove, mark on boomerang or shield.
boonbany *noun.* cabbage gum. *Corymbia confertiflora, C. grandifolia.*
Boonbawan *noun.* place name.
boonbemoorlardji *verb.* he wanted to HAVE them/it (non-singular). • *Nhawoona boonbemoorlardji dambi goomoonoongambi warrg-girrimbi.* He wanted that headdress to dance himself.
boonbiji *verb.* he wanted to HIT them/it non-singular.
boonbiyanya *verb.* wanted to PUT them/it (non-singular). • *Yanggi-wayi boonbiyanya goorndarrim-boorroo.* She must have wanted to ask them for fish.
boonbiyanyjende *verb.* he was wanting to PUT them/it (non-singular) (but didn't).
boonboomanyji *verb.* he wanted to GET them (but didn't).
boonboomoorloowardjende *verb.* he was wanting to HAVE/KEEP/LOOK AFTER them/it (non-singular).
boondalji, boondale SEE: **boorndalji**.
boondayi *coverb+SAY/DO_M.* be looking for a fight. • *Boondayi woomenyande wariwool dal.* That cheeky woman is looking for a fight.
boondayiwoony, boondayiwool, boondayiwoom *adjective.* someone looking for a fight. SEE: **boontherranybiny, boorlgarrijbeny**
boondayiwoorroony, boondayiwoorrool, boondayiwoorroom *adjective.* someone who doesn't look for a fight.
boonganynha *verb.* you SPEAR him/her/it!
boon'garr-boon'garr *coverb+SAY/DO.* come out (plural). • *Ngoomooloo dam boon'garr-boon'garr birrirn dam.* Those clouds will come out. SEE: **boon'gararr.**
booniny *noun.* name given to quite different

boon'gaj

Eucalyptus and Corymbia species by different people: hill bloodwood, *Corymbia aspera*; swamp bloodwood, *C. ptychocarpa*, *C. collina*; woolybutt, *Eucalyptus miniata*. [NOTE: name given to species growing on a rock face at Bream Gorge with small leaves by Hector Jandany, but also appears as *C. ptychocarpa*, 'swamp bloodwood', that has very big leaves]

boon'gaj *coverb+GO/COME.* appear. • *Boon'gaj boorroordboo.* They are coming out, appearing.

boon'gararr *coverb+SAY/DO.* come out (plural). • *Minyjoowoom dam-noowa nganyjoowarrji, ganggoom, thoowoo-thoowoom giyawoole boon'gararr berrani-ngiyi.* All the teeth from the snake, the spit and everything, the blood, all came out from her (when the man sang her to make her better). SEE: **boon'garr-boon'garr, boorarrgarr.**

boonoo *coverb+HIT.* paint someone/something. • *Boonoo benayidji warlawarr-bam garloomboom.* He painted the spears with white paint. • *Boonoo yindij goorayi!* Paint me, mother!

boonoo *coverb+SAY/DO_M.* paint someone/something. • *Boonooji-ngarri woomberrama.* When they painted (the rock).

boonoo REDUP: **boonoo-boonoo** *coverb+SAY/DO_REFL.* paint self. • *Boonoo berrangirriyinbende.* They used to paint themselves. • *Boonoo nginingirriyin.* He painted himself. SEE: **barrg, nyoon, yoorr.**

boonoomawoony, boonoomawool, boonoomawoom *adjective.* painted one (person who has painted himself/herself).

boonoo-boonoo *coverb+SAY/DO.* paint someone/something. • *Wayinigana boonoo-boonoo boorroorn, madiya.* That is how they paint, copying.

boonoo-boonoo *coverb+DO_REFL.* paint self. • *Boonoo-boonoo nginimiyinjende.* He used to paint himself. SEE: **barrg, nyoon, yoorr.**

boonoo-boonoo *coverb+CUT_REFL.* paint self. • *Yage goomboom-birri boonoo-boonoo ngenoowanke.* I just painted myself using my own urine.

boonoomoorloonji; benemoorloonji *verb.* he HAS them/it (non-singular).

boonoonggoony *noun masculine.* hill country goanna, rock goanna. *Varanus glauerti.*

Boonoonggoowirrin *noun.* Middle Brand (Branch). LIT: 'living place of the hill country goanna'.

boonooyooloonya *verb.* she is PUTTING them. SEE: **beniyooloonya, biniyilinya, binilinya.**

boonooyooloonyi *verb.* he is PUTTING them. SEE: **beniyooloonji, biniyilinji, binilinji.**

boonthal *noun feminine.* promised wife. • *Dany yagenginy jiyiliny, roord nyilangge-ni ngelela boonthal, ngalilel ngaginyil.* I promised my daughter to that other man.

boontham *noun.* promise. • *Boontham nyiliyangge-ni ngoorroonya lambarroonyga.* I promised her to that son-in-law there.

boonthany *noun masculine.* promised husband. • *Danya jiyiliny boonthany-ngooyoo.* That man is her promised husband.

boontherranybiny, boontherranybel, boontherranybem; bentherranybiny *adjective.* looking for fight. • *Nginyjiny joolany boontherranybiny.* This male dog is looking for a fight. See: **boorlgarrijbeny, boondayiwoony.**

boonthoorroo; boonyjoorroo *noun.* vagina. SEE: **milam.** [NOTE: swearing]

boony *coverb+PUT.* kiss someone. • *Boony-gala yindaj!* Kiss me!

boony-boony *coverb+SAY/DO_REFL.* kiss each other. • *Boony-boony berrangirriyan-joo.* They two are kissing each other.

boorab; berab *coverb+BE/STAY.* appear, come out. • *Nginya boorab gininiyin joowarrinyi.* This caveman appeared.

boorab; berab *coverb+BRING/TAKE.* make appear, bring out. • *Ngaaloom dam, ngela-yoorroong-ngarri boorroowoonbe, boorab-ayi nginanyji danyi, joowariny.* When that shade came over to the east that's the time that spirit brought him out. • *Booraba nyimberregbe joonbal dal.* Let them bring out that Joonba song and dance now.

boorab; berab *coverb+GO/COME.* appear, come out. • *Malalal berab nyidja ngelmang.* The sun is coming up from the east. • *Ngoowan yagengerram deg noonemen'gende boorroordboo, nhawoowoowam berab-bebe ngidjende yalginybe-moowany.* I don't see any other one coming, he is the only one that keeps coming out with his bony leg. [NOTE: talking about a bowerbird seen outside everyday]

boorab; berab *coverb+FALL/GO_DOWN.* appear, come out. • *Berab nginiwardji-ngiyi garndoorroonyga.* Suddenly Possum jumped out on her (from the spinifex).

boorab; berab REDUP: **boora-boorab; boorab-boorab.** *coverb+SAY/DO.* come out.
• *An dali woolgoomanel booraba nyanini jarlangga-biny.* And that old woman came out from the gully then. • *Yangel dal boora-boorab nyerne-ngiyi . . .* Some girl comes out to the other one . . . SEE: **berab**.

boorabwarloon; berabwarloon; boorabwarloojen *locative, temporal.* place where someone is about to/when ready to come out; when appearing, when coming out, when arriving.

booraj SEE: **beraj**.

boorarrgarr *coverb+SAY/DO.* come out, appear.
• *Boorarrgarr berrani, ngoorroo-ngoorroo-biny mawoongarrim.* The murderers came out from all over the place. SEE: **berab, boon'gararr**.

boorarrgarr *coverb+GO/COME.* come out, appear. • *Boorarrgarr boorroordboo goorndoorndoogamga men'gawiya.* The young men come out well and good. SEE: **berab, boon'gararr**.

boorlbawoog *interjection.* go get them (said to dogs).

boorlgarrijbeny, boorlgarrijbel, boorlgarrijbem *adjective* aggressive, one who looks for a fight, 'cheeky' (e.g. dog). • *Nginy wanyaginy joolany boorlgarrijbiny wariyam-boorroo.* This little dog is a cheeky one who looks for fights. SEE: **boontherranybiny**.

boorli-boorlirrg *coverb+DO_REFL.* start to rain.
• *Boorli-boorlirrg nginimiyin jadany.* It is starting to rain. SEE: **boorliyirrg**.

boorlirrg-boorlirrg *coverb+GO_ALONG.* start to rain. • *Jadam boorroordboo-ngarri, boorlirrg-boorlirrg wananyji berrema jalija ngerne yilag.* When the wet season comes, it starts to rain and the rain falls.

boorlirri *coverb + HIT.* clean off the skin of bush onions by rubbing between the hands.
• *Joorndambi gerd goorrayangbende, wayini boorlirri ngoorrayangbende, ramoob-ramooba woomberramande.–* They used to cook the bush onions in the hot sand, clean off the skin between their hands, then eat them by the handful.

boorliyi SEE: **booliyi**

boorliyirr *coverb+BECOME.* rain falling down.
• *Danya jadany boorliyirr waniyid ngirriban goowalen.* That rain is falling down, close up here on the little hill.

boorliyirrg *coverb+DO_REFL.* start to rain, rain come like smoke. • *Boorliyirrg nginimiyinji.* The rain is coming like smoke. • *Boorliyirrg nginimiyin gawarren.* It is starting to rain on the big hill.

boorljany, boorljam *noun.* football, ball.
• *Boorooj boorroorn boorljam, mool-moolji birrimiyanbe.* They are playing football, making each other happy. [NOTE: some people use this word freely to mean 'any kind of ball for ball games', others say that it really a men's word and should not be used]

boorloob *coverb+DO_REFL.* rain build up, little clouds come in. • *Boorloob nginimiyin jadam marrarnjaya jalij gerne.* The little rain clouds are coming in, it is already really raining.

boorloo-boorloony, boorloo-boorlool, boorloo-boorliny *adjective.* tricky, clever at doing things. • *Boorloo-boorloon-nga warrg-girrimga.* I'm a tricky fellow for dancing.
• *Dali wanggarnal boorloo-boorlool.* That crow is a tricky one.

boorlooj *coverb+FALL/GO_DOWN.* become angry with someone. • *Wayinigana boorlooj giniwardji-yarri na.* That is why he got angry with us then.

boorloorrji, boorloorroo *noun.* type of rough stone.

Boorlooroon *noun.* hill near Sophie Downs.

boorn *coverb+SAY/DO.* feel hot. • *Boorn ngenarn.* I feel hot.

boornarrany *noun masculine.* stick insect.

boornda-boorndabany, boornda-boorndabal, boornda-boorndabam *adjective.* prickly. • *Boornda-boorndabal; melagawoom-ngiyi boorndalega girlilga dal.* It is prickly, the bush tomato has lots of prickles.

boorndalba *coverb+BECOME.* become covered in prickles. • *Berdij nyaniniyinya, 'Marri boorndalba ngelayid!'* When she got up she said, 'Oh dear, I'm covered in prickles!'

boorndalji, boorndale *noun masculine.* prickle.
• *Boorndalji ngenangaboordji thambarlam.* A prickle poked me in the foot. • *Boorndalji, boorndal-ban-anyji-ngoo.* A prickle, you might have a prickle. SEE: **bagany, marlagal**.

boornmarrwoon *temporal.* hot time.
• *Boornmarrwoon-ngirri, ngoowan bagoo nginbin'ge.* I am hot at this time, I cannot sleep.

Boornoolooloo *noun.* Purnululu National Park, Bungle Bungles.

boornool, boornoom noun. fly. • Boornoombi wiwayi-wiwayi barrern-gili. *You all brush the flies away.* • Berrema melegawoom boornoom boorroordboo-yarri. *Here there are lot of fies coming to us.*

boornoongiliwoony, boornoongiliwoom noun. fly. mob of flies that you keep trying to chase away.

booroo coverb+BRING/TAKE. carry something hidden. • Booroo nginany. *She had carried him hidden (crow who put little boy in her vagina).*

booroo coverb+PUT. hide something. • Thoowoorra booroo noowajge-ni. *I want to hide this boy of his (her brother's child).* [NOTE: transitive 'hide']

booroo coverb+SAY/PLACE_REFL. hide face with hand. • Booroo naniyilin. *You hid your face. You put your hand over face.*

boorooj coverb+GO/COME. play. • Diyana boorooj yirriyande. *We will be playing there.*

boorooj; boorij REDUP: boorooj-woorooj. coverb+SAY/DO. play. • Nginya goorloony yilag boorooj-garri booroorn winyanyanggem. *This is the water down there where the children play (talking about part of a painting while sitting in a house near the real place).* • Boorooj barrern-gili ngaalooyan. *You play here in the shade.* • Boorij yarrani, warany dany ngarrgale-miliny nginiyin. *We were playing (cards) and that man who comes from the hills came along.* [NOTE: Is used to mean 'play cards'; is also used to mean to take part in a song and dance event]

boorooj coverb+GO_ALONG. play with something/someone. • Goorndoogal boorooj woomiyinya booboogarral. *The little girl is playing with a balloon.* [NOTE: mi- inserted before the verb stem refers to the balloon]

boorooj coverb+HIT. play with something/someone. • Joonggoobal boorooj giyinya Badebany. *Sylvia is playing with Badebany (dog's name).*

boorooj, boorij coverb+SAY/DO_M. play. • Boorooj-garri yirramande . . . *When we used to play . . .*

booroojbany coverb+GO/COME. go playing. • Marrarna ngenda booroojbany. *I'm going playing. (Kriol: 'play about').*

booroojwirrin noun. playground (e.g. for bowerbird). • Boolmamim-noongoo booroojwirrinbi-noo. *That construction is his playground.*

Booroorl noun. place name, personal name (a place painted by Madigan Thomas in the same area as Foal Creek and Charlie Bight Camp).

boorral coverb+GIVE_M. give someone a meal, fill up with food. • Boorral-gala woomberrayi-yoo yiwiny. *Let these two have a feed of lice.*

boorral coverb+EAT. eat something until full. • Deyenya boorral noongoon'ge. *That is what I fill myself up with.*

boorral coverb+SAY/DO_M. have a meal, fill up with food. • Boorral-bija booma! / Boorral-wija booma! *You eat! (You have a feed!)* • Boorral jarra-yoo. *You two eat.* • Boorral-wija jarra-kili. *You should all eat.*

boorrale noun. a good meal, a feed, something to fill one up. • Girli wananyji, biya-wiya nginini, boorrale-bawoorroo-jiyan. *He walked along, he was looking around, there was really nothing to eat.* • Gagoolanyil-ngooyoo diyala-nga boorralelga. *Little bush melons are what I fill myself up with.* • Marrarna nginbiyande joogboo boorrale-wanyji ninbinganyge. *I will go hunting, I might spear something for a filling meal.*

boorrayigthayoo pronoun. they two themselves. [NOTE: unusual pronoun form; translation provided by Rusty Peters and Eileen Bray]

boorr-boorr coverb+PUT. grind something, sharpen, file something to make it shine. • Boorr-boorr benayanyji-noo. *He sharpened it for him (to kill him).* SEE: **jalinggirig**.

boorr-boorr-girrem noun. grinder (workshop tool).

boorrg REDUP: boorrg-boorrg. coverb+SAY/DO. clap. • Boorrg-boorrg barrern-gili melagawiya. *All clap your hands!*

boorrg-boorrg coverb+GIVE. give a dog a pat. • Dany marloogany joolany boorrg-boorrga biyinnha. *Give that old dog a pat then.*

boorrgoorloorr; boowoorrgoorloorr directional. further to the north.

boorrijiny noun. diver jack, darter, snake bird. *Anhinga melanogaster.* SEE: **garrang-garranginy**.

boorriyangeny; boorriyangel; boorriyangem possessive pronoun. theirs.

boorriyin verb. they wanted to go/come.

boorrngoordge coverb+GET. give someone a

fright, make someone jump/twitch in fright.
• **Boorrngoordge ngemberramang.** *It gave me a fright.* SEE: **woorrngoord.**

boorrngoornji, boorrngoornngoornji, boorrngoorrngooroony *noun masculine.* hornet species. [NOTE: big black and orange one that builds mud nests]

boorrngooroony, boorrngooroom 1. *noun.* reddish yellow ochre. • **Nyalala wananyji bilij benayidji boorrngooroom. Biri nginiyin gananybe benamanyji. Ngoolnga-gal nyanini-ningi, 'Thoowoo-boorroo gananybe joonamennha?' 'Bilij-garri noonayid boorrngooroom. Woobooj-gala noondoom.'** *He was walking about and found some yellow ochre. He went back to get a digging stick. His wife asked him, 'Why do you want a digging stick?' 'I found some yellow ochre. I want to dig it up.'*
2. *adjective.* yellow. SEE: **goorndoorloo.**

-boorroo *suffix.* for, purposive suffix to nouns. SEE: **-geny.** [NOTE: homophonous with 3rd person non-singular benefactive enclitic pronoun]

-boorroo *benefactive enclitic pronoun.* for them, for it (non-singular). [NOTE: homophonous with nominal purposive suffix]

-boorroo-yoo *benefactive enclitic pronoun.* for them (dual)

boorrooben *pronoun.* they/them(dual).

boorroo-boorral *coverb+GO_ALONG.* have a meal, fill up with food. • **Mayimga-nga boorroo-boorral ngilin'gende.** *That is my food from which I make a good meal.* SEE: **boorral.**

boorroogoo *particle.* that now. • **Menkawoony boorroogoo miyalji dany.** *That meat (of the cat) is good then.*

boorroodboo SEE: **boorroordboo.**

boorrooloo *noun.* part of guts where food is minced up in bullock.

boorroombiny *noun.* bat species, ghost bat. [NOTE: bigger than *binyjirrminy*]

boorroomelewam *pronoun.* all the things from them.

boorroon *pronoun.* they, them.

boorroonany *noun masculine.* bull. *Bos taurus, B. indicus.* SEE: **boolngayirriny, booloomanji.**

boorroonbende *verb.* they ARE/KEEP ON STAYING.

boorroonboo *verb.* they ARE/ARE STAYING.

boorroongenji *temporal.* after that.

boorroongoo *coverb+SAY/DO_REFL.* hug each other.
• **Boorroongoo berrangirriyin.** *They hugged each other.*

boorroordbende *verb.* they keep on GOING/COMING.

boorroordboo *verb.* they are GOING/COMING.

boorroorn *verb.* they SAY, they DO.

boorroornji, boorrooroo *noun masculine.* club-leaf wattle. *Acacia hemignosta.* [NOTE: There are two types of this plant, one has very glaucous (grey coloured) leaves and the other one has green leaves.] SEE: **berewereny.**

boorroowany *pronoun.* they themselves, their turn.

boorroowardbe *verb.* they wanted to FALL/GO DOWN.

boorroowarriny *pronoun.* they themselves. SEE: **boorroowany.**

boorroowiyin *verb.* they should FALL/GO DOWN.

boorrwoorrji *noun masculine.* ground sugarbag, species of native bee living in anthills or in the ground, hive of that bee. *Trigona* spp. SEE: **gayirriny.**

boothal *coverb+SAY/DO.* feel bad, have no feeling for someone, to not want to be with someone.
• **Boothal ngenarn-narri.** *I don't want you all here. / I have a bad feeling about all of you.*

boothalge *coverb+GET.* put someone off when they are trying to do something, make someone have a bad feeling. • **Boothalge yinemanha. Ngenenggayana benennha. Nginbiyan-ngarri ngayoowanyda, bilij ninpijge.** *You put me off. You stay here. If I go by myself I might find something (e.g. kangaroo).*

boothalwoo *coverb+GET.* dislike someone, have no feeling for someone, to not want to be with someone. • **Boothalwoo nanemennha.** *I don't like you mob.* • **Boothalwoo nemenha-ngoo.** *I don't like you (one).*

boothalwoony, boothalwool, boothalwoom *adjective.* someone who doesn't want to talk to anyone.

Boowan'goorr *noun.* important place near Tableland. [NOTE: Rusty Peters says Ban'goorr]

boowarraj *noun.* painted marks used as decoration. • **Ngaginybe noonayangge-ni boowarraj.** *I put my decorative painted marks on it (hill in painting).* [NOTE: men's only word talking about country]

boowarre *verb.* you (one) BURN/BITE him/her/it.

boowoo *verb.* you (one) FALL/GO DOWN!

boowoob *coverb+GO/COME.* float. • **Thawalam**

boowoonnha

dam boowoob-merrarriny boorroordbende goorloon. *The flowers are all floating on the water.* • Lalanggarrany boowoob giniyinde laarne goorloonya. *The crocodile was floating on top of the water.*

boowoonnha *verb.* you (one) FALL/GO DOWN!

boowoorr; boowoorroogoo; boorroogoo *directional.* to the north.

boowoorroogoob
coverb+FALL/GO_DOWN. go north. • Biri yarrayi gerliyirr boowoorroogoob yarraward. *We went back to the west and then set off north.*

boowoorrgoorloorr; boorrgoorloorr *directional.* further to the north.

booyooj-booyooj *coverb+GO/COME* what the booyooj-booyoojgel lizard says or does.
• Ngarranggarninji, ngarranggarninji booyooj-booyooj nyaniyinya-ngarri. *From the dreamtime, from the dreamtime when the lizard called* booyooj-booyoojgel *was going along there.* [NOTE: this is a verse from the Dayiwool (barramundi) Moonga-moonga sung at Argyle Diamond Mine]

booyooj-booyoojgel; booyooj-booyoojjel; booyij-booyijgel *noun feminine.* lizard species, possibly a knob-tailed gecko. *Nephurus asper.* [NOTE: described as having a big head, big noise and no tail. Shirley Purdie describes this nose as 'pumping itself up'. This name is also given to the thorny devil, *Moloch horridus*, that lives in the desert south of Gija country.] SEE: **bedarrel, booyoord-booyoordjil.**

booyoolinnha *verb.* you should/must be PUTTING him/her/it! • Garninya, manim goorndoogal booyoolinnha mayim-boorroo. *What now, you should put in child money for food (speaking to father of child).*

booyoord-booyoordjil *noun feminine.* knob-tailed gecko. *Nephurus asper.* SEE: **booyooj-booyoojgel.**

Dd

daa-daa *coverb+SAY/DO.* camp habitually, live in a place. • *Berrema daa-daa berrani.* This is where they always used to camp/live.

daaloony; daloony *noun masculine.* green plum. *Buchanania obovata.*

daam REDUP: **daa-daam**. *noun.* camp, home, country.

daawany, daawal, daawam *noun.* country owner, one who belongs the country, one who has been taken to the country previously and properly introduced. SEE: **daawayalam**.

daawayalam *noun.* country owners. SEE: **daawam**. [NOTE: contrasts with *gamaliwam* 'strangers, new-comers']

daawirrin *noun.* traditional camping place.

dabaroony *noun masculine.* pelican. *Pelecanus conspicillatus.*

dab-dab *coverb+DO_REFL.* paint dots on self. • *Dab-dab nyanemiyinya-noongoo, danyga goorndoogany.* She painted herself with dots for that boy (i.e. for the ceremony remembering him.) SEE: **dag-dag**.

daboo *coverb+GET.* not share, starve someone, hide food. • *Thoowoorra-boorroo, daboo yimberramannha-boorroo miyali, ngayana thedji ngelanyge-noonggoo miyaliyi dam.* Why did you all refuse to share the meat with me, I'm the one who went along killing that meat for all of you. SEE: **dangoori**.

daboonggool *noun.* platypus. *Ornithorhynchus anatinus.* SEE: **nyoorroongool**. [NOTE: Gija people and neighbouring Miriwoong people are certain that platypus live or lived in the East Kimberley. Hector Jandany saw one in the Taronga Zoo in Sydney and said he ate one when young in the Bungles. Sophia Mung saw one near Frog Hollow in about 2012.]

Daboonggoole *noun.* Horse Creek on Texas Downs. [NOTE: bamboo, *gamanggerrji*, used for making spear shafts, grows there]

daboorlg *coverb+GO/COME.* family come together, 'big mob heap up'. • *Daboorlg yirrayin ngoorroon.* All us family moved in over there (to Frog Hollow when Jack Britten got the out-station).

daboorr *coverb+GO_ALONG.* go along stabbing the ground (e.g. when following a goanna tunnel or looking for water). • *Daboorr wananyande.* She kept going along stabbing the ground.

daboorr *coverb+HIT.* poke stick into hole (e.g. to get honey); open something with a crowbar. • *Daboorr ngoorrayidbende.* They used to poke a stick in (to get the honey).

daboorr *coverb+FALL/GO_DOWN.* get into hole, get into water. • *Daboorr ngenaward girli-ngarri ngelanyge.* I got in a hole when I was walking along. • *Danyi wegeny yilagja, daboorr ngoowoonji goorrngan.* That frog goes down then, he gets in the water.

dadigirrij *coverb+SAY/DO.* grind teeth. • *Dadigirrij ngerne.* He is grinding his teeth.

dag *coverb+SAY/DO_M.* push or hit something with the end of a stick. • *Garanybe dag woomberramande giningin-yoorroong.* They would push the hot stones inside (the kangaroo's gut cavity) with a stick. SEE: **tharn**.

dagalge *coverb+EAT.* make tongue/mouth

Figure 40. *Dabaroony: Dabaroony wad nginji therr ngingirriyin thoowerndem-birri.*

dagaragal

have strong sensation (e.g. by eating something bitter). • Gilyayal dagalge nyooloongoon'gende. *I always 'poison myself on the tongue' with that bitter one (small melons).*

dagaragal *noun feminine.* unidentified bird species.

dag-dag *coverb+SAY/DO.* paint dots, make white dots on painting with the end of a little stick. • Dag-dag ngenani men'gawoog-girrim. *I put dots on it to make it good.*

dag-dag *coverb+SAY/DO_REFL.* paint dots on self with the end of a little stick. • Dag-dag berrangirriyin mirrngim. *They painted their faces with dots.* SEE: **dab-dab, dilg-dilg.**

dagidji *coverb+HIT.* hit. • Garloomboo-bawoorroon-yoowoo, miya dagidji yambirrija ngarrgarliyam-birri wela. *We don't have a spear, we will just have to hit them with a stone, hey!*

dagidji *coverb+SAY/DO_M.* hit. • Dagidji wanema thoorrmal dal nyaniyanyji yageba-yoorroong. *He hit (the rock wallabies) and put all the fat females down next to him (on one side).*

dagoorlag; dagoorlagbe REDUP:

dagoorlagoorla. *coverb+GET.* make deep hole. • Dagoorlagbe benema. *He kept making the deep holes then (that are still there in the rocks in the riverbed).* • Dagoorlagoorla naw wayininy, dagoorlag-garri nginimanyjende, doorloorloog-garri wanemayinde, nhawoon. *Those are the deep holes he made when he kept coming out, him now (the moon who kept coming up and going down from the water).*

dagoorlaj *coverb+HIT.* put in hole. • Dagoorlaj janidji deyena. *He put her in there.*

dagoorlaj *coverb+FALL/GO_DOWN.* fall into a deep hole, e.g. in a car accident. • Berrema ngoorr-ngoorrgaja berrayi dagoorlaj berrewardbe. *This car came and they fell into a deep hole (had an accident).*

dagoorlam *noun.* hollow ground, basket.

dagoorlany, dagoorlan REDUP: **dagoo-dagoorlan.** *noun.* deep hole, deep waterhole, billabong.

dagoorr *coverb+PUT.* put in. • Dagoorr niniya. *I put it in.* • Dagoorr biyil! *Put it in!*

dagoorr *coverb+FALL/GO_DOWN.* get into something. • Ngerijin dagoorr-anyji nginiwardji, woo gendoowagoo nginiyin-

Figure 41. *Dag-dag: Lena Nyadbi, Goody Barrett, Shirley Bray: Dag-dag berrangirriyin mirrngim, merrgernbem jarloongoorroombi roord nyimberremoorloonbi-yoo ngalenganggal Nangaril.*

anyji ngenengga gendoowa. *Maybe he went into a hole on the south side or maybe he went upstream.* • Dagoorr ngenaward ngoorr-ngoorrgajin. *I got into the car.*

dagoorr *coverb+GO/COME.* get in (and go).
• Dagoorr ngenayin. *I jumped in (the car).*

daj REDUP: **daj-daj**. *coverb+HIT.* pound, smash, crush. • Gayi nyawanyi daj yarrooja? *Where can we smash up this tail?* • Daj benayidji. *He smashed it up.* • Ngenengga daj barrijtha-ngirri-yoo. *You two can smash it up here on my forehead.*

daj REDUP: **daj-daj**. *coverb+SAY/DO_M.* pound, smash, crush. • Daj woomberrama-ningi-yoo danyi nyawanyi moojooroog. *They two smashed up that tail on him (his forehead) mincing it up properly.*

dal *demonstrative.* that (feminine). • Dala jibilyoowool ngarag jilamangge. *That is a duck I painted.*

dalala *coverb+FALL/GO_DOWN.* fall into something.
• Dalala ngenawardge ngoowan deg noonamangge nawanbe. *I fell down in the hole, I did not see the hole.*

dalala *coverb+HIT.* stab ground and hit water, throw something in a well. • Dalalawoo nginiyidja. *She threw it down then (digging stick into ground when stabbing the ground for water).* [NOTE: -woo is the sequential suffix here]

dalaware *coverb+HIT.* bang something.
• Danya wanyageny dalaware beniyinji thoowoorranyji. *That little boy is banging something.*

Dalayiwan *noun.* place in Rammey Ramsey's country between Bedford Downs and Elgee Cliffs.

dalbarr *coverb+HIT.* smash. • Dalbarr nginiyidji. *He smashed it.*

dalberr *coverb+GET.* keep in mind. • Joonbamga dalberr yamberremnya-noowa. *We keep the Joonba song and dance in our mind (that we got/learned) from him.*

dal-dal *coverb+SAY/DO_M.* make noise by banging something. • Ngoorrinya dal-dal woomenjende. *That man is banging something, making a noise.* SEE: **daly**.

dalinyji *noun masculine.* big fork-tailed catfish. *Neorius graeffei, N. midgleyi.* • Dalinybe melagawoom noonamangge. *I caught lots of big catfish.* SEE: **binyjiwinyjiny**.

daliyany *noun.* sugar leaf (lerp) species. SEE: **thalngarrngarnany**. [NOTE: found on snappy gum, *thalngarr*]

Daloodaloo *noun.* Nine Mile Creek.

dalooj *coverb+HIT.* hit on head. • Ngenengga-wayi dalooj nginiyidja moowoole. *She hit him here like this on the forehead.*

daly *coverb+HIT.* make noise (e.g. by scratching on a stone). • Daly benayid. *He made a noise scratching the stone.* SEE: **dal-dal**.

dalyalya *coverb+BECOME.* hit the ground.
• Gerliwirring, ngerren-ngarri nginini, goowoo dalyalya waniyidji berrema yilag balawan. *It (lightning) has just struck the ground and lit a fire from up there.*

Dalyiwoon *noun.* place where rainbow snake drowned two boys.

dam *demonstrative.* those, that (non-singular).

damana *coverb+GO_ALONG.* be dazzled. • Damana wiyinji. *He was dazzled.*

damana *coverb+SAY/DO.* be dazzled. • Damana ngenarn. *I am dazzled by the glare.*

damarramarra *coverb+BE/STAY.* stay in big group.
• Damarramarra berraniyinde, Mirrilinggin. *They were all staying in a big group at Mirrilingki.*

dambang *coverb+GET.* catch in hand. • Dambang nginimanya. *She caught it in her hand.*

damberrji *noun masculine.* death adder. *Acanthophis* sp. [NOTE: Jawalyi skin] SEE: **ngadarrji**.

dandawa REDUP: **danda-dandawa**. *coverb+BE/STAY.* have one leg bent up over the other straight one. • Dandawa nginji. *He has one leg bent up against the other.* [NOTE: person can be sitting, standing or lying]

daminam *adjective.* being together.
• Berraniyinaa na daminam, ngarranggarnin. *They stayed there for good together then, in the dreamtime.*

daminemenag *coverb+BE/STAY.* group stay together, all stop together in one big camp.
• Daminemenag berraniyinde. *They all used to stay together in one camp.*

dan *demonstrative.* there, at that place.

danarrel *noun feminine.* Livistona palm. *Livistona* spp. [NOTE: some say this is a different variety of palm, some say it is the same as *yingajalil* but the word is used about plants that are the right height to cut to eat] SEE: **yingajalil**, **yangajalil**.

dangembi

dangembi *adverb.* then, after a while.

danggal, danggam *noun feminine.* red ochre. SEE: **badel**.

danggarriny *noun masculine.* waterlily flower stem. (Southern dialect).

dangoorayi *coverb+SAY/DO.* choose to stay somewhere, not want to go. • **Thoowoorra-boorroo dangoorayi nini?** *Why don't you want to go?* • **Dangoorayi ngenarn.** *I don't want to go.*

dangoori *coverb+HIT.* refuse to share with someone. • **Joolany dagoori-ngarri, ngoorrayidboo-gili-berroowa, roorrji-ngarri boorroonboo.** *They refused to share it (meat he had helped catch) with the dog when they are sitting there.* • **Dangoori ngoorrayidbende jiyirrem-boorroo.** *They refused to share the kangaroo.*

dangoori *coverb+SAY/DO.* keep for oneself. • **Dangoori ngenarn.** *I'm keeping it all for myself.*

dangoorinhawoony, dangoorinhawool, dangooringawoom *adjective.* person who does not share, person who keeps everything for himself/herself.

dany *demonstrative.* that (masculine).

danyja *coverb+FALL/GO_DOWN.* go flat (tyre). • **Yilgoowoorroo wanama danyja nyanooward damga wiyile.** *The car has a flat tyre.*

danyjag *coverb+BURN/BITE, coverb+SAY/DO_M.* go down (tyre). • **Danyjagboo nyoowarrenji ngoowananyji theb nyimberrayangbe wayinigana danyjag wanema.** *The tyre is going down now. Maybe they didn't put the valve in properly and that's why it has gone down.*

darag *coverb+GO/COME.* disappear, go out of sight. • **Darag-bija nirda.** *You should go out of sight.* • **Daragbe nginiyin thambarla-moowam ngininiyi thirringangab.** *Soon all of his body was inside, only his feet were sticking out.* • **Darag ngiwiyayi gooral-ngiyi, ngaboony-ningi.** *He will go out of sight to his mother and father (Christ when ascending to heaven).* • **Darag ngenardge ngayindi yilag boorooj-girrim.** *I am going to disappear down there to play.*

darag REDUP: **darag-darag**. *coverb+FALL/GO_DOWN.* disappear, go out of sight. • **Darag nginiwardji.** *He went out of sight.* • **Darag nyanoowardja birn'girrbal.** *The turkey went out of sight.* • **Daragboo-ngarri nyimboowoonya barndel.** *When the sun goes down.* • **Darag nanoowarda.** *You disappeared.*

darag *coverb+LEAVE.* go out of sight leaving someone behind. • **Darag benawoorroodji-yoo.** *He disappeared leaving the two of them behind.*

dard; dardaroo REDUP: **dardard**. *coverb+BE/STAY.* hanging up. • **Dard nginji.** *He/it (masculine) is hanging.* • **Miyingenbe dardaroo-ngarri boorroonboo mayaroon dan.** *All the flood rubbish that is hanging up on the house there.* • **Deg wanema, miyalel dardard janininya goowoole-yirrin.** *He looked and saw meat hanging up everywhere in the trees.*

dard *coverb+BURN/BITE_REFL.* get stuck up high, be hung up. • **Berdij-gala biyarr-noo danya boojigadji, dard giniwan laarne.** *Climb up and get that cat. He got himself stuck up there on top.*

dard REDUP: **dardard**. *coverb+PUT.* hang up. • **Dard benayanyji.** *He hung it up.* • **Dama dard benayanya laarne** *She hung it up there on top.*

darda-darda *coverb SAY/DO.* get the lumps out of something (e.g. ash, ochre). • **Darda-darda nyerne dam mawoondem.** *She is getting the lumps out that white clay.*

darda-darda *coverb+HIT.* separate rubbish from something, get the rubbish out of something (e.g. ash, ochre). • **Gooma dam darda-darda-ngarri yamberriyinya ajijboo wayina na.** *Just like we separate the ashes in that way now.* SEE: **thedayi**.

dardbany *coverb+GO/COME.* go along tangled up. • **Dardbanya yarrooya nyiyirri-yirrin ngabayi.** *We'll go along getting tangled in all the spinifex, Auntie (father's sister addressed as 'dad').*

Daremaren *noun.* place in Ngarrgooroon country between Goongewayin, Meriyin and Daboonggool.

dareng *coverb+PUT.* put head down/upside down. • **Ngarag janimanyji dareng nyaniyanya.** *He drew her head down (drawing of woman on wall in gorge)*

dareng *coverb+FALL/GO_DOWN.* be head down/upside down. • **Goonggooloom dareng nyanoowardja.** *She was (depicted) head down (upside down in rock painting).* SEE: **daying**.

darlam *noun.* wax lid in beehive.

darlg *coverb+HIT.* hit in eye. • **Darlg**

goorrayid-doo moorloo. *The two of them hit him in the eye (by throwing stones).*

darlg *coverb+GET.* poke in eye. • Darlg nimbimnha-ngoo. *It will poke you in the eye.*

darloo *coverb+SAY/DO.* throw rock in water. • Ngoowan darloo nimbirn; gamaliwan-ngoo. *Don't throw rocks in the water; you are a stranger.*

darndal *noun feminine.* turtle. SEE: **wayiwoorrool, bilidbal, balarnel.** [NOTE: *darndal* is the most common word for 'turtle' at Warrmarn]

daroogoo *noun.* sacred/secret things. [NOTE: Rusty Peters says he cannot say this word in front of women or he might be killed; others use it circumspectly (Kriol: 'sideways')]

darr *coverb+PUT.* cut umbilical cord. • Dinyjile, gad, ngayana darr ngenayanya. *She cut my umbilical cord.*

darradbem *noun.* boggy place. SEE: **yawool-yawooloo.**

Darrajayin *noun.* long hill on Springvale Station.

Darrarroo *noun.* Wyndham.

darreg *coverb+GO/COME.* come across plenty of something. • Darreg yiwiya-birri goorndarrimga. *We might run into plenty fish.*

darrgam *noun.* feathers used for dancing headdress. SEE: **birn'girre, ganalam.**

Darrjin *noun.* Water Spring (place name).

darrngig *coverb+FALL/GO_DOWN.* get stuck in mind. • *Well,* wayinigana ngayina darrngig berraward-girri Joonbam. *Well, that is how the song has become fixed in my mind now.*

darrooorl *coverb+SAY/DO_M.* belt someone with a stick. • Ngoorroo-ngoorroo-biny darroorl woomberrama-noo. *They belted him from all sides.*

darroorl *coverb+HIT.* hit someone with a stick. • Darroorl nginiyidja therlan. *She hit him on the back with a stick.*

dawadag *coverb+BRING/TAKE.* take to different place. • Daa-woorroon, ngagenyin, ngageny-woorroon-ngage yimberrennha dawadagboo,' nginini-yarri. *'This is not my place, I don't belong here, you are taking me far away to a different place now,' he said to us.*

dawadag *coverb+HIT.* take far away. • Dawadag yimberrayid-yoowoo. *They took us a long way from town.*

Dawarloowarlool *noun feminine.* name of a song cycle.

dawarr *coverb+SAY/DO_M.* hit. • Dawarr wanema-ngooyoo ngarrgalem-birri. *He hit her with a stone.*

dawarr *coverb+HIT.* hit. • Dawarr nginiyid. *He hit him.* • Goorlangginy, danya joolanyiyi, dawarr ngiyinji, roong-roong-girrinyi jiyilemboo-boorroo. *He is hitting that poor dog, who is (good) for barking at men (who might come at night to make trouble).*

dawarr *coverb+SAY/DO_REFL.* hit each other. • Dawarr berrangirriyinbi-yoo. *They two are hitting each other.* • Thoowoorrawoo dawarrji yarringirridja? *Why do we go on hitting one another then?*

dawiyan *noun.* word used by *garn'giny* the moon to speak indirectly about the black headed snake who was his mother-in-law. [NOTE: avoidance speech (Kriol: 'sideways mother-in-law talk')]

dawoogjil *noun feminine.* barramundi. *Lates calcarifer.* SEE: **balgal, dayiwool, nyilibal, wawoordjil.**

dawool *noun feminine.* black-headed python. *Aspidites melanocephalus.* SEE: **thoowerndemanbel.** [NOTE: Nambin skin]

dawoolan *coverb+FALL/GO_DOWN.* reach destination.

dawoong *coverb+BE/STAY.* be in love. • Yangelanyji dawoongboo-ngarri nyinyande-ningi ngarrgalen. *He must be in love (lit. 'He must have some woman in his heart').* SEE: **warda.**

dawoong *coverb+GET.* love, like, believe. • Raymondji dawoong nyanemanyji nhawiyangel gelengel bajinggelel. *Raymond loved his new bicycle.* • Ngoowan dawoong noonamen'ge dam rangga-ngarri noonaan'ge jarragboo. *I can't believe what I'm hearing. I don't like what I'm hearing.* SEE: **warda.**

dawoonyil *noun feminine.* bush potato species with very large root and short leaves. *Ipomoea costata.* [NOTE: talked about by people at Yarangga in 1988 as different from *larrwany* even though they are both listed as the same species in Purdie et al. (2018)] SEE: **berlayiny, bigoordany, larrwany, yalamarriny.**

dawoorrji *noun masculine.* top half of a kangaroo. [NOTE: the dreaming place is high up behind Elgee Cliffs where the top half of the kangaroo sits looking out from a cave in the side of the rock face, appears as a scene on a painted

dayi

board in the Goorirr-goorirr song cycle found by Rover Thomas, still staged at Warmun Art Centre]

dayi *coverb+GET.* learn. • Warna-warnarrayam ngininiyinde ngenenggaga wayinigana dayi benamanyji Gijambi jarragbi berrem. *He stayed here a long time and learned to speak this Gija language.* • Gijambi dayiwa bemberrembe wajbaloombi, gooma ngayin dayi-ngarri noonamangge wajbaloom-boorroowa jarragbi Yinggilij. *White people can learn Gija, just as I learn English from the white people.*

dayimbalji, dayimbale *noun masculine.* red-flowered kurrajong. *Brachychiton viscidulus.*

daying *coverb+PUT.* dislike, turn someone down, hang something upside down. • Daying ngoorrayangbe. *They hung him upside down.*

daying *coverb+BE/STAY.* be upside down. • Ngoorroonya daying nginji wanyageny. *That little boy is upside down.* SEE: **dareng**.

dayiwool *noun feminine.* barramundi. *Lates calcarifer.* SEE: **balgal, nyilibal, dawoogjil, wawoordjil**.

deberr *coverb+FALL/GO_DOWN.* break, fall and break. • Deberr nyanoowardja nganoonggoom. *She fell and broke her arm.* • Theberrjiya nginiward-yirroowa bardoon. *It has fallen down and really broken up since we were there.*

deberr *coverb+GET.* break, break off. • Goonyjam deberr benamanyjende ganarra-bam. *He used to break off sticks with leaves / leafy bits of bush.*

deberr *coverb+SPEAR.* spear and break. • Jirrawoony baliyarren deberr nyanengaboord. *The other one speared her and broke her leg.*

debereberr *coverb+SAY/DO_M.* break off. • 'Debereberr booma-boorroo wanyanyagem goorninyam,' wanamayinde nyaman. *'Cut it up small for the children, they're hungry,' the old lady used to say.*

deberrg *coverb+GET.* break off. • Deberrg ninemangge. *I broke it off.*

deberrngeny, deberrngel, deberrngem *adjective.* broken. • Deberrngel nganoonggoom. *She's got a broken arm.*

dedarleny, dedarlel, dedarlem *adjective.* being

Figure 42. *Dawoorrji: Chris Griffiths, Ralph Juli, Gabriel Nodea: Jaangariny wandaj ngerne dawoorrji Goorirr-goorirre.*

a strong singer. • Ngayin-ga dedarlen-nga. *I am a strong singer.*

deg *COVERB+SAY/DO_M.* watch and wait.
• Deg-gayan ngelamande:::, wanggooloo ngelanyge, marrarna nginbiyan bagoo-girrim. *I have been waiting all day, I'm sick of it and I am going home to sleep.*

deg *COVERB+DO_REFL.* look at self, look at each other. • Deg berramiyanbi-yoo. *They are looking at each other.*

deg REDUP: **derdeg**. *COVERB+GO_ALONG.* go along looking. • Deg wananya-boorroo. *She was going along looking for them.*
• Danya warlaginy deg wiyinji-ngooyoo goora-gal. *This puppy is looking for his mother.*
• Mendoowoon derdega woomberriyinbe dan, diyilijilin. *At night they (owls) look around there at all the bright lights.*

deg *COVERB+BRING/TAKE.* watch. • Deg nginanyji. *He was watching him.* • Deg-gela yamberregbany. *Let's all watch them.*

deg; dig *COVERB+SAY/DO.* look. • Danya yalarrngarnany deg ngerne-boorroo goorndarrim. *This jabiru is looking for fish.*
• Ngoowan deg nyanini gabi girli wananya. *She didn't look where she was walking.* • Deg ngenani girliwirringbiny. *I looked from up there.* [NOTE: alternate pronunciation is from the Southern dialect] SEE: **derdeg, derde-yerdeg**.

deg *COVERB+GET.* look at something, see something. • Deg benamanya-yoo bangariny-warriny, lalanggarra-warriny, barl-warl woomberranybi-yoo goorrngan. *She saw the two crocodiles swimming in the water.* • Deg bemberramenbe. *They are looking at them.*
• Ngeleli thengela, degba jemennha, jiregel dal? Ginyginy. *What kind is this feminine one? Can you see this bird (talking about a picture of a parrot)? It is a red-winged parrot.* • Deg ninemangge ngamarrany mendoowoon. *I saw a snake last night.*

deg *COVERB+FOLLOW.* follow and watch. • Deg yirramimanyjende. *We used to follow watching him.*

degbe *COVERB+SAY/DO_M.* look for. • Degbe wanamanyji-boorroo-yoo. *He looked for the two of them.* • Woorajanyji ngidji degboo woomenji-noonggoorroo. *He must be coming this way to look for all of you.*

degbe *COVERB +FOLLOW.* follow watching. • Degbe nginimemanyji. *He was following and watching him then.*

degerd *COVERB+HIT.* break/cut off part of something. • Thambarlam degerd, dangembi nyawam degerd boomberrayidbende. *They would take off the feet then cut off the tail (of kangaroo when cooking).*

degerd *COVERB+GET.* break/cut off part of something. • Degerd-gala nherem. *I'll have to cut a bit off (a spear that is too long).*

degijiya *COVERB+GET.* look at someone properly. • Degijiya nyanemanyji. *He looked at her properly.*

delanggerr *COVERB+SAY/DO_M.* keep talking loudly. • Delanggerr woomenyande. *She keeps talking loudly.*

dem-dem *COVERB+SAY/DO.* be jealous. • Dem-dem ngerne. *He's jealous.* • Dem-dem nyerne-ngage jarrag-ngarri ngenarn-ninggi. *She's jealousing me for talking to you.* SEE: **marroo, moongoorr, doom-doom**.

denggelalab *COVERB+BE/STAY.* be open, be clear, be a hole through a rock making a place like a window, be a window in a house.
• Dirranden, birrinybe goorloorroogoo, boorroonboo denggelalab. *Today the sky is open up there, there are no clouds.* • Ngoowan nyinjiny jinbimnha, dama denggelalab-garri boorroonboo theb benajtha. *Don't forget to close the window.*

denggerr *COVERB+GO_ALONG.* go along ripping up. • Denggerr wananyji:::, yoorlangoogoo, warany. *It went along downstream, ripping up everything (flood at Warrmarn in 2011).*

denggij *COVERB+GET.* break off, pull out branch or root, pick fruit off tree, pull off (like ticks off a dog). • Denggij benamanyji. *He broke it off.*

derawoog *COVERB+BRING/TAKE.* drown someone. • Wel derawoog benanyji-yoo birriyama na, nawarrangem jiyilem. *It drowned the two of them then, along with a big mob of people.*

derd *COVERB+FALL/GO_DOWN.* get stuck. • Derd nyanoowardja. *She got stuck (emu at Mount King in dreamtime).* • Derd nginiward-ninggi nhoowooloo goonthoorrji. *You have a bad cold (lit. 'A rotten cold is stuck in you').* SEE: **larr**. [NOTE: get jammed in a crack]

derderdeg *COVERB+SAY/DO.* look around. • Derderdeg nyanini, roord nginiyanya deyena. *She looked around and put it down there.* SEE: **deg, derde-yerdeg**.

derde-yerdeg

derde-yerdeg *coverb+SAY/DO.* look for. • Berab nginiyin, derde-yerdeg nginini-boorroo miyale, ngoowan. *He came out and was looking for his meat but there was none.* SEE: **deg, derderdeg.**

derinyberrwany *coverb+FALL/GO_DOWN.* be knocked down (e.g. accidentally by car).
• Derinyberrwany-ngarri boorroowoonboo ngoorr-ngoorrgajim-birri . . . *If they have a car accident . . .*

derinyberr, derinyberrwany *coverb+HIT.* knock down going along (e.g. floodwater, wind). • Wayinigana gibiwoonab, berrembi derinyberrwany benayid, mayaroombi goonjambi. *That is why it spread out and knocked down all the houses and trees.*
• Derinyberr benayidji waloorrji mayaroom doo goonjam. *The wind knocked down the houses and trees.* SEE: **woor.**

deriyid-deriyid *noun.* white-lined honeyeater, 'daaloony' bird. *Meliphaga albilineata.* [NOTE: calls out during *werrgalen*, the hot weather period when leaves sprout before the rain, to make the *daaloony*, 'green plum' fruit, fat and ripe.]

derlaj *coverb+SAY/DO_REFL.* be jealous, argue over country. • Derlaj yirringirriyan. *We are arguing over the country.*

derlawoog *coverb+BE/STAY.* smack the water to make a noise. • Derlawoog-gala ngenden-nenggab. *I'll make a smacking noise on the water with you.*

derlawoog-derlawoog *coverb+SAY/DO.* clap on thigh with one hand on top of the other to make the sound loud. • Derlawoog-derlawoog barroo-gili! *All clap on your thighs making a good sound!* SEE: **derlawoog.**

derlawoog-galem *adjective.* good at making sound by clapping thighs.
• Derlawoog-galen-yarre. *We are good at making a sound clapping on our thighs.* SEE: **derlawoog.**

derlbawoo *coverb+SPEAR.* pierce and make water spurt out. • Derlbawoo-ngarri nginingaboordja dandi, goorloonyi yilag. *When she pierced the ground and made the water come out at that place down there.* SEE: **doorlboog.**

derlbawoo *coverb+HIT.* shoot. • Derlbawoo nyilayid thamben-ngiyi. *I shot her in the side.*
• Derlbawoo nginiyid. *He shot him.*

derlbawoogajil *noun.* rifle. SEE: **doorlgajim, wan'gil.**

derlg *coverb+PUT.* cast away at high-water mark in flood, floodwater heap up rubbish/debris (flotsam). • Derlg ngenayanyji. *It took me and cast me up with the other rubbish.*

derlmenji *coverb+GET.* have eye on someone.
• Thoowoorra degji yinamennha? Derlmenji yinamennha. *Why are you looking at me? You've got your eye on me.*

dern *coverb+FALL/GO_DOWN.* hide behind, get behind something. • Dern nginiwardji. *He got in behind him.* SEE: **geren, waman.**

Deroogan *noun.* Nowhere Place (place name).

Deroorrji *noun.* Black Hills on Bow River Station.

derranel; derranil *noun feminine.* black cockatoo. *Calyptorhynchus magnificus.* [NOTE: young men are not supposed to say this word, they are supposed to say *mardangarril*]

derreb *coverb+SAY/DO.* be camping.
• Derreb-garri yarrirn, *When we camp,*

derreb *coverb+HAVE.* look after in camp. • Derreba ngenamoorlardji, nyigamirribja ngenanyji yoorlangoogoo Thalinyman-yoorroong. *He looked after me in the camp for the night and early in the morning took me down to Thalinyman.*

derreb *coverb+FALL/GO_DOWN.* make camp.
• Derreb nginiwardji. *He made camp.* • Derreb yarraward. *We made camp.*

derreb *coverb+GO/COME.* go and make camp.
• Derreb yardiya. *Let's go and camp.*
• Derreb-garri yoowiya. *When we go and camp*

derreb; derrebbe *coverb+BE/STAY.* camp, be camping. • Derreb yirraniyinde. *We were camping. / We used to camp.*
• 'Ngenenggayana derrebbe ngenan'ge-narroowa,' nyanini. *'I am camping here because of all of you,' she said (turkey when she made night-fall).*

derrerreb *coverb+BECOME.* go camping out.
• Marrarn nginiyi derrerreb wiyinji. *He's gone camping out.* SEE: **derreb.**

derrerreb *coverb+GO/COME.* go camping out.
• Derrerreb-garri narrayinnha. *When you all went camping out.* SEE: **derreb.**

derrerreb *coverb+GO_ALONG.* go camping out.
• Derrerreb yirranyji. *We went camping out.* SEE: **derreb.**

derrerreb *coverb+SAY/DO.* make camp.
• Wayinigana derrerreb yarroorn-ngiyiwa

dilg-dilg

birn'girrbal. *Because the turkey did that we all sleep at night.* SEE: **derreb**.

derrerreb *coverb+SAY/DO_M.* go camping out.
• Ngarranggarnin, derrerreb wanemayinde ngoorrinya na. *In the dreamtime that one used to camp all around here then.* SEE: **derreb**.

derrerrebany *coverb.* go camping out.
• Marrarna yamberrawoorroobja derrerrebany. *We will go away and leave them and go camping out.* SEE: **derreb**.

derrgerne *noun.* gorge.

derrmerle *noun.* narrow rocky place.

deyela *demonstrative.* that is the one (feminine). SEE: **diyala**.

deyema *demonstrative.* those are the ones, that's the one (non-singular). SEE: **diyama**.

deyena, deyana *demonstrative.* there, that is the place there. SEE: **diyana**.

deyenya *demonstrative.* that is the one (masculine). SEE: **diyanya**.

dibam *noun.* billy can. [NOTE: derived from English 'dipper'] SEE: **gardag**.

dig-dig *coverb+SAY/DO.* heart throbbing. SEE: **doob-doob**.

digoorlool *noun.* wild jack bean. *Canavalia papuana.* SEE: **woolngal**.

dijarr *coverb+SAY/DO.* make noise by breaking stick. • Rangga nginji dijarr-ngarri birrirn bardoobinyi dan. *He (kangaroo with ears up) is listening in case someone makes a noise by breaking a stick behind him there (in photo).*

dijarrji *noun masculine.* cat. *Felis catus.* SEE: **ngirrngiliny, ngirrngiliwoony, goordoony**.

dijboord *coverb+GO_ALONG.* be loaded with fruit/flowers (plant or tree). • Dijboord wanany nginyjiny thawalany thalngarrji. *This snappy gum tree is loaded with flowers.*

dijgawoorr *coverb+GET.* break off sticks.
• Dijgawoorr-gala benemnha goowoolem. *You break off the sticks.*

dilboony, dilbool, dilboom *adjective.* dry.
• Jirrayam berrema, dana roord boowoonha dilboom. *This place is alright, sit there, it's dry.*

dilboowoorroony, dilboowoorrool, dilboowoorroom *adjective.* wet. LIT: 'not dry'. SEE: **giyiny, jirlanyjany**.

dil-dil SEE: **thil-thil**.

dilg-dilg *coverb+BURN/BITE_REFL.* paint dots on self (for dancing). SEE: **dag-dag**.

dilg-dilg *coverb+PUT.* put dots on painting.

Figure 43. *Derranel: Lamba-lambarnbe ngoowan garij nyimbirrimbe derranel, googbel-birri.*

dilg-dilgbawoony, dilg-dilgbawool, dilg-dilgbawoom

• Dama dilg-dilg noonayangge men'gawoog-girrim daam dam. *I just put all the dots there on the country to make it look good.* SEE: **dag-dag.**

dilg-dilgbawoony, dilg-dilgbawool, dilg-dilgbawoom *adjective.* spotted, painted with dots.

diligajim *noun.* torch.

dim *coverb+PUT.* put on clothes. • Dim-gala benaj, wanyagem-anyji-ninggi. *Try this one, maybe it is too small for you.* • Dim noonayangge, wanyagem-ngirri, derd berraard-ngirri. *I tried it on but it was too small. It got stuck on me.* • Dim noonayangge joorrooloonggoombi, men'gawoom-ngirri. *I put on the trousers and they were good on me.*

dimal *noun feminine.* boat. [NOTE: old word used by Gija people derived from English 'steamer' because of the steam ships that used to take away countrymen as prisoners to Rottnest Island; word used in a Balga style song and dance about those people] SEE: **larndoorrool.**

dimalan *noun.* river red gum. *Eucalyptus camaldulensis.* SEE: **bilirn, garranggany.**

dimanal *noun feminine.* mare. *Equus caballus.* SEE: **yawardal.**

dimanany *noun masculine.* horse. *Equus caballus.* SEE: **yawardany.**

dimberralgarlgarlji; dimberralgarlji *noun masculine.* dollar bird. *Eurystomus orientalis.* [NOTE: this bird was a man who was always laughing when his relations were trying to catch kangaroos thus warning the kangaroos and making it impossible to catch them] SEE: **garl-garl.**

dimboom; dimboowoom *noun.* calf muscle.

dimboogaleny, dimboogalel, dimboogalem *adjective.* having nice legs, being a person with nice legs. • Dimboogaliyal ngelga. *This woman has really nice legs.*

dinbirril *noun.* little striped fish species. [NOTE: not the same as *goodabal*]

dinboolel; dindoowoolbel *noun feminine.* necklace vine. *Abrus precatrius.*

dindany REDUP: **dindanyindany** *coverb+GO_ALONG.* go along making a noise (e.g. bullock with creaking hooves). • Dindany wananyjende boorroonany. *The bull was going along making a noise (with his hooves as he walked along).*

dindinil *noun feminine.* black-tailed treecreeper. (Kriol: 'woodpecker'). *Climacteris melanurus.* SEE: **dinil.**

ding *coverb+HIT.* hit lightly on the head, tap someone's head. • Ding nginiyidji. *He tapped him on the head.*

dini-dininy *noun.* anything, everything. SEE: **thoowoo-thoowoom.**

dinil *noun feminine.* black-tailed treecreeper. (Kriol: 'woodpecker'). *Climacteris melanurus.* [NOTE: also recorded as meaning 'little woodswallow', *Artamus minor*] SEE: **dindinil.**

Dinil-wawoon-ngarri-wanema *noun.* place name. LIT: 'place on Springvale where the *dinil* bird was cooking'.

dinygoorleny, dinygoorlel, dinygoorle *adjective.* crooked, twisted, bent. • Ngoorroonya goowooloonyi dinygoorlenyiya. *That tree is really twisted.*

dinygoorlg *coverb+GO/COME.* turn off onto another path. • Dinygoorlg yarrayi Gerregerrewoon ngelmang ngela. *We turned off at Spring Creek for the east.*

dinygoorlg *coverb+BE/STAY.* be bent. • Ngarn dinygoorlg ginji men'gawoo joodiya ngarag-girrim. *That thing that is already bent is good for making (boomerangs) straight away.*

dinygoorlg *coverb+PUT.* bend something. • Ngoowan dinygoorlg ngoorrayangbende. *They never used to bend it.*

dinyjile *noun.* navel, umbilical cord.

dinyjirr *coverb+SAY/DO.* sneeze. • Dinyjirr-ngarri ngenarn, yangoorranyji gariji ngemberremenbe. *When I sneeze somebody is calling my name.*

dinyjirr *coverb+SAY/DO_M.* sneeze. • Goonthoorrgayan ngelamande dinyjirr ngelamande wayini. *I've been coughing and sneezing.*

dirdi *coverb+DO_REFL.* make pillow for self, rest head on something. • Warna-warnarramga, bagoo-ngarri yirraniyinde, dirdi yirramiyinde berriyama. *A long time ago, when we used to sleep, we would make pillow for ourselves with this.*

dirdi *coverb+BE/STAY.* rest head on something. • Dirdi-gala ngenden ngenengga. *Let me rest my head here.*

dirdim *noun.* pillow. SEE: **barndim, wanangem.**

Diringen *noun.* Greenvale, a place on western part of Bow River Station.

dirr *coverb+SAY/DO_M.* become bright (when the sun comes out). • Dirr wanema. *It became* *bright (when the sun came up).* SEE: **berr**.

dirr *coverb+PLACE_M.* become bright (when the sun comes out). • *Dirr wiyiloonya ngenengga laarne barndel. It becomes bright when the sun is here on top.* SEE: **berr**.

dirrandem; derrandem REDUP: **dirr-dirrandem**. *temporal.* daybreak, morning, daytime. • *Derrandem-birri / dirrandem-birri. One day.* • *Dirranden. In the daytime.*

dirrandeg; derrandeg *coverb.* do something all night until morning, be daybreak. • *Boorooj woomberramande dirrandeg. They were playing all night until sunrise.* • *Derrandeg-garri birrinbe, malalal berab-garri nyimbiyanya, marrarn yarrawan. When it is daybreak, when the sun comes out we will go away.*

diwinji *noun masculine.* wattle species common in the Halls Creek area. *Acacia* sp. aff. *lysiphloia*. SEE: **yarliyilji**.

diya-diya *noun feminine.* peewee, magpie lark. *Grallina cyanoleuca*. SEE: **birlirrijgel**.

diyala *demonstrative.* that is the one (feminine). SEE: **deyela**.

diyama; diyema *demonstrative.* those are the ones, that's the one (non-singular). SEE: **deyema**.

diyana; diyena *demonstrative.* right there. SEE: **deyena**.

diyanya *demonstrative.* that is the one (masculine). SEE: **deyenya**.

diyid *coverb+SAY/DO.* sound made by the katydid grasshopper, a flat green grasshopper called *girinyil*. • *Ngeleli diyid nyerne warn'gam. Warn'gama berremga jarrag 'diyid' nyerne. Diyidboo nyerne. This one calls out 'diyid' in the cold weather.* SEE: **giri, girinybe**.

diyile *noun.* light.

diyilijiliny *noun.* bright light. • *Mendoowoon, derdega woomberriyinbe dan, diyilijilin. At night they (owls) look around there in the bright light (for insects).*

doo *conjunctive particle.* and. SEE: **joo**. [NOTE: joins nouns]

-doo *suffix.* dual suffix to verbs. SEE: **-yoo, -joo**.

doob *coverb+HIT.* hit someone. • *Doob nginiyidji therlan. He hit him on the back.*

doob-doob *coverb+SAY/DO.* heart throbbing (from emotional feeling for someone or exercise). • *Danya doob-doob ngerne-ngooyoo giningim. That one's (man's) heart is beating for her (woman he loves).* • *Dooloom doob-doob ngenarn. My heart is beating (after running).*

doobam *noun.* grave. • *Gaboogana nyimberrajbe dooban-gili goorrgoo-yoorroong? When is her funeral?* (lit. 'When will they put her in the grave, in the hole in the ground?')

dooboorrngbeny, dooboorrngbel, dooboorrngbem; dooboorrbeny *adjective.* very hot. • *Ngoowan! Dooboorrngben-nga marne-jaya. No! I'm really hot like fire.* • *Dooboorrben-nga berab-gala ngenda ngarliyi. I am really hot, I should go out and cool down.* • *Dooboorrben. A really hot place.*

dooboo-yooboo *coverb+BECOME.* be sorry, be really upset. • *Dooboo-yooboo woomberrayidbe-boorroo mayaroom. They were all very sorry about their houses (being washed away by the flood).*

doog REDUP: **doog-doog**. *coverb+HIT.* hit with a stone to knock bark or gum off a tree. • *Doog benayidji. He hit it to get the bark.* • *Doog-doog beniyinji. He is hitting the bark to cut it off.*

doog *coverb+GET.* get bark or gum off a tree by hitting it. • *Doog-gala ngerem. Let him knock it (bark) off.*

doogoo-doogoo *coverb+SAY/DO_REFL.* feel for lice. • *Yiwimga doogoo-doogoo ngenengirriyan. I am feeling around for lice.*

Doogoorrenyinem *noun.* place near Red Butt in the northern part of Ngarrgooroon country.

doojood *coverb+GET.* hit. • *Dal nyamanil doojood nginema dany marloogany. That old woman hit that old man.*

doojood *coverb+HIT.* hit on neck or head with rock or stick. • *Mendoowiyan jara nginimanyji-noo doojood giniyidjende. Then he would sneak up on him in the middle of the night when he was asleep and kill him.*

doojoodbany *coverb+HIT.* go along hitting. • *Doojoodbany bemberrayid. They went along hitting them on their heads.*

doolbariny *adjective.* upright. [NOTE: swearing, from Jack Britten]

doolboom *noun.* heart. [NOTE: Southern dialect] SEE: **dooloom, giningim**.

doolgboo *coverb+BECOME.* just emerging. • *Gamoom doolgboo-ngarriya wimbirriyinbe. When they only have little breasts.*

dooljoog *coverb+SAY/DO_M.* smash.

doolmarinybany

- Boomberramangbende, dooljoog woomberramande. *They used to get them (green plum fruit) and smash them up.*

doolmarinybany *coverb+BE/STAY.* be a rising and falling line in country (like a winding road).
- Doolmarinybany-ngarri boorroonboo. *(Line in a painting that shows) where the country rises up and down, winding road everywhere.*

doolmoorroony *noun.* erection. [NOTE: swearing]

Doolngayim *noun.* Argument Gap, famous and important ceremonial meeting place near the borders of Miriwoong, Gajirrabeng, Ngarinyman and Jaminjung country, about 100 km east of Kununurra.

dooloo *coverb+PUT.* make smoke, smoke someone (ceremony). • Dooloo yamberraj, lingage yamberremnya. Deg-garri ngoorrimbe dooloo-ngarri ngoowirn, 'Dooloo woomberrayangbe dama biriwoo-wanyji boorroordboo.' *We'll make smoke, let them know. When they see the smoke (they will say), 'They have made smoke as a sign, they must be coming back.'* • Doorloog-garri ngelayidge, dama dooloo ngemberrayangbe, mabooram-birri gooroongem-birri. *When I was born they smoked me with conkerberry (konkerberry) and the kind of medicinal herb called* gooroongeny. SEE: **dooloorayi, dooloomayib.**

dooloo *coverb+PLACE_M.* make smoke. • Dooloo woomberrayangbe. *They made smoke as a sign.* SEE: **dooyoo-dooyoo.**

dooloo *coverb+SAY/DO.* be smoking. • Dooloo boorroorn. *It is smoking.* SEE: **dooloorayi, dooloomayib.**

dooloo *coverb+SAY/DO_M.* be smoking. • Dooloo wanemayinde warnarrayan. *It has been smoking for a long time.* SEE: **dooloorayi, dooloomayib.**

dooloodbinyji *noun.* olive python. *Liasis olivaceus.*

dooloom *noun.* heart. SEE: **giningim, doolboom.**

dooloomab *+BE/STAY.* be smoking (i.e. fire).

dooloomayib *coverb+BE/STAY.* be smoke rising, be dust rising like smoke. • Joordoombiya dooloomayib boorroonboo. *There is lots of dust getting up.*

dooloorayi *coverb+SAY/DO.* be smoking (fire).
- Dooloorayi boorroorn. *It is smoking (the fire).*

doombaj *coverb+GET.* knock down (e.g. trees by flood or with a bulldozer).

doomboo *coverb+GO/COME.* go through a gap.
- Doomboo yara woorayibenginy-nhi doomboon-ga. Yagenginy ngoorroony doomboo nyaliny yara. *Let's go through on this side of the gap. Then we'll go through that other gap.*

doomboo *coverb+FALL/GO_DOWN.* go through a gap. • Doomboo yarraward gerloowoorr. *We went up through the gap.*

doomboo-doomboo; doomboo-roomboo *coverb+SAY/DO.* go through gap between hills.
- Birriyama doomboo-doomboo-ngarri yarroorn, doomboo-doomboo-ngarri yirrani loonggoong, Ngiwoowa-biny. *Here is where we go through the gap, we used to go through the gap from down there, from Ngiwoowan.*

doomboolalib *coverb+BE/STAY.* be an opening through. • Ngoorriny ngarrgaliny doomboolalib nginji. *You can see right through that hill, there is a hole through it.*

doomboom *noun.* gap.

doomboomab *coverb+SAY/DO.* be a gap through hills. • Doomboomab-ngarri boorroonboo. *There is gap through over there.*

doomboony *noun masculine.* owl. *Ninox connivens, N. novaeseelandiae.*

doomboo-roombool *coverb+SAY/DO_M.* go though gaps in the hills. • Doomboo-roomboolboowa woomberramande. *They came along through the gaps in the hills then.*

doom-doom *coverb+SAY/DO.* be jealous, love very much. • Doom-doom ngerne-ngooyoo. *He loves her very much (and jealously holds onto her emotionally).* SEE: **dem-dem.**

doomooge *coverb+BE/STAY.* stay alone, stay by oneself. • Ngoon'goo yarraj vidiyoo-girrim. Doomooge nimbinha-yirrewa. *We are all moving off to go to a video. You will stay here by yourself after us.*

Doomoolji *noun.* place near Meriyin in Ngarrgooroon country.

doomoom *noun.* head. SEE: **goonggooloom.** [NOTE: sometimes used to mean 'hair']

doomoorriny, doomoorrinyji, doomoorrinyil, doomoorrinybe *noun.* spiritually dangerous place, important sacred place. • Ngelel doomoorrinyil, ngarranggarnil, girlib-garri nyaninya, ngoorrooma girliwirring nyaninya, tharrayimele. *This is the dreamtime place where* *the emu was walking over there coming down the gorge.* SEE: **joomoorrirriny**.

doomoorrngarnany, doomoorrngarnal, doomoorrngarnam *noun.* cousins from one family, children of mother's brother.

doomoorroo *noun.* chest. SEE: **manggam**.

doomoorroo *noun.* middle section of woomera.

doon *coverb+BE/STAY.* be bent around, be extended of hills, to run along in a range; to be bent like a boomerang (tree). • **Nginy ngarrgaleny doon nginji wayiniwa.** *This hill bends around in a line like that (talking about a painting).* • **Doon nginji goowooloony.** *The tree is bent.*

doonggood *coverb+BECOME.* be big shade, be really shady. • **Dama ngaaloom doonggood woomberrayid.** *That shade has increased (become very shady).* • **Goorndarrim jinbimnhande-ngarri, goowoolen dan, doonggoodgan roord nyimbinyande.** *When you are fishing, she (peaceful dove) will come and sit in the trees in the heavy shade.*

doonggoolbany, doonggoolbal *noun.* person who is in mourning, wearing necklace made of matted hair and observing dietary restrictions.

doonggoolji, doonggooloo *noun.* necklace made of matted hair. [NOTE: worn during times of mourning when people cannot eat meat, only fish, witchetty grubs and snake]

doonggoony *coverb+GO/COME.* come off (e.g. axe head off handle). • **Lawooggan-ga doonggoony nyimbiyanya.** *It (the axe head) will come off (the handle) while chopping.*

doongooroog *coverb+GET.* break into small pieces, mince up, make holes in something (e.g. rain in spinifex roof of bough shed). • **Jadam doongooroog ngoorrooma, wayinigana tharroorroo ngerne yilaga.** *The rain has broken it up and made holes in it, because of that it pours through.*

Doongoorriny *noun.* hill between Jin'gaweny and Ngindiwarriny in Ngarrgooroon country.

Doorawoorrji *noun.* place name. SEE: **Dooroorrji**.

doordoog *coverb+SAY/DO.* be handsome, be good-looking, be beautiful. • **Doordoog-ma ngenarn?** *Aren't I handsome?* • **Doordoog-ma yirrarn?** *Aren't we good-looking?*

doordoogany, doordoogal, doordoogam *adjective.* handsome, good-looking, pretty. • **Bangariny doordooga-warriny darnda-**

warriny nyirrega boorroorn-doo nawarran goorloon. *Two pretty turtles are swimming in the big water.*

doori; dooriyi REDUP: **dooriyi-dooriyi**. *coverb+GO_ALONG.* be thundering. • **Doori wiyinji / Dooriyi wiyinji.** *It is thundering.*

doorib *coverb+BE/STAY.* be in line, be long. • **Dooriba nginji danyga ngarranggarniny.** *That dreaming thing is long now.* • **Ngoorroona doorib-garri nginji ngarrgaleny diyena yarra.** *Over there where that rock is in one line we'll go there now.*

doori-doorib; doorib-doorib *coverb+GO/COME.* be thundering, anything go in a line one after the other. • **Doori-doorib ngidji.** *It is thundering.* • **Danya doorib-doorib ngidji jadany.** *That rain is thundering.* SEE: **doori**.

doorig-doorig *coverb+FALL/GO_DOWN.* to start thundering. • **Berrema, ngarnbe-ngarri doorig-doorig-garri ngoowoonji.** *This (painting) is when that thing, the thunder starts.* SEE: **doorib**.

doorlboog *coverb+BECOME.* bust out (e.g. water, blood), bust making a loud noise/deep sound. • **Dama doorlboog woomberrayid thoowiyanyji.** *Something busted out over there.*

doorlboog *coverb+HIT.* make spurt out (e.g. water, blood). • **Doorlboog bemberrayidbe-ni goorroobardoom-birri.** *They busted it and made the water spurt out of it (coolamon) with a boomerang.*

doorlboog *coverb+GET.* make spurt out (e.g. water, blood). • **Doorlbooga nginimanyi danyi goorrnganyi laarne.** *He made that water spurt out up there then.*

doorlboog *coverb+SAY/DO_M.* spurt out (e.g. water, blood), bust making a loud noise/deep sound, water come out from underneath when making a soak. • **Doorlboog wanema goorrngambi.** *The water spurted out.* • **Gaande Merrewoon jida nyanini, doorlboog wanema goorrngambi.** *Up at Merrewoon she stabbed the ground and the water gushed out.*

doorl-doorl *coverb+GO_ALONG.* turning while dancing. • **. . . doorl-doorl-ngarri wananyjende yoorroondoorroombi.** *. . . when he was turning and going in different directions while doing the dance like 'rock and roll'.*

doorlgajim *noun.* rifle. SEE: **derlbawoogajil, wan'gil**.

doorloog *coverb+BECOME.* grow, emerge, be

born. • *Garloonggoony doorloog waniyid-ni warlarriny.* The orchid is growing up in the white gum tree. • *Danya nyiyirriny doorloog waniyid ngarrgalen laarne.* This spinifex is growing up on the hill. • *Dany ngarrgaliny, danya doorloog-garri wiyinji ganarrany laarne.* That hill, that is where the leaves are growing up on top.

doorloonyil *noun feminine.* moving target made of bark used for spear throwing practice. • *Nginyjinya bilirnji doorloonyil bernngal boorij-girril-boorroo wanyanyagem.* This is the moving target made from red river gum tree-bark for the little boys to play with (play spearing).

doorloorloog *coverb+GO_ALONG.* emerge. • *Goorloony, winyjiny doorloorloog-ngarri wananyji.* This is water, spring water that comes out.

doorloorloog *coverb+SAY/DO_M.* be coming out, be emerging. • *Biya wananya-noo::: gedba nginiyid doorloorlooga wanamanyande na, ngalenganggany.* She (turtle) looked for him for a long time, then she saw her son (crocodile) and she came out (on the surface of the water).

doorloorloog *coverb+BECOME.* grow, emerge, be born. • *Berre-binyja doorloorloog janini, wayinigana doorloorloog-garri nyanini, barlberrwany nyaniyinya.* It started coming out from here now (dreamtime place of witchetty grub), because it came out it spread everywhere.

doorloorloog *coverb+HIT.* come out (flowers). • *Goorramindim thawalam ngarem-boorroo, doorloorloog ngiyinji thawalany melagawoony.* The flowers (of the snappy gum) called goorramirndim are good for bush honey. Many flowers come out (at the one time).

dooroog *coverb+SAY/DO_M.* tear sheets of paperbark from tree. • *Diyid-garri wanemanyande, merndama dooroog woomberramande wayininji.* When they hear it (the katydid grasshopper) call out 'diyid' they get their paperbark ready then (to use as blankets in the cold). [NOTE: this refers only to paperbark, not the bark of other trees]

dooroog *coverb+GET.* tear sheets of paperbark from tree. • *Dooroog barrem-gili merndany yoorn'goorr-girrim.* You all get paperbark sheets to cover the food cooking in the ground. [NOTE: this refers only to paperbark, not the bark of other trees]

Dooroorrji *noun.* place on Bow River Station. SEE: **Doorawoorrji**.

doorrbood *coverb+GET.* pull out of earth oven. SEE: **boog**.

doorrja-doorrjam *noun.* half-grown emu chicks.

doorrman *coverb+PUT.* put something inside (e.g. body in burial cave, clothes in cupboard). • *Yanggi noonayangge, 'Goorndarrim yimberriyinnha-gili ngenenggayanan, doorrman narroonnha.* I asked them all (deceased relations in country), 'Give us fish, you who are all buried right here.' SEE: **dooroon**.

dooroo-dooroo *coverb+SAY/DO.* put something on top of someone/something (when you empty something out, like rice or something on plates). • *Dooroo-dooroo nyanini-birri-yoo, ngarrgalem.* She put little rocks on top of the two of them.

doorroom *noun.* burial place, cemetery, graveyard. • *Doorroom-boorroo goonyingarre.* Burial place for dead bodies. SEE: **dooyoorroon**.

dooroon *coverb+PUT.* put away, hide something, place a corpse in a burial place. • *Dooroon benayanyji.* He put them away.

dooroon *coverb+DO_REFL.* put self at side. • *Dooroon-ayi nginimiyanya jawarlaliny, ngoorrooma na manjalji jawarlali nginji-ngarri.* The tata lizard put himself up on the side, the big white rock there now is where he stays.

dooroon *coverb+BE/STAY.* be placed. • *Ngoorriyane Warrmarne dooroon nyinya minyjiwarran.* She is (buried) right over there at Warrmarn near the black plum tree.

dooroo-woorroon *coverb+SAY/DO.* put deceased people inside. • *Deyena dooroo-woorroon berrani, yilgi-yilgoorroom, loosembany-ngarri berramiyinbende.* They used to put the old people there when they died.

doowab *coverb+GO/COME.* fly. • *Wanyanyagem moorrgoom doowab berrayi.* Lots of little grasshoppers (of the kind called *moorrgoony*) fly around. SEE: **doowarab**.

doowab *coverb+LEAVE.* fly away and leave someone. • *Gerloorroogoo doowab benawoorroordji-yoo na.* He flew away from the two of them up into the sky then.

doowageny; doowagoony *noun.* koel. *Eudynamys scolopacea.* • *Doowagoony dany wanggarnam dam ganggerre* ngoorroowarrenbe. Loorroobji ngoorroomenbende wayiniya thed ngoorriyinbe. *Crows don't like the koel. They chase him until they kill him.* [NOTE: the koel and the channel-billed cuckoo are both known as 'the storm bird' because they appear just before the wet season; their loud calls are sometimes described as 'swearing'] SEE: **girlgoowal, joowany**.

doowanggoonyji *noun.* rock wallaby. SEE: **woombardgoony, woonyjoorroony, woombarnoongoony**.

doowarab *coverb+GO/COME.* fly. • Wiji nyaliny nyanini goorloorroogoo na, doowarab::: nyaninya. *She ran along upwards then, she was flying (brolga in dreamtime).* SEE: **doowab**.

doowerrberr *coverb+SAY/DO_REFL.* wriggle. • Doowerrberr ngengirriyan-ninggi. *He (young energetic dog) is wriggling on you.*

doowerrberr *coverb+SAY/DO.* shake water off self. • Boorab nyidja, doowerrberr nyerne. *She comes out (mother emu from water) and shakes the water off.*

doowoo REDUP: **doowoo-doowoo**. *coverb+HIT.* hit tree with axe/rock. • Berrema doowoo nginiyid nginyjiny nyaarndiny gerloowoorrng, lemboo-lembood wanema-ni dambi, gerrij. *She knocked off some of this gum from up there and stuck it onto him.*

doowoo *interjection.* sound of hitting something.

doowoo REDUP: **doowoo-doowoo**. *coverb+GO_ALONG.* go along cutting trees. • Doowoo-doowoo-ngarri woomberranybende, ngoowan. *When they used to cut trees they didn't (cut big lumps to use as bowls as is done now for art shops).*

doowoodji *noun masculine.* black cormorant. *Phalacrocorax sulcirostris.*

doowoogboo *coverb+GO/COME.* go up. • Doowoogboo ngidji gerloowoorr ngarrgalen-gili. *He goes up (out of the water) up onto the rock.*

Doowoonan *noun.* Old Bedford. [NOTE: site of first Bedford Downs homestead]

doowoorrng *coverb+FALL/GO_DOWN.* turn around. • Yagenge-yoorroong na doowoorrng boowoo. *Turn around the other way now. / Turn towards the other way now.*

doowoorrng *coverb+PUT.* turn something over. • Doowoorrng beniyilinya. *She is turning them over (cooking damper).*

dooyoo-dooyoo *coverb+GO_ALONG.* make smoke. • Dooyoo-dooyoo waanyjende, ngoorroo-gayanya, gabinganyji. *He (marsupial mouse in dreamtime) used to go along making smoke everywhere.* [NOTE: Southern dialect]. SEE: **dooloo**.

dooyoorroon *noun.* burial place.

Ee

-e *suffix.* plural/non-singular suffix to nouns following stems ending in '*l*' or '*rr*' with vowels other than '*-oo*'. SEE: **-be, -m, -oo**.

-e *suffix.* at, in, on. SEE: **-n, -nyen, -jen**. [NOTE: locative suffix to nouns following consonant stems, allophone '*-oo*' follows nouns with '*oo*' vowels]

e-e; ee *interjection.* that's the thing and then. [NOTE: used as a kind of punctuation mark to say 'that happened and is completed' and then describe what happens next; discourse marker]

Gg

-g, -ge *suffix.* causative suffix, makes coverbs from nominals or other coverbs.

-ga *suffix.* emphatic marker on nouns, demonstratives and free form pronouns

gaageny, gaagel, gaagembi *noun.* poor thing. SEE: **goorlanggeny**. [NOTE: non-singular form *gaagembi* generally used as a kind of interjection expressing sympathy and affection]

gaag-gaag *coverb +GO_ALONG.* go along saying 'gaag-gaag'. • 'Gaag-gaag' wananyji, jirege nginiwamanyji. *He went along calling, 'Gaag-gaag' (the call of the wedge-tailed eagle) as he turned into a bird.*

gaagge *coverb+GET.* make someone say 'gaag'. • Gaagge ngoorramangbe dambi jalinggirimbi. *(When he sat down) the sharp point made him go 'Gaag!'*

gaalji, gaale *noun.* spinifex resin.

gaande *directional.* upstream, up there. • Gaande Merrewoon jida nyanini, doorlboog wanema goorrngambi. *She stabbed the ground upstream at Merrewoon and the water spurted out.* SEE: **gendewa**.

gaardaya *adverb.* slowly (referring to speed of action), softly (referring to other actions, e.g. hitting).

gabaanyji *interrogative.* something happening (I don't know what). [NOTE: Southern dialect] SEE: **gaboowanyji**.

gabagirrem, gabagerreny, gabagirrel *interrogative.* what for? what's wrong? • Gabagirrema? *What's wrong?* • Nyingen gabagirrenha-ngoo? *What is wrong with you?* • Gabagerrenyi danyi? *What is wrong with him?* • Gabagirrel dala? *What is wrong with her?* [NOTE: Southern dialect; agrees in gender with the person or thing being asked about]

gabi; gabiyi *interrogative.* where to? • Gabi nirda? *Where are you (one) going?* • Ngoowan deg nyanini gabi girli wananya. *She didn't look where she was walking.*

gabinga *interrogative.* where to? [NOTE: Southern dialect]

gabiyanyji; gabinganyji *interrogative.* to somewhere, it is unknown where to. • Gabiyanyji-birri yinginybiyi jiyilengembi. *I don't know the Aboriginal name for the place.*

gaboo *interrogative.* what? [NOTE: asks about verbs] • Gaboo ngenani ganggayi. *Sorry Nana (one person talking).* • Gaboo yarrani ganggayi. *Sorry Nana (more than one person talking).* [NOTE: special usage of 'what?' given by elders to translate 'sorry' said by a kid or kids when discussing how to say this in Gija]

gaboogana *interrogative.* when? [NOTE: Southern dialect] SEE: **gayigana**.

gaboogirriny, gaboogirril, gaboogirrim *interrogative.* what's wrong with him/her/them/it? [NOTE: agrees in gender with the person or thing being asked about] SEE: **gabagirrem**.

gaboo garningga; gaboo garnengga *interrogative.* what is it now? • Deg gerne, gaboo garningga, wooraygoo-yoorroong. *He is looking – what is the word now – this way.* • Ngiwin na berremboowa, gaboo garningga-wirrin, Ngirringirrinyin, Ngarrgooroon. *It is at that place there – what is it called now – Ngirringirrinyin in Ngarrgooroon country.* [NOTE: said to self when trying to think of the correct word]

gaboojana *interrogative.* how? • Gaboojana yoowoomnya? *How are we going to get it?*

gaboongarrigan *interrogative.* what is wrong? • Gaboongarrigan, thoowoo moojoong yarrengirriyan? Ngoowa jarrag yarrengirrij? *What is wrong, why do we feel funny with each other? We don't talk to each other?*

gaboongerreg *interrogative.* how many?

gaboo-ni garnengga *interrogative.* which one (masculine) was it now? [NOTE: said to self when trying to think of the correct word]

gaboowa; gaba *interrogative.* what? what is happening? what now? • Gaboowa boorroorn? *What are they doing?* • Gaboowa-girri-nha-ngoo gawayi? *What is wrong with you, Auntie?*

gaboowanyji *interrogative.* something happening (I don't know what).

gad *coverb+LEAVE_REFL.* leave each other, separate. • Gad-garri niniwoorroodge, gad-garri yirrawoorremiyinji-yoo, ngoorloorloog-gayan wanemayinde. *When I left him, when we left each other, because he was drinking too much.*

gad REDUP: **gad-gad**. *coverb+LEAVE*. leave someone/something. • Ngaginyji warlaginy gad genawoorrood, bardoon ngenan'ge-noowa. *My son left me and I stayed behind.* • Gad nginiwoorroodji. *He left him behind.* • 'Gadboo-ma yinawoorroona?' nyanini. 'Ngiyi.' *'So you're going to leave me?' she asked. 'Yes,' he said.* • Gad-garri yinawoorrood . . . *When you left me . . .*

gadij *coverb+FALL/GO_DOWN*. fall and cut self. • Ngoowan gadij nemboowoonnha! *Don't fall and cut yourself.*

gadij *coverb+BURN/BITE_REFL*. cut self. • Goorndoogaarriny dama nayifem, gadem-girrim jaabalam, gadija berrawoorranbi-yoo. *Those two kids cut each other with the sharp knife.* • Ngoowan gadij nimboowannha! *Don't cut yourself!* • Gadij ngenawoorran. / Gadij ngenawan. *I cut myself.* • Gadij birriwandi-yoo. *Those two will cut themselves.*

gadij *coverb+HIT*. cut, chop. • Waarrany gadijboo ngiyinji goowooloony ngarag-girrem baljarranggoom. *The boy is going to cut the tree to make boomerangs.*

gagoolanyil *noun feminine*. small, bitter bush melon, paddy melon. *Citrullus colocynthis*. [NOTE: eaten by kangaroos to clean out their guts, according to Hector Jandany]

gagoowany *noun*. silver-crowned friar-bird. *Philemon argenticeps*.

gaj *coverb+HIT*. chop, cut (e.g. tree). • Gaj-gala nherij. *I should chop it.* • Gaj benayidji. *He chopped it.*

gajam *noun*. shallow water.

-gajiny, gajil, -gajim *suffix*. used for. [NOTE: used to create neologisms, e.g. *ngoorr-ngoorrgajim* 'growl-used for', i.e. 'engines/cars']

gajig *coverb+GET*. make sore. • Gajiga yinama. *You made me sore then.*

gaji-gajibany *coverb*. have sores.

gajim REDUP: **gaji-gajim**. *noun*. sore. • Gajiban-anyji-ngoo. *You might have a sore.* • Marlam gajiban-nga. *I have a sore on my hand.*

gajoowoony, gajoowool, gajoowoom *adjective*. soft. [NOTE: swearing]

-gala; -gela *imperative/hortative suffix*. should, must, want to. [NOTE: follows coverbs before the verb in compound verbs and the verb in simple verbs]

galadil *noun feminine*. white paint. SEE: **mawoondool**.

galaleb *coverb+HIT*. race up and kill someone. • Galaleb-garri ngoorrayidbe. *When they raced up and killed him.*

galama *particle*. whether or not, wondering. (Kriol: what wrong). • Raymondji linga-linga nginini, galama barle nyimbijji bajinggelel. *Raymond was thinking about whether he (person who wanted to borrow it) was a good person to ride the bike.* • Galama barle nginboowoon-ngiyi. *I'm wondering why (I'm not allowed to / you won't let me) ride the bike? (Kriol: 'What wrong I can't ride it (the bike)?')* • Mooloorroo ngenarn-ngoo ngaboony. Galama biri nimbiyanha. *I feel sorry for you Dad (I miss you Dad). I wonder if you will come back.*

galamoordal *noun feminine*. bush turkey, bustard. *Ardeotis australis*. SEE: **birn'girrbal**. [NOTE: Southern dialect, Nyaajarri skin]

galarrwoorany *noun masculine*. scorpion.

galawarrjil *noun feminine*. spinifex pigeon. *Geophaps plumifera*. • Ngarranggarnin galawarrjil warrg-ngarri wanemanyande, warrggalel. *In dreamtime the spinifex pigeon was dancing, she is good at dancing.*

galayi *coverb+PUT*. put hand over forehead to shade eyes from sun while looking at something. • Galayi benajtha ngawooram ngoorroo-ngoorroola. *Put your hand over your forehead and look up at all those sugarbag bees.*

galayigajil *noun feminine*. helicopter. SEE: **birrinyoowoorlel**.

galayimarran *locative/temporal*. in the brightness at sunrise or sunset. • Galayimarran deg yamberramoodja. *Let's look at the sunset.*

galayimarrji, galayimarrel, galayimarre REDUP: **gala-galayimarrji**. *adjective*. bright-coloured as at sunrise or sunset. • Gerlenenyi dany gala-galayimarrji. *That tall, strong-smelling spinifex species is bright (light-coloured).*

galba-galbany *noun masculine*. spoonbill. *Platalea regia, P. flavipes*.

-galeny, -galel, -galem *suffix*. good at doing (coverb), good at getting/having lots of (noun stem). [NOTE: followed by gender suffixes, makes nouns, e.g. *mernmerdgalem* 'policemen' from *mernmerd* 'tie up' – 'people who are good at tying up'; *mayigalel*, 'female good cook, plant of feminine gender that gets lots of food'; *mayigaleny* 'male good cook, plant of masculine gender that gets lots of food']

galimbirrji, galimbirril, galimbirre adjective. red. • Ngoowan werrgalel, ani gelimbirrel. *Not the one with blue-green markings, only the red one (blue-tongue lizard species).* • Galimbirr waniyid. Galimbirrwany woomberrayid. *He became red. They all became red.* [NOTE: Rusty Peters says *galimbirrji*; his sister Mabel Juli says *gelimbirrji*]

galinggarra noun. clapsticks. SEE: **gil-gile, garnbagbe**. [NOTE: *gil-gil* is most commonly used]

galiwoony noun masculine. bloodwood gum, kino.

galja-galja coverb+PUT. put things separately. • Dam yajany-ngarri boorroonboo, galja-galja bimbirriyilinbe. *Those things that are the same, they put each separately.*

galja-galja coverb+GO_ALONG. go separately, do separately. • Ngoorrooma galja-galja woomberriyinbende. *That lot are all going (sleeping) separately over there (they don't want to sleep near us).*

galmang; galmangarri REDUP: **galma-galmang**. directional. to the east moving around from south to north or north to south (e.g. rain). • Galmangarriya wanyji jalij wiyinji. *The rain must be coming round over there to the east.*

galoowalel noun feminine. large pearl-shell pendant.

galyegbeg coverb+GET. make soft. • Yiwirnji jalij wanemayinde, galyegbeg benamanyji daam dam. *The set-in rain kept falling, making the ground soft.*

galyegbeny, galyegbel, galyegbem adjective. soft. • Galyegbeny danyga ngayawarlji. *That sand is very soft (at sugar leaf dreaming place).*

galyoolyoom noun. diarrhoea, stomach ache. • Galyoolyoobany-ngirri. *I have diarrhoea.* • Galyoolyool-ngarri woomberramenbe . . . *When they have diarrhoea . . .*

gama interrogative where? SEE: **gaya**.

gamaama coverb+GO_ALONG. be unable to see where to go. • Danyi warrarnanyi berab nginiyin, gamaama wananyji. *When the wedge-tailed eagle (eaglehawk) came out (of the cave), he could hardly see.*

gamalg coverb+SAY/DO. ask on behalf of someone. • Gamalg berne-birri thamboorroom merndam-boorroo. *Ask my mother-in-law (who I cannot speak to) for money.* [NOTE: mother-in-law is non-singular because of avoidance]

gamaliwany, gamaliwal, gamaliwam noun. stranger.

gaman coverb+SAY/DO_M. look around. • Nginyi gaman wanemayinde ngoorroon yiliginji, 'Gawoorra ngeli?' *This man looked around there inside (and said), 'Where is this woman?'*

gaman coverb+SAY/DO. look around, miss someone. • Marrge gaman yirrarn-boorroo daam. *We are still looking to them for our country.* • Gaman ngenarn-noongoo. *I miss him. / I am looking around for him.*

gamanggarrji, gamanggarre noun. bamboo. *Phragmites karka*. [NOTE: used as spear shafts]

Gamanggerrngarrin noun. Station Creek on Texas Downs.

Gamaninyin noun. place name.

gamany coverb+BECOME. fall down out of control. • Gamany ngelayidge. *I fell down out of control (I don't know what I did).* • Gamany woomberrayidbe ngoorr-ngoorrgaji-baya. *They fell down out of control in the motor car accident.* [NOTE: as in the car accident that killed the woman who came back and gave Rover Thomas the Goorirr-goorirr song cycle in his dreams]

gamanyjel noun feminine. boomerang type. SEE: **baljarranggool, garrabiril, goorroobardool, jaranggarril, jinybal**.

gamberarra-gamberarra adverb. go miles and miles, go very far. SEE: **ngirribawoorroon**.

gambirn noun. pus. • Moorloo gambirn-bal. *She has sticky eye/conjunctivitis.*

gamboord REDUP: **gamboo-gamboord**. coverb+GET. grab. • Gamboord nyanema. *He grabbed her.* • Gamboord benema. *He/she grabbed them.* • Boornoom-wanyji gamboord ninbimge. *I might grab some flies.* • Gamboo-gamboord-garri benamanyjende yilagga goorloo, nawane dan. *When he used to grab them down in the hole in the water there.*

gamboord coverb+PUT. grab and put. • Gamboord-ayi ngoorrayangbe wajbaloombi, ngaginya gelaginyima ngagenyji-ni. *The white men grabbed my grandfather with my father like that (and put him*

gamelanyel

in chains).

gamelanyel *noun.* mother's sister.

gamerrem *noun.* mother's father's country, the earth, the world. [NOTE: Hector Jandany said it meant 'this world Australia, this island']

gamingoorroom *noun.* everybody.

gamool *noun feminine.* slender skinks. *Carlia* spp., *Notoscincus ornatus.* [NOTE: when the tail comes off, a milky liquid comes out of the stump]

gamoolel *noun feminine.* camel. *Camelus dromedaries.* SEE: **yoobyoobgajil.** [NOTE: from English 'camel']

gamoom REDUP: **gamoo-gamoom.** *noun.* breast, milk.

-gan *adverbial_suffix.* makes adverbial forms from coverbs.

ganalam *noun.* feather. SEE: **birn'girre, darrgam.**

ganambiny *noun masculine.* river fig. *Ficus coronulata.* SEE: **jabayiny.**

ganany, gananyji *noun masculine.* digging stick.

ganarram REDUP: **gananarram.** *noun.* small leafy branches, leaves. [NOTE: used for putting food on or in ceremonies]

ganarram *noun.* paper money, cheque. [NOTE: Southern dialect]

ganarrangarnany, ganarrangarnal *noun.* mad person. LIT: 'one who dwells in the bushes'.

ganberaj *coverb+SAY/DO_M.* stand up aggressively in a threatening manner, stand on four legs lifting self up and down rocking (lizard).
• *Ganberaj woomenyande. She (a lizard puffing itself up) gets 'cheeky'.*

gang *coverb+SAY/DO.* choke. • *Gang ngenani. I choked.* SEE: **gim.**

gangalangaliny *noun.* red ant.

gangal garnengga *interrogative.* what (feminine) was it now? • *Ngela na biya ngenani-ngooyoo dal-ngiyi, gangal garnengga? This is the (feminine) one I was looking around for, which one was it now?*

gangal, gangel, gangangel *interrogative.* where is she, which feminine one?

Ganggamel *noun.* name of spirit woman.

ganggangel *noun feminine.* grey-crowned babbler. *Pomatostomus temporalis.* [NOTE: name has also been recorded as meaning the 'blue-faced honeyeater', *Entomyzon cyanotis*]

ganggal, ganggam *noun.* maternal grandmother, mother's mother, mother's mother's sister, woman's daughter's daughter, man's sister's daughter's daughter. (Kriol: 'granny') SEE: **ganggayi.**

ganggany, ganggam *noun.* mother's brother, woman's daughter's son, man's sister's daughter's son. (Kriol: 'granny') SEE: **ganggayi.**

ganggarrji, ganggarre *noun.* sugarbag wax, beeswax. SEE: **joornoogji.**

ganggayi *noun.* relationship address form used by people who are *ganggal* or *ganggany* to each other, what 'grannies' call each other; i.e. mother's mothers and mother's mother's brothers call woman's daughter's children and man's sister's daughters children and vice versa. (Kriol: 'granny')

ganggerr *coverb+GO/COME.* be angry.
• *... wayinigana ganggerr nginiyin ... because of that he was angry.*

ganggerr *coverb+SAY/DO_REFL.* be angry with each other. • *Ganggerr berrangirriyin. They were angry with each other.*

ganggerre *coverb+BURN/BITE.* dislike someone. • *Wanggarnambi ganggerre ngoorroowarrenbe. The crows do not like him (koel).*

ganggerre *coverb+CUT_REFL.* dislike each other.
• *Ganggerre berroowanboo-yoo. They don't like each other.*

ganggerr-ganggerr *coverb+SPEAR.* be angry with someone. • *Ganggerr-ganggerr nginengaboordji Chrisdobany. He was angry with Christopher.* SEE: **ganggerr-ganggerrgayan.**

ganggerr-ganggerrgayan *coverb.* be always angry with someone, one who always gets angry. • *Yagengerram boorooj boorroorn-ni, nawoonji ganggerr-ganggerrgayan. The others all have fun and he gets cranky all the time.* SEE: **ganggerr-ganggerr.**

ganggerrge *coverb+GET.* make someone angry.
• *Ganggerrge nginimanyji. He made him angry.*

ganggerrweny, ganggerrwel, ganggerrwem *adjective.* angry, cranky, grumpy. • *Ngoowana ganggerrweny ngiwinji. He was not a grumpy one then.*

ganggoom *noun.* spittle, saliva.

ganginy *coverb+HIT.* not to recognise/know someone. • *Ganginy nyaniyidji. He did not recognise her, he couldn't believe it was his* wife. • **Ngarranggarnim ngaginybe ganginy nimbirrijtha-boorroo.** *The dreamings from my country might not know you (and you might be in danger).*

ganjalji *noun masculine.* fork-tailed kite, black kite. *Milvus nigrans.* • **Danya ganjalji gerreleny, thoorroobgayi-nhawoony.** *That fork-tailed kite is a greedy one, he is always grabbing things.*

ganjiny, ganjim *noun.* seed, seed pod, bullet.

Gan'galin *noun.* place name.

gantheliny, ganthiliny *noun.* geebung, small tree with edible fruit. *Persoonia falcata.*

-gany, -gal, -gam *suffix.* his/her/their relation. • **ngaboo-gany** *his/her/their father* • **goora-gal** *his/her/their mother.* [NOTE: attached to relationship terms, agrees with the possessed relation, not the possessor]

-gany *suffix.* agent marker. • **Darndal-gany wanema-ni, 'Thoowoonha nimbinnha?'** *The turtle asked him, 'What will you be?'* • **'Yirrgawoo naniyanyji-ni lalanggarrany-gany,' wanema.** *'The crocodile was saying bad things about you,' he told him.* [NOTE: only in speech of people in the Southern dialect. Follows gender suffix to noun whereas homophonous relative possessive suffix *-ga-* precedes gender suffix; the final *-ny* is not a masculine gender marker.]

ganyarrany *noun masculine.* goanna. • **Mayim-boorroo, miyale-boorroo deg ngelanyge, ganyarram-boorroo, ngawoonybe-boorroo.** *I am going looking for vegetable food and meat, for goannas and pencil yams.* SEE: **garndoowoolany, jarrambayiny.** [NOTE: the three words *ganyarrany, garndoowoolany,* and *jarrambayiny* are used interchangably to mean any kind of goanna by many people. Dottie Wadbi said that *ganyarrany* is a specific type of small goanna of Jangala skin that is not eaten, *Varanus gilleni*; however, in the example sentence from Doris Fletcher in Halls Creek, *ganyarrany* is specifically noted as 'meat']

ganybel *coverb+SAY/DO.* be shy, embarrassed, ashamed. • **Ganybel nyerne.** *She is ashamed.* • **Ganybel ngenarn-noo.** *I'm too shy for it (to dance).*

ganybelbawoorroony, ganybelbawoorrool, ganybelbawoorroom *adjective.* having no shame. • **Ganybelbawoorrinyga jigili.** *He has no shame really, yuk!*

ganybelgbe; ganybelge *coverb+GET.* make someone feel shame. • **Ganybelgbe benamanyji.** *He made them feel ashamed/deeply embarrassed.* • **Ganybelge jamberramannha.** *You all made him feel shame (non-singular object in verb because speaker is talking about his brother-in-law sideways).*

ganybelgbe *coverb+GO/COME.* be made to feel shame/deeply embarrassed. • **Ganybelgbe nginiyin.** *He (the moon) was shamed (when the women berated him).*

ganyjalarrji *noun masculine.* cymbidium orchid. *Cymbidium canaliculatum.* • **Ganyjalarrji ngoowan maj jarrimnha yilgoowoorriny yagewalany.** *Don't touch that orchid, it is bad, no good.* [NOTE: found growing on Eucalyptus and Corymbia species trees. Sugarbag must not be cut from trees bearing this epiphyte; said to cause boils if touched or if honey produced by bees feeding on the flowers is eaten.] SEE: **garloonggoony.**

ganyjewoony; garnjiwoony *noun masculine.* caustic vine. *Cynanchum viminale.* [NOTE: used as fish poison, milky sap used to treat sores and ringworm]

gara *adverb.* later. SEE: **gerag.**

gara *temporal.* anytime, sometime SEE: **geragwaloon.**

garab-garab *coverb+SAY/DO.* be crunching something in the teeth.

garam *noun.* salt. SEE: **gilyam, girlarlam.**

Garaban *noun.* a place near Geminyban.

garajbe *noun.* corpse, dead body. SEE: **goonyingarre.**

Garanyba *noun.* gorge near Doon Doon.

garanybe *noun.* hot stones.

garawirrim *adjective.* many. SEE: **waringarri.**

garayarr *coverb+PUT.* spread out hot ashes to cook something. • **Garayarr noonayangge-noo ngela gerliyirr.** *I spread out the ashes for it (goanna) to the east and to the west.*

garayil *coverb+PUT.* hook something up. • **Garayil nginiya dalinyji.** *He hooked the catfish (up out of the water).* • **Garayil niniyangge lalanggarrany.** *I'm hooking up a crocodile.*

gardag, gardagboo *noun.* cup, pannikin, billy can.

garda-gardan *adverb.* take off fast. • **Garda-gardan marrarna wiji nginiyin.** *He took off as fast as possible.*

garda-gardawoo *adverb.* loud (of speech, singing), hard (of hitting), with all you've got

gardagarrji

(of dancing), the very best you can. • **Werd nyimberrayidbe ragim garda-gardawooya.** *The ants bit her really badly.* SEE: **lerra.**

gardagarrji noun. nankeen kestrel. *Falco cenchroides.* SEE: **marl-marlel, marrg-marrgjil, waaliny.**

gardawoorroom; gardawoorroon particle. possibly, maybe. (Kriol 'you never know').
• **Gardawoorroon jiyirremga gedba-wanyji noonbijge miyalega.** *You never know, I might find some kangaroos, some meat.*

gardij coverb+SAY/DO. cut, chop. • **Berrani-birri, 'Gardij barroo marnem.'** *They told them, 'You all cut fire wood.'*

gardiyany, gardiyal noun. white person. SEE: **wajbaloony.** [NOTE: the word *gardiya* is used throughout the Kimberley meaning 'white person' without -*ny* or -*l*, the Gija gender markers]

gardiyangem adjective. white person's way.

garerlel noun feminine. big bush cucumber. *Cucumis picrocarpus.*

gareng coverb+SAY/DO_M. speak with a hoarse voice.

garengbeny, garengbel, garengbem adjective. having a hoarse voice (e.g. from a sore throat). • **Danya garengbeny jarragbawoorroony, gareng woomenjende.** *That one has a hoarse voice and is not speaking properly, he is speaking with a gruff voice.* [NOTE: said about a dog or a human with a gruff voice]

garij coverb+DO_REFL. say each others name.
• **Ngajil ngoowan gariji narrimijtha-yoo.** *You and your sister cannot say each other's names.*

garij coverb+GET. say someone's name aloud, name someone, call out/sing the words of a song. • **Garij yimberrama-yoowoo.** *They called our names.* • **Garij nyimberrama-yoowoo.** *They called it (the Wangga song) out for us.*
• **Garij nyimbirrimbe.** *They will be calling it (the Wangga song) out.* • **Awoo! Ngaji! Ngaji! Garija nanema-ngoo ganybeliyi!** *Oh! Brother! Brother! I called your name then, shame!*
• **Garij biyim dal ngalil, gaboowa-ngiyi dal yinginybe, dal ngalil?** *Call that woman's name! What is her name, that woman?* [NOTE: people in relationships such as brother/sister, son- or daughter-in-law/parent-in-law are not allowed to pronounce their relation's name and the existence of this word reflects that it is a significant act to pronounce someone's name aloud; the act of singing and pronoucing the words of traditional songs is also referred to as *garij*]

garij coverb+SAY/DO_M. say someone's name aloud, name someone, call out/sing the words of a song. • **Garij-gala booma!** *Say the name!*

garijib coverb+GO/COME. saying name. • **Garijib berrayinde, 'Gaboowa yinemennha? Thoowoorra-boorroo?' woomberramande-birri.** *They call their names (people who have been given a sign – by a tingling feeling in the body – that their names have been spoken). 'What are you doing to me? What for?' they say to them.* • **Garijib giniyinde:::, janderre, yiligin dan, bernderre.** *He used to name all the rocks there under the burial plaform.*

garinybe coverb+BE/STAY. be on top of a hill.
• **Ngoorrinya garinybe nginjende.** *He is over there on top of the hill.*

gariyaliny noun. a goanna species.

garlabawoorroony, garlabawoorrool, garlabawoorroom adjective. someone who takes no notice of requests, one who can't listen. LIT: 'having no vagina'. [NOTE: swearing]

garlam noun. vagina. SEE: **milam.** [NOTE: swearing]

garl-garl coverb+SAY/DO. laugh. • **Garl-garl ngenarn.** *I am laughing.* • **Ngali-ngalim garl-garl berrani-noo Grisdobany.** *The women all laughed at Christopher.*

garl-garl coverb+SAY/DO_REFL. laugh at each other.
• **Garl-garl berrangirriyan-joo.** *They are laughing at each other.*

garl-garl-bawoorroony, garl-garl-bawoorrool, garl-garl-bawoorroom adjective. one who doesn't laugh. • **Nginyjinyi jiyilinyi barlij-bawoorroony, garl-garl-bawoorroony ngoowany.** *This man doesn't laugh, he is not a laughing person, no.*

garl-garlge coverb+GET. make laugh.
• **Garl-garlge ngemberremenbe dam jarragboo dam barlijbem.** *That joking story is making me laugh.*

Garlgarran noun. place name, Mount Amherst.

garlge noun. scar (from wound or sore, not tribal scar).

garli noun. man's sister's child, man's niece or nephew when spoken to.

garli-garli noun. woman's granddaughter's child, maternal great grandmother, maternal great grandmother's brothers. [NOTE: the fourth generation in the maternal line] SEE: **gamelany**.

garlil *noun feminine.* man's sister's daughter, man's niece.

garliny *noun masculine.* man's sister's son, man's nephew.

garlirrin *locative.* shallow edge of water, bank of river, on the side. • *Ngoowana berdij nginbiyan, ngoorroo-biny garlirri-biny girli ngilige. I will not climb up, I will walk along there along the side.* SEE: **lamban**.

garlirriny *noun.* shallow water, edge of water.

Garliwoorrangen *noun.* Carola Gully (Growler Gully).

garliyarlim *noun.* pancreas. SEE: **gerlalim**.

Garlmanderre *noun.* Elgee Cliffs, old station near Elgee Cliffs. SEE: **Gelawarli**.

garlmi REDUP: **garlmi-garlmi**. *coverb+SAY/DO_M.* push spinifex/grass through water to catch fish. • *Ngayin wanyagen ngenaniyinde-ngarri, garlmi yirramande. When I was small, we used to fish by pushing a wall of spinifex through the water.*

garlmi *coverb+SAY/DO.* push spinifex/grass through water to catch fish. • *Ngarranggarnin garlmi-ngarri nginini goorndarrimbi nhawiyangem-noo, ngagenyen . . . In the dreamtime when he was catching his fish (by pushing a wall of grass through water) in my country . . .*

garloomboo-bany *noun masculine.* boy. LIT: 'person who has a spear'. [NOTE: used when talking about whether a baby will be a boy or a girl; used by women to speak about a brother]

garloomboo-bawoorrool *noun feminine.* sister. • *Gangela-ninggi garloomboo-bawoorrool? Where is your sister (lit. 'she who has no spear')?*

Garloomboony *noun.* pointed hill to the east of Warmun Art Centre. LIT: 'place of the spear'.

garloomboony *noun masculine.* spear.

garloonggoony *noun masculine.* cymbidium orchid. *Cymbidium canaliculatum.* [NOTE: found growing on Eucalyptus and Corymbia species trees. Sugarbag must not be cut from trees bearing this epiphyte; said to cause boils if touched or if honey produced by bees feeding on the flowers is eaten]

Garlooroon *noun.* place name, big rockhole before the windmill near Six Mile, upstream from Warrmarn.

garlooroony *noun masculine.* male rainbow snake, waterhole, deep water. [NOTE: women should be careful of using this word to mean 'rainbow snake'] SEE: **goorlabal**.

garlooroom *noun.* deep water.

garlwanyil *noun feminine.* freshwater sawfish. *Pristis pristis.* [NOTE: Western dialect] SEE: **bayirrany**.

garn *coverb+HIT.* hit one stick down on the other. • *Garn-kala benij. Hit the stick down on the other stick.* • *Garn bemberrayid yangoorranyji. Someone hit a stick down on another stick.* SEE: **garn-garn**.

garnang *interrogative.* where is he/it (masculine)? • *Garnang, wanyagaarrinyi? Boorab biyil-ngirri! Where's the little boy? Bring him out to me!* [NOTE: Southern dialect] SEE: **garniwa**.

garnanganyjel, garnanganyjam *noun feminine.* emu. *Dromaius novaehollandiae.* SEE: **wiyarrel, ngarabarral**.

Garnanganyjen *noun.* Mount King, emu dreaming place on Bedford Downs.

garnawarrab *coverb+GO/COME.* go somewhere. • *Darag-garri, marri, garniwa garnawarrab ngoowiyin. When he disappeared, goodness, I don't know which way he could have gone.*

garnawoony *noun.* 'cheeky' yam. *Dioscorea bulbifera.* [NOTE: described as *ngoorroorn-bany*, i.e. 'having pubic hair' (Mabel Juli); slices rubbed in ash of *goonjiny*, 'bauhinia' before cooking]

garnbarrany; garnbidany *noun masculine.* wedge-tailed eagle (Kriol: 'eaglehawk'). *Aquila audax.* SEE: **warrarnany, girliwirringiny, wirli-wirlingarnany**.

garndarr-garndarre *noun.* windpipe.

garndarndarrji *noun masculine.* silver grevillea. *Grevillea refracta.* SEE: **tharriyarril**.

garndawarranginy *noun masculine.* silver wattle. *Acacia colei, A. holosericea.* [NOTE: has edible gum; stems used as hardwood spear parts]

garndiny, garndim *noun masculine.* root, butt of tree, part of tree right at ground level.

garndiny *noun masculine.* black-soil yam, type of plant with edible root. *Ipomoea abrupta, I. aquatica.* SEE: **yoowalany**.

Garndiwarle *noun.* place on Landsdowne Station.

garndiwarlel *noun feminine.* bat's wing coral tree. *Erythrina vespertilio.* [NOTE: woomeras are made from the wood of this tree]

garndoorroony *noun masculine.* rock ringtail

garndoowoolany

possum. *Petropseudes dahli*.

garndoowoolany *noun masculine*. goanna, sand goanna. *Varanus panoptes, V. gouldii*. SEE: **ganyarrany, jarrambayiny**. [NOTE: the three words, *ganyarrany, garndoowoolany*, and *jarrambayiny* are used interchangeably to mean any kind of goanna by many people while some say they are different]

garnengga; garningga; garnega; garniga *interrogative particle*. which/what/who/where then? [NOTE: follows interrogatives when the speaker is thinking about an answer to a question as if asking themselves 'Who/What/Where was that now?'; does not require an answer from a listener. The speaker often answers him/herself.]

garn-garn *coverb+SAY/DO*. be hitting one stick down on the other. • *Garn-garn boorroorn yangoorranyji*. *Someone is banging a stick on another stick*. SEE: **garn**.

garn'garr *coverb+SAY/DO*. show off; think oneself clever, knock something back. • *Garn'garr nginini-yarri*. *He thought he was a big shot on us*. • *Thoowoorra wela garn'garr narroorn? What now, you going to knock it back (you're too fussy to eat it)?*

garn'gim *noun*. month. • *Garn'gim jirrawoogoom*. *One month*.

garn'giny *noun masculine*. moon. • *Garn'giny nang-ngarri ngoowoonji, miyale ngoowan jambirrimnha*. *When the moon dies (full moon wanes) you can't catch meat*. SEE: **jawoorranyji**.

garn'giny *noun masculine*. moon grub. Lepidoptera, Cossidae larvae.

garn'giny *coverb+GET*. get a cramp, have a cramp. • *Garn'giny ngenamanyji*. *I have a cramp. / A cramp got me*. • *Garn'ginybe ngenemenji*. *I'm getting a cramp now. / A cramp is getting me*.

garn'ginybe *coverb+SAY/DO*. have a cramp. • *Wanyanyagem garn'ginybe boorroonboogili*. *The children will have a cramp (said of children held on pause on a video)*.

garn'girrayijirran *locative/temporal*. in the moonlight. • *Roord nginji garn'girrayijirran*. *He is sitting in the moonlight*.

Garn'goorlbany *noun*. Jack Flood, a place in

Figure 44. *Garn'giny: Wirringgoon Mabel Juli. Nyawoorrool deg nyerne ngaji-gany garn'giny garlmi-ngarri nginini goorndarrim ngarranggarnin.*

garral-garralji; garrarl-garrarlji

Paddy Bedford's father's country.

garn'goorlji *noun masculine.* wattle species with curly seed pods. *Acacia tumida, A. holosericea, A. platycarpa.* [NOTE: the seed is ground and made into damper (Hector Jandany); pods used as fish poison, swished around in water to make it soapy; wood can be used to make *jiwiny*]

Garn'goowan *noun.* place upstream from Garanyba.

garni *interrogative particle.* where/what? • *Garni berra, garni? Where? Where? Nothing here! (he said.)*

garni; garniwa *interrogative.* where is he/it (masculine)? • *Garni-ngirri ngaboony? Where is my father?* • *Garni-ngirri garloomboony? Where is my spear?* • *Garniwa-ninggi ngaboony? Where is your father?*

garningga, garniga, garnega, garnengga *interrogative particle.* which/what/who/where then? [NOTE: follows interrogatives when the speaker is thinking about an answer to a question as if asking themselves 'Who/What/Where was that now?'; does not require an answer from a listener. The speaker often answers him/herself.]

garninya *interrogative.* what now? do you have anything? • *Garninya miyale? Any meat?* [NOTE: often used as a greeting]

garniwa, garni *interrogative.* where is he/it (masculine)? • *Garniwa-ninggi ngaboony? Where is your father?*

garnbag, garnbagbe *noun.* clapsticks. SEE: **gil-gile**.

garnbagji *noun masculine.* milkwood tree. *Wrightia saligna.* SEE: **gil-gilji**. [NOTE: species used to make clap sticks]

garnjalji SEE: **ganjalji**.

garrabiril *noun feminine.* boomerang. SEE: **baljarranggool, gamanyjel, goorroobardool, jaranggarril, jinybal**.

garraginy, garragim *noun.* bag. SEE: **wananginy**.

Garragin *noun.* Lansdowne.

garragoonbe *noun.* type of bush salt that animals like kangaroos come to lick.

garral-garralji; garrarl-garrarlji *noun masculine.* tall, hard spinifex species. *Triodia racemigera.* [NOTE: big brown type that stings if it pokes you, seen near Gawarre.]

Figure 45. *Garrang-garranginy: Wirringgoon Mabel Juli: Nyawoorrool madi ngiyinya garrang-garranginy doorloog-ngarri wananyji goorloo-biny.*

garranggany

SEE: **jirriny-jirrinyji**.

garranggany *noun.* river red gum. *Eucalyptus camaldulensis*. SEE: **bilirn, dimalan**.

garrang-garrang; garrang-garrang-garrang *coverb+SAY/DO.* call of the diver jack.

garrang-garranginy *noun.* diver jack, snake bird, darter. *Anhinga melanogaster*. SEE: **boorrijiny**. [NOTE: this word is used to mean 'old noisy car' by people in the Hall's Creek area because the bird's call sounds like that]

garrany *coverb+BE/STAY.* be in a hurry. • *Garrany ngininiyin biri-girrem daa-yoorroong.* He was in a hurry to go back.

garrara *coverb+SAY/DO_M.* throw a boomerang.
• *Garrara wanema, men'gerr nginiyid.* He threw a boomerang and hit him.

garraroon; garrwaroon *temporal.* at sunset, afternoon.

garraroony; garrwaroony REDUP: garra-garraroony. *coverb+FALL/GO_DOWN.* be getting dark, be becoming afternoon.
• *Garraroonyboo berroowoonboo.* It is getting dark now. / Night is falling.

garrarram *noun.* ear wax. • *Dama wanyanyagem melagawoo-bam garrarram yiligin yardem-birri. Yardebawoorroom.* Those children have lots of wax inside their ears. They cannot hear.

garrawiny *noun.* emu berry, 'dogs balls', small plant with edible fruit. *Grewia retusifolia*. SEE: **gawoorroony, ngoojal, ngoowardiny**.

garrayile *noun.* wrist.

garrayilel REDUP: garra-garrayile. *noun feminine.* adult woman.

garrayilgbe *coverb+GO/COME.* become adult, mature. • *Linga-linga-ngarri ngenani, garrayilgbe-nga ngenayin, 'Aa, wayinijarrany-aya, wayinijarrany,' ngenani.* When I thought about it when I became grown up, 'Ah, that's the kind he is, he's like that,' I said.

garrayilji REDUP: garra-garrayile. *noun masculine.* young adult man with pierced nose.

garrayilji, garrayilel, garrayile REDUP: garra-garrayile. *adjective.* adult, responsible person, grown up.

garrenbawoorroom *noun.* old people.

garr-garr *coverb+GO_ALONG.* jog along.
• *Garr-garr wiyinji joolany.* The dog is jogging along

garrgbayiny, garrgbayil, garrgbayim *adjective.* having a thin waist.

garrgoowal *noun feminine.* rifle fish, archer fish. *Toxotes chatareus*. SEE: **loowarrel**.

garrid-garrid *coverb+SAY/DO.* be looking for scraps, eat leftover bits, scavenge.
• *Ngoorrinya ngarem garid-garid ngerne.* This fellow is scavenging about for sugarbag.

garriyil, garriyiny *noun.* black bream, sooty grunter. *Hephaestus jenkinsi*. SEE: **jambinbaroony**. [NOTE: word also used for long-nose or Butler's Grunter, *Syncomistes butleri*]

garrjany *noun masculine.* waterlily. *Nymphaea violacea*. [NOTE: has bulbs like a hard-boiled egg] SEE: **gelewoorrji**.

garrwarla-warlany, garrwarla-warlal, garrwarla-warlam *adjective.* tall and very thin.

garrwaroon REDUP: garrwa-garrwaroon. *coverb+GO_DOWN_M.* be afternoon. • *Marrarna garrwaroon wanooward.* It is already afternoon. SEE: **garraroon**.

garrwaroowany *coverb+GO/COME.* go in the afternoon, go while it is getting dark, go at sunset. • *Garrwaroowany-gala ngenda.* I should go round in the late afternoon.
• *Garrwaroowany ngenardge gerliyirr.* I am going west into the sunset.

garrwim *noun.* armpit.

gathathag *coverb+GO_ALONG.* go along slowly (walking or driving). • *Danya gathathag wiyinji bardoon.* He's coming along slowly behind.

gawal REDUP: gawal-gawal. *coverb+HIT.* singe fur/skin off. • *Gawal ngoorrayid-doo warloom-ni dam.* They (two) singed its fur. • *Gawal beniyinji.* He is singing the fur off it (kangaroo).
• *Gawal niniyidge.* I singed it (goanna).

gawalalanygarre *locative.* side of hill.
• *Ngarrgalem jamboorn-jamboorn benayanyji ngarnega gawalalanygarre gawarren.* He (eagle) piled a lot of stones up there on the side of the hill so he could climb up.

gawangel *noun.* aunt, father's sister, mother's brother's wife.

gawara *coverb+PUT.* make fire flare up with big flames. • *Gawara bamberraj.* Make the fire flare up brightly.

gawarab REDUP: gawara-warab. *coverb+GO/COME.* go up high. • *Ngoorroonayi gawarab giniyi laarne.* He went right up high on top like that over there. • *Ngoorrooma gawarabbany boorroonboo-gili laarne.* They are all sitting up high over there.

gayilarriny

gawarabaran *locative.* up on top, up high.
• *Gawarabaran yarroonya.* We are sitting on top (up high on elevated verandah).

gawarangbeny, gawarangbel, gawarangbem *adjective.* white. SEE: **lawagbeny, waagoom, wagoony**.

Gawarlgan *noun.* place name.

gawarnbe *noun.* black soil.

gawarnngarnany *noun masculine.* rufous songlark. *Cincloramphus mathewsi.* SEE: **binyjirrmiyanma**.

gawarrangbiny *locative.* in a high place.

Gawarre *noun.* Bungle Bungle Outcamp, Gija outstation living area on the northern side of Purnululu National Park, Kawarre.

gawarriny, gawarrem *noun.* cliff, steep bank, range of steep hiills.

gawayi *noun.* auntie, father's sister, mother's brother's wife (address form used when speaking to the relation). SEE: **gawangel**.

gawayin; gawayinde *particle.* never mind, doesn't matter. • *Gawayinde gool-goolji ninbiyajgende.* Never mind, I'll have to keep trying.

gawil *noun feminine.* any very small fish, tiny fish like a bony bream, rainbow fish. *Melanotaenia* sp., north-west glass fish. *Ambassis* sp. (West Kimberley)

gawilge; gawilig; gawilige *coverb+FALL/GO_DOWN.* become cold, get cold.
• *Gawilge ngenawoon'ge.* I'm getting cold.
• *Gawiligboo boorroowoonboo mayim.* The food is getting cold. • *Mayiny gawilige-ngarri nginoowoon yiligin.* The food got cold (should be made cold) inside the fridge.

gawilig *coverb+BURN/BITE.* become cold. • *Mayiny gawilig nginiwoorran yiliginy fridge.* The food got cold in the fridge. • *Miyali gawilig benawoorran yiligin.* The meat got cold inside the fridge. • *Gawiligiya nginiwoorran.* He got really cold.

gawilig *coverb+PUT.* make cold. • *Gawilig-gala benaj!* Cool it down!

gawiliny, gawilil, gawilim *adjective.* cold.
• *Nyirrega yarrani gawiliyiny-ni goorrngan.* We had a swim in the really cold water.

gawingel; gawiyingel *noun feminine.* very large snake species with yellow belly, 'big like a tyre' (Peggy Patrick). [NOTE: Rusty Peters says this is the Gooniyandi equivalent of *goorlabal*; 'Gija plants and animals' (Purdie et al. 2018) has it as 'keelback', 'freshwater snake', *Tropidonophis mairii*]

Gawinyen; Gawoonyen; Gawinyji *noun.* Cattle Creek rockhole on Texas Downs.

gawoo *interrogative.* where? • *Goo gawoo-ngirri merndambi?* But where is my money?

gawoom *noun.* lungs. SEE: **ranggoo**.

gawoornbe *noun.* ash.

Gawoornben; Gawoornboon *noun.* Texas Downs Station.

gawoorra *interrogative.* where are they? where is it (non-singular)? • *Gawoorra yawardambi? Where are the horses?* • *'Gawoorra-ninggi miyale?' nyamanil nyanini. 'Where is the meat?' said the old woman.* • *Gawoorra-ninggi-yoo wigi-warrinyji? Where are your two sons?*

gawoorrngarndil; gawoorrngarnil *noun.* female plains kangaroo, female antilopine wallaby. *Macropus antilopinus.* [NOTE: mother of *jarlangarnany/warlambany*, Nyawana skin; Madigan Thomas said *gawoorrngarnil*.]

Gawoorrngarndin *noun.* Blackfella Creek north-east of Warrmarn.

gawoorroony *noun.* emu berry, short plant with edible fruit, 'dogs balls' plant. *Grewia retusifolia.* SEE: **garrawiny, ngoojal, ngoowardiny**. [NOTE: eaten by turkey in dreamtime, *gawoorriny*; almost the same word said to be a name for 'pink river apple', *Syzygium eucalyptoides* ssp. *eucalyptoides*] SEE: **roonggoony**.

gawoothany, gawoothal, gawootham *adjective.* champion, one who comes out in front in the Wangga. [NOTE: used to describe King Kong in the movie]

-gayan *coverb suffix.* continuous action suffix to coverbs.

gayana *demonstrative.* here. SEE: **ngenenggayana**.

gayanyji *interrogative.* somewhere.

gayawoony, gayawool, gayawoom *adjective.* sexy (Kriol: 'tickly'). SEE: **yoowarroony**.

gayi; gayiwa *interrogative.* where (location)?
• *Gayiwa derreb yarrinya daambi? Where shall we camp?* • *Gayi nyawanyi daj yarrooja? Where will we smash up this tail?*

gayigan; gayigana *interrogative.* when? *'Gayigan biri ngiwiyayi?' berrani. 'When will he come back?' they said.* SEE: **gaboogana**.

gayigananyji *interrogative.* sometime unknown.

gayilarriny *noun masculine.* rubber yam, edible root species. *Typhonium lilifolium.* [NOTE:

gayirra-goolaniyid

must be repeatedly cooked and smashed, all day until the sun goes down and it (yam) turns black before it can be eaten (Hector Jandany). Worn on the head by the brolga with *garrjany* the waterlily from in the dreamtime, *ngarranggarnin*]

gayirra-goolaniyid *adverb.* very far away. [NOTE: Jaru, talking about distant fire in song]

gayirriny *noun masculine.* ground sugarbag, species of native bee living in anthills or in the ground, and their hives. [NOTE: Joowoorroo (Joolama) skin]

Gayirriwarrin *noun.* place north of the Bungle Bungles / Purnululu.

gayiyanyji *interrogative.* somewhere.

-ge, -g *suffix.* causative suffix, makes coverbs from nominals or other coverbs. Can be attached to coverbs or nominals to form incoative coverbs that combine with the verb FALL/GO_DOWN.

geberd *coverb+FALL/GO_DOWN.* hurt self. • Geberd ngenawardge wenggarrem. *I hurt my neck.* SEE: **mirl-mirlge, thalijbel**.

Geboogan *noun.* Nowhere Place (place name). [NOTE: dreaming place of the greater spotted cuscus]

ged *coverb+FALL/GO_DOWN.* go around. • Gerlirrang-biny ged-garri yarriwoon . . . *If we go around from the west . . .* SEE: **wambalayiny**.

gedba *coverb+HIT.* see, find. • 'Nga! Ngoorroona lalanggarrany gedba yirrayidji,' woomberrama. *'Hey! We saw a crocodile over there,' they said.* • Berrayin-gili gedba ngoorrayidbe. *They all went and found him.*

ged-gedgoowany *coverb+GET.* make go around and around. • Ged-gedgoowany ngoorramangboo goowooloon ngoorroonji. *They made him go around and around the tree over there.*

gejig *coverb+DO_REFL.* tickle each other. • Gejig yaremij. *You and me tickle one another.*

gejig *coverb+GET.* tickle someone. • Ngoowan gejig yinbimnha! Yagengerram gejig benemnha! *Don't tickle me! Tickle someone else!*

-gela, -gala *imperative/hortative suffix.* should,

Figure 46. *Gayirriny: Dirrmingali Barradjil Peggy Patrick: Naangaril woobooj nyerne gayirriny jamernden.*

must, want to. [NOTE: follows coverbs before the verb in compound verbs and the verb in simple verbs]

gelagi *noun.* address form used by people who call each other *gelaginy* or *gelagiil*.

gelagil, gelagim; gelaagil, gelaagim *noun feminine.* father's father's sister, man's son's daughter.

gelaginy, gelagim; gelaaginy, gelaagim *noun masculine.* father's father, man's son's son.

-gelaj *suffix.* like, similar to.

gelaroogool; goolaroogool *noun feminine.* bar-shouldered dove. *Geopelia humeralis.* SEE: **marrawayil**.

Gelawarli *noun.* Elgee Cliffs. SEE: **Garlmanderre**.

gelengawoony, gelengawool, gelengawoom REDUP: **gelelengawoom**. *adjective.* new. • Gelengawoola noomoorloona-ngal ganggayi janiyida-ngiyi Joonggoobalgawa. *You keep a new one for my granny Sylvia now.* • Ngoowan yarren, dam warna-warnarram, yarren gelelengawoon, ngoowan-yarre. *Not us, those old people, us new people we don't do it (make ground dried fish).* SEE: **gelengeny**.

gelengeben *temporal.* not too long ago.

gelengen *temporal.* today, now.

gelengeny, gelengel, gelengem REDUP: **gelelengem**. *adjective.* new, fresh, green (plant). • Gelelengem damga ngarag yarroorn. *We are making all the new things.*

gelengiyana *temporal.* really today.

gelengiyana *adverb.* the first time. • Gelengiyana beroowal nyilayid. *This is the first time I made a mistake.*

gelengoowoony, gelengoowool, gelengoowoom *adjective.* new, not ready. SEE: **gelengeny**.

gelengoowoorroony, gelengoowoorrool, gelengoowoorroom *adjective.* old. LIT: 'not new'. • Gelengoowoorroon-nga. *I'm old.* SEE: **gelengeny**.

gelewoorrji *noun masculine.* waterlily root. SEE: **garrjany**.

gelng *coverb+GET.* rub to increase game, all hunt game together in a group. • Gelng ngoomberramangbe, boorroowiyin-anyji-wa jarlangarnany-ningi. *They wanted to rub it (the dreamtime rock) so that maybe plains kangaroos would come.*

gelyeg-gelyeg *coverb+GO_ALONG.* go along saying '*gelyeg-gelyeg*' (call of eagle). • Danyi warrarnanyi gelyeg-gelyeg wananyji, jirege nginiwamanyji. *That eagle flew off crying 'gelyeg-gelyeg' (the call of the eagle) and turned into a bird.*

gemag *coverb+PUT.* put aside, put away from action, put outside. • Gemag-ngarri niniyangge gadij-girrema, gadijboowa niyin'ge. *I put it aside to cut it up and now I am cutting it up.*

geman *locative.* outside, away from action.

gemerlawoorroony *noun.* magpie. *Gymnorhina tibicen eylandtensis.* SEE: **goorrooranggoolji**. [NOTE: some people use this word for *wirrindiny*, 'pied butcherbird']

gemerre REDUP: **gemerr-gemerre; geme-gemerre**. *noun.* cicatrice, tribal scar.

gemerrem-nhawoony, gemerrem-nhawool, gemerrem-nhawoom *adjective.* jealous. • . . . gemerrem-nhawoon-ngoongoo . . . *you are jealous*

Geminybany *noun.* cave with paintings, in limestone hills near Argyle Diamond Mine.

Geminymiyan *noun.* Bull Hole near Saddler's Jump-Up.

-gen *adverbial_suffix.* in the time of.

gendaloogany, gendaloogal, gendaloogam *adjective.* short and fat. • Ngayinji jiyilen-nga gendaloogan. *I am a short, fat man.*

gendang *directional.* from upstream.

gendayingen *directional.* on the higher side.

gendayingibiny *directional.* from the higher side. • 'Gabiyi-binya naniyinnha?' 'Gendayingibiny bardib ngelanyge, goowooloony wandarra-ngarri nginji.' *'Where did you come from?' 'I came from higher up walking along the edge of that tree that is lying across (the path).'*

gendewa, gendoowa *directional.* upstream, up hill, up into (e.g. cave). • Marrarn gendewa ngoorranybe-yoo, joolooj wanamanyande gendewagoo. *They two kept carrying him upstream, she carried him upstream.* • Nginya nawarragawoony nginji, wayini gendoowa balmendeg ginini. *This is the river, it forms a junction upstream like this (from a painting description).*

gendewagoo, gendoowagoo REDUP: **gende-gendewagoo; gendendewagoo**. *directional.* upstream; up into (e.g. cave).

gendoowajarriny *directional.* further upstream.

gengereb

gengereb *coverb+BRING/TAKE.* stop breathing in fright. • Thoowoo-berra gengereb joonanynha? *Why have you stopped breathing?*

-geny *suffix.* purposive suffix to nouns. SEE: **-boorroo**.

ger REDUP: **ger-ger**. *coverb+SAY/DO.* blow wind. • Ger boorroorn. *It is blowing.* • Waloorrji ger ngerne warn'gabany. *The cold wind is blowing.* • Ger-ngarri boorroorn wanyagibawa waniyid warrarnanyi. *When the cold wind blows the eagle has little ones.* • Warn'ganya nginya ger ngerne, wayinigana warlarlayimga nyoorlg-nyoorlg boorroorn. *When the cold wind blows, then the little puppies are whimpering.*

gerag *temporal.* later. • Welangen biyarra, gerag nginbiyan-nenggewa bardoon. *Go ahead, I'll follow you later.* • Marrge, gerag-gili birrinbe-gala, bib noonbimge. *Leave it for later, I'll get it then.*

geragwaloon *temporal.* anytime, sometime. • Geragwaloona biri nginboowoon ngeriga ngenenggaga. *Anytime I will come back right here from the south.* SEE: **garawanyji**.

geraj-geraj *coverb+SAY/DO.* sharpen something. • Geraj-geraj nyanini. *She sharpened it.* SEE: **jalinggirig**.

geraj-geraj *coverb+PUT.* sharpen something. • Gananyji geraj-geraj nginiyanyande booloorroo. *She sharpened her digging stick on the sandstone.* SEE: **jalinggirig**.

gerarr *coverb+SAY/DO.* crawl. • Gerarr ngenani nawarra ngenayin deyena. *I started to crawl when I grew bigger there.*

gerawarrel *noun.* hailstones. SEE: **gooroowarrbany**.

gerd *coverb+HIT.* cook on coals, get burned (e.g. on hot stones). • Gerd gimberrayidbewe garany-jam, yilgoowoorroom, marne-bam; warrag-garri ngilige-birri. *Those bad hot stones like cooking stones would burn me if I walk on them.* • Yarrangirriyin birn'girrbal gerd jimberrayid diyana wawoo-wawoog yarranya . . . boog jimberramang. *We waited for the turkey to cook there where we were cooking and we pulled it out.*

gerd *coverb+PUT.* cook on coals. • Gerd ngiyilinya garriyiny. *She is cooking the bream.* • Gerd biyil gernjil-yoorroong. *Cook it in the hot earth.* • Gerd ngoorraya-yoo. *The two of them cooked it.* • Gerd boombarraya yagebawirri wayini-gelaj. *They each cooked them in their own separate fireplace.*

gerd REDUP: **gerd-gerd**. *coverb+SAY/DO_M.* cook on coals. • Gerd-gerd woomberramande. *They used to cook.*

gerdadal *noun feminine.* insect gall species found on the Eucalyptus species called *booniny* and *mawoorroony*, 'bush coconut'. Hemiptera, *Cystococcus* ssp. SEE: **barlabil**.

gerdanji *noun masculine.* frillneck lizard. *Chlamydosaurus kingii*. SEE: **wawooleny**.

gerdgardbe; gerdardboo *noun.* country with lots of little stones, sugar. SEE: **roongalga**.

gerdgeny, gerdgel, gerdgem *adjective.* cooked.

gerd-gerd *coverb+SAY/DO.* cooking on coals. • Ngoorriyana gerd-gerd nginbirn gaande ngaaloon goorloon-ga-wanyji. *I will cook right over there, upstream in the shade, maybe somewhere near the water.* • Goorloon gerd-gerd-garri nyanini. *She was cooking near the water.*

gered *coverb+HAVE.* have in the mouth. • Gereda nyoomoorloonji. *It is holding it (fish) in its mouth.*

gered *coverb+GET.* pick up with the mouth. • Gered benemenji. *He (bowerbird) gets them (stones) in his beak.*

gered *coverb+BRING/TAKE.* carry in the mouth. • Joolany gered biniyinji miyale. *The dog is carrying it (the meat) in its mouth.*

ger-ger *coverb+GO/COME.* wind blow. • Ger-ger nginiyi-yarri. *The wind blew on us.* SEE: **ger**.

geren *coverb+FALL/GO_DOWN.* go behind tree. • Geren nginiwardji. *He went behind the tree.* • Jiyiliny geren nginiwardji goowooloon. *The man hid behind a tree.* [NOTE: can be used to talk about lizards on the side of the tree that move around behind as the person looking tries to move around towards them] SEE: **dern, waman**.

gererreb *coverb+BE/STAY.* be all dead. • Ngagenybe wool-woolbalam, gererreb berraniyin, ngoowangarnan jirrawoogoo-moowan ngenan'ge. *All my old people have passed away, I am the only one still alive.*

gererreb *coverb+BURN/BITE.* be burned right up in a fire. • Gererreb benawoorranyji. *They (dogs and ghosts) were all burned right up.*

gerewoolel; gerewelel *noun feminine.* egg. • gerewoole. *eggs.* SEE: **goomboonyel**.

gerge *coverb+GET.* blow wind (transitive). • *Gerge benamanyji waloorroo biyoorroong.* The wind is blowing from the north. [NOTE: impersonal type construction, the wind is the object of the verb]

gerijaleb *coverb+GET.* chuck in the fire and burn off the hair, singe skin (e.g. of goanna). • *Gerijaleb nginemanyande dany jarrambayiny, gerijaleb, gerd.* She used to singe the goanna and cook it on the coals.

gerlalbam *noun.* thigh, thigh bone, leg.

gerlalbam *noun.* big mob of people, group acting as backstop for someone. • *Dama gerlalbam benanyji ngayin-ga gerlalba-bawoorroon-nga.* He has a big group as backstop, I have no backstop.

gerlalim *noun.* pancreas, bauhinia seed pods. SEE: **garliyalim**. [NOTE: seed pods on the bauhinia, *goonjiny*, are called *gerlalim*]

gerlambawoony *noun masculine.* type of large grasshopper seen in August, late in the cold weather time.

Gerlarren *noun.* place name, ridges upstream from Warmun Art Centre.

gerlarreny *noun.* tree species with long thin leaves and edible roots.

Gerlawarliny *noun.* a hill near Elgee Cliff. [NOTE: has a cave with a dreamtime rock that looks like the top half a kangaroo standing there looking out from the side off the cliff]

gerlenggeny; gerlengginy; gerlinggeny *noun.* penis. SEE: **nyawam**.

gerlerneny *noun masculine.* tall, soft spinifex species. *Triodia pungens.* SEE: **miloowoony**. [NOTE: resin called *gaalji* is made from this type of spinifex that grows on hills]

Gerlgany *noun.* a sharp hill down from Moonlight Valley.

gerlgayi *coverb+SAY/DO.* push wall of grass or spinifex through water to catch fish. • *Ngoorroo-binya jarrg giniwardji ngoorroo minyberne-yoorroong, gerlgayi-ngarri berrani.* He jumped from there over the dry grass when they were pulling it through the water for fish.

gerlgayi *coverb+GO/COME.* go pushing wall of grass or spinifex through water to catch fish. • *Gerlgayi-gela yarra.* Let's go and push grass through the water to catch fish.

gerlgayi *coverb+GET.* catch fish by pushing wall of grass/spinifex through water. • *'Nginyjiyanya gerlgayi yarrem, goorndarrinya,' berrani.* 'Here we will catch fish with grass,' they said.

gerlgayi *coverb+GO_ALONG.* push wall of grass/spinifex through water to catch fish. • *Gerlgayi woomberranybende.* They were fishing with a wall of grass.

Gerlinggengayin *noun.* Blue Dress. [NOTE: The name 'Gerlinggengayin' refers to men's private parts because there is a tall thin dreamtime rock there that 'stood up when it saw all the girls'. It is near the border of Paddy Bedford's country and that of fellow artist Rusty Peters. Peters explained that the European name is really 'Blue Dress' because old stockmen found a blue dress there. Because the English words 'dress' and 'trees' sound very similar when pronounced by a Gija speaker and the seeming unlikelihood of a name 'Blue Dress', two early Bedford works were titled 'Blue Trees']

gerliny-gerlinyil, gerliny-gerlinybe *noun feminine.* galah. *Cacatua roseicapilla.*

gerlirrang *directional.* from the west.

gerlirrijarriny *directional.* further over to the west, up that way.

gerlirrin *directional.* in the west.

gerlirringarri *directional.* in the west moving around from south to north or south to north (e.g. rain).

gerlirroogoo REDUP: **gerli-gerlirroogoo**. *directional.* to the west. SEE: **gerliyirr, girliyirr**.

gerliwirring; gerloowirreng; girliwirring; gerloowoorring *directional.* down from top. • *Goorloony gerliwirring ngidji. Jamboorn ngoowoonji. Nginya gerliwirring wiji ngerne, goorloony, fil-em-ab giyilinji, jamboorn ngiyilinji dan yilag gidji, jamboorn ngenengga.* The water runs down from on top. It fills (the rockhole). This is the water running down from on top filling up the waterhole down at the bottom here. SEE: **gerloowoorrng**.

gerliyirr; gerlirr REDUP: **gerli-gerliyirr**. *directional.* to the west. SEE: **gerlirroogoo, girliyirr**.

gerliyirrgoorloorr *directional.* further to the west.

gerlmarr *coverb+SAY/DO.* feel proud, show off. • *Gerlmarr ngerne.* He feels proud.

gerloorroogeb *coverb+PUT.* put stomach up, put facing up (i.e. on back). • *Wayi gerloorroogeb nyimberriyajbe.* They will/should put it (echidna)

gerloorroogoo, gerloowirrgoo

with stomach up.
gerloorroogoo, gerloowirrgoo *directional.* up.
gerloowoorr; gerloorr; goorloowoorr; goorloorr; gerloowoorroogoo *directional.* up. • Gerloowoorra berdij jidja. *It (road) climbs up there then.* • Gerloowoorr berdij woomenya. *She is climbing up.*
gerloowoorrng; gerloorroong; gerloowoorreng; gerloowoorreng; gerloowirring *directional.* from up there.
gernalil, gernalim *noun.* net used for fishing, mosquito net.
gernanyjel *noun feminine.* echidna, 'porcupine'. *Tachyglossus aculeatus.* SEE: **bagabal**.
Gernawarliyan *noun.* Camel Gap, a place in Paddy Bedford's mother's country.
gerndab *coverb+PUT.* roll something up in paperbark making a bundle. • Gerndab-gala noondaj ngagenybe berrem boolbam mernda-yoorroong. *I should wrap up these things of mine in paperbark.*
gerndeng *coverb+SAY/DO_M.* be out of breath. • Gerndeng wanemayinde yagoorn. *He was pretending to be out of breath.*
gerndiny, gerndi-werndiny, gerndi-werndim *adjective.* male.
gerneg *coverb+DO_REFL.* hold each other. • Marlam gerneg berramiyanbe-yoo. *They are holding each other's hands.*
gerneg *coverb+HAVE.* hold something. • Gerneg ngoomoorloonji. *He is holding him/it (masculine).* • Dala wanyagel gerneg benemoorloonya boorljam. *This little girl is holding a football.* • Gerneg bemberremoorlenbe goowooloom marnebam. *They are holding burning sticks.*
gerneg *coverb+GET.* hold on to someone/something. • Gerneg yimberrem-joo, bardal ngenboowoo. *You two hold me, I might fall.*
gernemboowoorriny *noun masculine.* wattle species used to make hard spear points. *Acacia* ssp. SEE: **jiwiny**.
Gernimboowoorriny *noun.* a long hill east of highway north of Lissadell turn-off.
gerniny-gerniny *coverb+SAY/DO.* draw in sand. • Nginyjiny gerniny-gerniny ngerne. *This man is drawing in the sand.*
gernjile *noun.* hot dirt. • Gerd biyil gernjil-yoorroong. *Cook it in the hot dirt.*
gern'galeny; gern'galiny *noun masculine.* ordinary wind. SEE: **waloorrji**.

gern'gag *coverb+FALL/GO_DOWN.* die. • Gern'gag nginiward. SEE: **nang, goonyingarrg**.
gern'gany, gern'gal, gern'gam *adjective.* raw, unripe, dead meat, dead. • Gern'gam berremga miyale. *This meat is raw.* • Danyga joomooloony gern'gany. *Those boab nuts are not ready yet.* • Nyamananim gern'gaya jang-jang woomberramande. *Old women used to eat them raw.*
gerrayiny, gerrayim *noun masculine.* a tree-living native bee species, tree 'sugarbag' species that has a long wax entrance hole. *Tetragonula* ssp. [NOTE: young man in dreamtime, Joongoorra skin; Southern dialect] SEE: **nhawiny**.
gerrayim *noun.* honey. [NOTE: Southern dialect] SEE: **ngarem**.
gerrbij *coverb+HIT.* cut up. • Gerrbij-gala benij miyale! *Cut up the meat!*
gerrbijgajiny *noun masculine.* knife. SEE: **barrajgajiny, begerrgajiny**.
gerrbij-gerrbij *coverb+DO_REFL.* cut self. • Gerrbij-gerrbij giningirriyin. *He cut himself.*
Gerregerrewoon *noun.* Fletcher Creek; known to Hector Jandany and Left Hand George as Stoney Creek.
Gerregerrewoon *noun.* place with waterfall near Argyle Diamond Mine. [NOTE: people from the Argyle Diamond Mine used to go swimming there]
gerrejbe *coverb+EAT.* eat/drink all of something. SEE: **girrijbe**.
gerreleginy, gerrelegel, gerrelegem *adjective.* greedy. • Thoorroob benamanyji mayim gerreleginyaya. *He snatched the food, he is a greedy one.* • Ngayin-ga gerreleginyga. *I'm a greedy one.*
gerrelem *noun.* rectum.
gerreleny, gerrelel, gerrelem *adjective.* greedy. • Mayimbi gerrelinyaya nyaganyjiga nginy. *This uncle here is really greedy for food.* SEE: **gerrelem, gerrijbendeny**.
gerrerlel *noun feminine.* red root of shrub, *Haemodorum ensifolium.* SEE: **minyngil**. [NOTE: can be used to dye fibres]
gerreranggoolji; goorrooranggoolji *noun.* magpie. *Gymnorhina tibicen eylandtensis.* SEE: **gemerlawoorroony**. [NOTE: some people use this word for *wirrindiny*, the pied butcherbird]
gerrewool REDUP: **gerre-gerrewoom**. *noun feminine.* freshwater mussel. *Velesunio wilsonii.*

[NOTE: word not supposed to be said by young men; they can say *goorloongarnal* 'water dweller']

gerr-gerr *coverb.* roll something. • Gerr-gerr benaj-girri. / Gerr-gerr beniyi-ngirri. *Roll it to me.*

gerrij *coverb+EAT_MID.* eat something up oneself. • Ngoowan gerrij jarrimiyangnha-yoo. *Don't you two eat it all up yourselves.*

gerrij; girrij; gerrej *coverb+GET.* finish something. • Gerrij benama! *You finish it!* • Gerrej benamanyji diyanya jalariyany. *That egret (white crane) had finished the lot.* • Ngelmang berrema ngarranggarnim gerrij-garri yirrimji ngoorroom ngela galma-galmang Jadidin wingini-merrarriny birrim jiyilemga. *When we have finished this Good Friday ceremony, on Saturday all those men will be drunk over there to the east (at the rodeo ground).* • Gerrij-gela yirrim gerniny-gerninybe. *Let's finish the drawings.*

gerrij; girrij; gerrej *coverb+BECOME.* finish, end. • Gerrej woomberrayidbe-yoo ngaaloo-giny wanda-wandaj berrani-yoo. *When they finished killing all the rock wallabies they carried them into the shade.* • Girrij-ngarri waniyid, bagoo ngineward. *When he had finished he went to sleep.* • Marra biyarra, girrija ngelayidge. *Go away! I've finished.* • Marloogany doo waarrany gerrij woomberrayid-joo baljarranggoombi. *The old man and the young boy finished (making) the boomerangs.* • Warrg berrani gerrij. *They danced, then finished.* • Garlirrin-gili gerrij woomberrayid. *They came right up to the bank (ripples on water).*

gerrij; girrij; gerrej *coverb+GO/COME.* finish. • 'Yage girrij genayi,' marloogany nginini. *'I finished it,' said the old man.* • Derrerreb-garri narrayinnha ngoowana miyale joonanynha-ngage wawoorrmarndiny gerrij narrayinha. *When you went camping you did not bring me any meat, you all finished up the crocodile.* • Nginyjinya gerrij giniyi wayiningerreg. *This man finished this many.*

gerrij *coverb+FALL/GO_DOWN.* finish. • 'Garninya? Gerrijboo-ma ngoowoonji?' 'Ngoowan, nyirlginy.' *'How is it? Is it just about finished?' 'No, it can't stop.'*

gerrij; girrij; gerrej *coverb+EAT.* finish by eating. • Gerrij nyilangoon'ge gerrewool. *I finish* up all the mussels (by eating them). • Gerrij-gala nherang, goorninyan-ngage. *I'll have to finish it up, I'm hungry.* • Ngoowan gerrij ginbiyangnha-nga berrebe-nga. *Don't eat up all of this on me.*

gerrij *coverb+BURN/BITE.* finish by burning. • Gerrija benawoorranyji. *They were all burnt up in the fire.*

gerrij *particle.* finish.

gerrij; girrij *coverb+SAY/DO.* finish, die. • Girrij berrani marrarn, ngoowangarnabelala. *The people (from there) are all gone/finished, nobody left.*

gerrij *coverb+HIT.* finish something up.

gerrijbendeny, gerrijbendel, gerrijbendem *adjective.* greedy. LIT: 'one who finishes the lot'. • Ngoorroonyayi mangoony woomenjende, gerrijbendenyga. *He's over there eating, he is really greedy.* • Jang jemanande gerrijbenden-ngoo. *You keep eating, you are really greedy.*

gerrijbendiny *noun masculine.* murderer. SEE: joowarrigaleny, mawoongarriny.

gerrji *coverb+GO/COME.* keep still, stay very quiet. • Ginyany gerrji nginiyi. *The heron is keeping very quiet/still.*

gerrmabany *coverb.* having sores and lumps sticking out. • Gerrmabany gaji-gajibany. Ngarri narroorn-ni-ngarri-gili berdij barrij-gili. *I am the one with sores everywhere. You all said it, stand up and fight.*

gerrma-gerrma *coverb+SAY/DO.* say someone has sores. • Yangirni jarroongambiny-gili, gaji-gajiban-ngarri yimberranynha-gili, gerrma-gerrma-ngarri narrani-ngerri-gili. *(He said), Who can spear me, the one with all the sores, you all said I had a backside covered in sores.*

gerrmam *noun.* ringworm, sores.

gethed *coverb+GO/COME.* go and cut. • Nginyi jirrgany nginiyin dany mawoorroony, gethed giniyi. *This hill kangaroo went and cut that bloodwood tree.*

-gi *suffix.* having large body part. [NOTE: followed by gender suffix agreeing with the gender of the owner of the body part, often included in very rude swearing, e.g. *milagil*, 'big vagina'; *ngarndaginy*, 'big semen']

gibigel *noun feminine.* earwig. Dermaptera.

gibin *locative.* in the bush. [NOTE: *gibin*, 'dry land' contrasted with *ngabarl-ngabarl*, 'sea']

gibi-ngarnany, gibi-ngarnal, gibi-ngarnam *adjective.* belonging to the bush, living in the bush. • Lawoony nginyjinyga, yoowoorriyangeny gibi-ngarnany men'gawoog-girreny moorl-moorl yambirrimoorliya-ngarri. *This lemonwood is our bush medicine when we have little sores.*

gibiwoonab *coverb+GO/COME.* spread over bush (floodwater), overflow. • Gibiwoonab nginiyi warrambany. *The big floodwater spread all over the bush.*

gibi-yibin *locative.* right in the bush, all along in the bush, all over the bush.

gig *coverb+SAY/DO_M.* be full of food. • Gig wanema. *He is full. / He filled himself up.* • 'Ngoowan, ngoowan, gig ngelama,' yagoorn nginini dany jalariny. *That egret (white crane) told a lie, he said, 'I'm really full now.'*

gig *coverb+EAT.* eat until full up with food. • Gig ninoongoon ganyarrany men'gawoony. *I'm full up with good goanna.* • Gigboo joonoongoona. *You are full now.*

gig *coverb+SAY/DO.* be full of food. • Goorndarri-moowam gig genarn. *I just fill myself up with fish.*

gigbawoony, gigbawool, gigbawoom *adjective.* full of food. • Gigbawoona, biri biyarra daa-giny bagoowa benennha. *Now you are full, go back to the camp and sleep.*

gij *coverb+GO/COME.* climb to top, reach top of hill. • Ngoorrinya berdijbe woomenji, gijaa nginiyin laarne. *That man has climbed to the top of the hill.* • Ngoorriyana gij ginbiyan laarne. *I'll come out right on top there.* • Gij nginiyi. *He came out on top.*

gij *coverb+SAY/DO_M.* climb to top, reach top of hill. • Gijboowaa ngelemen'ge laarne. *I'm climbing to the top now.*

Gija *noun.* language name. [NOTE: the language name has also been spelled 'Kija'; community educators requested a spelling change after a meeting of stakeholders at Warrmarn in 2012; this word appears in Ray (1897) list meaning 'speak']

Gijabany, Gijabal, Gijabam *noun.* Gija person. LIT: 'having Gija language'.

gil *coverb.* click clapsticks once. SEE: **gil-gil**.

Gilban *noun.* Mabel Downs, hill near Mabel Downs station gate that is the dreaming place for the rasp-tailed goanna.

gilbany *noun masculine.* rasp-tailed goanna. *Varanus acanthurus, V. storri.*

gilemberrji *noun masculine.* long sugar grass. *Mnesithea rottboellioides.*

gil-gil *coverb+SAY/DO_M.* play clapsticks. • Gil-gil-moowamda gil-gil woomberramande. *They just used to play clapsticks.*

gil-gil, gil-gile *noun.* clapsticks. SEE: **garnbagbe**.

gil-gilji *noun.* milkwood tree. *Wrightia saligna.* SEE: **garnbagji**. [NOTE: is used to make clap sticks]

-gili *plural suffix.* many (suffix to verbs and enclitic pronouns). [NOTE: homophonous with one of two allative suffixes]

-gili *suffix.* towards. [NOTE: homophonous with plural suffix to verbs and enclitic pronouns, only used with direction 'towards', whereas *-yoorroong* can also be used meaning 'into', 'onto'] SEE: **-yoorroong**.

gilingin, gilyingen *temporal.* today, now. SEE: **gelengen**.

gilin'goowoony *noun.* sesbania bean, type of annual plant that has tall stems used as spear shafts. *Sesbania cannabina, S. simpliciuscula.* SEE: **barragal**.

giljerrengginy *noun.* tadpoles.

gilyalal *noun feminine.* small bitter melon. *Citrullus colocynthis* SEE: **gagoolanyil**.

gilyam *noun.* salt, salty. • Gilyam goorloom. *Salty water.* SEE: **garam, girlarlam**.

gim *coverb+GET.* choke someone. • Gim nginima. *He choked him.* SEE: **gang**.

giningim; giningem *noun.* heart. SEE: **doolbem, dooloom**.

giningoob *coverb+GO/COME.* be short of breath. • Wanyjinawa, giningoob naniyinnha goorloon yiligin. *Maybe you were getting short of breath there under the water then.* SEE: **reminy**

ginyan; ginyanbe *temporal particle.* that time when. • Ginyanbe dam yaniyiya-ngarri deg-garri yanemanya ginyam melagawoom. *You know that time when you and I went and saw lots of white-faced herons.* [NOTE: example sentence dictated by Rusty Peters to show contrast between *ginyan*, 'that time when' and *ginyam*, 'white-faced herons']

ginyane *locative.* in/at the same place. • Nyarliwiny jimarrawoogda ngiwinjinde ginyane. *He's crippled, he has to stay always in* *the same place.* • 'Gayiwa booroojgirrembi?' Ginyane-gili ngaginyin daan. *'Where's the party?' / 'Where's the card game?' In the same place, at my place.* SEE: **giyale**.

ginyany *noun masculine.* white-faced heron, 'blue crane'. *Egretta novaehollandiae.*
• Melagawoom ginyam ngoorrooma, deg yimberremenbe-yoowoo. *There are lots of white-faced herons over there, they are looking at us.*

ginyginyel *noun feminine.* red-winged parrot. *Aprosmictus erythropterus.* [NOTE: word not supposed to be said by young men, who say *thirrilngarnal* instead]

ginyirriny, ginyirril *noun.* someone who takes someone else's wife or husband, enemy. • Berrembi, warim, warim dam wari-wari-ngarri berramiyinbende, thoowiya-berrewa dam, ginyirrim-anyji ngalim-berrewa. *Here is where they use to fight, fight over things maybe like men taking other men's wives.*

girewany *noun.* willy-willy. SEE: **jalawoonany**.

giri *coverb+SAY/DO.* sound made by the flat green katydid grasshopper called *girinyil*. • Girinyil giri nyerne. *The flat green katydid grasshopper calls out 'giri'.* SEE: **diyid, girinybe**.

girinybe *coverb+SAY/DO_M.* sound made by the flat green katydid grasshopper called *girinyil*.
• Belegawirrin merdbe-merdbe-ngarri berroowoondi wayinigana girinybe woomenya. *When it gets dark in the middle of the night she (katydid grasshopper) calls out.*

girinyil *noun feminine.* katydid grasshopper, flat green grasshopper species. *Caedicia* sp.

giriyig-giriyig *coverb+SAY/DO.* sound made by the flat green katydid grasshopper called *girinyil*. SEE: **diyid, giri, girinybe**.

girlarlam *noun.* salt. SEE: **garam, gilyam**.

girlgoowal *noun feminine.* female koel. *Eudynamys scolopacea.* [NOTE: the koel and *goorragoorral*, 'channel-billed cuckoo', are both known as the storm bird because they appear just before the wet season] SEE: **doowagoony, joowany**.

girli *coverb+GO_ALONG.* walk along. • Girli wananyji, biyawiya nginini, boorrale-bawoorroo-jiyan. *He walked along, he was looking around, there was really nothing to eat.*
• Girli-girri-woorroony. *Someone who does not want to walk.* • Jaroongem dal wanyagarral girli nyaliny wananya. *Yesterday that little girl walked too.* • Girli yirrinji wayirran. *We walk along the side of the hill.* • Ngoowan girli ngiliyande mendoowoon. *I don't want to keep walking at night.* SEE: **girliwany; girlirli, girlirlib, girlirliwany, warrag**.

girli *coverb+SAY/DO.* walk. • Ngarriwarlan-anyji girli nyimbirn. Mamberre girli-ba-woorrool. *She might walk later. She can't walk yet (because she is too little).* SEE: **girliwany; girlirli, girlirlib, girliwany, warrag**.

girlib *coverb+GO/COME.* walk. • Nyigamirribdawa girlib yarraya. *We will go early in the morning.*
• Jang-jang yarrama marrarn nyaliny girlib yarrayi ngelamoogoo. *We ate and then we kept driving to the east.* [NOTE: speaker uses *girlib* even though we were driving]

girlib *coverb+LEAVE.* walk away leaving someone.
• Girlib yinawoorroodji-yarre. *He walked away and left us.*

girligewa *coverb+GET.* make walk.
• Goorndoogany dany girli-girri-woorroony, girligewa ninemangge. *That little boy did not want to walk but I made him walk.* SEE: **girli, girliwany; girlirli, girlirlib, girlirliwany**.

girli-girlirrangem *noun.* people from the west. • Joonbam deg yirramanyjende girli-girlirrangem berrayinde-ngarri-yirri. *We used to watch Joonba when the people from the west came to visit us.*

girlil *noun feminine.* bush tomato, wild gooseberry. *Solanum echinatum.*
• Melakawoom-ngiyi boorndalaga girlilga dal; mayilga-yoowoo jang-girrilga gig-girrem. *That bush tomato is very prickly; it is bush tucker for us to eat and get full on.*

Girlingmanji *noun.* Twenty Mile.

girliny-girliny *coverb+BECOME.* go blue/green (meat when rotten). • Miyale girliny-girliny woomberriyinbe. *The meat has gone blue/green.*

girliny-girlinyji; girliny-girlinyel; girliny-girlinybe *adjective.* blue/green (e.g. rotten meat).

girlinyiny *noun masculine.* eel-tailed catfish (large species), Rendhal's catfish. *Porochilus rendahli.* SEE: **woorlengerriny**.

girlirli *coverb+SAY/DO_M.* walk. • Girlirli woomberramande-yirrab yiligibinyda. *They used to walk with us down that way.*

girlirli *coverb+SAY/DO.* be walking.

girlirli

• **Goorndoorndoogan girlirli yirrani-birri.** *We were walking there when we were children.* [NOTE: can mean 'travelling' of animals, e.g. an owl flying around at night]

girlirli *coverb+GO_ALONG.* be walking.

• **Jirrawoom-birri goorndoorndoogam girlirli woomberranybe dirrandem-birri girlarla-ba-yoorroong goorloon.** *One day the children went out walking to the salt lake.* • **Marrarn girlirli wananyji wirrijga wananyji.** *He went walking away by himself with no friends.*

girlirlib *coverb+SAY/DO.* walk along. • **Girlirlib narrani.** *You were all walking along.*

girlirremiliny, girlirremilil, girlirremilim *adjective.* someone from the west.

girlirrin *directional.* in the west.

girliwany REDUP: **girlirliwany.** *coverb+GO_ALONG.* walk along. • **Ngarayi nyaniyid jirrawool ngalil, girliwany wananya.** *He found one woman walking along.*

girliwirringiny *noun masculine.* wedge-tailed eagle, (Kriol: 'eaglehawk'). *Aquila audax.* LIT: 'one who is up high'. [NOTE: Southern dialect] SEE: **warrarnany, garnbarrany, garnbidany, wirli-wirlingarnany.**

girliyirr; girlirr *directional.* to the west. SEE: **gerlirroogoo, gerliyirr.**

girndilji *noun.* medium-sized brown grasshopper species, similar to *malnginyji* and *birlbirljil.*

girr *coverb+DO_REFL.* scratch self. • **Girr-gala ngendemij.** *I want to scratch myself.* • **Girr ngenamiyan'ge yiwiyam.** *I am scratching my head lice.* • **Girr barremijtha doomoom.** *Scratch your heads.*

girrangem *noun.* honey. • **girrangegaliny** *big honey*

girranynhawoony, girranynhawool, girranynhawoom *adjective.* one that scratches.

-girrem; girrim *coverb suffix.* gerundive, purposive on coverbs.

girrem *coverb+PUT.* light fire, strike a match.
• **Girrem benayanya nyamanil.** *The old woman lit the fire.* • **Girrem-gala benaj!** *Light the fire!*

girremgajim *noun.* matches. • **Yindiyi gala girremgajim.** *Give me the matches.* SEE: **girrem.**

girrganyji *noun masculine.* brown falcon. *Falco berigora.* [NOTE: was burned brown in dreamtime when he stole fire from the frillneck lizard; he threw *goonggalany*, 'fire stick tree',

all over the country. Same word also recorded meaning 'brown goshawk', *Accipiter fasciatus.*]

girr-girr *interjection.* call of *girrganyji*, 'brown falcon'.

girr-girr *coverb+DO_REFL.* scratch self. • **Girr-girr ngendemij yayi ngenan.** *Let me scatch myself. / I'll have to scratch myself I'm itchy.* • **Joolany girr-girr ngimiyanyji.** *The dog is scratching itself.*

girr-girr *coverb+GET.* scratch someone/something. • **Girr-girr yindemnha!** *Scratch me!*

-girrim; -girrem *coverb suffix.* for doing . . ., gerundive, purposive on coverbs, can be used to generate new nouns by adding to coverbs (e.g. *goorloorrgirrem* 'injection', LIT: 'for poking with a stick').

girringilyim *noun.* rocks and leaves put in stomach cavity when cooking (e.g. of a kangaroo after guts are removed to make it cook well and smell good).

girriyag *coverb+HIT.* to not like something and tell someone off about it, dislike. • **Danya roorrajnhawoony, girriyag-gala barrij.** *That man is always swearing, you all go and tell him off. You mob go tell em off he like swearing all the time.*

girriyiny, girriyil, girriyim *adjective.* brave.

girrji *coverb+GO/COME.* stay quiet. • **Nhawoondi thadaa nginjende, girrji nginiyi.** *He (owl) keeps on standing (sitting upright) staying very quiet.*

giwaj *coverb+PUT.* show. • **Giwaj noowiyajge-birri-gili.** *I will show it to them all.* SEE: **jirri.**

giwinarlany, giwinarlal, giwinarlam *adjective.* blonde hair.

giwinboorrel *noun.* rough bluebell, camel bush. *Trichodesma zeylanicum.*

Giwirnbi *noun.* a place on Mabel Downs west of the place called Joorlboon.

giyale *noun.* same place, place one has been to before, favourite place. SEE: **ginyane.**

giyawoole *noun.* blood. SEE: **goongoorloom.**

giyawoolge *coverb+DO_REFL.* make self bleed.

giyim *noun.* wet sand. • **Giyim-baya.** *It is wet.*

giyiny, giyil, giyim *adjective.* wet. • **Jilam dama giyim yilag.** *That ground is wet.* • **Giyin-ngage marra ngenardge.** *I am wet, I am going.*
• **Dala giyil nyirreg-garri nyanoowardja.** *That woman is wet from bathing.* • **Danya giyiny, nyirreg-garri nginiwardji.** *That man is wet from bathing.*

goo; goowoo *particle.* only, just, or, but. SEE: **goowa**. [NOTE: dubitative linking particle]

goobil *noun feminine.* nankeen night heron. *Nycticorax caledonicus.* SEE: **jawoombal**.

goodabal *noun feminine.* small striped fish species. *Amniataba percoides.* [NOTE: Nyaajarri skin; mother of *garriyiny*, 'black bream']

goodaj REDUP: **goodaj-goodaj**. *coverb+SAY/DO_M.* knead. • *Mayim goodaj wanema. She kneaded the bread.*

goodaj-goodaj *coverb+GET.* knead. • *Goodaj-goodaj bemberramangbende mayim. They were kneading damper.*

goodaj-goodaj *coverb+GO_ALONG.* make young men. • *Werlweli, goorndoorndoogam goodaj-goodaj-garri wananya. She became that dreaming place from the time when she used to carry the law for the young men.* [NOTE: *goodaj* meaning 'knead dough' is used as a euphemism for circumcision]

goodam *noun.* hair belt.

goodawoodany *noun.* northern shovel-nosed snake. *Brachyurophis roperi.* [NOTE: striped snake species, one of three striped snake species called 'emu killer' by Gija people, other two are *jarloongoorroobarndegji* and *joowarri-barndegji*]

goodoo coverb+SAY/DO grind.
• *Ngarranggarnin-ga manggerregerreny goodoo ngini minyjiwarrany. In the dreamtime the big tata lizard ground-up black plums.* SEE: **goodoorr**.

goodoo *coverb+GO_ALONG.* grind. • *Badem gooyarrg yirranyjende, goodoo yirranyjende. We used to collect red ochre and grind it.*

goodoo *coverb+PUT.* grind. • *Goodoo nginiyanyji ngarag ginimanyji nanggeriny. He ground them (black plums) up and made them into a big cake.* • *Goojimga-ngiyi goodoo nyimberrayangbende ngaande-ngaande-baya. They used to grind up the bones together with all the flesh (of fish caught by poisoning, to dry and keep).*

Goodoogoodoo *noun.* place near Saltpan / Mount Evelyn on Lissadell Station. [NOTE: mentioned in one of the verses of the Dayiwool Moonga-moonga]

goodoo-goodoo *coverb+SAY/DO_M.* grind.
• *Goodoo-goodoo woomberramande. They used to grind it.*

goodoo-goodoogirriny *noun.* grindstone. LIT. 'thing for grinding'.

goodoongeny, goodoongel, goodoongem *adjective.* something that has been ground up. • *Diyena na dawoorrgoo nyimberrayangbende goodoongelga dal. They used to put it in there now, that ground-up (fish).*

goodoorr *coverb+SAY/DO_M.* grind. • *Jidi ngoorrayangbende, goodoorr woomberramande, wayina jang woomberramande. They used to join it together, grind it up and eat like that (mashed cooked roots of hairy kapok bush and cooked boab seeds).* SEE: **goodoo**.

goog *coverb+DO_REFL.* be forbidden to do something. • *Ngoowana miyale jang yarrirn, goog yarremija. Goorndarri-moowam jang yarrirn. We are not allowed to eat meat. It is forbidden to us. We can only eat fish.*

googan *particle.* just for nothing, for no particular purpose. • *Berrema googan ngarag noonamangge, bidjam, deg-girrim, googan. I just made this as a picture, just to look at.*
• *Googan ngenayin-ninggi jarrag-girrem. I just came to talk to you.* • *Googan jarrag ngenarn-ninggi, thoowoo-boorroo lerndej joonooyilinha. I'm just telling you, why do you have to write it down? / You don't have to write it down.*

googbeny, googbel, googbem; googboom *adjective.* forbidden. • *Ngoowan yarriyan yoorloo, googboom dan-ga. We shouldn't go downstream, that place is forbidden.*
• *Googboom-birri ngalim. Forbidden to women.* • *Googboom-birri jiyilem. Forbidden to men.*

googoonjal *noun feminine.* sheep. *Ovis aries.* [NOTE: sheep were brought to Gija country by the original invaders but they are not kept there anymore; a sheep features in the Christmas Joonba that used to be staged at Gawoornben, Texas Downs Station] SEE: **jiyigjel, yiwoolthelel**.

gooj *coverb+SAY/PUT_REFL.* make trouble for self.
• *Gooj yarrayilin-noowa. We made trouble for ourselves because of it (bullock that was killed).*

gooj *coverb+PUT.* make trouble for someone.
• *Gooj ngenaya. He made trouble for me.*

gooj *coverb+HIT.* blame someone. • *Ngoowana gooj jarriyinnha dany Marloogany Joolany. Don't blame Old Dog.*

gooj *coverb+BECOME.* be the person to blame, be

goojim

at fault. • *Ngayana gooj ngelayidge.* I am the one to blame. It is my fault.

goojim noun. bone. SEE: **mayiwarndem**.

goojinji noun. bandicoot. *Isoodon* sp. [NOTE: used for 'wombat' in a 1988 school program when teachers brought out photos of Australian animals not occuring in Gija country] SEE: **jinberrji, nyarlgool**.

goojoog *coverb+GET*. break up into pieces. • *Goojooga barremnhawa-yoo.* You two break it up! • *Goojoog benamanyji.* He broke it up.

gool REDUP: **gool-gool** *coverb+PUT*. try. • *Ngaga, gool yamberraja dam men'gawoom-anyji.* Well, we should try if it is any good. • *Gawayinde gool-goolji ninbiyajgende.* I'll just have to try my best/keep trying.

gool REDUP: **gool-gool**. *coverb+SAY/PUT_REFL*. try self. • *Gool nyaniyilin yilag.* She tried herself out in the water. • *Googan gool-gool nginbiyilijge jarrag-girrim.* I will just try talking myself.

goolaroogool; gelaroogool noun. bar-shouldered dove. *Geopelia humeralis*. SEE: **marrawayil**.

goolboorr *coverb+HIT*. smash. • *Goolboorr nyimberrayidbe ngoorr-ngoorrgajil.* They smashed the car. • *Goolboorr ngoorrayidbe bajalarri.* They ran over the billy can and smashed it.

gooldany-gooldanyel noun. northern rosella. *Platycercus venustus*.

goolibil noun feminine. bush banana. *Marsdenia viridiflora*. [NOTE: vine with long fruit containing edible seeds like peas]

goolijil noun feminine. **1.** buff-banded rail. *Gallirallus philippensis*. **2.** Eurasian coot. *Fulica atra*.

gooliyi-gooliyi *coverb+GO_ALONG*. move bottom from side to side like a willie wagtail or mistletoe bird. • *Gooliyi-gooliyi wiyinya werlemernel.* The teenage girl is walking along moving her hips from side to side.

gooliyi-gooliyinhawoony, gooliyi-gooliyinhawool, gooliyi-gooliyinhawoom adjective. someone who moves their bottom from side to side like a willie wagtail or mistletoe bird, sexy one.

goolmaj *coverb+SAY/DO_M*. squeeze together with fingers. • *Goolmaj woomberramande, jang woomberramande.* They used to squeeze it (mashed green plum) together with their fingers and eat it.

gooloo *coverb+SAY/DO_M*. be happy. • *Gooloo-gooloowoony jiyiliny, boorooj-girrim gooloo wanema wanyanyagem-boorroo.* He was a happy man then, he was happy for the children to play.

gooloogoo *coverb+GET*. make happy. • *Gooloogoo yinamannhande gamingoorroom.* You used to make all of us happy.

gooloo-gooloo *coverb+SAY/DO_M*. be happy. • *Wanyanyagem gooloo-gooloo yarrama-ngooyoo.* We children are all happy about her (because she is coming, *wanggarnal* at Christmas time).

gooloo-gooloo *coverb+SAY/DO*. be happy. • *Melagawooya gooloo-gooloo berrani.* They were all happy. • *Yagenginy dany gooloo-gooloo nginini.* That other one was happy.

gooloo-gooloowoony; gooloo-gooloowool; gooloo-gooloowoom adjective. happy.

gooloomarram noun. prickle bush. *Dichrostachys spicata*.

gooloomboong, gooloomboongnyel noun feminine. didjeridoo. SEE: **jooboony**. [NOTE: people used to say that this word was Miriwoong and the Gija word was *jooboony*; in the 2000s it has become the only word commonly used]

gooloongarriny, gooloongarril, gooloongarrim adjective. happy, young, new. • *Ngoowan gooloongarrin-nga gelengoowoorroon-nga.* I'm not young, I am old. • *Ngoowan jana joowida, gooloongarri-beben-ngoo.* Don't go prowling around in the night, you are too young.

gooloongarriny, gooloongarril, gooloongarrim noun. younger sibling.

gooloong-gooloong noun. armband. • *Garijgawoorroom damga, googbem ngalimga-birri.* Women can't say this word; it is forbidden to them. [NOTE: Rusty Peters said it should not be mentioned as it is men's business, but others use it freely]

gooloowala *coverb+SAY_REFL*. be happy together. • *Warn'gany ngidji-ngarri, melagawoom, labam doo derranbe gooloowala berriliyanbe.* When it is cold all the corella and black cockatoo are happy together.

goolyany, goolyam noun. testicles.

SEE: **ngalyarr**.

goolyoolyool *noun feminine.* budgerigar. *Melopsittacus undulates.*

gooma *conjunctive particle.* just as, just. • Gijambi dayiwa bemberrembe wajbaloombi; gooma ngayin dayi-ngarri noonamangge wajbaloom-boorroowa jarragbi Yinggilij. *The white people learn Gija, just as I learn English from them.* • Goonthoorrban-nga nyenge-jan gooma goonthoorrban-ngoo. *Got a cold just like you.*

goombam *noun.* short spear.

goombarriyil *noun.* yellow paint. [NOTE: Western dialect] SEE: **goorndoorloo**.

goomboo *noun.* urine. [NOTE: Kriol, pan-Kimberley word] SEE: **jarnangarre**.

goomboo *coverb+SAY/DO.* urinate. • Danya yawardany goomboo ngerne. *That horse is urinating.*

goomboolangil, goomboolanginy *noun.* cockroach. *Cosmozosteria* spp. SEE: **jarnangarre**.

goomboonyel, goomboonyji *noun.* egg. • goomboonybe *eggs* SEE: **gerewoolel**.

goomboornany *noun masculine.* nail-tailed wallaby. *Onychogalea unguifera.* SEE: **goon'goodoogoodoony gooroorroonggoony, woorrood-woorroodji, woordoorr-woordoorrji.** [NOTE: left-handed from the dreamtime, *ngarranggarnin*; Janama skin; brother-in-law of the moon]

goomboowany *coverb+GO/COME.* go urinating. • Goomboowany ngenda. *I'm going to urinate.* [NOTE: not polite; polite usage is *Ngenardge jaam-boorroo.* 'I am going for stomach.']

goomoonoongam *noun.* tall conical paperbark headdress. • Goomoonoonga-bany warrg-ngarri nginini . . . *When he was dancing wearing a paperbark headdress . . .* • Ngara-ngarag ngerne goomoonoongam. *He is making paperbark headdresses.*

goomoorroo *coverb+BECOME.* become worn out with no-good legs. • Goomoorroo ngelayid girli-ngarri ngelanyge ngirribawooroon. *My legs are worn out because I was walking a long way.*

Figure 47. *Gooloomboongnyel: Henry Wambiny: Jawalyiny boomi nyiyooloonji gooloomboongnyel.*

goomoorroony, goomoorrool, goomoorroom *adjective.* having no-good legs. • Goomoorroon-yarre. *Our legs are worn out.*

goomoorroowoo *coverb+GO_ALONG.* become old and have no-good legs. • Goomoorroowoo wiyinya. *She is getting old and can't walk properly.*

goonanderoony; goornandooroony *noun masculine.* tree species, nulla-nulla tree. *Acacia coriacea, Hakea macrocarpa.* [NOTE: used to make nulla-nullas (fighting sticks), boomerangs, axe handles and digging sticks]

goonangginy *noun.* cluster fig, fruit of cluster fig. *Ficus racemosa.* SEE: **jawoonany, ngalalabany.** [NOTE: fruit on trunk and branches, tree found near water]

Goonanggoowany *noun.* Pigeon Spring, a place in George Mung Mung's country.

goonarre *noun.* rotten meat. SEE: **nhoowoole.**

goondoony *coverb+GET.* claim someone, love/want someone. • Ngelela goondoony nginimanya. *She loved him from when she was a baby.*

goongarr *coverb+SAY/DO.* go up and down, wander about (many). • Goo googan, goongarr-ngarri berrani. *They were all wandering about for nothing.*

Goongewayin *noun.* a place in Ngarrgooroon country.

goonggalam, goonggalany *noun.* firestick, stick used to make fire. [NOTE: *Premna acuminata* and *Clerodendrum floribundum* can be used]

goonggalany *noun masculine.* firestick tree. *Clerodendrum floribundum.* [NOTE: one growing near the highway in front of the Warmun Roadhouse]

goonggooloom; goonggoongoom *noun.* brain, head. SEE: **doomoom.**

goonggoon *coverb+GET.* cook in ground, roast in earth oven. • Ngoowan ngenengga wooboo, goonggoon yambirrimnya berremga goorndarrim? *Can't we cook these fish here?*

goonggoon REDUP: **goonggoo-goonggoon, goonggoo-woonggoon.** *coverb+HIT.* cook in ground, roast in earth oven. • Goonggoon bemberrayidbe-yoo. *The two men are cooking (something).* • Goonggoonbe yirriyinji. *We are cooking it in an earth oven.*

goonggoon *coverb+PUT.* cook in ground, roast in earth oven. • Goonggoonbe beniyilinya. *She is cooking (something) in the earth oven.*

goonggoonngem *adjective.* cooked in ground, roasted. • goonggoonngem miyale. *roast meat.*

goonggoorr *noun.* cough. [NOTE: Southern dialect] SEE: **goonthoorr.**

goongoo *coverb+BRING/TAKE.* carry something (e.g. tobacco) in the side of the mouth. • Dal binggoonyel goongoo nyimberranybende thoowernden. *They used to go along with that bush tobacco tucked inside the cheek at the side of the mouth.*

goongooloo *noun.* smoke.

goongoorloom *noun.* blood. • Goongoorloom bimbirriyajbe-ninggi deg-girrem menkawoom-anyji yilgoowoorroom-anyji. *They will put it on your blood to see if it is good or bad (description of blood pressure machine).* SEE: **giyawoole.**

gooni REDUP: **gooni-gooni.** *coverb+GET.* dream. • Gooni noonamangge yilgoowoorroom. Goonimka dam yilgoowoorrejiyam. *I had a bad dream. That dream was very bad.* • Diyanya gooni-gooni ngemenya. *That is the one (man) she is dreaming about.*

goonijib *coverb+GO/COME.* be dreaming. • Goonijib-anyji ngenardge. Rangga ninan'ge jarraggan Jambinji. *I must have been dreaming. I thought I heard Jambinji talking.*

gooniny, goonil, goonim *noun.* dream, personal dreaming. • Ngaginyil goorndoogal goonim benamanya yilgoowoorroom. *My little girl had a bad dream.* [NOTE: if you dream of someone's dreaming then that person will soon arrive] SEE: **gooningarriny.**

gooningarriny, gooningarril, gooningarrim *noun.* dream, personal dreaming, dreamtime thing. SEE: **gooniny.**

goonjal *noun.* kapok bush, edible root of kapok bush. *Cochlospermum fraseri* v. *fraseri.* [NOTE: roots of young plants cooked and eaten, ends of sticks frayed for spoons and brushes, and fibres used to make string]

goonjiny *noun.* bauhinia. *Lysiphyllum cunninghamii.* [NOTE: ash used with chewing tobacco and for detoxifying *garnawoony*] SEE: **wanyarriny.**

goon'gany-goon'gany *coverb+HIT.* give someone goosebumps. • Goon'gany-goon'gany niyinji-ni. *He is giving you goosebumps.*

goon'goodoogoodoony noun. nail-tailed wallaby. *Onychogalea unguifera*. SEE: **goooorroonggoony, woorrood-woorroodji, woordoorr-woordoorrji**. [NOTE: left-handed from the dreamtime, *ngarranggarnin*]

goonthoorr; goothoorr coverb+SAY/DO. cough. • Goonthoorr-gela ngenda-. *I'll have to cough.* • Goonthoorr ngini. *He coughed.* • Wela goothoorrgayan. *Goodness (I) keep on coughing.*

goonthoorrg coverb+SAY/DO_M. be coughing. • Goonthoorrg ngelamande rangarrwanyge. *I was coughing all night until sunrise.*

goonthoorri coverb+GET. get flu. • Wayinigana goonthoorri yamberramenya ngard-ngarri boorroorn. *We are all getting flu from that bad smell (burning rubbish).*

goonthoorrji, goonthoorroo noun. cold (illness), phlegm. • Goonthoorr-bawoorroon-nga. *I don't have a cold.* • Goonthoorrjiga gerrij waniyidji. *The cold has finished now. / He got better from his cold.* • Goonthoorr-ban-nga. *I have a cold.*

goony coverb+GET. give someone a chance/time to do something. • Marrge goony yimbirrimbi-yoowoo jarrag-jarrag-garri yarroorn. *Wait, they are just giving us a chance to get on with talking.*

goonyingarre noun. corpse, dead body. • Goonyingarre wirli-wirlin thedji-ngarri berrani, wethedji berrani. *They threw all the bodies on top when they killed them.* • Wandaj nyananyji ngoorroona goonyingarrel, dagoorr nyaniyidji. *He carried the woman's body over there and put her in (burial place).* SEE: **garajbe**.

goonyingarrg coverb+FALL/GO_DOWN. die.

goonyingarrg coverb. kill.

goonyjany, goonyjal, goonyjam noun. tree, stick. SEE: **goowooleny**.

goonyjiri 1. coverb+GET. tease, make fun of someone. • Goonyjiri nemenha-ngal yoowarrge nemenha-ngal. *She's flirting with you.* **2.** coverb+SPEAR. tease, make fun of someone. • Danya goonyjiri nengamboornji-ningi. *He is teasing you.* SEE: **birriman, birrga-wirrga, jing**.

goonyjiriwoony, goonyjiriwool, goonyjiriwoom adjective. person who goes stealing other people's husbands or wives, a flirt. • Danya goonyjiriwoony. *That man goes stealing every woman.* • Dala goonyjiriwool. *That woman goes stealing every man.*

Goonyoorrban, Goonyirribany noun. Eagle Hawk Bottle Tree, a place in Paddy Bedford's mother's country.

goonyoorrji noun masculine. ant species, stink ants.

goonyoorroo noun. bits of rubbish in bush honey.

goorabel noun. older sister. [NOTE: can be used to speak to or about an older sibling whom a younger sibling cannot name] SEE: **booloongool**.

goorabeny noun. older brother. [NOTE: can be used to speak to or about an older sibling whom a younger sibling cannot name] SEE: **booloongoony**.

goorag coverb+PUT. change. • Yage-yoorroong goorag beniyilinya. *She changed colours.* SEE: **goornag**.

gooraj coverb+SAY/DO_REFL. pick each other out. • Gooraj berrangirriyin boorij-girrim. *They pick em out for playing.*

gooraj-gooraj coverb+SAY/DO. pick out someone (e.g. football team) /something. • Gooraj-gooraj berrani. *They picked them.*

gooral noun feminine. mother.

goorara coverb+SAY/DO. speak to country asking for help, ask dreaming place or spirits of ancestors for help; dreaming place tells people to do something. • Dama da-ngarri nginini, goorara-ngarri nginini 'Wawoo:::!' *That is the place where he (moon in dreamtime) spoke to the country, saying 'Wawoo!'*

goorara coverb+PUT. speak to country asking for help, ask dreaming place or spirits of ancestors for help; dreaming place tells people to do something. • Goorara nyilayangge, 'Yindiyinnha-boorroo ngawooji-goorroo-wanem,' ngenani-ngiyi. *I asked her (the spirit of my relation who lived at that place before), 'Give me (fish) for all your son's children,' I said to her.* • Goorara yinayanya-yarre, 'Men'gawiya barrennha-ngerroowa ngayin gooma,' nyanini-yirri. *She (our dreaming, the rainbow) used the kind of powerful speech that we use to speak to our dreaming places. 'You live in a good way just by my rules,' she told us.*

goorara coverb+SAY/DO_REFL. speak to heal self in country. • Deberr ngoorrayidbe leg-jin, bat goorara nginingirriyinjende, gibiyan

goorayi

ngininiyin men'gawoo waniyidji. *They shot him in the leg but he spoke to himself to fix himself up and he stayed right out in the bush until it healed.*

goorayi *noun.* mother (address form), mum.

goord *coverb+FALL/GO_DOWN.* die suddenly in group. • Goord berraward ngoorr-ngoorrgaji-baya. *They all died in a car accident.* • Gaboo-ngiyi woolgoomanel neyimbe-ngiyi ngoorrool gendoowa goord-garri nyanoomooward? *What is the name of that old woman who died together with those others up there (in a car accident)?*

goord *coverb+GET.* kill many at one time. • Wanda-wandaj woomberramande melakawoom goord bemberramangbende. *They were carrying large numbers of fish/animals that they kept killing.* [NOTE: plural object]

goord *coverb+HIT.* kill many at one time. • Joomooloony-noo jarrag-garri nginbirn-berra ganggam goord-garri bemberrayidbe jawoojim, ganggam, nyaganybe, gooram. *I am going to speak about the boab tree where they killed my mother's mother, her sisters and brothers, my mother's father and his brothers, my uncles and my mother's little sisters.* [NOTE: plural object]

goord *coverb+WOUND.* kill many people. • 'Wel joowembad doonamangge mernmerdgalem, wayiningerrega goord doonawoon'ge wajbaloomga,' nginini. *'I showed the police, I killed this many white men (showed marks he made on his arm for each one killed),' he said.* • Wayinigana goordbe benawoonji. *Because of that he killed them all then.* [NOTE: plural object]

goord *coverb+WOUND_REFL.* many people kill each other. • Goordboo berrawooranbende jiyile-warriny ngarranggarnin. *Then many Aboriginal people killed each other here a long time ago.*

goordangalam *noun.* top muscly part of arm.

Goordbelayin *noun.* place where many were killed at one time, massacre site. [NOTE: used to refer to places such as the Bedford Downs massacre site and the Mistake Creek massacre site]

goordiny *noun.* small rock goanna. *Varanus glebopalma.*

goordirdal *noun feminine.* bush orange. *Capparis umbonata.* [NOTE: word used to mean 'bush orange' by young men who are not allowed to say *joogoorrool*; leaves can be used as a steaming medicine to treat colds; also used to mean 'bush coconut', *barlabil*, by some people]

goordoony *noun.* round thing, ball, marble.

goordoony *noun.* cat. *Felis catus.* [NOTE: used to mean 'cat' because of their round heads] SEE: **ngirrngiliny, dijarrji.**

goordooroom *noun.* big nulla-nulla, fighting stick.

Goorirr-goorirr *noun.* name of a song and dance cycle in 'balga' style with painted boards carried on shoulders. [NOTE: dreamed by Rover Thomas in mid 1970s, word is said to be Worla as the person who gave him the song was a Worla woman killed in a car accident near Turkey Creek; Peggy Patrick says two big rocks near the highway north of the Lissadell/Argyle Diamond Mine turn-off are two men called Goorirr-goorirr; has also been spelled Gurrirr-gurirr]

goorl REDUP: **goorlool.** *coverb+SAY/DO.* stretch arms out. • Goorl nginini. *He stretched out his arms.*

goorlabal *noun feminine.* female rainbow snake. SEE: **garlooroony.**

goorladany *noun.* large wooden spear.

goorlam *noun.* dark-coloured rubbish found in native beehives. SEE: **jaroom.**

goorlanggeny, goorlanggel, goorlanggem, goorlangginy *noun.* poor thing. • Nyanini, 'Ngoowan goorlanggel-ngage, yambarra-gilaya.' *She said, 'No, (don't kill her on me) poor thing, she has lots of hair.'* SEE: **gaageny.**

Goorlany *noun.* **1.** place belonging to the wedge-tailed eagle somewhere near Fletcher/Stoney Creek south of Warrmarn. **2.** place near Carola Gully (Growler Gully) with many springs.

goorlany *noun masculine.* kangaroo tail cooked then pounded together with blood and put into raw guts. • Goorlayi-yoorroong ngoorraya-yoo. *They made it into* goorlany.

goorlawoorlal *noun feminine.* water goanna species. [NOTE: mother of *wigamany*]

goorlawoorlal *noun feminine.* restless flycatcher, scissors grinder. *Myiagra inquieta.* [NOTE: stress on second syllable *goo'rlawoorlal*; cousin for willie wagtail, this bird looks like the willie wagtail but has white under the chin]

Goorlawoon *noun.* a place near Nyidbarriya in Purnululu National Park. [NOTE: Janama skin]

goorlgoom *noun.* waist.

goorlgoon coverb+BRING/TAKE. carry in hair belt.
- Goowooloom benamanyji mangadam-birri, goorlgoon benanyji-ngarriya. *He got a sharp stick that he had in his hair belt on his hip.*
- Thed janiyidji jirrawoogool, goorlgoon nyananyji. *He killed one and put it in his hair belt.* • Nginiyin, thed-jaliny nyaniyi, goorlgoon nyaliny nyanany. *He kept going, he killed another one and put it in his hair belt too.*

goorlgoon coverb+PUT. put in hair belt.
- Goorlgoon benayanyjende bangariny jiyirri-warriny. *He used to put a kangaroo on each side in his hair belt.*

goorlgoon coverb+DO_REFL. have hands on hips, stand with hands on hips. • Goorlgoon nginimiyinji. *He is standing with his hands on his hips.*

goorlgoordoogoordoo noun. conical paperbark headdress. SEE: **goomoonoongam**.

goorlirlij coverb+SAY/DO. have stomach rumbling from hunger. • Goorlirlij ngenarn jaam, goorninyan-nga. *My stomach is rumbling, I am hungry.*

goorliyirrel noun feminine. peewee, magpie lark. *Grallina cyanoleuca.* SEE: **birlirrijgel**.

goorloog coverb+GO/COME. die, die while walking in bush, die of thirst. • . . . goorloog-garri berrayinde-birri, bemberrayangbende-ngarri joowarrim berndere . . . *when people used to die and they put the dead bodies on the burial platform.* [NOTE: Shirley Purdie uses the word to mean 'die' by any means; Rusty Peters said it meant 'die from no water'] SEE: **nang**.

goorloog coverb+SAY/DO_M. water become small in dry time. SEE: **lintharrg**.

goorloom noun. water. SEE: **goorrngam**.

goorloongarnany, goorloongarnal, goorloongarnam adjective. water dweller.

goorloordoogjel; goorloordoordoogjel noun feminine. peaceful dove. *Geopelia striata.*

goorloony noun masculine. water in a specified place. SEE: **goorrngany**.

goorloorrgirrem noun. injection.

goorloorr-goorloorr coverb+PUT. poke with stick. • Goorloorr-goorloorr ngoorrayangbende, ngardawoogoowany yiligindi thaloorroone. *They were poking him, making him cry inside the hollow log.*

goorloowanginy; goorloowabany noun masculine. cold-season rain.

Goorloowarren noun. name sometimes given to the Northen dialect of Gija.

goorloowoorloony, goorloowoorlool, goorloowoorloom adjective. watery one, fluid in movement (of person). • Goorloowoorloony mayiny bendereg boomannha. *Make that watery dough more sticky.* • Dala goorloowoorlool warrg-garri nyerne. *That woman twists herself around when she is dancing.* • Danya goorloowoorloo wiyinji madi nyiyinji. *He twists his backside around, copying her.*

goorloorroogoo directional. up.

goornag coverb+FALL/GO_DOWN. change.
- Goornag nginiward. *He changed.* SEE: **goorag**.

goornag coverb+SAY/DO_REFL. take turns.
- Goornagji berramiyinbende-yoo, ngajiboo. *The two brothers used to take turns (at looking after us in two different places).*

goornag coverb+GIVE. change, translate, exchange. • Berrem ganarram goornag beniyinha merlga-yoorroong. *Cash this cheque.* LIT: 'Take this cheque/large note and exchange it for individual notes'. • Berrem jarragboo goornag beniyinha Gija-yoorroong. *Translate these words into Gija.*

goornawool REDUP: **goornawoornawoom**. noun feminine. little girl before puberty.

goornawoorriny noun masculine. little boy.

goorndarril, goorndarriny, goorndarrim noun. fish (generic). [NOTE: generic is feminine *goorndarril*, if species is known the word agrees with the gender of that species]

goorndoogal noun feminine. child, little girl.

goorndoogany noun masculine. child, little boy.

goorndoorlbal noun. yellow ball flower, small tree with yellow fruit. *Mallotus nesophilus.* [NOTE: fruit described as having 'yellow stuff' that needs washing off, washed by putting the fruit in a soak hole and allowing it to float to the top; when eaten fruit makes the mouth red]

goorndoorlji, goorndoorloo REDUP: **goorndoorl-goorndoorloo**. noun. yellow ochre.

goorndoorlji, goorndoorlool, goorndoorloo; goorndoo-goorndoolool, goorndoo-goorndooloo, goorndoorl-goorndoorloo adjective. yellow.
- Goorndoorloo dam thad benajtha. *Stand up those yellow ones.*

goorndoorndoogam noun. children. SEE:

goorn'gany

goorndoogany, goorndoogal.
goorn'gany *noun.* bull ant species.
goorninya *coverb+SAY/DO.* be hungry.
- Goorninya berrani-yoo miyale-boorroo. *They were hungry for meat.*

goorninyag *coverb+GET.* make hungry.
- Goorninyag gemberremenbe dam ngardboo-garre boorroordboo miyale. *That smell coming from the meat is making me hungry.*

goorninyag *coverb+FALL/GO_DOWN.* make self hungry. • Goorninyag barrewoonha-gili. *Make yourselves hungry.*

goorninyany; goorninyal; goorninyam *adjective.* hungry. • Gerrij-gala nherang goorninyan-ngage. *I'll have to finish it up, I'm hungry.* • Goorninyal wanyji. *She might be hungry.*

goornoogal *noun feminine.* rosella yam. *Abelmoschus ficulneus.* [NOTE: listed in Purdie et al. (2018) as 'rosella yam' with the description: 'this small plant grows on black soil areas that become boggy in the wet season, it has pretty pale pink hibiscus flowers'; possibly also used to refer to a different species as it has been described as 'a plant species with white flowers and edible root that if eaten raw makes lots of spit come to the mouth']

gooroogoorany REDUP: gooroo-gooroogooram. *noun masculine.* old man.

goorooj *coverb+GET.* scoop up something with hand. • Marlam-birri goorooj nherem yawoony-yoorroong. *I'll have to scoop it up into the coolamon with my hand.*

gooroomboorrg *coverb+GET.* get a big mob of something. • Majoorroom-ngarri yarranya nawarram gooroomboorrg yambarrama booloomanbi. *Out of that muster we got a lot of bullocks for the meatworks.* • Gooroomboorrg bemberrayidbe goorndarrim. *They got a big mob of fish.*

Gooroongoon *noun.* place near the airport at Warrmarn.

gooroongool *noun feminine.* dangerous night bird that takes away the spirits of children. SEE: **doowagoony**

gooroongoony *noun masculine.* name given to a number of small, strongly smelling herbs. *Pterocaulon serrulatum, Stemodia* ssp. [NOTE: smoke used to bring back spirit of child stolen by dangerous night bird called *gooroongool* or *doowagoony*; can be placed under child's pillow to prevent the spirit being stolen; medicinal, good for colds] SEE: **manyanyiny**

Gooroorrbin *noun.* Chamberlain Gorge.

gooroorrji *noun.* winged terminalia, also other terminalia species. *Terminalia platyptera.* [NOTE: name also given to different *Terminalia* species trees growing near sign north of community saying '5 miles to Warmun']

gooroorroonggoony *noun masculine.* nail-tailed wallaby. *Onychogalea unguifera.* SEE: **goon'goodoogoodoony, woorrood-woorroodji, woordoorr-woordoorrji.** [NOTE: left-handed from the dreamtime, *ngarranggarnin;* Janama skin; brother-in-law of the moon]

gooroorroony *coverb+FALL/GO_DOWN.* all die.
- Daawirrine-boorroo gooroorroony-ngarri berraard, ngoorrooma wirli-wirlin. *It is the place where all the people who have passed away used to camp, up there on top.* SEE: **goord.**

gooroorrooroorrool *noun.* termites, white ants. SEE: **moonggoorlool.**

gooroowal *noun.* stone spearhead. SEE: **jimbirlal.**

gooroowarrbany *noun.* hailstones. SEE: **gerawarrel.**

goorra-goorral *noun.* channel-billed cuckoo, storm bird. *Scythrops novaehollandiae.* [NOTE: The koel and the channel-billed cuckoo are both known as 'the storm bird' because they appear just before the wet season; their loud calls are sometimes described as 'swearing']

Goorra-goorran *noun.* place on Bow River, place of the channel-billed cuckoo or storm bird

goorralg-goorralg *coverb+GO_ALONG.* brolga call made while flying along, storm bird call.
- Marrarn goorrarndale goorralg-goorralg wananyande goorloorroogoo. *The brolga was already going along up there calling 'goorralg-goorralg' as she went along.*

goorramindiny, goorramindil, goorramindim *noun.* flowers of the snappy gum tree, *thalngarrji.*

goorrandal; goorrarndal *noun feminine.* brolga. *Grus rubicunda.* [NOTE: interview with Rusty Peters and Eileen Bray suggests this is really *goorrandal;* the *rn* spelling is included as it has been spelled that way for a long time and in several publications]

goorrandal; goorrarndal *noun feminine.* type of grasshopper with green and yellow stripes down its long body. • Merewangarril gerlalbamga wayinigana goorrandal boorroorn-ngiyi. *They call it (the same name as) the brolga because it has long legs.* [NOTE: see *marl-marl* for another example sentence]

goorrarrg *coverb+SAY/DO.* call made by blue-winged kookaburra. SEE: **jawoorrg-jawoorrg**.

goorrg *coverb+GET; coverb+SAY/DO_M.* pull out (e.g. kidney fat from kangaroo, seeds from cycad palm). • Goorrg bemberramangbende. *They used to pull it (the kidney fat) out.* • Goorrg woomberramande dam ganjim. *They used to pull out those seeds (from the cycad).*

goorrgoom *noun.* hole in ground used for cooking.

goorrgoorrjil *noun feminine.* tawny frogmouth. *Podargus strigoides.*

goorr-goorr *coverb+GO_ALONG.* go along saying *goorr-goorr* (the sound made by the tawny frogmouth). • Goorrgoorrjil, goorr-goorr-ngarri wiyinyande. *The tawny frogmouth goes along saying 'goorr-goorr'.* • Goorr-goorr woomberriyinbe-boorroo, ngalany-ngarri boorroorn. *They go along saying 'goorr-goorr' to them (people) when they sing.*

goorrijil *noun feminine.* mother-in-law/daughter-in-law relationship.

goorrijiny *noun.* woman's mother-in-law's brother.

goorriya *particle* keep doing then, just do then • Goorriya ninanyge. *I took him then.* • Goorriya George, 'Niwige'. *Then George said, 'I will take him.'*

goorrjalji *noun masculine.* small black biting march fly. [NOTE: found near water at the same time as *minyjiwarrany*, 'black plum' fruit]

goorrjibbany *coverb+HIT.* knock something (e.g. flying fox with a stick). • Goorrjibbany-gala barrij goowoolem-birri. *You all go along knocking it down.*

goorrngam *noun.* water. SEE: **goorloom**.

goorrnga-girrem dam bemberrooloonboo-ngarri-ngiyi. *noun.* car radiator (that place where they put water for her)

goorrngany *noun masculine.* water in a specified place. SEE: **goorloony**.

-goorroo *suffix.* your relation. [NOTE: attached to stem of relationship terms and followed by gender marker; gender agrees with relation possessed, e.g. *ngaboo-goorroony*, 'your father'; *goora-goorrool*, 'your mother']

goorroobardool, goorroobardoony *noun.* boomerang. SEE: **baljarranggool, gamanyjel, garrabiril, jinybal**.

goorrooj *coverb+HIT.* carry with hands down. • Goorndoogal goorrooj ngiyinya rarribany. *The little girl is carrying a basket*

Goorroomooloo *noun.* big rockhole on Stoney Creek upstream from old mining place. [NOTE: Anglo American later reopened the mine as Sally Mallay then the name was changed to Savannah Nickel Mine.]

goorrooranggoolji; gerreranggoolji *noun.* magpie. *Gymnorhina tibicen eylandtensis.* SEE: **gemerlawoorroony**. [NOTE: some people use this word for *wirrindiny*, the pied butcherbird]

goorroorroo *coverb+SAY/DO_M.* throw stick. • Dama yagenginyi wiji nginiyin, goorroorroo wanema, jad, aa, dama na. *That other one ran away, (this one) threw a stick and it was stuck on him (that other one) then.*

goothoongoony; goothoongool; goothoongoom *adjective.* short. SEE: **goothoongoowarra-**.

goothoongoowarrany; goothoongoowarral; goothoongoowarram *adjective.* short. SEE: **goothoongoony**.

goowa *particle.* just, or, but. • Gawoorra yagengerram? Goowa gayiyanyji. *Where are all the others. I just don't know where they are.* • Goowa gayi. *I just don't know where.* • Goowa gaboo ngenarn. *I just don't know what I'm doing.* SEE: **goo, goowoo**. [NOTE: emphatic form of *goo, goowoo*; dubitative linking particle, often precedes interrogatives]

goowaleny REDUP: **goowale-walem**. *noun.* small round hill. [NOTE: often used by Yalarrji Jack Britten to describe the small round hills in the country he painted]

goowarri *coverb+PUT.* block someone by holding a fighting stick at both ends to ward off blows. • Goowarri benajtha. *You block him/her.*

goowarrigalel *noun feminine.* woman who is good at fighting with a nulla-nulla holding both ends of the stick to block the other person's blows. • Goordooroom goowarrigalel-anyji. *She might be good at holding both ends of the* stick and blocking the other person's blows.

goowarroolji *noun masculine.* white currant. *Flueggea virosa.* SEE: **ngoorrwany, roonggoony, berenggarrji.** [NOTE: shrub bearing masses of small edible white fruit in the wet season; names *goowarroolji* and *berenggarrji* also given to the 'black currant', *Antidesma ghesaembilla*]

Gooweriny *noun.* Mad Gap, place in Paddy Bedford's mother's country.

gooweriny *noun.* cypress pine. *Callitris intratropica.* [NOTE: a tree with fragrant wood; its ash smeared on babies' heads]

goowirriny *noun.* coolamon. • Bib-gala yarrem dany goowirriny joomboony-ngirri. *Help me pick up (let's pick up) that coolamon, it is too heavy for me.* SEE: **larndoorrji, yawoonyji.**

goowoo; goo *particle.* only, just, or, but. SEE: **goowa.** [NOTE: dubitative linking particle, often precedes interrogatives]

goowooleny, goowoolem; goowooloony, goowooloom *noun.* tree, stick, plant. SEE: **goonyjany.**

Goowoorljin *noun.* Six Mile.

gooyarrg *coverb+SAY/DO.* pick up, collect.
• Gooyarrg berne marloorloom. *Pick up some kindling.* • Woorrg-garri boorroowoonbe, gooyarrg boorroorn. *When they all fall down they pick them up.* • Goorndoorndoogambi gooyarrg berrani ngarrgalem. *All the children were gathering rocks.*

gooyarrg *coverb+GET.* pick up, collect.
• Goorndarrim gooyarrg benamanyji. *He is collecting fish.*

gooyarrg *coverb+GO_ALONG.* go picking up, go collecting. • Jimbirlambi dambi ngarrgalembi gooyarrg ngiliyin'ge. *I (bowerbird) go along collecting those stone spearheads.*

gooyoorrg *coverb+SAY/DO.* spit. • Nginyjinyi lawoony bed woomenji balawan dany garn'giny gooyoorrg-garri nginini, lawoony-lawoony nandiji-ningi. *This lemonwood grows on the flat ground from when that moon spat and said, 'You will be white like that.'*

gooyoorrgboo *coverb+HIT.* speak with power to change state/country. • Wayinigana gooyoorrgboo benayidji. *Because of that he (moon) spoke and changed them forever.* SEE: **wiyawoog.**

I i

-i, -iyi *suffix.* topic/focus marker. SEE: **-bi, -ji.**

Jj

-ja *suffix.* like, similar to. [NOTE: suffixed to nominals, followed by gender suffix]

jaa *coverb+BURN/BITE.* heat something. • Jaa-gala bendoowarre. *Put the water on to boil.*

jaa REDUP: **jaa-jaa**. *coverb+PUT.* put something on fire to heat, warm something. • Jaa-gala benaj nalijam-boorroo. *Put on some water for tea.* • Berrema jaa boomberrayangbe gardagbi nalijam-boorroo. *They are boiling the billys for tea.*

jaam *noun.* stomach. • Jaam mooloorroo nginini. *He was sad.* [NOTE: part of body where emotions are felt]

Jaangari *noun.* a skin name (when spoken to).

Jaangariny *noun masculine.* a skin name (when spoken about).

jaawag *coverb+SPEAR.* made pregnant. • Jaawag boomberrangaboord werlerlemenbega. *The young women all got pregnant.*

jaawany; jaawawany *coverb+BECOME.* become pregnant. • Moorniny-moorninygan wayinigana jaawawany woomberrayid. *They keep fucking and so they become pregnant.*

jabananggany *noun masculine.* rain from the south. • Danya ngerig ngidji jabananggany, boorliyirr waniyid ngoorrinya. *That big rain is coming from the south.*

jabarr *coverb+SAY/DO.* make a noise behind someone. • Jabarr-anyji berrani gayany. *Maybe they made a noise somewhere behind him.* SEE: **jagard**.

jabayiny *noun.* river fig. *Ficus coronulata*. SEE: **ganambiny**. [NOTE: grows near river but has fruit on ends of branches, unlike *jawoonany*, 'cluster fig', *F. racemosa*, that bears fruit along the trunk and main branches and is often found in similar habitat]

jabig *coverb+GO/COME.* go up to the end (source) of the river or right on top of something (e.g. hill or tree). • Jabig yarrayi gaande. *We will go upstream to the end (i.e. source) of the river.* • Danya jabig nginiyi goowoolen. *He climbed right on top of the tree.*

jabijbe *coverb+GO/COME.* go as high as possible in a tree. • Jabijbe nginiyin. *He climbed right up the tree as far as he could go.*

jabirriny, jabirrim *noun masculine.* spearhead made from iron (e.g. horse shoe or shovel blade).

jaboogool, jaboogoom *noun.* deep dish, tin, basin, rubbish bin.

jaboolany *noun.* subincision. [NOTE: swearing]

jaboorr *coverb+GO_ALONG.* walk in water splashing feet. • Jaboorr wiyinji goorrngan. *He went along splashing his feet in the water.*

jad *coverb+FALL/GO_DOWN.* stand up (e.g. grey hair standing up), take a standing position. • Marrarn boolgambi jad berraward-ninggi. *You already have grey hair (lit. Grey hair has already stood up on you).*

jad *coverb+PUT.* place something in an upright position, stand something upright in ground. • Jad benayanyji. *He stuck it upright in the ground.* • Jad nheraj. *Let me stand it upright.*

jad REDUP: **jad-jad**. *coverb+BE/STAY.* be standing upright. • Berrema yilag ngarrgalem berrem jad-garri boorroonboo. *Down here at the bottom (of the painting) some hills are standing upright.*

jad *coverb+GO_THROUGH.* place something in an upright position in ground. • Nginyjiny woordoorr-woordoorrji, jiyirriny dany wanyaginy, jad-garri woongamenji dam-ningi, manam, ngenengga jilan tharriyarrem boorab boorroordboo-yarri. *This nail-tailed wallaby, a kind of little kangaroo, puts his tail down here in the ground and rainbows come out on us.*

jadagen; jadagin *temporal.* wet season. • Jadagi-moowan bawoo-wawoo ngenarn. *Only in the rain time, I call out.*

jadag-jadag *coverb+FALL/GO_DOWN.* cloud build-up in hot time, be the time when little bits of cloud start coming in one by one (not when they come as big storm clouds). • Jadag-jadag-garri ngoowoonji dany ngoomoolji, barndem dam loordboo-ngarri woomberriyinbe, linyjil-ningi dany bin'gany. *When the clouds start to build up and the sun becomes very hot,* linyjilji, *the smoky cabbage gum, is laden with* bin'gany, *sugar leaf (lerp species).* SEE: **jawoorl-jawoorl**.

jada-jadawany *coverb+SAY/DO_M.* be raining.

- Nginya jada-jadawany woomenji danyga. *This (painting shows) when it is starting to rain.*

jadany *noun masculine.* rain. • *Danya jadany ngidji-yarri ngirribag ngini-yarri. That rain is coming, it is getting close to us.* [NOTE: Rammey Ramsey used this word to mean 'waterfall'; more common word for 'waterfall' is *thoolooloorrji*]

jadayadab *coverb+GO/COME.* come down and run along (e.g. brolga). • *Jadayadab noombanha-ngoo. You are down running along now.*

Jadibany *noun.* Hadler Spring near Kilfoyle.

jadiwiriny *noun.* western brown snake. *Pseudonaja nuchalis.*

jag *coverb+GO/COME.* appear in sky (e.g. one cloud, new moon). • *Jag giniyin ngenengga ngoomoolji. One cloud came out here.*

jagard REDUP: **jagard-jagard.** *coverb+SAY/DO.* move behind someone. • *Rangga nginji gayi jagard-garri birrirn. He (wallaby) is listening for anyone coming up somewhere behind him.* SEE: **jabarr.**

Jagarra *noun.* a skin name (when spoken to).

Jagarrany *noun masculine.* a skin name (when spoken about).

jagij REDUP: **jagij-jagij.** *coverb+SAY/DO.* poke/stab something. • *Ngarayi benayid, jagija nyerne, dama waanyim yilag. She (crow) found them and is now stabbing them (with her beak), those maggots down there.*

jagij *coverb+SPEAR.* stab. • *Ngaliyangem-birri thoowerndem jagij benangaboordja, yiligi-biny, berrema. She (emu chick) was stabbing with her beak from inside.*

jagij *coverb+SPEAR_REFL.* poke self/each other. • *Dama jangada-warriny jagij birringanybi-yoo. Those two little boys will poke each other with a stick.* • *Jagij birringandijbe. They will poke each other.*

jagirr *coverb+GO_ALONG.* be jabbing at something while going along. • *Jagirr wananyjende-ngooyoo doomoo-moowan. It was jabbing at her head all the way (snake wrapped around woman who was walking along).*

jagoola *noun.* subincision. [NOTE: swearing]

jagoorlil, jagoorlim REDUP: **jagoo-jagoorlim.** *noun.* pearl shell. *Pinctada maxima.* [NOTE: used to be traded from the west on the *wirnan* exchange and was an important part of men's ceremony]

jaj *coverb+PUT.* dip (e.g. bread in soup). • *Jaj benayanya mayim wooroo-yoorroong. She dipped the bread in the soup.*

jaja *noun.* maternal grandfather. SEE: **thamanyji, jawoojiny.** [NOTE: Jaru address form sometimes used by Gija people, used in Gija Kriol]

jalabgany, jalabgal, jalabgam *adjective.* straight as a post, tall and straight, nice looking. • *Jalabgan-ngoo. You are as straight as a post.*

jalag *coverb+SAY/DO_M.* open something out (e.g. when digging something). • *Ngarrgale-bany-anyji woorrgaj-gala noondaj, jalag ngelema-ni. If there is a big rock I'll have to pull it out and open it (the hive when digging ground sugarbag).*

jalariny *noun.* egret, (Kriol 'white crane'). *Ardea alba.* [NOTE: star separate from Milky Way; relates to story in which *jalariny* says, 'no fish'; other story features egret (white crane) and wedge-tailed eagle (eaglehawk)]

jalawer *coverb+SAY/DO_M.* being straight (stems of a bush). • *Jalawer wanema nginya jiwiny. This small Acacia shrub has straight stems.*

jalawoonany *noun.* willy-willy. • *Jalawoonany ngidji-yarri, nawarranyi. A willy-willy is coming to us, a big one.*

jalawoorr *coverb+SAY/DO.* water run down, big pouring rain, be storm coming. • *Jalawoorr ngerne. The water runs down.*

jalayi *coverb+HIT.* get halfway from/to somewhere. • *Jalayi nginiyidji Fig Tree Hole-biny. He was halfway out from Fig Tree Hole.*

jalba REDUP: **jalba-jalba.** *coverb+GET.* catch up with someone both in the literal sense and in the sense that one was born and knew an older person while they were still alive. • *Ngoowan jalba yirramanyi. We could not catch up with it (something that was too fast).* [NOTE: *jalba* can also be used to talk about the next child born after someone. • *Jalba nginimanya. She caught him up (i.e. she was born next after him).*]

jalbaga-woorroony, jalbaga-woorrool, jalbaga-woorroom *adjective.* one that can't be caught up with.

jaleng *coverb+PUT.* heap firewood. • *Jaleng benayanyji marnem. He is heaping up firewood.*

jalgirrigirriny *noun.* long tom, freshwater garfish. *Strongylura krefftii.* SEE: **bayirrany.**

jalgoorrg

jalgoorrg REDUP: jalgoo-jalgoorrg. *coverb+GO/COME*. stars twinkling. • Ngelela wardal, jalgoo-jalgoorrg-garri nyaniyi wardal. *This is the starry night, when all the stars are twinkling (talking about a painting).*

jalgoorrji *noun masculine*. sharp hill, pointed hill.

jalij *coverb+SAY/DO*. rain fall, be raining. • Jadany jalij-garri nginini-yarri, daambi men'gawoog benamanyji-yoowoo. *When it rained on us, it made the country good for us.* • Jalij gerne. *It is raining.*

jalij *coverb+BECOME*. rain fall, be raining. • Jadany jalij wiyinji. *It is raining.*

jalij *coverb+FALL/GO_DOWN*. rain fall, be raining. • Jalij nginiwardji-yarri jadany mendoowoon. *It rained last night.* • Jalijboo ngoowoonji. *It is raining now.*

jalij *coverb+SAY/DO_M*. rain fall, be raining. • Jalij wanemayinde, jalij, jalij. *It kept on raining and raining and raining.*

jalijgel *noun feminine*. freshwater prawn, cherabin. *Macrobrachium spinipes*.

jalinggirig *coverb+PUT*. sharpen. • Jalinggirig benayanyji. *He sharpened it.* SEE: **boorr-boorr, gooraj-gooraj**.

jalinggirig *coverb+GET*. sharpen. • Gooraj-gooraj nyanini, jalinggirig nginimanyande. *She sharpened it until it was sharp.* SEE: **boorr-boorr, gooraj-gooraj**.

jalinggiriny, jalinggiril, jalinggirim *adjective*. sharp.

Jalinggirringen *noun*. Five Mile, a place where Ganggamel, a spirit woman, rested in dreamtime.

jaliny SEE: **nyaliny**.

jaliwoob *coverb+HIT*. poison fish by soaking large amounts of spinifex or other vegetation in water. • Goorndarril, jaliwoob nyimberrayidbende. *They used to poison fish.* SEE: **jaloowib**.

jaliwoob *coverb+GET*. get fish by poisoning. • Jaliwoob ngoorramangbende danyi goorndarriny, mangoonybe-birri. *They used to get fish by poisoning with river mangrove.* SEE: **jaloowib**.

jalmoorrg *coverb+HIT*. smash. • Jalmoorrg nimbiyinha-ngoo. *I'll smash you.* [NOTE: Southern dialect]

jaloob *coverb+GET*. soak something. • Goorloom jaloob-gala benem. *Soak this in the water.*

jaloorl-jaloorl *coverb+BE/STAY*. scrape and make smooth. • Jaloorl-jaloorl boorroonboo damga, ngara-ngarag-garri boorroorn, larndoorrja-yilim. *They scrape it (lump off tree, burl) out and make it smooth inside like a coolamon.*

jaloowib; jaloowoob *coverb+GET*. poison fish by soaking large amounts of spinifex or other vegetation in water. • Jaloowib-ngarri ngoorramangbende, nyeg woomberramande-ni garn'gool dam-birri, nyeg goorrayangbende, wanyji lenggale-birri, wanyji doowoo-doowoo ngoorrayidbendi dam, doowoo ngoorrayidbende dam-ni. *When they poison fish, they hit the water with the curly wattle branches, sometimes they hit the water with the roots (of the river mangrove), sometimes they chop off the bark and use that.* [NOTE: people used to have big meetings at Blue Hole in the Purnululu National Park to do this; they used *gerlerneny*, 'tall spinifex', ordinary tree branches, *garliwoony*, 'bloodwood gum' or *garn'goolji*, 'Acacia species with curly seed pods and large flat hairy leaves'. Three men did the breaking up.]

jalyberrnga *coverb+FOLLOW*. come behind someone and catch/attack. • Jalyberrnga nyimberramiyanboowoo / Jalyberrnga nyimberramayanbe. *They came along behind and caught up with her and attacked her.*

jama *coverb+SAY/DO*. put things together, get things ready for an event. • Baalem jamangarri -nyanininoowa-. *When she bundled the ceremonial goods together for him (grandson who was going to initiation ceremony).*

jamarndaji *noun*. cluster fig, fruit of cluster fig. *Ficus racemosa*. SEE: **jawoonany, goonangginy, ngalalabany**. [NOTE: has fruit on trunk and branches, found near water]

jambalgeny, jambalgel, jambalgem *adjective*. sticking out. • Warna-warnarral ngarranggarnil dala, gernanyjel, berrema bagam jambalgem. *She is from long ago in the dreamtime that porcupine (echidna), she has prickles sticking out here.* [NOTE: Southern dialect]

jambalngarriny REDUP: jamba-jambalngarrim. *noun*. young man.

jamberramannha *verb*. you all were GETTING them/it (non-singular).

jamberramannhande *verb*. you all kept on

GETTING them/it (non-singular).
jamberramennha verb. you all are GETTING them/it (non-singular).
jamberramoorloowarda verb. you HAD/KEPT them/it (non-singular).
jamberrayanande verb. you all kept on PUTTING them/it (non-singular).
Jambin; Jambirn noun. a skin name (when spoken to).
Jambinji; Jambirnji noun masculine. a skin name (when spoken about).
jambinbaroony noun masculine. black bream. SEE: **garriyil**.
jambirrany, jambirral, jambirram REDUP: jambi-jambirram. adjective. pretty. • Jambirral ngagenyil. *My pretty one (feminine).*
jambirrimnha verb. you all will GET them/it (non-singular).
jambirrimnhande verb. you all will keep GETTING them/it (non-singular).
jambooggany, jambooggal, jambooggam REDUP: jamboo-jambooggam. adjective. bumpy, lumpy. • Berrema-noo bagoo-ngarri nginji wanyaginy, jamboo-jambooggam. *The little boy's bed here is too bumpy.*
jamboorn REDUP: jamboorn-jamboorn. coverb+PUT. heap up/ fill up. • Yilag boomberrayangbe-yoo gerlernem jamboorn. *They heaped up the tall spinifex at the bottom.* • Ngarem-ninggi jamboorn-ngarri dam gardagbe, gadagjen joolooj goorrayangbende. *You should have seen how much honey they used to fill the billy can with and then carry it along. / You should have seen how full with honey the billy can was when they carried it along.* • Ngarrgalem jamboorn-jamboorn benayanyji ngarnaga gawalalanygarre gawarren. *He piled a lot of stones up the side of the hill.*
jamboorn coverb+HAVE. be full. • Daliyi wilbarrali jamboorn benemoorloonya ngarrgalem. *The wheelbarrow is full of rocks. (lit. The wheelbarrow keeps the rocks.)* [NOTE: inanimate subject of transitive verb]
jamboorn REDUP: jamboorn-jamboorn. coverb+BE/STAY. be full (e.g. waterhole, receptacle), be heaped up (e.g. stones). • Jamboorn nginji. *It is full.*
jamboorn coverb+FALL/GO_DOWN. go down and fill, fill deep hole (water running). • Goorloony girliwirring ngidji, jamboorn ngoowoonji.

The water is going down from up there filling it (waterhole). • Berrema dagoorlan jamboorn ngoowoonji. *Here is the deep rockhole, it is filling up (with water).* • . . . yoorloo ngidji, dagoorlan-noo, jamboorn ngoowoonji goorloony . . . *it goes down to the deep rockhole and fills it with water.*
jamboorn coverb+SAY/PUT_REFL. fill deep hole (water running). • Nginya gerliwirring wiji ngerne, goorloony, jamboorn ngiyilinji dan yilag gidji, jamboorn ngenengga. *This (water shown in a painting) runs down from on top and fills the waterholes, it fills it there and then goes down and fills this one here.*
jamboorn REDUP: jamboorn-jamboorn. coverb+GET. gather and fill up. • Jamboorn nyimberramangbende goonjal, biriwoorrg berrayinde-yirri daan. *They used to gather them (kapok bush roots) filling (their containers) and come back to us in the camp.*
jamboorral noun feminine. slippery lizard. *Ctenotus robustus*, and other skinks with 'shiny' skin.
Jamelayigoon noun. Fig Tree Hole, a place in Paddy Bedford's father's country. [NOTE: has also been recorded as 'Victory Hole'; Victory Hole and Fig Tree Hole sound the same when pronounced using the Gija sound system]
jamerndel noun. ant hill, termite mound, antbed. [NOTE: old Gija men in Halls Creek said that they were not allowed to say this word or a big cyclone would come; Gija men in Warrmarn used to say the word but warned that young men were not allowed to touch or eat the termite larvae.] SEE: **ngawagool**.
jamoo coverb+GO/COME. lots come together. • Jamoo berrayin melagawoom. *Lots of people all came in together. (Kriol: 'They all bin heap up.')* SEE: **nyawoorn, jamboorn**.
jamoone particle. not ready, not yet. • Jamoone yarra marrge. *We are not ready, wait.*
jamoonin; jaminin particle. soon, not yet.
jamoorr noun. lap. SEE: **birrmale**.
jamoorrg coverb+PUT. put on lap (e.g. child). • Jamoorrg noonayangge ngagenybe ganggam. *I put my grandchildren on my lap.*
jamoorrg coverb+FALL/GO_DOWN. get on lap. • Jamoorrg nginiwardji-ni. *He sat down on his lap.*
jana coverb+GO_ALONG. prowl, walk around at night, hunt at night. • Jana wananyji

janaj

mendoowoon. *Someone (male) was prowling around last night.* • Jana wananya. *She was prowling about.* • Jana woomberranyboo. *They two were prowling about.*

janaj *coverb+PUT.* put honey in stringy beaten inner bark of eucalypt, *bijam*, to strain or suck. • Jirrayam janaj benaj. *Alright put it to strain it (honey in pieces of coolibah string,* bijam*).*

janaj *coverb+GET.* mix together stringy beaten inner bark of eucalypt, *bijam*, with honey to suck or extract. • Goorloom jaloob-gala benem, janaja benem. *Soak it with water and then mix it with the honey.*

janaj-janaj *coverb+SAY/DO.* put honey in stringy beaten inner bark of eucalypt, *bijam*, to strain or suck. • Janaj-janaj boorroorn ngarem bijam-birri thoong boorroorn. *They strain the honey with the beaten inner bark of the coolabah and suck it.*

Janama *noun.* a skin name (when spoken to). [NOTE: Miriwoong; used by some Gija]. SEE: **Jawan**.

Janamany *noun.* a skin name (when spoken about). [NOTE: Miriwoong; used by some Gija]. SEE: **Jawanji**.

jananynha *verb.* 1. you (one) were GOING ALONG. 2. you (one) were BRINGING/TAKING him/her/it.

jananynhande *verb.* 1. you (one) kept GOING ALONG. 2. you (one) kept on BRINGING/TAKING him/her/it.

janawany *noun masculine.* goanna species. [NOTE: 'Gija plants and animals' (Purdie et al. 2018) lists this as alternate name for 'water goanna'; Mabel Juli says it is a relation of *boonoonggoony*, 'hill country goanna' and lives in the hills.] SEE: **wigamany**.

janawoorran *verb.* you (one) BURNED/BIT him/her/ it.

janbaroorrg *coverb+BE/STAY.* be all standing together. • Ngarrgale-woorrarrem janbaroorrg boorroonboo. *All kinds of rocks are standing up all together.*

janbaroorrg *coverb+GO/COME.* all go out together (e.g. in back of truck). • Janbaroorrg boorroordboo ngoorr-ngoorrgajin gabiyanyji birriyan. *They are all in the truck, they must be going somewhere.*

jandamaji *noun.* boot (Jaru).

jandanbeny *adjective.* bony. • Tharrayabthitha wayiniya jandanben-ngoo. *You are a bony one with bones sticking out everywhere.*

janderre *noun.* rocks under a burial platform that are named to find out who killed the dead person.

Janderrji *noun.* Dolly Hole, a place in Paddy Bedford's mother's country.

jandiyandiny *noun masculine.* straw-necked and white ibis. *Threskiornis molucca, T. spinicollis.* SEE: **joodoojgajil**.

janema; janama *verb.* you SAID/DID.

janewan *verb.* you (one) WOUNDED him/her/it.

jang REDUP: **jang-jang**. *coverb+SAY/DO.* eat. • Goorndoorndoogam jang boorroorn minyjiwarrany. *The children are eating black plums.* • Jang berrani-gili mayim. *They ate food.* • Joorndam men'gawoom jang-girrim. *Bush onions are good to eat.* • Ngoowan dam jang nimbirn, yoorlag dimbirn. *Don't eat that, you will vomit.* • Jang-jang ngenarn. *I am eating.* • Jang-jang boorroorn-gili. *They are all eating.*

jang REDUP: **jang-jang**. *coverb+SAY/DO_M.* eat. • Jang jara. *You (one) can eat.* • Jang jarra-gili. *You all can eat.* • Jang-bija booma. *You (one) should eat.* • Jangboo woomenji. *He is eating now.* • Jang-gayan woomberramande, gigbawoom-anyji wanyagem. *Those kids have been eating all day, they must be full now.* • Jang-jang woomberrama. *They all ate.*

jang *coverb+BURN/BITE.* eat. • Jang-ayi ngoorrawoorranbende-yoo. *The two of them pretended to eat.*

jang *coverb+GO_ALONG.* go along eating.

jangadany, jangadal, jangadam REDUP: **jangangangadam**. *noun.* child, little one. [NOTE: Southern dialect] SEE: **goorndoogany**.

Jangala *noun.* a skin name (when spoken to).

Jangalany *noun masculine.* a skin name (when spoken about).

jangalangalany *noun masculine.* very small goanna species. *Varanus kingorum.* [NOTE: can't grow big from the dreamtime, *ngarranggarnin*] SEE: **lirri-lirriny**.

jangalangaliny *noun.* red ant species that goes in lines. SEE: **gangalangaliny**.

Jangalgin *noun.* Emu Island, a place in George Mung Mung's country.

jangal-jangal; janga-jangal *noun.* chains. SEE: **merdgajil**.

jangarrgany, jangarrgal, jangarrgam *adjective.* generous. • Danya jangarrgany wajnhawoony. *That one is a generous man, he*

jarlayi

is a person who gives things. • Dala jangarrgal wajnhawool. *That one is a generous woman, she is a person who gives things.* [NOTE: opposite of *dangoori*]

jangga-jangga *noun.* an internal body part described as 'little round guts'. [NOTE: big in bullock, small in kangaroo]

janggan *adverb.* when eaten. • Mirlim men'gawoom janggan. *Liver is good to eat.* • Dalga ngimirlil men'gawool janggan-ga. *That Leichhardt tree fruit is good when eaten.*

janggarr; janggarrg *coverb+HIT.* be new moon. • Garn'giny janggarr nginiyid. *The new moon came out.* • Janggarrg benayidji-birri-yoo, men'gawoo berrani-yoo. *When the new month came the two of them got better.*

janil, janim *noun feminine.* small mistletoe species. *Lysiana subfalcata.* • Berrem janim, boorroonboo-ngarri-wa ngarem-boorroo, ngarem-anyji boorroonboo ngenengga goowoole-yirrin. *When these little mistletoes called* janim *are there they are a sign of bush honey, there is probably honey here in all the trees.*

janigim *noun.* pubic covering. SEE: **jarnim**.

janiyida *verb.* you (one) HIT him/her/it, you (one) GAVE him/her/it.

jany *coverb+GET.* squeeze. • Jany benamanyji. *He squeezed it.*

jany; janynga *coverb+SAY/DO_M.* squeeze. • Gayirrim jany woomberramande wayini. *They used to squeeze out the ground sugarbag like this.* • Janynga woomberramande goowirri-yoorroong. *They used to squeeze it into the coolamon.*

janyoowoony *noun masculine.* grasshopper species, small pretty grasshopper like *moorrgoony* but bigger.

jara *verb.* you (one) should SAY/DO.

jara *coverb+GET.* sneak up on someone. • Mendoowiyan jara nginimanyji-noo. *He sneaked up on him in the middle of the night.* SEE: **bandaj, mari-mari, mariwoo**.

jara-jara *coverb+GO_ALONG.* go loafing about, bludging, go from camp to camp asking. • Ngiyi, ngiyi jara-jara wimbirrinbe ngoorroon-ngoorroon yagengen daan boorroordboo. *They go loafing about all over the place (kids whose parents are playing cards).*

jaramberle *noun.* big guts (internal body organ).

jaranel *noun.* marsupial mouse. *Pseudomys nanus, P. desertor.* [NOTE: makes mist like smoke on the hills in the wet time; also used for house mouse, *Mus musculusi*, and introduced rat, *Rattus rattus*.] SEE: **nyilimbiny, yiroowoonji**.

jaranggarril *noun feminine.* boomerang type. SEE: **baljarranggool, gamanyjel, garrabiril, goorroobardool, jinybal**.

jard *coverb+PUT.* put wood in place for fire. • Nyaman jard benaya marnem. *The old woman made a fire.* SEE: **jardgi**.

jarda *coverb+PLACE_M.* come upon something suddenly and get a shock. • Jarda waniyanyji-ni. *He came out and found him and was shocked. He was shocked (when he came and found him dead).*

jardgi *coverb+SAY/DO_M.* set wood in place for fire. • Jardgi woomberramande. *They made a fire.*

jardgi *coverb+SAY/DO.* set wood in place for fire. • Jardgi nginbirn. *I will make a fire.*

jardgi *coverb+PUT.* set wood in place for fire. • Jardgi binilinya marnem. *She is making fire.*

jardiny, jardinyji *noun masculine.* itchy grass, wallaby grass. *Chrysopogon fallax.* • Jardimbaya berrembi. *There is itchy grass here. / These have itchy grass.* [NOTE: Janama/Jawan skin]

jaringindij *coverb+BE/STAY.* standing up all around. • Gendoowagoo jaringindij ginji. *There is a line of hills standing up there.*

jariyi *coverb+GET.* save. • Jariyi-ngarri jambirrimnha dam ngerrenbe-boorroo, maroolooya yamberramoorliya daam, men'gawiya berrenbe. *By saving electricity you are helping the environment.*

jarl *coverb+PUT.* push quickly, give a shove, try to push someone into fighting. • Jarl nginiyanyji. *He pushed him to try to get him to fight.*

Jarlaloon *noun.* area near crossing of Ord River south of Warrmarn, an estate name.

jarlaloony *noun.* shitwood, helicopter tree. *Gyrocarpus americana.* [NOTE: wood used to make coolamons and, in recent times, other carved objects]

jarlangarnany *noun.* plains kangaroo, antilopine wallaby. *Macropus antilopinus.* LIT: 'plains dweller'. [NOTE: Jagarra skin] SEE: **warlambany** (male), **gawoorrngarndil** (female).

jarlanggam REDUP: **jarla-yarlanggam**. *noun.* creek, gully, break away.

jarlayi *noun.* friend. [NOTE: address form

Jarlbooroon

of *jarlijiny*]

Jarlbooroon noun. place between Bungle Bungles and Texas.

jarlboorr coverb+FALL/GO_DOWN. become blind.
- Moorliyi dam jarlboorr nginiwardji. *He was going blind.*

jarlboorrji, jarlboorrel, jarlboorroo adjective. blind. • Moorloo jarlboorroo. *Blind eye.*

jarlijiny, jarlijil, jarlijim noun. friend.
- Jirrawoonyga binarriwoorroony boorooj-girrimbi jarliji-gam-birri. *This one doesn't know how to play with his friends.*

jarlinybaroom; jarlinyjaroom noun. generational moiety. • Nginyjiny Jagarrany, Jaangariny, Jawalyiny, Jambinji, wayiningerreg jarlinybaroowarriny. *This Jagarra, Jaangari, Jawalyi and Jambinji, that many are one group together.* [NOTE: See Figure 9 Gija skin names, page 12] SEE: **yinara**.

jarl-jarl coverb+SAY/DO_REFL. give each other a shove, try to push each other into fighting. • Jarl nginiyanyji jarl-jarl-jaya birringirriyan-joo. 'Jilba-ma nirni-ni?'. *He is pushing the arm of the other man, they are pushing each other like that to fight, (and asking) 'Are you frightened of him?'*

jarloongoorroony, jarloongoorrool, jarloongoorroom adjective. good-looking.

jarloongoorroobarndegji noun. ringed brown snake, 'emu killer'. *Pseudonaja modesta*. [NOTE: one of three striped snake species called 'emu killer' by Gija people, other two are *goodawoodany* and *joowarribarndegji*] SEE: **jilyiwoony**.

Jarloowany noun. black hill on old Greenvale Station.

jarn coverb+HIT. cut sugarbag. • Jarn nyaniyidja ngarel. *She cut the sugarbag (feminine species).* • Jarn-gala biyij-ngiyi. *You cut the bush honey for her.*

jarnangarr coverb+GO/COME. urinate.
- Jarnangarr-gala ngenda. *I want to urinate.* [NOTE: not polite; *Ngenardge jaam-boorroo* 'I am going for stomach' is the polite form in mixed company]. SEE: **goomboowany**.

jarnangarre noun. bladder, urine.

jarnangarre noun. cockroach. *Cosmozosteria* spp. SEE: **goomboolanginy, goomboolangil**.

jarnim, janim noun. pubic covering, 'cock-rag'. SEE: **janigim, warlboorroo, nyagoom**. [NOTE: Rusty Peters says made from string but more like a present-day loin cloth, a 'naga' or 'cock-rag' (Kimberley Kriol terms), made from material other than that used for the type of pubic tassel, *nyagoom*, that is smaller]

jarn'girriny, jarn'girrim noun masculine. kind of grass, stick used for painting made from that grass. • Jarn'girrim men'gawoom dag-dag-girrem. *That little grass is good for painting dots.* [NOTE: has been recorded as another name for *beremerrel*, 'cumbungi, bullrush', *Typha domingensis* but Eileen Bray and Rusty Peters say it is a grass with stems that can be used for painting dots]

Jaroo noun. language spoken south of Gija, usually spelled 'Jaru'.

jaroogoony, jaroogool, jaroogoom adjective. fat person, person having big stomach. [NOTE: *goowooloony jaroogoony*, 'tree with a big stomach' can be used to mean *joomooloony*, 'boab tree']

jaroom noun. stomach (internal), large intestine. [NOTE: word also used to mean 'light-coloured rubbish found in native beehives', see Purdie et al. (2018:195)]

jaroongem temporal. yesterday, next morning. SEE: **ngooloo-ngooloon**.

jaroowenyji noun masculine. black box tree. *Eucalytus obconica*.

jarr coverb+BECOME. heal. • Jarr waniyidji gajimga, men'gawoo waniyid. *The sore healed up and he got better.*

jarr coverb+SAY/DO. heal. • Jarr nanini gajim. *Your sore has healed.* • Jarr ngenani gajimga, men'gawoo ngelayid. *My sore healed up and I got better.*

jarr coverb+PUT. recover, get better. • Jirrayam, jarr benayanyji-ngirri giningim. *I am alright. My heart has recovered (after a fright from nearly drowning).* [NOTE: impersonal construction with 'heart' as the object of the verb]

-jarra suffix. like that. [NOTE: attached to interrogatives and adverbials, followed by gender suffixes]

jarra verb. you all should SAY/DO.

jarrag REDUP: *jarrag-jarrag*. coverb+SAY/DO_M. talk. • Jarraga yirramanya daam-boorroo jirram na, wajbaloom bemberrangbe. *We talked about the country in the proper way and the whitemen put it (wrote it) down.*
- Jarrag-jarrag wanemayinde-yirri. *He used to*

talk to us.

jarrag *coverb+GET.* tell someone.
- Ngarranggarnin jarrag ngemberramande-yirri, gooram-birri, ganggam-birri. *In the old times our mothers and grandmothers told us.*

jarrag *coverb+SAY/DO.* talk. • Jarrag nginini. *He spoke.* • Jarrag-ma nerne-birri-yoo Gijam-birri? *Do you talk to the two of them in Gija?* • Yijiyan ngenarn-ninggi jarrag. *I am telling you the truth.* • Birrinybiyoo berrem yarroonya-ngarri-birri gamerrem jarrag ngerne-boorroo. *He talks about the sky and the earth here where we live.* • Jarrag yarrani daam-boorroo. *We talked about the country.* • Ngarrgalembi yambirrimnya-ma berrem jarrag-garri yarroorn manoom? *Will we get money for these words we are talking?*

jarrag *coverb+GO_ALONG.* speak language.
- Malngin joo Ngarinyman dal Gara-garag jarrag wananyande. *Queenie McKenzie used to speak Malngin and Ngarinyman.*

jarrag *coverb+BE/STAY.* speak, be speaking.
- 'Ngenden'ge ngayin-ga belegan jarrag ngenden, ngayin-ga Gijamayinde-nga,' nyanini. *'I'll stay here in the middle (in between), I'll speak Gija,' she said.*

jarrag REDUP: **jarrag-jarrag.** *coverb+SAY/DO_REFL.* talk to self/each other.
- 'Gaboowa narrangirriyin-joo?' 'Googan, jarrag yirrangirriyin-joo'. *'What have you two been talking about doing?' 'Nothing, we were just talking to each other.'* • Jarrag-jarrag giwingirrij-nenggab. *I will talk with you.* • Jarrag-jarrag yirringirriyan Gija-bayan-yarre yarren-ga. *We talk to each other, we really know our Gija language.*

jarragbawoorriny, jarragbawoorrool, jarragbawoorroom *adjective.* being unable to speak. • Jarragbawoorriny gamama ngerne. *He couldn't speak. He didn't know what to say.*

jarragbe; jarragboo *noun.* word, story, language, speech. • Berremga jarragbe-ngiyiwa gernanyjel. *This is the (dreamtime) story of echidna.* • Berrembi jarragbe noonayangge Gijam. *These are the words I put into Gija.* • Goonijibanyji ngenardge, rangga ninan'ge jarraggan Jambinji. *I must have been dreaming, I thought I heard Jambin talking.* • Miya ngenda-narri-gili; nawarram-ngirri jarragbooga linga-linga-ngarri ngenarn. *I just had to come to all of you because I have been thinking of something important to say.* • Reminy benanya jarragenaa-woorrool. *She was gasping for breath and could not talk (after being chased by a yoonggoony, 'hairy man').*

jarraggajim, jarraggajiny *noun.* radio, phone, microphone. • Marra ngenardge jarrag-jarrag-girrem, jarraggajim-birri dam, jadam-anyji ngoowiyan goo thoowoorranyji-boorroo. *I am going to talk on that radio about the weather (the rain or whatever).*

jarrag-jarrag *coverb+GO/COME.* talk.
- Nawarra-ngarri nyinya, daam-boorroo jarrag-jarrag-garri nyiniya, yanggiji-ngarri yinhemen-yoowoorroo daam-boorroo yoowoorriyangem. 'Gayi-ngarna-noongoo, nyingiyang-goorroombi dambi daambi?' *She (KLC employee) is the one who has the job of talking about country, the one who asks us about our country. 'Where do you belong, where is your country?'*

jarrama; jarrema *verb.* you all GOT him/her/it.
jarrama; jarrema *verb.* you all SAID/DID.
jarramanande *verb.* you were all SAYING/DOING.
jarramanha; jarremannha *verb.* you all were GETTING him/her/it.

jarrambayiny *noun masculine.* goanna, sand goanna. *Varanus panoptes, V. gouldii.*
- jarrambayim. *goannas.* jarrambayi-woorrarrem. *all kinds of goannas.* SEE: **ganyarrany, garndoowoolany.** [NOTE: the three words *ganyarrany, garndoowoolany,* and *jarrambayiny* are used interchangably to mean any kind of goanna by many people]

jarramennha; jarremennha *verb.* you all are GETTING him/her/it.

jarranang *coverb+BE/STAY.* sitting down looking straight ahead, be sitting down with knees up, be crouching. • Jirrgany jarranang nginji nawane. *The hill kangaroo is sitting down looking straight ahead in the cave.* [NOTE: old people used to say that young people should not sit down like this in front of them] SEE: **jarrboolab.**

jarranynha *verb.* you all were GOING ALONG.

jarrarrawoorl *coverb+GO/COME.* have body part twitching because of a relation. • Gamoom, jarrarrawoorl-ngarri birriyan ngalengangem-boorroo. *When they feel twitching in the breasts it is for their own children.*

jarrawoorl

jarrawoorl REDUP: **jarra-jarrawoorl**. *coverb+SAY/DO*. have some part of body throbbing tells you that some relation is coming, have nerves in body part jumping (different body parts remind you of different relatives). • Barnale jarrawoorl ngenarn ngaboony-anyji-noo. *The back of my shoulder is twitching, it must be for my father.*
• Jarra-jarrawoorl ngenarn. Yangoorranyji boorroordboo. Ngidji wanyji-nga goorndoogany. *My flesh is throbbing. Someone must be coming. Maybe it is my son.* SEE: **jarrarrawoorl, jirreg, woorlmooj-woorlmooj**.

jarrayilge *coverb+EAT*. make oneself really full by eating something.

jarrbaroog. *coverb+GET*. cover a long distance, travel far. • Daamga merewam-yoowoo jarrbaroog yamberremnya. *That country is a long way from us, we will have to go far to get there.* (Kriol: 'We got to catch up that far-away country.')

jarrbird *coverb+FALL/GO_DOWN*. jump and bite someone, jump up and grab someone (e.g. dog, snake). • Jarrbird nginiwardji-ngirri joolany. *The dog grabbed me.* • 'Jarrbird ginboowoon-ngiyi gamoom gamoom,' wanemayi nginyi yiroowoon. *'I jump and bite her on the breast,' said this marsupial mouse.*

jarrboolab *coverb+BE/STAY*. be squatting.
• Jarrboolab nyinya. *She is squatting on her haunches.* • Ngoowan jarrboolab nimbinnha ganybele-ninggi. Deg-anyji nimbirrimnha-boorroo. *Don't squat down like that, it would be shame for you. People might look at you.* [NOTE: old people used to say that young people should not sit down like this in front of them and that young boys could not say the word.] SEE: **jarranang**.

jarrboo-yarrboolab *coverb+BE/STAY*. be squatting (plural). • Jarrboo-yarrboolab boorroonboo. *They are all squatting on their haunches.* SEE: **jarrboolab**.

jarreda *verb*. you all will TAKE him/her/it.
jarrem *verb*. you all will SAY/DO.
jarrema; jarrama *verb*. you all GOT him/her/it.
jarrema; jarrama *verb*. you all SAID/DID.
jarremiyinnha *verb*. you are all DOING to yourselves/each other.
jarrg *coverb+BE/STAY*. be jumping. • Jarrg nyanininyande. *She was jumping.*

jarrg REDUP: **jarrg-jarrg**. *coverb+FALL/GO_DOWN*. jump, jump down, cross (creek etc.), get on a horse, get/go down. • Jarrg nginiward. *He jumped.* • Jarrg berrawardbe-birri-yoo yawarda-warriny. *They both got on the horses.*
• Jarrg nginewardji goorloo-yoorroong. *He jumped down into the water.* SEE: **jarrgooroog**.

jarrg *coverb+SAY/DO*. jump down. • Jarrg ngerne. *He jumps down.*

jarrg *coverb+BRING/TAKE*. take down.
• . . . jarrg-garri benanyji . . . *where he took them down*

jarrg *coverb+FALL/GO_DOWN_WITH*. cross over with someone. • Warrambam berrayin-ngarri-ya, jarrg nginimoowardji goorndoorndoogam. *He crossed over with the children just as the floodwater was coming.*

jarrga *coverb+PUT*. block off something, make a windbreak, stop something coming. • Jarrgaa boonbiyanyjende. *He wanted to try to stop the wind.*

jarrga; jarrgab *coverb+PUT*. block off fish using grass wall, make a windbreak. • Gerlernem jarrga benayanyji goorndarrim-boorroo. *He set up a wall of spinifex to block off the fish.*
• Dama jarrgab benayanyji minybernem. *He made a wall of dry grass.*

jarrga-jarrga *coverb+SAY/DO_M*. block off something, make a windbreak. • Ngoorrooma jarrga-jarrga woomberrama. *They set up a windbreak there.*

jarrgam *noun*. windbreak, wall. • Ngarag benamanyji jarrgam. *He made a windbreak.*

jarrgooroog *coverb+SAY/DO*. be jumping (plural). • Goorndoorndoogam jarrgooroog boorroorn. *All the children are jumping.* SEE: **jarrg**.

jarrij *coverb+SAY/DO*. dig. • Jarrij nginini. *He was digging. / He dug down.* • Jarrij boorroorn men'gawoog. *They are digging making it good/fixing it.*

jarrij *coverb+GET*. dig up. • Jilam jarrij benamanyji. *He is digging the sand.*

jarrij *coverb+GET_HIT*. dig up. • Jarrij ngendamawa. *I'll dig it up.*

jarrij *coverb+GO_ALONG*. go along digging. • Jarrij wiyinya grader-el. *The grader is going along digging.*

jarrij *coverb+GO/COME*. dig. • Jarrij-gela ngenda mayil. *I will have to dig yams.*

jarri-jarrirrij *coverb*. be striped marks on side

of hill.

jarri-jarrirrijmawoom *adjective.* striped.
- Deg gala benem dam ngarrgalem jarri-jarrirrijmawoom. *Look at those stripey rocks.*

jarrijbany *coverb+GO/COME.* go digging.
- Jarrijbany yarra goonjam. *Let's go digging kapok bush roots.*

jarrij-jarrij *coverb+SAY/DO.* be digging. • Dana banane jarrij-jarrij berrani mayaroom-boorroo. *There on the road where they were digging (a place) for a house.* [NOTE: answer to question 'Where did you find it?']

jarrijtha *verb.* you all will HIT him/her/it.

jarringgel *noun.* black flying fox. *Pteropus alecto.* [NOTE: the black flying fox is found only in the northen part of Gija country; the little red flying fox, *walimalil, Pteropus scapulatus*, is more common throughout Gija country.]

-jarriny *suffix.* further on. [NOTE: attached to directional words]

jarrinybany, jarrinybal, jarrinybam *noun.* person who is the reincarnation of someone who has died, one who carries the *jarriny* or spirit of the deceased person. SEE: **jarrinybe**.

jarrinybe *noun.* spirit of person that is reborn after death. [NOTE: spirit is reborn and the new person who has the spirit is the *jarrinybany, jarrinybal* of the person who was the previous incarnation]

jarrinyin, jarrinyinji *noun masculine.* devil dog, ghost dog. [NOTE: can be used to refer to the thylacine, *Thylacinus cynocephalus*, that lived across northern Australia until about 3000 years ago (Purdie et al. 2018)] SEE: **mooloogoorrji**.

jarriwoorroobda *verb.* you all will LEAVE him/her/it.

jarriyajtha *verb.* you all will PUT him/her/it.

jarriyanande *verb.* you all will be SAYING/DOING.

jarriyi *verb.* you all will GIVE him/her/it.

jarriyinha *verb.* you are all BECOMING.

jarrngarengaj *coverb+BE/STAY.* standing close all around. • Berre-binyga, Bernngaware-biny, jarrngarengaj-garri nginji nginya, boowoorrgoorloorr. *From here, from the place called Bernngawaren is where the hills are standing close all around going to the north (what is shown in a painting).*

jarranyngoorlg *coverb+BE/STAY.* talk loudly (plural). • Jarranyngoorlg boorroonboo melagawoom. *They are all talking loudly.*

jarroomboony, jarroombool, jarroomboom *adjective.* pointed, sharpened. • jarroomboo-woorrarrem *lots of pointed ones (e.g. sharpened pencils)*

jarroongambi; jarroongambiny; jarroongambeny *verb.* you should all spear it.

jarroongany *verb.* you will spear him/her/it.
- Yangirni jarroongany? *Who among you all will spear him? Which one of you will spear him?*

jarrward *coverb+GET.* lift. • Ngoorramangbe-yoo jarrward mernda-yoorroong, nginiyanya manggerregerreny. *She (turtle) and the shaky paw lizard lifted him onto some paperbark.* SEE: **jarrbird**.

jarrward-girrem *noun.* car jack. LIT: 'thing for lifting'.

jawa-jawayi *coverb+SAY/DO.* stop someone fighting. • Jawa-jawayi ngenani. *I stopped the fighting.* • Jawa-jawayi ngenarn-birri melagawoom wariny berrimiyanbe-ngarri. *I stop all of them when they are fighting.*

Jawalyi *noun.* a skin name (when spoken to).

Jawalyiny *noun masculine.* a skin name (when spoken about).

Jawan *noun.* a skin name (when spoken to). SEE: **Janama**.

Jawanji *noun masculine.* a skin name (when spoken about). SEE: **Janamany**.

Figure 48. *Joondalji: Mick Jawalji: Jawalji roord nginji joolabany nhawiyangeny joondalji.*

jawaren

Jawaren *noun.* place on Springvale Station.
jawariny *noun.* shaky paw lizard, 'tata' lizard. *Lophognathus temporalis, Diporiphora lalliae, D. magna.* SEE: **manggerregerreny, jawarlaliny**.
jawarlaliny *noun.* shaky paw lizard, 'tata' lizard. *Lophognathus temporalis, Diporiphora lalliae, D. magna.* SEE: **manggerregerreny, jawariny**.
Jawigin *noun.* Billy Mac Spring.
Jawinjan *noun.* place close to Old Halls Creek, north from Boorlooroon.
jawirij *coverb+DO_REFL.* make fun together.
 • Jawirij berramiyanbi-yoo. *Two of them are making fun together.* SEE: **barlij, mool-moolji, ngoolya-ngoolya**.
jawoogbe REDUP: **jawoog-jawoogbe**. *coverb+BE/STAY.* be white. • Jawoogbe-ngarri nginji. *The thing that is shining white (that is the sand, that is the sugar leaf that they tipped out in dreamtime).* • 'Marra ngoorrool jawoog-jawoogbe nyinya,' yirramande. *'Oh there they are all white there (group of goats on hills),' we said.*
jawoojiny *noun.* maternal grandfather, mother's father, mother's father's brother. (Miriwoong but word used by Gija) SEE: **thamanyji**.
jawool REDUP: **jawool-jawool**. *coverb+SAY/DO_REFL.* all talk together. • Jawool yarrengirrij wara-waranggan. *We will all talk together really quickly.*
jawooloo-wooloony *noun.* grass-leaf yam, edible plant species with food 'like a peanut'. *Curculigo ensifolia.* [NOTE: same sort of food as *wawalji* but grows in dry ground; grows underground and has soft shell; lots at Violet Valley, *ngoorroornbany*, 'having hairs like pubic hair']
jawoolyiny *noun masculine.* corkwood. *Hakea lorea.* [NOTE: name also used for the beefwood tree, *Grevillea striata*, and the fern-leaf grevillea, *G. pteridifolia*, which grows only in the northern part of Gija country; all three species are used to make boomerangs and carved boards]
jawoombal *noun feminine.* nankeen night heron. *Nycticorax caledonicus.*
Jawoombalnginy *noun.* next mountain north of Mount King. LIT: 'place of the nankeen night heron'.
jawoonany *noun.* cluster fig, fruit of cluster fig. *Ficus racemosa.* SEE: **goonangginy, ngalalabany, jamarndaji**. [NOTE: has fruit on trunk and branches, found near water]
Jawoonarrany *noun.* place near Queensland Creek on Bedford Downs, in Paddy Bedford's father's country.
jawoorijbe *coverb+DO_REFL.* be joking together, be having fun together. • Jawoorijbe berremiyanbende. *They are always joking together.* SEE: **barlij, birriman, ngoolya-ngoolya**.
jawoorl-jawoorl *coverb+SAY/DO_M.* clouds build up before rain, new fruit growing on tree. • Winyjiny yarroordja-ngarri dam, jawoorl-jawoorla-ngarri woomenji. *When we go to the spring and the clouds are making up ready for rain (is what is seen in the painting).* SEE: **jadag-jadag**.
jawoorlji *noun.* first fruit of black plum (*minyjiwarrany / minyjaarrany*). • Woorrg nginiwardji jawoorlji. *The first fruit of the black plum has fallen.*
jawoorr *coverb+BE/STAY.* soak self in water, be in water. • Jawoorr ngenaniyin. *I soaked myself. / I was sitting in the water.* • Jawoorr nyinya. *She is soaking in the water. / She is sitting in the water.*
jawoorr *coverb+PUT.* soak, put in water to soak.
 • Jawoorr booyool! / Jawoorr biyil! *Soak it!*
 • Jawoorr noonayangge goorndarrim. *I soaked the fish.*
jawoorr REDUP: **jawoorroorr**. *coverb+SAY/DO.* get into water. • Goorloon jawoorroorr ngenarn-noo ngayiwanyda gooyarrg ngiliyin'ge. *I get into the water for it and get it myself.*
jawoorr REDUP: **jawoorr-jawoorr**. *coverb+HIT.* drive into water. • Yilag jawoorr nyaniyidji gawayinda. *He just drove it down into the water.* • Jawoorr-jawoorr nyaniyidji. *He drove it (car) on into the water (when drunk).*
jawoorr REDUP: **jawoo-yawoorr**. *coverb+FALL/GO_DOWN.* get into water. • Jawoorr nginiwardji. *He got into the water.*
Jawoorraban *noun.* McPhee Hole, a cockatoo dreaming place in Paddy Bedford's father's country.
jawoorranyji *noun masculine.* moon, month.
 • merrgernbe jawoorranybe *three months* SEE: **garn'giny**.
jawoorrg-jawoorrg *coverb+SAY/DO.* call made by blue-winged kookaburra.

jigi-jigili

jawoorrinyalg *coverb+SAY/DO_M.* get into water (plural). • Jawoorrinyalg woomberrama. *They jumped into the water (e.g. from tree or bank).*

jawoorroony, jawoorrool *noun.* blue-winged kookaburra. *Dacelo leachii.*

jawoorroorr *coverb+SAY/DO_M.* get into water. • Jawoorroorrnga wanemayinde-boorroo. *He used to get in the water for them then.*

jawoorroorr *coverb+HIT.* throw into water. • Yarren-ga jawoorroorr yinayidjende-yarre-gili. *He would throw us all in the water too.*

jayi *coverb+SAY/DO_REFL.* share out. • Ngoorrooma jayi berrimingirriyan. *They are sharing with each other.*

jemenande *verb.* you (one) keep on SAYING/DOING.

jemenngarram *noun.* stranger. SEE: **gamaliwany, ngayanboo.**

jemennha; jemenha; jimenha *verb.* you are GETTING him/her/it.

jem-jem *coverb+HIT.* chip off wood. • Jem-jema ngoorrayidbende dali-ngiyi ngarneli, manyjangal. *They used to chip away at it with that thing, a stone axe then.*

-jen, -jin *suffix.* locative marker used with nominals ending in stop sounds (e.g. *gardag-jen*, 'in the cup/billy can'). SEE: **-n, -e, -nyen, -oo.**

jengamboornnha *verb.* you (one) are SPEARING him/her/it.

Jengoowoon *noun.* Binays Pocket north of Violet Valley. SEE: **Marle.**

jererd *coverb+PUT.* join strips of something to make (it) long. • Benayanyjende dam, mooloonggoom dam jererdbebe benayanyande. *The woman put lots of strips of fat together, joining them to make a long thing.* • Jererd benaya. *She joined them to make it long.*

jerreb *coverb+GET.* scoop up water. • Jerreb benamanya goorrngam yawinybe-birri. *She scooped up the water in a coolamon.* • Berrema-gili goorloom jerreb ngoorramangbe. *All of these children are scooping up water.*

jerr-jerr *coverb+SAY/DO.* be shaking. • Jerr-jerr boorroorn. *They are shaking.*

jibigel *noun feminine.* quail. *Coturnix ypsilophora.*

jibilyoowool, jibilyiwoony *noun.* duck.

-ji *suffix.* masculine suffix following stems ending in consonants. SEE: **-ny**

-ji *coverb suffix.* sequential suffix to coverbs, and then. SEE: **-boo.**

-ji *suffix.* topic/focus marker following -ny. SEE: **-iyi, -i, -bi.**

jid *coverb+HIT.* drop. • Jid benayidji. *He dropped it.*

jid *coverb+FALL/GO_DOWN.* drop off. • Jid giniwardji. *It dropped off.*

jida *coverb+SAY/DO.* stab ground (e.g. to look for water). • Belegan jida nyanini. *She stopped halfway to stab the ground for water.*

jida *coverb+SAY/DO_M.* stab ground (e.g. to look for water). • Jida wanamanyande loonggoong; jida-gayan, jida-gayan, jida-gayan, jida-gayan, ngoowa-ngarnan, goorloo goorloo-woorroon. *She went along the river bed from downstream, stabbing the ground for water, she kept on stabbing the ground over and over, nothing, there was no water.*

jida REDUP: **jida-jida.** *coverb+GO_ALONG.* go along stabbing ground (e.g. to look for water).

jida-jida *coverb+GO_THROUGH.* stab the ground with a digging stick looking for something. • Wayini jida-jida wanangaboord. *She stabbed the ground as she went along until she found a good spot (to dig yams).*

jidali *coverb.* use a walking stick.

jidali-girrem *noun.* walking stick.

jidi *coverb+HIT.* join in with someone/ on to something, meet someone/something. • Jidi benayidji-doo . . . *He joined those two (in the action).*

jidi *coverb+BURN/BITE_REFL.* meet. • Berrema marramelemga, jidi yirrawooran. *Here are all the people from far away; we are all mixed up together.* • Jidi berrawoorranbe. *They met them. / They met each other.*

jidi *coverb+PUT.* teach. • Gijam jidi noonayangge wajbaloom-boorroo jarrag-girrem. *I teach the white people to talk Gija.* SEE: **binarrig, dayi.**

jigerl *coverb+PUT.* draw someone in sorcery. • Ngoolngaganyga jigerl nyaniyanyji. *Her husband put the drawing of her there.* [NOTE: said about a little painting of an upside-down woman in the gorge called Boolanji on the Frank River]

jigerrel *noun.* kingfisher. *Todiramphus sanctus.*

jigij *coverb+GET.* tickle. • Jigij nginimanyji. *He tickled him (once).*

jigi-jigili *coverb+PUT.* dislike someone. • Ngoowan, jigi-jigili yimberriyajtha-yarre, *You don't like us (you been talking about us in a*

jigij-jigij

rude way).

jigij-jigij *coverb+GET.* tickle. • Jigij-jigij ngenemenyji. *He's tickling me.* • Jigij-jigij yindemnha. *Tickle me!*

jigij-jigij *coverb+DO_REFL.* tickle each other.
• Jigij-jigij yirramiyiny-joo. *We tickled each other.*

jigili *interjection.* yuk!

jigiliny, jigilil, jigilim *adjective.* horrible, revolting, yukky, ugly. • Ngoowan deg ninamangge wayinijarrany jigilin-ngoo. *I've never seen a man as ugly as you.* • Jigilim ngalimga berremga. *All these women are no good.*

jigirridji; jigirrid-jigirridji *noun.* willie wagtail. *Rhipidura leucophrys.*

jijberrg *coverb+HIT.* throw into water. • Jijberrg nginiyid yilag. *She threw him down into the water.*

jijberrg; jijboorrg REDUP: jijbi-jijberrg. *coverb+FALL/GO_DOWN.* dive (into water).]
• Jijboorrg berraward-joo. *The two of them dived into the water.* • Jijbi-jijberrg nginiwardji. *He dived in.* SEE: **jilyboorrg**.

-jijiny, -jijil, -jijim *suffix.* his/her/their relation. [NOTE: attached to relationship terms; agrees with relation possessed, not the possessor; rare suffix, described by Rusty Peters as 'high Gija'] SEE: **-gany, -gal, -gam**.

jilam *noun.* ground. [NOTE: used by some people to mean 'sugar'; also used to mean 'funeral']

jilangarnal *noun feminine.* ochre. LIT: 'ground dweller'.

jilangarnal *noun feminine.* small sand frog. LIT: 'ground dweller'. SEE: **nangala-nangalal**.

jilarrg *coverb+HIT.* squash. • Jilarrgboo beniyinji. *He's just about squashed it.* • Jilarrg benayidji. *He squashed it.*

jilarrgeny, jilarrgel, jilarrgem *adjective.* squashed. • Jilarrgem ngarriyan. *It's already squashed.*

jilba *coverb+SAY/DO_M.* be afraid, be frightened.
• Goowool-boorroo jilba wanemanyande 'Ngoowan birriyan goowool-yoorroong,' nyanini-yirri. *She was afraid of (letting us go to school). 'Don't go to school,' she told us.*

jilba *coverb+HIT.* be afraid of someone/something, be frightened. • Wayinili barra jilbama nyooloojge? *Do you think I'm afraid of that kind of woman?* • Wayininy barra jilbama noowoojge. *I'm not afraid of that kind of man.*

• Jilbama jiyinnha? *Are you afraid?* • Jilba benayidjende wajbaloom. *He was afraid of the white people.*

jilba *coverb+SAY/DO.* be afraid, be frightened.
• Jilba ngerne. *He is frightened.*
• Melagawooya jilba berrani. *They were all frightened.* • Jirrawoonginy girriyiny ngoowan jilba nginini. *One brave one was not frightened.*
• Jilba-wanyji nerne. *Maybe you are afraid.*

jilbage; jilbaga *coverb+GET.* frighten, cause to be afraid. • Jilbage benamanyji. *He made them afraid.* • Jilbaga ngoorrooma yoonggoonyga. *They (engines and noise) frightened the big ghost (so that he does not come round anymore).*

jilbawoony, jilbawool, jilbawoom *adjective.* frightening, scary.

jilemberre *noun.* ribs, rib bone. • 'Berrembi jilemberre noonbiyajge-ma marnen? Woolthoob-gala noondaj marnen.' 'Ngiyi, bendewarre-gala gerag-gili.' *'Will I put this rib bone in the fire? I'll chuck em in the fire.' 'Yes, let it cook for later.'* SEE: **walamboom**.

jililib *coverb+BURN/BITE.* get burned in fire.
• Marnena jililib benawoorranji. *They were burnt up in the fire.*

jililiny, jililim *noun.* boab seeds. [NOTE: not the whole big nuts, just the seeds inside. When green nuts are roasted seeds can be eaten as part of the nut; when dry the seeds can be cracked one by one and eaten or cooked, pounded and winnowed in a coolamon to remove skin.]

Jilinyangarriny *noun.* name of a devil dog.

jilinggoowiny *noun masculine.* curl snake, little spotted snake. *Suta suta, S. punctata.*

jilinybel *noun feminine.* bush cucumber. *Cucumis melo.*

jilirr-jilirrji *noun masculine.* long yam, vine species with edible roots. *Dioscorea transversa.*

jilyboorrg; jilyberrg *coverb+FALL/GO_DOWN.* dive into water. • Goorloon jilyboorrg-garri nyimboowoonya, jalbagawoorrool. *When it jumps in the water you can't catch it.* SEE: **jijberrg**.

jilyirr *coverb+SAY/DO.* be unable to light fire.
• Ngoowan mirlim jinbiyangnha-ni jarrambayiny. Goonggalamga jilyirr birrirn-ninggi. *Don't eat goanna liver or your firestick won't light.*

jilyiwoog *coverb+PUT.* burn someone/something with the end of a stick. • Jilyiwoog nimbiyajtha-ngoongoo goowoolem-birri marnebam. *I'll burn you with the end of a fire stick.*

jilyiwoony noun. small snake species. [NOTE: has a mark on the head, can kill young people quickly] SEE: **jarloongoorroobarndegji**.

jily-jily coverb+SAY/DO. burn with the end of a stick, brand cattle. • Dambi majoorroom-ngarri yarranya, waranya jily-jily yarrani. *After the mustering we did the branding.*

jimarniny; jemarniny noun. wild taro. *Colocasia esculenta*. [NOTE: small roots can be roasted and eaten; were eaten by kangaroo in the dreamtime after which he couldn't talk, only say 'sss, sss' (McConvell notes)]

jimarri noun. age mate, person of the same age (when spoken to).

jimarriny, jimarril, jimarrim noun. age mate, person of the same age.

jimbi-jimbij coverb+SAY/DO_M. be spitting/sprinkling rain. • Jimbi-jimbijboo woomenji. *It is sprinkling now (rain).* [NOTE: in Halls Creek sometimes used as a euphemism for urinating]

Jimbirlan noun. 1. O'Donnell Range just north of Crocodile Hole. 2. Dicky Spring on Bedford Downs. LIT: 'place of the stone spearhead'.

jimbirlany, jimbirlal, jimbirlam noun. stone spearhead. SEE: **gorooowal**.

jimerrawoon adverb. always, for good, forever.

Jimingarrinyin noun. Charlie Bight Camp.

Jiminjerl noun. a place on Mabel Downs.

jimirlbel noun. wild grape, brown grape. *Jasminum molle, Ophilia amentacea*.

jimirlbiny noun. rock fig. *Ficus atricha, F. brachypoda, F. platypoda*. SEE: **banggoornji**.

jina-jinam noun. dress.

Jinanggany noun. place on Cattle Creek south of Bedford Downs station and east of Mount King.

jinba-jinbalel, jinba-jinbalji noun. white-breasted woodswallow. *Artamus leucorynchus*.

jinberrji noun. bandicoot. *Isoodon* ssp. [NOTE: word recorded in 1980s when looking at book of mammals; not seen in Gija country for many years] SEE: **goojinji, nyarlgool**.

jinbijtha verb. you (one) will HIT them/it (non-singular).

jinbimnha verb. you (one) will GET them/it (non-singular). [NOTE: alternate form *jimbimnha* is either a different mood or a dialectal difference]

jinbiyajtha verb. you (one) will PUT them/it (non-singular).

jinbiyangnha verb. you (one) will EAT them/it (non-singular).

jinbiyinha; jinbiyinnha verb. you (one) will GIVE them/it (non-singular).

jindag-jindag coverb+GO_ALONG. be leaking. • Jindag-jindag waanya goorrnga-girrem dam bemberrooloonboo-ngarri-ngiyi boonany-boonanya nyerne yilgoowoorrool. *It (the car) is leaking water from the radiator, and the water in the radiator is boiling, it is no good.*

jinderre, jindirrji noun. clitoris. [NOTE: swearing]

jindiwirrij noun masculine. willie wagtail. *Rhipidura leucophrys*. SEE: **jigirridji**.

jing coverb+GET. tease. • Jing nginimanyji. *He teased him.* SEE: **birrga-wirrga**.

jingganyarrany, jingganyarral, jingganyarram noun. premature baby, child spirit that can be reborn, foetus.

jinggerawoogoony noun masculine. little friar-bird. *Philemon citreogularis*.

jinggoolji noun masculine. freshwater mangrove, river mangrove. *Lophostemon grandiflorus*.

jingirri-ngirrim noun. headband with curtain of long knotted strings hanging in front of the face worn by women dancing Moonga-moonga.

jinilinnha verb. you (one) are PUTTING them/it (non-singular).

jininy SEE: **jirniny**.

jiniyinnha verb. you (one) are HITTING him/her/it.

jinjilji noun masculine. type of small paperbark tree. *Melaleuca acacioides*. [NOTE: small paperbark tree with hard bark that cannot be peeled off the trunk like some of the other paperbarks]

Jin'gaweny noun. Ashburton Range.

jin'gerdi coverb+SAY/DO_M. spear properly, kill with one blow. • Jin'gerdi woomberrama-noo gendoowagoo. *They tried to spear him properly up there.*

jinybal noun feminine. boomerang type. SEE: **baljarranggool, gamanyjel, garrabiril, goorroobardool, jaranggarril**.

jirawoorr coverb+GET. make long scratches on someone (e.g. wild cat, angry man). • Ngirrngiliny jirawoorr ngenamanyji. *The cat*

jirawoorr

made long scratches on me.

jirawoorr *coverb+DO_REFL.* make long scratches on self. • *Jirawoorr nyimiyanya. She made a long scratch on herself.*

jirege *coverb+BECOME_REFL.* become bird. • *Jirege nginiwamanyji. He turned into a bird.*

jiregel, jiregem *noun feminine.* bird (generic).

jirlanyel, jirlanybe *noun feminine.* water leech.

jirlanyjag *coverb+GET.* make wet. • *Jadam doongooroog ngoorrooma, tharroorroo ngerne yilaga, jirlanyjag benemenyji daam. The rain has minced it up (roof on bough shed) and it pours through and makes everything wet.*

jirlanyjag *coverb+HIT.* make wet. • *Jadamga jirlanyjag yinbiji-yoowoo. The rain will make us wet.* • *Jirlanyjagboo biniyinji merndamga. The paper nearly got wet.*

jirlanyjag *coverb+BECOME.* get wet. • *Jirlanyjag wimbiji jadany. He will get wet in the rain.*

jirlanyjany, jirlanyjal, jirlanyjam *adjective.* wet. SEE: **dilboowoorroony, giyiny.**

jirlbeg *coverb+FALL/GO_DOWN.* jump into water. • *Bangariny dany jirlbeg berraward. They jumped in the water at the same time.* [NOTE: singular 'two' no dual marker on non-singular verb to express 'same time'] SEE: **jijberrg, jilyberrg.**

Jirlilirliny *noun.* name of Osmond River area near Gawarre.

jirliwoorril *noun feminine.* flowers of *mawoorroony* 'bloodwood tree'.

jirlewoorrji, jirlewoorre REDUP: **jirle-jirlewoorre.** *noun.* red-coloured soil type.

jirliwoorrji *noun.* red water (i.e. from rotting vegetation, or from algae late in the dry season).

Jirljin *noun.* Red Pocket, a place on Bedford Downs.

jirlmirndiny *noun masculine.* mistletoe bird. *Dicaeum hirundinaceum.* SEE: **jiwirnbeny.**

jirlwam; jirloowam *noun.* sinew, something used as string, feelings. [NOTE: kangaroo sinews are used for for binding spearheads to spears; word also used as metaphor for feelings] SEE: **nganyjoom.**

jirniny *coverb+SPEAR.* be cranky with someone. • *Jirniny nanengaboordji-ni. He was cranky with you.* • *Jirniny yinbinganynha. You are cranky with me.* • *Jirniny-wanyji ngenengambennya. She might be jealous of me, of my boyfriend at home.*

jirniny *coverb+HIT_REFL.* be cranky with each other. • *Jirniny-ngarri nirrij-thoo. You might be cranky with each other.*

jirniny *coverb+SAY/DO_M.* get cranky, take offence and sulk. • *Jirniny wanema nginyi jiyiliny. This man got cranky.*

jirniny *coverb+SAY/DO_REFL.* be cranky with each other. • *Jirniny-anyji berrangirriyinbende ginyirrim warnarram. Maybe they used to be cranky with each other because of things like wife-stealing in those days.*

jirninybiny, jirninybel, jirninybim *adjective.* grumpy, cranky.

jirniny-jirniny *coverb+GO_ALONG.* be cranky. • *Jirniny-jirniny wananyji. He was cranky.*

jirn'gawool *noun.* plant species with edible root. *Vigna lanceolata* var. *lanceolata.* [NOTE: leaves like *ngawoonyji* but are greasy; easily pulled up, roots 'as long as your arm', cook in hot earth and hit with a stone before eating (Hector Jandany); lots at Bedford Downs]

jiroo-girrim *noun.* last one before leaving. • *'Warrg-gala yarra Joonbam,' berrangirriyin, 'jiroo-girrim.' 'Let's dance Joonba (a song and dance style),' they said to each other, 'last one before leaving.'*

Jirragen *noun.* place name. LIT: 'the place of the frog'. [NOTE: there are various different places called Jirragen, e.g. one near Norton Bore, one between Moola Bulla and Springvale, and another in the Bungles.]

jirraginy *noun masculine.* small frog species, rocket frog, sharp-nosed frog. *Litoria nasuta.*

jirra-jirrawoom *adjective.* a few. • *Gooragal dal garnanganyjel ngoowana jirra-jirrawoom, melagawoom benamoorloonya. The mother emu does not have just a few chicks, she has lots of them.*

jirrawoogen barnden *temporal.* for one day.

jirrawoogem jadam *temporal.* for one year. • *Jirrawoogem jadam benamoorlardja-birri ngaliyangem ninggoowoom. She stayed with her relations for one year.*

jirrawoogeny, jirrawoogel, jirrawoogem; jirrawoogoony *adjective.* one. • *Lamany-ngirri jirrawoogoony ngirriminy. I have one loose tooth.* SEE: **jirrawoony, jirrawoonginy.**

jirrawoo-moowam *adverb.* once. • *Thed-gala biyij jirrawoo-moowam! Hit him once!*

jirrawoonginy, jirrawoongil, jirrawoongim; jirrawoongeny *adjective.* one. SEE:

jirrawoony, jirrawoogeny.

jirrawoony, jirrawool, jirrawoom *adjective.* one. • *Jirrawoo-moowany deg nemen'gende.* I always see that same one. • *jirrawoom-birri* for one day SEE: **jirrawoongi-, jirrawooge-**.

jirrayam *interjection.* alright, OK. SEE: **nyoonggayam**.

jirrayany, jirrayal, jirrayam; jirram *adjective.* alright. • '*Jirrayan-ma-noonggoorroo-gili?*' '*Ngiyi! Jirrayan-yarre-gili.*' 'Are you all alright?' 'Yes. We are all alright'. • '*Ngoorroonya wariwoony-ma?*' '*Ngoowan, jirrayany men'gawoony, werd-bawoorroony.*' 'Is that a cheeky one?' 'No, he's alright, he's a good one, he won't bite.' SEE: **nyoonggayam**. [NOTE: alternate elided form *jirram* from Southern dialect; *nyoonggayam* much more frequent in the Southern dialect]

jirrayirriyan *coverb+BE/STAY.* be all together in one place. • *Jirrayirriyan-joorroo boorroonbende.* They all keep piling up together in the one place (talking about an intermarrying family).

jirreg *coverb+BECOME.* feel a nerve jump. • *Jirreg ngelayid, yangoorranyji birriyan-yarri.* I felt a nerve jump, someone must be coming to us. SEE: **woorlmooj-woorlmooj**.

jirrgaj REDUP: **jirrgaj-jirrgaj** *coverb+BRING/TAKE.* follow someone. • *Jirrgaj ninanygende ngagenyji ngaboony thambarlam-ningi.* I was following my father's footprints.

jirrga-jirrgaj *coverb+DO_REFL.* follow seach other in line. • *Jirrga-jirrgaj yarremija-gili.* We will all follow each other in a line (group of cars going bush).

jirrgany *noun.* male hill kangaroo, common wallaroo, euro. *Macropus robustus.* SEE: **moordany**.

jirrgawoorr *coverb+SAY/DO.* drop out (e.g. seeds from pod), drop down (e.g. black plum when ripe). • *Mayi jirrgawoorr berrani, mayibawoorroon. Lirlmi-moowam. Gelengebany mayibawa wimbiji.* The edible seeds have dropped out, there is no tucker in (the kurrajong pod). Only the dry pod. When it is green it will have tucker.

jirrgawoorrg *coverb+HIT.* make something drop out. • *Dayiwool, berrembi lirlmim jarrg-garri nyanoowardja jirrgawoorrg benayidja, ngenengga laarne, woobooj-garri boorroorn.* These are the barramundi scales that she caused to drop, when she jumped over, high up there where they are digging (diamonds at the Argyle Diamond Mine in Lena's country).

jirrgilji *noun masculine.* blackmast, strawman, small fish species. *Craterocephalus stramineus.*

jirrgoolji *noun masculine.* eel-tailed catfish, black catfish, Hyrtl's catfish, Rendhal's catfish. *Porochilus rendahli, Neosilurus ater, N. hyrtlii.* [NOTE: Western dialect; word nearly the same as that given for blackmast, *Craterocephalus stramineus*, in the eastern part of Gija country] SEE: **girlinyiny, ngirndany, woorlengerriny**.

jirri *coverb+PUT.* show, point out something, point at. • *Jirri-gala benaj.* Show it. • *Jirri noonaya-ngiyi.* I aimed (the rifle) at her ('porcupine', echidna) / I pointed the rifle at her. • *Jirri nyiliyajke-birri-gili.* I will show her to them. [NOTE: this combination of *jirri* with PUT is the most commonly found combination; the thing being shown is the direct object] SEE: **bina, jirri, giwaj**.

jirri *coverb+HIT.* show. • *Jirri benayidji-birri-yoo dam nawarram goorloom, ngoowan.* He did not show them the big water. SEE: **giwaj**. [NOTE: unusual in that the negative particle is at the end; uses HIT instead of the usual PUT with *jirri*]

jirri *coverb+BRING/TAKE.* show. • *Jirriji nyilige ngayin.* I will show her, me! SEE: **giwaj**.

jirri *coverb+GET.* show. • *Jirriji ngenamanyande dam ngarranggarnim-boorroo, gerlirroogoo.* She used to show me all those dreaming places to the west. [NOTE: uses GET instead of the usual PUT with *jirri*]

jirril *noun.* white substance used for love magic. • *Jirril dalga ngoolnga-ngoolnga-girril.* Jirri is that white thing used for getting lovers. [NOTE: commonly referred to as *jirri* without the gender marker in Kimberley Kriol]

jirriliny *coverb+GO/COME.* to sweat. • *Loordbenybe nginiyinji, jirriliny ngenayin.* It is getting hot, I am sweating.

jirriliny *coverb+GET.* to sweat. • *Jirriliny-ngarri benamanyjende, balarr-moowam ngard woomberramande.* When they (hunters) sweat, they (kangaroos) only smell the mud (that the hunters have painted themselves with). SEE: **malngoony**.

Jirrindingarrin *noun.* place near Billy Mac Spring.

jirrindiny *noun.* boomerang tree. *Hakea*

jirriny-jirrinyji

arborescens. [NOTE: used to make boomerangs]

jirriny-jirrinyji *noun.* hard tall spinifex species, limestone spinifex. *Triodia* sp. SEE: **garral-garralji**. [NOTE: seen on track to Goondooloo, waterhole upstream from highway on Spring Creek south of Warrmarn]

jirrinyngalil *noun feminine.* fairy martin. *Hirundo ariel.*

jirr-jirr *coverb+SAY/DO.* feel sad, feel upset. • Jirr-jirr ngenarn jaam-ngooyoo. *I feel sad and upset in my stomach about it (Joonba song and dance – because young people don't learn it).* [NOTE: *Joonba* takes feminine agreement]

jirr-jirrge *coverb+GET.* make someone feel sad/sorry, make someone feel upset. • Jirr-jirrge ngenamanyji. *He makes me feel sorry (can be said as a kind of expression of affection for a loved small dog who is staring at the speaker when he is eating meat).*

jiwerd-jiwerdji *noun.* whitewood, tree species used to make fighting sticks. *Atalaya hemiglauca.* SEE: **loowarriny**.

jiwibal, jiwibany *noun.* morning star, Venus, Haley's Comet.

jiwijtha *verb.* you will HIT him/her/it.

jiwijthande *verb.* you will keep HITTING him/her/it.

jiwimnha *verb.* you (one) will GET him/her/it.

jiwiny *noun masculine.* hardwood part of spears, wood used for hard pointed part of spears and the hook on woomeras, any tree species from which the wood comes. SEE: **gernemboowoorroony**. [NOTE: short hardwood part joined to bamboo either sharpened as the spear point or can have a spearhead joined onto the wooden part, species used include *Acacia acradenta, A. cowleana, A. lamprocarpa, A. tumida, Grevillea miniata* and *G. wickhamii*; some of these species have edible gum]

jiwirnbenji *noun masculine.* mistletoe bird. *Dicaeum hirundinaceum.* SEE: **jirlmirndiny**.

jiwiyajtha *verb.* you (one) will PUT him/her/it.

jiwoore *coverb+SAY/DO.* feel strange, feel funny. • Jiwoore ngenarn-ninggi. Ngirribag daniyi-ngirri. *I feel funny with you. You are coming too close to me.*

jiyi *coverb+DO_REFL.* comb hair. • Jiyi ngemiyanyji. *He is combing himself.* • Jiyiwa nginbimij. *I will comb myself then.*

jiyigajim *noun.* comb.

jiyigjel *noun feminine.* sheep. *Ovis aries.* [NOTE: sheep were brought to Gija country by the original invaders but they are not kept there anymore; a sheep features in the Christmas Joonba that used to be staged at Gawoornben,

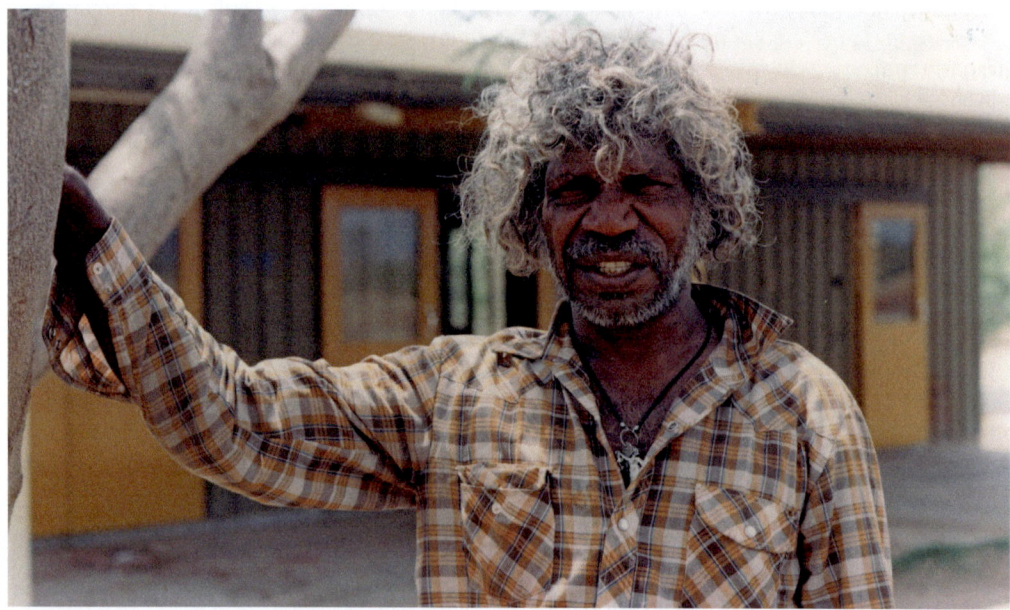

Figure 49. *Jiyiliny: Yoonany Churchill Cann: Jiyiliny thad nginji.*

Texas Downs Station] SEE: **googoonjal, yiwoolthelel**.

jiyig-jiyiggel; jiyig-jiyigjil *noun feminine*. rufous whistler. *Pachycephala rufiventris*.

jiyilengem *adjective*. in the Aboriginal way.

jiyilengoonybel *noun*. woman who cannot do without a man. SEE: **ngalingoonybiny**.

jiyilem *noun*. Aboriginal people.

jiyilil; jiyilel *noun*. Aboriginal woman.

jiyiliny; jiyileny *noun*. man, Aboriginal man.

jiyinhande, jiyinande *verb*. you (one) keep going along.

jiyinnha; jiyinha *verb*. **1.** you (one) are HITTING him/her/it. **2.** you (one) are becoming.

jiyirriny, jiyirrel, jiyirrem *noun*. kangaroo (generic). [NOTE: generic is masculine; if species is named the generic acts as a classifier and agrees in gender with the species]

joo *conjunctive particle*. and. SEE: **doo**. [NOTE: joins nouns following -*ny*]

-joo *suffix*. dual suffix to verbs. SEE: **-doo, -yoo**.

jooboony, jooboonyel, jooboonyboo *noun feminine*. didjeridoo. • *Garniny-ayi jooboonyboo? Is there a didjeridoo?* SEE: **gooloomboong**.

jood *coverb+HIT*. drop, put down. • *Jood benayid. He dropped it.*

joodiya *adverb*. straight up ahead, immediately.

joodoob *coverb+BURN/BITE*. teach properly.
• *Joodoob joonawoorrany. You taught them really properly (they can really do it)*

joodoobiny *locative*. on the right, to the right.
• *Joodoobiny mira barroo! Put your hands out to the right!*

joodoog REDUP: **joodoog-joodoog**. *coverb+PUT*. straighten, make correct, make sure information is right. • *Joodoog-gala nandaj-noonggoo. I'll try to put you all straight (at the meeting).*

joodoog *coverb+DO_REFL*. straighten self.
• *Marrge joodoog-gala ngendamij therlam. Wait till I straighten my back.*

joodoojgajil *noun feminine*. straw-necked and white ibis. *Threskiornis molucca, T. spinicollis*. SEE: **jandiyandiny**.

joodoombarrany, joodoombarral, joodoombarram *adjective*. long and straight.
• *Nginyjiyanya joodoobarrany. This is a long straight one.*

joodoony, joodool, joodoom *adjective*. straight, correct (e.g. word or story).
• *Moorloo joodoon-nga. I have good eyesight.*
• *Joodoombiya bananbe. A really straight road.*

joog *coverb+FALL/GO_DOWN*. ambush, double-bank, gang up on. • *Joog berrawardbe-ni-yoo. They two double-banked him*

joog *coverb+BE/STAY*. ambush, double-bank, gang up on. • *Joog berraniyin-ni-yoo. They two double-banked him.*

joogboo, joogbany *coverb+GO/COME*. go hunting. • *Joogboo nginiyin joolany. A dog went hunting.* • *Jambalngarri-warriny joogboo berrayin-doo. The two young men went hunting.* • *Joogboo ngenardge miyale-boorroo. I'm going hunting for meat.*
• *Nginyi jiyiliny joogbany nginiyi. The man has gone hunting.* SEE: **joog**.

joog-joog *coverb+GO/COME*. trot along, jolt along (on horse). • *Joog-joog ngenardge dimanan. I'm trotting along on a horse.*

Joogoomoorndin *noun*. Carola Gully (Growler Gully).

Joogoorreyirrin *noun*. Battery Creek.

joogoorrool *noun feminine*. bush orange. *Capparis umbonata*. [NOTE: young men are not supposed to say this word, they say *goordirdal* instead; leaves can be used as a steaming medicine to treat colds]

joolal *noun feminine*. female dog, bitch. *Canis familiaris*.

Joolama *noun*. a skin name (when spoken to). [NOTE: Miriwoong equivalent of 'Joowoorroo', also often used by Gija people] SEE: **Joowoorroo**.

Joolamany *noun masculine*. a skin name (when spoken about). [NOTE: Miriwoong equivalent of 'Joowoorroony', also often used by Gija people] SEE: **Joowoorroony**.

joolany *noun masculine*. dog. *Canis familiaris*. SEE: **ngarriyanyji**.

jooliya *adverb*. keep up with. • *Nyingindi miyi jooliyan nirdande-boorra. You too, you had to keep going after them.* • *Jirrgaj-jirrgaj beneda jooliya. You go together with them, follow them.*

jooloog *coverb+SAY/DO*. bend down, bend and put head down. • *Jooloog nyerne. She (brolga) puts her head down.*

jooloogbayiny, jooloogbayil, jooloogbayim *adjective*. bent down, having head down.
• *Berrem-ngiyi joorloogbayim, therlam. Here she (brolga) is with her back bent down.*

joolooj *coverb+SAY/DO*. carry under arm

joolooj

sometimes supported by a strap over the shoulder. • **Marrarna joolooj nyanini, nyaniyinya-ngarri goonja-giny.** *She set off carrying it under her arm when she went to get kapok bush roots.*

jooloo REDUP: **jooloo-yoolooj.** *coverb+SAY/DO_M.* carry under arm sometimes supported by a strap over the shoulder. • **Marrarn gendewa ngoorranybeyoo, jooloo wanamanyande gendewagoo.** *They two set off upstream carrying him, she went along up the river carrying him under her arm.* • **Dangembi jooloo-yoolooj woomberramande joowegbe.** *Then they went along carrying their swags under their arms.*

jooloo REDUP: **jooloo-jooloo.** *coverb+BRING/TAKE.* carry under arm. • **Jooloo nginanyande.** *She was carrying him along under her arm.*

jooloo *coverb+FALL/GO_DOWN_WITH.* take away carrying under arm sometimes supported by a strap over the shoulder. • **Wiji nyanoomoowardja jooloo janoomoowardjande-ni warlagarriny goordooroony-berra goordooroony.** *She ran away carrying that supplejack tree used to make fighting sticks.*

jooloo REDUP: **jooloo-jooloo.** *coverb+PUT.* put under arm to carry. • **Ngarem-ninggi jamboorn-ngarri dam gardagbe, gardagjen jooloo goorrayangbende.** *You should have seen how much honey they used to fill the billy can with and then carry it along under their arms. / You should have seen how full with honey the billy can was when they carried it along under their arms.* • **Gooral ngaginyel boorroordboo-yoo wiginy ngaboony jooloo-jooloo ngeneyooloonya.** *My mother goes along with my father and her son putting me under her arm to carry me (in a coolamon?).*

jooloooong *coverb+BRING/TAKE.* bring young man out to family after the stage of initiation when he receives a headband. • **Diyena merre-merreb wanemayinde, dangembi jooloooong ngoorranybe.** *He was hidden there and afterwards they brought him out to his family.*

Jooloorroo *noun.* song and dance type that is a bit spiritually dangerous.

jooloorrooj *coverb+BE/STAY.* bend over.
• **Jooloorrooj boorroonboo-yoo.** *Those two are bending over.*

joombayiny, joombayil *noun.* caterpillar. SEE: **booboogarral, boomboongel.**

joombiyajtha *verb.* you will PUT them/it (non-singular). • **Gerdgardboo joo gamoom joombiyajtha nalija-yoorroong.** *You put sugar and milk in the tea.*

joomboo *coverb+BRING/TAKE.* be heavy. • **Joomboo**

Figure 50. *Joolany: Joolany girli wiyinji baroowoorroon.*

ngenanyji doomoon-ga-ngany ngarrgalejany. *My head was heavy like a stone (after I hurt my neck in a car accident).*

joomboony, joombool, joomboom *adjective.* heavy (physical, e.g. load, log, or metaphorical, e.g. language). • Joomboon-ngage doomoon. *I have a hangover (lit. 'My head is heavy').*

joomboorrirrig *coverb.* being a spiritually dangerous place, important sacred place.

joomboorrirriny *noun.* spiritually dangerous place, important sacred place. SEE: **doomoorriny.**

joomboowoo; joomboog *coverb+GO/COME.* have a hangover. • Joomboowoo ngenardge. / Joomboog ngenardge. *I have a hangover.*

joomenha *verb.* you are GETTING him/her/it.

joomool *noun feminine.* spirit of dead woman.

joomooloony *noun.* boab tree, boab nuts. *Adansonia gregorii.* [NOTE: Jangala skin]

joomoorloonha *verb.* you HAVE him/her/it.

joomoorr-joomoorre *adjective.* having a rough surface (e.g. like a rasp). • Joomoorr-joomoorre ngarrgalem. *Raspy stones.* • Ngelel bardigel joomoorr-joomoorre-ngiyi bernngam. *This nutwood tree has rough bark.*

joomoorrirriny, joomoorrirrim *noun.* spiritually dangerous place, important sacred place. • Nginyi yilag dagoorlan goorloony joomoorrirriny ngarranggarniny. *This down here (in the painting) is a deep waterhole that is a spiritually dangerous place from dreamtime.* SEE: **doomoorriny.**

joonamannha *verb.* you were GETTING them/it (non-singular).

joonamennha; joonemenha; joonoomenha; jenemennha *verb.* you are GETTING them/it (non-singular).

joonamoorloonha *verb.* you HAVE them/it (non-singular).

joonangoon *verb.* you ATE them/it (non-singular).

joonanynha *verb.* you were BRINGING/TAKING them/it (non-singular).

joonawoorrany *verb.* you (one) BURNED/BIT them/it (non-singular).

joonaya *verb.* you (one) PUT them/it (non-

Figure 51. *Joomooloony: Joomooloony thawala-bany jadagen.*

singular).

joonayanha, joonayannha *verb.* you (one) were PUTTING them/it (non-singular).

joonayida *verb.* you (one) were HITTING (non-singular).

joonayinha *verb.* you are BRINGING/TAKING them/it (non-singular). [NOTE: Southern dialect]

Joonba *noun.* type of song and dance event. (Kriol). SEE ALSO **Joonbal**.

Joonbal, Joonbam *noun feminine.* type of public song and dance event sung by men and women accompanying themselves with boomerangs or clapsticks, word is used by some people to mean any song and dance event. • Ngarranggarnin joonbam warrg berrani binyjirrminy, warrarnany, manggerregerreny. *In dreamtime the bat, the eagle and the shaky paw lizard were dancing Joonba.* • Ngelelga Joonbal Thawooloongarnal; nanbardi berrawoorran-doo Gija-bany doo Jaroo-bany. *This is the song and dance belonging to Hann Spring; (the place where) the Gija man and the Jaru man knocked each other down (in dreamtime).* [NOTE: referred to as *Joonba* in Kriol; in a full Gija sentence becomes a feminine noun *Joonbal* when talking about a complete song and dance cycle, or a non-singular noun *Joonbam* when talking about a part of a performance]

joonbamirrib *coverb+BE/STAY.* gather together for Joonba song and dance. • Joonbamirribga berranin. *They were all gathered together then to dance Joonba.*

joonbangnha *verb.* you will EAT them/it (non-singular).

joonbida *verb.* you will TAKE them/it (non-singular).

joonbijtha *verb.* you will HIT them/it (non-singular).

joonbimnha *verb.* you will GET them/it (non-singular).

joonbimnhande *verb.* you will keep on GETTING them/it (non-singular).

joonbiyajtha *verb.* you will PUT them/it (non-singular).

joonboomanha *verb.* you should GET them/it (non-singular).

joonboomoorlarda *verb.* you should have HAD them/it (non-singular), if you HAD them/it (non-singular).

joonboomoorloonha *verb.* you will HAVE/KEEP them/it (non-singular).

joonbooroong *coverb+BE/STAY.* sit with head down for a long time. • Joonbooroong barrennha-gili! *Stay with your heads down.* • Joonbooroong nginji. *He has his head down.* SEE: **yoodoong**.

joondalji, joondalel *noun.* domestic dog of which one is very fond, special pet dog.

joondoo REDUP: **joondo-joondoo**. *coverb+SAY/DO_M.* make camp. • Joondoo woomberrama daam. *They made camp.* • Joondoo wanema daam. *He made camp.* • Joondoo yarrem ngenengga. *Let's make camp here.* • Joondoo-joondoo yarrimnya daam. *Let's camp at this place.*

joondooj *coverb+BECOME.* make camp. • Joondooj waniyidja berrema daam. *She made camp here in this place.*

joonggoom *noun.* elbow.

joong-joong *coverb+SAY/DO.* suck. • Joong-joong ngini mooloonggoom gooji-milim. *He is sucking the marrow from the bones.* SEE: **joony-joony**.

joongoorleny, joongoorlel, joongoorlem REDUP: **joongoo-joongoorlem**. *noun.* crawling baby.

Joongoorra *noun.* a skin name (when spoken to).

Joongoorrany *noun masculine.* a skin name (when spoken about).

jooniyinnha; jooniyinha *verb.* you (one) are HITTING them/it (non-singular); you (one) are bringing/taking them/it (non-singular).

joonjoonel SEE: **joornjoornel**.

joonjoonoonoojgel *noun.* pardalote species. *Pardalotus spp.* SEE: **binbininidgel**. [NOTE: very small bird that nests in holes in the ground]

joon'goo REDUP: **joon'goo-joon'goo**. *coverb+BE/STAY.* be heaped up. • Jarlangarnam nawarrarram roord, ngoorrooma joon'goo berraniyin. *Lots of plains kangaroos were sitting over there heaped up together.*

joon'goo REDUP: **joon'goo-joon'goo**. *coverb+PUT.* heap up. • Wayiniya ngarrgalem boorroonboo-noowa googana joon'goonga benaya. *The stones are like that because of him, from when he just put them in a heap.*

joon'goo-joon'goo *coverb+SAY/DO_M.* heap up. • Berrayin-ayi werrgale bemberramangbende, joon'goo-joon'goo berra woomberramande. *They used to go like that and get lots of green*

stuff and they used to heap it up there.
joonoomoorloonnha verb. you HAVE them/it (non-singular).
joonoongoona verb. you (one) ATE them/it (non-singular).
joonoowoorroonha verb. you are LEAVING them/it (non-singular).
joonooyilinha verb. you (one) are PUTTING them/it (non-singular).
joony-joony coverb+SAY/DO. suck. • Joony-joony ngerne mooloonggoom gooji-milim. *He is sucking the marrow fat from the bones.* SEE: **joong-joong**.
joony-joony coverb+GET. suck something out. • Dali-ngiyi barlabil, wilyawoom damga jang woomberramande, menkawool, joony-joony nyimberramangbende. *That thing (grub) from the 'bush coconut', insect gall, that thing is sweet, they used to eat it, they used to suck it out.* [NOTE: even though this is translated as 'suck' it is more like 'picking out with the lips' when demonstrated by Shirley Purdie on video]
joorarrg coverb+GO/COME. have hair standing on end. • Joorarrg ngenayi. *My hair is standing on end.*
joord coverb+GO_ALONG. eat. • An danji yirraniyin-ngarri Bow-Rivan, gibi-ngarnam mayim joord yirranyjende yarrewanyga. *And when we were living there at Bow River, we used to eat our own bush food.* SEE: **jang**.
joord coverb+SAY/DO. eat. SEE: **jang**.
joordoob coverb+HIT. throw dust at something (e.g. spirit or ghost). • Joordooba benayidja. *She threw dust at them (mermaids) then.*
joordoobany, joordoobal, joordoobam adjective. dusty, dirty.
joordoom noun. dust.
Joorlboon noun. place on Mabel Downs.
joorlgoony, joorlgool noun. fat toddler. [NOTE: Southern dialect]
joorlgoorlgoom noun. little round things, tablets. [NOTE: Southern dialect]
joorl-joorloo noun. burl, lump on tree.
joornanygarreg coverb+DO_REFL. make pretty, make good-looking. • Berrebaarrinyga joornanygarregboo birrimiyanbe. *Those two are making themselves pretty now (by combing their hair).*
joornanygarreny, joornanygarrel, joornanygarrem; joornanygarrany adjective. pretty, good-looking, delicious.

joorndaj coverb+SAY/DO. look for food, dig little bush onions called *joorndam*, peck with beak (brolga). • Ngoorroola goorrarndal joorndaj nyerne mayim-boorroo. *That brolga is digging for bush onions.*
joorndajgoowool coverb+SAY/DO. all look for food, dig little bush onions called *joorndam*. • Joorndajgoowool boorroorn goorrarnda-woorrarrem joorndam-boorroo. *All the brolgas are looking for bush onions.*
joorndany, joorndam noun. bush onion, little round edible bulb about size of a peanut. *Cyperus bulbosus*. [NOTE: 'Where you find *joornda* you usually also find brolgas' (Hector Jandany); cooked by putting hot ash/earth on them in a coolamon and then winnowing all the ash and the skins away]
joornjoornel; joonjoonool noun. tree species. *Vachellia valida*. [NOTE: used to make woomeras; name also given to *Carallia brachiata* and *Timonius timon* in 'Gija plants and animals' (Purdie et al. 2018)]
joornoogji, joornoogbi noun. sugarbag wax, beeswax. SEE: **ganggarre**.
jooroomoorroo noun. mist/heat haze. SEE: **yaale**.
jooroony noun masculine. tree species found at Bream Gorge.
joorra coverb+PUT. chase game, muster. • Joorra yirrayanyji biriwoorrg Kilfoyle-gili. *We were going to muster back to Kilfoyle's Yard.* • Gendang-biny joorra nginiyanyji. *From upstream he was chasing it down.*
joorra coverb+SAY/DO. drive (car or truck). • Joorra nyerne. *She is driving.* • Joorra berne ngoorr-ngoorrgalil. *Drive the car.*
joorra coverb+BRING/TAKE. drive, chase. • Loonggoong-binyda joorra ngoorranybe nginyjinyga, aa, boomberranybe berremga jiyilem. *They chased him from down here, no, they chased these men.*
joorraj coverb+HIT/CUT. come upon someone and harrass them, bail someone up. • Jaroobam-anyji jiyilem dam, joorraj goorrawoonbe. *Those men who came upon him and growled at him were possibly Jaru people.*
joorr-joorr coverb+SAY/DO_M. scrape. • Joorr-joorr woomberramande bagam-ngiyi. *They used to scrape off its (echidna's) prickles.* [NOTE: using a movement towards the actor, contrasts with *wij-wij* that uses a movement away; a hand

joorr-joorrngiliwool

movement like this is a Gija hand sign for 'echidna']. SEE: **therr-therr.**

joorr-joorrngiliwool *noun.* thing that is scraped (i.e. echidna).

joorroo *coverb+PUT.* put down. • Belegan jida nyanini, joorroo-booboowayi nginayanyande. *She put him down for a little while while she stabbed the ground halfway along.* • Joorroo niniyangge geman ngarliyig-girrem. *I put it down outside (away from the fire) to cool down.*

joorroob REDUP: **joorroorroob, joorroob-joorroob.** *coverb+SAY/DO_M.* come together in line, come in to one place, go in one line. • Rangga yirranyjende nawarra-noo wajbaloom, joorroob-garri woomberramande. *We used to hear it (white people's music) when a big mob of white people came together there.* • Deg-ayi nyimberramangboo, yage ngeli melagawool joorroob-joorroob woomenyande. *They all looked and saw a big mob (of ants) coming in one line.*

joorroob REDUP: **joorroob-joorroob.** *coverb+SAY/DO.* go together in one line. • Joorroob-joorroob berrani Bedford Downs-yoorroong. *They were all walking along in one line to Bedford Downs.* • Joorroob-boorroob boorroorn booloomanbe yilag nawarragawoo-yoorroong goorloom-boorroo. *The bullocks are all walking in a line down to the river for water.* • Joorroob nginini-berrab-gili mernmerdgaleny ngoorrooma, Ord Riva-yoorroong, boorarrgarr benanyji, dangembi Mistake Creek-jen boorarrgarr. *The policeman walked along with them in a line, taking them right over there to Ord River Station and on to Mistake Creek.*

joorroob-joorroob *coverb+GO/COME.* go in one line. • Joorroob-joorroob yarra ngoowan barlberrwany. *Let's go together in one line, don't turn off.*

joorrooji *coverb+SAY/DO.* put down, pour, lay eggs, give birth. • Dama jiregem goomboonybe joorrooji boorroorn. *Those birds lay eggs.*

joorrooloonggoom *noun.* trousers.

joowaj-joowaj *coverb+HIT.* disparage somone, talk about someone claiming they have no culture. • Joowaj-joowaj ngemberriyinbe. *They are saying bad things about me claiming I don't practise my culture.*

joowamennha *verb.* you are GOING AND GETTING him/her/it.

joowangnha *verb.* you (one) will EAT it. • Joowangnha-ma ngabayi? *Do you want to eat, Dad?*

joowany, joowal *noun.* koel, bird that calls out in the night and steals children's spirits. *Eudynamys scolopacea.* • Ngardawoo-ngarri boorroorn, bawoo nyaliny ngini laarne, biniyinji-birri birlirre goorndoogam-birri. Marrarn biniyinji-birri birlirre joowany. *When children cry he calls out at the same time and takes away their spirit. The koel takes away their spirit.* [NOTE: spirit may be brought back by using the smoke of the medicinal plant *gooroongoony*. Some people use *joowany* to mean the koel, also known as 'the storm bird'. Rusty Peters says that *joowany* is a night bird or dangerous spirit bird that calls out in the night and the koel, *doowageny*, drives the *joowany* away. The koel and the channel-billed cuckoo are both known as 'the storm bird' because they appear just before the wet season; their loud calls are sometimes described as 'swearing'.] SEE: **doowagoony, girlgoowal.**

Joowarlgerrji *noun.* hill close to Texas Station homestead. [NOTE: Texas had three names: *Joowarlgerrji, Gawoornboon* and *Ngarrgooroon*]

joowarrg-joowarrg *coverb+GO_ALONG.* go to speak to family after a death. • Joowarrg-joowarrg ngelinke-narri binarri-woorroon-nga. *I am coming to speak to all of you after the death, I don't know anything about it.* SEE: **thayad.**

joowarribarndegji *noun.* northern snake lizard, 'emu killer'. *Delma borea.* [NOTE: one of three striped snake or lizard species called 'emu killer' by Gija people; the other two are *goodawoodany* and *jarloongoorroobarndegji*]

joowarrigaliny *noun.* murderer. LIT: 'ghost/devil-good-at'. SEE: **gerrijbendiny, mawoongarriny.**

Joowarringayin *noun.* Donkey Spring. [NOTE: dangerous 'devil-devil' country in the Leopold Ranges near the old Elgee Cliffs Station.

joowarriny, joowarril *noun.* ghost, spirit, devil, spirit of dead person.

joowawoog *coverb+GO_ALONG.* bird called *joowany* call out. • Belewawirrin joowawoog wiyinya wanyanyagem benamenya-ngarri ngarnbe, giningem. *She (joowany) calls out joowawoog in the middle of the night and takes away children's spirits.*

joowida *verb.* you will TAKE him/her/it. • *Rangga joowida. You will hear him.*

joowijgarneny *noun masculine.* greater bowerbird, 'stealing bird'. *Ptilonorhynchus nuchalis.*

Joowijgarnin *noun.* hill west of Osmond Creek.

joowimnha; joowoomnha *verb.* you (one) will GET him/her/it. [NOTE: alternate form may be a different mood]

joowinganynha *verb.* you will SPEAR him/her/it.

Joowinma *noun.* Gum Hole, country to the north of Bedford Downs in Paddy Bedford's father's country.

joowiyajtha *verb.* you will PUT him/her/it.

joowiyanande *verb.* you (one) will be SAYING/ DOING. • *Nyigawa wiji joowiyanande. Tomorrow you will be running.*

joowiyinnha *verb.* you (one) may be HITTING him/her/it. • *Bilij-anyji joowiyinnha na. You might find it then.*

Joowoolewa *noun.* place name.

Joowoorlinyji; Joowoorlinybany *noun.* Bow River Station.

joowoorlinyji REDUP: **joowoo-joowoorlinybe.** *noun.* boulder, very big round stone.

Joowoorroo *noun.* a skin name (when spoken to).

Joowoorroony *noun masculine.* a skin name (when spoken about).

Ll

-l, -el, -il, -ool *suffix.* feminine suffix to nouns, adjectives and demonstratives. [NOTE: *-l* follows stems ending in vowels, epenthetic vowel added after consonant stems]

laarne *locative.* on top, up high, up on the hill. • *... malala laarne ... midday*

laarn-ngarnany *noun masculine.* green tree frog. *Litoria caerulea.*

lab REDUP: **lab-lab**. *coverb+BE/STAY.* welded/joined together (e.g. hills). • *Lab boorroonboo-gili wayini, lab-lab boorroonboo. They are joined together like that, all joined together.*

labag *coverb+GET.* catch in fingers. • *Labag boomanha. Catch it in your fingers.*

labany, labal *noun.* little corella. *Cacatua sanguinea.* SEE: **ngayilanji**. [NOTE: the little corella is called 'white cockatoo' in Kriol, *ngamarriny* the sulphur-crested cockatoo is called the 'top-knot cocky' in Kriol]

laberd *coverb+BE/STAY.* be behind something like a tree or termite mound so as to not be seen, be camouflaged against the side of the tree. • *Wawooleny laberd nginji goowooloon. The frillneck lizard is just hanging on behind the tree.*

laberd *coverb+FALL/GO_DOWN.* go behind tree. • *Laberd nginiwardji. He went behind the tree.*

laberd-laberd; labe-laberd *coverb+SAY/DO.* attach self to the side of a tree so as to not be seen, stay camouflaged up on the side of the tree. • *Ngarayi-ngarri nimbiyinnha-ngal labe-laberd nyimbirn goowoolen dan. When she (woodswallow/tree creeper) sees you she will put herself against the side of that tree.* • *Wayinigana ngarag dinemangge dany goowooleny thalngarrji laberd-laberd-garri nyerne. That is why I painted that snappy gum tree where she clings close to the side.*

labij *coverb+FALL/GO_DOWN.* clamp self onto something, latch on. • *Warooban dana, ngela deyena, ngarne nawane, labij giniward, gendoowa walig giniyi. He went up there to the east to that cave there at Warooban, he went in there and latched onto the cave wall like a bat.*

lag *coverb+GO/COME.* split (intransitive). • *Lag nginiyin goonyjany. The stick split.*

lag *coverb+HIT.* split (transitive). • *Lag benayidji goowooloom. He split the tree.*

lagarnel, lagarnbe *noun.* witchetty grub, edible grub. Lepidoptera, Cossidae larvae. SEE: **barlganyel, lajel**. [NOTE: not allowed to be eaten or touched by young people]

lagarr *coverb+HIT.* chop tree. • *Wanyanggen-ga ngenengga jirrawoony, yilgoowoorroony, lagarr nyaniyidjende, goowoolem benemanyjende wayinijarram, nhen nyaniyanyjende, beralg nyanemanyjende. When I was a little girl here, one old man used to chop (turpentine wattle trees) for them (witchetty grubs), get sticks like that, poke them in for them and pull them out.*

lagarr *coverb+SAY/DO.* cut/split open. • *Wanggarnal lagarr nyerne nyaliny ngarembi-ningi, benengoonya-ningi. The crow splits it (cabbage gum) open too and eats bush honey from it.*

lagarr; lagarrwany *coverb+GO_ALONG.* go along cutting. • *Ngarranggarni-minyin-anyji lagarr wananyande diyana. Maybe (when she was a woman) in dreamtime she went along cutting it (bush honey) there.* • *Nyaninyande ngarem-boorroo, lagarrwany wananyande. She went along for bush honey, she went along chopping (trees to look for it).*

lagim *noun.* crack. • *Lagin-anyji nginji. He must be in the crack.*

Lagoowan *noun.* place name mentioned by Madigan Thomas.

laj *coverb+PUT.* put on clothes. • *Laj doonbiyajge goothoongoom joorrooloonggoom. I'll put on my short trousers.* SEE: **dim**.

laj *coverb+BRING/TAKE.* wear clothes. • *Laj benanyande mayaroom gooma barndi-warndimga dam. The clothes she used to wear were just that traditional skirt made of spun fur.*

lajel *noun feminine.* witchetty grub. Lepidoptera, Cossidae larvae. • *Ngayin-ga lajen-ngage. I am a witchetty grub.* SEE: **lagarnel**. [NOTE: not allowed to be eaten or touched by young people]

Lajiban *noun.* place on Texas Downs Station.

lalalinybalg *coverb+BE/STAY.* bones lying around. • *Goojina lalalinybalg-garri boorroonboo. All* *the bones are lying there.* SEE: **lalinyparr**.

lalanggarrany *noun masculine.* freshwater crocodile. *Crocodylus johnstonii*.
- Lalanggarram melagawoom. *Many freshwater crocodiles.*

lalawoorroony, lalawoorroom *noun masculine.* heavy wet-season rain (e.g raining all night), heavy fall of rain mixed with big wind like a tornado.

lalinybarr *coverb+BE/STAY.* bones fall to pieces.
- Goojimbi nhawiyangem lalinybarr-ngarri ngininiyin tharloorroon. *His bones fell to pieces in the hollow log.* SEE: **lalalinybalg**.

lamany *adjective.* be loose (tooth).
- Lamany-ngirri jirrawoony ngirriminy. *I have one loose tooth.* [NOTE: word and example provided by Paddy Williams in 1988; younger people are not familiar with this word] SEE: **leg-legnginy**.

lamba-biny, lambag *coverb+GO/COME.* go on side of hill.
- Gaardaya lambag yarroo. *Let's go slowly along the side of the hill.*
- Lamba-biny yarraya gawarre. *We will go along the side of the cliff.*

lamba-lambarrji, lambarr-lambarrji *noun.* bush tea plant, wedelia. *Apowollastonia verbesinoides.*
- Nginyjinya thawalam-ni lamba-lambarrji, winyjingarnany. *Here are the flowers of the bush tea plant, a spring country plant.* [NOTE: also used by some people to refer to *Sesbania cannabina*.] SEE: **manyanyiny**.

lamban *locative.* side of hill.

Lambanjangiliwoon *noun.* place near Norton Bore.

lambarnji, lambarnbe REDUP: **lamba-lambarnbe**. *noun masculine.* young man, youth with a headband aged about sixteen.
- Nginya lambarnji jirrawoony roord nginji lamban. *This is one young man sitting on the side of the hill.*
- Lamba-lambarnbe boorroordboo lamba-yoorroong. *The young men are going to the side of the hill.*

lambarram *noun.* daughter-in-law of man. [NOTE: non-singular agreement used because of avoidance]

lambarrany *noun.* father-in-law of woman, son-in-law of man.

Figure 52. *Lalanggarrany: Danya lalanggarrany barndeg nginji ngarrgalen.* (Photo Jan van der Kam.)

lambood

lambood *coverb+BE/STAY.* be hanging on the side of something (e.g. lizard on tree, bat in cave).
• **Nawane binyjirrminy lambood nginji.** *The bat is hanging up on the side of the cave.*

lamerndarlel *noun feminine.* paperbark. *Melaleuca leucadendra.* [NOTE: said to be an old name not used much in recent times] SEE: **merndany**.

lanany *noun.* yellow pollen sacs in native beehives (sugarbag). SEE: **lernjim**.

lanboodany *noun masculine.* lily species. *Crinum angustifolium.* SEE: **baljanggarrji**. [NOTE: has white flowers in the wet season, not edible]

landiny *noun.* beetle. • **Melagawoom landim.** *Many beetles.* SEE: **lirn'girre**. [NOTE: in dreamtime, *ngarranggarnin*, tries to get in your ear and bore into your brain]

-lang *suffix.* shared relationship (e.g. *thamany-lang*, two people who call each other *thamany*).

lang *coverb+GO/COME.* go along staring.
• **Ngoorroonya lang ngidjinde bardoon ngoorr-ngoorrgajin.** *He's travelling along in the back of the car staring out.*

lang REDUP: **lang-lang**. *coverb+BE/STAY.* stare off into the distance. • **Ngoorroonya lamban lang nginjinde.** *He's looking out from the hillside.*
• **Waringarriny lang-lang-ngarri ngininiyin ngoorroo-biny, ngoorroo-biny.** *Where the big mob were staring out from here and there.*

Langaban *noun.* place in Paddy Bedford's mother's country. [NOTE: 'the place that has lots of puffball fungus' is a dreaming place for that kind of fungus. There are lots of little caves there linked by bush tracks; today there is a bore with a windmill there called Jack Amble Bore. The modern road to Bedford Downs passes close by.] SEE: **langany**.

langabany, langabal, langabam *adjective.* mouldy. SEE: **langany**.

langany *noun.* mould, puffball fungus. [NOTE: puffball used for making yellow paint]

langany-langany *coverb+GET.* be made dry white bones. • **'Langany-langany nandemji-ni,' wanema-birri.** *'Your bones will be white in the sand,' he told them (Moon telling humans they would die).*

langgenybany *coverb+GET.* go grey/get old.
• **Nginyjiny yilag langgenybany nginima.** *This down here has gone grey (cycad seeds).*

langgoornool; langgoornel *noun.* woman, wife. • **Melagawoom langgoornbe** *many women.* SEE: **ngalil, ngoolngal**.

lan'gerrji *noun.* king brown snake. *Pseudechis australis.* SEE: **loonboorroony, booloorrji**.

Lanyin *noun.* place in Rammey Ramsey's country.

lanyiny *noun masculine.* eel. *Ophisternon gutturale.* • **Melelagawoom lanyimga.** *Very many eels.*

lard REDUP: **lalard**. *coverb+GO/COME.* have a headache. • **Lard nginiyi.** *He has a headache.*
• **Lardba naniyi doomoomga?** *Do you have a headache?* • **Doomoom lard genayi.** *I've got a headache.*

lardbe *coverb+SAY/DO.* have a headache.
• **Goonggooloo lardbe ngenarn.** *I have a headache now.*

lare *coverb+HIT.* get fright. • **Lare nginiyid.** *He got a fright.* [NOTE: impersonal, the person frightened is the object]

larl *coverb+BE/STAY.* open legs.

larndoorrji, larndoorroo *noun masculine.* flat coolamon.

larndoorrool *noun feminine.* boat, truck.

laroog *coverb+SAY/DO_M.* tear off pieces of paperbark. • **Merndanyga laroog-gala booma, banjale miyale-boorroo.** *Tear off the pieces of paperbark and spread it out to put the meat on.*

larr *coverb+FALL/GO_DOWN.* get stuck in corner, be trapped. • **Larr nginiwardji.** *He got stuck.* • **Larr nyanoowardja.** *She got stuck (in dreamtime).* SEE: **derd**. [NOTE: get stuck sideways, e.g. water toy in swimming pool]

larrag *coverb+FALL/GO_DOWN.* stick in mind.
• **Larrag berraward-ngirri joonbam goonggooloon.** *The Joonba songs stuck in my mind.* SEE: **larrngig**.

larra-larraj *coverb+GO_ALONG.* go along rattling.

Larrayinji *noun.* place on Texas Downs Station.

Larrelarren *noun.* place on Springvale Station near moon dreaming in Little Panton River.

Larreniny *noun.* Clifton Hole.

larrgardiny, larrgardim *noun.* boab nuts (whole). • **Larrgardim-ni joomooloony.** *The nuts of the boab tree.* [NOTE: Eileen Bray says that the word comes from Derby side but used by Gija, the word *joomooloony* also means 'boab nuts' and 'boab tree']

larrg-larrg *coverb+SAY/DO.* rain in big drops.
• **Larrg-larrg gerne nawarrarrany.** *It is raining*

in great big drops.

larrngib *coverb+FALL/GO_DOWN.* stick in mind.
- *Wayinigana Joonbam thoowoo-thoowoom larrngib berraward-girri.* That is why all the Joonba songs stuck in my mind. [NOTE: Peggy Patrick sometimes says *darrngib*]

larroo *coverb+HIT.* empty something, tip something out, make someone lose something. • *Larroo benayid.* He emptied it. • *Larroo benayidji goorrngam.* He tipped out the water. • *Joowarriny-anyji larroorroo nginiyidji.* Maybe that spirit made him mad (lose his brains).

larroorroo *coverb+SAY/DO.* drip off, drip down.
- *Goorrngajiya larroorroo berrani-birri-yoo boodoonggili.* The sweat was dripping off the two of them like real water.

larroorroo *coverb+GO_ALONG.* sweat drip off, drip down. • *Larroorroo ngeliyin'ge boodoonggooloo.* My sweat is running down.

larrwany *noun masculine.* bush potato species. *Ipomoea costata.* • *Geraj berrani larrwam melagawoom.* They dug up lots of bush potatoes. [NOTE: word used at Yarangga in 1988 where it was considered different to *dawoonyil*] SEE: **berlayiny, bigoordany, dawoonyil, yalamarriny.**

lawag REDUP: **lawa-lawag.** *coverb+BE/STAY.* be white. • *Ngoorroola lawagboo nyinya ngoorroola.* There she is, white over there now (stone that was a female kangaroo in dreamtime). • *Berrem lawa-lawag-garri boorroonboo.* Here when they are all getting white (grey hair).

lawagbeny, lawagbel, lawagbem *adjective.* white.

lawagjil *noun.* white woman.

lawaral *noun feminine.* type of small termite mound, antbed. [NOTE: Southern dialect; young men are not allowed to touch or eat the larvae or big rain will come] SEE: **jamerndel.**

lawardem *noun.* shoulder blade.

lawarrbal, lawarrbany *noun.* long-necked turtle. *Chelodina rugosa.* • '*Ngoowan biri ngenda daa-yoorroong,*' *wanema ngeleli, lawarrbali.* 'I can't go home,' she said, the long necked turtle. [NOTE: *ganggal*, i.e. 'granny' for *darndal*] SEE: **weloowoomoorany, wirriwoonany, woorlemerewal.**

lawoog REDUP: **lawoog-lawoog** *coverb+SAY/DO.* chop with axe, chop sugarbag, cut off roots (e.g. of kapok bush). • *Ngarema lawoog barrern-yoowoo.* You all chop sugarbag for us. [NOTE: usually done by women]

lawoog *coverb+BE/STAY.* be chopping sugarbag.
- *Woolangen ngenardge ngarem lawoog giniyin'ge ngaaloon-kili.* I'm going ahead, chopping sugarbag in the shade. • *Lawoog-gala yade.* Let's chop sugarbag.

lawoog *coverb+GO_ALONG.* go chopping sugarbag.
- *Lawoog woomberranybende-yarre gooramga.* Our mothers used to chop sugarbag for us.

lawoogbany *coverb+GO/COME.* go chopping.
- *Gabiyi lawoogbany ngoonba?* Where will I go cutting? • *Gabiyi lawoogbany yarrwaya?* Where will we go chopping sugarbag?

lawoony *noun.* lemonwood. *Dolichandrone heterophylla.* [NOTE: medicinal, bark used to make a decotion for washing sores]

lawoony-lawoony *coverb+HIT.* cause to become white bones. • *Goojoo lawoony-lawoony nandiji-ni.* Your bones will become white in the sand (said the moon to humans who would not give him the woman who was his mother-in-law).

lawoorany *noun masculine.* white gum, ghost gum. *Corymbia bella.* [NOTE: when burnt provides good ashes for chewing tobacco] SEE: **warlarriny.**

lawoorr *coverb+GET.* put arms around someone.
- *Lawoorr biyim.* Put your arms around him/her.

lawoorr *coverb+DO_REFL.* put arms around self.
- *Joomooloony lawoorr-ngarri nginimiyinji moorlbany laarne dany.* The boab tree has its branches twisted around itself and eyes up at the top (said of a boab tree photographed on the road past Violet Valley on the way to Greenvale).

leb *coverb+FALL/GO_DOWN.* get close behind, crowd in on, sit in a gap (e.g. doorway). • *Leb nyaniward-ngiyi bardoobiny.* She sat close behind her. • *Leb nginiwardji-boorroowa, thed-anyji binbiji.* He got behind them, he might be going to kill someone. • *Leb nginiwardji.* He sat in the doorway. SEE: **leb-leb.**

leb-leb *coverb+GO/COME.* go in a crowd (e.g. cars). • *Leb-leb boorroordboo-gili ngoorr-ngoorrwajim.* There's a traffic jam.

leb-leb *coverb+DO_REFL.* crowd together, crowd in

leg

on each other, get close together. • Ngoowan leb-leb yarrimij, loordbem-yarri. *Don't crowd together, it's too hot for us.*

leg coverb+GO/COME. tooth fall out.
• Minyjoowoom leg ngenayi. *My tooth fell out.* • Jirrawoogoony leg nginiyi-ngirri minyjoowoom. *One of my teeth fell out.*

leg-legginy, leg-leggil, leg-leggim adjective. having no teeth. SEE: **loowoo-loowooginy**.

lembood coverb+PUT. stick something on.
• Lembood-bija benaya therlan, lembood benaya ngenengga, gool nyaniyilin yilag. *She stuck it on her back, and here (on her front) and tried herself out in the water.* SEE: **lambood**.

lemboo-lembood coverb+SAY/DO_M. stick something on. • Lemboo-lembood wanema-ni dambi, gerrij. *She (turtle) stuck it onto him (stuck gum on back of dead crocodile), that was it.* SEE: **lambood**.

lendij; lendej; lerndij REDUP: **lendi-lendijbi**. coverb+PUT. write, read, pressure-flake stone.
• Googan jarrag ngenarn-ninggi. Thoowoo-boorroo lendej joonooyilinnha? *I'm just talking to you. What are you writing it down for?* • Goorayi men'gawoombayi lendej joonayanha. *You wrote that very well, Mother.*
• Lendejboowa nooniyilin'ge ngayin-gawa. *I'm writing it all down now.* • Lendi-lendijbi benayanyji garloomboom jimbirlam, thoord ginimanyji. *He made spearheads and joined them on to his spears.* [NOTE: word used to mean 'writing' because the old people saw writing as a similar action to pressure-flaking stone spearheads, also done with a small hard stick, *mangadany*]

lendij; lendej coverb+GO/COME. write, pressure-flake stone. • Lendij yirrayinji merndam, ngarrgalem-boorroo. *We signed a paper for money.*

lendij; lendej coverb+SAY/DO_M. read, write, pressure-flake stone. • Wayiniya nyinyande lendej woomenyande. *She over there, still reading.*

lendij; lendej coverb+SAY/DO. read, write, pressure-flake stone. • Warnarran lendij berrani gooroogooram jimbirlam. *Long ago the old men used to pressure-flake stone to make spearheads.*

lendijgaleny, lendijgalel, lendijgalem noun. school teacher. SEE: **merndagaleny**.

lengag coverb+SAY/DO. have the hiccups.
• Lengag-jaliny ngenarn. *I have the hiccups again.*

lengagge coverb+EAT. get the hiccups.
• Lengagge noonangoon. *I got the hiccups.*

lenggale noun. woomera handle.

lenggale, lenggam noun. roots. • Rerroob-gala booma lengga-baya. *Pull it out with the roots.*

lenggale noun. ankle. SEE: **boodoom, madaroom**.

lenggeb coverb+SAY/DO_M. flood come and block access, come behind and block off.
• Warrambany loorlg-garri ngoowiyayi lenggeb wimbimji-ngirri mendoowoon-ga. *If the flood comes down in the night it will cut off my access (across the creek).*

lenggeb coverb+GO/COME. flood come and block access, come behind and block off. • Lenggeb goowiyayi goorloony warraminany nawarrany. *The big running floodwater will come and cut us off.* • Nawarrany, nawarrany lenggeb giniyi. *A big one, a big one (flood) came (and cut the road).*

lenggeb coverb+BECOME. come behind someone and block their way. • Lenggeb waniyidja daan nhawiyangen. *She came to his camp behind his back (and blocked his way).*

lenggeb coverb+HIT. come behind and take over. • Lenggeb gemberrayid Yinggilim goonggooloon-ga. *Too much English has come over my brains.*

lerawoog coverb+BE/STAY. lever out, rip off.
• Lerawoog boorroonboo, woobooj-garri woomberrama nyamananim, dal jamerndel dal, barnde-warndeg jimberrayangbe dan, larndoorroo. *The old women lever out the termite larvae and put it to dry out in the sun in a coolamon.*

lerd REDUP: **lerd-lerd**. coverb+FALL/GO_DOWN. become cracked (e.g. ground when dry). • Lerd berraward. *It became cracked.* SEE: **lerlerd**.

lerd; lerlerd coverb+HIT. crack something, bust something open. • Lerlerd boomberriyinbe waranya jamerndel dal gerewoolel gooyarrg boorroorn. *They bust open the anthill, alright then they gather those termite eggs.*

lerd-lerd coverb+SAY/DO. be cracked. • Lerd-lerd ngerne yalamarriny. *The bush potato is cracked.*

lerd-lerd coverb+GO/COME. be cracks. • Lerd-lerd berrayi jilam. *There are cracks in the ground.*

lerlb *coverb+GET.* peel. • Lerlb nyerne goonjal. *She is peeling a kapok root.*

lerlbag *coverb+GO/COME.* come off (e.g. eggshell, damaged fingernail). • Lerlbag nginiyin dambi, boorab nyaniyinya. *The shell comes off and it (baby emu) comes out (from egg).* SEE: **lerlg**.

lerlbag *coverb+GET.* open (egg shell), take off covering (e.g. blanket). • Lerlbag benamanya, booraba nyaninya berrembi. *She (baby emu) opened it (egg from inside) and then she came out here.*

lerle *coverb+HIT.* shiver. • Lerle ngiyinji warn'gany. *He is shivering from cold.* • Lerle nginiyinji. *I am shivering.*

lerle *coverb+SAY/DO.* shiver. • Lerle ngenarn, ngoowanja warn'gam. *I am shivering, oh no, it is cold.*

lerlerd; lerl-lerd *coverb+GO/COME.* become cracked (e.g. ground when dry). • Berrema balawam lerlerd berrayi, dilboo-ngarri woomberrayidbe. *This ground became cracked when it dried out.* • Thambarlam lerl-lerd naniyi gawarn-jaya. *Your feet are cracked like black soil.*

lerlerl *coverb+HIT.* make a ringing sound (e.g. bell). • Marrarnjiya lerlerl boomberrayid. *They already rang the bell to go home.*

lerlg *coverb+BE/STAY.* hatch (egg). • Goomboonyboo dam, lerlg-ngarri boorroonboo, wayinigana warnkany nawarrany ngidji-yarri. *Those eggs (eagle), when they hatch (are peeled), that is the time big cold comes to us.*

lerlg *coverb+GO/COME.* come off (e.g. diseased fingernail). • Yarnderre lerlg ngenayi. *My fingernail came off.* SEE: **lerlbag**.

Lerndijwanema *noun.* Lightning Creek.

lernjim *noun.* yellow pollen sacs in native beehives (sugarbag). SEE: **lanany**. [NOTE: *lernjim* from *gayirriny*, ground sugarbag is sometimes considered medicinal because of the strong taste; *lernjim* from *beranggool* and *nhawiny* tree-living species is a really good food source]

lernngej *coverb+HIT.* collide with something, bump into something. • Lernngej-girrem. *Bull bar* SEE: **linggood**.

lerra REDUP: **lerra-lerra.** *coverb+SAY/DO.* speak

Figure 53. *Lerlb: Birrmarriya Shirley Purdie: Naangaril lerlb nyerne goonjal.*

lerreg

loudly. • *Ngoowan jarrag nimbirn lerra.* Don't speak loudly. • *Ngoowan lerra-lerra nimbirn yage thamboorroo.* Don't speak loudly, your mother-in-law is near.

lerreg *coverb+EAT.* eat until full, fill self with food. • *Lerreg yarrang.* Let's fill ourselves up. • *Lerreg yirrangoon.* We filled ourselves up. SEE: **boorral**.

lerrij *coverb+SAY/DO.* have contractions (childbirth). • *Lerrija nyanini na.* She started to have contractions then.

lerrma *coverb+GO/COME.* keep looking at someone. • *Ngalil lerrma nyaniyi.* The woman was staring. • *Wanyage-warriny lerrma berrayi-noowa-yoo.* The two children kept looking at him.

lig *coverb+BE/STAY.* have head to one side, have head cocked sideways on shoulder. • *Ngoorroonya jiyiliny wenggarrem lig nginji.* That man has his head to one side.

lig *coverb+GO/COME.* go along with head on one side. • *Wenggarrem lig ngidji.* He has his head cocked sideways. • *Lig nyinya wenggarrem yilgoowoorrool.* She has her head sideways because of her bad neck.

liga *coverb+BE/STAY.* wait. • *Liga ngenan'ge-ngooyoo ngenengga.* I am waiting for her here.

ligbayiny, ligbayil, ligbayim *adjective.* having head to one side, shy, tired.

ligirriny, ligirril, ligirrim *adjective.* cross-eyed. • *Moorloo ngelela ligirril.* She is looking at you with one eye.

lilgoonel *noun feminine.* bilby, type of small animal with white tail. *Macrotis lagotis.* [NOTE: buries itself in the bush like a goanna; big mob get into one hole; used to be found in the southern part of Gija country]

lilinyil, lilinybe *noun feminine.* bony bream. *Nematalosa erebi.* SEE: **wirabal**. [NOTE: name also given to similar species, oxeye herring, *Megalops cyprinoides*]

limbalbiny *locative.* side way, on the side. • *Limbalbiny biyarra dala thamboorroo-goorrool roord nyinya.* You go round side way, that is your mother-in-law sitting there. • *Danya wanyageny girli wiyinji limbalbiny banan.* That little boy is walking on the side of the road.

limboog *coverb+PUT.* stick on. • *Limboog benaya therlan.* She stuck them on her back. SEE: **limboord**.

limboord REDUP: **limboord-limboord**. *coverb+PUT.* put something on top of something.

Figure 54. *Lernjim: Lernjim men'gawoom jang-girrem.*

Lirrga, Lirrgal

- **Limboord bemberrayangbe-ni.** *They put it (flat stone) on top of it (small spring).* SEE: **limboog.**

limimim *noun.* cheek. SEE: **ngan'gerre.**

linga *coverb+PUT.* make someone think about something, remind, put thoughts in someone's mind. • **Warna-warnarramga linga benayanyande jiyilemga ngalim.** *In earlier days it (flat green grasshopper calling out) used to put thoughts (of the cold weather) in the minds of all the men and women.*

linga *coverb+GET.* think about someone. • **Linga yimberramanha.** *You should think about us.* • **Linga yinamanha.** *You should think about me.*

linga REDUP: **linga-linga.** *coverb+FALL/GO_DOWN.* remember. • **Linga ngenawoon'ge-boorroo mawoondoom thoowoo-thoowoom, woobooj-garri woomberranybende-yarre, gibi-yibin.** *I remember how they used to take us digging white clay and everything all over the bush.* • **Wayinigana linga-linga ngenaard-ngooyoo joonbal.** *That is how I remember all the songs now.*

linga *coverb+BE/STAY.* be thinking. • **Linga ngenan'ge.** *I started thinking.*

linga REDUP: **linga-linga.** *coverb+SAY/DO.* be thinking. • **Raymondji linga-linga nginini, galama barle nyimbijji bajinggelel.** *Raymond was thinking about whether he was a good person to ride the bike.* • **Linga-linga yirrarn-ngoongoo gilingin-ga.** *We've been expecting you. / We have been thinking about you today.*

lingage *coverb+GET.* remind, draw attention to something, make someone think about something. • **Wayiniya lingage ninimanggende Jambinji, Patrickji.** *I used to point out that sort of thing to Patrick.* • **Lingage benemanyande giri-ngarri wanamanyande.** *It (green grasshopper species called* girinyil*) used to remind them when it called out 'giri'.* • **Lingage boomannha-yarre.** *Remind him about us.* SEE: **liya.**

linga-linga *coverb+GET.* think about someone/something. • **Linga-linga yindemnha-yarre.** *You think of us.* • **Linga-linga nemennha-ngoo.** *I am thinking of you.*

lingam *noun.* thoughts.

Lingga *noun.* Palm Spring (out from Halls Creek).

linggara-gara *coverb+SPEAR.* refuse to answer someone, ignore someone.

- **Jarrag-jarrag-gela ngelamande-ni. Ngoowany. Linggara-gara ngenangaboordjende.** *I wanted to talk to him but no, he wouldn't answer me.* SEE: **nyire-nyire.**

linggara-gara *coverb+BECOME.* not answer someone, go along ignoring people. • **Thebanyji nginini yardembi. Ngoorroonyayi linggara-gara wiyinji.** *His earholes must be blocked up. He can't answer.* SEE: **nyire-nyire.**

linggara-gara *coverb+SAY/DO.* be someone who keeps to him/herself and does not listen to others (a loner).

linggood *coverb+HIT.* collide with something, bump into something. • **Ngoorr-ngoorrgajil linggood nyimberrayidbe.** *They bumped into the car.* SEE: **lernngej.**

linggood *coverb+CUT_REFL.* collide with each other, bump into each other. • **Dama-yoo linggood berrawooranbi-yoo ngoorr-ngoorrgajim-birri.** *They bumped into each other with their cars.*

lintharrg *coverb+GO/COME.* dry up (water in dry season). • **Lintharrga boorroordboo.** *It (water) is drying out (in the dry time).* • **Ngoowan lintharrg giniyinde, danyi goorrnganyi ngininiyinde barranggan.** *It does not dry out, that water stays there all the time as 'living water'.*

linyjilji *noun masculine.* silver cabbage gum. *Eucalyptus pruinosa.* [NOTE: **bin'gany** type of sugar leaf (lerp) found on this tree]

lirlij *adverb.* quickly in a good way.

lirlmim *noun.* dry bark, empty pod, dry skin, fish scale. • **Mayi jirrgawoorr berrani, mayi-bawoorroon, lirlmi-moowam.** *All the food is gone. There is no food, only the dry pod.* SEE: **lirn'girre, nyilim.**

lirn'girre *noun.* shell (of egg, pupa), dry bark, scales, skin of bush onion. • **Ngoowanya lirn'girr-bawoorroony. Belag nginya.** *It has no skin now. It is clean.* SEE: **lirlmim, nyilim.**

lirn'girrel *noun feminine.* water-walking bug.

lirn'girrel, lirn'girril, lirn'girrji, lirn'girrbal *noun.* beetle, ladybird.

Lirrga, Lirrgal *noun.* song and dance style. [NOTE: originated from north of Port Keats; men play didjeridoo and clapsticks, men and women dance; different rythmn from Wangga. Referred to as Lirrga in Kriol. Becomes a feminine noun *Lirrgal* when occurring in a full Gija sentence.]

lirrgarn

lirrgarn *coverb+GET.* explain to someone, instruct someone. • **Lirrgarn yirramanyende.** *We explained to them.* • **Lirrgarn benamanyji goorndoorndoogam.** *He is explaining to the children.* • **Wanemayinde-yirri lirrgarn-ngarri yinamanyjende-yarre-gili yarrewan na.** *He always used to talk to us and tell us all the proper way to live.*

lirrij *coverb+BECOME.* be staring, be wide-eyed. • **Moorloo lirrij waniyid.** *He's got big staring eyes.* • **Lirrij waniyidji-ngiyi ngelela.** *He looked at her hard. / He stared at her.* • **Thoowoo-boorroo lirrij janiyida-ni?** *Why are you looking at him real hard? Why are you staring at him?*

lirrijbayiny, lirrijbayil, lirrijbayim *adjective.* wide-eyed, staring (i.e. one who is staring). • **Moorloo lirrijbayiny.** *He is wide-eyed.* • **Moorloo lirrijbayil.** *She is wide-eyed. Big eyes* SEE: **lirrijgeny.**

lirrijgeny, lirrijgel, lirrijgem *adjective.* wide-eyed, staring (i.e. one who is staring). SEE: **lirrijbayiny.**

lirri-lirriny *noun.* type of very small goanna. *Varanus kingorum.* SEE: **jangalangalany.**

lirring *locative.* sideways.

lirring *coverb+GET.* look at someone/something from side. • **Lirringa ngemenya wayini wad jinya.** *She is looking at him from the side with her head turned back.*

lirring *coverb+SAY/DO.* look sideways not moving head, look askance. • **Lirring nyerne-ngiyi.** *She's looking sideways at her.*

lirring *coverb+SPEAR.* glance sideways. • **Lirring nginingaboordja.** *She glanced at him from the side.*

lirrinil, lirrinbe *noun feminine.* cicada.

liwarag *coverb+SAY/DO_M.* think about something. • **Thoowoo barra liwarag jemenande?** *What are you thinking about?*

liwaya-bawoorroony, liwaya-bawoorrool, liwaya-bawoorroom *adjective.* having no friends or relations. • **Liwaya-bawoorroon-ngoo ninha nyengoowany.** *You have no mate, you stay by yourself.* • **Ngiyi, liwaya-bawoorroon-nga ngayiwanyda ngenan'ge.** *Yes, I have no mate, I stop by myself.* SEE: **melgabawoorroony, wawoonggany.**

liwij, liwooj *coverb+SAY/DO_M.* suck out, slurp up juice/soup/fat. • **Liwija wanemayinde-ni mooloonggoom garrwi-milimbi.** *He was sucking the fat from his armpits.*

liwij *coverb+BE/STAY.* suck out, slurp up juice/soup/fat. • **Liwija ngenden.** *I'll suck it up then.*

liya REDUP: **liya-liya**. *coverb+PUT.* give sign by feeling in body part, remind someone. • **Berrem dam jemenngarram-boorroo, berrayinde- ngarri, bemberramangbende-ngarri, ngenengga-wanyji manyjoorroo, liya bemberrayangbende.** *This (painting) is about when strangers are travelling, when they get them, here in the knees, they give them a sign.* • **Liya-liya bamberremnha yagengerram.** *You all remind that other lot.* SEE: **lingage.**

liyanbe *noun.* feeling in guts.

liyirrim *noun.* intestines.

loobag-loobag *coverb+PUT.* stick gum on (to make heavy). • **Dangembi loobag-loobag benayanya-ni nyaarndembi dany-ni lalanggarrany-ni.** *Then she stuck gum everywhere on the crocodile.*

loob-loob *coverb+GO/COME.* come out in lumps, swell up (from insect bite). • **Loob-loob nimbiyanha.** *You will come out in lumps / swell up.*

loob-loob *coverb+SAY/DO.* come out in lumps, swell up (from insect bite). • **Loob-loob nimbirn-noowa.** *You will get lumps from it (thengawiny ant, if it bites you).*

loogaj *coverb+SAY/DO_M.* feel in mud with hands and pull up something (e.g. waterlily roots, crabs). • **Marlam-birri loogaj-gala ngenda garrjam-boorroo nhoonban.** *I want to feel in the mud with my hands for water-lily roots and pull them up.*

loogoorr *coverb+DO_REFL.* wash self. • **Loogoorr-gala ngendemij.** *Let me wash myself!* • **Loogoorr nimbimjtha, men'gawoog nimbimji-ni nginyjinyga goowooloony.** *Wash yourself (with the water from boiling these leafy branches) and this tree will cure you.* • **Loogoorr nginimiyin.** *He washed himself.*

loogoorr *coverb+GET.* wash. • **Loogoorr-gela nherem.** *I'll have to wash it first.* • **Loogoorr nginimanya.** *She washed him.*

loogoorr *coverb+SAY/DO_M.* do washing. • **Birriyama-birri, loogoorr yirramande.** *These (sinks) are where we used to do the washing.*

looj *coverb+SAY/DO.* be smoking a long way off, be smoke rising far away. • **Marnem looj boorroorn.** *The fire is smoking a long way off.*

loojem, loosem *coverb+SAY/DO_REFL.* die. • **Diyana**

loojem nyanemiyinya. *She died there.* [NOTE: Kriol from English 'lose' but the word most commonly used to mean 'die' by Gija people today] SEE: **nang.**

loojem *coverb+GET.* lose someone through death. • **Warrern berrani-yoo, loojem noonamangge-yoo marlayan ngagenybiyi.** *They two were sick and I lost them from my own hand (i.e. I cared for them through their illness and I held their hands in mine while they were dying).* [NOTE: Kriol from English 'lose']

looloo *coverb.* sit down. SEE: **roord.** [NOTE: Miriwoong]

loomayi *coverb+GO_ALONG.* rock up and down, move from side to side to show off when walking, swagger. • **Loomayi jiyinhande girligan-ga.** *You go rocking all the way when walking.* SEE: **yigily-yigily.**

loomboord REDUP: **loomboo-loomboord.** *coverb+BE/STAY.* lie flat on stomach. • **Wiyarrel loomboord nyinya goomboonyboo.** *The emu is sitting stomach-down on her eggs.*
• **Loomboo-loomboord boorroonboo.** *They are lying stomach down.*

loomoogool *noun feminine.* blue-tongue lizard. *Tiliqua scincoides.*

Loomoogoon *noun.* Osmond Valley.

loomoorrmoorr *coverb+SAY/DO.* come out in lumps or rash. • **Nimbiyanha-ngarri nhawiyangen daan, loomoorrmoorr nimbirn-noowa.** *When you go under his (hairy caterpillar's) camp, you'll get lumps / come out in a rash.*

loomoorrmoorr-nhawoony, loomoorrmoorr-nhawool, loomoorrmoorr-nhawoom *adjective.* one that causes swelling, irritation, lumps or rash (e.g. hairy caterpillar). • **Nyingginy yilgoowoorroony loomoorrmoorr-nhawoony.** *The hairy caterpillar is bad, it causes lumps / gives a rash.*

loonboorroony *noun masculine.* king brown snake. *Pseudechis australis.* SEE: **lan'gerrji.**

loonggaya *coverb+BE/STAY.* be naked.
• **Loonggaya nginbin'ge.** *I'll be walking around naked.*

loonggaya *coverb+GO/COME.* go naked.
• **Loonggaya yirrayinde warnarramga.**

Figure 55. *Loomoogool: Dala loomoogool merreb nyinya ganarran.*

loonggiyengen

Ngoowan drawoojam. *We used to go naked long ago. No trousers.*

loonggiyengen *directional.* go down across
• Bardib wiyinji loonggiyingen goowooloony. *He is going along the edge, down across the tree (log lying down).*

loonggoong *directional.* from downstream.
• Loonggoong girli woomberranybe. *They were walking from downstream up the river.*
• Deg-gala bemij loonggoong-ninggi. *Look at your bottom! (swearing)* • Dal loonggoong-milil nyaninya lawagjil. *That white woman from downstream (i.e. Wyndham) came.*

loonyoorr *coverb+HIT.* spear. • Loonyoorr nginiyid. *He speared him.* • Nginy jiyiliny, dany jiyirriny loonyoorra ngoowiji, ngoowangarnana. *This man wanted to spear that kangaroo but he didn't manage it.*

loordbe *coverb+BECOME.* become hot. • Loordbe ngelayid. *I am hot.* SEE: **loordboog**.

loordbeny, loordbel, loordbem *adjective.* hot.
• Loordbem berrembi daam. *This place is hot.*

loordboog *coverb+BURN/BITE.* get hot.
• Mooloonggoom loordboog benewarrenji mayim-boorroo. *The fat is getting hot for the damper.*

loorlg REDUP: **loorl-loorlg**. *coverb+GO/COME.* floodwater come down creek/river bed, floodwater spread. • Warrambany loorlg nginiyin-yarri rangarrwan. *The big floodwater came down early this morning.* • Loorl-loorlg giniyin gibi-yibin. *It (floodwater) came all over the bush.* • Loorlg nyaliny-ngarri ngoowiyan-yarri, jirrayama dambi nyirregawa narrirn-ni. *When it comes down again, it will be alright for you to swim.*

loorlg *coverb+GET.* wash something away (flood).
• Loorlgoo benamanyji warrambany. *The floodwater washed it away then.* • Loorlg nyimberrangbe. *She got washed away.*

loorlg REDUP: **loorl-loorlg**. *coverb+BRING/TAKE.* floodwater come and carry things away.
• Warrambany nginy loorlg-garri yinanyji-yarre Warrmarne. *This is the flood that washed us away at Warrmarn.*

loorlgoodaj *coverb+SAY/DO.* make a grinding noise, grind seeds in stomach. • Jawarlaliny loorlgoodaj ngerne jaan-ga. Minyjiwarrany ngiyilinji loorlgoodaj. *The shaky paw lizard makes a noise like loose stones rubbing in his stomach. He is thinking of grinding up the*

black plums.

loorndoomooroom *noun.* lower back. SEE: **moon'goom**.

loorndoony; loorndiny *noun.* tree trunk, foot of tree. • . . . nyaarnden loorndoon . . . *at the foot of the Nyaarndiny tree.* [NOTE: *loorndiny* is Southern dialect]

loorr *coverb+SAY/DO.* rush. • Goorloonyi danyi loorr nginini warangganda. *That water rushed fast.*

loorrloorrjaya *coverb+SAY/DO.* make hollow sound (when hit). • Nga, loorrloorrjaya nyerne. Mayi-galelga nginiyala. *Ah, that makes a hollow sound (when I hit it). There must be plenty of tucker on this one.*

loorrma-loorrma *noun.* big tick, kangaroo tick. SEE: **birlinyil, wegerlel**.

loorroob *coverb+HIT.* chase. • Nawarrany danya loorroobji ngiyinji wanyjany. *The big man is chasing the skinny man.*

loorroob *coverb+SAY/DO.* chase. • Joolany loorroob nginini jiyirriny. *The dog chased the kangaroo.* • Ngayin-ga wawooloon-nga. Girndili loorroobji ngenarn. *I am a frillneck lizard. I chase grasshoppers.*

loorroob *coverb+GET.* chase.
• Ngali-ngalim-boorroo, loorroobji-ngarri benamanyjende. *(He was sulking because of) the women he had been always chasing.*

loorroob *coverb+FOLLOW.* chase after someone. • Wajbaloom loorroobji bemberramimangjende ngalim, ngalim-boorroo manbem. *White men used to chase after women, black women.*

loorroob *coverb+GET_HIT.* chase. • Ngoorroo-binya loorroob goorramoowoonbe. *They chased him from there.*

loorroobbany *coverb+HIT.* go chasing someone/something. • Dany loorroobbany nyaniyidji. *He chased her.* • Loorroobbany nginiyidja. *She chased him.* • Dany loorroobbany nyaniyidji gooroogoorany dany. *That old man chased after her.*

loorroob-nhawoony, loorroob-nhawool, loorroob-nhawoom *adjective.* one who chases. • Loorroob-nhawool wariwool gooragalga. *Its cheeky mother (crocodile) will chase you.* [NOTE: unusual in that *nh* follows *b*; would normally become *th* following a stop sound]

looward *coverb+GET.* lever out, dig out put aside.
 • **Looward-gala benem.** *Dig it out and throw it to the side.* SEE: **thera.**

loowarrel *noun feminine.* rifle fish, archer fish. *Toxotes chatareus.*

loowarriny *noun.* tree species, whitewood. *Atalaya hemiglauca.* SEE: **jiwerd-jiwerdji.** [NOTE: used to make fighting sticks]

loowoo *coverb+GET.* take out teeth.
 • **Baroomanbem loowoo ngoorrama minyjoowoomga.** *The doctors took out his teeth.*

loowoo-loowoonginy, loowoo-loowoongil, loowoo-loowoongim *adjective.* someone who has no teeth. SEE: **leg-legginy.**

loowoo-loowoorrel *noun feminine.* bronzewing pigeon. *Phaps chalcoptera.*

loowoongoo *directional.* down there.
 • **Ngoorroona loowoongoo roord nginji.** *He is sitting down over there.*

loowoontherr-loowoontherr *coverb+GO/COME.* suck up. • **Wayinigana loowoontherr-loowoontherr nginiyi dama mooloonggoombi.** *(He) was sucking up that fat like that.*

Mm

-m *suffix.* plural/non-singular suffix to nominals. SEE: **-be, -boo, -e, -oo.**

ma *interjection.* come on.

-ma *suffix.* interrogative suffix.

mabarn *noun.* clever person, doctor, sorcerer, 'magic man'. SEE: **baremanbeny, mooroonggoorrony, nyangoobany.**

maboorany *noun.* conkerberry (konkerberry). *Carissa lanceolata.* SEE: **biriyalji.** [NOTE: said to be Jaru but used by many Gija]

mad *coverb+GET.* pretend to hit, be about to hit. • *Mad nginimanyji. He pretended to hit him.* • *Mad-ayi nginemanyji joolany. He held up the stick as if he was going to hit the dog.* • *Gerloowoorr mad ginimanya. She was about to hit him up there.*

madaroom *noun.* ankle. SEE: **boodoom, boodoom.**

madarrgoony *noun masculine.* brown plum. *Zizyphus quadriloculans.* [NOTE: only the cooked skin of the *madarrgoony* is eaten; same word used for myoporum tree, *Myoporum montanum*, that has small fruit eaten by emus]

madi REDUP: **madi-madi.** *coverb+HIT.* copy someone, imitate someone. • *Joowijgarneny jarrag-jarrag-garri boorroorn, madi biniyinji. The bowerbird copies them when he talks.* • *Madi-madi nyimberrayidbende. They all used to copy her.*

madi REDUP: **madi-madi.** *coverb+SAY/DO.* copy, imitate.

madiwoony, madiwool *noun.* mimic, someone who is good at copying others. • *Danyi joowijgarneny madiwoony danyga. That bowerbird is a mimic.*

magardal *noun feminine.* hat.

magarne *temporal.* tomorrow, the next day. SEE: **nyigawa.**

magoo-magoo *coverb+SAY/DO.* hurry. • *Magoo-magoo boorroorn-gili. They are all hurrying up.*

Magoombarrany *noun.* place name, ancestral being.

maj REDUP: **maj-maj** *coverb+GET.* touch. • *Maj-garri joowimnha woonggariny-ngiyi, birlg nimbiyanha. If you touch that baby kangaroo you will swell up.* • *Ngoowan maj yinbimnha. Don't touch me.* • *Yangoorra berra damba maj-maj bemberrama? Who were those people putting their hands on them?*

maja *coverb+GET.* like, love, want. • *Thoowoorra-boorroo maja benamanya? Why did she love him?* SEE: **warda.**

majalji, majale *noun.* green grass, scrub country. • *Banan-bawoorroon-yarri, majale-yarri, ngoowan yarriyan. There is no path for us, there is scrub, we can't go.* SEE: **werrgalji.**

majany, majal, majam *noun.* boss. [NOTE: Mabel Juli says this word comes from the Worla side]

majarr *coverb+SAY/DO.* be hurting in body part. • *Gaya majarr nerne? Where do you hurt?* SEE: **mirl-mirl, woorrngoord.**

majoorroom *coverb+GO_ALONG.* muster. [NOTE: from English 'muster']

majoorroom *coverb+SAY/DO.* muster. [NOTE: from English 'muster']

malalal *noun feminine.* sun. SEE: **barndel, malwalal.** [NOTE: *malalal* not accepted by Queenie McKenzie but used by lots of other people at Warrmarn]

malaliny *noun.* rosewood. *Terminalia volucris.* [NOTE: has edible gum in wet weather time; probably Southern dialect] SEE: **marlarriny.**

mala-malab *coverb+BE/STAY.* be burning far away, be a fire in the distance at night, glow in the dark far away. • *Mala-malab boorroonboo marnem. The fire is lighting up over there.*

Malamalayi *noun.* place name.

malanyjarrji *noun.* furry-leaved kapok bush, edible root species that resembles *goonjal* but is bitter. *Cochlospermum fraseri* v. *heteronemum.* [NOTE: has similar flowers to *goonjal* but has hairy leaves and different growth pattern. Cooked in the coals and then pounded together with cooked boab seeds, *jililiny*; lots found on Texas Downs] SEE: **ngalwany, warndiwal.**

malawany; malawarn *noun masculine.* freshwater mangrove. *Barringtonia acutangula.* SEE: **mangoonyji.** [NOTE: used as fish poison, roots called *werlarlambalji*]

malawoorrgoony SEE: **marlawoorrgoony**.

malgirrambal *noun.* crow. *Corvus orru.* [NOTE: old word from Shirley Purdie's grandmother at Mabel Downs] SEE: **wanggarnal**.

malirrany *noun masculine.* man who doesn't know or doesn't like women (thinks they cause trouble).

malirri *coverb+HIT.* like something, want something. • Gardiyamga-birri, malirri bembirriyinbe men'gawoombaya-birri. *White people liked it (the country, so they built their houses in it), it was very good for them.*

malirri *coverb.* want to join in. • Ngayin-ga malirri noonoomiyin'ge, wayinigana deg ngelemen'gende. *I'd like to join in with you, that is why I am looking.*

mal-malel SEE: **marl-marlel**.

malmalji *noun masculine.* bush lemon grass, citronella grass. *Cymbopogon bombycinus, C. procerus.* SEE: **ngarrngarrji**.

malmoorrji *noun masculine.* short fighting spear. SEE: **ngoorniny**.

Malngin *noun.* language spoken east of Gija.

malnginyji, malnginybe *noun masculine.* very large grasshopper species.

malngirriny *noun masculine.* lightning.

malngoonybe *noun.* sweat, smell of body sweat.

malwalal *noun feminine.* sun. SEE: **malalal, barndel**.

malwalan *temporal.* hot season. SEE: **barnden**.

mam *coverb+GET.* put hands on someone, feel someone's heart. • Giningin mam barrem-gili. *All of you feel his heart* • Mam nginimanyji barnale. *He put his hands on his shoulders.*

mamag *coverb+HIT.* pour/sprinkle water on someone/something. • Mamag beniyinya werrgale mayim. *She is watering the vegetables.* • Mamag ninbijke. *I will sprinkle water on him.* • Mamagbe ngoorriyinbe roorrany. *They are watering the grass.* • Berremka ngaginybe daam joomoorrriri, marra barriyany-gala, mamag dandiyi-noonggoorroo. *This country of mine is dangerous. Come here! I'll have to put water on you all.* [NOTE: means protection from supernatural harm and also ordinary garden watering]

mamag *coverb+BRING/TAKE.* pour/sprinkle water on someone/something. • Mamag nginanyji. *He was pouring water on him.*

mamag *coverb+SAY/DO.* be watering. • Mamag boorroorn roorrany. *They are watering the grass.*

mambanel *noun feminine.* bush potato species. [NOTE: said to be similar to *banariny*]

mambarnel *noun feminine.* type of black plum. *Vitex acuminata.*

mamberre *interjection.* wait.

mamoorroongan *locative.* spiritually dangerous place. [NOTE: men's word]

man *coverb+GO_DOWN_M.* get dark. • Man wanawoon. *It is about to get dark (night).*

man REDUP: **man-man**. *coverb+FALL/GO_DOWN.* get dark. • Man berraward daam. *It got dark.* • Manbe berrewoonbe daam. *It's getting darker and darker.* SEE: **ngij**.

manam *noun.* anus, faeces, backside. [NOTE: can be a cause for laughter but not really swearing; can be used to refer to the whole area of anus and buttocks]

manambarrany, manambarral, manambarram REDUP: **mananambarram**. *noun.* senior person, leader, important person, holder of the law, person who is in charge of a particular piece of land, elder.

manana *coverb+SAY/DO_M.* play around. • Balgayan manana woomenyande. *She is playing around on the flat.* • Ngenengga manana wanemayinde-yarri-yoo::: yooroorr. *He kept dancing and playing around us two.*

manaroony, manarool REDUP: **mana-manaroom**. *noun.* parents and their siblings, relationship term used to refer to people of the correct skin to be mother, uncle, father or aunt (e.g. what Nambin calls Naminyji, Joongoorra, Nangala and Jangala), senior people. • mana-manaroom *parents, uncles and aunties*

manarr-manarr *coverb+SAY_REFL.* talk together with family after a death to sort out what happened. • Warna-warnarram manarr-manarr-ngarri berrangirriyinbende-berra. *Old people used to talk together to sort out how the person from them (their family) had died.* [NOTE: some say this is Jaru] SEE: **thayad**.

manbe; maanbi *coverb+FALL/GO_DOWN.* become dark. • Danya ngoomoolji manbe ngoowoonji. *That cloud is getting black.* • Manbe berrawoonbe-yarri. *It is getting dark (on us).* SEE: **man, man-manbe**.

manbe *coverb+BECOME.* become black. • Wayinigana manbe waniyid. *That is why he*

manbeg

became black.
manbeg *coverb+BURN/BITE.* make/become black in fire. • Manbeg nginiwoorranji marnem-berrewa. *He had got black from the fire.*
manbeg *coverb+BRING/TAKE.* make black. • Manbeg nginanyji. *It made him black.*
manbeg *coverb+GET.* make black. • Nyoon nginanya welerrem-birri, manbeg nginemanya, merreb nginiyanya. *She rubbed the baby with charcoal, she made him black and hid him*
manbegayiny *noun.* black person. [NOTE: Goody Barrett talking about African people in the street at Footscray, Melbourne]
manbe-manbe *coverb+BE/STAY.* be black. • Danya yingarrjiny manbe-manbe nginji. *That sandpaper fig fruit is black.* SEE: **man, manbe, man-manbe**.
manbeny, manbel, manbem REDUP: manbe-manbem] *adjective.* black. • Bib-gala benemnha dam manbe-manbem. *Pick up the black ones.* • Danya goorloony yilag dagoorlan manbeny yilag. *That is the water in the deep hole, the black part at the bottom (of the painting).*
manbooloo-wooloo *adjective.* be blackened by smoke, be dirty from smoke. [NOTE: said of *girrganyji*, 'brown falcon', who stole fire from *nyinyil*, 'zebra finch', in the dreamtime]
manboorlool *noun feminine.* rock pigeon. *Petrophassa albipenis.* SEE: **ngarrgalengarnal**.
mandegerreny, mandegerrel, mandegerrem *adjective.* dark.
mandirri *noun.* woman's husband's brother/sister, brother-in-law/sister-in-law (spoken to). SEE: **ngawooji, wardoo**.
mandirril *noun feminine.* woman's husband's sister, sister-in-law. SEE: **ngawoojil, wardool**.
mandirriny *noun masculine.* woman's husband's brother, brother-in-law. SEE: **ngawoojiny, wardoony**.
mangadany *noun masculine.* short stick of very hard wood used to pressure-flake stone making the teeth on 'Kimberley points'; small sharp stick, trimmer for making spearheads; species of small shrubs with very hard wood used to make the spearhead-making tool of the same name. Turkey bush, *Calytrix brownii, C. exstipulata* or dodonea, *Dodonea polyzga*. [NOTE: four-inch nails were also used to pressure-flake stone when they arrived in the Kimberley; the word is used to mean 'pencil' at Warrmarn]
mangan REDUP: **mangan-mangan**. *coverb+SAY/DO.* wave. • Mangan ngerne. *He is waving.* • Mangan-mangan nginini manggerregerreny. *The tata lizard was waving.*
mangan-mangan *coverb+GO_ALONG.* go along waving. • Mangan-mangan ngiliyande. *I will keep waving my hand.*
mangij *coverb+FALL/GO_DOWN.* get stuck in the mind. • 'Mangij birriwoon-narri gerag,' nginini-yirri. *'It (song) will get stuck in your mind later,' he told us.*
mangi-mangi *coverb+GO_ALONG.* be walking having a strange feeling of being like a spirit. • Mangi-mangi ngelanyge gaboowanyji ngenarn. *I am walking as a spirit not knowing what I am doing. / I have a bad feeling about something.* SEE: **rawoorl**.
manggam *noun.* chest. SEE: **doomoorroo**.
Manggerlen; Manggarlan *noun.* place where the bat hid in a cave in dreamtime.
manggerregerreny, man'gerregerreny, manggirrigirriny *noun.* shaky paw lizard, tata lizard. *Lophognathus temporalis, Diporiphora lalliae, D. magna.* SEE: **jawarlaliny, jawariny**.
manggoom *noun.* shade. SEE: **ngaaloom**.
mangoony *coverb+SAY/DO_M.* gobble, eat

Figure 56. *Mangan: Dindanyji Ashley Clifton, Manyjoorrbal Berylene Mung Mung: Jangala mangan ngerne.*

by stuffing handfuls of food in mouth. • **Mangoony jemenande.** *You are gobbling food.* • **Ngoorroonyayi mangoony woomenjende gerrijbendenyga.** *He's gobbling his food over there, he's really greedy.* SEE: **jang, ramoob.**

mangoonyji, mangoonybe *noun.* water weeds like grass. • **Goorndarrim walilig berrayin yiligin mangoonyen.** *The fish have gone in under the water weeds.* • **Bib bemberramangbe mangoonybe gerlgayi-girrim.** *They got the water weeds to roll up to push through the water to catch fish.*

mangoonyji, mangoonybe *noun.* freshwater mangrove. *Barringtonia* sp. SEE: **malawany.** [NOTE: used as fish poison]

Manjalban *noun.* place on Bow River Station.

manjalji, manjale *noun.* white stone, quartz.

Manjalji *noun.* place with a white hill in George Mung Mung's country.

Manjalngarriny *noun.* place west of March Fly Creek on Bow River Station.

man'garraya *adverb.* suddenly. • **Dooriyi wanema man'garraya.** *There was a sudden crack of thunder.*

manmad *coverb+GET.* try out something, test something. • **Manmad-garri ninemangge garloomboony, 'Ngoowanjaya merewany, degerd-gala nherem.' Jirrayanya. 'Werndij-gala nheraj. E-e jirrayanya.'** *I tried out the spear, 'Not like that, it's too long, 'I'll have to cut a bit off.' (I tell myself,) Then it's OK. 'I'll try throwing it.' 'Yes, it's OK now.'*

man-manbe *coverb+FALL/GO_DOWN.* be getting dark. • **Ngoomoolji man-manbe ngoowoonji, men'gawoo-men'gawoo wiyinji.** *The clouds are getting dark, it is becoming very good.*

manoom *noun.* word, story. SEE: **jarragboo.**

manoo-manoo *coverb+DO_REFL.* • **Manoo-manoo-gala yarremij.** *Let's talk to each other.*

manoomarnoony *noun.* wood of the conkerberry (konkerberry) bush. *Carissa lanceolata.* [NOTE: smoke when wood is burned smells good, it repels mosquitoes and protects children] SEE: **biriyalji.**

mantha *coverb+PUT.* introduce someone to country or food, to conduct a ceremony that allows someone to eat a particular type of food or enter a part of the country safely. • **Miya mantha narajtha-ngoongoo ngagenybe-berroowa daam.** *I would just like to introduce you to my country properly so that you will come to no harm.* • **Mantha-ngarriga nimbiyajtha-ngoo men'gawiya girli nimbirn.** *When you've been welcomed in this way you will be able to visit in safety.*

mantha *coverb+FALL/GO_DOWN.* be introduced to country or food, undergo a ceremony that allows one to eat a particular type of food or enter a part of the country safely. • **Mantha-ngarri nanoowoon-ngoongoo men'gawiya girli nimbirn berremga-birri daam.** *When you've been welcomed in this way you will be able to walk around safely in this country.*

manthan *coverb+GO/COME.* meet someone, meet halfway. • **Manthanbe ngenardge-boorroo.** *I'm going to meet them.* • **Manthan nginiyinde-ngooyoo.** *He kept going to meet her halfway.*

manthan *coverb+PUT.* go to meet someone, meet halfway. • **Manthan nginiyanyji.** *He went to meet him.*

manthan *coverb+HIT.* go to meet someone, meet halfway. • **Marrarn joogboo ngenardge, manthan barrijtha-ngage.** *I'm going hunting, come to meet me halfway.*

manthoornji *noun masculine.* mistletoe. SEE: **janim.**

manyanyiny *noun masculine.* **1.** wild tea. *Ocimum tenuiflorum, Apowollastonia verbesinoides.* SEE: **barnabeliny, lamba-lambarrji. 2.** small medicinal herb, smelly bush. *Streptoglossa bubakii, S. odora.* SEE: **gooroongoony**

manyawoorlale *noun.* scales of rainbow snake.

manyjangal *noun feminine.* axe. SEE: **ngajiral, thalerrel, woomal.** [NOTE: young men have to say *mayinggal* (Rusty Peters)]

manyjangalam *noun.* skin.

Manyjoorroo *noun.* hill near Balan'gerr on Texas Downs.

manyjoorroo *noun.* knee.

manymaj *coverb+SAY/DO_REFL.* put hands on self, feel self (e.g. to see which pocket a wallet may be in). • **Manymaj genangirriyin, 'Goowoo gawoo-ngirri merndambi?'** *I felt myself (my pockets), 'Hey, where is my money?' (I said to myself.)*

manymaj *coverb+GET.* put hands on, feel something. • **Manymaj nyanemanyande, bilirnbe benamanya-ngooyoo, therlan, dinyjile gerd-gerd nyanemanyande**

maraloo

ganarram-birri. *She would put her hands on her, she got river red gum leaves for her to warm her back and navel.*

maraloo coverb+GET. get a song from a spirit.
- Maraloo nemenha-ngoo dam joonbam. *I just want to get that song from you (Buttercup speaking to the spirit of her dead sister).*

maram noun. hot dirt, hot sand.

marayam noun. light.

mard coverb+SAY/DO_M. dry out. • Jawarlaliny mard wanema yilwarraya. *The tata lizard dried up completely (said of dry dead lizard).*

mardangarril noun. black cockatoo. *Calyptorhynchus magnificus.* [NOTE: word used by young men who are not supposed to say the word *derranel*.]

mardany noun. small tree with green shiny leaves, smooth yellowish bark and white flowers. *Gardenia megasperma, G. dacryoides.* [NOTE: gives good flavour to meat if it is wrapped in the leaves of this tree before cooking; can be put in kangaroo's guts with *thalngarr*, 'snappy gum', before cooking. Young men take leaves of this tree to the main waterhole and chop them up with their own sweat so that they are safe and they can then talk to the water. Leaves used to make smoke to stop heavy rain.]

Mardarrnginy noun. place near Gum Hole on Bedford Downs.

mari REDUP: **mari-mari** coverb+HIT. sneak up on someone/something. • Gaboowanyji danya mari-mari yiniyinji-yoowoo. *Something is happening, that one is sneaking up on us.*
- Mariwoo niyin'ge jiyirriny. *I am sneaking up on the kangaroo.* • Mariwoo ngoorriyinbe melagawoom. *They are sneaking up on him, all of them.* SEE: **bandaj**.

mari-mari coverb+BRING/TAKE. sneak up on someone. • Mari-mari yimbirrigbe-yoowoo googan. *They will just be sneaking up on us.*

marlagal noun. prickle. • Marlagal-ban-nga thambarlam. *I have a prickle in my foot.*
- Marlagal ngoorroongany-gala thambarlam. *Let the prickles poke him in the foot.* SEE: **bagany, boorndalji**.

marlalji coverb+DO_REFL. grab from each other.
- Marlalji barremijtha-gili. *You all grab from each other.*

marlam noun. hand.

marlam coverb+PUT. help, lend a hand.

- Goorndooganyi yambilji wanggarlwoony, ngoowan marlam benayanyji. *One little boy was slow and lazy, he didn't put his hand to it.*
- Men'gawiya marlam yinayannha-yarre biya-wiya-girrem dany Marloogany-noo Joolany. *It is good you were helping us to look for Old Dog (i.e. thank you for helping us).*

marlam coverb+HIT. help, lend a hand, help as part of the State Emergency Services.
- Dam jiyilem werrgam-ngarri boorroorn, bimbirriyinbe-ngarri marlam, boorroorn-yarri, 'Yiligin barrennha, dany jadany beraj-ngarri ngiwiyan.' *Those men who work as part of the State Emergency Services (putting their hands on things) tell us, 'Stay inside until the rain passes.'*

marlambeny noun. scraggy bloodwood. *Corymbia abbreviata.*

marlarriny noun. rosewood, tree species. *Terminalia volucris.* SEE: **malaliny**. [NOTE: shavings were used for body decorations]

marlawoorrgoony, marlawoorrgool, marlawoorrgoom; marlawoorrji, marlawoorrool, marlawoorre adjective. having a lot of fat (animal/meat).
- Mooloonggoogalel marlawoorrgool miyalelga dal goorndarril garriyil. *That bream is a fish that is really fat, it has really fat meat.*
- Gernanyjel marlawoorrgool. *The echidna has fat meat.* SEE: **mooloonggoogaleny**.

Marle noun. Binays Pocket. SEE: **Jengoowoon**.

marlil noun feminine. nuisance grass. *Heteropogon contortus.* [NOTE: female version of 'bush sugarcane', *H. triticeus*; seeds from this grass are a nuisance at the end of the wet and the early dry season as they poke into your clothes and swag]

marliny noun masculine. **1.** cane grass, wild sorghum, spear grass. *Sorghum timorense, S. stipoideum.* [NOTE: grows at the end of the wet season, time of *marligen*, 'knock-em down rains'] **2.** bush sugarcane. *Heteropogon triticeus.* [NOTE: a large grass that has sweet watery juice]

marlirn, marlirnji noun. water weeds, long green algae in water, green slime, water hair. *Chara* spp.

marlirnbany noun. newborn baby. LIT: 'having green water weeds' (as its spirit has just come from the water). SEE: **nyarlimbiny**.

marliwal; marloowal noun feminine. fat female

rock wallaby. *Petrogale brachyotis.* • *Wa, marliwa-gayin-jaya-ninggi nyengen-gawa, ngayin-ga gerndi-werndi-gayin-ngirri. Hey, you've got all the fat girl ones, but me, I've got all the bony boy ones!.* • *Diyanya walaji nginiyidji marliwam-berrewa. He was jealous and made trouble for him because of the fat female rock wallabies.* SEE: **thoorrmal.**

marl-marl *coverb+GO_ALONG.* flap wings, fly. • *Goorrarndal, goorrarnda-jal marl-marl-ngarri wiyinya. The grasshopper species called goorrarndal (the same name as the brolga) is like a brolga because it flaps its wings.* • *Marl-marl ngerne danya laarne. It (kestrel) is flapping its wings up high.*

marl-marlel *noun feminine.* nankeen kestrel. *Falco cenchroides.* SEE: **gardagarrji, marrg-marrgjil, waaliny.**

marloogany REDUP: **marloo-marloogam**. *noun masculine.* old man, elder. • *Marloo-marloogam berraniyinde-ngarri. Where all the old men used to stay.*

marloorloom *noun.* kindling, little sticks.

marloowoorroo *noun.* lips.

mar-maroora *coverb+SAY/DO.* finish ceremony. • *Diyena mar-maroora berrani, diyena merre-merreb wanemayinde. They finished the ceremony and hid him away (from women).*

marnale *noun.* nose. SEE: **nyoomboorroo.**

marndi *coverb+BECOME.* leave for later. • *Marndi waniyidjende. It can stay until later.*

marndi *coverb+HIT.* put off until later, leave until later. • *Marndi benayidji. He left them/it (non-singular) for later.* • *Marndi-wanyji nyaniyid. The man must have left (the echidna) until later.*

marnebany, marnebal, marnebam *adjective.* hot, burning. LIT: 'having fire'.

marnel *noun feminine.* dynamite.

marnem, marneny *noun.* fire, firewood. SEE: **mawarrji.**

maroolooya *coverb.* look after someone/something. • *Maroolooya yamberramoorliya daam. We will look after the country.*

maroongoony, maroongool, maroongoom *adjective.* low. • *Ngelel-ngooyoo maroongool maroongool ngelga ngoorr-ngoorrool. This car is very low (i.e. the clearance underneath).*

maroorr *coverb.* look after someone, keep someone/something to oneself. • *Maroorr biyi! Look after him!* • *Maroorr-maroorr biyida goorlangginy. You keep looking after him*

poor thing. • *Maroorr ngimberriyinbi-yoo men'gawiya. They two look after me very well.*

marra *adverb.* already. SEE: **marrarn.**

marra *adverb.* far. • *Marra looj boorroorn-ni ngoorriyama, miny-miny nginini. He saw smoke rising in the distance and the flickering light.*

marra *coverb+GO/COME.* set off, go away. • *Marra biyarra, girrija ngelayidge. Go away! I've finished* • *Marra boorroordboo-yoo girlirliwany. The two of them went walking away.* • *Marra yidja nyirrega-giny, ngaji. Let's go swimming brother!* • *'Marra biyarrmawa!' nginini-ngiyi. 'You'll have to get out of here now,' he said to her.* SEE: **marrarn.**

marra *coverb+LEAVE.* go away and leave someone. • *Marra ngenawoorroodji. He went away and left me.* • *Marra yinboowoorroobja-yoowoo. She will be leaving us.* SEE: **marrarn.**

marra *coverb+BRING/TAKE.* take away. • *Beneda marra Pandanus Yard-yoorroong yawardamga. You can take those horses down to Pandamus Yard.* SEE: **marrarn**

marra *interjection.* come on. SEE: **marrarn.**

marragoowoorroon *locative.* not far away.

marraj *coverb+HIT.* go past. • *Marraj nginiyidja dany jiyiliny. She went past that man.*

marrajgany, marrajgal, marrajgam *adjective.* sticking far out.

marralam *noun.* part of the stomach of cattle that grinds up grass.

marralan *noun.* flat country. • *Berrema goowooloo-merrale marralan Loomoogoon-ga. Here are all the trees on the flat country at Loomoogoon.*

marranyil; marranyel *noun feminine.* fruit species, bush pawpaw. *Capparis lasiantha.* SEE: **bambilyiny.** [NOTE: very prickly creeper with edible fruit, does not look anything like a pawpaw in spite of the common name]

marranyji *noun masculine.* dingo. *Canis lupus dingo.* • *Marranybe. Dingoes.* SEE: **merlarrji.**

marrarab *coverb+BE/STAY.* glow (bushfire at night over the horizon). • *Marrarab nginji marneny. The bushfire is glowing in the distance.*

marraram *noun.* glow (of bushfire at night over the horizon). • *Deg woomberrama 'Marri marraram boorroonboo wirli-wirlin.' They looked, 'Oh, the bushfire is glowing on top of the hills' (they said).*

marrarn *adverb.* already time passed/gone

marrarn

away. • *Banyma yiniyinnha, marrarn nyamani jiyinnha.* You can't say you are getting young, you are becoming an old woman. SEE: **marra**.

marrarn *coverb+BRING/TAKE*. take away.
• *Goora-woorrarrem woolgoowool-gooman, marrarn yimberranybende-yarre.* All our mothers and other old women like them used to take us.

marrarn *coverb+LEAVE*. go away and leave someone. • *Marrarn ngemberrawoorroodbe warnarrayam.* They left me a long time ago.
• *Marrarna nhewerranha-ngoo goonja-giny.* I'm leaving you to get kapok bush roots.

marrarn *coverb+FALL/GO_DOWN*. go away, die.
• *Marrarn nyanooward.* She went away (i.e. she died). [NOTE: idiomatic coverb-verb combination recorded in Halls Creek]

marrarn *coverb+GO/COME*. go away. • *Marrarn thewerr nginiyin-berrewa-yoo wigi-warriny.* He went away following his two sons. • *Marrarn nginiyin danyi jalariny.* That egret (white crane) went away. • *Nyoonggayam na marrarn nginbiyan-ninggi diyena.* Alright I had better go to you at that place. [NOTE: adverbial in many cases, unlike other coverbs]

marrarn *coverb+HIT*. take away. • *Marrarn nginiyid.* He/she took him away. • *Marrarn niyinnha-ngoo.* I am taking you away.

Marraroon *noun*. place name.

marrawayil *noun feminine*. bar-shouldered dove. *Geopelia humeralis*. SEE: **gelaroogool, goolaroogool**.

marrga *coverb+GET*. like someone, praise someone. • *Marrga yarremenya.* We like him/her/it.

marrge *interjection*. wait.

marrge *particle*. still, yet.

marrg-marrgjil *noun feminine*. nankeen kestrel. *Falco cenchroides*. SEE: **gardagarrji, marl-marlel, waaliny**.

marri *interjection*. oh dear!, hey! goodness what a lot! (expression of amazement/surprise).

marrirri *coverb+HIT*. love, like. • *Men'gawoom, werrgale marrirri benayidja berrem daam.* She really loved this good green grass place. SEE: **maja, malirri, warda**.

marr-marr *coverb+GO_ALONG*. go along being greedy. • *Gerrelel, marr-marr wiyinya, dama waanyim ngarayi-ngarri benayid.* A greedy one, she (crow) is going along being greedy (eating everything) when she found those maggots/worms.

marr-marr *coverb+SAY/DO*. wanting everything, be greedy. • *Dama marr-marr nyerne-birri jangaa woomenyande.* She (crow) is greedy for those things (worms) and is eating then.
• *Dama wanyanyagem marr-marr boorroorn-boorroo thoowoo-thoowoom gedba-ngarri bemberrayid.* Those children want everything they see. [NOTE: Eileen Bray explains that it is like kids going into the shop and their eyes light up and they want everything]

marrmoogji *noun masculine*. collared sparrow hawk. *Accipiter cirrocephalus*.

marrngen *coverb+SAY/DO*. murder. • *Marrngen nginini-ni.* He murdered him.

marroo REDUP: **marroo-marroo**. *coverb+GET*. be jealous, want to keep something oneself, like, love. • *Marroo-marroo ngoorramang-boorroowa ngalim-boorroo.* They were jealous for the women (so they killed all the men).
• *Marroo-wanyji ngenemenya.* She might be jealous about him. She wants to keep him/it (masculine) for herself. • *Marroo-wanyji ngenemenyji.* He might be jealous about him. He wants to keep him/it (masculine) for himself.
• *Marroo-ngarri yimberramangbende-yarre woolgoolgoomenbega.* The old women used to want to keep us themselves (and not let the Yarrali spirit woman take us). • *Marroo nyiliyin'ge.* I love her. / I like her. [NOTE: gloss as 'like, love' from Doris Fletcher from Halls Creek]

marroo-marroo *coverb+SAY/DO*. be jealous, want to keep something oneself. • *Marroo-marroo nyerne-noo daanyga dany.* She's jealous for that place. She wants that place for herself.

marroo-marroo *coverb*. be jealous, want to keep something oneself. • *Marroo-marroo woombiyanyande-noo.* She is jealous for it all the time. (She (emu) keeps it (egg) to herself all the time.)

marroorool; marrooral *noun feminine*. Leichhardt tree. *Nauclea orientalis*. SEE: **ngimilil, ngimirlil**. [NOTE: has edible fruit]

mathe *coverb+GET*. say goodbye to someone.
• *Mathe nginimanyji.* He said goodbye to him.

mathe-mathe *coverb+SAY/DO_M*. be saying goodbye. • *Ngoowan mathe-mathe joowiyanande warren-warren-nhawoon-ngoo.* You don't want to talk about going away, you get sick.

mathe-mathe *coverb+SAY/DO_REFL*. say goodbye

to each other. • *Mathe-mathe berrangirriyin.* *They said goodbye to each other.*

mawarr coverb+PLACE_M. light a bushfire.
• *Mawarr-gela ngelaj, booj noondaj-birri. Let me light a bushfire and burn up everything.*

mawarrji noun. bushfire. • *Nginiwarrenji marneny mawarrji. The bushfire is burning.*

mawij coverb+SAY/DO. get skinny. • *Wayinigana, mawij berrani-yoo dambi gerlalbambi. Because of that the two of them became very skinny in the legs.*

mawiyab REDUP: **mawoo-mawiyab**. coverb+SAY/DO_M. poison someone.
• *Mawoo-mawiyab woomberramande. They (early invaders of Gija country) used to poison people.*

mawiyab coverb+CUT_REFL. poison self.
• *Mawiyab-wanyji yirriwan. We might poison ourselves.*

mawiyam noun. poison.

mawoo-mawoonde coverb+SAY/DO_REFL. kill each other.
• *Mawoo-mawoonde berrangirriyinbende. They used to kill each other.*

mawoondool, mawoondoom, mawoondem noun. white paint, white clay. SEE: **galadil**.

mawoondoongarnayin noun. murderer. SEE: **mawoongarriny**.

mawoongarriny, mawoongarril noun. murderer, dangerous person. SEE: **mawoondoongarnayin**.

mawoorooriny noun. diver jack, snake bird, darter. *Anhinga melanogaster.* SEE: **garrang-garranginy**.

mawoorrboonybe coverb+FALL/GO_DOWN. getting dark. • *Mawoorrboonybe berrewoonbe-yarri. It is getting dark on us now.*

mawoorrg coverb+FALL/GO_DOWN. stay for good.
• *Ngenenggayana mawoorrg barriwoo! 'You should all stay right here' (he said to them).*

mawoorroo coverb+SAY/DO. be sunset.
• *Mawoorroo boorroorn. It is sunset.*
• *Mendoowoon marrarna mawoorroo. Just still a little bit bright.*

mawoorroony, mawoorrool noun. bloodwood. *Corymbia dichromophloia, C. terminalis.* [NOTE: the ash is chewed with tobacco; flowers called *jirliwoorril* let people know that the cold weather is coming; has sugar leaf (lerp) species called *wanamarriny*. Name also recorded applying to *C. polycarpa* and the ironbark, *Eucalyptus jensenii*. Blood-red gum or kino, *galiwoony*, is used in painting and on artefacts. Most commonly heard in the masculine singular form, *mawoorroony*.]

mayajarrg coverb+SAY/DO. be unable to walk.
• *Mayajarrg ngenarn. I can't walk.*

mayam noun. magic power, strength. • *Dambi mayam-ngiyi, mayam-ngiyi merrngag-merrngaga nyanini. She (rainbow snake) flashed a light using her magic power then.*

mayabany, mayabal, mayabam adjective. strong, having magic power. • *Danyga mayabany. That one is strong.*

mayaroom, mayaroony noun. house, clothes. [NOTE: rarely in the masculine singular form]

mayawanji noun. willy-willy. SEE: **jalawoonany**.

mayigalel, mayigaleny noun. 1. plant bearing lots of food. LIT: 'good at food'. • *Mayigalelga nginiyala. There must be plenty of tucker on this one.* 2. person who is a cook. LIT: 'good at food'.

mayim, mayiny, mayil noun. non-meat food, vegetable food, bread. • *Danya joomooloony mayi-bany. There is fruit on that boab tree.* • *Melakawoom-ngiyi boorndalega girlilga dal; mayilga-yoowoo jang-girrilga gig-girrem. That bush tomato is very prickly; it is bush tucker for us to eat and get full on.* [NOTE: agrees in gender with the plant referred to]

Mayimboorroon noun. Spring Creek Station; a place at Spring Creek Station, with name like Nancy Nodea and Churchill Cann's uncle.

mayinggal noun feminine. axe. [NOTE: avoidance word supposed to be used by young men who are not allowed to say the other words] SEE: **manyjangel, ngajiral, woomal**.

mayiwarndem noun. bone. SEE: **goojim**.

melagawiya adjective. everyone, all, the whole lot. • *Nyirreg-gala barrawoo-gili melagawiya! You all dive in the water, the whole lot of you!* SEE: **waringarriya**.

melagawoom, melagawoony, melagawool, melagam REDUP: **melelagawoom**. adjective. many, all, plentiful. • *Melagawoomga woorrjib boorroonboo-ngirri. Everyone sits down with with me.* • *Ngiyi, jirrayam melagawoo-ban-nga berrthaban ngelayid. It's alright, I've got lots of mates.* • *Biri ninbige melagawoom-anyji jiyirrem-anyji thed-garri ninbijge wan'gim-birri. I might bring back lots of kangaroos that I will kill with the*

melaya

rifle. • Wanda-wandaj woomberramande melagawoom goord bemberramangbende. *They were carrying lots (of game) that they kept on killing in a large number.* SEE: **waringarrim**.

melaya *adjective.* all. • Boorroowiyina-gili melaya walig! *They should all go in.* SEE: **melagawiya**.

melele *coverb+SAY/DO_M.* smile. • Melele-ngarri jemanande gooloogoo yinamannhande. *When you smiled you used to make us happy.*

meleliny *coverb+SAY/DO.* be shining, be smooth. • Meleliny ngerne dambi ganarram-ngiyi ngelel goonjal. *The leaves of the real goonjal type of kapok bush are shiny.* [NOTE: contrasts with the furry leaves, *nyinggi-nyinggiwoony*, of the subspecies called *ngalwany*] SEE: **mililiny**.

melera *coverb+SAY/DO.* talk sideways about mother-in-law, speak using respect forms of language as when a man uses the third person non-singular when addressing or talking about his brother-in-law. • Melera nginini, 'Dawiyan, dawiyan'. *He (the moon) spoke 'sideways' using respect language (about the black-headed snake) saying, 'Dawiyan, dawiyan' (instead of the usual word* dawool*).*

melgam *noun.* mates, friends, someone to accompany you.

melgabawoorroony, melgabawoorrool, melgabawoorroom *adjective.* having no friends. • Garninya? Ngoowan, melgabawoorroon-nga. *What now? Oh no, I have no mates.* SEE: **liwayabawoorroony**.

melgabawoorroony, melgabawoorrool, melgabawoorroom *noun.* person whose name someone can't say (e.g. mother-in-law, father-in-law, son-in-law, daughter-in-law, person with no spouse).

mel-mel *coverb+SAY/DO_M.* shake chest. • Mel-mel barroo-gili manggam-birri! *You all shake your chests!*

melng *coverb+GO/COME.* daybreak come. • Ngelmang melng berrayin daam. *Daybreak comes over the land from the east.*

melngarribal *noun.* feminine. female doctor.

Figure 57. *Mayim: Wirrid Mona Ramsey: Nyawoorrool gerneg nyoomoorloonya nawarrany mayiny, ngarag-garri nyanini.*

[NOTE: Southern dialect]

melngarribany *noun.* doctor, bush doctor, clever man. [NOTE: Southern dialect] SEE: **baremanbeny, mabarn, nyangoobany**.

Menaliyan *noun.* place where *thoogool*, 'goanna with eggs' became part of the country.

menan *coverb+GO_ALONG.* go along flashing (lightning). • Malngirriny menan wananyji. *The lightning was flashing.* • Nginya miyi ngelmang menan wiyinji. *It (lightning) is also flashing coming from the east.*

menan REDUP: **menan-menan**. *coverb+SAY/DO.* sparkle/flicker (stars), flash (lightning). • Ngoorrinyayi menan ngerne ngagenyen daan. *Lightning is flashing over there like that at my place.* • Deg-garri nimbirn laarne menan-menan-ngarri birrirn dam wardam wel, damboowa loordben. *When you look up high and the stars are flickering, well it getting hot then.*

menan REDUP: **menan-menan**. *coverb+SAY/DO_M.* sparking lightning. • Menanji wanema. *Lightning was sparking.*

Mende-menden *noun.* Island Yard.

mendoowiyan *temporal.* in the very middle of the night.

mendoowoomoowan *temporal.* every night, only at night. • Mendoowoomoowan nginjinde. *He is here every night. He comes every night.* • Mendoowoomoowan girlrli nyerne gerrewoombi-boorroo. *Only at night it goes hunting for mussels.*

mendoowoon *temporal.* at night, darkness.

mendoowoongarnam *noun.* night dwellers, people travelling in the dark (i.e. dark spirits).

mendoowoony *noun masculine.* gecko. *Gehyra australis.* SEE: **moondoowoony; nyigany**.

mendoowoony *coverb+FALL/GO_DOWN.* be nightfall. • Mendoowoonyboowa boorroowoonbe marrarna yarraya daan-gili. *Night is falling now, we will go home.*

mendoowoonybe REDUP: **mendoo-mendoowoonybe**. *coverb+FALL/GO_DOWN.* be nightfall. • Mendoo-mendoowoonybe berroowoonbe. *Night is falling.* • Mendoowoonybe berroowoonbe-yarri. *It is getting dark on us.*

mendoowoonyboo REDUP: **mendoo-mendoowoonyboo**. *coverb+FALL/GO_DOWN_M.* become night-time, get dark. • Mendoowoonyboo-ngarri winan, mendoowoony-ngarri berrooward. *When it is night-time it gets dark.* • Mendoo-mendoowoonyboo-ngarri waniniwan berrem. *When night was falling here.*

Mendoowoorrji *noun.* Medicine Pocket on Bedford Downs.

mengelarr *coverb+PUT.* open out flowers and put in tongue to get honey (flying fox). • Ngayinga walimalin-ngage. thawala-moowam mengelarr nooniyilen'gende. *I am a flying fox. I suck honey from all the flowers.*

mengerr *coverb+GO/COME.* push self back, move self over. • Mengerr-anyji naniyi jarlayi. *Maybe you pushed backwards on your bottom, my friend.* SEE: **rerreg**.

mengerr *coverb+PUT.* push someone back, move someone/something over. • Mengerr naniyanyji-ni. *He moved you over.* SEE: **rerreg**.

menhang *coverb+SAY/DO_REFL.* lick. • Menhang ngenangirriyan. *I lick myself.*

menherrgarr *coverb+GO/COME.* enjoy taste, find that something is sweet. • Ngiyi, men'gawool, menherrgarr yarra-ngooyoo. *Yes, it (kapok bush root) is good, we find it nice and sweet.*

menherrgayiny, menherrgayil, menherrgayim *adjective.* tasty, sweet.

men'gawiya *coverb+BE/STAY.* be good (be good to people). • Men'gawiya barrennha-yoo. *You two be good.* • Men'gawiya benennha-ngirri. *You all be good to me.*

men'gawoo REDUP: **men'gawoo-men'gawoo; men'gawoo-men'gawoogbe**. *coverb+BECOME.* become good, get better. • Belayig-belayig nginimanyji bardoon men'gawoo-ngarri waniyidji. *When he (eagle) got better he followed him (egret).* • Bagoo ngenan'ge, wayinigana men'gawoo-ngarri ngiliyin'ge. *I lie down and get better now.* • Men'gawoogboo wiyinji. *It is getting good (country from rain).*

men'gawoo *coverb+SAY/DO.* become good, get better. • Men'gawoo berrani-yoo. *They two became good, they two got better.*

men'gawoog *coverb+GET.* make good. • Men'gawoog nginimanyji jaam. *It made him feel good.* • Men'gawoog yindemnha. *Make me good.* • Men'gawoog ninima-ngoo. *I made it good for you. / I fixed it for you.* • Jadany jalij-garri nginini-yarri, daambi men'gawoog benamanyji-yoowoo. *When the rain rained (on us), it made the country good for us.*

men'gawoog

men'gawoog *coverb+SAY/DO_REFL.* make self good/clean. • Boorroonboo, men'gawoog berremiyanbe, marrarn boorroordboo yoongoombi, goorrnga-binyi dam. *The spirits stay and make themselves clean then go away from the water.*

men'gawoog *coverb+SAY/DO_M.* be cured, be fixed up, be made good. • Men'gawooga ngelama. *I was cured.*

men'gawoog *coverb+HIT.* make good. • Men'gawoog nyiyinya wirli-wirlin jadagen jalij-garri nginiyi. *She (blue-tongue lizard) makes it (rainbow) good up high (in the sky) when it rains in the wet season.*

men'gawoog *coverb+BE/STAY.* be becoming good. Men'gawoog nginjende ngarrgaliny. *The hill is becoming good (starting to look good in the sunset).*

men'gawoony, men'gawool, men'gawoom REDUP: **men'ga-men'gawoom.** *adjective.* good.

men'gerr *coverb+HIT.* hit. • Men'gerr nginiyid. *He hit him.*

men-men *coverb.* run flat out.

menyawenya *coverb+SAY/DO.* be lonely. • Menyawenya ngelemen'gende ninggoowoo-bawoorroon-nga. *I am lonely, I have no relations.* SEE: **barndawarlawarla, wanga-wanga.**

meraangarriny, meraangarril, meraangarrim *adjective.* long, far, tall. [NOTE: Southern dialect] SEE: **merewany, merewangarriny.**

merala *coverb+GO/COME.* be at dawn (when just able to see). • . . . merala-ngarri berrayin . . . *when dawn was just breaking*

merandam *noun.* hip.

merd REDUP: **mernmerd.** *coverb+GET.* tie up. • Merd nginimanyji. *He tied him up.* • Jiyilemga wayinigana mernmerd bemberramangbende, thedji woomberramande. *That is how they used to tie up Aboriginal people and hit and kill them.* • Merd ginimangjende marrarn rerr, joolajaya. *He tied him up and took him away, dragging him like a dog.*

merd *coverb+DO_REFL.* tie on self. • Dala ngalil yambarram merd nyanimiyin. *This woman is tying up her hair.* • Ganarra-bam gerlalban merd nginimiyin warrg ngerne. *He tied leafy bushes on his legs and he is dancing.*

merdbe-merdbe *coverb+FALL/GO_DOWN.* get dark. • Belegawirrin merdbe-merdbe-ngarri berroowoondi wayinigana girinybe woomenya. *When it gets dark in the middle of the night the katydid grasshopper calls out.*

merdben *temporal.* night-time, at night. • Merdbenanyji nginbiyan. *I might come tonight.*

merdbenybe *coverb+FALL/GO_DOWN.* getting dark. • Merdbenybe berroowoonbe daam. *The country is getting dark.*

merdgajil *noun.* neck chain. • Barndeli nyanewoorranjende-ngarri-ni dali merdgajil, janga-jangal, baberrgi nginanyjende wenggarrenji-ni. *When that metal neck chain was heated up by the sun, it burned him on the back of his neck.* SEE: **jangal-jangal.**

mereleg *coverb.* make someone feel sorry.

merelegbeny, merelegbel, merelegbem *adjective.* person one is sorry for, poor thing. SEE: **gaageny, goorlanggeny, werlerlewoony.**

merenyji, mirinji *noun masculine.* salt wattle. *Acacia ampliceps.* [NOTE: seeds are ground and made into damper]

merewagawoony, merewagawool, merewagawoom *adjective.* long, far. SEE: **merewany, merewangarriny.**

merewagboo *coverb+GET.* make long (action). • Merewagboo benemenya dam jarragboo. *She's making it a long story.*

merewan *adverb.* further.

merewangarriny, merewangarril, merewangarrim *adjective.* long, far. SEE: **merewany, meraangarriny, merewagawoony.**

merewany, merewal, merewam REDUP: **mererewam.** *adjective.* long, far, tall. • Goowooloom mererewam gerneg bemberremoorlenbe, goowooloom marne-bam. *They are holding long sticks, burning sticks.* SEE: **merewangarriny, meraangarriny, merewagawoony.**

Meriyin *noun.* long hill on Texas Downs Station with caves that were traditional camping areas, place with rock art.

merlarn *coverb+SAY/DO.* be mad. • Ngoowan merlarn yirrarn. *We are not mad.*

merlarn *coverb+SAY/DO_M.* go mad. • Merlarn-ngarri wanamanyande . . . *When she went mad . . .*

merlarnji, merlarnel, merlarnbe *adjective.* mad, mad person. • Nyingen miyi

merlarne-ngoongoo. *You, too, you are mad.*
• Merlarne-noonggoorroo. *You are all mad.*
• Merlarniya-ngoo nyaganyji. *You are really mad, Uncle.*

merlarrji, merlarrel *noun.* dingo. *Canis lupus dingo.* SEE: **marranyji**.

merlgam *noun.* coins, change, loose notes. [NOTE: Southern dialect]

merliny-merliny SEE: **miliny-miliny**.

merlngard *coverb.* make em full up (swearing).

mern *coverb+HIT.* bludge, sit about waiting for a feed, sponge on someone. • Mern nginiyid. *He/she begged him (for something) / sponged on him.* • Mern benayidji. *He begged from them. / He sponged on them.*

mern *coverb+SAY/DO_M.* beg. • Mernji wanamanyande boorrale-boorroo wanggarne-jaya. *She was begging like a crow for a meal to fill her stomach. (Kriol: 'He bin wait abat for tucker like a crow.')*

merndagaleny, merndagalel, merndagalem *noun.* school teacher, bookkeeper. LIT: 'one who is good at paper'. [NOTE: *merndam*, 'paperbark, paper, books, paper money']

merndany, merndam *noun.* paperbark, paper money, paper, books. *Melaleuca leucadendra.* [NOTE: flowers are called *yilengerrngerrel*; this word can be used by a father-in-law to speak indirectly about a daughter-in-law]

mernderr-mernderr *adjective.* striped, diamond-patterned. [NOTE: like *dawool* 'black-headed python']

mernmerd *coverb+SAY/DO.* tie up. • Ngoowan mernmerd boorroorn. *They don't tie them up now.*

mernmerd *coverb+SAY/DO_M.* tie up. • An yamberram-birri gad, gadem-nga woomberramande, wiyird woomberramande boorriyana na ngarn mernmerd woomberramande-birri, warna-warnarramga dam. *And they used hair, they would cut it, spin it and tie up that thing (feathers onto headdress) long ago.*

mernmerdgaleny *noun.* policeman. LIT: 'one who is good at tying up'. SEE: **ngerlabany**.

Figure 58. *Merndany: Merndany bed woomenji yilag nawarragawoon.*

-merrale

-merrale *suffix.* in all that kind. • *Daamga-nga berrema nyiyirri-merrale.* My home is here in all the spinifex (spinifex pigeon).

merreb REDUP: **merrerreb**. *coverb+PUT.* hide (transitive). • *Berrem yiligin ngaginyin daan, walig doonbajge, merreb doonbajge.* I will have to put this inside my place and hide it.
• *Merrerreb nginiyanyjende-birri-yoo.* He always used to hide it from them two. SEE: **booroo, moorndoog**.

merreb *coverb+BE/STAY.* be hiding (intransitive).
• *Merreb ginji.* He is hiding.

merreb *coverb+FALL/GO_DOWN.* hide (intransitive).
• *Merreb nginiward.* He hid. • *Merreb-gala yarrewoo!* Let's hide!

merrembernel *noun.* paper wasp. [NOTE: makes large round nests on the side of sheltered cliffs]

merre-merreb *coverb+SAY/DO_M.* hide.
• *Jilba-wanyji nerne; merre-merreb jimanande.* You must be frightened, you always hide yourself.

merrerreb *coverb+SAY/DO_M.* be hiding, stay in hiding. • *Merrerreb wanemayinde.* He stayed in hiding.

merrerreb *coverb+GO_ALONG.* go along hiding.
• *Merrerreb wananyjende gibi-yibin.* He went along hiding right out in the bush.

merrerreb *coverb+BE/STAY.* be hiding, stay in hiding. • *Merrerreb berraniyin.* They were hiding.

merrerrebbe *coverb+SAY/PUT_REFL.* hide self.
• *Merrerrebbewa ngimiyanyjende gibi-yibin.* He used to hide himself in the bush.

Merrewoon *noun.* deep waterhole on upper Ord, the place made when turtle stabbed the ground in dreamtime.

merrgeb *coverb+HIT.* be throbbing (body part from exercise). • *Girli-ngarri ngenayin, merrgeb ngenayid.* My flesh is throbbing inside from walking. / The walking made my flesh throb.

merrgernbe; merrgernbem *adjective.* three. SEE: **moorrgoornboo**.

merrjil, mirrjil *noun.* boil. • *Merrji-ban-nga.* I have a boil. • *Mirrji-ban-nga manam.* I've got a boil on my backside. [NOTE: *mirrjil* is Southern dialect]

Merrmerrji *noun.* place in the area of Queensland Creek on Bedford Downs.

merrngag *coverb+GO_ALONG.* be flashing lightning. • *Merrngag wiyinjende malngirriny boowoorroogoo.* The lightning was flashing to the north.

merrngag REDUP: **merrngag-merrngag**. *coverb+SAY/DO.* flash lightning.
• *Ngarranggarninji, ngarranggarninji, malngirrinyiyi merrngag-garri ngerne.* From in the dreamtime, from in the dreamtime, when the lightning flashes.

merrwardge *coverb+GET.* make think about someone/something. • *Goorlabal jirri nyaniyanyji-ngirri yijiyan merrwardge ngenamanyji.* He showed me the rainbow, truly and made me think about him.

mibiny, mibil, mibim *adjective.* closed and dry. • *Mibin-nga thoowerndemga.* My mouth is closed and dry (from talking). • *Manambi mibin-ngoo.* You have a little tight arse (something old people used to say).

miginy *noun.* black ant species (bigger than *thengawoony*). [NOTE: name also given to red meat ant]

milam *noun.* vagina. SEE: **boonthoorroo**.

-miliny, -milil, -milim; -milem *suffix.* from, originating from. [NOTE: used to form nominals with places, locatives, directional and demonstratives, followed by the gender suffixes]

mililiny REDUP: **mili-mililiny**. *coverb+SAY/DO.* be shining (little points of light). • *Men'gawoom mililiny-ngarri boorroorn berrem daam.* It is good when this country is shining. • *Danya nyaarndiny, mili-mililiny ngerne laarne goowooloon.* There is the gum shining up high on the tree. SEE: **miliny-miliny**

mililinybeny, mililinybel, mililinybem *adjective.* shining.

mililinygany, mililinygal, mililinygam *adjective.* shining. • *Danyga minyjoowoom mililinygany.* That one has shining teeth.

mili-milil; milmilel *noun feminine.* very small lizard, type of little skink, slender snake-eyed skink. *Proablepharus tenuis.*

milin *coverb+BE/STAY.* be alive. • *Ngoowan milin yoorraniyin-joo.* We two might have not been alive. [NOTE: Southern dialect] SEE: **mooliny**.

milinyin, milinyinji *noun masculine.* large bamboo type. *Bambusa arnhemica.* [NOTE: does not grow in Gija country but used to be traded on the *wirnan*, 'traditional trade' routes]

miliny-miliny *coverb+SAY/DO.* be shining.
• *Nginya, ngaarriny miliny-miliny ngerne.* This

stone is shining. SEE: **belany-belany, mililiny, minin-minin**.

miloowoony *noun.* spinifex species, tall soft type of spinifex used to make spinifex resin, *gaalji. Triodia pungens, T. stenostachya.* SEE: **gerlerneny**.

miliwoorrangel; miloowoorrangel *noun feminine.* black-faced cuckoo shrike. *Coracina novaehollandiae.* SEE: **yirringaragjel**.

mil-mil SEE: **mirl-mirl**.

mily *coverb SAY/DO_M.* make dried fish into powder, heap the dried fish after grinding.
- Barnde-warndeg, mily woomberramande. *They used to dry it out and make them into small bits.*

mindalngarriny *noun masculine.* small wattle species. [NOTE: used to make *jiwiny*, the hard wooden part of spears]

mindi-mindil *noun.* kerosene wood, tree with small edible red fruit. *Erythroxylum ellipticum.*
- Ngelela dal mindi-mindil dal, ngagenyin daan. *This tree (shown in a painting) is the fruit tree called Mindi-mindil growing in my country.* [NOTE: small red fruit put in water, the ripe ones, *baabji*, sink and are then eaten.] SEE: **binyji-binyjil**.

mingany-mingany *coverb+DO_REFL.* wave branches (e.g. palm fronds on Palm Sunday).
- Thoowoo-berra mingany-mingany jarremiyinnha danyjiwa? Ngoowan, ngarranggarniny mingany-mingany yirremiyinji. *Why are you waving that thing? Oh, we are waving with the dreamtime (talking about people waving palm fronds on Palm Sunday).*

mingany-mingany *coverb+SAY/DO.* wave.
- Woomberramande-yirri danyi manggerre-gerrenyi, mingany-mingany dandi, ngalim-boorroo-wayi mingany-mingany wanemayinde. *They used to tell us that tata lizard, when waving there, he was waving for women like that.* SEE: **mangan**.

mingayoorroom, mingayoorriny *noun.* holiday feast, large quantity of food prepared for special occasion.
- Ngirribagboo boorroordboo mayiny mingayoorriny. *The holiday feast time is coming close (Christmas dinner).*

minilg-minilg SEE: **mirnilg**. [NOTE: Rusty Peters said both *n* and *rn* were acceptable]

minin-minin *coverb+SAY/DO.* shine.
- Goonji-ngarnam gerlalim-ni. Gerlali-ba-ngarri wiyinji, marrarna woorrg boorroowoonboo, minin-minin boorroorn barndem. *The red shiny seed pods growing on the bauhinia trees are called* gerlarlim. *When they have the seeds and they start to fall they shine in the sun.*
- Gerlaliba-ngarri wiyinji goonjiny-ni minin-minina nyimbirn barndeli. *When the bauhinia seed pods appear on the tree they shine in the sun.*

min'giri *coverb+SAY/DO_M.* dodge.
- Werndij-garri wanema, gawayinda min'giri ngelema. *He threw a spear, never mind, I dodged it.*

minyal *noun.* green ant. SEE: **waawal**. [NOTE: Mabel Juli says *minyal* is red and *waawal* is green; squeezing the juice from the ant's body into the throat is good for helping singers to have a good voice]

minyanyany *noun.* plant used to put on coals when cooking black plum, *minyjaarrany. Euphorbia ssp.* [NOTE: found growing along the side of the highway north of the turn-off to Alice Downs]

minyarr-minyarreny, minyarr-minyarrel, minyarr-minyarre *adjective.* smelly, sweaty.

minybernem *noun.* dry grass. [NOTE: some people use this word to mean any kind of grass]

-minyin *suffix.* in the time of.
- Girli yirramande wanyage-minyin. *We used to walk when we were little.*

minyjaarrany *noun.* black plum. *Vitex glabrata.* [NOTE: Southern dialect pronunciation, and in fast speech in Northern dialect] SEE: **minyjiwarrany**.

minyjiwarrany *noun.* black plum. *Vitex glabrata.* [NOTE: pronunciation used by some in Northern dialect] SEE: **minyjaarrany**.

minyjiwoorrji *noun.* limestone.

minyjoowoom; minyjoom *noun.* teeth. SEE: **ngirrimem**.

miny-miny *coverb+SAY/DO.* be flickering light (e.g. of fire).
- Marra looj boorroorn-ni ngoorriyama, miny-miny nginini. *(He saw) the smoke (of his fire) already rising in the distance and its flickering light.*

minymirdginy; minymijginy *noun masculine.* peregrine falcon. *Falco peregrinus.*

minyngil *noun feminine.* red root of shrub. *Haemodorum ensifolium.* SEE: **gerrerlel**. [NOTE: can be used to dye fibres]

minyoolang-minyoolang *coverb+SAY/DO.* flick

mira

tongue in and out. • Minyoolang-minyoolang ngerne garndoowoolany. *The goanna is flicking its tongue in and out.*
mira *coverb+SAY/DO.* stretch arm out to one side. • Mira barroo! *You all stretch out one arm to one side!*
mirdal *noun feminine.* shield. • Mirdal dal yindiyi-gala. *Give me that shield.*
mirinji; merenyji *noun masculine.* salt wattle. *Acacia ampliceps.* [NOTE: seeds ground and made into damper; collected at Chinamans Garden]
Miriwoong *noun.* language spoken north of Gija.
mirlim *noun.* liver.
mirli-mirlim; merle-merlem *noun.* book. • Mirli-mirli-yoorroong bemberrangbende wajbaloom. *The white people were putting it into the book/onto paper.* [NOTE: common Kimberley word for 'book'. Rusty Peters says it is also the word for a type of rock seen on the back road to Purnululu in 1988 (now closed) which was very flaky, lying on its sides looked like book leaves; this has not been confirmed with any other speaker.]
mirlirdiny *noun masculine.* hook on woomera.
mirl-mirl *coverb+SAY/DO.* be hurting, feel sore. • Mirl-mirl ngenarn. *I feel sore. / I am hurting.* SEE: **majarr**.
mirl-mirlge *coverb+FALL/GO_DOWN.* fall and hurt oneself. • Nyaj-garri ngenoowardge, mirl-mirlge ngenawardge. *When I tripped over, fell and hurt myself. I got hurt.* SEE: **geberd, thalijbel**.
mirnilg *coverb+SAY/DO_M.* blink both eyes. • Mirnilg booma. *You blink both eyes.*
mirnilg-mirnilg *coverb+SAY/DO.* flicker (e.g. stars), be blinking (eyes). • Wardam mirnilg-mirnilg boorroorn. *The stars get brighter and flicker (in the cold time).*
mirr REDUP: **mirr-mirr**. *coverb+SAY/DO.* shake (e.g. from cold or fever), shiver. • Mirr ngirni. *He is shaking.* • Mirr-mirr berrani. *They are shaking.* • Warn'gam mirr-mirr ngenani belegawirrin. *I was shivering with cold in the middle of the night.* [NOTE: reduplicated form *mirr-mirr* is more common]
Mirrilinggi (Mirrilingki) *noun.* place near Warmun Roadhouse where Catholic missionaries conduct alcohol awareness camps and other meetings and hire out rooms; Mirrilinggi is the Gija name.
mirr-mirrge *coverb+GET.* make someone shake with fright. • Mirr-mirrge ngemberrama. *They made me shake with fright.*
mirrngem, mirrngim *noun.* face.
miya *particle.* never mind, just. • Miya, biri nginiwardji daa-yoorroong. *Never mind, he just went back to his camp.* • Gayigana miya yamberrannya mayimga ngaaloon yarroon? *Can we just take this food and sit in the shade?*
miyale, miyalji, miyalel *noun.* meat, edible animal.
miyaloob *coverb+BE/STAY.* be without meat.
miyawanya *adverb.* still. • Jang berrani-yoo, miyawanya ganggerr-ganggerr nginingaboordji. *They were both eating the rock wallabies, but he was still sulking.*
miyi *particle.* also, too. • Ngayindi miyi. *Me too.*
miyi-miyi *coverb+GET.* think about someone. • Miyi-miyi yindemnha-yarre. *You should think about us/remember us.* • Miyi-miyi-ma jemennha danyi wajbaloony wariwoony? *Are you thinking about that 'cheeky' white man (talking about a man who came to the Kimberley from Germany and shot people and was eventually shot by police)?*
miyi-miyi *coverb+SAY/DO.* think about someone. • Miyi-miyi ngenarn-ngoo. *I am thinking of you.* • Miyi-miyi ngenarn-noonggoowa. *I am thinking about you. / I remember you.*
miyingenbe *noun.* flotsam, driftwood.
Miyirrawoon *noun.* place to the east of Waren-waren, Calico Springs.
miyinggajil *noun feminine.* goat. *Capra hircus.*
moog *coverb+BE/STAY.* lie flat on stomach. • Moog nginji. *He is lying flat on his stomach.* SEE: **moord**.
moogoogoob *coverb+SAY/DO.* be locked up. • Moogoogoob yarrern. *We are all locked up.*
moogoonybe *noun.* skin, greenhide. • . . . moogoonybe-ni jiyirriny . . . *kangaroo skin* SEE: **wangarrem**.
moojoong *coverb+SAY/DO.* be shy, be embarrassed. • Thoowoo-boorroo moojoong nerne? *Why are you shy?* SEE: **ganybel**.
moojoongbeny, moojoongbel, moojoongbem *adjective.* shy. • Moojoongbi-yilin-jaya-noonggoorroo; jarrag-bawoorroon-noonggoo. *You are all the same you, too shy, you can't talk.* • Moojoongbenyiya. *He is really shy.* • Moojoongbiyam. *They are all*

mooloonggoo-galeny, mooloonggoo-galel, mooloonggoo-galem

really shy.

moojoonggoolg *coverb+GET.* make someone feel shamed, embarrass someone.
• Moojoonggoolg joonoomenha waringarrim. *You are making them all feel embarassed.*

moojoonggoowool *coverb+SAY/DO.* be all shy, be embarrassed (plural). • Thoowoo-boorroo moojoonggoowool narroorn? *Why are you all shy?* SEE: **ganybel**.

moojooroog *coverb+GET.* mince. • Daj-garri ngenani moojooroog noonemangge. *When I had smashed it, I minced it up.*

Moolanyin *noun.* place name.

mooliny, moolil, moolim *adjective.* alive, awake.
• Ngoowan-anyji moolin yirraniyin-joo. *We were not awake.* SEE: **milin**.

moolirrji *noun.* roly-poly. [NOTE: has also been recorded with the meaning 'bindi-eye'; roly-polys are very prickly]

mool-moolji *coverb+DO_REFL.* have fun, make each other happy. • Mool-moolji birrimiyanbe. *They are having fun together.* SEE: **barlij, jawirij, ngoolya-ngoolya**.

mooloogoorrji *noun masculine.* devil dog, spirit dog. [NOTE: eyes can look like motor car lights, it can appear as a horse or a lion] SEE: **jarrinyinji**.

mooloogoonbe *noun.* glass. • Mooloogoon deg girrem. *Eye glasses, spectacles.*
• Yirranybebeny mooloogoonji. *Sunglasses.*
• Mooloogoonjam deg-girrem goorloon yiligin. *Thing like glass for looking under water (i.e. diving mask).* [NOTE: said to be originally from Jaru meaning 'spearhead'; word used because glass was used to make spearheads] SEE: **jimbirlam**.

moolooloongboo *coverb+BE/STAY.* feel sad inside.
• Gardiyamga, jiyilemga moolooloongboo boorroonboo-noonggoowa. *White people and Aboriginal people all feel sad inside because of you (dying) (words dictated to be said at a funeral).*

mooloonggoo-galeny, mooloonggoo-galel, mooloonggoo-galem *adjective.* fat. • Mooloonggoo-galel malawoorrgool miyalelga dal goorndarril garriyil. *The bream is a fish with really fat meat.* • Ngiyi yirramanyji

Figure 59. *Miyale: Rossi Ramsey: Goorndoogany gooloo-gooloo ngerne-boorroo miyale.*

mooloonggoom

mooloonggoo-galem. *We caught lots. They were really fat.* SEE: **marlawoorrgoony**.

mooloonggoom noun. fat.

mooloorroo coverb+BECOME. become sad.
- Goorndoogany mooloorroo waniyid. *The boy was sorry for them.*

mooloorroo coverb+SAY/DO_REFL. feel sorry for each other. • Mooloorroo berrangirriyin-joo. *They feel sorry for each other.*

mooloorroo coverb+SAY/DO. be sad, feel sorry about someone/something, miss someone.
- Mooloorroo ngenarn-noowa ngayin-gawa Jandaloowoon-nga. *I, Jandaloo, feel sorry about him. / I miss him.*

mooloorroog coverb+GET. make sad. • Daam dam mooloorroog ngemberramangbe. *That country made me feel sad.*

moom coverb+GET. put hand over mouth.
- Moom nginimanyji. *He put his hand over his (another person's) mouth.*

moom coverb+DO_REFL. put hand over mouth (self). • Moom nginimiyin. *He put his hand over his mouth.* • Moom nyanemiyin. *She put her hand over her mouth.*

moondarij coverb+BE/STAY. be sitting slouched forward (kangaroos, cattle). • Booloomanel moondarij-ngarri nyinya warnkam-anyji-birri. *When the cattle are sitting slouched forward, maybe they are cold.*

moondoorr coverb+PUT. heap up in one place, place together. • Binarri-woorroom marnemga dam, moondoorr-ngarri bemberrayangbe. *They didn't know what the wood they were heaping up was for.*
- Moondoorr noonayangge. *I heaped it up.*

moondoorr coverb+BE/STAY. be heaped up in one place. • Moondoorra boorroonboo-noowa. *They are all heaped up there now from him (where he left them).*

moondoorr; moondoorrwany coverb+GO/COME. many come to one place. • Moondoorrwany berrayin. *Many people came all to the one place (they bin all heap up).* SEE: **nyawoorn**.

moondoorroong coverb+BE/STAY. lie down on stomach, lie face down. • Moondoorroong nginji. *He is lying on his stomach.*

moondoowoony noun masculine. gecko. *Gehyra australis*. SEE: **mendoowoony, nyigany**.

Moonga-moonga noun. public song and dance style danced by women. [NOTE: men often lead the singers but do not dance]

moongerri coverb+PUT. trap fish. • Moongerri yamberraj garlirrin-gili. *We'll have to drive them into the trap in the shallow water.*

moonggoolji noun. melaleuca species. *Melaleuca nervosa, M. acacioid, M. minutifolia.*

moonggoorlool noun feminine. termites. SEE: **gooroorrooroorrool**.

moongooli-moongooli coverb+GO_ALONG. go along wriggling big bottom. • Moongooli-moongooli wiyinya mana-galel. *She is walking along moving her big bottom.*

moongoorr coverb+SAY/DO_M. be jealous, be jealously possessive of someone/something.
- Moongoorr woomenyande-noongoo. *She is jealous of him (does not let him look at anyone else).* • Moongoorr woomenjende-ngooyoo, joonboorroong nyinyande, ngoowan derdeyerdeg nyerne. *He guards her jealously, she sits with her head down, she doesn't look around.*

moongoorr coverb+GET. act in a jealous way to someone, jealously refuse to share. • Danya-ninggi jiyiliny moongoorr nemenji-ningi ngoolngagal-ngooyoo jarrag-garri nerne-ngiyi. *Look out! That bloke is jealousing you for talking to his girlfriend.* • Moongoorr nimbirrimnha-boorroo. *They will be jealous and not give you (anything).*

moon'goom noun. lower back. • Moon'goom yilgoowoorroon-nga. *My lower back is sore/bad.* SEE: **loorndoomoorroom**.

moon'goom noun. part of woomera from curve to handle.

moonoorroony coverb+BURN/BITE. die down to coals (fire). • Moonoorroony-ngarri binbiwarri warany gerd noowiyajge. *When the fire dies down I will cook it (food or meat).*

moonthoorroogaleny, moonthoorroogalel, moonthoorroogalem adjective. good at finding meat. • Moonthoorroogale-woorron-noonggoorroo-yoo. *You two are no good at finding meat.*

moord coverb+HIT. press on something.
- Moord-gayan bemberrayidbende thambarlam-birri. *They kept on pressing it with their feet.*

moord coverb+PUT. press, put weight on. • Moord nginiyanyji. *He put weight on him.*

moord coverb+BE/STAY. lie stomach-down (e.g. fish, lizard). • Danya nyagoornany moord nginji nhoonban. *The rock cod is lying on the mud.*

SEE: **moog**.

moord *coverb+PLACE_M.* place heavy object, put weight on something. • Moord waniyanya-birri-yoo ngarrgaleny nawarrany barlaliny. *She put a big heavy flat rock on top of the two of them.*

moordany *noun.* hill kangaroo, common wallaroo, euro. *Macropus robustus.* SEE: **jirrgany**.

moordoorram REDUP: moordoo-moordoorram. *noun.* traditional men's hairdo with hair tied with grass and mud made up to a point. • Boorarrgarr berrayi-yarri moordoo-moordoorra-bam warrg-girrem. *They all came out to us with traditional hair styles to dance.*

moorlgoorrool *noun feminine.* freshwater crab. Potamonidae.

moorl-moorl *coverb+HAVE.* have little sores.
• . . . moorl-moorl yambirrimoorliya-ngarri . . . *when we have little sores*

moorlji, moorloo *noun.* entrance of native beehive.

moorloo *noun.* eye.

moorloogoorndoorlgoorndoorlji *noun masculine.* spectacled hare wallaby. *Lagorchestes conspicillatus.*

moorndood *coverb+BE/STAY.* be a high hill that is stretched out. • Nginya gendoowajarri ngoorroonya moorndood-garri nginji danya ngerigjende. *This (painting) is where that hill is stretched out from the south.*

moorndoog *coverb+FALL/GO_DOWN.* hide. • Wiji nginiyin, moorndoog nginewardji gibin. *He ran and hid in the bush.* SEE: **booroo, merreb**.

moorndoog *coverb+PUT.* hide something.
• Moorndoog biyila wan'gilga! *Hide the rifle!*

moorniny-moorniny *coverb+HIT.* fuck, have intercourse with someone. • Roowaj ninemangge, 'Wajbaloon-ngoo ngenhengben-ngoo gerlenggem', ngenani-ni. 'Ngalim moorniny-moorniny jooniyinnha manbem,' ngenani-ni. *I swore him, 'You are a white man red prick,' I told him. 'You fuck black women,' I told him.* [NOTE: swearing]

moorniny *coverb +SAY/DO_REFL.* have sex together. • Jiyilem ngalim moorniny-ngarri berringirriyan. *When men and women have intercourse together.* • moorniny-moorninygan *when having sex.* [NOTE: swearing] SEE: **tharriny**.

moornmoordel; moornmoordool, moornmoordbe *noun feminine.* spangled perch, golden spotted perch, gudgeon, spangled grunter. *Leiopotherapon unicolor.*

mooroonggoorroony *noun.* clever person, doctor, sorcerer, 'magic man'.
• Mooroonggoorroon-ngoo joonanynha wanyji. *You might be a 'clever man' and have brought something good.* SEE: **baremanbeny, mabarn, nyangoobany**.

mooroorlbany, mooroorlbal, mooroorlbam *adjective.* having watery eyes, teary eyed.
• Moorloo mooroorlbal. *She has watery eyes.*

mooroorl-mooroorl *coverb+GO/COME.* tears run down. • Mooroorl-mooroorl nginiyi. *Tears ran down his cheeks.*

mooroorl-mooroorl *coverb+SAY/DO.* have tears running, eyes watering. • Mooroorl-mooroorl ngenarn moorloo. *My eyes are watering.*

mooroorloo *noun.* tears.

moorr *coverb+DO_REFL.* clench fists tightly.
• Marlam-birri wayini moorr nginimiyinji. *He has his fists clenched tightly like that (wallaby in photo.)*

moorrga *coverb+PUT.* transport.
• Moorrga-ngarri ngoorriyangbe yoorloo-yoorroong, ngoowan gendoowa-yoorroong. *They should have moved it (big log left on the bridge by the floodwater) downstream, not upstream (when they cleared it off the bridge).*

moorrga *coverb+BRING/TAKE.* take, transport.
• Marrarna moorrga-wooja yindegbany ngoorroon-gili galma-galmang? *Will you take me to the other side?* • Wara moorrga-wooja nharegbany-ngoo. *Yes, I'll take you.*

moorrgoony *noun masculine.* grasshopper species, very small pretty grasshopper.

moorrgoonboo *adjective.* three. SEE: **merrgernbe**.

moorrji *noun.* mushroom/fungus found growing on cow dung. SEE: **binoowoonggool**. [NOTE: both words given when Peggy Patrick and Paddy Bedford were eating mushrooms for breakfast and discussing Gija words for different types]

moorroo REDUP: moorroo-moorroo. *coverb+GET.* mind, look after. • Moorroo yindemnha daan nyinanggoorroon. *You look after me at your place.* • Mayaroom moorroo-moorroo ninbimge. *I must mind the house.*

moorrooloomboony

moorrooloomboony *noun masculine.* prickly wattle. *Vachellia farnesiana.* [NOTE: sticks of this plant are used to poke the foot of the dead in *bernderre* so that their spirit will not follow] SEE: **bagawagany.**

-moowa *suffix.* only. [NOTE: attached to stems of nouns, adjectives, pronouns, demonstratives, locatives and temporals, followed by the gender or locative suffixes]

moowalangel *noun feminine.* spangled perch, golden spotted perch, gudgeon, spangled grunter. *Leiopotherapon unicolor.* SEE: **moornmoordool.**

moowany, moowal *noun.* sugarbag bee, bush honey bee. • Ganggarre-ngiyiwa moowal nhem woomberrama-ngirri jang-ngarri ngenani. *The wax from the bush honey bee got stuck on me when I was eating.* • Moowany derd giniwardji-ngirri minyjoowoon gayirriny-noowa. *The wax from the ground sugarbag species is stuck in my teeth.* SEE: **ngawooral.** [NOTE: gender agrees with species; *beranggool* is feminine, *gayirriny* and *nhawiny* masculine]

moowoog *coverb+SAY/DO.* whine, howl (dog/dingo). • Danya moowoog ngerne. *That one is howling/whining (dog).*

Moowoolan *noun.* place upstream from Springvale.

moowoolooloob *coverb+SAY/DO.* calling out (dogs, dingoes, cattle). • Marranybe moowoolooloob boorroorn. *The dingoes are calling out.*

moowooloom *noun.* forehead.

mooyooloo *noun.* wrist.

mooyoony, mooyoom *noun.* sleep. • Noongoog-anyji ninbiyangge mooyoomga. *I might have a good sleep.*

Nn

Naangari, Nangari *noun.* a skin name (when spoken to).

Naangaril, Nangaril *noun feminine.* a skin name (when spoken about).

nadiling, nandeling REDUP: **nadi-nadiling.** *coverb+FALL/GO_DOWN.* kneel down. • Jiyiliny nadeling nginiwardji. *The man knelt down.* • Nadi-nadiling berroowardbe. *They all knelt down.* • Goorndoogany nandelingboo ngoowoonji. *The little boy is kneeling down now.* • Nadelingbany berrawardbe. *They were all kneeling down (taking a kneeling position).* SEE: **balmarr, yerderr.**

nadiling, nandeling *coverb+BE/STAY.* be kneeling down. • Nadiling nginji. *He is kneeling down.* SEE: **balmarr, yerderr.**

nag REDUP: **nag-nag** *coverb+GO/COME.* be quiet, stay still, stop. • Nag barriyinha-gili, ngoowan ngarl-ngarl barrern. *Be quiet, don't make noise.* • Nag barriyi joolan! *Stop, quiet you dogs!* • Nag nyaniyinya ngoorr-ngoorrool. *The car went and stopped.* • Nag-nagboo-ma narroorda? *Are you all about to stay quiet now?* SEE: **nagarr.**

nag *coverb+BECOME.* become quiet, stop (making noise). • Nag waniyid. *It has stopped (the lawn mower noise).* SEE: **nagarr.**

nag *coverb+FALL/GO_DOWN.* stop. • Ngoorr-ngoorrool nag nyanoowardja. *The car stopped.*

naga *noun.* pubic covering, (Kriol: 'cock-rag, naga'). SEE: **janigim, jarnim, warlboorroo, nyagoom.**

nagarr, nagarrg *coverb+GO/COME.* be quiet, stay still, stop talking. • Ngenani-birri, 'Nagarrg barriyinha.' *I told them, 'Stop fighting and be quiet.'* • Nagarr barrinha-gili, gamaliwa-noonggoo! *Be quiet, you are strangers!*

Figure 60. *Nalijam: Boorljoonngali Phyllis Thomas: Nagarra ngoorloog nyerne nalijam.*

Nagarra

- Nagarr berrayid, ngoowan ngarl-ngarl boorroorn. *They're quiet (presumed asleep), they are not making a noise.* SEE: **nag**.

Nagarra *noun.* a skin name (when spoken to).

Nagarral *noun feminine.* a skin name (when spoken about).

naj *coverb+SAY/DO.* smash up as with a mortar and pestle, hit leaves to extract fish poison. • Naj nginini. *He hit the leaves to extract the poison.*

naj *coverb+HIT.* smash something, hit leaves to extract fish poison. • Naj benayidji mangoonybe. *He hit the leaves of the river mangrove to extract the poison.* • Danya nyaganyji naj benayidji mawoondoom. *That uncle pounded the white ochre to make it into fine powder.*

naleg *coverb+GO/COME.* stop. • Wayinigana dany naleg giniyin jadanyi dany yarrewoorri. *That is why the rain stopped on us.* SEE: **nag**.

nalijam *noun.* tea.

naloog *coverb+WOUND_REFL.* join together (e.g. rivers). • Nawarragawoom dama nalooga berroowanbi-yoo. *The two rivers joined up (met at a junction) then.*

naloog-naloog *coverb+PUT.* join something together • Naloog-naloog benajtha! *Join those things together!*

namalji *noun.* bird species. SEE: **nganyjiwoorany**. [NOTE: lives in caves]

naman *coverb+DO_REFL.* be exhausted. • Naman ngenamiyin'ge ngenayin. *I was completely exhausted going along.*

nambalg REDUP: nambal-nambalg *coverb+PUT.* put weight on something, put something on top of something, join something on. • Nambal-nambalg benayanya-ni nyaarndem. *She (turtle) put gum on him (crocodile, in dreamtime to make him heavy and stay in the water).* SEE: **limboord**.

nambalg *coverb+FALL/GO_DOWN.* put heavy foot in something (e.g. when walking in mud). • Nambalg ngenaward nhoonban. *I put weight in the mud.*

nambarr *coverb+DO_REFL.* gather together. • Nambarr-gala yarremij jarrag-girrim. *Let's get together and talk.* • Nambarr-gala yarremij, ngoorrooma gooma nambarr berrayiliyin. *Let's get together, just like that big mob over there has got together.*

namberraj-boorroo *verb.* they will PUT you all.

namberrajtha-boorroo *verb.* they will PUT you all.

namberranynha-boorroo *verb.* they will BRING/TAKE you all.

namberremnha-boorroo *verb.* let them all GET all of you.

namberrijtha-boorroo *verb.* they will HIT you all. • Thed namberrijtha-boorroo-yoo. *They will kill you two.*

namberriyinnha-boorroo *verb.* they are HITTING you all.

Nambin; Nambirn *noun.* a skin name (when spoken to).

Nambinil; Nambirnil *noun feminine.* a skin name (when spoken about).

nambirrimnha-boorroo *verb.* they will GET all of you.

nambirriyinnha-boorroo *verb.* they are HITTING you all.

namboorroongoony, namboorroongool, namboorroongoom; namboogoorroongeny *adjective.* very big.

namboorrarrim *noun.* all the adults in a family, big family. • Namboorrarrim-birri deyema boorarrgarr berrayi. *All the adults in the family are the ones who come (to talk about a death).*

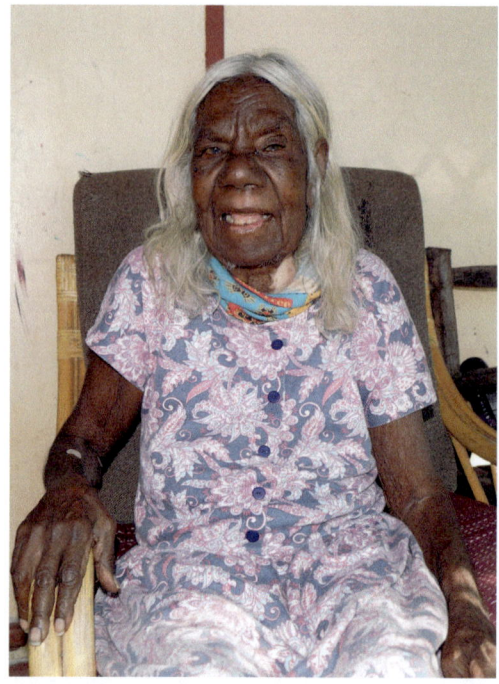

Figure 61. *Nambin: Yooroojil Lulu Trancolino: Nambinel deg nyerne.* (Photo Josua Dahmen)

Naminyji *noun.* a skin name (when spoken to).
Naminyjili *noun feminine.* a skin name (when spoken about).
namoorl *coverb+HIT.* swallow. • Namoorl benayid. *He swallowed it.* • Yilaggarnany namoorl ngerayji. *Let a crocodile swallow it.* SEE: **ngeltheg**.
nanandeda-noonggoo *verb.* I will TAKE you all.
nananyji-ni *verb.* he was BRINGING/TAKING all of you.
nananynha-ngoo *verb.* I BROUGHT/TOOK you.
nanbardi *coverb+WOUND_REFL.* hit each other over head. • Nanbardi berrawooran-doo Gijabany doo Jaroobany. *The Gija man and the Jaru man were hitting each other over the head.*
nanbewoorrooda-ngarri-noonggoo *verb.* if I leave you all.
nanbida; nanbitha; nanbida-noonggoo *verb.* I will TAKE you all.
nanbida-yoo; nanbitha-yoo *verb.* I will TAKE you two.
nanbimji-ni *verb.* he/it (masculine) will GET you all.
nanbimnha-noonggoo *verb.* I will GET you all.
nanbimnha-yoo *verb.* I will GET you two.
nanbitha; nanbida; nanbida-noonggoo *verb.* I will TAKE you all.
nanbitha-yoo; nanbida-yoo *verb.* I will TAKE you two.
nanbiyin-ni *verb.* he/it (masculine) will GIVE you all. • Nanbiyin-ni thedbany yimele-ngarri narrirn. *He will hit you all if you steal.*
nandaj-noonggoo; nandaj-doonggoo *verb.* I will PUT you all.
nandeda *verb.* I should TAKE you all. • Nandeda-yoo biri ngoorroon-gili ngagenyen yoorloo. *I should take you two back down there to my place.*
nandegbany *verb.* I will TAKE you all.
nandeg-gala-yoo *verb.* let me TAKE you two.
nandemji-ni, nandimiji-ni *verb.* let him/it masculine GET you all.
nandem-ngal *verb.* let her GET you all.
nandem-noonggoo *verb.* let me GET you all.

Figure 62. *Naminyji: Marayal Betty Carrington, Wayne Nulgit, Willy Carrington, Gordon Churchill, Cassius Nulgit, Patrick Gallagher: Naminyjili roord benoomoorloonya ngaliyangem wanyanyagem.*

nandiji-ni

nandiji-ni *verb.* he will HIT you all.
nandiji-ni-yoo *verb.* he will HIT you two. • Yilag-ayi nandiji-ni-yoo. *He will teach you two down there like that.*
nandiyin *verb.* I should GIVE you all, let me GIVE you all.
nandiyi-noonggoorroo *verb.* I should GIVE you all.
nanema-ngoo *verb.* I GOT you all. [NOTE: example from a sentence where speaker is talking about saying her brother's name by mistake; probably has plural object prefix because of this]
nanemennha *verb.* I am GETTING you all.
nanengaboordji-ni *verb.* he was SPEARING/POKING you all.
nanewoonji-ni *verb.* he was WOUNDING you all.
nanewoorroonnha *verb.* I am LEAVING you all.
nang *coverb+FALL/GO_DOWN.* die. • Nang nginiward. *He died.* • Nang nimboowoonhan. *You will die.* • Nang nyanoowardja. *She died.* • Nangboo-wanyji nyoowoonya. *She might be dying.*
nang *coverb+SPEAR.* kill by spearing. • Nang yarrengaboord. *We speared him and he is dead.*
nangag *coverb+GO/COME.* be stopped. • Wiyawoog nyerne, nangag ngidji, danyi jadany. *She hunts the rain away and it stops.*
nangarrg-nanggarrg *coverb+GO/COME.* be dying, be getting killed. • Nangarrg-nangarrg boorroordbende-wanyji. *Maybe they (fish) are getting killed (by cane toads).*
Nangala *noun.* a skin name (when spoken to).
Nangalal *noun feminine.* a skin name (when spoken about).
nangala-nangalal *noun.* small sand frog species. *Platyplectrum ornatus.* [NOTE: found buried near water in dry season]
nanggalag *coverb+BURN/BITE_REFL.* paint face white. • Nanggalag ngenawoorran. Menkawoon-ma? *I painted my face white. Does it look good?*
nanggalagmawoony, nanggalagmawool, nanggalagmawoom *adjective.* having a white face (e.g. painted with white paint). • Nanggalamawoony, boonoo-ngarri nginiwoorran moowoolem. *He has a white face, having painted himself.* [NOTE: can be said of a horse with a white face; refers to putting white paint all over the face, not white paint

Figure 63. *Nangala: Josie Farrer: Nangalal gerneg ngoomoorloonya jarrambayiny, mooloonggoogaleny.*

dots as with *dilg-dilg* or *dab-dab*]
nanggayig, nanggayib *coverb+GO/COME.* die (plural). • Nanggayig berrayin. *They all died.* • Pshaa, nanggayib barrinnha-gili. *Go now, you all can't come back, you have to be dead for good (said by the moon).*
nanggeg *coverb+HIT.* kill, knock down. • Ngarnji dany goonthoorrji nanggeg yinayidji-yarre. *That cold (sickness) cut us down.* • Gooral ngagenyel ngaboony ngenenggayana nginiwardji dimana-baya nanggeg ngoorrayidboo. *My mother's husband, my father, fell down here with a horse and he was killed.* [NOTE: type of impersonal construction, literal translation of verb is 'they killed him']
nanggeg *coverb+EAT.* eat until can't eat anymore. • Mooloonggoogoom nanggeg benangoonji. *There was so much fat, he ate until he couldn't eat any more.*
nanggegboo *coverb+GET.* kill, make die. • Waranyjara, nanggegboo yinamena. *That's enough, you are killing me.*
nanggeriny *noun.* big cake made of ground black plum, *minyjaarrany.*
nanggerrg *coverb+GO/COME.* stop (rain).

- Jadanyga nanggerrg nginiyi-yarri gelengen-ga. *The rain has stopped now.*

nanggoony *noun masculine.* brushtail possum. *Trichosurus vulpecula.* [NOTE: also word used by old people for photograph of koala even though they do not live in Gija country]

nanggooroo *noun.* chin.

nangoolooloob *coverb+BE/STAY.* be smelly, be smelly from far away. • Roord-garri ngoowinji-ninggi, nangoolooloob ngiwinji-ninggi. *If he sits down near you he'll be smelly to you.* SEE: ngardbiny.

nanina *verb.* I am TAKING you all. • Marra, marrarn nanina-yoo. *Come on, I'll take you two.*

nanini *verb.* you (one) SAID/DID.

nanininnha *verb.* you (one) WERE/WERE STAYING.

naniniyin *verb.* you (one) WERE/STAYED.

naniya-ngoo *verb.* I PUT you (one).

naniyanha-ngal *verb.* she was PUTTING you.

naniyanyji-ni *verb.* he was PUTTING you.

naniyi *verb.* you (one) CAME/WENT.

naniyilin *verb.* you (one) PUT ON YOURSELF, you (one) SAID TO YOURSELF.

naniyindi *verb.* you (one) kept COMING/GOING.

naniyinha *verb.* you (one) were GOING/COMING.

naniyida-ngoo *verb.* I HIT you (one).

nan'goon *noun.* hole in bank, roots at edge of water. • Nan'goone walig nyoowoonya derrandenji, mendoowoo-moowan girlirli nyerne gerrewoombi-boorroo. *In the daytime it (platypus) goes into a hole in the bank. Only at night it goes hunting for mussels.* • Nan'goonbe goorloon boorroonboo-ngarri . . . *The roots at the edge of the water . . .*

nanoojboo *coverb+BECOME.* become stiff.
• Nanoojboo ngelayid manyjoorroo. *I'm getting stiff in the knee.*

nanooward *verb.* you (one) FELL/WENT DOWN.

nanoowarda *verb.* you (one) were FALLING/GOING DOWN.

nany *coverb+BE/STAY.* straighten one's back.
• Nany ngininiyin. *He straightened his back.*
• Nany ngenaniyin. *I straightened my back.* SEE: nanybayiny.

nanybayiny, nanybayil, nanybayim *adjective.* having bottom stuck out. • Nanybayil dala. *She walks with her bottom stuck out.* • Nanybayiny danya. *He walks with his bottom stuck out.*

nanyjoorroo *noun.* nose peg. SEE: **ninjirri**.

narloob *coverb+WOUND_REFL.* get together, meet.
• Narloob yarrewa. *We'll get together, we meet.*

• Narloob berrawooran. *They got together.*

narloog *coverb+BE/STAY.* bend legs up, be good for dancing. • Ngayin-ga miyi narloog ngenan'ge-ngooyoo Wanggalga. *Me too, I'm bending up my legs for that Wangga.*

narrangirriyin *verb.* you all DID TO YOURSELVES/EACH OTHER.

narremiyinnha *verb.* you are all DOING TO YOURSELVES/EACH OTHER.

narrani *verb.* you all SAID/DID.

narrayi *verb.* you all WENT/CAME.

narrayinnha; narrayinha *verb.* you all were GOING/COMING.

narreninha *verb.* you all WERE/WERE STAYING.

-**narri** *indirect object enclitic pronoun.* to you all.

narrimijtha *verb.* you all will DO TO YOURSELVES.

narrini *verb.* you all want to say/do.

narrinnha; narrinha *verb.* you all will BE/STAY.

narrirn *verb.* you all will SAY/DO.

narriyana; narriyannha; narriyan *verb.* you all will be GOING/COMING.

-**narri-yoo** *indirect object enclitic pronoun.* to you (two).

narroogoo REDUP: **narroo-narroogoo**. *noun.* person having the same name, sharing a name derived from a dreaming animal that is the same as the person's skin. • Thawooloon nginyji melelagawoom ngarrgaleny narroo-narroogoo-bany Thawooloonji. *Lots of people have the same name as Hann Springs.*

narrooni *verb.* you all wanted to SAY/DO.

narroonnha *verb.* you all ARE/ARE STAYING.

narroorda *verb.* you all are GOING/COMING.

narroorn *verb.* you all are SAYING/DOING.

-**narroowa** *ablative enclitic pronoun.* from/after/because of you all.

nawan, nawanji, nawanbe *noun.* hole, cave.

nawarra REDUP: **nawarrra**. *coverb+BE/STAY.* be big, be important.

nawarra *coverb+GO/COME.* become big, become important. • Nawarra-ngarri ngiwiyayi, nawarrany-anyji ngiwirnji. *If he grows up he'll be a big man (i.e. working for or part of the government).* • Ngayin wanyage-joolan ngenaniyin, nawarrawoo ngenayindi mayarooyiyan, ngaginyen mayaroon Ngarraarnji, nawarra ngenayin. *When I was a little girl I grew up right at the house, the house at my place Moola Bulla, that's where I grew up.* • Nawarra-ngarri birriyan-joo, girliwa woomberridbendi-yoo, jangada-warriny

nawarra

bangariny. *When the two little ones get big they will walk.*
nawarra REDUP: **nawarrarra**. *coverb+SAY/DO.* grow. • *Nawarrarra yirrani Gilbayan. We all grew up right at Mabel Downs.*
nawarragam *noun.* many. SEE: **nawarrangim, melagawoom.**
nawarragawoony; naarragawoony. *noun.* river, creek. SEE: **nyanagawoony.**
nawarrangim *noun.* many. SEE: **nawarragam, melagawoom.**
nawarrany, nawarral, nawarram REDUP: **nawarrarram.** *adjective.* big, many, important.
nawarrawoo *coverb+GO/COME.* become big. • *Nawarrawoo nyidja, werlemenel. Goornawool werlemen-boo nyidja. She is getting big. The little girl is becoming a young woman.* • *Nawarrawoo boorroordboo. They are getting big now.*
nawarraya *coverb+BRING/TAKE.* bring a big lot. • *Nawarraya benanynha nawarran bajalarrin. Bring a big lot in the big bucket.*
nawiri-wirib *coverb+EAT.* all eating. • *Yirrayinde nawiri-wirib, yirrangoonjinde dambi miyali gig. We all started eating and had a good feed of the meat.* SEE: **nawooririb.**
nawooloony, nawooloom *noun.* nulla-nulla, fighting stick [NOTE: smaller than *goordooroom*]
nawooririb *coverb+SAY/DO.* eating all around. • *Ngoorrooma melalagawoom nawooririb boorroorn werrgale woongga-woonggare-bal. All the mother kangaroos with their babies are eating grass.*
neg *coverb+BURN/BITE.* get burnt, burn self. • *Marnemga neg ngenawoorranyji marlanga. The fire burned my hand.*
nemberrayanynha-boorroo *verb.* they were PUTTING you (one). • *Ngoorriri nemberrayanynha-boorroo. They were talking about you behind your back.*
nemberriyinnha-boorroo *verb.* they are HITTING you (one). • *Dama-ninggi mariwoo nemberriyinnha-boorroo jiyilem. People are there sneaking up on you.*
nembiyinnha-ngoo *verb.* I GIVE to you (one). • *Thalalam nembiyinnha-ngoo. I give you (one) your tongue (to sing with).*
nemboowoonnha *verb.* you (one) will FALL/GO DOWN.
nemenha-ngal; nemennha-ngal *verb.* she is GETTING you (one).
nemenji-ni; nemenji-ningi *verb.* he is GETTING you (one).
nemen'ge *verb.* I am GETTING him/it (masculine).
nemen'gende *verb.* I keep on GETTING him/it (masculine).
nemennhande-ngoo *verb.* I keep on GETTING you (one).
nemennha-ngoo; nemenha-ngoo *verb.* I am GETTING you (one). • *Ngoowan dawoong nemenha-ngoo. I don't love you.*
Neminoowarlin *noun.* Pompey's Pillar and country around. [NOTE: name given by Peggy Patrick to the Neminuwarlin Dance Group that staged 'Fire, fire burning bright', 'Neminuwarlin' is an earlier spelling]
nenbega-gili melagawiya *verb.* I should TAKE them all.
noonbanyge-gili *verb.* I wanted to bring them/it (non-singular)
nendegbany-noonggoo *verb.* I should TAKE you all
nendegge *verb.* I should TAKE them/it (non-singular).
nengamben'ge *verb.* I SPEAR him/it (masculine).
nenggerreben *pronoun.* you two.
nenggerren; nenggerren-gili *pronoun.* you all.
nenggerrewany *pronoun.* you yourselves. • *Jarrag-jarrag barrern nenggerrewany wela reminy ngenayin wela. You all talk, it is your turn, goodness, I am short of breath, goodness me.*
nenggerriyangeny, nenggerriyangel, nenggerriyangem *possessive pronoun.* yours (plural). SEE: **nenggeriyany.**
nenggerriyany, nenggerriyal, nenggerriyam *possessive pronoun.* yours (plural). SEE: **nenggerriyangeny.**
-nenggoowa *ablative enclitic pronoun.* from/after/because of you (one).
nerne; nirne; nirni *verb.* you are SAYING/DOING.
-ni; -ningi *indirect object enclitic pronoun.* to him.
nimberrayitha-boorroo *verb.* they HIT you (one).
nimberremnha-boorroo *verb.* they will GET you (one).
nimbida-ngoo *verb.* I'll TAKE you (one).
nimbida-ngal *verb.* she will TAKE you (one).
nimbijtha-ngal *verb.* she will HIT you (one).
nimbimge *verb.* I will GET him/it (masculine).
nimbimijtha *verb.* you (one) will DO TO YOURSELF.

nimbimji-ni; nimbimnha-ni *verb.* he/it (masculine) will GET you.
nimbimnha-ngal *verb.* she will GET you (one).
nimbimnha-ngoo *verb.* I will GET you (one).
nimbinnha; nimbinha *verb.* you will BE/BE STAYING.
nimbirn *verb.* you (one) will SAY/DO.
nimbirndi *verb.* you (one) will keep on SAYING/DOING.
nimbirrijtha-boorroo *verb.* they will HIT you (one), it (non-singular) will HIT you (one).
  • Daam ngaginybe ganginy nimbirrijtha-boorroo. *My country will not recognise you (if you go there without proper introduction ceremony).* [NOTE: this example sentence shows a compound verb that combines the coverb '*ganginy*' with a HIT inflecting verb. The verb is acting as an event classifier and the HIT meaning is subsumed in the compound.]
nimbirrimnha-boorroo *verb.* they will GET you (one), it (non-singular) will GET you (one).
  • Jad-garri bemberriyajbe laarne, jarrag-garri nimbirn jarraggajim-birri gara nimbirrimnha-boorroo ngirribawoorroo-biny. *When they put that thing up high, and you talk on the phone, then they will get you (what you say), from far away (talking about a satellite phone).*
nimbirriyinha-boorroo *verb.* they are HITTING you (one).
nimbiyaji-ni *verb.* he/it (masculine) will PUT you (one).
nimbiyajtha-ngal *verb.* she will PUT you (one).
nimbiyajtha-ngoo *verb.* I will PUT you (one).
nimbiyanha; nimbiyana; nimbiyannha *verb.* you (one) will be COMING/GOING.
nimbiyinnha-ngal *verb.* she is HITTING you (one).
nimbiyinnha-ngoo; nimbiyinha-ngoo *verb.* I want to HIT you (one). I will GIVE it to you (one).
nimboomoorloonha-ngoo *verb.* I will HAVE/KEEP you (one).
nimboowannha *verb.* you (one) will BURN/BITE yourself.
nimboowoonha *verb.* you (one) will FALL/GO DOWN.
nimboowoorroob-ngoo *verb.* I will LEAVE you (one). • Darag nimboowoorroob-ngoo. *I'll go away and you won't see me again.*
nimbiwoorroobtha-ngoo *verb.* I will be LEAVING you (one).
ninande *verb.* you (one) are BEING, you (one) keep on STAYING.
ninanyge *verb.* I was BRINGING/TAKING him/it (masculine).
ninbige, ninbigge *verb.* I will BRING/TAKE him/it (masculine).
ninbijge *verb.* I will HIT them/it (non-singular).
ninbijyajgende *verb.* I will keep PUTTING him/it (masculine).
ninbimge *verb.* I will GET him/it (masculine).
ninbinganyge *verb.* I will SPEAR him/it (masculine).
ninbiyajgiyi *verb.* I will PUT them (dual).
ninbiyangge *verb.* I will EAT him/it (masculine).
ninema, ninima *verb.* I GOT him/it (masculine).
ninemangge; ninimangge *verb.* I GOT him/it (masculine).
-ninggi *indirect object enclitic pronoun.* to you (one)
ninggerriyany, ninggerriyal, ninggerriyam *possessive pronoun.* yours (plural). [NOTE: Southern dialect] SEE: **nenggerriyany**.
ninggoowoony, ninggoowool, ninggoowoom *noun.* person or persons belonging to the same country. [NOTE: alternate form *ninggiwiny* from Halls Creek]
nini; nirni; nerne *verb.* you (one) are SAYING/DOING.
ninima *verb.* I GOT him/it (masculine).
ninimanggende; ninemanggende; ninamanggende *verb.* I kept on GETTING him/it (masculine).
niningoon; ninoongoon *verb.* I ATE it (masculine).
ninirl *coverb+SAY/DO.* make sparks. • Marnem ninirl boorroorn-yarri. *The fire is making sparks.* • Ninirl boorroorn marnemga dam. *That fire is sparking everywhere on us.* SEE: **nhil**.
niniwoorroodge *verb.* I LEFT him/it (masculine).
niniyangge *verb.* I PUT him/it (masculine).
niniyid *verb.* I HIT him/it (masculine).
niniyidge *verb.* I HIT him/it (masculine).
niniyidgende *verb.* I kept on HITTING him/it (masculine).
ninjirri *noun.* nose peg, fibula. SEE: **nanyjoorroo**.
niny *coverb+DO_REFL.* bite lower lip in anger or expectation that something bad might happen, grit teeth. • Niny nginimiyinji. *He is biting his lip.* • Danya jiyiliny niny nginimiyinji warim-boorroo. *This man is gritting his teeth for a fight.*
nirda *verb.* you (one) are GOING/COMING.
nirdande *verb.* you (one) keep GOING/COMING.

nirij

nirij REDUP: **niri-nirij** *coverb+GET.* pinch someone. • *Nirij nginimanyji.* He pinched him. • *Niri-nirij nginimanyjende.* He kept on pinching him.

nirrij-doo *verb.* you two will HIT EACH OTHER.

niwige *verb.* I will TAKE him/it.

niwijge *verb.* I will HIT him/it.

niwoomoorloowoonde *verb.* I will be KEEPING him.

niwoorroobge *verb.* I will LEAVE him/it (masculine).

niyilen-ngoo *verb.* I am PUTTING you (one).

niyilinji-ni *verb.* he/it (masculine) is PUTTING you (one).

niyilin'ge *verb.* I am PUTTING him/it (masculine).

niyinji-ni *verb.* he/it (masculine) is HITTING you (one).

niyin'ge *verb.* I am HITTING him/it (masculine).

niyinnha-ngoo *verb.* 1. I am BRINGING/TAKING you (one). 2. I am HITTING you (one).

niyinyil; nyinyil *noun.* zebra finch. *Taeniopygia guttata.* [NOTE: stole fire in the dreamtime; word used for all other finches as well]

nooloonha-ngal *verb.* she is PUTTING you (one).

nooloonha-ngoo *verb.* I am PUTTING you (one). SEE: **niyilen-ngoo**.

noombimge-yoo *verb.* I might GET them (dual).

noomboorn *verb.* you (one) want to SAY/DO. • *Mirlimbi jang-ma noomboorn?* Do you want to eat liver?

noomboowoonnha *verb.* when/if you (one) FALL/GO DOWN.

noomoorloona-ngal *verb.* she HAS/KEEPS you (one).

noomoorloonha-ngoo *verb.* I am KEEPING you (one), I have you (one).

noonaj REDUP: **noonaj-noonaj**. *coverb+SAY/DO.* nod head. • *Dala goorndoogal noonaj nyerne.* This little girl is nodding her head. • *Noonaj-noonaj barroo-gili!* All nod your heads!

noonaan'ge *verb.* I am BRINGING/TAKING them/it (non-singular). [NOTE: Southern dialect]

noonama; noonema *verb.* I GOT them/it (non-singular).

noonamang *verb.* I GOT them/it (non-singular).

noonamangge; noonemangge *verb.* I was GETTING them/it (non-singular).

noonamanggende *verb.* I kept on GETTING them/it (non-singular).

noonamoorloon'ge *verb.* I HAVE them/it (non-singular).

noonamoorloowardgende *verb.* I used to HAVE/KEEP/LOOK AFTER them/it (non-singular).

noonangoon *verb.* I ATE them/it (non-singular).

noonangoon'ge *verb.* I EAT them/it (non-singular).

noonanyge *verb.* I was BRINGING/TAKING them/it (non-singular).

noonanygende *verb.* I used to BRING/TAKE them/it (non-singular).

noonawoon'ge *verb.* I WOUNDED them/it (non-singular).

noonawoorrood *verb.* I LEFT them/it (non-singular).

noonawoorroodge *verb.* I left them/it (non-singular).

noonaya *verb.* I PUT them/it (non-singular).

noonayangge *verb.* I PUT them/it (non-singular).

noonayid *verb.* I HIT them/it (non-singular).

noonayidge *verb.* I HIT them/it (non-singular).

noonbajge *verb.* let me PUT them/it (non-singular).

noonbemge; noonboomge *verb.* I should GET them/it (non-singular).

noonbijge *verb.* I will HIT them/it (non-singular).

noonbimge *verb.* I will GET them/it (non-singular).

noonbiyajge *verb.* I will PUT them/it (non-singular).

noondaj *verb.* let me PUT them/it (non-singular).

noondajge *verb.* let me PUT them/it (non-singular).

noondem; noondoom *verb.* I want to GET them/it (non-singular).

noondemge *verb.* let me GET them/it (non-singular).

noondijge *verb.* let me HIT them/it (non-singular).

noondoogoo *verb.* I want to/should TAKE them/it (non-singular).

noondooj *verb.* let me HIT them/it (non-singular).

noondoomoorloo *verb.* I want to/should HAVE/KEEP them/it (non-singular). • *Noondoomoorloo-noonggoowa Joonbambi dambi jimerrawoon.* I want to keep those Joonba of yours forever.

noondoowam *verb.* I want to GO AND GET them/it (non-singular), I'll have to GO AND GET them/it (non-singular).

noonemen'ge *verb.* I am GETTING them/it (non-singular). • *Nhoonbam ngarag noonemen'ge*

nooyooloonnha-ngoo; nooyoolennha-ngoo

daamga-nga goowooloon laarne. *I (peewee) make my home from mud at the top of the tree.*

noonemen'gende *verb.* I keep on GETTING him/it (masculine).

noonemoorloon'ge; noonoomoorloon'ge *verb* I HAVE him/it (masculine).

noongoog *coverb+EAT.* have a good lot of something (e.g. food, sleep). • Mooyoonyga noongoog niningoon ngoorroon yarraniyin-ngarri. *I had a good sleep at the place where we stopped.*

noongoon'ge *verb.* I EAT him/it (masculine).

nooniyilin'ge; nooniyilen'ge; nooniyooloon'ge; noonilin'ge *verb.* I am PUTTING them/it (non-singular).

nooniyilin'gende; nooniyilen'gende *verb.* I kept on PUTTING them/it (non-singular).

nooniyin'ge *verb.* I am HITTING them/it (non-singular).

nooniyin'ge *verb.* I am BRINGING/TAKING them/it (non-singular)'. [NOTE: Northern dialect]

nooniyooloon'gende; nooniyilin'gende *verb.* I keep on PUTTING them/it (non-singular).

noonoongoon'ge *verb.* I EAT them/it (non-singular).

noonoongoon'gende *verb.* I EAT them/it (non-singular) always/habitually.

noonoord *coverb+GO_ALONG.* bite on something (e.g. boab seed). • Noonoorda woomberranybende woo thil-thil ngoorramangbende, gooma dam binadbe. *They used to bite them with their teeth or crack them like peanuts.* SEE: **noord**.

noord REDUP: **noonoord** *coverb+SAY/DO.* bite something small. • Noord nginini jililim. *He was biting (boab seed).* • Dala noonoord nyerne yiwim. *That woman is biting lice.*

noord REDUP: **noonoord** *coverb+BURN/BITE.* bite on something, bite something between teeth. • Goorndoogany noord nginiwoorranji jililiny. *The little boy is biting the boab seeds.* • Noord benawoorranyji. *He is biting them.* • Ngoowan-nga noord-girrimga. Minyjoowoo-bawoorroon-nga leg genayi. *I can't bite. I have no teeth.* • Wanyagem noord-bija benewarre-birri. *Bite off a little bit.* SEE: **noonoord**.

noorroo *coverb.* whistling in ears. SEE: **nhoorr, nyoore-nyoore**.

-noowa *ablative enclitic pronoun.* from/after/because of him/it (masculine).

noowidge *verb.* I wanted to HIT him/it (masculine).

noowige *verb.* I will TAKE him/it (masculine).

noowimge; noowemge *verb.* I will GET him/it (masculine).

noowiyajge *verb.* I will PUT him/it (masculine).

noowiyanda *verb.* I will EAT him/it (masculine).

noowoojge *verb.* I might HIT him/it (masculine.

nooyooloonnha-ngoo; nooyoolennha-ngoo *verb.* I am PUTTING you (one).

Ng ng

nga *interjection.* ah!, yes!, I see!

-nga; -ngage; -ngageny *benefactive enclitic pronoun.* for me.

-nga *suffix.* sequential suffix to coverbs.

ngaaloo REDUP: **ngaaloo-ngaaloo**. *coverb+BE/STAY.* rest in shade. • Berrema ngaaloo ngininiyindi yilag warlarrin. *This is the place (shown in a painting) where he used to sit in the shade down near the river beside a white gum tree.*

ngaaloom *noun.* shade, shadow, photograph. • Benanynha-ngoo dam ngaaloom-boorroo joonbimnha-ngarri, nyaman. *Bring your camera (that thing for getting shadows), Ms Chen.*

ngaandem *noun.* flesh.

ngaarriny, ngarreny REDUP: **ngaarriny-ngaarrinybe**. *noun.* stone, hill. • Ngarriny-ngarrinybeny-anyji. *Maybe two stones. / Maybe lots of little stones?* SEE: **ngarrgaleny**.

ngabarl-ngabarl *noun.* sea water, waves. • Marra yarroordja ngabarl-ngabarl-yoorroong. *We are going away to the sea.*

ngabarl-ngabarl *coverb+SAY/DO.* be waves on water. • Ngabarl-ngabarl ngerne goorlinyga. *The water is making waves.*

ngabayi *noun.* father; son/daughter of father, niece/nephew of aunt (father's sister); address form, 'dad', used by father to speak to son or daughter, child to speak to father, and aunt to speak to her nieces and nephews. • Mirlimbi jang-ma noomboorn ngabayi? *Do you want to eat liver, Dad?* [NOTE: has been recorded as used by a niece or nephew to address an aunt (father's sister) who can also be addressed as '*gawayi*']. SEE: **ngaboony**.

ngabibij *coverb+SAY/DO.* smell, give off an aroma.

Figure 64. *Ngaaloon: Jibilyiwoony Doug Macale: Ngaaloon roord nginji Jambinji.*

- Aa, thoowoo ngabibij boorroorn. *Ah, something is making a smell here.*

ngabool *noun.* female child of father, woman's brother's daughter. SEE: **ngabayi**.

ngaboony *noun.* father, child of father, woman's brother's son. SEE: **ngabayi**. [NOTE: used by Catholics to mean 'God']

ngaboorayi REDUP: ngaboo-ngaboorayi. *coverb+SAY/DO.* yawn. • Ngaboorayi nginini. *He was yawning.* • Ngaboorayi nini ngayijan gooma ngaboo-ngaboorayi ngenarn. *You are yawning just as I am yawning.* • Marloogany ngaboorayi ngerne. *The old man is yawning.*

ngadarrji *noun masculine.* death adder. *Acanthophis* sp. [NOTE: Jawalyi skin] SEE: **damberrji**.

ngadi *coverb+PUT.* put something back.
• Ngoowan ngadi nyaniyanyji. *He didn't give it (borrowed bicycle) back.*

ngadi *coverb+PLACE_M.* stay behind. • Ngadi waniyanya birn'girrbal. *The turkey stayed behind.*

ngadidi *coverb+SAY/DO.* stay behind.
• Ngarranggarnin ngadidi nyanini birn'girrbal. *The turkey stayed behind in dreamtime.* [NOTE: stay behind even when being asked to go]

ngag *coverb+GO/COME.* come all of a sudden, happen upon someone/something, arrive suddenly close to someone. • Nginiyin, ngag giniyin-ni nginyjiny jirraginy, goorlangge. *He was going along, he happened upon this frog, poor thing.* • Ngag giniyin-ningi. *He (the king brown, Jambin skin) came upon him (water python, Joongoorra skin) all of a sudden.*

ngaga *interjection.* oh no!

Ngagarramarn *noun.* place on Lansdowne Station.

-ngage, -ngageny, -nga *benefactive enclitic pronoun.* for me.

ngaginyji, ngaginyil, ngaginybe; ngagenyji, ngagenyil, ngagenybe *possessive pronoun.* my, mine.

ngagoony *interjection.* exclamation made if speaker's brother-in-law or sister-in-law is sworn. SEE: **yigelany, warri-warri**.

ngaj *coverb+FALL/GO_DOWN.* mistake, not recognise.
• Ngaj ngenaward-ngooyoo. *I did not recognise her. (I should have gone over to her in the first place.)* SEE: **ngany**.

ngajarrg-ngajarrg *coverb+GO/COME.* share food.

• Ngajarrg-ngajarrg berrayinjende. *They gave a little bit beef round to every camp.*

ngaji *noun.* brother; sister (address form).

Ngajibawoobgernem *noun.* place on Newry Station. [NOTE: place where a little boy called out for his brothers and was taken by an old spirit woman]

ngajiny, ngajil, ngajim *noun.* brother, sister, sibling.

ngajiral *noun.* stone axe. SEE: **manyjangal, woomal**. [NOTE: young men are not supposed to say this word, they have to say *mayinggal*]

ngalagangarril SEE: **ngarlagangarril**.

ngalalabany *noun.* cluster fig, fruit of cluster fig. *Ficus racemosa*. SEE: **jawoonany**.

ngalanga *noun.* child (said by mother when speaking to him/her). SEE: **ngalangany, ngalangal**.

ngala-ngala *coverb+SAY/DO.* be greedy.
• Ngala-ngala boorroorn-joo. *They two are really greedy.*

ngala-ngala *coverb+SAY/DO_M.* be greedy.
• Ngala-ngala jemenande. *You are really greedy (you eat like a dog).* • Dali ngalil ngala-ngala woomenyande, welang-welang woomenyande. *That woman is greedy, she finishes before everyone.* • Danyi jiyiliny ngala-ngala woomenjende. *That man is really greedy.*

ngalangangeny, ngalangangel, ngalangangem REDUP: ngala-ngalangangem. *noun.* son/daughter of mother. • Ngalangangboom. *Mother and child, mothers and children.* [NOTE: 'Ngalangangpum' is the name of the school at Warrmarn, using the old spelling system]

ngalany *coverb+GET.* sing someone.
• Ngalany nanbimnha-yoo. *I'll sing you two.* • Diyalawanyoowa ngalany nyimberramangbe Goordbarriyal ngoorroona Red Butt-e nyinya. *She is the one they sang, Goordbarriya who stays at Red Butt now.*

ngalany *coverb+DO_REFL.* sing self. • 'Gaboowa narrani-gili?' 'Ngoowan. Ngarranggarniny ngalany yirremiyinji'. *'What will all of you do?' 'Oh, we will sing to ourselves about the dreamtime.'*

ngalany REDUP: ngalany-ngalany. *coverb+SAY/DO.* sing. • Ngalany barrern-gili! *You all sing!*
• Melagawoom ngalany-merrarriny berrani.

ngalany

All of them were singing together, the whole lot.
ngalany coverb+WOUND. sing someone. • *Ngalany nyanewoonji danyga. That man sang her.*
ngalany coverb+SAY/DO_M. sing. • *Warrg-garri woomberramande, ngalany-ngarri woomberramande deg yirramanyjende. We used to watch them when they were dancing and singing.*
ngalany coverb+GO_ALONG. sing. • *Ngalany ngiliyin'ge. I sing.*
ngalanybe noun. song.
ngalanygaleny, ngalanygalel, ngalanygalem noun. good singer.
ngalayi noun. son of woman, woman's grand-mother's mother's brother (address form).
ngalayiny REDUP: **ngala-ngalayim**. noun. son of woman, woman's grand-mother's mother's brother. [NOTE: can also used to refer to 'father-in-law' by women]
ngalemelewam pronoun. all the things from her. • *Liyanbe-ngiyiwa ngalemelewam waj-garri nyanini-yirri, wel, nawarrarra yirrayin na. We grew up with the good feeling for life and all that she gave us.*
ngalen pronoun. she, her.
ngalerr coverb+SAY/DO. scold, shout at someone. • *Ngelela gooragal ngalerr nyerne-ningi ngoowan jang nginini nhawiyangem mayim. His mother is scolding him because he did not eat his food.* • *Ngalerr nyanini-ningi. She scolded him.*
ngalewany; ngalewarriny pronoun. she in turn, her turn, herself.
ngaliba coverb+BECOME. get married. • *Ngaliba waniyid. He became a married man, he got married.*
ngalil, ngalim REDUP: **ngali-ngalim**. noun. woman.
ngalingoonybiny noun. man who cannot do without a woman. SEE: **jiyilengoonybel**.
ngaliyana pronoun. she is the one.
ngaliyangeny, ngaliyangel, ngaliyangem possessive pronoun. hers. • *Ngaliyangeny-ngooyoo danygawa. That is hers.*
Ngaljirriwany noun. Five Mile on Moola Bulla.
ngalwany noun. furry-leaved kapok bush, edible root species that resembles *goonjal* but is bitter. *Cochlospermum fraseri* v. *heteronemum*. [NOTE: has similar flowers to *goonjal* but has hairy leaves and different growth pattern. Cooked in the coals and then pounded together with cooked boab seeds, *jililiny*; lots found on Texas Downs] SEE: **malanyjarrji, warndiwal**.
ngalyarr, ngalyarre noun. testicles. SEE: **goolyany**.
ngam coverb+BE/STAY. have mouth open. • *Goorndoogany ngam nginji. The little boy has his mouth open.*
ngamal coverb+GET. bless someone. • *Ngamal nemennha-ngoo ngaji. I bless you, sibling.*
ngamalan SEE: **ngamarlan**.
ngamalil noun. cabbage palm. *Livistona victoriae*. SEE: **yangajalil, yingajalil, danarrel**.
ngamanang coverb+GET. carry on both arms in front of body (as on a tray). • *Ngamanang nginimanyji. He is carrying it on his arms in front of him.*
ngamanang coverb+BRING/TAKE. carry on both arms in front of body. • *Damboowa goorndooganya ngamanang nginanyjende na, warrga wanemayinde. Then he carried the child on his arms in front and was dancing.*
ngamanang coverb+HAVE. hold in arms in front of body. • *Goorndoogal ngamanang ngoomoorlinya ngirrngiliny. The little girl is carrying a cat.*
ngamanyiny, ngamanyil noun. person whose parent, uncle or aunt has died.
ngamanyigboo coverb+GO/COME. being a person whose parent, uncle or aunt has died.

Figure 65. *Ngalany: Gamaliny Timmy Timms, Deanne Ramsey: Ngalany-galeny ngalany ngerne.*

ngambarnji

Figure 66. *Ngamarran: Warlagarriny Rammel Peters, Lawrence Peters: Ngaboo-lang thad boorroonboo-yoo Ngamarran yilag Balinyin.* (Photo Rusty Peters.)

- Ngamanyigboo-ngarri nirda . . . *You being a person whose parent, uncle or aunt died . . .* [NOTE: referring indirectly to the person who died, who would be known to the speaker and addressee, instead of naming them]

ngamarlam *adjective.* soapy, frothy. SEE: **nyoomarlim**.

ngamarlan *coverb+PLACE_M.* be frothy like soap.
- Nginyjinyi boonbany dambi thawalam ngarem, ngamarlan woomberriyilinbe. Menkawoom. *This cabbage gum tree, the honey from those flowers is frothy like soap. It is good.*

ngamarr *coverb+SAY/DO_M.* wanting to be looked after all the time (child), wanting to be carried, wait for others to do things. • Ngamarr-ma jeminande? *Do you want to be looked after all the time? (e.g. kid being sooky, person who can't work for themselves).* • Gaboo barra ngamarr jarremenande-yoo, ngarranggarnin-noonggoorroo-yoo. *What then, you two can't look after yourselves, you are old enough (said as a joke by Rusty Peters to Eileen Bray and Nancy Nodea).*

Ngamarran *noun.* snake dreaming place in the river bed near Springvale Station homestead.

ngamarrany *noun.* snake (generic).
Ngamarrany-wad-garri-nginini *noun.* place name. LIT: 'the place where the snake looked back'.

ngamarriny *noun.* sulphur-crested cockatoo. *Cacatua galerita.* SEE: **ngayirr-ngayirrji**.

ngamarrwoony, ngamarrwool, ngamarrwoom *adjective.* lazy, want to be carried all the time (child). • Nyengen ngamarrwoonjaya-ngoo. *You always want looking after.* • Ngamarrwoonyiya. *A really lazy one.* • Ngamarrwooyan-ngoo. *You always want to be carried.*

ngambarl *coverb+GET.* bless. • Ngoorroom mayaroom ngelmangboo Yisdam-boorroo, ngaboony ngoowiyayi, ngambarl binbimji ngoorloorloog-girrim-boorroo. *Those buildings over there around to the east (made ready) for Easter (Gymkhana), Father (the priest) will go and bless them for drinking (used to be a licensed bar at Turkey Creek at the Easter Gymkhana).* SEE: **mam**.

ngambarnji *noun masculine.* juvenile freshwater crocodile. *Crocodylus johnstonii.* SEE: **lalanggarrany**.

ngambooroony

Figure 67. *Nganthanji: Nganthanji bed woomenji ngarrgalen.*

ngambooroony *coverb+GO/COME.* eat something by the handful (e.g. honey). • Ngambooroony-gala ngenda marlam-birri. *I'm going to eat it with my hand.* • Ngambooroony-gala jara. *You eat it by the handful.* SEE: **ramoob**.

ngamibany, ngamibal, ngamibam *adjective.* liar, one who tells lies. SEE: **ngarlibany**. [NOTE: swearing, also means having a big wet arse]

ngamoonayi *coverb+SAY/DO.* drown, struggle in water. • Belegawirrin nginiyin garlooroon. Ngamoonayi nginini. *He went right into the middle of the deep waterhole. He was drowning (struggling in the water).* [NOTE: this word doesn't mean that the person necessarily died, just had difficulty in the water]

ngamoongoom, ngamoongoony, ngamoongool; ngamoo-ngamoom REDUP: ngamoo-ngamoongoom. *adjective.* previous, from long ago, older. • Jiregam berraniyin, ngamoo-ngamoom jiyilem ngalim berraniyin. *The birds lived here, they were men and women previously.* • Jangadany dany ngamoongoony nginiwardji-ngarri bangariny jada-warriny. *That little boy was born two years ago.*

ngamoongoon REDUP: ngamoo-ngamoongoon. *temporal.* previously, long ago.

Nganbenan *noun.* place on Mabel Downs with a permanent spring.

ngang *coverb+SAY/DO.* sob. • Goorndoogany ngang ngerne. *The little boy is sobbing.*

nganggerrge *coverb+GET.* give someone a fright. • Dany ngamarrany nganggerrge binbimji-yoo. *That snake will give those two a fright.* SEE: **boorrngoordge**.

Ngangamany *noun.* big hill near Killarney Bore.

Nganirrin *noun.* place on Springvale Station.

ngan'gerre *noun.* cheek. SEE: **limimim**.

nganoonggoom *noun.* arm.

nganthanji *noun masculine.* cycad palm. *Cycas pruinosa.*

ngany *coverb+HIT.* not recognise. • Ngany benayidji. *He didn't recognise them.* SEE: **ngaj**.

nganyjalany *noun masculine.* type of small goanna.

nganyjarlil *noun feminine.* type of bush tomato. *Solanum chippendalei.*

Nganyjarriwoony *noun.* McKenna Spring, family outstation near Argyle Diamond Mine for Goody Barrett and Lena Nyadbi.

nganyjiwoorany *noun.* bird species. SEE:

namalji. [NOTE: lives in caves]

nganyjoom noun. nerves, feelings, sinew.
• Nganyjoom woorrngoord ngenarn yiligin. *My nerves are hurting inside (from people who keep on asking non-stop.)* • Gawoo-birri nganyjoombi? *Where are their feelings?* SEE: **jirlwam.**

nganyjoowarrji noun. snake. [NOTE: word used on Texas Downs] SEE: **ngamarrany.**

ngar coverb+SAY/DO. have teeth on edge. • Ngar ngenarn minyjoowoom. *My teeth are on edge.*

ngarabarral noun feminine. emu. *Dromaius novaehollandiae*. [NOTE: word from Bedford Downs way] SEE: **garnanganyjel, wiyarrel.**

ngarag REDUP: ngara-ngarag. coverb+DO_REFL. be making self up (e.g. clouds). • Ngarag nginimiyinji. *(The clouds) are building up.* [NOTE: Phyllis Thomas talking about clouds]

ngarag REDUP: ngararag. coverb+SAY/DO. be making/repairing something. • Ngarag yirrarn. *We are making*

ngarag coverb+GET. make. • Ngarag nginima nawooloony. *He made a nulla-nulla.* • Dama yoorayimem ngarag bemberramangbe. *They made this soak.* • Ngawalel ngarag nyimberremenbe. *They are making woomeras.* • Dala jibilyoowool ngarag jilamangke. *I made/painted that duck (in the painting).* • Yirrangirriyin, 'Ngarag yamberrem daam-yoowoo.' *We said to each other, 'Let's make ourselves a cubby!'*

ngarag coverb+SAY/DO_M. make. • Jiregam dam ngarag woomberramande-ni nhoonbam. *Those birds make mud (nests) on it.*

ngarag coverb+HIT. make. • Mayaroom ngarag boomberrayid gimoonyidi na. *They built community houses then.*

ngarag coverb+GO_ALONG. go along making. • Garloomboom ngarag woomberranybende, garrabirim. *They used to go along making spears and boomerangs.*

ngarag coverb+BECOME. be made. • Ngarranggarniny, Deroorrji ngaraga woomberrayidbe. *It was the dreamtime, you know, the Black Hills were made then.*

ngarajbe coverb+BE/STAY. pose with arms folded. • Ngarajbe nyinya werlemenel. *The young girl is sitting with arms folded.*

ngaram coverb+BE/STAY. squat. • Ngaram boorroonbe-gili. *They are all squatting.*

ngara-ngarag coverb+SAY/DO. be making. • Ngara-ngarag ngenani-boorroo-gili dagmanbe dinaan. *I was making dinner for all the stockmen.* • Thoowoorranyji ngara-ngarag nyerne. *She is making something.* SEE: **ngarag.**

ngarayi coverb+PUT. find, see. • Wanyja yagenge-yoorroong ngaraga noonboomge, an boorroon, ngarayi-ngarri bimbirriyajbe, 'Yangoorra ngarag berrani daam yoorriyangem?' *Supposing I paint other people's country, when they see it (they will say), 'Who made this picture of our country?'*

ngarayi coverb+HIT/CUT. find, see. • Ngarayi bemberrawoonbi-yoo wajbaloo-warriny nang-ngarri berrawardbi-yoo yiligin. *They found the two white men dead inside the house.*

ngarayi coverb+HIT. find, see. • Ngarayi nyaniyid jirrawool ngalil, girliwany wananya. *He found one woman walking along.* • Ngoowan biri nginiyi, gerag miyale ngarayi-ngarri binbijji. *He didn't come back when he found some meat later on.* • Jarrambayiny ngarayi-wanyji nginiyid joolany. *The goanna must have seen the dog.*

ngarayiwarran locative. be silhouetted in a gap. • Doombooman thad ginji ngarayiwarran. *He is standing up, a silhouette in the gap.*

ngard coverb+SAY/DO. smell. • Nhoowoole ngard boorroorn. *There is a rotten smell.* • Ngard-garri ngerne dambi yagewoo, yilgoowoorriny, yilgoowoorriny, warrern'ge yinema-yarri. *From his really bad, bad, different smell, it made us sick.* SEE: **ngard-ngard.**

ngard coverb+GO/COME. smell. • Bagabalaya ngardjiyijande. / Ngard berrayi bagabamanyji. *It smells like a 'porcupine' (echidna).* • Ngard berrayi nhoowoole. *It smells rotten.*

ngard coverb+GET. smell. • Ngard noonama. *I smelled it.* • Joolany ngardanyji nginima jarrambayiny. *The dog must have smelled the goanna.* • Ngard noonemen'ge nhoowoole. *I can smell the rotten meat.*

ngard coverb+SAY/DO_M. smell. • Balarr-moowam ngard woomberramande. *They only smell the mud (kangaroos, when hunters paint themselves with mud).*

ngarda-ngardawoo coverb+SPEAR. cry at someone. • Ngoowan ngarda-ngardawoo yinbengany-ngage. *Don't keep on crying at me. Don't assault me with your crying.*

ngardawoo

ngardawoo REDUP: **ngarda-ngardawoo**. *coverb+SAY/DO*. cry. • Ngardawoo nyanini. *She started to cry.* • Ngoowan warrmaj joowida, ngardawoo nyimbirn. *Don't hit her, she will cry.* • Wanyanyagem ngarda-ngardawoo berrani nawarrarram. *All the children were crying.*

ngardawooge; ngardawoogoo *coverb+GO/COME*. be made to cry. • Ani, marrarn-ayi goorloo-giny nyaninya, ngardawoogoowaya ngenardge-ngiyiwa bardoon. *But when she went to get the water, I started crying just after she left.*

ngardawooge *coverb+HIT*. make someone cry. • Degijiya nyanemanyji, jarrg-garri nyanewardja, ngardawooge-ngarri nyimberrayidbe. *He looked at her properly as she was jumping and they (ants) were making her cry.*

ngardawooge, ngardawoogoo REDUP: **ngardawoo-ngardawoogoowany**. *coverb+GET*. make someone cry. • Ngardawoogoo ngoorroomenbe gajim. *He (lizard) was crying because of the sores (on the crocodile) (the sores made him cry).* • Ngerr-ngerrji woomberrama, ngardawoo-ngardawoogoowany ngoorramangbe. *They were throwing things at him, making him cry.*

ngardbiny, ngardbel, ngardbim *adjective*. smelly.

ngardboo *coverb+GO/COME*. smell. • Goorrag benayidji na, malngoonybi-birri ngardboo-ngarri nginiyinde. *He half killed them with the bad smell of his sweat.*

ngard-ngard *coverb+SAY/DO*. sniff. • Joolany ngard-ngard ngerne. *The dog is sniffing.*

ngaregalel *noun*. good at getting bush honey.

ngarem, ngariny, ngarel *noun*. bush honey, native beehive, sugarbag (generic). • Nginya ngariny bilij-garri niniyid. *This is the sugarbag (ground sugarbag) I found.* [NOTE: the generic is non-singular; if species is named, the generic acts as a classifier and agrees in gender with the species, e.g. *ngarel* refers to *beranggool*; *ngariny* refers to *nhawiny* or *gayirriny*]

ngarij *coverb+GO/COME*. arrive, meet. • Yaad-yoorroong yirrayin-ngarri ngarij giniyin manijany. *When we went to the yard, the manager arrived.*

ngarij *coverb+GET*. meet someone. • Diyena ngarij benamanyji-yoo ngaji-ga-warriny. *He met his two brothers there.*

ngarl *coverb+FALL/GO_DOWN*. feel sick in stomach, not feel like eating. • Ngarl nginiwardji. *He felt sick. / He did not feel like eating.* • Ngarl ngenaward jaam. *I felt sick in my stomach.*

ngarlagangarril, ngarlagangarriny *noun*. magpie goose. *Anseranas semipalmata.*

ngarlalmanginy *noun masculine*. lizard species, little white lizard that lives in trees, like a *moondoowoony*, 'gecko', but with a big head.

ngarla-ngarla *coverb+SAY/DO*. ripple. • Ngarla-ngarla boorroorn goorloon. Thoowiyanyji. *There are ripples on the water. It must be something.*

ngarlarrang *coverb+BE/STAY*. be lying on back. • Ngarlarrang nginji gerloorroogoo nginji. *He is lying on his back, facing up.*

ngarlibany, ngarlipal, ngarlibam *adjective*. liar, one who tells lies. SEE: **ngamibany**.

ngarli; ngarliyi *coverb+FALL/GO_DOWN*. cool down, settle down after being angry/upset. • Gerag ngarli nyimboowoonya ngaliwanyda. *After a while she'll settle down again.*

ngarli; ngarliyi *coverb+SAY/DO*. cool down, settle down after being angry/upset. • Goonyjiri-ngarri jengaboornnha wariwoom-birri warinyboo ngemenji ngoowan ngarliwoo ngoowirn. *When you tease that bloke in a cheeky way he'll get wild and he won't settle down.*

ngarliyig *coverb+FALL/GO_DOWN*. be cooled. • Ngarliyigboo boorroowoonboo ngabibij boorroorn daam. *The country has been made cool, it smells good.*

ngarliyig *coverb+BURN/BITE*. cool down, pain ease. • Ngarliyig nginoowoorran. *I already cooled down.*

ngarliyig *coverb+HIT*. cool something/someone down. • Ngarliyig-gela yindij-yoowoo. *Let it (wind) cool us.*

ngarliyig *coverb+GET*. make cool. • Nalijam loordboom, ngarliyig-gala noondem goorloom-birri. *The tea is hot, let me cool it with water.*

ngarliyiny, ngarliyil, ngarliyim *adjective*. cool (of food, fire, etc.). • Ngarliyim gawoornbe. *Cold ashes.* • Ngarliyim gere boorroorn-yarri berrema gen'galem. *This cool wind is cooling us down.* SEE: **gawiliny**.

ngarl-ngarl *coverb+SAY/DO*. make noise. • Ngarl-ngarl boorroorn waringarrim. *They are all making noise when they talk.*

ngarlngarlban *temporal.* early evening, 'after supper' (i.e at the time when everyone is still awake and talking).

ngarlngarlbawoorroon *locative.* a quiet place.

ngarloo *coverb+SAY/DO.* feel like not eating.
- Thoowoorre-boorroo ngarloo nerne? *Why don't you feel like eating?*

ngarloo *coverb+SAY/DO_M.* feel like not eating.
- Ngarloo ngelemen'gende. *I don't feel like eating.*

ngarloogoo *coverb+EAT.* eat too much and fall asleep. • Ngarloogoo noonangoon'ge. *I ate too much and fell asleep.*

ngarloogoo *coverb+FALL/GO_DOWN.* fall flat with guts down. • Ngarloogoo nginiward. *He fell down flat. He fell down winded.*

ngarn *pronoun, locative, coverb (space filler, a word used in place of a word that the speaker cannot immediately think of).* that thing, that stuff, that place, that action (that I cannot say or cannot think of right now). • Jaam ngarn ninemangge dany jarrambayiny. *I did that thing to the goanna's stomach (i.e. I gutted it).* [NOTE: gender forms *ngarnji*, 'that masculine thing'; *ngarnel*, 'that feminine thing'; *ngarnbe*, 'those things, that non-singular thing'; the locative suffix *-e* giving *ngarne*, 'at that place' and can act as a coverb 'to do that thing']

-ngarnany, -ngarnal, -ngarnam *suffix* denizen of, dweller • Ngayin-ga nyiyirri-ngarnan-nga galawarrjin-nga. *I am someone who lives in the spinifex, a spinifex pigeon.*

ngarndaginy, ngarndagel *interjection.* big semen. [NOTE: swearing, masculine form said about men, feminine form about women]

ngarndam *noun.* semen. • Ngarndam gajoowoom-birri. *Soft semen (swearing).*

ngan'goo *noun.* bull shark. *Carcharhinus leucas.* [NOTE: Western dialect]

ngaroom *noun.* front of lower part of the body, kangaroo's pouch. • Barawool woonggariny ngiyinya ngaroon. *The female hill kangaroo has a baby in her pouch.*

ngarr *coverb+GO/COME.* get angry, go off in a huff.
- Ngarr nginiyi. *He became angry and went away.* SEE: **roog**.

ngarr *coverb+SAY/DO.* have a stomach ache, have a pain. • Ngarr ngerne. *He has a stomach ache.*

ngarra REDUP: **ngarra-ngarra.** *coverb+GET.* know someone/something, recognise. • Ngarra ninemangge. *I know him.* • Girinyil dal ngarra-ngarrawoo benamenya warn'gam. *The katydid grasshopper knows about the cold.* SEE: **ngoongoo**.

ngarra *coverb+DO_REFL.* know each other.
- Ngoowan ngarra berramiyinbe. *They did not know each other. / They did not recognise each other.*

ngarra *coverb+SAY/DO_M.* know.
- Doori-doorib-ngarri ngidji, ngarra wanema jalij-girrem. *When it thunders, it is the right time for rain (it is known that).*

ngarranggarnin *temporal.* dreamtime, creation time, long ago, time when the landscape took its present form and the rules for living came into being.

ngarranggarniny, ngarranggarnil, ngarranggarnim *adjective.* belonging to the dreamtime. *noun.* dreamtime thing.

ngarranggarniny *coverb+GET.* become part of country during the time when the landscape took its present form, become part of the dreaming. • Ngarranggarniny nginimanyji na, ngoorrooma laarne. *Then he became part of the dreaming high up there.* SEE: **werlwe**.

Ngarraarnji; Ngarrawarnji *noun.* Moola Bulla.

ngarrarlg; ngarrag *coverb+PUT.* stop someone doing something by talking to or shouting at them. • Ngarrarlg benayanyji-yoo. *He stopped them fighting.* • Wanyageny gerarr wiyinji marne-yoorroong, gooragal ngarrarlg nginiya. *The little boy is crawling towards the fire and his mother is shouting at him to come back.* • Joolam-birri berrayinde ngarrarlg ngoorrayang. *The dogs went and stopped him.* • Ngarraga yimberraya-yarre wajbaloombi. *The white people stopped us then (walking around our country).*

ngarrarlg-ngarrarlggem *adjective.* kind of people who stop someone.

ngarrarlji *coverb+GET.* stop someone doing something by talking to or shouting at them.
- Thoowoorra ngarrarlji yimberramannha? *Why did you all stop me?*

ngarrgalel *noun feminine.* gold. [NOTE: alluvial gold as found around Halls Creek]

ngarrgaleny; ngarrgalem REDUP: **ngarrga-ngarrgalem.** *noun.* stone, rock, hill, money. [NOTE: also used to mean 'heart' by some Southern dialect speakers]

Ngarrgooroon *noun.* country east of Warrmarn, an estate name.

-ngarri

-ngarri *suffix.* subordinate suffix to verbs. [NOTE: attached to the coverb in compound verbs and the verb in simple verbs; realised as *-garri* following stop sounds]

-ngarrim; -ngarrem *suffix.* and all that kind, and all that lot. [NOTE: used when giving a list of participants in an event *-garrim, -garrem* following stop sounds]

ngarri *particle.* as a result, and then, right then [NOTE: used to introduce a sentence]

ngarrij *coverb+SAY/DO.* have a rest. • Waranya ngarrij yarrani *Town-*yoorroong yarraya. *Then we had a break in town.*

ngarrij *coverb+BE/STAY.* have a rest. • Ngarrij-gala yade. *Let's have a rest.*

ngarrirrij *coverb+BE/STAY.* be resting.
• Gelengenaga ngarrirrij yarroonya. *We are resting today.*

ngarrirrij *coverb+FALL/GO_DOWN.* have a rest.
• Ngarrirrij berrooward. *They had a rest.*
• Ngarrirrijboo berroowoonboo. *They are going to have a rest now.*

ngarriwarloojen *temporal.* couple of years ahead, after a long time. • Ngeleli Nambinel boorab nyaniyi ngarriwarloojen. *This Nambijin arrived (here) after a long time.*
• Ngarriwarloojen bilij nyilayidge. *I found it after a long time.* • Ngarriwarloonjen boorabwarloon boorab giniyi. *He was away for a long time then he came back.*

ngarriwarloon *temporal.* later.

ngarriyan *adverb.* already, properly, almost.

ngarriyanyji *noun masculine.* dog. *Canis familiaris.* SEE: **joolany**.

ngarrjan *coverb+BE/STAY.* be well grown, be a good-sized child. • Ngayindi goornawoona ngenaniyin ngarrjan. *I was a little girl about six, a good size.*

Ngarrmaliny *noun.* Police Hole near Foal Creek. [NOTE: birthplace of artist Freddie Timms who was named after the place]

ngarrngarrji *noun.* bush lemon grass, citronella grass. *Cymbopogon bombycinus, C. procerus.* [NOTE: medicine; decoction drunk (may be mixed with *gerlerneny*, according to R. Fry)] SEE: **malmalji**.

ngathoogooj; ngalthoogooj
coverb+SAY/DO. suck something up (e.g. honey), slurp something. • Ngathoogooj-girriny gayirriny. *Ground sugarbag is for sucking up / slurping up.* • Ngalthoogooj ngerne. *He is sucking it up.*

ngawagool *noun feminine.* edible larvae from termite mound. SEE: **jamerndel**.

ngawalel *noun feminine.* woomera.

ngawalem *noun.* jaw bone.

ngawarrang REDUP: ngawa-ngawarrang. *coverb+BE/STAY.* lean back looking up, put head right back to look up. • Ngawarrang barrenha-gili! *All lean back!* • Nginyjinygawa jawarlaliny gooni-gooni ngemenji minyjiwarrany, wayinigana ngawarrang nginji. *This shaky paw lizard is dreaming about black plums, that is why he is looking up at the sky.* • Ngawa-ngawarrang boorroonboo. *They are all leaning back looking up.*

ngawaying *coverb+BE/STAY.* be nothing there.
• Daa-moowam ngawaying boorroonboo, ngoowangarnan, mayaroo-bawoorroon. *Only the country is there empty, nothing, no houses.*

ngawooji *noun.* father's mother, sister-in-law of man, woman's son's daughter, woman's son's son, brother-in-law of woman, father's mother's brother. [NOTE: form used to address someone of that relationship (Kriol: 'oji, awooj, awooji']

ngawoojil *noun feminine.* father's mother, sister-in-law of man, woman's son's daughter. [NOTE: form used when speaking about the relation]

ngawoojiny *noun masculine.* woman's son's son, brother-in-law of woman, father's mother's brother. [NOTE: form used when speaking about the relation]

ngawoombij *coverb+GO/COME.* smell (intransitive), give off an aroma. • Ngawoombij-wayi nyaninyande-ngiyi bagabal-aya. *It smelled like a porcupine.* • Ngawoombij-garriya berrayin giga ngelama. *I am full from the smell.*

ngawoombij *coverb+SAY/DO.* smell (intransitive), give off an aroma. • Ngawoombij boorroorn men'gawoom. *It smells good.* SEE: **yirrinyngoorlg**.

Ngawoongooliwoon *noun.* place in Paddy Bedford's country near Merrewoon.

ngawoonyji *noun masculine.* pencil yam, plant with edible roots. *Vigna lanceolata latifolia.*
• Melagawoom ngawoonybe. *Many pencil yams.* [NOTE: plant looks like a bean plant, lives in sandy soil (Kriol: 'sand ground')]

ngawooral *noun feminine.* native bee. • Galayi benajtha ngawooram ngoorroo-ngoorroola. *Shade your eyes with your hand over your* forehead and look up at all those sugarbag bees there. SEE: **moowal**.

ngawoorr; ngawoorrg *coverb+BURN/BITE.* become cooked, get ripe. • *Ngawoorrboo benawarrenji.* It got cooked. • *Minyjiwarrany gern'gany, gelengoowoony ngawoorrgboo ngoowarrenji.* The black plums are unripe, they are only just about to get ripe.

ngawoorrg *coverb+SAY/DO.* get burned. • *Ngawoorrg berrani.* They all got burned.

ngawoorroorroom; ngawoorroo-woorroom *noun.* flame. • *Ngawoorroo-woorroon thaloorrg biyij.* Throw it on the flame.

ngayalel *noun feminine.* melon. [NOTE: includes edible, inedible and exotic]

ngayana *pronoun.* I'm the one.

ngayanboo *noun.* stranger. SEE: **gamaliwany, jemenngarram**.

Ngayarlwaren *noun.* place name.

ngayarrg *coverb+SAY/DO.* corella calling out.

ngayawarlji, ngayawarle *noun.* river sand.

Ngayewoorre *noun.* Dick Yard.

ngayi *interjection.* hey.

ngayijan *pronoun.* like me.

ngayilanji, ngayilanil *noun.* corella, 'white cockatoo'. *Cacatua sanguinea.* SEE: **labal, labany**. [NOTE: not the sulphur-crested cockatoo – see *ngamarriny, ngayirr-ngayirrji*]

ngayin *pronoun.* I, me.

ngayirr *coverb+SAY/DO* breathe. • *Ngayirr ngerne.* He is breathing.

ngayirr REDUP: **ngayirr-ngayirr**. *coverb+GO_ALONG.* pant, gasp for breath, breathe heavily, e.g. when running or thirsty. • *Gaboo jarranynha ngayirr-ngayirr?* Why are you panting?

ngayirrg-ngayirrg *coverb.* cockatoo call.

ngayirr-ngayirrji *noun.* sulphur-crested cockatoo. *Cacatua galerita.* SEE: **ngamarriny**.

ngayiwany; ngayoowany *pronoun.* myself, by myself.

ngayiwarriny *pronoun.* myself, by myself.

Ngayiwoorroo *noun.* place between Bow River Station and Lissadell Station.

ngel *demonstrative.* this (feminine). SEE: **ngelel**.

ngela *verb.* I will SAY/DO.

ngela *directional.* to the east. SEE: **ngelamoogoo**.

ngelagoorloorr *directional.* further to the east.

ngelaj *verb.* I should PLACE.

ngelama; ngelema *verb.* I SAID/DID.

ngelamande *verb.* I kept on SAYING/DOING.

ngelamiyan'ge *verb.* I am FOLLOWING.

ngelamoogoo REDUP: **ngela-ngelamoogoo**. *directional.* to the east. SEE: **ngela**.

ngelamoogoog *coverb+SAY/DO.* do in the east.

ngelanyge *verb.* I was GOING ALONG.

ngelanygende *verb.* I used to GO ALONG.

ngelaya *verb.* I TOOK UP A POSITION.

ngelayangge *verb.* I was TAKING UP A POSITION.

ngelayid *verb.* I BECAME.

ngelayidge *verb.* I BECAME.

ngelegbany *verb.* I should GO ALONG.

ngelel *demonstrative.* this (feminine). SEE: **ngel**.

ngelem *verb.* let me SAY/DO.

ngelemangge; ngelamangge *verb.* I was SAYING/DOING.

ngelemen'ge *verb.* I am SAYING/DOING.

ngelemen'gende *verb.* I keep on SAYING/DOING.

ngelgany, ngelgal *adjective.* smart, good at something. • *Danya booleman ngelgany-ngooyoo.* That man is good at looking after cattle. • *Dala ngelgal woobooj-girrem.* That woman is good at cooking.

ngelinggel *noun feminine.* hairy water yam. *Aponogeton euryspermus.* [NOTE: word used to mean 'waterlily root' in 'Gija plants and animals' (Purdie et al. 2018)]

ngelmang *directional.* from the east.

ngelmibiny; ngilmibiny *directional.* from the east. SEE: **ngelmang**.

ngelmin; ngilmin *directional.* in the east.

ngeltheg *coverb+HIT.* swallow. • *Ngiliyal-anyji ngeltheg benayidja-yoo goorlabayal lambarn-warrinyji.* It must have been her, the rainbow snake, who swallowed up the two young men.

ngelyagbeny, ngelyagbel, ngelyagbem REDUP: **ngelyelyagbem**. *noun.* white person, person of mixed descent. [NOTE: reddish white colour]

ngelyarrge *coverb+GET.* give someone a fright/shock. • *Ngelyarrge benamanyji-yoo na.* He gave the two of them a shock then. SEE: **ngarlg, ngirlarr, nganggarrge**.

ngemberrama *verb.* they GOT me.

ngemberramande-yirri *verb.* they used to GET us.

ngemberramang *verb.* they GOT me.

ngemberramangbe *verb.* they were GETTING me.

ngemberramangbende *verb.* they were GETTING me.

ngemberramenbe, ngemberremenbe

ngemberramenbe, ngemberremenbe *verb.* they are GETTING me.
ngemberramimangbende *verb.* they used to FOLLOW me.
ngemberranybe *verb.* they BROUGHT/TOOK me.
ngemberranybende *verb.* they used to BRING/TAKE me.
ngemberrawoorroodbe *verb.* they LEFT me.
ngemberrayangbe *verb.* they were GETTING me.
ngemberrayangbe-yarre *verb.* they were GETTING us.
ngemberrayid *verb.* they HIT me.
ngemberrayidbe *verb.* they were HITTING me.
ngemberremoorloonbe *verb.* they HAVE/KEEP/LOOK AFTER me.
ngemberriyilinbe *verb.* they are PUTTING me.
ngemenji *verb.* he is GETTING him/it (masculine).
ngemenya *verb.* she is GETTING him/it (masculine).
ngemiyanyji *verb.* he is DOING TO HIMSELF.
ngen *coverb+SAY/DO.* have headache, rock from side to side. • Ngen ngerne. *He has a headache.* • Deg-garri yinemenji-yoowoo, ngen ngerne. *When it (preying mantis) sees us it rocks from side to side.* SEE: **lard, ngen-ngen**.
ngenama *verb.* he/she/it GOT me.
ngenamanya; ngenemanya *verb.* she/it (feminine) GOT me.
ngenamanyande *verb.* she/it (feminine) used to GET me.
ngenamanyjende *verb.* he/it (masculine) used to GET me.
ngenamanyji *verb.* he/it (masculine) GOT me.
ngenamiyan'ge *verb.* I am DOING TO MYSELF.
ngenamiyin'ge *verb.* I was DOING TO MYSELF.
ngenamoorlardji *verb.* he/it (masculine) HAD/KEPT ME.
ngenamoowardge *verb.* I WENT DOWN WITH SOMETHING.
ngenangaboordjende *verb.* he/it (masculine) kept on SPEARING/POKING me.
ngenangaboordji *verb.* he/it (masculine) SPEARED/POKED me.
ngena-ngenangarriga *locative.* here all around.
ngenangirriyan *verb.* I SAY/DO to myself.
ngenangirriyin *verb.* I SAID to myself.
ngenani *verb.* I SAID/DID.
ngenaniyin *verb.* I WAS/WAS STAYING.
ngenaniyinde *verb.* I used to BE/STAY.
ngenan'ge *verb.* I AM/STAY.
ngenan'gende *verb.* I AM always, I always STAY.
ngenanya *verb.* she/it (feminine) BROUGHT/TOOK me.
ngenanyande *verb.* she/it (feminine) used to BRING/TAKE me.
ngenanyji *verb.* he/it (masculine) BROUGHT/TOOK me.
ngenard *verb.* I GO/COME.
ngenardge *verb.* I am GOING/COMING.
ngenarn *verb.* I SAY/DO.
ngenaward, ngenaard *verb.* I FELL/WENT DOWN.
ngenawardge, ngenoowardge, ngenaardge, *verb.* I was FALLING/GOING DOWN. • Ngenengga yilag, berrema born ngenoowardge. *Down here, this is where I was born.* • Gerrij ngenaardge. *I've finished.*
ngenawoon'ge; ngenoowoon'ge; ngenewoon'ge *verb.* I am FALLING/GOING down.
ngenawooran *verb.* he/she/it (masculine) CUT/WOUNDED me. • Thenbel ngenawooran. *It cut me. / I cut myself.*
ngenawoorran *verb.* he/she/it (masculine) BURNED/BIT me. • Babij ngenawoorran. *I got burned.*
ngenawoorranji; ngenawoorranyji *verb.* he/it (masculine) was BURNING/BITING me.
ngenawoorrood *verb.* he/she/it LEFT me.
ngenawoorroodji *verb.* he/it (masculine) LEFT me.
ngenaya *verb.* he/she PUT me.
ngenayanya *verb.* she PUT me.
ngenayanyji *verb.* he PUT me.
ngenayi *verb.* I WENT/CAME.
ngenayid *verb.* he/she/it HIT me.
ngenayidjende *verb.* he was HITTING me.
ngenayidji *verb.* he HIT me.
ngenayin *verb.* I was GOING/COMING.
ngenayinde *verb.* I used to GO/COME.
ngenayinji *verb.* he is HITTING me.
ngenboowardge *verb.* I wanted to FALL/GO DOWN, I thought I would FALL/GO DOWN (but didn't).
ngenboowoo *verb.* I might FALL/GO DOWN.
ngenda *verb.* I can GO/COME, I should GO/COME.
ngendan *verb.* I should be GOING.
ngendamawa *verb.* I should GO and GET.
ngendemij; ngendamij *verb.* I want to DO TO MYSELF, let me DO TO MYSELF.
ngenden *verb.* I should BE/STAY.

• Jarrag-gela-wayi ngenden-birri Gijam-birri gayi born ngenawardge. *I should talk to them like that in Gija about where I was born.*

ngende-ngenderrmawoony, ngende-ngenderrmawool, ngende-ngenderrmawoom *adjective.* striped, having a diamond pattern, pretty.

ngenden'ge *verb.* I should BE/BE STAYING.

ngenderr-ngenderrel *noun feminine.* barred grunter. *Amniataba percoides.* SEE: **goodabal**.

ngendoowoo; ngoondoowoo *verb.* I should FALL/GO DOWN.

ngenega *demonstrative.* here. [NOTE: Southern dialect] SEE: **ngenengga**.

ngenel *demonstrative.* this (feminine). SEE: **ngel, ngelel**.

ngenemenji *verb.* he/it (masculine) is GETTING me.

ngenemenya *verb.* she/it (feminine) is GETTING me.

ngenengambennya *verb.* she is SPEARING/POKING me.

ngenengga REDUP: **ngenenengga**. *demonstrative, locative.* here.

ngenenggayana *demonstrative, locative.* right here.

ngenengirriyan *verb.* I am SAYING/DOING to myself.

ngenewarrenji *verb.* he/it (masculine) is BURNING/BITING me.

ngenewoorranjende *verb.* he was BURNING/BITING/CUTTING himself, the fire was still BURNING.

ngeneyooloonya *verb.* she is PUTTING me.

ngengirriyan *verb.* he is SAYING/DOING to himself.

ngenhengbeny, ngenhengbel, ngenhengbem REDUP: **ngenhenhengbem**. *adjective.* red. • Ngenhenhengbem dam belegan benajtha-birri dam yagengerram. *Put the red ones in the middle of the other ones.* [NOTE: sometimes considered as swearing] SEE: **galimbirrji**.

ngenhenhengge *coverb+HIT.* make red (with blood by flogging). • Berrema ngenhenhengge ngoorrayidbende-yoo. *Here the two of them used to make him red with blood.*

ngenilinji *verb.* he is PUTTING me.

ngen-ngen *coverb+SAY/DO.* shake head from side to side, shake head to say 'no'. • Ngen-ngen barroo-gili. *Shake your heads from side to side.*
• Ngen-ngen ngini. *He is shaking his head from side to side.* • Thoowoo ngen-ngen nini? *What is making you shake your head from side to side?* SEE: **ngen**.

-ngeny, -ngel, -ngem *suffix.* that kind.

nger *coverb+SAY/DO_M.* feel glad. • Nger woomberrama-yoo giningin, werlge-werlge woomberramandi-yoo bajalarrin. *Those two are happy now, they were stuck in the bucket (two turtles that were let go in a pond.)*

ngerd *coverb+HIT.* cut stick (e.g. for spear).
• Ngerd nginyidji goowooleny. *He cut a stick.* SEE: **lagarr**.

ngere *coverb+SAY/DO_M.* recover, get better.
• Ngere wanema. *He/she got better.*

ngereb-ngereb *coverb+SAY/DO.* be feeding, be eating (group). • Ngenengga gerliyirr ngenda-gala lamban googajoorroon ngereb-ngereb-ngarri birrirn werrgalega gagoolany. *I will go here to the west along the side of the hill where they (kangaroos) will all just be eating green grass and little melons together.*

ngeremji *verb.* he wants to GET him/it (masculine).

ngererr *coverb+HIT.* shave hair. • Danya ngererrnginy, yambarram ngererr ngoorrayidbe. *That one has a shaved head, they shaved his hair off.* SEE: **birlijig**.

ngererrnginy, ngererrngil, ngererrngim *adjective.* bald, having a shaved head.
• Yambarram ngererrnginy doomoom. *'Knobby head'.*

ngerig *directional.* from the south.

ngeriji-biny *directional.* from the south. SEE: **ngerig**.

ngerijin *directional.* in the south.

ngerijingarriya *directional.* around from the south. • Jadany jalij wiyinji ngerijingarriya. *The rain is coming around from the south.*

ngeriyany *verb.* let him COME, he should COME, he wants to COME.

ngerlabany *noun masculine.* policeman. LIT: 'string/rope-having'. SEE: **mernmerdgaleny**.

ngerlam; ngerlarrem *noun.* string, wire, fishing line, fence, rag used to tie something.

ngerne *verb.* he/it (masculine) SAYS/DOES.

ngeroowi *verb.* let him/it (masculine) FALL/GO DOWN.

ngerr REDUP: **ngerr-ngerr**. *coverb+HIT.* throw.
• Goordoony ngerr-ngerr ngoorriyinbe. *They*

ngerr

are throwing the ball. • **Ngerr biyijtha-ngirri ngayin.** *Throw it to me!* • **Boorljany ngerr niyin'ge-ninggi.** *I am throwing the football to you.*

ngerr *coverb+SAY/DO_M.* throw. • **Warinyanyji danya garrabirim ngerr wanema marrarn nginiyid.** *That man must have been angry, he threw boomerangs and went away.*

ngerr *coverb+BRING/TAKE.* throw. • **Ngerra noowige-narri-gili.** *(Let me pick up this ball) then I will throw it to you mob.*

ngerr *coverb+SAY/DO.* throw. • **Ngerr nginini, ngoowan.** *He threw it but missed.*

-ngerra *ablative enclitic pronoun.* from/after/because of me. [NOTE: Southern dialect] SEE: **-ngerroowa. -ngerreg** *suffix.* as many as, as much as, as far as. • **berre-ngerreg** *as far as here.* • **dama-ngerreg** *as far as that.* • **wayini-ngerreg** *like this much, this many.*

ngerren *coverb+SAY/DO.* flare up (flames). • **Dama marnem ngerren boorroorn.** *This fire is flaring up.*

ngerren *coverb+PUT.* make fire flare up, make fire light, make fire catch alight. • **'Ngerren nyaliny bamberraj-noo marnem,' berrani dany-noo.** *'Light a fire for him again,' they said about him.* • **Ngerrena yamberraj.** *Let's light a fire then.* • **Ngerren gala benaj.** *Light the match.*

ngerrg *coverb+BURN/BITE.* be all burned. • **Ngerrgboowa ngoowarrenji.** *It is being burned out by the fire now.*

ngerrenbe-boorroo *noun.* generator, electricity. LIT: 'for making light'.

ngerren'gajim *noun.* battery. • **Nangooroog nyaniyi-ngirri ngerren'gajim ngoorr-ngoorrool-ngooyoo.** *The car battery went flat on me.*

ngerr-ngerrji *coverb+PUT.* throw things at someone. • **Gooloorr-gooloorr ngoorrayangbe, ngerr-ngerrji ngoorrayangbe wanyanyanggembi dam.** *Those children were poking him with a stick and throwing things at him.* [NOTE: trivalent (three participant) verb with the 'things' part of the coverb and the object at which the things were thrown as part of the verb]

ngerr-ngerrji *coverb+SAY/DO_REFL.* throw to each other. • **Ngerr-ngerrji yarremengerrij.** *Let's throw it to each other.*

-ngerroowa *ablative enclitic pronoun.* from/after/because of me. SEE: **-ngerra**.

ngerroowoogoo *coverb+GET.* make fire blow up (e.g. lighting gas when it is turned up too high). • **Laarne benayanyji wayini gerroowoogoo benamanyji boodooj-garri benayanyji.** *He put it too high and made it blow up when he lit it.*

ngidiyi *verb.* let him/it (masculine) BE/STAY.

ngidjende *verb.* he/it (masculine) keeps on GOING/COMING.

ngidji *verb.* he/it (masculine) is GOING/COMING.

ngij *coverb+FALL/GO_DOWN.* get dark. • **Ngij berraward daam.** *It got dark.*

ngilige; ngelege *verb.* I will be GOING ALONG. • **Ngoowana girli ngilige.** *I can't walk.*

ngilijge *verb.* I will BECOME.

ngilimke *verb.* I will SAY/DO. SEE: **ngelem**.

ngili-ngiliwoob *coverb+DO_REFL.* copulate (dog style), have sex. • **Goorloo-goorloorroogoob-garri berraniyindi-yoo, ngili-ngiliwoo berrangirriyinboo-yoo.** *When they (moon and girl in dreamtime) kept coming up (from under the water) they kept having sex together (in the dog style).* SEE: **moorniny**.

ngili-ngiliwoob *coverb+WOUND_REFL.* have sex, (Kriol: 'make love one another' (dogs and other animals)). • **Ngili-ngiliwoob berroowanbe.** *They two are having sex (talking about two pelicans at Roogoon).*

ngilin'ge *verb.* I am GOING ALONG.

ngilin'gende *verb.* I keep GOING ALONG.

ngiliwool *noun.* dog that is on heat. • **Dala joolal ngiliwool.** *That dog is on heat*

ngiliyal *demonstrative pronoun.* this (feminine). • **Ngiliyal-anyji.** *It might be her. It might be this woman.*

ngiliyande *verb.* I will keep GOING ALONG.

ngiliyanyji *verb.* he is PUTTING himself.

ngiliyin'ge; ngeliyin'ge *verb.* I am GOING ALONG.

ngiliyin'gende *verb.* I keep GOING ALONG.

ngimberrayidbe *verb.* they HIT me.

ngimbiji *verb.* he will HIT me.

ngimbirringanybe *verb.* they will SPEAR me.

ngimbirriyinbe *verb.* they are GIVING me something.

ngimilil; ngimirlil *noun feminine.* Leichhardt tree. *Nauclea orientalis*. SEE: **marrooral**. [NOTE: has edible fruit]

ngimiyaji *verb.* he will DO TO HIMSELF.

ngimiyanyjende *verb.* he keeps on DOING TO HIMSELF.

ngimiyanyji *verb.* he is DOING TO HIMSELF.

ngim-ngim *coverb+SAY/DO*. dance moving knees in and out (woman's dance movement). • *Dala ngalil ngim-ngim nyerne.* This woman is dancing, doing the movement called ngim-ngim.

ngim-ngim *coverb+SAY/DO_M*. clap knees together. • *Ngim-ngim barroo-gili.* You all clap your knees together.

nginaardji *verb*. he FELL/WENT DOWN. [NOTE: elided form of *nginiwardji* used in Southern dialect]. SEE: **nginiwardji**.

nginanya *verb*. she BROUGHT/TOOK him/it (masculine).

nginanyande *verb*. she kept on BRINGING/TAKING him/it (masculine).

nginanyjende *verb*. he used to BRING/TAKE him/it (masculine).

nginanyji *verb*. he BROUGHT/TOOK him/it (masculine).

nginayanyande *verb*. she kept on PUTTING him/it (masculine).

nginbija *verb*. she will HIT me.

nginbiji *verb*. he will HIT me.

nginbimij *verb*. I will DO TO MYSELF.

nginbimji *verb*. he will GET me.

nginbimoowoon *verb*. I will GET AND HIT it.

nginbin'ge *verb*. I will BE / STAY.

nginbin'gende *verb*. I will BE / BE STAYING.

nginbirn *verb*. I will SAY/DO.

nginbiyaja *verb*. she will PUT me.

nginbiyan *verb*. I will GO/COME.

nginbiyande *verb*. I will be GOING/COMING.

nginbiyilijge *verb*. I will PUT myself.

nginbiyinya *verb*. she will GIVE me.

nginboowan *verb*. I will CUT myself.

nginboowoon *verb*. I will FALL/ GO DOWN.

ngindany SEE: **ngirndany**.

Ngindiwarriny *noun*. holiday camp at a spring on Texas. [NOTE: next hill from Doongoorriny]

nginemanya *verb*. she was GETTING him/it (masculine). SEE: **nginimanya**.

nginemoorlardji *verb*. he HAD, was HOLDING/KEEPING him/it (masculine).

ngingim *noun*. fontanelle. [NOTE: part where spirit lives]

ngingirriyan *verb*. he is SAYING/DOING TO HIMSELF.

ngini; ngirni *verb*. he SAYS/DOES. [NOTE: seems to be a variant form of *ngerne*]

nginima; nginema *verb*. he/she/it GOT him/it (masculine).

nginimanya *verb*. she was GETTING him/it (masculine). SEE: **nginemanya**.

nginimanyande; nginemanyande *verb*. she used to GET him/it (masculine). • *Gaalji-ni ngarag nginimanyande-boorroo marloo-marloogam.* She used to make spinifex resin for the old men.

nginimanyjende *verb*. he/it (masculine) used to GET him/it (masculine).

nginimanyji; nginimanyji; nginimangji; nginemangji *verb*. he/it (masculine) was GETTING him/it (masculine).

nginimemanyji *verb*. he/it (masculine) FOLLOWED him/it (masculine).

nginimin *verb*. he DID TO HIMSELF. SEE: **nginimiyin**.

nginimiyin *verb*. he DID TO HIMSELF.

nginimiyinjende *verb*. he used to DO TO HIMSELF.

nginimiyinji *verb*. he was DOING TO HIMSELF.

nginimoorlardjende *verb*. he kept on HAVING/HOLDING/KEEPING him/it (masculine).

nginimoorloowardja *verb*. she HAD him/it (masculine), she was HOLDING/KEEPING him/it (masculine).

nginimoowardji *verb*. he WENT DOWN WITH someone/something

nginingaboord *verb*. he/she SPEARED him/it (masculine).

nginingaboordja *verb*. she SPEARED him/it (masculine).

nginingaboordji *verb*. he SPEARED him/it (masculine).

nginingirrija *verb*. he will SAY/DO TO HIMSELF.

nginingirriyin *verb*. he SAID/DID TO HIMSELF.

nginingirriyinjende *verb*. he used to SAY/DO TO HIMSELF.

nginingoonjende *verb*. he was EATING him/it (masculine).

nginini *verb*. he SAID/DID.

nginiiniyi *verb*. he WAS / STAYED.

nginiiniyin *verb*. he WAS / was STAYING.

nginiiniyinde *verb*. he used to BE / STAY.

nginiwamanyji *verb*. he/it (masculine) WENT AND GOT him/TOOK him away, he BECAME (i.e. another form overtook him).

nginiward; ngineward *verb*. he FELL/WENT DOWN.

nginiwardjende *verb*. he/it (masculine) kept on FALLING/GOING DOWN.

nginiwardji; nginewardji *verb*. he was FALLING/GOING DOWN.

nginiwarenji

nginiwarenji *verb.* he/it (masculine) is CUTTING him/it (masculine).
nginiwarrenji *verb.* he/it (masculine) is BURNING/BITING him/it (masculine).
nginiwooran *verb.* he/it CUT him/it (masculine).
nginiwoorran *verb.* he/she/it BURNT/BIT him/it (masculine).
nginiwoorranji; nginewoorranji *verb.* he BURNT HIMSELF, it BURNED him.
nginiwoorranjende *verb.* he/it used to BURN him/it (masculine).
nginiwoorroodja *verb.* she LEFT him/it (masculine).
nginiwoorroodji *verb.* he LEFT him/it (masculine).
nginiya *verb.* he PUT him/it (masculine).
nginiyala *demonstrative.* this is it (feminine), here it is (feminine). • Degboo woomberramangbende, 'Marri nginiyala!' *They would look, 'Goodness, here it is,' (they would say when they found the dried ground barramundi stored for a year in an anthill).*
nginiyanya *verb.* she PUT him/it (masculine).
nginiyanyande *verb.* she was PUTTING him/it (masculine).
nginiyanyjende *verb.* he used to PUT him/it (masculine).
nginiyanyji *verb.* he PUT him/it (masculine).
nginiyi *verb.* he/it (masculine) WENT/CAME.
nginiyid *verb.* he/she HIT him/it (masculine).
nginiyidja *verb.* she HIT him/it (masculine).
nginiyidjande *verb.* she used to HIT him/it (masculine).
nginiyidjende *verb.* he used to HIT him/it (masculine).
nginiyidji *verb.* he HIT him/it (masculine).
nginiyiliyin *verb.* he PUT HIMSELF.
nginiyin *verb.* he was GOING/COMING.
nginiyinde *verb.* he used to GO/COME.
nginiyinji *verb.* he/it (masculine) is HITTING me.
nginjende *verb.* he/it (masculine) IS/KEEPS ON STAYING.
nginji *verb.* he/it (masculine) IS/IS STAYING.
nginoowoon *verb.* he/it (masculine) should FALL/GO DOWN. • Mayiny gawiligi-ngarri nginoowoon yiligin. *The food got (should be made) cold inside the fridge.*
nginy; nginyjiny *demonstrative.* this one (masculine). • Nginya goorloony yilag. *This is the water down here.* • Nginya nawarragawoony nginji. *This is the river here.* • Nginyji yagenge yoorloo nginji. *This other one (river) is going downstream (talking about painting).* • Nginyjiny manbiny Jarloowany. *This black hill is called Jarloowany.*
nginyjiyanyaya *demonstrative.* this one indeed (masculine).
nginymelemeleb *coverb.* grinning showing teeth with open mouth.
ngirem *verb.* let him/her GET him/it (masculine).
ngiri-ngirigbe *coverb+BE/STAY.* coming from south, facing speaker from the south. • Nginyga thamanyji ngirribawoorroon nginji berrema ngiri-ngirigbe boorroonboo mayaroomga-noo. *This grandfather lives far away, here is his house facing (us) from the south.*
ngiriny *coverb+SAY/PLACE_REFL.* grumble at each other. • Dama ngoowan ngiriny berrayiliyinbende warna-warnarrambi. *They never used to grumble at each other, those old people long ago.*
ngirlarr *coverb+SAY/DO.* get a fright, get a shock. • Ngeleli darndal ngirlarr nyanini. *The turtle got a fright.*
ngirndany *noun.* small catfish species. *Neosilurus hyrtlii*. [NOTE: lives in springs, has poisonous spike and flat tail, often goes in big groups]
Ngirndirriman'gen *noun.* Waterfall Creek near Boolmiwoon in Ngarrgooroon country.
ngirndirring *coverb+BE/STAY.* be leaning, be lying sideways. • Danya jiyiliny ngirndirring nginji mayaroon. *This man is leaning on the house.* • Ngoowan ngirndirring nimbinha-ngirri, wanggarlgoo yinimenha. *Don't lean on me, you make me slack.*
ngirndirring *coverb+PUT.* lean something on something else. • Ngirndirring niniyangge. *I leant it on something.*
ngirndirring *coverb+FALL/GO_DOWN.* take a leaning position. • Goonyjany ngirndirring nginiward. *The tree has fallen into a leaning position.*
ngirni; ngini *verb.* he SAYS / DOES. [NOTE: seems to be a dialect alternate of *ngerne*]
-ngirri *indirect object enclitic pronoun.* to me.
ngirribag *coverb+BRING/TAKE.* take/bring closer. • Benanyji-yoo ngirribag. *He took the two of them closer.*
ngirribag REDUP: **ngirrirribag** *coverb+GO/COME.* come/go close. • Ngirribag daniyi-ngirri. *You are coming too close to me.*

ngirribag *coverb+FALL/GO_DOWN.* go down close, come close (in time or place). • Berdijboo-wayi ngininiyin, ngarrgalembi marrarn ngirribag berroowardbe-ni. *When he tried to get up all the hills were already coming down close on him.* • Ngoowan, ngoowan, ngirribagboo ngoowoonji-yarre-gili danyga. *No no, he is coming close to us that one.*

ngirribagboo *coverb+GO/COME.* be coming closer (in time or place). • Ngirribagboo boorroordboo mayiny mingayoorriny. *The holiday feast time is coming close.* • Ngirribagboo-wanyji nyidja. Jaam-birri nyilemen'ge. *She must be coming close. I can feel her with my stomach.* • Ngirribagboo boorroordboo. *They are coming close.* • Garn'giny ngirribagboo ngidji-ngooyoo. *The time (next month) for it (the* wanggarnal *visit at Christmas) is coming close.*

ngirribagboo *coverb+SAY/DO_M.* move closer (in time or place). • Ngirribagboo wanemanya. *She came close.*

ngirriban *adverb.* close.

ngirribany, ngirribal, ngirribam REDUP: **ngirrirriban**. *adjective.* close. • Tharreb barren-gili ngenengga ngirrirriban. *You all stand up here really close.*

ngirribawoorroon *adverb.* far away. • Ngirribawoorroon yarriyan-gili, ngoorroon-gili. *We are going a long way over there.*

ngirril *coverb+SPEAR.* look/glance sideways at someone. • Thoowoo-boorroo ngirril yinangaboorda? *Why did you glance at me?* • Ngirril-ngarri nyanengaboordjende dali thamboorroogali. *When he used to keep on looking at his mother-in-law from the side.*

ngirrimem; ngirriminy *noun.* teeth. SEE: **minyjoowoom**.

Ngirriny-ngirrinyin *noun.* place in Ngarrgooroon country.

ngirrirribag *coverb+GO/COME.* move closer, come closer. • Ngirrirribag barriyany! *You all come close!* SEE: **ngirribag**.

ngirrngiliny *noun.* cat. *Felis catus.* SEE: **ngirrngiliwoony, goordoony, dijarrji**.

ngirrngiliwoony *noun.* cat. *Felis catus.* SEE: **ngirrngiliny, goordoony, dijarrji**.

ngirrngirril *noun.* wasp species, sand wasp.

ngiwayi *verb.* he will CUT himself. Thenbel ngiwayi. *He will cut himself.*

ngiwija *verb.* she will HIT him/it (masculine).

• Werd-anyji ngiwija. *She might bite him.*

ngiwiji *verb.* he will HIT him/it (masculine).

ngiwingirrij *verb.* he will SAY/DO to himself.

ngiwinji *verb.* he will BE/BE STAYING.

ngiwinjende *verb.* he will keep on BEING/STAYING.

ngiwiny, ngiwil *noun, interjection.* hey you! hey man! hey woman! hey you! [NOTE: not really polite, can be said to *ngawooji, ganggayi* or *thamany*]

ngiwirn *verb.* he will SAY/DO.

ngiwiwarri; ngiwiwarriyi *verb.* he/she will BURN/BITE him/it (masculine). • Werd-anyji ngiwiwarri. *She might bite him.*

ngiwiyayinde *verb.* he/it (masculine) will be GOING/COMING ALONG.

ngiwiyi; ngiwooyi *verb.* he will FALL/GO down.

Ngiwoowan *noun.* Flat Rock, place on Mabel Downs.

-ngiyab *commitative enclitic pronoun.* with her.

-ngiyi *indirect object enclitic pronoun.* to her.

ngiyi *interjection.* yes, that is right. • Ngiyi-ma? *Isn't that right?*

ngiyilinji *verb.* **1.** he is PUTTING him/it (masculine). **2.** he is PUTTING himself.

ngiyilinya *verb.* she is PUTTING him/it (masculine). SEE: **ngiyooloonya**.

ngiyinjende *verb.* he keeps on HITTING him/it (masculine).

ngiyinji *verb.* he is HITTING him/it (masculine).

ngiyinya *verb.* she is HITTING him/it (masculine).

-ngiyiwa *ablative enclitic pronoun.* from/after/because of her/it (feminine).

ngiyiwayi *verb.* he will cut himself

ngiyooloonya *verb.* she PUTS him/it (masculine). SEE: **ngiyilinya**.

-ngoo, -ngoongoo *benefactive enclitic pronoun.* for you (one).

ngooboongool *noun.* labia. [NOTE: swearing]

ngooj *coverb+GET.* pluck (feathers), pull out hair. • Ngooj benamanyji-ngiyi yambarram. *He pulled out her hair.* SEE: **ngoojoorr**

ngoojabal; ngoojam *noun.* emu feathers.

ngoojal, ngoojany *noun.* emu berry, 'dogs balls' plant with small edible fruit. *Grewia retusifolia*. [NOTE: roasted together with *garnawoony* by the turkey in the dreamtime (Hector Jandany); plant seen at Palm Springs called *ngoojany* said to be 'tucker for turkeys'] SEE: **gawoorroony, garrawiny, ngoowardiny**.

ngoojoorr

ngoojoorr *coverb+SAY/DO_M.* pull up grass, pull out hair, pluck. • Ngoojoorr woomberrama-yoo gerlernem boorroom. *They pulled up long soft spinifex.* SEE: **ngooj**.

ngoojoorr-ngoojoorr *coverb+GET.* pull up grass, pull out hair, pluck. • Wayiniyana ngoojoorr-ngoojoorr benama gerlernem danyi jalariny. *While he (eagle) was inside, the egret started pulling out spinifex.*

ngoolmoorroony, ngoolmoorrool, ngoolmoorroo; ngoolmoowoorroo *noun.* stranger. • Ngoolmoorroo dama berrayi-yarri gayimilem-anyji. *There are strangers coming to us from somewhere.* SEE: **gamaliwany**.

ngoolnga REDUP: ngoolnga-ngoolnga. *coverb+PUT.* make love. • Ngoolnga nyaniyanyji. *He made love to her.* • Ngoolnga-ngoolnga benayanyjende dany garawirrimbi. *He always made love to a big mob.*

ngoolnga-ngoolnga *coverb+SAY/DO_REFL.* make love. • Ngoolnga-ngoolnga yaringirrij. *Let's (you and I) make love.*

ngoolnga-ngoolnga-nhawoony *noun.* man who likes loving up to women.

ngoolngany, ngoolngal *noun.* spouse, husband, wife, brother-in-law, sister-in-law, man who looks after initiates. • Ngoowan! Ngoolnga-ban-nga ngayin-ga! *No! I am already married! (she said)* • 'Ngayin-ngoongoo ngoolngagan-ga!' wanemayi-ngiyi. *'I am your husband now!' he shouted at her.*

ngoolngawoogbeliny *coverb.* having no husband. • Ngoolngawoogbeliny jaawany woomberrayid. *They get pregnant without any husband.*

ngooloongooloomenbe *coverb+GET.* get ready, collect stuff ready together for an event. • Ngooloongooloomenbe yamberremnya wayiniyana joonbam-boorroo ngela yarriyan. *We will get everything ready and then go to the east for the Joonba song and dance event.*

ngooloo-ngooloon *temporal.* afternoon, yesterday.

ngooloo-ngooliyan *temporal.* late afternoon, yesterday.

ngoolwa, ngelwa *verb.* I should SAY/DO. • Goowoo gaboo ngoolwa? *What should I do?*

ngoomoolji, ngoomooloo *noun.* cloud.

ngoomoorlinji *verb.* he HAS him/it (masculine).

ngoomoorlinya *verb.* she HAS him/it (masculine).

ngoomoorloonji *verb.* he HAS/IS HOLDING him/it (masculine).

ngoon *coverb+PUT.* speak about someone in a jealous way behind their back. • Ngoon ngemberrayangbe. *They were talking about me jealously behind my back.* SEE: **ngoorriri**.

ngoonba *verb.* I should GO.

ngoonbe *noun.* jealous talk about people behind their back. • Ngoonbe-birri thed yimberriwoonnha. *You are talking about me behind my back (killing me with that thing).*

ngoonbija *verb.* she wanted to HIT me.

ngoonbirn *verb.* I should SAY/DO, I wanted to SAY/DO.

ngoonbiyin *verb.* I WAS not/did not STAY.

ngoonboomge *verb.* I should GET it, let me GET it.

ngoonboorn *verb.* I should SAY/DO, I want to SAY/DO. • Jarrag-ma ngoonboorn-ninggi? *Should I speak to you?*

ngoonboowoon *verb.* I will (should/want to?) fall/go down.

ngoongoo *coverb+GET.* love, believe, know. • Ngoongoo nyanemanyji ngoolnga-girrim. *He loved her and wanted her to be his wife.* • Ngoowan ngoongoo nimbimge-narri dambi jarragboo. *I don't believe your story.* • Ngoongoo bamberremnha berrembi ngirribawoorroo-ngarnan. *You should know/recognise these strangers.* [NOTE: Shirley Purdie's father used to say this to the country when welcoming/introducing strangers with a *mantha* 'welcome ceremony'.]

Ngoonjoowa *noun.* place near the main roads' depot in Halls Creek; name of the Ngunjuwa resource centre in Halls Creek.

ngoon'goo *coverb+SAY/PLACE_REFL.* move away. • Ngoon'goo yarraj video-girrim. • Doomooge nimbinha-yirrewa. *We are all moving off to go to a video. You will be left here by yourself.* • Wariwoony ngoon'goo yarraj. *He's a cheeky one, let's move away.*

ngoon'goo *coverb+GET.* move away from someone. • Ngoon'goo yimberremenbe. *They are moving away from us.*

ngoonoomoorloonya *verb.* she is keeping me.

ngoony *coverb+FALL/GO_DOWN.* become angry, sulk. • Ngoony nginiwardji. *He became angry.* • Goonyjiri-ngarri jengamboornnha warim-birri ngoony nyinboowoonya. *If you tease that girl in a cheeky way she'll sulk.* SEE: **roog**.

ngoonjoo-ngoonjoom *noun.* moustache.
- *Ngoonjoo-ngoonjooba wiyinji.* *He came to have a moustache.*

ngoonyjoom *noun.* tobacco. [NOTE: word used for any tobacco as well as the native tobacco species, Nicotiana benthamiana] SEE: **binggoonyel, binggoonyji.**

ngoord *coverb+SAY/DO.* say 'eh?', say 'I beg your pardon'. • *Ngoord nginini.* *He said, 'Eh?'*

ngoorinyja *coverb+PUT.* chew tobacco.
- *Binggoonyel dal ngoorinyja nyimberrayangbe.* *They used to chew that bush tobacco.*

ngoorlan'gayiny *adverb.* again. SEE: **ngoorlanyaliny.**

ngoorlanyaliny *adverb.* again. SEE: **-nyaliny.**

ngoorlooba *coverb+SAY/DO.* tell lies. • *Ngoolooba nginini.* *He was telling lies.* [NOTE: considered swearing as it can also mean 'having a dirty bottom'] SEE: **yagoorn.**

ngoorlooba *coverb+SAY/DO_M.* be lying.
- *Ngoorlooba wanemayinde.* *He was lying.* SEE: **yagoorn.**

ngoorlooba *coverb+PUT.* lie to someone.
- *Ngoorlooba nyaniyanyji.* *He lied to her.* [NOTE: considered swearing as it can also mean 'having a dirty bottom'] SEE: **yagoorn.**

ngoorlooba *interjection.* liar.

ngoorloog *coverb+SAY/DO.* drink. • *Jiyiliny ngoorloog ngerne nalijam.* *The man is drinking tea.* • *Ngoorloog nyerne.* *She is drinking.* • *Ngoorlooga nimbirndi goorrngam, minyjoowoo-bawoorroon nimbirn-ayi joodooyoon.* *When you drink the water (of that particular tooth place) you will be like that, having no teeth, straight away.*

ngoorloog *coverb+FALL/GO_DOWN.* go down to drink. • *Ngoorloog janooward Woojaninin.* *She wanted to go down to drink at the spring called Woojaninin.*

ngoorloog *coverb+SAY/DO_M.* drink. • *Goorloom birriyama-boorroo wanyagem ngoorloogbija booma.* *Here is water for the children, you (child) should drink.*

ngoorloog-bayilim *noun.* drunkards.
- *Ngoorloog-bayilim yilag nyirrega berrani-gili.* *All the drunkards were down there swimming.*

ngoorloongginy *noun.* lily species. [NOTE: edible lily root] SEE: **ngelinggel.**

ngoorloony, ngoorlool *adjective.* successful, one who has just done something difficult successfully, what a clever one, 'praise-em up'. [NOTE: heard often as exclamations when someone has done something good; can also mean 'liar', some people consider this to be swearing] SEE: **nyarlany.**

ngoorloorloog *coverb+HIT.* give someone a drink, get someone to drink. • *Ngoorloorloog ngiyinya dali nyaman.* *The old woman is giving him a drink.*

ngoorloorloog *coverb+SAY/DO_M.* be drinking. • *Ngoorloorloog wanemayinde, ngoorloorloog wanemayinde, ngoorloorloog wanemayinde.* *He was drinking and drinking and drinking.*

ngoorloorloog *coverb+SAY/DO.* be drinking.
- *Yagoowalany dany ngoorloorloog-garri boorroorn, wangalag benemanyji goonggoorloom.* *They have been drinking that beer (that other kind of thing) and lost their brains.*

ngoorloorloog *coverb+GO_ALONG.* go along drinking. [NOTE: see example under *wanganyge*]

ngoorniny *noun masculine.* short fighting spear. SEE: **malmoorrji.**

ngoorn-ngoorn *coverb+SAY/DO.* talk quietly (group). • *Ngoorrooma ngoorn-ngoorn boorroorn.* *The group of people are talking quietly in the distance.* [NOTE: drone of conversation as heard from distance]

ngoorr *coverb+GO_ALONG.* buzz, growl. • *Ngoorr wiyinya moowal.* *The sugarbag flies are buzzing.* SEE: **ngoorr-ngoorr.**

ngoorr *coverb+SAY/DO.* buzz. • *Moowal ngoorr nyerne.* *The sugarbag flies are buzzing.*

ngoorr REDUP: **ngoorr-ngoorr.** *coverb+SAY/DO.* have buzzing/whistling in ears. • *Ngoorr ngenarn yardem.* *I have whistling in my ears (from the dreamtime water).* • *Ngoorr-ngoorr boorroorn-ngirri thoowoorranyji yarden.* *Something is whistling in my ears.*

ngoorrama; ngoorramang *verb.* they GOT him/it (masculine).

ngoorramande *verb.* they were GETTING him/it (masculine).

ngoorramangbe; ngoorramangboo *verb.* they GOT him/it (masculine).

ngoorramangbende *verb.* they used to GET him/it (masculine).

ngoorramenbe *verb.* they are GETTING him/it

ngoorramingaboordboo

(masculine).

ngoorramingaboordboo *verb.* they SPEARED him together with someone/something.

ngoorramiyid *verb.* they HIT him together with someone/something.

ngoorramiyidbe *verb.* they HIT him together with someone/something

ngoorramoorloowardbe; ngoorramoorlaardbe *verb.* they HAD/WERE HOLDING him/it (masculine).

ngoorramoorloowardbende; ngoorramoorlaardbende *verb.* they used to HAVE/HOLD/KEEP him/it (masculine)

ngoorramoowangbende *verb.* they used to GO AND GET him/it (masculine).

ngoorramoowoonbe *verb.* they GOT AND HIT him/it (masculine).

ngoorrangaboord *verb.* they SPEARED him/it (masculine).

ngoorrangaboordbe; ngoorrangaboordboo *verb.* they were SPEARING him/it (masculine).

ngoorrangaboordbende *verb.* they kept on SPEARING him/it(masculine).

ngoorrangambenbe *verb.* they are SPEARING him/it (masculine).

ngoorrangamboord *verb.* they SPEARED him/it (masculine).

ngoorrangamboordboo *verb.* they SPEARED him/it (masculine).

ngoorrangirriwardboo *verb.* they WAITED for him/it (masculine).

ngoorrangoonbe *verb.* they were EATING him/it (masculine).

ngoorranybe *verb.* they BROUGHT/TOOK him/it (masculine).

ngoorranybende *verb.* they used to BRING/TAKE him/it (masculine).

ngoorrawamangbe *verb.* they WENT AND GOT him/it (masculine).

ngoorrawamangbende *verb.* they used to GET him/it (masculine).

ngoorrawoon *verb.* they WOUNDED him/it (non-singular).

ngoorrawoonbe *verb.* they WOUNDED him/it (non-singular).

ngoorrawoorranbende *verb.* they were BURNING/BITING him/it (masculine).

ngoorrawoorroodbe *verb.* they LEFT him/it (masculine).

ngoorraya *verb.* they PUT him/it (masculine).

ngoorrayang *verb.* they PUT him/it (masculine).

ngoorrayangbe; ngoorrayangboo *verb.* they were PUTTING him/it (masculine).

ngoorrayangbende *verb.* they used to PUT him/it (masculine).

ngoorrayid *verb.* they HIT him/it(masculine).

ngoorrayidbe; ngoorrayidboo *verb.* they HIT him/it (masculine).

ngoorrayidbende *verb.* they used to HIT him/it (masculine).

ngoorrayoo *verb.* they two PUT him/it (masculine). [NOTE: elided form of *ngoorraya-yoo*]

ngoorrigbe; ngoorrigboo *verb.* they will TAKE him/it (masculine).

ngoorrijbe; ngoorrijboo *verb.* they will HIT him/it (masculine).

ngoorrilinbe; ngoorrilinboo *verb.* they are PUTTING him/it (masculine).

ngoorrimbe; ngoorrimboo *verb.* they will GET him/it (masculine).

ngoorriri *coverb+PUT.* talk about someone behind their back, plot against someone.
• Ngoorriri nimbiyajtha-ngoo. *I'll talk about you.* • Nyengen-ga miyi ngoorriri nimbiyajtha-ngoo bardoon-ga-nenggoowa. *I'll talk about you too after you are gone.* • Bardoobiny ngoorriri yarraja, thelngoorroob-garri noomboowoonnha. *We'll talk about you when you turn your back.*

ngoorriyajbe *verb.* they will PUT him/it (masculine)

ngoorriyana *locative demonstrative.* right over there.

ngoorriyangbe *verb.* they wanted to PUT him/it (masculine)

ngoorriyangbende *verb.* they used to want to PUT him/it (masculine).

ngoorriyinbe *verb.* they are HITTING him/it (masculine).

ngoorrg-ngoorrgjil *noun.* pig. *Sus scrofa.* SEE: **bigi-bigil**. [NOTE: a few feral pigs live in Gija country]

ngoorr-ngoorr *coverb+SAY/DO.* growl.
• Ngoorr-ngoorr ngerne joolany. *The dog is growling.*

ngoorr-ngoorrgajil; ngoorr-ngoorrwajil *noun feminine.* car, truck, motor bike. LIT: 'something used for growling'. SEE: **ngoorr-ngoorrgalil**.

ngoorr-ngoorrgalil *noun.* car. LIT: 'good at growling'. SEE: **ngoorr-ngoorrool**,

ngoowiyi

ngoorr-ngoorrgajil.

ngoorr-ngoorrge-girrem *noun.* car key. LIT: 'thing that makes something growl'. SEE: **nyarlarlam.**

ngoorr-ngoorroo *noun.* engine. [NOTE: from the sound *ngoorr-ngoorr*, 'to growl']

ngoorr-ngoorrool *noun.* car, truck. SEE: **ngoorr-ngoorrgajil, ngoorr-ngoorrgalil.** [NOTE: from the sound *ngoorr-ngoorr*, 'to growl']

ngoorrool REDUP: **ngoorroo-ngoorrool.** *demonstrative.* that one over there (feminine)
• Galayi benajtha ngawooram ngoorroo-ngoorroola. *Put your hand over your forehead (to shade your eyes) and look up at all those sugarbag bees right over there.*

ngoorroom REDUP: **ngoorroo-ngoorroom.** *demonstrative.* those over there, that over there.

ngoorrooma *verb.* they GOT him. SEE: **ngoorrama.**

ngoorroomboo *verb.* let them GET him/it (masculine).

ngoorroomenbe *verb.* they are GETTING him/it (masculine).

ngoorroomenbende *verb.* they keep on GETTING him/it (masculine).

ngoorroongany *verb.* let them SPEAR/POKE him/it (masculine).

ngoorroongoonbe *verb.* they are EATING him/it (masculine).

ngoorroon *demonstrative.* over there, at that place.

ngoorroo-ngoorroon *locative.* everywhere, all over the place. • Jiyirrem jarrg-jarrg boorroorn ngoorroo-ngoorroon. *Kangaroos are jumping everywhere.*
• Ngoorroo-ngoorroo-milem jarrag berrani boorriyangem jarragboo. *People from everywhere used to speak their own language.*
• Nyigawa ngoorroo-ngoorroo-biny birriyan boorij-girrem boorljanyji. *Tomorrow they will be coming from everywhere to play football.*

ngoorroony; ngoorriny *demonstrative.* that there (masculine). • Ngoorrinya nawarragawoony yoorlangoogoo nginji. *That (image in the painting) is the river going down.*

ngoorroornbe *noun.* pubic hair.

ngoorroowarrenbe *verb.* they are burning/biting him/it (non-singular).

ngoorrwangarnal *noun feminine.* fire fly.

ngoorrwany *noun masculine.* white currant. *Flueggea virosa.* • Ngoorrwany dany ninamanggende, gool-ngarri niniyangge ngarijayin. *I tried the ngoorrwany fruit I was picking and they were really sweet.* SEE: **roonggoony, berenggarrji, goowarroolji.** [NOTE: shrub bearing masses of small edible white fruit in the wet season]

ngoowag *coverb+SAY/DO_M.* be nothing, be not there, be gone. • Ngoowag wanema. *He was not there anymore.*

ngoowan *particle.* negative particle.

ngoowan *interjection.* no.

ngoowangarnany, ngoowangarnal, ngoowangarnam *adjective.* having nothing, knowing nothing.

ngoowangarnan *interjection.* not at all, nothing.

ngoowa-ngoowag *coverb+SAY/DO.* be unable to do something, be unsuccessful. • Ngoowa-ngoowaga narrooni-yarre. *Then you would have looked for us but we would not have been there.* • Degbe wanamanyji-boorroo-yoo ngoowa-ngoowag nginini-boorroo-yoo. *He looked for the two of them but he couldn't find them.*

ngoowany, ngoowal *adjective.* someone who doesn't do something, nothing.

ngoowardiny *noun.* plant with edible fruit. *Grewia polygama.* SEE: **gawoorroony, garrawiny.**

ngoowarrenji *verb.* he/it (masculine) is about to BURN/BITE him/it (masculine). SEE: **ngiwarrenji.**

ngoowarri *verb.* he will BURN it.

ngoowayinjende *verb.* he keeps on BITING himself.

-ngoowiny, -ngoowil, -ngoowim *suffix.* similar to, resembling.

ngoowiji *verb.* he wants to HIT him.

ngoowirn *verb.* he/it (masculine) should DO, if he DOES.

ngoowiya *verb.* he will GO/COME.

ngoowiyaji; ngiwiyaji *verb.* he will PUT him/it (masculine).

ngoowiyan *verb.* he will GO/COME.

ngoowiyanya *verb.* she wanted to PUT him/it (masculine).

ngoowiyayi; ngiwiyayi *verb.* he/it (masculine) will go.

ngoowiyayin *verb.* he/it (masculine) will be GOING

ngoowiyi *verb.* he/it (masculine) will FALL/GO DOWN.

ngoowiyi

ngoowiyi *verb.* he might GO/COME.
ngoowiyin *verb.* he wanted to GO/COME.
ngoowoob REDUP: **ngoowoob-ngoowoob**. *coverb+SAY/DO.* be steaming, be radiating.
• Barndinyboo winan wayinigana daambi ngoowoob boorroorn. *It is getting hot and because of that the country has a heat haze.*
• Jalij-ngarri nginini, daam ngoowoob boorroorn-noowa bardoon. *After the rain, the country is really hot and steamy.* • Ngoowoob nyerne malala. *The sun is radiating heat.*
• Maram ngoowoob-ngoowoob boorroorn. *The hot dirt is steaming.*
ngoowooni *verb.* he wanted to SAY/DO.
ngoowooniyin *verb.* he should have STAYED.
ngoowoonji *verb.* he/it (masculine) is FALLING/GOING DOWN.

ngoowoorn *verb.* he wanted to SAY/DO.
ngoolya-ngoolya *coverb+SAY/DO_REFL.* have fun together. • Ngoolya-ngoolya yarrengirrij gawayinda. *We still have good fun together.* SEE: **barlij**.
ngooyarr *coverb+SAY/DO.* pick up. • Ngooyarr boorroorn nyamananim minyjiwarram. *The old women are picking up the black plums.*
-ngooyoo *benefactive enclitic pronoun.* for her, for it (feminine).
ngooyoo *noun.* emu apple. *Owenia vernicosa.* SEE: **nyarerrji**.
ngooyood *coverb+SAY/DO_REFL.* belt each other with sticks. • Deyena ngooyood berrangirriyinbende-yoo. *The two of them kept on belting each other with the sticks there.*

NH nh

-nha *suffix.* you.
Nhanban *noun.* Wesley Spring.
nharajgoo *verb.* let me PUT you.
nharajtha *verb.* let me PUT it.
nharayig-ngoo *verb.* let me TAKE you (one).
nhared *coverb.* make a sound as in speech. • Nhared berrawerriyin. *They are making speech sounds to each other.* • Nhared-biny-da-birri jarragbooga Gijam. *That is the way Gija sounds.*
nharedbem *noun.* sounds of a language. • Yoowoorriyangem nharedbem Gijam. *Our Gija language sounds.*
nharegbany-ngoo; nharegbany *verb.* let me TAKE you along. • Nharegbany-gala-ngoo. *I want to take you away.*
nharem *verb.* let me GET him/it (masculine).
nharem-ngoo; nharem-ngoongoo *verb.* let me GET you (one).

nharemnha-ngoo *verb.* let me GET you (one).
nharida-ngoo *verb.* let me TAKE you. • Mamberre jarrag berne-ngirri rangga nharida-ngoo. *Speak slowly so I can hear you (let me listen to you).*
nharrimijtha *verb.* you all will do to self/each other.
nhawany, nawany *pronoun.* he himself. SEE: nhawiyan, nhawoowany.
nhawiny *noun masculine.* a tree-living native bee species, tree sugarbag species that has a long wax entrance hole. Tetragonula sp. [NOTE: young man in dreamtime, Joongoorra skin] SEE: gerrayiny.
nhawiyan *pronoun.* he's the one.
nhawiyangeny, nhawiyangel, nhawiyangem *possessive pronoun.* his.
-nhawoony, -nhawool, -nhawoom, -thawoony, -thawool, -thawoom *suffix.* one who does that kind of thing. [NOTE: attached to coverbs forming nouns]
nhawoomelewam *pronoun.* all the things from him.
nhawoomoowam *pronoun.* him only.
nhawoon *pronoun.* he, him. • 'Nhawoonji nginiyinde ngenenggayana niwoomoorloowoonde,' wanamayinde. *'He will be staying here, I will be keeping him,' she said.* • Nyingang-goorriny nyagany-goorriny danyi, nhawoon ngoowirn-ninggi 'garli'. *That man is your uncle. He has to call you 'garli' (niece/nephew).* • Yagengerram boorooj boorroorn-ni, nhawoonji ganggerr-ganggerrgayan. *The others all have fun and he gets cranky.*
nhawoowany *pronoun.* he in turn, his turn, himself.
nhawoowarriny *pronoun.* he himself.
nhayirril *noun feminine.* small spearhead used for revenge killing. • Dal ngardawoo-ngarri wanamanyande goora-gal, dal nhayirril, waj nyimberrayidbe-ni dany. *When his mother has been crying (for the dead man), they give that little spearhead for him (the murderer of the one she is crying for to someone who will carry out the revenge killing).*

Figure 68. *Nhawiny*: Dardayal Shirley Drill: Ngare-galel thad ngoomoorloonya nhawiny ngareny goowoole-ngarnany men'gawoony.

Gija Dictionary 243

nhegbayiny, nhegbayil, nhegbayim

Figure 69. *Nhen-nhen: Nhennhen-gala booma ngarem-boorroo.*

nhegbayiny, nhegbayil, nhegbayim *adjective* having partly closed up eyes, slant-eyed.

nheleb *coverb+DO_REFL.* masturbate. • **Nhelebjiwa yirremiji-ngiyiwa-yoo.** *We two will just have to masturbate because of it (bus).* [NOTE: joke by Peggy Patrick about what she and Paddy Bedford would have to do if they missed the bus (-*ngiyiwa* – *feminine*)] • **Danya nhelebji ngimiyanyji-ngiyiwa.** *That one is masturbating because of her.* [NOTE: what is said about a man if his wife leaves him]

nhem *coverb+GET.* stick on/together. • **Nhem benama. Nhem benamanyji.** *He stuck them on. He was sticking them on.* • **Nhem nimbirrimnhawoo.** *It/they will stick on you then.*

nhembad *coverb+BE/STAY.* be stuck. • **Nhembad ninande ngamarrwoon-ngoo balg naniyindi manam-ninggi dam.** *You are stuck there, you always want to be carried and sit down, that bottom of yours and won't get up.*

nhembad *coverb+FALL/GO_DOWN.* get stuck. • **Nhembad nginiwardji.** *He got stuck.*

nhembadbe; nhembadboo *coverb+FALL/GO_DOWN.* get stuck (e.g. in mud or quicksand). • **Nhembadbe ngenewoon'ge.** *I'm getting stuck.* • **Nhembadboowaa yirrewoonye-yoo yilwarraya!** *We are both completely stuck now!* • **Nhembadboowaa berrewoonbe-yoo.** *They were both stuck.*

nhen REDUP: **nhenhen**. *coverb+PUT.* poke. • **Nhen ngoorrayangbe.** *He got poked. / It (non-singular thing) poked him.*

nheng-nhegany, nheng-nhegal, nheng-nhegam *adjective.* bung-eyed, slant-eyed, eyes partly stuck together. SEE: **nhegbayiny.**

nhen-nhen *coverb+SAY/DO_M.* poke stick into hole. • **Nhen-nhen-gala booma.** *Poke it (sugarbag in hole) with a long stick.*

nheraj *verb.* let me PUT him/it (masculine).

nherajge *verb.* let me PUT him/it (masculine).

nherang *verb.* let me EAT him/it (masculine).

nheregelij *verb.* I'll LEAVE it.

nherem *verb.* let me GET him/it (masculine).

nheremge *verb.* let me GET him/it (masculine).

nherij *verb.* I should HIT him/it (masculine).

nheroowam *verb.* I want to GO AND GET him/her/it. SEE: **nhiyiwam.**

nherraj REDUP: **nherrerraj**. *coverb+FALL/GO_DOWN.* spurt out (water). • **Nherraj nginiwardji na goorloonyi dany yilang.** *That water spurted out from underneath then.*

nherraj *coverb+SAY/DO.* rush out (water). • **Nherraj nginini yilanggan.** *It (water) rushed up from the bottom.* SEE: **boonany.**

Figure 70. *Nhoonbam: Warlbawoony-ni thambarlam nhoonban.*

nhij REDUP: nhij-nhij; nhiny-nhij. *coverb+SAY/DO.* have backache. • Marrge joodoog-gala ngendamij therlam, nhiny-nhij ngenarn. *Wait till I straighten my back, it aches from sitting.*
• Therlam nhij nginini marloogany. *The old man has a backache.*

nhil, nhil-nhil *coverb+SAY/DO.* make spark.
• Nhil-nhil-ngarri nginini dany marniny, jarrg-garri nginayinde, thoorroob ginimanyji, marniny dany nhil-ngarri nginiyin. *When he (little grasshopper) was making that fire spark, when he (falcon) swooped down, he snatched the fire that was sparking.* SEE: **ninirl.**

nhiny *coverb+DO_REFL.* go into hole (e.g. goanna).
• Thoogool nhiny nyanemiyin. *The female goanna went into the hole / took herself into the hole.* SEE: **therramij.**

nhirim *verb.* let me GET him/it (masculine). • Deg nhirim-ngage goomoonoonga-bany. *Let me have a look at that one wearing the paperbark hat.*

nhiyimge *verb.* I should GET him/it (masculine).
• 'Tharrboorda nhiyimge,' nyanini. *'I'll have to spear him,' she said.* SEE: **nhirim.**

nhiyiwam *verb.* let me GO AND GET him.

nhoonbam *noun.* mud.

nhoonmoony, nhoonmool, nhoonmoom *adjective.* blunt.

nhoony *coverb+BE/STAY.* bend down. • Nhoony ngininiyin. *He was bending down.* • Rega, ngoowan nhoony nimbinnha, dama-ninggi bardoobiny roord boorroonboo. Deg nimbirrimnha-boorroo. *Don't do that, don't bend over, that lot are sitting behind you. They might look at you.*

nhoorany *verb.* let me BRING him/it (masculine).

nhoorr REDUP: nhoorrngoog. *coverb+PUT.* nudge someone secretly (with elbow), give a secret sign. • Nhoorr nginiyanyji. / Nhoorrngoog nginiyanyji. *He nudged him secretly.*

nhoorr *coverb+HIT.* nudge someone secretly (with elbow), give a secret sign. • Nhoorr ngenayid. *He/she nudged me.*

nhoorrngoog *coverb+HIT.* nudge someone secretly (with elbow), give a secret sign.
• Nhoorrngoog nyaniyidji. *He jabbed her with his elbow.*

nhoorrngoog *coverb+SAY/DO_REFL.* nudge each other. • Nhoorrngoog birringirriyan-joo. *They are nudging each other (e.g. to tell the other to*

nhoorr-nhoorr

go and fight.) SEE: **nhoorr-nhoorr**.

nhoorr-nhoorr *coverb+SAY/DO.* have a premonition, feel something in the ears.
 • **Nhoorr-nhoorr ngenarn yardem.** *My ears are tingling, I have a feeling about something.*

nhoorr-nhoorr *coverb+SAY/DO_REFL.* nudge each other. • **Nhoorr-nhoorr birringirriyan-joo.** *They are nudging each other (e.g. to tell the other to go and fight.)* SEE: **nhoorrngoog**.

nhoowoolji, nhoowoolel, nhoowoole *adjective.* bad smelling (e.g. rotten meat).
 • nhoowoole goomboonyboo *bad eggs*

nhoowoolgbany *coverb+GO/COME.* become stinking, go bad. • **Ngoowa nhoowoolgbany nyimbiyanya, ngoowangarnan.** *It doesn't go bad, not at all (speaking about dried ground barramundi stored for a year in an ant hill).*

nhoowooljiny *coverb+GET.* go bad, begin to stink.
 • **Ngoowan ngenengga wooboo, goonggoon yambirrimnya berremga goorndarrim. Ngoowan nhoowooljiny binbimji-yarri.** *Can't we cook these fish here, they might go bad on us.*

nhoowoorrenha-ngoo; nhewerranha-ngoo *verb.* I'll have to leave you, let me leave you, I'm leaving you.

NY ny

-ny *suffix.* masculine suffix following stems ending in vowels. SEE: **-ji**.

Nyaajarri; Nyawajarri *noun.* a skin name (when spoken to).

Nyaajarril *noun.* a skin name (when spoken about).

nyaarndem *noun.* edible gum found on the river gum tree. *Terminalia platyphylla.*
- ... nyaarnde-ngarran-noonggoorroo-yoo. *(You two can't find a feed), you are only good for eating gum.* SEE: **nyaarndiny**.

nyaarndiny *noun masculine.* river gum, tree species that has edible gum. *Terminalia platyphylla.* SEE: **nyarlany, thaleginy, nyaarndem**. [NOTE: common tree with dark bark and big leaves found along creeks, called a 'gum tree' by Gija people because of the edible gum]

nyaarrji, nyaarel, nyaarre *noun.* spirit, angel, ghost of dead person who comes back and shows self. SEE: **yoongoom**.

nyad REDUP: **nyad-nyad**. *coverb+GET.* stick something on. • *Nyad nginimanyji. He stuck it (masculine) on.*

nyad *coverb+SAY/DO_M.* stay one place.
• *Ngoorrinya jalij ngerne nyad wanema. It is raining over there, stopping in one place.*

nyade *verb.* let her BE, let her STAY.

nyadinya *verb.* let her/it (feminine) BE/BE STAYING.

nyaganyji *noun.* uncle, mother's brother, father's sister's husband. SEE: **nyagayi**.

nyagayi *noun.* uncle, mother's brother, father's sister's husband (when spoken to). SEE: **nyaganyji**.

nyagoom *noun.* type of pubic tassell. SEE:

Figure 71. *Nyaajarri: Dottie Wadbi: Nyaajarril roord nyinya barnden.*

nyagoornany

warlboorroo, jarnim.

nyagoornany *noun.* rock cod, giant gudgeon. *Oxyelotris selheimi.*

nyaj *coverb+FALL/GO_DOWN.* trip over. • *Danya goorndoogany nyaj nginiwardji ngarrgalen.* That little boy tripped over the stone.

nyalala *coverb+GO_ALONG.* go slowly walking about. • *Nyalala wiyinya.* She is walking about slowly.

nyalalawany *coverb+GO/COME.* go hunting. • *Gabinganyji nyalalawany nginiyi.* I don't know where he went hunting. • *Nyalalawany-gala yarra boorrale-boorroo.* Let's go hunting for a good meal.

nyalg *coverb+FALL/GO_DOWN.* kick something accidentally. • *Dala ngalil nyalg nyanooward.* That woman kicked something (by accident). SEE: **berd.**

nyaliny *particle.* also, again. [NOTE: frequently occurs following coverbs in verb compounds, becomes *jaliny* following stop consonants.]

nyalngawoog *coverb+SAY/DO_M.* go walking all night. • *Nyalngawoog woomberremenbe girlirrin.* They walk around all night in the west.

nyaloonggooj *coverb+SAY/DO.* be curled around (snake). • *Dawool nyaloonggooj nyinya.* The black-headed python is curled around.

nyam REDUP: **nyam-nyam.** *coverb+SAY/DO.* whisper. • *Dama melgabarroom boorroordboo boorij-girrem-anyji, nyam-nyam berne.* That is my in-law (cousin) coming, you have to whisper.

nyam REDUP: **nyam-nyam.** *coverb+PUT.* whisper to someone. • *Nyam nginiyanji.* He whispered to him. • *Dala goorndoogal nyam nginiyanya.* That little girl was whispering to him. • *Binginya nyam nginiya, dany binginy dany, yilgoowoorriny raginy.* And the red ant told tales (whispered to him), that little ant, that bad one.

nyamani *coverb+BECOME.* become an old woman. • *Marrarna nyamani jiyinnha.* You are already an old woman.

nyamanil; nyamanel REDUP: **nyamananim.** *noun.* old woman. [NOTE: also used with the meaning 'white woman' or Kriol 'missus']

nyambarrginy *noun.* river gum, edible gum, tree species with edible gum. *Terminalia platyphylla.* SEE: **nyaarndiny, nyarlany, thaleginy, nyaarndem.** [NOTE: common tree with big leaves found along creeks]

nyamiginy, nyamigil, nyamigim *adjective.* short-sighted. • *Moorloo nyamigil.* Short-sighted woman.

nyamooloong *coverb+BE/STAY.* be coiled (as a snake). • *Ngamarrany nyamooloong nginji.* The snake is coiled up. SEE: **nyamoolyoo.**

nyamoolyoo *coverb+BE/STAY.* be coiled (as a snake). • *Nginya ngamarrany nyamoolyoo nginji nawane.* The snake is coiled up in the hole. SEE: **nyamooloong.**

nyanaardjande *verb.* she used to FALL/GO DOWN. [NOTE: Southern dialect] SEE: **nyanoowardjande.**

nyanagawoony *noun.* river. [NOTE: Southern dialect] SEE: **nawarragawoony.**

nyanany *verb.* he/she BROUGHT/TOOK her/it (feminine).

nyananya *verb.* she BROUGHT/TOOK her/it (feminine).

nyananyande *verb.* she was BRINGING/TAKING her/it (feminine).

nyananyjende *verb.* he was BRINGING/TAKING her/it (feminine).

nyananyji *verb.* he BROUGHT/TOOK her/it (feminine).

nyanema *verb.* he/she GOT her/it (feminine).

nyanemanya *verb.* she GOT her/it (feminine).

nyanemanyande *verb.* she was GETTING her/it (feminine).

nyanemanyji *verb.* he/it (masculine) GOT her/it (feminine).

nyanemiyin *verb.* she DID to herself.

nyanemiyinya *verb.* she was DOING to herself.

nyanemoorlaardja *verb.* she HAD/KEPT her/it (feminine).

nyanengaboord *verb.* he/she/it SPEARED/POKED her/it (feminine).

nyanengaboordji *verb.* he/it (masculine) SPEARED/POKED her/it (feminine).

nyanengirriyin *verb.* she SAID/DID to herself.

nyanewoorranyja *verb.* she BIT her, she/it (feminine) BURNED her.

nyanewoorranyji *verb.* he BIT her, he/it (masculine) BURNED her/it (feminine), she got BURNED.

nyanewoorranyjende *verb.* he/it (masculine) was BURNING her/it (feminine), she/it(feminine) was getting BURNED.

nyanggernam *noun.* hooked stick, long stick with hook used for getting honey.

nyangoobany, nyangoobal noun. doctor. SEE: baremanbeny, mabarn.

nyangoolyoo-ngoolyoog; nyangoolyooyoogoo coverb+BURN/BITE. get really soft (meat). • Nyangoolyoo-ngoolyoog nginiwoorrany miyalji. *The beef got really soft/overcooked.* • Nyangoolyoo-ngoolyoog-gala bendoowarre miyale. *Let the meat get really cooked.* • Nyangoolyoolyoogoo nyanewoorranyja. *It was really cooked.*

nyaniminyande; nyanimiyinyande verb. she was DOING TO HERSELF.

nyanini verb. she SAID, she DID.

nyaninin, nyaniniyin verb. she WAS/STAYED.

nyanininya verb. she WAS/WAS STAYING.
• Gernanyjelga ngalil nyanininya ngarranggarnin. *The echidna was a woman in dreamtime.*

nyanininyande verb. she was/used to BE, BE STAYING.

nyaninya verb. she was GOING/COMING.

nyaninyande verb. she kept on GOING/COMING.

nyaniyanya verb. she PUT her/it (feminine).

nyaniyanyjende verb. he used to PUT her/it (feminine).

nyaniyanyji verb. he PUT her/it (feminine).

nyaniyi verb. she/it (feminine) WENT/CAME.

nyaniyid verb. he/she/it HIT her/it (feminine).

nyaniyidja verb. she HIT her/it (feminine).

nyaniyidjende verb. he was HITTING her/it (feminine).

nyaniyidji verb. he HIT her/it (feminine).

nyaniyilin verb. she PUT it on herself.

nyaniyinde verb. she/it (feminine) kept GOING/COMING.

nyaniyinya verb. 1. she/it (feminine) is HITTING her/it (feminine). 2. she/it (feminine) was GOING/COMING.

nyaniyinyande verb. she/it (feminine) kept on GOING/COMING.

nyanmaj coverb+PUT. stick on, sticker. • Ngayin-ga wijigalen-nga benaj-girri nyanmaj. *I am a good runner. Put a sticker on me.*

nyanoomooward verb. she WENT DOWN WITH someone/something.

nyanoomoowardja; nyanemoowardja verb. she WENT DOWN WITH someone/something.
• Berab janemoowardja-birri waringarrim. *She came out to the big mob of people.*

nyanoomoowardjande verb. she kept on GOING DOWN WITH someone/something.

nyanooward; nyaneward verb. she FELL/WENT DOWN.

nyanoowardja; nyanewardja verb. she FELL/WENT DOWN.

nyanoowardjande verb. she used to FALL/GO DOWN.

nyanoowoonji verb. he WOUNDED her/it (feminine).

nyanoowoorrood verb. he/she/it LEFT her/it (feminine).

nyanoowoorroodji verb. he/she/it LEFT her/it (feminine).

nyaraji verb. let him PUT her/it (feminine).

nyaranya verb. let her COME.

nyarerrji noun masculine. emu apple. *Owenia vernicosa.* fish poison plant. *Nomismia (Rhyncosia) rhomboidea.* [NOTE: both species used as fish poison]

nyariyanya verb. let her COME.

nyarlanam noun. hook.

nyarlany noun masculine. river gum. tree species that has edible gum. *Terminalia platyphylla.* SEE: nyaarndiny, thaleginy, nyaarndem. [NOTE: common tree with dark bark and big leaves found along creeks]

nyarlany, nyarlal, nyarlam adjective. one who is very clever at something. • Ngagenybi gangga-warriny nyarlam-joo. *My two grandkids are both clever.* [NOTE: often used as exclamation *Nyarlany! Nyarlal!* when someone does something very well]

nyarlarlam noun. key. • Yindiyi-gala dam nyarlalam ngoorr-ngoorrool-ngooyoo. *Give me that car key.* SEE: ngoorr-ngoorrge-girrem.

nyarlgool noun feminine. golden bandicoot. *Isoodon auratus.*

nyarli coverb+SAY/DO_M. become crippled.
• Nyarli wanama ngoowan girli ngiwirn. *He's crippled, he can't walk.*

nyarlimbiny, nyarlimbel noun. newborn baby. SEE: marlirnbany.

nyarliwiny, nyarliwil, nyarliwim adjective. crippled. [NOTE: Southern dialect]

nyarlool coverb. shed skin and have a new one (e.g. snake, goanna, cicada). • Dala lirrinel nyarlool wanema. Berrema lirn'girre-ngiyiwa. *That cicada has shed its skin. Here is her old skin (that she shed).*

nyare coverb+FALL/GO_DOWN. be hot time of day.
• Nyare nyaneward-yarri malalal. *The sun is hot on us.*

nyarewarloon

Figure 72. *Nyawana: Yarangalil Mary Thomas: Nyawanal thad nyinya manyanyi-bany.*

nyarewarloon *temporal.* midday.

nyawam *noun.* tail. [NOTE: gender varies with gender of referent if detached from body: *nyawany, nyawal*; euphemism for 'penis'] SEE: *gerlenggeny.*

Nyawana *noun.* a skin name (when spoken to).

Nyawanal; Nyawanel *noun feminine.* a skin name (when spoken about).

Nyawawoorroon *noun.* place where Mabel Juli's *thamanyji* died on Springvale Station.

nyawoorn *coverb+GO/COME.* gather together in large group. • Berdij nginiyin. 'Marri nyawoorn berrayi dambi woombarnoongoom.' *When he climbed up (he said), 'Goodness, so many rock wallabies have gathered there in the one place.'*

nyawoorn *coverb+PUT.* put together in large group. • Nyawoorn yinayanyjende-yarre fayablejin woorrg yirraniyinde jarrag wanemayinde-yirri. *He used to get us all to gather around and sit by the fireplace and talk to us.*

Nyawoorroo *noun.* a skin name (when spoken to).

Nyawoorrool *noun feminine.* a skin name (when spoken about).

nyawoorroorroo; nyawoorroo-woorroo *coverb+GET.* gather together on something. • Boornoom nyawoorroorroo ngoorroomenbe, ngardawoogoo ngoorroomenbe gajim. *The flies were all gathering on him (crocodile), and the sores were making him (lizard) cry.*
• Nyawoorroo-woorroo ngoorramangbe dam boornoom. *Those flies all gathered on him.* [NOTE: old people used to say that young boys could not say this word]

nyawoorroo-woorroo *coverb+BRING/TAKE.* gather together on something. • Nyawoorroo-woorroo ngoorranybe. *They (flies) all gathered on him (crocodile).*

nyeg *coverb+HIT.* pound (soft thing, e.g. meat).
• Ngelela ngalil nyeg benayidja miyale. *This woman is pounding the meat.*

nyemenjende *verb.* he keeps on GETTING her/it (feminine).

nyemenji *verb.* he is GETTING her/it (feminine).

nyemenya *verb.* she is GETTING her/it (feminine).

-nyen *suffix.* in, at, on. SEE: **-n, -e, -jen, -oo**. [NOTE: locative following stop sounds or words ending in *-ng*, frequently found following loan words]

nyenberrg *coverb+GO/COME.* go away and take a long time to come back. • **Garniwa, garniwa, yage nyenberrg giniyi.** *Where is he, where is he? He's been gone a long time, he should be back now.* [NOTE: you send somebody and they are a long time coming back, they should be back by now]

nyengen; nyingen; nyingin *pronoun.* you (one). [NOTE: *nyingin* is Southern dialect]

nyengirriyan *verb.* she SAYS/DOES TO HERSELF.

nyengoowany *pronoun.* you yourself. SEE: **nyingoowany**.

nyerne *verb.* she/it (feminine) SAYS/DOES.

Nyidbarriya *noun.* significant rocky place in Purnululu National Park. [NOTE: Nyawana skin]

nyidim *noun.* coccyx, tail bone.

nyidja *verb.* she/it (feminine) is going/coming. • **Dala roadel nyidja Garlmarnderr-biny.** *That road comes from Landsdowne.*

nyidjande *verb.* she/it (feminine) keeps on GOING/COMING.

nyigamirrib; nyigamirribda; nyigamirribja *temporal.* early morning.

nyigan *temporal.* night-time, tomorrow.

nyigany *noun masculine.* gecko. *Gehyra australis.* SEE: **mendoowoony, moondoowoony**.

nyiganybe REDUP: **nyiga-nyiganybe**. *coverb+FALL/GO_DOWN.* get dark. • **Nyiganybe berroowoonbe-yarri.** *It is getting dark on us.*

nyiga-nyigawa *temporal.* early morning, this morning.

nyigawa *temporal.* tomorrow, the next day. SEE: **magarne**.

nyilaj *verb.* I will PUT her/it (feminine).

nyilajge *verb.* I will be PUTTING her/it (feminine).

nyilama *verb.* I GOT her/it (feminine).

nyilamangge *verb.* I GOT her/it (feminine).

nyilamanggende *verb.* I was GETTING her/it (feminine).

nyilamen'ge; nyilemen'ge *verb.* I am GETTING her/it (feminine).

nyilamoorlaardge *verb.* I HAD/WAS KEEPING/ HOLDING/ LOOKING AFTER her/it (feminine).

nyilangoon'ge *verb.* I EAT her/it (feminine).

nyilanyge *verb.* I was BRINGING/TAKING her/it (feminine).

nyilawoorroon'ge *verb.* I am LEAVING her/it (feminine).

nyilayangge; nyiliyangge; nyilangge *verb.* I PUT her/it (feminine). [NOTE: elided form *nyilangge* is Southern dialect]]

nyilayid *verb.* I HIT her/it (feminine).

nyilayidge *verb.* I HIT her/it (feminine).

nyilem *verb.* let me GET her/it (feminine).

nyilemoorloo *verb.* I will HAVE/KEEP/HOLD/ LOOK AFTER her/it (feminine).

nyilemoorloon'ge *verb.* I HAVE/KEEP/HOLD/ LOOK AFTER her/it (feminine).

nyilenggam *noun.* end of spear, part of spear made of bamboo.

nyilibal *noun.* barramundi. *Lates calcarifer.* LIT: 'having scales'. SEE: **dayiwool, dawoogjil, balgal, wawoordjil**.

nyilige *verb.* I will TAKE her/it (feminine).

nyiligende *verb.* I will keep on TAKING her/it (feminine). • **Ngayin wandaj nyiligende.** *I will carry her on my shoulder as we go along.*

nyilij *verb.* I will HIT her/it (feminine).

nyilim *noun.* scales. SEE: **lirlmim, lirn'girre**.

nyilimbil, nyilimbiny *noun.* marsupial mouse. *Pseudomys nanus, P. desertor.* [NOTE: makes mist like smoke on the hills in the wet time; also used for house mouse, *Mus musculus*, and introduced rat, *Rattus rattus*; Southern dialect.] SEE: **jaranel. yiroowoonji**.

nyilimge *verb.* I will GET her/it (feminine).

nyiliyajge *verb.* I will PUT her/it (feminine).

nyiliyanya *verb.* she is PUTTING herself.

nyiliyi *verb.* I will GIVE her.

nyiliyin *verb.* I am HITTING her/it (feminine).

nyiliyin'ge *verb.* I am TAKING her/it (feminine).

nyiliyin'gende *verb.* I keep TAKING her/it (feminine).

nyiman'gool *noun feminine.* green pigmy goose. *Netapus pulchellis.*

nyimbe *coverb+GO/COME.* close in on someone 'like a clamp' (e.g. dangerous country). • **Nyimbe ngiwiyayinde nyigan-ga nimbiyannha-ngarri.** *(The country) will close up behind you if you go there at night.*

nyimbelawoony, nyimbelawool *noun.* baby.

nyimberrama; nyimberramang *verb.* they GOT her/it (feminine).

nyimberramangbe; nyimberramangboo *verb.* they GOT her/it (feminine).

nyimberramangbende *verb.* they kept on GETTING her/it (feminine).

nyimberramenbe

nyimberramenbe *verb.* they are GETTING her/it (feminine).
nyimberramenbende *verb.* they keep on GETTING her/it (feminine).
nyimberramiyanboo *verb.* they were FOLLOWING her/it (feminine).
nyimberramiyidbe *verb.* they HIT her/it (feminine) together with him.
nyimberramiyidbende *verb.* they kept on HITTING her/it (feminine) with him.
nyimberramoorlaardbende *verb.* they always used to HAVE/KEEP her/it (feminine).
nyimberramoorloowardbe *verb.* they used to HAVE/KEEP her/it (feminine).
nyimberramoowoonbe *verb.* they are GETTING AND HITTING her/it (feminine).
nyimberrangaboordbe *verb.* they were SPEARING her/it (feminine).
nyimberrangoonbe *verb.* they were EATING her/it (feminine).
nyimberranybe *verb.* they were BRINGING/TAKING her/it (feminine).
nyimberranybende *verb.* they used to BRING/TAKE her/it (feminine).
nyimberrawoonbe *verb.* they were WOUNDING her/it (feminine).
nyimberrawoorrood *verb.* they LEFT her/it (feminine).
nyimberrayangbe *verb.* they PUT her/it (feminine).
nyimberrayangbende *verb.* they used to PUT her/it (feminine).
nyimberrayid *verb.* they HIT her/it (feminine).
nyimberrayidbe *verb.* they HIT her/it (feminine).
nyimberrayidbende *verb.* they used to HIT her/it (feminine).
nyimberregbe *verb.* let them TAKE her/it (feminine).
nyimberrengoonbe *verb.* they are EATING her/it (feminine). • Gerrejbe nyimberrengoonbe gamoomga. *They (puppies) are drinking all her (mother dog's) milk.*
nyimberriyajbe; nyimbirriyajbe *verb.* they will PUT her/it (feminine).
nyimberriyinbe *verb.* they are BRINGING/TAKING her/it (feminine). SEE: **nyimbirriyinbe**.
nyimbewarri *verb.* he/she will BURN/BITE her/it (feminine). • Werdanyji nyimbewarri. *He might bite her.*
nyimbijji *verb.* he will HIT her/it (feminine).
nyimbimji *verb.* he will GET her/it (feminine).

nyimbinya *verb.* she will BE/STAY.
nyimbirn *verb.* she will SAY/DO.
nyimbirridbe *verb.* they wanted to HIT her/it (feminine).
nyimbirrimbe *verb.* they will be GETTING her/it (feminine).
nyimbirriyinbe *verb.* **1.** they are BRINGING/TAKING her/it (feminine). **2.** they are HITTING her/it (feminine).
nyimbiyanya *verb.* she will GO/COME.
nyimboowardja *verb.* she/it (feminine) would have FALLEN/GONE DOWN.
nyimboowoonya *verb.* she/it (feminine) will FALL/GO DOWN.
nyimeniny *coverb+WOUND_REFL.* drown. • Dama nyirreg-garri boorroonboo wanyanyagem, yilak goorrnga-yoorroong, nyimeniny berroowan. *When those children go swimming down at the water they might drown themselves.*
nyimeniny *coverb+HIT.* drown something/someone. • Nyimeniny nyimberrayidbe-nga ngenengga yilag Warrmarne. *They drowned it on me (my car) down here at the creek at Turkey Creek.*
nyimininybe *coverb+FALL/GO_DOWN.* be sinking, be drowning. • Nyimininybe nginewardji. *He was sinking under (the water).*
nyimiyanya *verb.* she DID TO HERSELF.
nyimiyinya *verb.* she is DOING TO HERSELF.
nyimoog *coverb+HIT.* drown something, put into water. • Dal ngoorr-ngoorrgirrel nyimoog nyimberrayid yilag nyanagawoon. *They 'drowned' the car in the creek.*
nyimoog REDUP: **nyimoog-nyimoog**. *coverb+FALL/GO_DOWN.* dive in, get into water. • Nyimoog-anyja ngenboowardge. *I thought about going swimming (getting in the water) (but didn't).* • Nyimoog-nyimoog boowoo. *You get into the water.*
nyimooga *coverb+SAY/DO.* dive in, get into water. • Nyimooga boorroorn. *They get into the water.* • Nyimooga-ngarri boorroorn, men'gawoog benemenji. *When they get into the water, it makes them (feel) good.*
nyin *coverb+BE/STAY.* forget. • Nyin-ngarri narreninha-ngage ngenayin-narri boorab. *When you had all forgotten about me I came to you all.* [NOTE: also heard as *nyirn*, *nyen*, and *nyern*]
nyin *coverb+SAY/DO.* forget, have funny feeling in ears. • Nyin ngenani yardem. *I have a funny*

Figure 73. *Nyinyil: Nyinyil yimele benamanya marnem ngarranggarnin.*

feeling in the ears.
nyin *coverb+LEAVE.* forget and leave something.
• *Walig-garri noonaya, nyinji-ngarri noonawoorroodge berrema belegan. When I put it inside, I forgot then and left it here in the middle.* [NOTE: also heard as *nyirn*, *nyen*, and *nyern*]
nyin *coverb+GET.* forget. • *Jalarinyi nyina nginimanyji. The white crane forgot about it then.* • *Nyin noonamangge. I forgot them.* [NOTE: also heard as *nyirn*, *nyen*, and *nyern*]
nyindoorrg *coverb+SPEAR.* spear right through.
• *Werndij wanema-noo. Wayi! Nyindoorrg giningaboord. He (bat) threw a spear at him. Oh goodness! He speared him right through.*
nyinge-nyingeg *coverb.* annoy. • *Ragim nyinge-nyingeg-ayi, berde-werdij woomberramande-birri . . . Ants were annoying them like that, climbing all over them . . .*
nyinggelarre *noun.* snot. • *Berrema nyinggelarre-ningi nyoomboorroo. This snot is dripping from his nose.*
nyingginy *noun masculine.* hairy caterpillar, itchy grub. *Euproctis lutea.* [NOTE: also recorded meaning 'scabies', *Sarcoptes scabiei*]
nyingginy, nyinggil, nyinggim *noun.* people in avoidance or restricted relationship.
• *Ngoowan garij joonbimnha thamboorroom, ngajim, nyinggim damga. Don't say the names of mothers-in-law or sisters, it is forbidden, they are to be avoided.*
nyinggiwoony, nyinggiwool, nyinggiwoom REDUP: **nyinggi-nyinggiwoom**. *adjective.* hairy (like an itchy grub), furry (like the leaves of the furry-leaved kapok bush), wooly.
nyingirrinji *verb.* he is WAITING for her.
nyingirriyan *verb.* she is DOING TO HERSELF.
nyingiyana *pronoun.* you are the one, really you (one).
nyingiyangeny, nyingiyangel, nyingiyangem *possessive pronoun.* yours (one).
nyingoowany *pronoun.* you (one) in turn, your turn, yourself. SEE: **nyengoowany**.
nyini *verb.* she SAYS/DOES. SEE: **nyerne**.
nyiniya *verb.* she PUT her/it (feminine).
nyinjinybany *coverb+GET.* start forgetting.
• *Nyinjinybany-ngarri yamberramenya thoowiyanyji. When we start forgetting anything (due to old age).*
nyin'ge *coverb+HIT.* make deaf, make someone forget. • *Berremawa yardem nyin'ge ngenayidji. This (bad cold) made me deaf then.*
nyiny *coverb+SAY/DO.* blow nose. • *Nyiny nginini. He blew his nose.* SEE: **nyoony**.
nyinya *verb.* she IS, she is STAYING.
nyinyande *verb.* she IS, she keeps on STAYING.
nyinyil; niyinyil *noun.* zebra finch. *Taeniopygia guttata.* [NOTE: stole fire in the dreamtime; word used for all other finches as well]
nyireg REDUP: **nyire-nyireg**. *coverb+SAY/DO.* be quiet (e.g. when game is sighted). • *Nyireg-*

nyireg

gala barrern-gili thoowooyanyji boorroordboo-yarri. *All be quiet, something is coming towards us.*

nyireg *coverb+BE/STAY.* stay quiet. • **Nyireg benenha!** *You keep quiet!*

nyiremoorl *coverb+HIT.* take someone down.
• **Nyiremoorl benayidji.** *It (boab tree that had opened for people running from a cyclone in dreamtime) took them down. / It sank down with them.*

nyire-nyire *coverb+SAY/DO.* be lonely, be quiet.
• **Nyire-nyire ngenarn.** *I'm lonely.*

nyirerrege *coverb+FALL/GO_DOWN.* get hit (e.g. by something small like a stone), get stung.
• **Wardawoo nyirerrege ngenaward.** *Ouch, I got hit.*

nyirerrege *coverb+HIT.* hit someone with something small like a stone, sting. • **Danya nyirerrege ngenayidji ngarrgalem-birri.** *That one hit me with a stone.*

nyirl *coverb+GO/COME.* go for a long time. • **Nyirl nginiyi gabinganyji.** *He's been gone a long time, where can he have gone?*

nyirle-nyirleg *coverb+GET.* keep asking someone for something. • **Nyirleg-nyirleg yimberremenbe-yoowoo.** *They keep asking us.* SEE: **beringye, nyirli-nyirligboo.**

nyirlginy, nyirlgil, nyirlgim; nyirlgeny, nyirlgel, nyirlgem *adjective.* persistent, one who forces someone else to keep doing something, someone who can't stop and just keeps going (at Turkey Creek), someone who keeps doing something in spite of being asked to stop. • **Nyirlginy danyga jiyiliny.** *That man is really persistent in asking.* • **Dalga ngalil nyirlgil, loorroobjinhawool jiyilem.** *That woman is really persistent chasing after men.* • **Nyirlginy yardewoorriny rangga-girri-woorroony. Thoorlg ginini.** *He won't listen, he is deaf and keeps doing his own thing (in spite of what anyone tells him). His ears are blocked.*

nyirli-nyirli *coverb+SAY/DO.* wanting to walk, having itchy feet. • **Nyirli-nyirli ngenarn thambarlamga.** *I have itchy feet (in the idiomatic sense). / My feet are pushing me to keep walking.*

nyirli-nyirligboo *coverb+GET.* want someone to do something everywhere. • **Nyirli-nyirligboo yimberremenbi-yoo.** *They want you and me everywhere (for interviews during the production of 'Fire, fire burning bright').*

nyirli-nyirliwoom *adjective.* people who keeps pushing someone to do something.
• **Nyirli-nyirliwoom gardiyam.** *White people who keep pushing someone to do something.*

nyirndiwarliny *noun.* a tree species. *Phyllanthus reticulatus.*

nyirreg *coverb+HIT.* make bathe, drown someone.
• **Nyirreg ninbijge.** *I will make him bathe. I will make him get into the water.* • **'Googben. Nyirreg dimbirrijtha-boorroo thoowiya,' yirrani-ni.** *'It is a dangerous place. Something might drown you,' we told him.*

nyirreg *coverb+BE/STAY.* be swimming. • **Dama nyirreg-garri boorroonboo wanyanyagem, yilag goorrnga-yoorroong, nyimeniny berroowan.** *When those children go swimming down at the water they might drown themselves.*

nyirreg *coverb+FALL/GO_DOWN.* dive into water, go swimming, get into water, bathe. • **Danya jiyiliny nyirreg nginiwardji goorloon.** *This man dived into the water.* • **Jirrawoony nginini, 'Nyirregboo ngenoowoon'ge'.** *One said, 'I'm going to dive in.'* • **Nyirreg-gala barrawoo-gili melagawiya.** *You all dive in, the lot of you.*
• **Ngoowan nyirreg yirraardjende rarrinybe yirrayinde-berra.** *We did not swim along in the water, we just hung on behind them (hair belts of people wading through the water pushing spinifex to catch fish).*

nyirrega *coverb+SAY/DO.* be swimming. • **Dala ngarlagangarril nyirrega nyerne goorloon.** *This magpie goose is swimming in the water.*
• **Yilag nyirrega berrani-gili.** *They were all down there swimming.* • **Nyirrega yarrani gawiliyiny-ni goorrngan.** *We had a swim in the cold water.*

nyirrega *coverb+SAY/DO_M.* be swimming, be bathing. • **Berrema nyirrega-garri woomberramande.** *This (in the middle of the painting) is where they went swimming.*

nyirrng *coverb+BRING/TAKE.* grab someone from two sides, 'double-bank em'. • **Nyirrng ngoorranybe jirrawoony.** *They grabbed the one man from both sides.*

nyiwiny, nyiwinyji *noun masculine.* mosquito.
• **Nyiwiny-moowam boorralega-nga.** *My only food is mosquitoes (binyjirrminy the bat talking).*

nyiwirle *noun.* tip of tail of goanna or snake.
• **Nyiwirle dama.** *That is the tip of the tail.*

nyiyilinji *verb.* he is PUTTING her/it (feminine).

nyiyilinyande *verb.* she keeps on PUTTING her/

Figure 74. *Nyirreg: Garnanil Helen Clifton: Nyawanal nyirreg nyanewardja goorloon.*

it (feminine).
nyiyinjende *verb.* he keeps on HITTING her/it (feminine).
nyiyinji *verb.* he is HITTING her/it (feminine).
nyiyinya *verb.* she keeps on HITTING her/it (feminine).
nyiyirringarnany *noun masculine.* spinifex snake-eyed skink. *Proablepharus reginae.* [NOTE: harmless small lizard that looks like a snake, lives in spinifex country]
nyiyirriny *noun masculine.* spinifex. *Triodia sp.* [NOTE: word used for all smaller common spinifex species; contrasts with *miloowoony* or *gerlerneny*, the tall strong-smelling types used to make resin, *gaalji*, and the large, very hard species *garral-garralji* or *jirriny-jirrinyji*]
nyiyooloonji *verb.* he is PUTTING her/it (feminine).
nyood *coverb+PUT.* make rain. • Gaboo-wanyji nyood-anyji ngoorrayangbe ngoowan. *Maybe someone made the rain or maybe not.*
nyooloojge *verb.* will I HIT her, I want to/should HIT her.
nyooloongoon'gende *verb.* I always want to EAT it (feminine).
nyoomarlig *coverb+HIT.* make soapy. • Ngali-ngalim nyaj ngoorroomenbe dany mangoonyji nyoomarlig dambi goorloom thedji-girrim dam goorndarrim. *Women use the bark of the* mangoonji *(freshwater mangrove) tree to make a soapy lather, to kill and catch fish.*
nyoomarlim *noun.* soap. [NOTE: wattle species like *gan'goorlji* that have curly seed pods that make soaplike suds when swished through water]
nyoombany *noun.* grass yam, type of edible root. *Ipomoea sp. aff graminea.* • Ngeleli nyamanel jarrij nyanini melagawoom nyoombam. *This old woman dug up many* nyoombany *roots.* [NOTE: was dug by echidna in dreamtime; found in sandhill country, has leaves and vine like a sweet potato but different from *garndiny*; some people say *nyoombany*, others say *yoombany*]. SEE: **yoombany**.
nyoomberridbe *verb.* if they had HIT her. • Waj-ngarri nyoomberridbe-ni dal thamboorroo-gal . . . *If they had given him that woman of his mother-in-law skin . . .*
nyoombiyidja *verb.* she wanted to HIT her.
nyoomboojji *verb.* he should/could HIT her/it (feminine).
nyoombooninya *verb.* if she WAS/WAS STAYING.
nyoomboorriwidbe *verb.* if they had HIT her, if they had GIVEN her. SEE: **nyoomboorriyidbe**.

nyoomboorriyinbe

Figure 75. *Nyoon-nyoon: Lena Nyadbi: Nyawoorrool girr woomenya nyoon-nyoon-girrem.*

nyoomboorriyinbe *verb.* if they are HITTING her, if they are GIVING her.
nyoomboorroo *noun.* nose. SEE: **marnale**.
nyoomboowardja *verb.* she nearly FELL/WENT DOWN.
nyoomoog *coverb+HIT.* drown someone, knock someone into water. • Nyoomoog-anyji nyoombiyidja. *She (rainbow snake) must have wanted to drown her (woman who took a photo).*
nyoomoorloonji *verb.* he HAS her/it (feminine).
nyoomoorloonya *verb.* she HAS her/it (feminine).
nyoon *coverb+BRING/TAKE.* rub something on someone or something (e.g. paint). • Nyoon nginanya. *She rubbed it on him.*
nyoon *coverb+GET.* rub something on someone or something (e.g. paint). • Danya doomboony nyoon nginimanyji gooma nhawoon. *That is the owl he painted just like him (talking about photo of Hector Jandany's painting).* SEE: **barrg, boonoo, yoorr.**
nyoon-nyoon *coverb+SAY/DO.* rub something on someone or something (e.g. paint). • Nyoon-nyoon boorroorn. *They are painting.* SEE: **yoorr.**
nyoonggayany, nyoonggayal, nyoonggayam *adjective.* alright.
• Nyoonggayan-ma-ngoo? *Are you alright?* SEE: **jirrayam**.
nyoonggayam *interjection.* alright, OK. SEE: **jirrayam**. [NOTE: much more frequent than *jirrayam* in Halls Creek]
nyoongoon *coverb+SAY/DO.* be moving, be shaking (e.g. country when it is thundering, leaves when the wind blows). • . . . nyoongoon birrirn-ninggi, daambi . . . *the country will be shaking on you (moving, ready for the rainbow snake at the beginning of the wet to pull you in).* • Dam bimbirriyinbe-ngarri mirrngim nyoongoon-ngarri boorroorn. *Video camera (i.e. that thing that will be giving faces when they are moving).*
nyoony *coverb+SAY/DO.* blow nose. • Nyoony nginini. *He blew his nose.* SEE: **nyiny**.
nyoore-nyoore *coverb.* whistling in ears as a sign. • Nyoore-nyoore ngenarn yardem

ngagenybe daam bawoo-wawoo boorroorn-ngirri. *I hear whistling in my ears, my country is calling me.* SEE: **nhoorr, noorroo.**

nyoorl *coverb+SAY/PLACE_REFL.* give up hope, realise one is about to die, give up in a fright. • Ngoowana nyoorl berrayilin-doo boorroowanyda na. *They (the young men) were not told to do it, they did it themselves.* • Nyoorl yarrayilinnya. *We are going to die.* [NOTE: Peggy Patrick said of the people who died in the Bedford Downs massacre when they realised they were doomed]

nyoorlg-nyoorlg *coverb+SAY/DO.* whimper. • Warlarlayimga nyoorlg-nyoorlg boorroorn. *All the puppies are whimpering.*

nyoornayi REDUP: **nyoornayi-nyoornayi.** *coverb+SAY/DO_M.* scavenge, eat old bones with no beef (e.g. crow).

nyoorrg *coverb+BE/STAY.* snore. • Nyoorrg ginji nyoorrmirlib. *He is snoring.* SEE: **nyoorrmirlib.**

nyoorrmilib *coverb+BE/STAY.* snore. • Nyoorrmilib ngininiyin. *He's snoring.* • Nyoorrmilib berraniyin-gili. *They are all snoring.* SEE: **nyoorrg.**

nyoorrnga *coverb+BE/STAY.* hill coming down to a point. • Nyoorrnga nginji. *It (hill) is standing with the end pointing in a particular direction.*

nyoorroongool, nyoorroongoony *noun.* platypus, *Ornithorhynchus anatinus*; water rat. *Hydromys chrysogaster.* SEE: **daboonggool.** [NOTE: Rusty Peters and Hector Jandany said the platypus in Sydney Zoo was *nyoorroongool*; Rusty Peters did not think the water rat in Territory Wildlife Park was *nyoorroongool*. Sophia Mung saw a platypus in a creek near Woorreranginy in about 2008; feminine gender suffix used more frequently than masculine]

nyoorroorn-nyoorroornel *noun feminine.* small thing like a crab that lives at the edge of the water. [NOTE: eaten by *bilinyirrinyirril*, 'dotterel', that lives at the edge of the water]

nyoowool; nyoowooloogoo REDUP: **nyoowool-nyoowooloogoo.** *directional.* to the south.

nyoowoolgoorloorr *directional.* further to the south.

nyoowooloogbany, nyoowooloogbal, nyoowooloogbam *adjective.* south going. • Dala nyoowooloogbal. *That one has gone south herself.*

nyoowoonya *verb.* she is FALLING/ GOING DOWN.

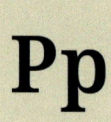# Pp

pshaa, shaa *interjection.* said when speaking to country, word said to cause important effect.

Rr

raginy, ragil, ragim noun. ant.

raj coverb+GO/COME. be thirsty. • Raj nginiyi. *He is thirsty.* • Raj ngenayi. *I am thirsty.*

ral coverb+SAY/DO. pull out (grass).
• Goorndoogany ral ngerne minybernem. *The little girl is pulling out grass.*

rambe-rambem; ramboo-ramboom adjective. light (weight). SEE: **rarangem**.

ramoob REDUP: **ramoob-ramoob**. coverb+SAY/DO_M. eat by stuffing handfuls of food in mouth. • Joorndambi men'gawoom ramoob woomberramande. *They used to eat bush onions by stuffing handfuls in their mouths.* SEE: **mangoony, ngambooroony**.

randany coverb+GET. pull out. • Jarlangarnany baarn-moowam, randany benamanyjende. *The plains kangaroo kept pulling out only spiders.*

rang coverb+PUT. put sticking up. • Ngelga woorranggool, rang, nyimberrayangbende-ngarri ngenengga-yoorroong. *This is the kind of headdress with wool and sticks sticking up they used to put on here (shows putting vertical things around the head).*

rangarrg; ranggarrg coverb+FALL/GO_DOWN. be dawn. • Jadany nawarrany nginiwardjende-yarri, rangarrg nginiward. *Big rain fell on us right up until daybreak.*

rangarrg coverb. be dawn. • Rangarrg wanini. *It is just on dawn.*

rangarrwam noun. dawn.

rangarrwan temporal. at dawn. • Warrambany loorlg nginiyin-yarri rangarrwan. *The floodwater came down on us early in the morning.*

Figure 76. *Ragim: Ragim rarrawooloob boorroorn.*

rangarrwanyge

rangarrwanyge *coverb.* do something all night until dawn. • *Goonthoorrg ngelamande rangarrwanyge.* I was coughing all night.

rangarrwayan *temporal.* just at dawn, right at dawn.

rangga *coverb+SAY/DO_REFL.* listen to/hear each other. • *Rangga berrengirriyan-doo.* They were listening to each other.

rangga REDUP: **rangga-rangga**. *coverb+SAY/DO.* hear, listen, understand.
• *Yagengam jarragboo dam, ngoowan rangga ngenarn.* That is a different language; I can't understand it.

rangga *coverb+BRING/TAKE.* hear, listen, understand. • *Thoorranyji rangga nooniyin'ge.* I can hear something.
• *Rangga-ma yimbirrinha jarrag-garri ngenarn-narri?* Do you listen when I talk to you? • *Rangga-ngarri nyimberriyinbe, mooloonggoo-galem-anyji miyalega.* When they hear it (katydid grasshopper), all the game will be fat. • *Ngoowan, ngoowan rangga ngoorranybe gaboowa nginini-birri.* No, they could not understand what he said to them.

rangga *coverb+GET.* hear, listen. • *Rangga nginimanyji.* He heard him.

ranggab *coverb+BE/STAY.* listen. • *Ranggab nyanininya.* She was listening. • *Ranggab barrenha-boorroo-yoo.* You listen to the two of them.

rangga-rangga *coverb+GO_ALONG.* go along listening. • *Wananyanggem-boorroo rangga-rangga wiyinjende danyga joowany.* That dangerous night bird always goes along listening for children.

ranggarrg *coverb+BECOME.* be a bit of light (just after sunrise or just before sunset).
• *Ranggarrg waniyid.* It is still light. SEE: **rangarrg**.

ranggoo *noun.* lungs. SEE: **gawoom**.

Ranijan *noun.* Fig Tree Gorge.

rany *coverb+GET.* make a rude hand sign at someone. • *Rany nginimanyji.* He made a rude sign at him.

rarangeg *coverb+GET.* make something light (weight). • *Rarangeg jimberramenbe.* They make it light (termite larvae that has been cleaned).

rarangem *adjective.* light (weight). SEE: **rambe-rambem**.

rard *coverb+FALL/GO_DOWN.* trip over.
• *Minybernem rard nginiwardji.* He tripped over in the grass.

rardbany *coverb+GO/COME.* trip over while going along (e.g. in long grass). • *Ngoowan nginya, goothoongoony, rardbany ngoowiyi, yiroowoonji-ni goothoongoony.* No, this one is too short, he might get tangled up (in the grass) as he goes, this mouse is a short one.

rardbany *coverb+FALL/GO_DOWN.* trip over. • *Danya goothoongoony rardbany ngoowoonji.* That little short one is tripping over.

rarr *coverb+GO_ALONG.* pull something up.
• *Diyama rarr woomberranybendi-yoo.* That's what they two were pulling up.

rarrawoolib *coverb+GO/COME.* run/move around in a group (e.g. ants or shoal of fish).

rarre-rarriny *coverb+SAY/DO.* be hanging.
• *Rarre-rarriny boorroorn goowoole-yirrin.* They (black cockatoos and little corella) are hanging in all the trees.

rarrgalen *temporal.* at sunrise.

rarrgalil *noun feminine.* sunrise.

rarrgaliyan; rarrgalewaniny *temporal.* time when it is still light just before the sun goes down

rarribany *noun masculine.* basket. LIT: 'hanging having something, hanging having string'.

rarrim *noun.* string, human hair handle of water container. • *Doomoomga wiyird boomberrayidbende yambarramga rarrima ngarag boomberramangbende.* They used to spin hair to make handles.

rarriny REDUP: **rarri-rarriny**; **rarre-rarriny**. *coverb+BE/STAY.* be hanging. • *Rarriny-ngarri boorroonboo-nga daamga ngaginybega laarne goowooloon.* My home is hanging up there in the tree (willie wagtail).

rarriny REDUP: **rarre-rarriny**. *coverb+HAVE.* hold something that is hanging down. • *Rarriny ngoomoorloonji.* He is dangling him/it (masculine), he is holding it up while it hangs down. • *Rarriny nyoomoorloonya.* She is dangling her/it (feminine), she is holding it up while it hangs down.

rarriny REDUP: **rarre-rarriny**. *coverb+HIT.* carry something that is hanging down.
• *Goorndoogany rarriny nyiyinji darndal bajalarribaya.* The little boy is carrying a turtle in a bucket.

rarrinybe *coverb+GO/COME.* go along hanging on.
• *Rarrinybe yirrayinde-berra.* We just went

Rawooliliny

Figure 77. *Rarrwayi*: John Gallagher: *Rarrwayi boorroonboo goorndarrim.*

along hanging on behind them (onto the hair belts of old people fishing by pushing a wall of spinifex through the water).

rarrinyboo *coverb+SAY/DO.* be hanging.
- *Rarrinyboo nginji laarne.* It is hanging up there.

rarrirrij *coverb+GET.* pull something out.
- *Rarrirrij bemberramangbende liyirrem.* They used to keep pulling out the guts.

rarrwayi *coverb+SAY/DO_M.* hang on.
- *Rarrwayi yirramande bardoobiny.* We used to hang on behind (to old people's hair belts when they were pushing spinifex through the water to catch fish).

rarrwayi *coverb+BRING/TAKE.* carry something hanging.
- *Rarrwayi benanyji.* He was carrying it hanging down.

rarrwayi *coverb+GO_AFTER.* have something hanging.
- *Dama rarrwayi ngelamiyan'ge, ngamanang ngelamiyan'ge.* I have something hanging in my hands, I have it in my hands in front of me.

rarrwayi *coverb+PUT.* hang something up.
- *Rarrwayi nooniyilen'ge ngaginybe.* I'm hanging up my things.

rarrwayi *coverb+SAY/DO.* carry something hanging.
- *Rarrwayi boorroorn-doo jaboogoom.* They two are carrying the rubbish bin (hanging between them).

rarrwayi *coverb+BE/STAY.* be hanging.
- *Rarrwayi boorroonboo goorloo-yoorroong.* They (flowers) are hanging down towards the water.

rawalgbany *coverb+GET.* collect big mob of fish that have been poisoned by *jaloowib*, 'heaping a pile of grass and other vegetation in the water'; said to be 'like pulling a net'. [NOTE: different from *garlmi*]

rawoolilib *coverb+GO/COME.* go making a rustling noise through grass.
- *Deyena benennha, thoowoo rawoolili nirdande?* You stay there, why are you going through the grass making a rustling noise?

Rawooliliny *noun.* Mount Buchanan. [NOTE: in the dreamtime Rawooliliny was a man who spoke Gija, who stood near Warnambany

rawoorl

(Glass Hill), a man who spoke Miriwoong]

rawoorl *coverb+SAY/DO.* have goosebumps.
- Rawoorl ngenarn. *I've got goosebumps.*

rawoorlgoowany *coverb+GET.* make someone have goosebumps.
- Rawoorlgoowany yindemnha. *You are giving me goosebumps (by tickling).*

rayiny *noun.* little spirit man that lives in the water in springs. [NOTE: can take people away and make them 'clever']

rebej *coverb+GET.* scoop up, dig up.
- Goorndoogany rebej benamanyji roongalga. *The little boy is scooping up the sugar.*

rega *interjection.* don't do it, stop.

reganyda; reganyja *coverb+GO/COME.* sneak up without letting anyone know, come secretly.
- Reganyda yirrayin-ninggi, ngoowan nimbirn-birri. *We came to you secretly, don't tell any one.*

rega-rega *interjection.* stop, wait, no no.

rembarrg *coverb+PUT.* open something to look around.
- Rembarrg biyil dal banjalgjel, noonayangge wanyji dana. *Lift off that blanket, maybe it is there (e.g. when getting help to look for something).*

rembelenga *coverb+FALL/GO_DOWN.* roll over.
- Rembelenga yarriwoo. *We'll roll over soon (said of car on a steep slope).*

reme-remeny-nhawoony, reme-remeny-nhawool, reme-remeny-nhawoom *adjective.* one who gets thirsty.
- Reme-remeny-nhawoon-nga. *I am a person who gets thirsty.*

reminy *coverb+BRING/TAKE.* gasp for breath.
- Reminy benanya jarraggenaa-woorrool. *She was gasping for breath and could not talk (after being chased by a yoonggoony, 'hairy man ghost').*

reminy *coverb+GO/COME.* be thirsty.
- Reminybi yirrardji. *We (singers) are getting short of breath.*
- Reminy ngenayi. *I was thirsty.*
- Reminy yirrayi. *We were thirsty.*
- Reminy berrayi. *They were thirsty.*

reminyge *coverb+EAT.* make self thirsty.
- Reminyge niningoon. *I made myself thirsty (by eating lots of honey).*

reminyge *coverb+PUT.* make thirsty, make gasp for breath.
- Reminyge nginiyanyji laarne dana gamanggarrjiga dany dabaroony gamanggarrji. *The bamboo up there made the pelican thirsty (made him gasp for breath?).*

rendany *coverb+GET.* pull something like a fishing line.
- Gaardaya rendany-gala benem. *Pull it (line) slowly.*
- Wil-wil woomberrama nyamanimbi, nginyi, rendanyji benema garlooroonyi thoorroorroog. *The old women were dancing (in the style with a jumping movement) and this rainbow snake pulled them along then, making the water run (and they drowned).*

rererrij *coverb+GET.* pull out.
- Liyirrim mooloonggoom rererrij bemberramangbende gema-yoorroong. *They used to pull out the intestines and fat.* SEE: **rerr, rerroob** and other reduplicated forms **rererr, rerr-rerr.**

rerr REDUP: rerr-rerr; rererr; rerrerr. *coverb+GET.* pull.
- Rerr boomberramangbende jiwimbi. *They pulled out their spears.*
- Rerrerr nyilamangge. *I pulled her/it (feminine).* SEE: **rererrij, rerroob.**

rerr REDUP: rerr-rerr; rererr. *coverb+SAY/DO_M.* pull.
- Ngelel nyaninyande-ngarri yardemerewany rerr-ngarri wanimayinde mayim-boorroo nawarran-gili booyoorroongboo. *It (wagon/dray) used to go along when the donkey was pulling it to bring food to the big place coming from the north.* SEE: **rererrij.**

rerr REDUP: rerr-rerr; rererr; rererrg. *coverb+SAY/DO.* pull.
- Jiyiliny rerr ngerne jiyirriny. *The man is pulling the kangaroo.*
- Rererrgayi ngenani-ningi liyirrim thoowoo-thoowoom dam jaa-biny. *I pulled out the intestines and everything from its stomach.* SEE: **rererrij.**

rerr *coverb+BRING/TAKE.* pull along.
- Rerr yimberranybende-yarre. *They pulled us along.*

rerreb *coverb+SAY/DO.* pull.
- Rerreb-ngarri nimbirn goonggooloo-biny bib boomanha. *If you pull it by the head you can get it.*

rerreg *coverb+GET.* move something.
- Rerreg benem wayini. *Move it (over there) like that.*

rerreg *coverb+GO/COME.* go backwards, move over.
- Wayinigana ngeleli rerregbe nyidja wayini, gaardaya. *That is how she goes backwards like that, slowly.*
- Rerreg biyarr wayini-bebe. *You move up a bit.*

rerreg *coverb+GO_ALONG.* move backwards, move back sitting on buttocks, shuffle on buttocks.
- Rerreg wiyinji manam-birri. *He is moving*

Figure 78. *Roogoon: Gilmarriyi Joe Thomas, Susan Henry, Delena Henry: Jaangariny roord nginji nhawiyangen daan Roogoon.*

himself backwards on his buttocks.
rerregjel *noun feminine.* small fish species. SEE: **goodabal.** [NOTE: Nyaajarri skin, moves backwards in the mud]
rerroob; roorroob *coverb+GET.* pull up.
 • *Rerroob bemberramangbende deg bemberramangbende.* They used to pull them out and look at them. • *Roorroob nyanema. Deg nyanemanya.* She pulled it (root of kapok bush) up. She looked at it.
Rijarr *noun.* Turner River.
Ringgirriny *noun.* place in Ngarrgooroon country.
ring-ring *coverb+SAY/DO.* sob. • *Goorndoogal ring-ring nyerne.* The little girl is sobbing.
Rinjan *noun.* place near Greenvale.
rinyiny *noun.* idea. • *Rinyim melagawoom.* Lots of smart ideas. [NOTE: 'Rinyim melagawoom' is the name of the Warmun Art Centre–Melbourne University partnership.]
 • *Goonggooloo-bany rinyi-bany men'gawoony.* Brainy one.
riyi REDUP: **riyi-riyi.** *coverb+BE/STAY.* peeping.
 • *Nganyjoowarrji biriwoo nginiyin, riyi ngininiyin.* A snake came back and was peeping in.

riyi REDUP: **riyi-riyi.** *coverb+SAY/DO.* peep.
 • *Berrem ngarrgale-joorroong, girli-ngarri yirrarn, riyi-riyi-ngarri yirrarn bagabam-boorroo.* Here are lots of rocks where we walk along peeping around for echidnas.
roo *coverb+DO_REFL.* hold self. • *Roo ngemiyanyji wayini, jaa-yoorroong.* He is holding himself like this, towards the stomach (said about a photo of a wallaby).
roo *coverb+GET.* hold something. • *Nhenhen ngoorrayangbende:::, wel, roo benamanyjende-birri.* They would poke it in and he would hold it on them. SEE: **gerneg.**
roog *coverb+HIT.* sulk, be offended by someone and sulk (Kriol: 'take a sulk'). • *Wawooleny roog giniyidji mayim-boorroo.* The frillneck lizard was upset and sulked (took a sulk) because of the food (that was stolen by the brown falcon). SEE: **ngoony.**
roog *coverb+GO/COME.* go and sulk, (Kriol: 'take a sulk'). • *Goorndoogal roog nyaniyi.* The little girl went and sulked. • *Nginyi binyjirrminyi roogaa nginiyin.* This bat was sulking then. SEE: **ngoony.**
Roogoon *noun.* Crocodile Hole.
rooloo *coverb+BRING/TAKE.* take someone's place.

roong

Figure 79. *Roord*: Dooldool Norah Bedford: *Ngoorroona roorran roord nyinya Nambinel.*

• Rooloo nginanyji. *He took his place.*
roong *coverb+SAY/DO.* bark. • Roong ngerne joolany. *The dog is barking.*
roongalga *noun.* sugar. SEE: **gerdgardboo, warrayele**.
roonggerr *coverb+SAY/DO_M.* be panting.
• Roonggerr wanemayinde. *He was panting.*
roonggoony *noun.* white currant. *Flueggea virosa.* SEE: **ngoorrwany, berenggarrji, goowarroolji**. [NOTE: shrub bearing masses of small edible white fruit in the wet season, name also used for 'pink river apple', *Syzygium eucalyptoides* ssp. *eucalyptoides*]
roong-roong *coverb+SAY/DO.* bark (dog).
• Joolany roong-roong ngerne. *The dog is barking.* • Roong-roong boorroorn joolam melagawoom. *All the dogs are barking.*
roong-roong *coverb+SAY/DO_M.* bark (dog).
• Roong-roong wanemayinde. *He kept barking.*
roong-roong *coverb+HIT.* bark at someone (dog).
• Roong-roong nyimberrayidbe. *They barked at her.*
roord *coverb+BE/STAY.* be sitting. • Danya woogoony roord nginji. *That is a frog sitting there.* SEE: plural subject **roorrjib**.
roord *coverb+FALL/GO_DOWN.* sit down.

• Nginiyin roord nginiwardji. *He went and sat down.* • Ngoorrool ngalil thad-gayan nyanininyande, ngoowan roord joowoonya? *That woman has been standing up all day, why can't she sit down now?* • Marrge! Roord-gala nginboowoon. *Wait! I want to sit down.*
roord *coverb+HAVE.* sit looking after someone (e.g. children). • Naminyjili Janamany doo Nyawanel roord benemoorloonya-yoo. *Naminyjili is sitting looking after Janama and Nyawana.* • Gangga-gal roord benemoorloonya-yoo berremga. *Their grandmother is sitting with these two looking after them.*
roord *coverb+HIT.* put down. • Bib barrem-joo nawarrany dany lalanggarrany, roord barrij-joo yilag. *You two pick up that big crocodile and put him down there.*
roord *coverb+PUT.* put down, bury person (put in ground at funeral). • Dama wirlmerrem roord boomberrayangbe ganarran. *They put this kidney on the leaves.* • Marrarn roord yirrayanyji yilag jilan. *We buried her (at the funeral). / We already put her down in the ground.* [NOTE: funeral example from Southern dialect]
roord *coverb+PUT.* promise daughter to man.

roowaj-nhawoony, roowaj-nhawool, roowaj-nhawoom

- Dany yagenginy jiyiliny, roord nyilangge-ni ngelela boonthal, ngalilel ngaginyil. *I promised my daughter to that other man (I put her to him).* SEE: **boonthal**.

roorraj *coverb+GET.* swear at someone. • Roorraj benamanyjende, *He used to swear at them.* SEE: **roorrij, roowaj**.

roorrany *coverb+SAY/DO_REFL.* scratch self. • Aa, ngoorroola ngaginyel roorrany nyingirriyan, yayi wanyji nyerne. *Ah, mine over there (female dog) is scratching herself, she must be itchy.* SEE: **girr, therr**.

roorrany *coverb+GET.* scratch a hole (e.g. in ground). • Roorrany gala benem dam yoorayimem-boorroo goorloom. *Scratch a hole in the ground for soak water.*

roorrany, roorram *noun masculine.* grass. • Ngoorroona roorran roord nyinya Nambinel. *Nambin is sitting over there on the grass.* SEE: **minybernem**.

Roorrany; Roorraroorrany *noun.* Jeffrey Well.

roorrij *coverb+SAY/DO_M.* swear. • Marra biyarra roorrij jemenande. *You go away, you keep on swearing.* SEE: **roorraj, roowaj**.

roorrij *coverb+DO_REFL.* swear at each other.
- Bangariny-warriny roorrij berramiyanbi-yoo. *Those two are swearing at each other.* SEE: **roorraj, roowaj**.

roorrijbe *noun.* swearing. • Marrarn berdij nginbiyan, ngoowan rangga nenbega, roorrijbe dam. *I will get up and go away, I can't listen to that swearing.*

roorrjib, roorrji, roorrjeb *coverb+BE/STAY.* sit (plural – more than three). • Roorrjib boorroonboo-gili. *They are all sitting.* SEE: **roord**.

roorroob *coverb+GET.* pull up. SEE: **rerroob**.

roowaj *coverb+SAY/DO.* swear. • Ngoowan roowaj narrirn-doo men'gawoom jarragbega bamberrajtha-yoo. *Don't you two swear, you should use good words.*

roowaj *coverb+GET.* swear someone. • Roowaj yinamenji-yayi. *He is swearing at you and me.*

roowaj-nhawoony, roowaj-nhawool, roowaj-nhawoom *adjective.* one who swears. [NOTE: unusual because suffix is not *th* following *j*]

TH th

thaarr *coverb+BE/STAY.* stand (plural). SEE: **thayarr, tharrb; thad.**

thaa-thaa *coverb+SAY/DO_M.* winnow, shake coolamon to get rid of rubbish. • *Gooral dal thaa-thaa wanemayinde. That mother was winnowing it.* SEE: **therra-therra.**

thab *coverb+GIVE.* put food in someone's mouth (e.g. bird feeding its baby). • *'Gayigana thaba nginbiyinya mayimbi?' ngirni-ngiyi. 'When will she put food in my mouth?' he says to her.*

thad REDUP: **thad-thad.** *coverb+BE/STAY.* to stand (one, two or three people), to be upright.
• *Ngelela Nyidbarriya thad nyinya belegan. This is the hill called Nyidbarriya standing in the middle.* • *Nginyjinya jiyirriny thad nginji. This kangaroo is standing up.* SEE: plural subject **thayarrwa.**

thad *coverb+FALL/GO_DOWN.* stand up, take up a standing position, stay in a standing position.
• *Thad-gala barrewoo. You all stand there.*

thad *coverb+HAVE.* to stand holding something. • *Danya thada ngoomoorloonji jarrambayiny. He is standing holding the goanna.*

thad *coverb+PUT.* to stand something up, to place in an upright position. • *Jiyirriny thad goorrayangbe dawoorrji. They put the upper part of a kangaroo upright there.*

thadboo REDUP: **thathadboo.** *coverb+BE/STAY.* to be standing to be upright. • *Boorrijiny thadboo nginji. The diver jack is standing up (on the branch in an illustration).* • *Darrarroon malngirriny thathadboo nginji girliwirring joodiya. The lighting is standing very straight (from up in the sky) at Wyndham (talking about a photo).*

thagalge *coverb+BECOME.* get poisoned.
• *Thagalge ngelayid. I got poisoned.*

thagalge *coverb+HIT.* poison someone.
• *Thagalge ngoorrayid, ngoowan warda ngoorriyinbe. They poisoned him, they don't like him.*

thagalge *coverb+EAT.* eat something and get poisoned. • *Jang-ngarri nginini, thagalge benangoonji. When he ate it, he was poisoned by it.*

thalalam *noun.* tongue.

thalebal *noun.* woman whose child has died.

thalebany *noun.* man whose child has died.

thalebagboo *coverb+GO/COME.* being a person whose child has died. [NOTE: refers indirectly to the person who died instead of naming them; they would be known to the speaker and addressee]

thaleginy *noun masculine.* river gum, large tree species that has edible gum. *Terminalia platyphylla.* SEE: **nyaarndiny, nyambarrginy, nyarlany, nyaarndem.** [NOTE: common tree with dark bark and big leaves found along creeks, called a 'gum tree' by Gija people because of the edible gum]

thaleng *coverb+PUT.* light fire. • *Thaleng-gala bamberraj. You all light fires.* • *Thaleng benayanji. He lit a fire.*

Figure 80. *Thalngarrji: Thalngarrji thad nginji thawala-bany.*

thamalarrg

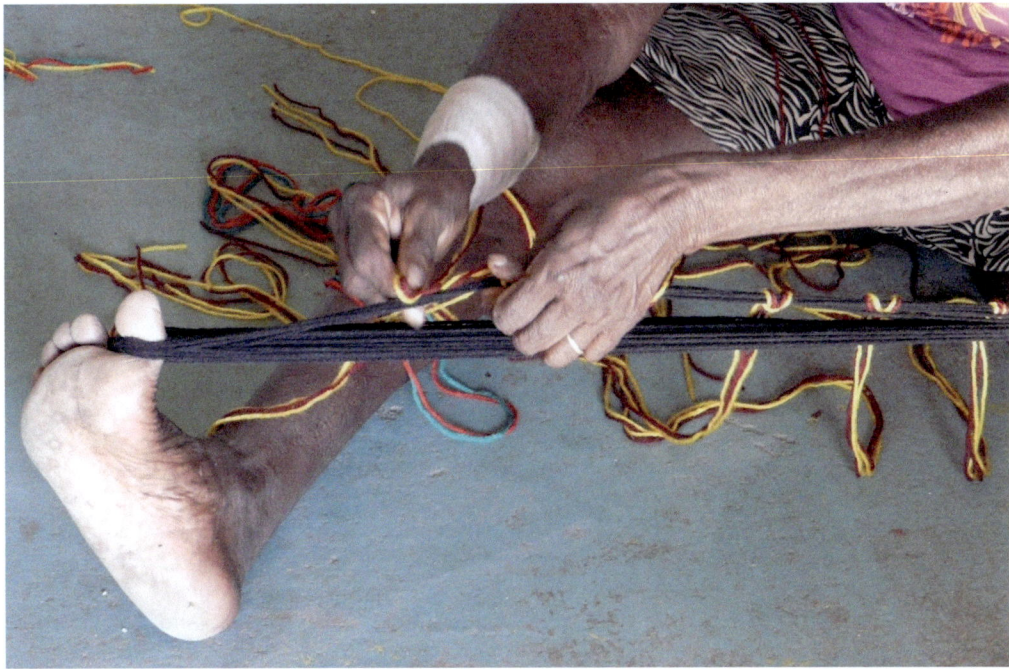

Figure 81. *Thambarlam: Ngarag nyerne goodam thambarlan-ngiyi.*

thalenggeny, thalenggel, thalenggem *adjective.* having no taste, tasteless.
• Men'gawoog-girrimbi miyale, thalenggem-anyji dam giyawoole-yoorroong yirrayinjende jaan-ni. *To make meat good if it has no taste, we used to put the stomach in blood.*

thalerr *coverb+HIT.* chop bark with a sharp stone.
• Berrema-birri thalerr ngoorrayidbe. *They chopped it with this (a sharp stone used as an axe to remove bark from a tree).*

thalerrel *noun feminine.* sharp stone used as an axe to knock bark from tree.

thalg *coverb+GET.* hook up a spear in woomera.
• Thalg nginima, werndij wanema, nginingaboord jiyirriny. *He hooked up his spear in the woomera, he threw it, he speared the kangaroo.*

thalijbel *coverb+FALL/GO_DOWN.* fall and hurt self.
• Thalijbel ngenaward manyjoorroo. *I fell and hurt my knee.* SEE: **geberd, mirl-mirlge**.

Thalinyen *noun.* place in Rusty Peters' country.

Thalinyman *noun.* place in Rusty Peters' country in Springvale. SEE: **Warloo**.

thaliwarn, thaliwarnji *noun masculine.* mountain bloodwood, Kimberley bloodwood, silver-leaved bloodwood. *Corymbia collina.* [NOTE: wood very resistant to white ants; used by Rusty Peters to make posts for the bough shed at the original Ngalangangpum school at Warrmarn in about 1979]

Thalngarrgen; Thalngarrgenyen *noun.* place in black soil country near Wooneba Spring.

thalngarrji *noun masculine.* snappy gum. *Eucalyptus brevifolia, E. confluens.* [NOTE: flowers called *goorramindil*; wood used to make digging sticks and makes good coals for cooking; *daliyany* type of sugar leaf, (lerp) is found on *thalngarr*; leaves used in cooking and in smoking ceremonies to send spirits away]

Thalngarrngarrem *noun.* Red Hill, place just out of Halls Creek.

Thalngarrwany *noun.* Saddler's Jump-Up.

thalooj SEE: **dalooj**.

thaloorrg *coverb+FALL/GO_DOWN.* fall and be burnt up. • Thaloorrg berraward. *They fell and were all burnt up.*

thaloorrg *coverb+HIT.* throw something on fire.
• Ngawoorroowoorroon thaloorrg barrij. *You all throw it on the flames!*

thaloorroony, thaloorroom *noun.* hollow log.

thamalarrg *coverb.* be glad inside. [NOTE:

thamany

Southern dialect]

thamany *noun.* relationship address form used by people who are *thamanyji* or *thamanyel* to speak to each other.

thamanyel, thamanybe *noun.* maternal grandfather's sister, man's daughter's daughter.

thamanyji, thamanybe *noun.* maternal grandfather, maternal grandfather's brother, man's daughter's son. • *Thamany-lang.* The people who are thamany to each other.

Thambanyen *noun.* place in Ngarrgooroon country.

thambarlam *noun.* foot, footprint.

thambem *noun.* side of body. • *Thambejiyan nyanengaboord.* He speared her right in the side.

thamboong *coverb+BE/STAY.* be sticking out. • *Wayiniya thamboong nyinya bring-bi-ngiyi dam.* Its (wagon) springs are still sticking out there.

thamboorrool *noun feminine.* mother-in-law of man.

thamboorroony *noun masculine.* son-in-law of woman, man's mother-in-law's brother.

thamoonmoorroo *noun.* rocky/holey country in gorge.

Thanbinin *noun.* place on Texas Downs.

thard *coverb+HIT.* poke. • *Thard ngenayidjende marlan.* I got poked on the hand (it poked me).

Tharemariny *noun.* Texas Fish Hole. [NOTE: spring with yellow water]

tharimbirij *coverb+GET.* clever at learning, know how to speak, learn language quickly. • *Tharimbirij benamanyji-ngirri jarragbega.* He picked up that story from me quickly.

tharleny, tharlel, tharlem *adjective.* wrinkled (e.g. skin), shrivelled. • *Tharleliya ngoorrooli.* That woman's skin is really all wrinkled. • *Tharlenyi ngoorroonyi.* That man's skin is all wrinkled up.

tharn *coverb+HIT.* hit with something. • *Tharn nginiyid.* He hit him/it (masculine). • *Tharnbe beniyinji.* He is hitting them/it (non-singular) now. • *Tharn benayid.* He hit a peg into the ground. SEE: **dag**.

tharn'geny *noun masculine.* silky wattle. *Acacia acradenia.* [NOTE: stems used to make *jiwiny*, hardwood spear ends; can also mean 'hill kangaroo', *jirrgany*, in some contexts]

tharr *coverb+PUT.* fill up, pour something into something else. • *Tharr noonaya.* I filled it. • *Tharr benayanya.* She poured it in. • *Gardagboo benany tharr-gala benaj.* Bring cups and fill them. SEE: **jamboorn, tharroo, tharroorroo**.

tharranggal *coverb+HIT.* throw a spear at someone, hit with a spear. • *Tharranggal benayidji-birri garloomboom.* He threw a spear at them. / *Ngoorrinya tharranggal nginiyid.* That man threw a spear and hit him.

tharrayab *coverb+GO/COME.* go showing an open space. • *Tharrayab nirda wayiniya jandanben-ngoo.* You are going along showing an open space between your legs, because you are so skinny. (Kriol: 'They can see em you right through la you two leg, you properly bony one.') [NOTE: swearing]

tharrbelil *coverb+BE/STAY.* stand straight and tall. • *Tharrbelil benennha.* You stand up straight and tall ('proper handsome bloke').

tharrboolirr *coverb+BE/STAY.* stand with arms out and chest straight. • *Thaboolirr ngininiyin.* He was standing with his arm held out and his chest straight (in Joonba).

tharrbood *coverb+SAY/DO_M.* pierce. • *Gelengiyana berab giniyi nyangoobam-birri ngininiyin-ngarri tharrbood woomberramang.* Today he came to the doctors and they put a needle in him.

tharrbood *coverb+GET.* spear, poke. • *Tharrbood-garri benamenyji dany-gany, garij-garri bemberremenbe thamboorroo-gam warangganja, dambi ngarliyi na.* When that thing (small catfish spine) pokes them, they call their mother-in-law's name quickly and the pain eases.

tharrbood *coverb+SPEAR.* spear, poke. • *Tharrbood goorrangaboordbende.* They were spearing him.

tharrboodji *coverb+BRING/TAKE.* spear/poke while being taken along. • *Ngayin wanyagen ngenaniyinde-ngarri garlmi yirramande dambi jangangangadan yirraniyin-ngarri, tharrboodji-gayan yimberranybende-yarroo.* When I was little, we used to push spinifex through the water to catch fish, we were children and it (the spinifex) used to poke us as we took it along.

tharreb *coverb+BE/STAY.* stand (plural). • *Ngoorrooma tharreb boorroorn.* There they are standing. SEE: **thayarr, thaarr; thad**.

Figure 82. *Tharriyarrel: Tharriyarrel thad nyinya laarne birrinyen.*

tharreyimerle *noun.* gorge, valley. SEE: **yawilan**.
tharrgi *coverb+SAY/DO_M.* fill up. • Tharrgi wanamayinde-yarri nalijam doo ngoonyjoom blawa benayanyjende-yarri. *He would give us our rations of tea, tobacco and flour.*
tharrgi *coverb+SAY/DO.* fill up. • Tharrgl nginini. *He filled it up.* Tharrgi boorroorn jaboogoo-yoorroong. *They are filling up the bucket. / They are pouring it into a deep dish.*
tharrimin *noun.* hook spear.
tharriny *coverb+SAY/DO.* copulate. • Tharriny-ma nanini garli? *Were you fucking, Niece? (joke among friends)* SEE: **moorniny**.
tharriyarril; tharriyarrel *noun feminine.* rainbow.
tharriyarril *noun feminine.* silver grevillea. *Grevillea refracta.* SEE: **garndarndarrji**.
tharrmoong *coverb+PUT.* put food into mouth. • Wayini niliyin'ge marlan-ga-birri nawarrayaya tharrmoong niyilin'ge thoowernde-yoorroong mayin-ga rayijga. *I put the rice with my hand like this and stuff it in my mouth.*
tharroo REDUP: **tharroo-tharroo**. *coverb+PUT.* pour water. • Tharroo benayanyji. *He poured away the water.* • Tharroo beniyilinya bajalarri-yoorroong. *She is pouring it (water) into the tin.* SEE: **tharr, tharroorroo**.
tharroorroo *coverb+SAY/DO.* drip through (rain); come in and out of hole (bees); water run down. • Jadanyga tharroorroo ngerne-birri girliwirring. *The rain is pouring down on them from up there.* • Ngawooram tharroorroo boorroorn. *The sugarbag bees are coming in and out of the hole.*
thawalam REDUP: **thathawalam**. *noun.* flower.
thawoolarrji, thawoolarrel, thawoolarrem *adjective.* skiting fellow, braggart. • Nyengen-ga thawoolarre-ngoo. *You are a skiting fellow.* • Ngayin-ga miyi thawoolarre-nga. *I'm a skiting fellow too.* • Nginyga miyi thawoolarrji. *He's a skiting one too.* • Ngelelga miyi thawoolarrel. *She is a*

Thawooloon

skiting one too.

Thawooloon *noun.* Hann Spring.

Thawoon'goorroo *noun.* Elbow Hole.

-thawoony, -thawool, -thawoom, -nhawoony, -nhawool, -nhawoom, *suffix.* one who does that kind of thing. [NOTE: attached to coverbs forming nouns]

thawoorem; thawooroom *noun.* beard, moustache.

thayad *coverb+GO/COME.* go and talk to family after a death. • *Thayad-gala yarra-birri namboorrarrim. Let's go and talk to all the family who have lost their relation.*

thayarr *coverb+BE/STAY.* stand (non-singular). • *Thayarrwa yirraniyin-gili. We were all standing up then.* • *Joomooloom berrema melagawoom thayarr boorroonboo welangen. Lots of boab trees are standing here in front.* SEE: **tharrb, thad.**

thayarr; thaarr *coverb+FALL/GO_DOWN.* stop and stand (plural, more than three). • *Goowoo, (berrem-doo) thayarr berrawardbi-yarri. They have just come and stopped near us (car full of people looking at two wallabies) (say those two wallabies in the photo).* SEE: **thad, tharrb.**

thayin *locative.* side of something, edge of something. • *Danya bardib wiyinji thayin. That one is walking on the edge of the bank.* • *Goowooleny bardal-ngarri nginiward, ngoorrinya girli wiyinji thayin. That man is walking along the side of the tree that has fallen down.*

thayinbe *coverb+GO_ALONG.* go along the side or edge of something. • *Danya thayinbe wiyinji banderre. That one is walking on the edge of the bank.*

theb *coverb+SAY/DO.* deaf, have blocked ears. • *Theb-anyji nginini yardembi. His earholes must be blocked up. He must be deaf. He maybe didn't hear.*

theb *coverb+PLACE_M.* shut, block off. • *Theb waniya-ngiyi. / Theb waniyanyji-ngiyi ngarrgalem-birri. He shut her up with a stone (blocked the passageway).* • *Theb waniya-noowa yiligin. He blocked it up behind him (leaving him stuck inside).*

theb *coverb+PUT.* close, shut, block off. • *Theb benaya. He/she closed it.* • *Theb-gala nheraj. Let me close it. / I'll close it up.* SEE: **berreb.**

theb *coverb+SAY/PLACE_REFL.* close self up (e.g. inside house). • *Theb berrayilinbe. They shut themselves up (inside the house).*

thebag *coverb+SAY/DO_M.* spit. • *Thebag woomenyande. She is spitting all the time.* • *Thebagma jemenande. Why are you spitting all the time?* • *Thebag-gala ngenda. I want to spit. / I'll have to spit. / Let me spit.* SEE: **thoobag.**

thebbany *coverb+BE/STAY.* be deaf. • *Garawirrim thebbany-ngarri berraniyin jiyilem joo wagoom. Lots of (old) people are deaf, black and white.*

theberr, theberrg SEE: **deberrg.**

thed *coverb+HIT.* hit and kill. • *Jarloongoorroom jiyilem-ngage gooningarrim, ngaboom-berra joowarrim, jarloongoorroom thed-garri bembirriyinbe ngaginybe goonim. My dreaming is the spirit of a handsome man that has been killed, that is the dreaming from my father.* • *Ngawoojiny diyena thed goorrayidbe-nga ngalim-berra. They killed my ngawooji (father's mother's brother/husband's brother/woman's son's child) at that place because of women.* • *Jigirridji thed nyaniyidji warlimarrgool. The willie wagtail killed the butterfly.* • *Thed namberrijtha-boorroo-yoo. They are going to kill you two.*

thed *coverb+FALL/GO_DOWN.* kill self. • *Marra thed nyanoowardja ngaloowanyda. She killed herself.*

thed *coverb+CUT_REFL.* kill self. • *Thed giniwarenji nhawoowarriny. He killed himself.*

thed *coverb+GO/COME.* hit and kill. • *Nginiyin:::, thed-jaliny nyaniyi, goorlgoon nyaliny nyanany. He kept going, he killed another one and put it in his hair belt too.*

thed *coverb+WOUND.* hit and kill. • *Thed-anyji-wa goorrawoonbe. They must have wanted to kill him.*

thed *coverb+SAY/DO_M.* hit and kill. • *Thed woomberramande-boorroo. They used to kill them.*

thedayi *coverb+SAY/DO.* winnow. • *Thedayi berrani minyjaarram larndoorre-birri. They cleaned the rubbish from the black plums by shaking them in a coolamon.* SEE: **therra.**

thedbany *coverb+HIT.* hit. • *Thedbany nyimberrayidbe gananybe-birri. They hit her with a digging stick.*

thedbany *coverb+HIT/CUT.* kill together. • *Thedbany nyimberramoowoonboo wigibaya. They killed her together with her* daughter. [NOTE: *moo-* inserted before the stem shows action together]

thedginy, thedgil, thedgem *adjective.* one that has been hit and killed, dead one.

thedji *coverb+GO_ALONG.* go along killing. • Thedji ngilin'gende nyiwiny-moowam. *I go along killing only mosquitoes.*

thedji *coverb+SAY/DO.* hit and kill.
• Woorajbana yirrayin-ngarri damboowa garnanganyjambi:::, galamoordambi thedji nginini-yarre Joongoorranyi. *When we were coming back this way Joongoorra killed emus and turkeys for us.*

thedji *coverb+SAY/DO_REFL.* hit and kill each other. • Warna-warnarram thedji-ngarri berrangirriyinbende wajbaloom, jiyilem, gibingarnam. *It was a long time ago when white men and Aboriginal people living in the bush were killing each other.*

thedji *coverb+GET.* kill. • Wentha berrembi wajbaloom berrayin-ngarri, thedji bemberramangbende raivele-birri, poisonabat woomberramande na. *Well, when the white men came they were killing them with rifles and poisoning them then.*

thedji *coverb+SAY/DO_M.* hit, hit in the mind and make mad. • Nawane yarra ngoorramangboo berrembi, ngelgawayi warrg-garri woomberramande joowarrim goowi thedji woomberramande yarden. *They took him away to this cave, it was when they were dancing with this kind of Joonba headdress, the spirits just hit him in the ears (and made him mad / made him listen to them only).*

thel *coverb+HIT.* cut down tree, cut off at base.
• Thel biyij! *Cut down the tree!* • Thel benayid. *He cut down the tree.* • Thel ngoorrayidbe wenggarrem. *They cut off his head (lit. 'They cut his neck').* • Theloowoo ngiyinji garndiny goowooloony chainsaw-em-birri. *He is cutting down the tree, right at the base with a chainsaw.*
• Thel gala noondij begerrgajim-birri mayim nginy goodoojany. *I'm going to cut up this round tucker (pumpkin) with a knife.*

thel *coverb+SAY/DO_M.* cut down. • Ngoorroo-ngoorroo-biny thel woomberrama-noo. *They cut him down from every side.*

thelberr *coverb+GET.* open stomach, gut something. • Thelberr yirramangjende. *We used to cut open the stomach to get the guts out.*

thelberr *coverb+HIT.* open stomach. • Thelberr nginiyid. *He opened up the stomach.*
• Thelberra beniyinji. *He cut open their stomachs then.*

thelberr *coverb+SAY/DO_M.* cut up meat.
• Jirrayanyaya ngarliyi, warany thelberr booma. *It's alright, it is cool now you can cut it up (cooked meat).*

thelbij *coverb.* pull out guts. • Berrema thelbij yirrani wayinigana bagabam, melagawoom. *Here we gutted lots of echidnas.*

thelinyjany *noun.* water sedge, reed. *Cyperus vaginatus.* SEE: **theltheny**.

theliny-thelinyji, theliny-thelinyel *noun.* Eucalyptus species, Halls Creek white gum. *Eucalyptus cupularis.*

thelngim *adjective.* something that has been cut down (e.g. a tree that has been cut down for a long time).

thelngoorroob *coverb+BE/STAY.* be with back to someone/action. • Thelngoorroob nginji. *He has his back to someone (sitting or standing).* • Thelngoorroob nyinya. *She is sitting or standing with her back to someone.*
• Thelngoorroob boorroonboo. *They are sitting or standing with their backs to someone*

thelngoorroob *coverb+FALL/GO_DOWN.* turn back on someone/action. • Bardoobiny ngoorriri yarraja, thelngoorroob-garri noomboowoonnha. *We'll talk about you when you turn your back.*

theltheny *noun.* water sedge, reed. *Cyperus vaginatus.* SEE: **thelinyjany**.

themberrbe *coverb+BECOME.* be really smelly.
• Themberrbe ngelayid. *I'm really smelly.*

themerr *coverb+FALL/GO_DOWN.* die.
• Themerr-ngarri boorroowoonbe, boorroonboo-ngarri yoongoom marrarn boorroordboo gerloorroogoo barlberrwany. *When people die and are lying there, their spirits float away.*

thenbel REDUP: thenbel-thenbel. *coverb+HIT.* pull out guts, gut something. • Thenbel niniyid jarrambayiny. *I pulled out the goanna's guts.* • Thenbel ngoorrayid-doo mirlim doo thoowoo-thoowoom. *The two of them gutted it (kangaroo) pulling out the liver and everything.* • Thenbel-thenbel niniyidge jarrambayiny dany. *I gutted that goanna.*

thenbelbany *coverb+GO/COME.* come out.
• Warlawoorroowoorroo thenbelbany nginiyi miloowoony-ningi, nyiyirriny-ningi, marliny-

thengam

ningi. *The tall grass flowers are coming out on the long spinifex, the shorter spinifex or the cane grass.*

thengam noun. foot. [NOTE: said to be 'heavy Gija'] SEE: **thambarlam**.

thengangelanyji interrogative. some kind of female or feminine one, I am not sure which kind she is. • Thengangelanyji, Nagarralanyji. *I am not sure which skin she (black cockatoo) belongs to, maybe Nagarra.*

thengawiny noun. black ant species that bites and makes you swell. SEE: **binginy**.

thengela interrogative. what is this thing of feminine class? • Thengela ngeli? *What is this feminine thing?*

thengenge REDUP: **thengeyenge**. *coverb+SAY/DO.* make buzzing noise and be unable to speak (hornet in dreamtime), feel shame and be unable to speak. • Thengenge ngerne dany boorrngoornngoornji. *That hornet could only make a buzzing noise.* • Thoowoo-boorroo thengenge narroorn, ganybele? *Why can't you all talk properly, do you feel ashamed?* • Thoowoo-boorroo thengeyenge-ma nerne? *Why do you feel ashamed?* SEE: **moojoong, ganybel**.

thenggerrb-ngem; thenggerrngem adjective, noun. torn, a tear (something torn). • Thenggerrb-ngem-baya joorrooloonggoombi-ninggi bardoon-ninggi. *You have a tear in your trousers at the back.*

thera *coverb+PUT.* lever something out. • Thera-gala noondaj-ngiyi. *I'll have to lever it (to get) her (echidna) out.*

thera *coverb+GO/COME.* go levering something out. • Gananybe-birri ngaliyangem thera nyaninyande jamernde-biny. *She used to lever it out from the antbed with her digging stick.*

thera *coverb+SAY/DO_M.* lever something out, turn something over with a long stick. • Ngenayin dijgawoorr goowooloony theraji ngelema dany gerlerneny nawarrarrany. *I went with a long stick and then I turned over that big spinifex.*

therdboo *coverb+HIT.* pull up spinifex. • Therdboo ngiyinji Jagarrany gerlerneny warij-girrim. *Jagarra is pulling up the type of spinifex used to make resin, to hit it to get the resin.*

thereg *coverb+SAY/PLACE_REFL.* bury self. • . . . thereg-garri nyiliyanya . . . *where she buries herself (sand frog)*

thereg *coverb+BE/STAY.* be covered up, buried. • Therreb berraniyin-doo deyena. *They were both covered up there.*

thereg *coverb+DO_REFL.* bury self. • Dala nangala-nangala thereg nyanimiyinya jilan. *That sand frog is burying herself in the ground.*

thereg *coverb+PUT.* bury, cover with dirt. • Thereg-jaliny ngoorrayangboo. *They covered him up again.*

thereg REDUP: **theriyereg**. *coverb+BE/STAY.* be buried. • Goo yangirni dany boonban thereg-garri nginji. *But who is that buried near the cabbage gum?* • Goord berraard melagawiya, berrembe theriyereg boorroonboo na. *They are all dead and buried now.*

thereg *coverb+PUT.* bury, cover with dirt. • Thereg benayanyji. *He covered it with dirt.*

therema *coverb+SAY/DO_M.* camp alone. • Jimbirla-gariny therema wanemayinde. *He camped by himself for a long time, all through his country called Jimbirla (north from Crocodile Hole).*

therl *coverb+HIT.* bust em bottle. • Therl nyimberrayidbe. *They knocked her/it (feminine) down.* • Therl bemberrayidbe mooloogoonbe. *They smashed the glass.* SEE: **woor, woonboorr**.

therlad *coverb+BRING/TAKE.* hit accidentally. • Therladji nyinanyande milan. *She was accidentally hitting herself on the vagina then (when making the drumming sound by hitting the space between crossed legs while sitting and singing – said as joke when talking about an old woman making the sound).*

therlad *coverb+FALL/GO_DOWN.* get hit by something. • Therlad nyanewardja ngarrgalen. *She hit herself (accidentally) on a rock.*

therlad *coverb+HIT.* hit someone/something. • Therlad nyimberrayid goonyjam-birri. *They hit her with a stick.*

therlam noun. 1. back, backbone. 2. underside of woomera.

thern *coverb+GO/COME.* be unable to look back (e.g. because of stiff neck). • Thern nginiyi, wad-girriwoorroony. *He ran away with a stiff neck without looking back.*

therr REDUP: **therr-therr**. *coverb+DO_REFL.* scratch self. • Therr ngimiyanyji. *It is scratching itself (animal).* • Danya joolany therr-therr ngimiyanyji birlinybany-anyji. *That dog is scratching itself, maybe it has ticks.*

therr *coverb+SAY/DO_REFL.* scratch self. • Therr ngingirriyin jiyirriny. *The kangaroo is scratching itself.* SEE: **therr-therr**.

therra-therra *coverb+SAY/DO.* be winnowing, be shaking something to clean out all the rubbish and leaves. • Therra-therra nyerne gawoornbe. *She is cleaning the rubbish out of the ash by winnowing (shaking in a container).*

therra-therra *coverb+GET.* winnow, shake, clean out all the rubbish and leaves from something by shaking. • Larndoorroo bemberriliyinbe-ngarri minyjaarram-anyji, therra-therra bemberremenbe ganarram. *When they put something in a coolamon, maybe black plum, they shake it to clean out all the rubbish.*

therraj *coverb+HIT.* defecate. • Berlgerren-ngarri wimbiji-ngirri, miyawa therraj diwijge. *When my stomach is completely stuffed I'll have to shit it out.* SEE: **therrilaj**.

therramij *coverb+SAY/PLACE_REFL.* cover self up (e.g. goanna in hole, grub in tree). • Ngayin-ga lajen-nga. Googanda therramij nginbiyilijge. *I am a witchetty grub. I'm only good for covering myself up in trees.*

therranggelji *noun.* kurrajong species. *Brachychiton viscidulus.* SEE: **banjaroony**.

therrbag REDUP: **therrbag-therrbag**. *coverb.* cut up something. • Therrbag-therrbag yarridja mayinyi dany garnawoonyga. *We cut up the cheeky yam roots.* • Therrbag nginiyi goowooloony. *He cut a stick.*

therrbeg *coverb+FALL/GO_DOWN.* get stuck, become stuck, be bogged. • Therrbeg nyaneward ngoorr-ngoorrgajil. *The car got bogged.* • Therrbeg nyaneward jilan. *It got stuck in the ground.*

therrendang *coverb+BE/STAY.* be facing someone, turn to face someone.

therrendang *coverb+GO_ALONG.* go along facing someone. • Therrendang wiyinjende gangganyi. *Grandson is going along facing this way.*

therrendang *coverb+PUT.* put something facing someone. • Therrendang benaj gooma-birri. *Put them (paintings that are part of the dance event) facing straight up to them (the singers) like that.*

therrij; therrijboo *coverb+FALL/GO_DOWN.* sun go down. • Ngoorroola yilag therrijboo-ngarri nyoowoonya malalal men'gawoom. *When that sun is going down it is good.*

therrilaj *coverb+HIT.* defecate. • Ngayin-ga birn'girrbal-nga. Bela-ngarri ngemberramenbe, therrilaj nooniyin'ge manampi-ngirri. *I am a turkey. When they frighten me, I shit myself.* SEE: **therraj**.

therrilim *noun.* cooked boab seeds from green/young fruit/nuts. SEE: **jililiny**. [NOTE: white and soft after roasting whole nuts in hot coals or hot sand]

therrilimbi SEE: **thirrilimbi**.

therrmawiya REDUP: **therrmawiya-therrmawiya**. *coverb+GO/COME.* pull back hard against something 'like you jam on the breaks'. • Therrmawiya-therrmawiya ngenayinde. *I kept pulling back hard against it (a water python that was wrapped around her legs).*

therrngarn *coverb+SAY/DO.* shake, twitch in agony from poison, be writhing in pain. • Marri ngoorriny therrngarn ngerne. *Goodness that man over there is shaking (he is twitching).* • Therrngarn ngerne yiligin. *He seemed as though he was shaking from being hit inside there.*

therrngarn'ge *coverb+GET.* cause to shake with pain, cause to writhe in agony (poison). • Yilgoowoorriny-anyji mawiyab, therrngarn'ge yinbimji-yoowoo. *It (poisonous plant) might be bad and poison us (if we eat it), causing us to writhe in agony.*

therroowoog *coverb+BRING/TAKE.* take someone away (e.g. cyclone).

therr-therr *coverb+GET.* scrape. • Therr-therr-gala benem-ngiyi bagam. *Scrape all those prickles off it (echidna).* [NOTE: using a movement towards the actor, contrasts with *wij-wij* that uses a movement away] SEE: **joorr-joorr**.

therr-therrb *coverb+SAY/DO.* scrape. • Therr-therrb nimbirn-ngiyi dam bagam. *You scrape all those things off it (echidna), those prickles.*

thewerr *coverb+GO/COME.* follow, hurry off after someone. • Marrarn thewerr nginiyin-berrewa-yoo wigi-warriny. *He went away following his two sons. / He hurried off because of those two.*

thewinyji *noun.* dodonaea plant. *Dodonaea oxyptera.*

Thildoowan

Thildoowan *noun.* Lissadell Station. [NOTE: often called 'No Name' in the 2000s because a Gija person with the same name died]

thil-thil *coverb+SAY/DO_M.* crack skin off seed.
• Thil-thil boorroorn jililim. *They are cracking boab seeds.*

thini; thiniwa *interrogative.* what is this thing of feminine class? • Thiniwa nginyjinyji? *What is this masculine thing?*

thiniwawanyji *interrogative.* some kind of thing (masculine). • Thiniwawanyji danygawa yagoowalanyanyji. *He must be some other kind of thing.*

thiny *coverb.* to fart, to pass wind. SEE: **thirriny**.

thirndil *noun feminine.* northwest glass fish. *Ambassis* spp. [NOTE: grandmother of *dayiwool*, 'barramundi']

thirrilimbi *coverb+SAY/DO.* use a little stick to pick out seeds from something or as a toothpick to get stuff from between the teeth.
• Thirrilimbiwa yirrarn-ningi dambi, ngarnbe ganjim, lawa-lawagbem. *We use a little stick then to pick out the those white seeds (in cooked green boab nuts).*

thirril-ngarnal *noun feminine.* rainbow lorikeet or red-winged parrot. [NOTE: young men are supposed to use this word instead of *ginyginyel* or *wirrilijgel*]

thirringangab *coverb+BE/STAY.* be sticking out.

thirringgenji *noun masculine.* owlet nightjar. *Aegotheles cristatus*.

thirriny *coverb.* to fart, to pass wind. SEE: **thiny**.

thiwingenha-ngoo *interrogative.* what kind are you? What skin are you?

thiwingenyanyji *interrogative.* some kind of masculine one.

thoobag *coverb+GO/COME.* spit.
• Thoobag-nhawoon-ngage ngayin-ga. *I am spitting. I am one who spits.* • Thoobag ngini. *He was spitting.* SEE: **thebag**.

thoo-berra; thoowoo-berra; thoowoorra-berra *interrogative.* why?

thood *coverb+FALL/GO_DOWN.* go down.
• Thood-garri yarroowoo. *When we go down.* • Thood giniwardji. *He got off (a horse).* • Thood nanarde. *You went down.* • Thood yarraward. *We all went down.*

thoodboo *coverb+FALL/GO_DOWN.* be going down.
• Thoodboo boorroowoonboo-gili. *They are all going down.* • Thoodboo nyoowoonya barndelka. *The sun is going down.* • Thoodboo ngoowoonji girliwirring. *He is going down from on top.* • Thoodboowa ngiyardjende yilag nyanagawoo-yoorroong, Joowoolewa-gili. *He kept going down to the river to Joowoolewa.*

thoodboo *coverb+FALL/GO_DOWN_WITH.* go down with someone/something • Thoodboo nginimoowardji. *He was going down with it.*

thoodboo *coverb+GO/COME.* go down.

thoogool *noun feminine.* female goanna wth eggs.

thool SEE: **thoorl**.

thoolg *coverb+SAY/DO.* be blocked (ears), be unable to go through. • Nyaniyinya-ngarri thoolg janini Nhanba-yoorroong. *When she (dreamtime barramundi woman) was trying to go through the gap at Nhanba she couldn't get through.* • Thoolg nanini yardemga yilwarraya. *You must be really deaf (yours ears must be completely blocked up).*

thoolngoony REDUP: **thoolngoo-thoolngoony**. *coverb+SAY/DO.* smoke (cigarettes, tobacco, ganja). • Thoolngoony ngerne dam yilgoowoorroom yagewalam. *He's smoking that lousy ganja.*

thoolngoonyji, thoolngoonybe *noun.* cigarette. • Thoolngoony nginini jirrawoony thoolngoonyji. *He smoked one cigarette.*
• Thoolngoony wanemayinde melagawoom thoolngoonybe. *He was smoking lots of cigarettes.*

thoolngoorroo *coverb+GO/COME.* go away turning back on someone/action. • Thoolngoorrooboo berrayin. *They were going away with their backs to him then.*

thoolngoorroob REDUP: **thoolngoo-yoolngoorroob**. *coverb+BE/STAY.* sit with one's back to someone.

thoolngoo-yoolngoorroob *coverb+BE/STAY.* sit with one's back to someone (plural subject).
• Thoolngoo-yoolngoorroob boorroonboo. *They are all sitting with their backs (to us).* SEE: **thoolngoorroob**.

thooloob *coverb+HIT.* blow out fire. • Thooloob benayidji. *He blew out the fire.* SEE: **thoomooj**.

thoolooloorrji, thoolooloorroo *noun.* running water, current, waterfall. SEE: **thoorroorroo**.

thoolthoolji *noun masculine.* pheasant coucal. *Centropus phasianinus*.

thoombawoogboo *coverb+GO/COME.* being a person whose spouse has died.

thoombawool *noun feminine.* widow.

thoombawoony *noun masculine.* widower.

thoomboonyboo *noun.* anus. SEE: **manam**.

thoomboonygoo *coverb+HIT.* be very cold, eat so that one's anus sticks out and hence one is cold. • Thoomboonygoo ngiyinji doomboony. *The owl is feeling cold.* • Thoomboonygoo ngiyinji warn'gany. *He is cold (lit. 'It is making his anus stick out').* • Thoomboonygoo naniyin-ngoo garli. *You are cold, Niece.* [NOTE: swearing]

thoomboonygoo; thoomboonyboo *coverb+EAT.* eat so that one's anus sticks out and hence one is cold. • Thoomboonygoo benang. *Eat more!* • Thoomboonygoo joonangoon. *You eat.* • Jang-ngarri nginini thoomboonyge benangoon. *When you ate it made your anus stick out.* [NOTE: swearing]

thoomooj *coverb+FALL/GO_DOWN.* go out (fire).
• Thoomooj giniwardji. *It's gone out.*
• Thoomoojboo ngoowoonji marnenya dany. *The fire is almost gone out.* • Moorliyi thoomooja nginiwardji. *He closed his eyes (to shut out bright headlights).* SEE: **thooloob**.

thoomooj *coverb+PUT.* put fire out. • Thoomooj-gala joondaj. *Put out the fire!* • Thoomooj-gala bamberraj. *Put out the big bushfire.*

thoonbam *noun.* fire, firewood. SEE: **marnem**.

Thoonbi *noun.* gorge on upper reaches of the Ord River near Dolly Hole on Bedford Downs.

thoondooloom *noun.* hollow log. [NOTE: Southern dialect] SEE: **thaloorroony**.

thoong *coverb+SAY/DO.* suckle, drink milk from mother. • Thoong ngini-ngiyi gooragal. *He is drinking milk from his mother.*

thoong *coverb+BURN/BITE_REFL.* suck. • Thoong ngoowayinjende marlam. *He is sucking his hand.*

thoong *coverb+HIT.* kiss. • Thoong nyiyinjende. *He is kissing her.* SEE: **boony**.

Thoonggoonybel *noun.* place in Mick Jawalji's country.

thoong-thoong *coverb+SAY/DO_REFL.* suck.
• Marlam thoong-thoong ngenangirriyan. *I am sucking my hand.*

thoony *coverb+HIT.* make go fast. • Thoony benayid ngarndam. *He (moon) made his semen go fast (ejaculated when looking at the pretty woman).*

thoony *coverb+GO/COME.* run away fast.

thoonyga *coverb+HIT/CUT.* make run away fast.
• Thoonyga bemberrawoonbe. *They belted them and made them take off.*

Figure 83. *Thoonbi: Berrembi thamoonmoorroo Thoonbin ngirriban Janderrji.*

thoord

thoord REDUP: **thoord-thoord**. *coverb+GET*. stick spearhead to spear with wax. • *. . . marnen jaa yijib jimbirla bemberrayangbende thoord . . . heat properly in the fire then they used to stick the spearheads on.* [NOTE: see example with verb under *lendij*]

thoord-thoord *coverb+SAY/DO_M*. stick spearhead to spear with wax. • *Thoord-thoord-garri wanemayinde garloomboom thoowoo-thoowoom deg yirramimanyjende. When he was joining up his spears and everything we used to watch him.*

thoorl *coverb+GET*. wash away. • *Thoorl benamanyji warrambany bananbe. The floodwater washed the road away.*

thoorl *coverb+GO_THROUGH*. make a hole through. • *Thoorl wanengaboordja-ni gananybe-birri. She made a hole through it with a digging stick.*

thoorlboog *coverb+SPEAR*. spear in heart, spear right through. • *Thoorlboog giningaboord. He speared him in the heart.*

thoorlngem *noun*. hole in something. • *Thoorlngembaya-ninggi joorrooloonggoombi. You have a tear in your trousers.* SEE: **thenggerrb-ngem**.

thoorr *coverb+SAY/DO_M*. come down. • *Ngoorroo-biny thoorr woomberramande. They used to come down from over there.* SEE: **thood**.

thoorranyji; thoowoorranyji *interrogative*. something.

thoorrbool *coverb+BRING/TAKE*. bring/take something through. • *Thoorrbool-gala yarregbany-gili Garanyba-yoorroong. Let's bring it through to Garanyba.*

thoorrbool *coverb+GO/COME*. go through. • *Thoorrbool nginiyi. bindid-gala benaj, goorndarrim thoorrbool birriyan. Block up the holes or the fish will go through.* • *Lirn'girre-ngiyi thoorrbool nyaniyinya mernda-yoorroong. Her scales came through the paperbark.*

thoorrbool *coverb+GO_THROUGH*. break through. • *Thoorrboola wanengaboord yilangoogoo ngoorroon, gerlgayi-ngarri berrani goorndarrim, ngarranggarnin. He broke through, going down there when they were getting fish with a wall of grass in dreamtime.*

thoorrboong *coverb+FALL/GO_DOWN*. dive in. • *Thoorrboong nginiward. He dived in.*

thoorrboord *coverb+SAY/DO*. dig out. • *Ngayin-ga gernanyjen-ngage. Miyalega-nga jamerndem.* • *Wayinigana thoorrboord ngenarn jamerndemga. I am an echidna. My food is termites. Because of that I dig out the termite mounds.*

thoorrmal *noun feminine*. fat female rock wallaby. *Petrogale brachyotis*. SEE: **marliwal**.

thoorroo *coverb+PUT*. spread sand, flatten out and clear place in sand (e.g. to make a place for a fire or to sleep). • *Thoorroo benayanyji ngayawarle bagoo-girrem-noongoo. He spread the sand to make a place to sleep.*

thoorroo *coverb+HIT*. put something on top of someone/something. • *Thoorroo benayidja-ngirri jilam. She put dirt on me.* SEE: **thoorroo-thoorroo**.

thoorroob *coverb+GET*. snatch. • *Thoorroob benamanyji. He snatched it.* • *Thoorroob benamanyji-ngiyi. He snatched it from her.* • *Thoorroob benamanya-ningi. She took it from him.*

thoorroobji *coverb+SAY/DO_REFL*. grab things from each other. • *Thoorroobji-ngarri berrengirriyan. When they are grabbing things from each other.*

thoorroogboo *coverb+BRING/TAKE*. try to drown someone. • *Thoorroogboonga benanyji-gili. It (rainbow serpent) tried to drown them all.*

thoorroojga *coverb+SAY/DO*. play. • *Thoorroojga boorroorn-gili goorloon. They are playing about in the water.* SEE: **boorooj**.

thoorrooleb; thoorrooloob *coverb+GET*. pull something out (e.g. from hole or ground). • *Men'gawoom jang-girrim dam garndim-ningi thoorrooloob-garri ngoorroomenbe. Its (boab's) roots are good to eat when they pull them out.*

thoorroorooroo *coverb+SAY/DO*. have a stroke. • *Yilgoowoorroo nginini thoorroorooroo nginini. He got bad, he had a stroke.*

thoorroorroo *coverb+FALL/GO_DOWN*. pour. • *Gera thoorroorroo nyoowoonya rarangeg-garri nyimberramenbe. Later it pours through when they make it light (in weight, having cleaned termite larvae).*

thoorroorroo *coverb+SAY/DO*. water running (e.g. a waterfall). • *Ngarranggarninji, ngarranggarninji, goorloonyi thoorroorroo-ngarri ngerne. In the dreamtime, in the dreamtime when water runs in the waterfall (at Gerregerrewoon).* • *Thoolooloorroo goorloony thoorroorroo ngini. The waterfall is water* *running down.*

thoorroorroog *coverb+HIT.* make water run and drown someone. • Wayinigana thoorroorroog benayidji-yoo garlooroonyi, jang-ngarri berrani dany, jamerndel. *Because of that the rainbow snake drowned those two when they ate the termite larvae.*

thoorroo-thoorroo *coverb+SAY/DO.* put something on top of someone/something (e.g. when putting something like rice on plates). • Thoorroo-thoorroo nyanini-birri-yoo, ngarrgalem. *She put little rocks on top of the two of them.* SEE: **thoorroo.**

thoothood *coverb+SAY/DO_M.* be going down. • Bananbe thoothood-garri woomberramande Thawooloo-yoorroong. *They are the roads going down to Thawooloon.*

thoowerndem *noun.* mouth.

thoowerndemanbel *noun feminine.* black-headed snake, black-headed python. *Aspidites melanocephalus.* SEE: **dawool.**

thoowiya *interrogative.* something, anything. • Thoowiya dam ngarayinga, deg-garri benamanyjende, garl-garl wanemayinde-boorroo. *When he (dollar bird) sees something, he laughs at it.* • Ngoorroo-milim bemberranybende thoowiya, wayina waj berrangirriyinbende. *They bring something from over there then they give it to each other.* SEE: **thoowoo.**

thoowiyanyji; thoowanyji; thoowooyanyji; thoowoowanyji *interrogative.* something (don't know what thing). SEE: **thoowoorranyji.**

thoowoo; thoowi *interrogative.* what? • Thoowoo linga-linga narroorn? *What (thing) are you all thinking about?* • 'Thoowoo-ninggi berrembi?' nginini. *'What's that all over you!'* he said. • Thoowi-bam-anyji berrembi mayim. *There must be something in this food.* SEE: **thoowoorra.**

thoowoog *coverb+BE/STAY.* fly high, jump up in the air. • Goorloorroogoo berdij ginini, thoowoog ngininiyin, thoowoog, thoowoog goorloorroogoo. *He got up and flew away up into the sky.*

thoowool REDUP: **thoowool-thoowool.** *coverb+SAY/DO.* go up and down the same track. • Ngagenybe damga bananbe thoowool-thoowool ngenarn. *This is my track where I go up and down.* • Thoowoorra-boorroo thoowool-thoowool narroorn? *Why do you all keep going up and down every day?* • Nginya ngagenyji nginini-boorroo daa-yoorroong-da thoowool-girrim bananbe. *This man of mine said that this is the track where they go up and down all the time.*

thoowool-thoowool *coverb+SAY/DO_M.* go up and down the same track. • Ngirribawoorroo-biny nirda-ngarri biyoorroong, thoowool-thoowool jemenande. *When you come from far away from the north, you keep going up and down the same track.*

thoowoongenha-ngoo *interrogative.* what are you? what kind are you? (i.e. What is your skin?) [NOTE: Southern dialect] SEE: **thoowoonha-ngoo.**

thoowoonggeny, thewengginy *noun.* celtis tree. *Celtis strychnoides.* [NOTE: dark-leaved fig-like species growing on the side of rocky places, has small edible fruit]

Thoowoonggoonarrin *noun.* Tunganary, place on Bedford Downs in Paddy Bedford's mother's country.

thoowoonha *interrogative.* what about you? • 'Thoowoonha nimbinnha?' *'What will you be?'*

thoowoonha-ngoo *interrogative.* what are you?

thoowoone *coverb+SAY/DO.* feel dizzy, black out. • Thoowoone ngerne danya. *That man feels dizzy. / He has blacked out.* SEE: **wingini.**

thoowoore *coverb+SAY/DO.* hungry, be shaking from hunger. • Goorninyany thoowoore nginini. *He is hungry, shaking from having no food.*

thoowoorra *interrogative.* what are they? what thing (non-singular)? • Thoowoorra berrembi? *What are these things?* • Thoowoorra jang nanini. *What were you eating?* SEE: **thoowiya.**

thoowoorra-boorroo *interrogative.* what for? (asking about things). • Thoowoorra-boorroo nimbiyanha? *What (thing) are you going for?*

thoowoorrag *coverb+SAY/DO_M.* burp. • Thoowoorrag jemenande. Jaam yilgoowoorroon-anyji-ngoo. *You are burping. You must be no good in the guts.*

thoowoorranyji *interrogative.* something (don't know what thing). SEE: **thoorranyji, thoowiyanyji.**

thoowoo-thoowoom *noun.* everything.

Ww

wa *interjection.* hey.

-wa, -a, -aa *suffix.* sequential suffix to coverbs.

-wa, -a *suffix.* topic/focus marker on nominals.

-wa *nominal suffix.* big, attached to body parts; followed by gender suffix agreeing with the gender of the owner of the body part.

waagoom *adjective.* white. SEE: **wagoom, lawagbem**.

waag-waag *interjection.* call made by crow. • Dangembi 'waag-waag' wananya wanggarnali dali. *After that the crow went along saying 'waag-waag'.*

waag-waagjil *noun feminine.* crow. *Corvus orru.* SEE: **wanggarnal**. [NOTE: wanggarnal is the word most commonly heard]

waaliny *noun masculine.* nankeen kestrel. *Falco cenchroides* [NOTE: one who was too lazy to hunt in the dreamtime and ate a strip off his own leg] SEE: **gardagarrji, marl-marlel, marrg-marrgjil**.

waanya *verb.* she WENT ALONG. [NOTE: Southern dialect] SEE: **wananya**.

waanyim *noun.* worms, maggots. • waanyibany *something with maggots*

waanyji *verb.* he WENT ALONG. [NOTE: Southern dialect] SEE: **wananyji**.

waarrany REDUP: **waawaarram**. *noun.* adolescent boy.

waawalji, waawalel, waawale *noun.* green ant. SEE: **minyal, wawalji**.

wabagoorreny, waboogoorroony *noun masculine.* small nulla-nulla. [NOTE: held in one hand and used to whack something (Kriol: 'belt em down')]

wad *coverb+BE/STAY.* be looking back, be the next sibling born after another to whom he/she 'looks back' in time. • Wad nginji. *He is looking back.* • Ngoorrool yoorloo wad gininiyin-ngooyoo. *He looked back to that female one (my sister whose name I cannot say), who lives at bottom camp (who was born after him) (i.e. He was the next born after that sister).*

wad REDUP: **wad-wad**. *coverb+SAY/DO.* look back. • Dala wad nyanini. *That girl looked back.* • Wad-wad boorroorn. *They are looking back.*

wadboo-wadboo *coverb+GO/COME.* go along looking back. • Wadboo-wadboo-ngarri nimbiyannha . . . *When you go along looking back . . .*

wadoo-wadoo *coverb+GET.* think someone can't do something. • Wadoo-wadoo-ma yinemenha (warrg-girrem, warim-boorroo)? Wanyagen-ma-ngage? *You think I'm no good (at dancing, for fighting)? Am I a little kid?*

wad-wadgewany *coverb+GET.* keep on making someone look back. • Wad-wadgewany nginemanya. *She kept making him look back.*

wag *coverb+BE/STAY.* have a twisted neck. • Wag ngininiyin. *He has a twisted neck. / He twisted his own neck.*

wag *coverb+GET.* twist someone's neck. • Wag nginimanyji. *He twisted his (i.e. someone else's) neck.*

wag *coverb+SAY/DO.* have a cramp in the neck. • Ngoowan, wag nginini wenggarrem. *No, he has a cramp in his neck.*

Wagaban *noun.* Wuggubun Community. [NOTE: small community 140 kilometres north of Warrmarn, spelled 'Wuggubun' by the community using 'u' to represent the sound that is spelled with 'a' in the Gija spelling system]

Wagalooloo *noun.* name of an old song and dance event [NOTE: was like Moonga-moonga with men and women singing but only women dancing; they used to wear only a loin cloth. It used to be performed at Texas Downs. Also referred to as 'Buttercup's old Moonga-moonga' because she used to stage it before she found the Woorra-woorral Moonga-moonga, i.e. the mermaid Moonga-moonga.]

wagirr *coverb+SAY/DO_M.* ask a question to which one should know the answer already, say one doesn't know, keep on asking the same thing, ask 'who's that person over there – someone we don't know' (but we really do know who they are). • Wagirr-ma jemanande? *Why do you keep asking that question you should know (the answer to)?*

wagirrwoony, wagirrwool, wagirrwoom *adjective.* one who asks questions all the time. • Wagirrwoon-ngoo. *You are a question asker.*

You keep on asking the same thing.

wagoony, wagool, wagoom *adjective.* white. SEE: **waagoom, lawagbeny**.

waj *coverb+HIT.* give, throw, blow (wind). • Waj benayidji-ngirri. *He gave it to me.* • Waj benayid. *He threw them/it.* • Wanyagel waj joonayida-ngiyi, ngelel ngenenggawoom-boorr. *You should give the things from here to this little girl.* • Waloorroo waj benayidji biyoorroong. *The wind was blowing back this way.* • Gara waj noonbiyi-ninggi. *I will give it to you later.*

waj *coverb+SAY/DO_REFL.* give each other. • Waj berrangirriyin-joo boolbam jarliji-gany-ningi. *The two friends are giving presents each to the other.*

waj *coverb+GET.* pay. • Gaboongerrega waj noonbemge-ninggi ngarrgalem? *How much do I owe you?*

waj *coverb+SAY/DO.* give. • waj-garri nyanini-yirri *(the things that) she gave us*

waj *coverb+SAY/DO_M.* give. • Mawoondool, gamanggarr, ngenengga-yoorroong wirnanboo waj woomberramande, warna-warnarran. *They used to give that white paint and the bamboo here as trade presents long ago.*

wajawoorroo *noun.* skin.

wajbaloony, wajbalool *noun.* white person. SEE: **gardiyany**. [NOTE: from English 'white fella']

wajbe *coverb+HIT.* be throwing. • Wirli-wirlim wajbe yirriyinji wirnbe-merrale. *We are throwing our fishing lines in amongst all the pandanus.*

wala *coverb+HIT.* leave something behind. • Ngoorriyana wala nyilayidge ngagenyil. *I left mine (mobile phone) behind right over there.* SEE: **gad**.

walaji *coverb+HIT.* hassle in menacing way, attack, attack through jealousy, look for trouble. • Diyanya walaji nginiyidji marliwam-berrewa. *He had made it (fire to burn the eagle) because he was jealous of him having all the fat female wallabies.* • Thoowoo-boorroo walaji jooniyinha? *Why are you looking for trouble?*

walaji *coverb+SAY/DO_M.* attack, menace, demand with menaces. • Walaji wanemayinde-boorroo ngali-ngalim. *He kept on hassling all the women.*

walaji *coverb+WOUND.* attack someone, menace someone. • Wawawoonggam walaji benawoonji gangga-woorrarrem goorlanggem, yoorn'goorr-yoorn'goorr-ngarri berrani jiyirrem, ngarabarram. *They were minding their own business and he attacked them all, my mother's mother and all her sisters and brothers poor things, when they were cooking kangaroo and emu in the ground.*

walamboom *noun.* 1. rib bone. 2. side of woomera.

walanarriny *noun masculine.* type of coolamon, type of wooden dish, big one used for carrying babies. • Walanarriny dany nawarrany joolooj-girrem wanyageny. *The coolamon called* walanarriny *is a big one for carrying babies.*

walangany *coverb+GET.* make a mistake about something. • Walangany nyanemanyji. *He made a mistake about her. He mistook her for something else.*

walangem SEE: **warlangem**.

Walarrwan *noun.* Moonlight Bore.

walganji, walganel *noun.* mad person. • Merlarn-anyji nginyjinyga nyaganyji, ganarra-ngarnany walganji. *This uncle might be mad, a bush dweller, a madman.*

walig *coverb+GO/COME.* go in. • Nawan-yoorroong walig nyaniyinya. *She went into a cave.* • Waliga nginiyin thoondooloom, goowoolem nawarram, nawan-jam. *He went into the hollow log then, a big tree like a cave.*

walig *coverb+FALL/GO_DOWN.* go in. • Walig ngenawardge. *I went in.* • Walig nanooward. *You went in.* • Walig nyanoowardja. *She went in.* • Boorroowiyina-gili melagawiya walig. *They should all go in.*

walig *coverb+FALL/GO_DOWN_WITH.* go in together, enter together. • Walig berramoowardbe ngooloo-ngooliyan. *They all went in yesterday (late afternoon).* • Walig birrimoowoon nyigawa. *They might be going in tomorrow.* • Waligboo berremoowoonbe-gili. *They are all just going in.* [NOTE: verb is FALL/GO_DOWN with *moo-* inserted before stem showing action together]

walig REDUP: **walilig**. *coverb+PUT.* put in. • Berrem yiligin ngaginyin daan, walig doonbajge, merreb doonbajge. *I will put this inside my place and hide it.*

walig *coverb+HIT.* wrap, put in.
• Mernda-yoorroong walig nyaniyinya. *She is wrapping them in the paperbark.*

walig *coverb+BRING/TAKE.* take in. • Walig goorranyboo yiligin nawane. *They took him inside the cave.*

waligboo *coverb+GET_HIT.* take in. • Waligboo ngenamoowoon'ge ngayiwany. *I'm taking him in myself.* • Nawane-gili waligboo yirremoowoonji melaya. *We are all taking it in the house.*

walilig *coverb+GO/COME.* go in. • Nawane walilig berrayin gawarrena. *They all went into a cave in the hillside.*

walilig *coverb+SAY/DO_M.* go in. • Walilig wanemayinde nawane ngenengga. *She kept on going into the cave here.*

waliligboo *coverb+FALL/GO_DOWN.* going in (plural). • Wanyanyagembi, wanyanyagembi, waliligboo yarroowoonya-gili. *Children, children, let's all go in.*

walimalil, walimaliny *noun.* flying fox, little red flying fox. *Pteropus scapulatus.*

waloob *coverb+HIT.* spirits looking after someone's camp make people sick if they go there and take something. • Ngoowan nimbiyannha dan mayaroon, waloob nimbirriyinnha-boorroo. *Don't go to that house, the spirits looking after it will make you sick.* SEE: **winyjirrab**.

waloom *noun.* spirits looking after someone's place. • Waloom boorroonboo ngenengga daan, maroorr-girrem. *The spirits stay here to look after the camp.*

Waloorrji *noun.* wind dreaming place on Bedford Downs. SEE: **Doowoonan**.

waloorrji, waloorroo *noun.* wind, wind that comes after the rain. SEE: **gern'galeny**.

waltherre *adjective.* half raw, half cooked.
• Waltherre-bebeya yamberrangoonya miyale. *We eat the meat half cooked.*

walwajbarrany, walwajbarral, walwajbarram *adjective.* having a sore or injured leg that causes one to hobble, having a bad leg that makes it hard to walk properly (Kriol: 'hobbly leg'). • Thambarlam walwajbarrany girli-ngarri wiyinji. *His feet and legs are wobbly when he walks.* • Walwajparral ngelela. *She has a hobbly leg.*

waly *coverb+FALL/GO_DOWN.* have slurred speech, be unable to talk properly. • Waly nginiward. *He had slurred speech. / He could not talk properly.*

waman *coverb+GO/COME.* go around to the other side. • Waman nginbiyan-noongoo deg-girrem. *I will go around to the other side to look for him.*

waman *coverb+FALL/GO_DOWN.* go around corner, get behind something. • Waman nginiward. *He went around a corner.* SEE: **dern, geren**.

wambalayiny, wambelayig *coverb+GO/COME.* go around a turn on the road. • Wambalayiny yarroonya. *We go around there.* • Ngelmi-biny wambelayiny yarran ngoorroom gendoowa Baloobaloon. *We go around from the east there upstream at Baloobaloon.* • Wambelayig-gala yarroo galmang-biny. *Let's go around, moving along in the east.*

waligge *coverb+HIT.* make someone go in. • Waligge ngoorrayidbe yiligindi thandooliyin. *They made him go right inside a hollow log.*

waloog, waloogbany *coverb+PUT.* claim something belonging to someone else, sing something incorrectly (using incorrect words). • Bilij nyilayidge, ngoowan waloog nyilayangge, ngaginyel-ngage. *I found it (song), I didn't claim someone else's, it is mine.* • Waloogbany nyiliyilinke joonbalga ngelela. *I was singing this Joonba song incorrectly.*

Wamboorrbany *noun.* place somewhere near Fletcher/Stoney Creek south of Warrmarn, near a place belonging to the wedge-tailed eagle.

wanamarriny *noun.* species of sugar leaf (lerp) found on bloodwood *mawoorroony*. SEE: **mawoorroo-ngarnany**. [NOTE: sugar leaf (lerp) is an edible sweet white flaky substance which appears on the leaves of some eucalypt species during the dry season; made by insects that are relatives of the scale insects]

wana-wana *coverb+BE/STAY.* be in one line.
• Wana-wana yarroonya, deg yarrija thambarlam-anyji-noowa gedba-ngarri yamberrija. *We can form one line (a search line), and look for him, maybe we will find his tracks.*

wanan *coverb+BE/STAY.* be stretched across (clouds across sky, long hill across the landscape, snake across the road). • Danyi ngamarrany wanan nginji banane. *There is a snake there stretched across the road.* SEE: **wandarra**.

wananbany *coverb+FALL/GO_DOWN.* spread across.
• Wel ngenengga-biny, ngenengga-biny

wandaj

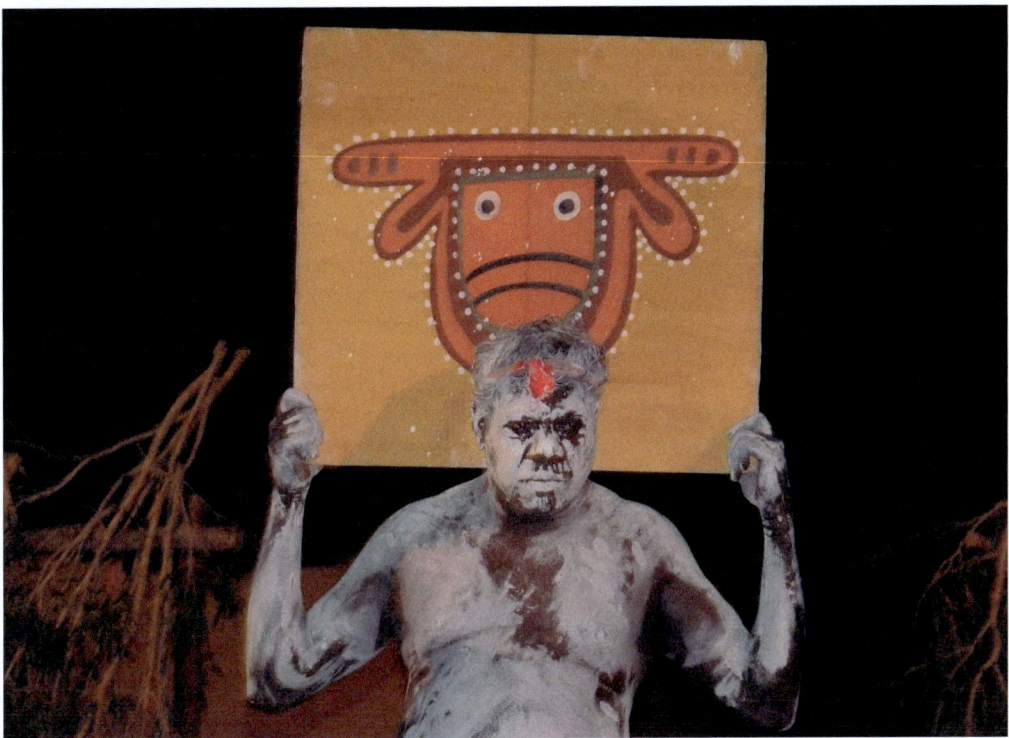

Figure 84. *Wandaj: Jangardi Gabriel Nodea: Wandaj ngerne woorranggool Goorirr-goorirrel warrg-garri ngerne.*

gerliwirring, ngamarra-jaya warrambany wananbany nginiwardji-yirri, walig yiligin. *Well from here, down from up here, it (floodwater) came along to us like a snake and spread out and came inside (our houses).*
wananginy, wanangem *noun.* bag. SEE: **garraginy.**
wanangem *noun.* pillow. SEE: **barndim, dirdim.**
wanany *verb.* he/she/it WENT ALONG.
wananya *verb.* she WENT ALONG.
wananyande *verb.* she used to GO ALONG.
wananyjande *verb.* she kept GOING ALONG.
wananyjende *verb.* he kept GOING ALONG.
wananyji *verb.* he WENT ALONG.
wanarrji *noun.* bush peanut, cowpea yam. *Vigna vexillata* [NOTE: grows on the black soil]
wanawoon *verb.* it should FALL/GO DOWN.
Wanbin *noun.* Wooneba (Winiper, Wirneba) Spring.
wanboorrbany, wanboorrbal, wanboorrbam REDUP: **wanboo-wanboorrbam.** *adjective.* having webbed skin as in a duck's feet, have skin hanging down (as in a flying fox wing). • Yilgoowoorrinayi-ngoo, wanboorrban-ngoo! *You are no good like that, you have skin hanging down (like a flying fox)!* • Nyoorroongool thambarlambi wanboorrbal. *The platypus has webbed feet.*
wandaj REDUP: **wanda-wandaj.** *coverb+SAY/DO.* carry on shoulder (humans), carry (birds, e.g. bowerbirds). • Wandaj ngerne. *He is carrying on his shoulder.* • Thoowerndem-birri wanda-wandaj ngerne. *He (bowerbird) carries it with his mouth.* • Gerrej woomberrayidbe-yoo ngaaloo-giny wanda-wandaj berrani-yoo. *When they finished (killing all the rock wallabies) they carried them into the shade.*
wandaj REDUP: **wanda-wandaj.** *coverb+PUT.* put on shoulder and carry. • Wandaj benayanyji. *He is carrying it on his shoulders.* • Wanda-wandaj ngoorriyangbende. *They were putting it on their shoulders to carry.*
wandaj *coverb+BRING/TAKE.* carry on shoulder. • Wandaj banynha. *You carry it here on your*

wandajboo

shoulder. • Goorlgoon ngenengga-biny noonanyke, joodoobiny, waroogoobiny goorlgoon noonanyge, warany jirrawoogooli wandaja nyilanyge. *I hooked one (porcupine) here on my hair belt on the right, one here on the left and the other I was carrying on my shoulder.*

wandajboo *coverb+GET.* be carrying on shoulder. • Goorndoorndoogam wandajboo ngoorramangbe ngarrgaleny. *The children were carrying heavy rocks.*

wandandaj *coverb+GO_ALONG.* go along carrying something on shoulder. • Ngarranggarniny jiyiliny ngininiyinde-ngarri, goonggala-bany danya jiyilinya wandandaj wananyjende, miyale. *In dreamtime when he (dingo) was a man, he had firesticks and went along carrying meat on his shoulder.* [NOTE: recorded in Halls Creek]

wanda-wandaj *coverb+SAY/DO_M.* carry on shoulders. • Wanda-wandaj woomberramande. *They used to carry them on their shoulders.*

wandarra *coverb+PUT.* make hole in the ground in a straight line to cook goanna, put a long rail across. • Wandarra niniyangge yilag. *I put it straight across down there.*

wandarra *coverb+BE/STAY.* be stretched across something in a line (e.g. rainbow across the sky). • Wandarra nyinya-boorroo na. *It is stretched out across (the sky) for them now (rainbow for young men at law time).* SEE: **wanan**.

wandawandal *noun.* black whip snake. *Demansia vestigiata.* • Dal wandawandal woorlagal. Gamboord nimbimnha-ngal. *That whip snake is a whore. She will grab you.* SEE: **wijgel**. [NOTE: Nambin skin; this word has also been recorded as the name of the 'yellow tree snake', *Dendrelaphis punctulata* and the 'brown tree snake', *Boiga irregularis*]

Wandawandangarri *noun.* hill on Old Texas.

-wanem *suffix.* that kind together (relations, group of humans). • ngaji-wanem *all the brothers/sisters* • warnarre-wanem *all the people from long ago, all the old people*

wanema *verb.* he/she SAID/DID. SEE: **wanemayi**. [NOTE: when asked about the difference between *wanema* and *wanemayi*, Rusty Peters, Eileen Bray and Mabel Juli said that they mean the same: one version is longer]

wanemany REDUP: **wanenemam**. *noun masculine.* man who has been through all law.

wanemanya *verb.* she was SAYING/DOING.

wanemanyande *verb.* she used to SAY/DO.

wanemanyji *verb.* he was SAYING/DOING.

wanemayanyande *verb.* she used to be SAYING/DOING.

wanemayi *verb.* he SAID/DID. SEE: **wanema**.

wanemayin *verb.* he used to SAY/DO.

wanemayinde *verb.* he/she used to SAY/DO.

wanemiyanya *verb.* she was DOING something at the same time as something else.

wanemiyanyande *verb.* she used to DO something at the same time as something else.

wanengaboord *verb.* he/she/it WENT THROUGH.

wanengaboordja *verb.* she WENT THROUGH.

wanengaboordji *verb.* he WENT THROUGH.

wangala *coverb+SAY/DO_M.* forget. • Wangala ngelemen'gende. *I have forgotten.*

wangala *coverb+BECOME.* go mad, get cranky with someone. • Wangala waniyidja. *She went mad.* • Wangala waniyidji-ngirri. *He got cranky with me.*

wangalag *coverb+GET.* make someone lose their brain/mind, make mad. • Yagoowalany dany ngoorloorloog-garri boorroorn, wangalag benemanyji goonggoorloom. *They have been drinking that beer (that other kind of thing) and lost their brains (it made them mad).*

wangalany, wangalal, wangalam *adjective.* mad. • Ngoowan linga-linga nerne, jilba-wanyji nerne wangalan-anyji-ngoo. *You are not thinking, you might be afraid, you might be mad.*

wangalawoo *coverb+BECOME.* become mad. • Wangalawoo-wanyji ngiliyin'ge. Goowoo gaboo ngenarn. *I must be going mad. I don't know what I'm doing.* • Wangalawoo-wanyji jiyinha. *You must be going mad.*

wangalji *noun.* name given to more than one tree with edible gum, a plant. [NOTE: listed in a Purnululu list as *Calytrix exstipulata* but this shrub does not have edible gum; plant shown to F. Kofod by Hector Jandany and called *wangalji* is not *C. exstipulata*. According to Hector Jadany charcoal from this tree was used to make self black. Listed in 'Gija plants and animals' (Purdie et al. 2018) as 'cockroach bush', *Senna notabilis*.]

wanganga *coverb+SAY/DO.* be lonely, having nobody. • Wanganga ngenarn. *I am lonely.*

SEE: **barndawarlawarla, minyawenya, wanga-wanga**.

wanganyge *coverb.* become blurry eyed. • Wanganyge ngoorrangoonbe ngoorloorloog-anyji woomberranybende ngeriga. *They couldn't see properly because they must have been drinking all the way along the road coming from the south.*

wangarr *coverb+SAY/DO.* forget.

wangarrag, wangarrg REDUP: **wangarrarrag**. *coverb+FALL/GO_DOWN.* get lost. • Milgin'gawool wangarrag janooward. *The milking cow got lost.*

wangarrag, wangarrg *coverb+HIT.* lose. • Wangarrg noonayid goonggooloombi. *I lost my brain (i.e. I went mad).* • Gayiyanyji wangarrag doonayid garragim. *I lost my bag somewhere.*

wangarrem *noun.* skin, hide, leather. SEE: **moogoonybe**.

wangarrg *coverb+GET.* forget, lose memory, go mad. • Goonggooloom dam wangarrgboo-ngarri yamberramenya. *When we lose our brains (memory) and start forgetting.*

wangarrg *coverb+GO/COME.* get lost. • Wangarrg goowiyi. *He will get lost.*

wangarrgbanynhawoony, wangarrgbanynhawool, wangarrgbanynhawoom *adjective.* forgetful

wangarrge *coverb+GET.* make forget. • Wangarrge ngenemanya. *She made me forget.*

wangarrgoowany *coverb+GET.* make forget. • Wangarrgoowanya nginimanyji nginya wanyagoowarrany. *He made this little boy forget.*

wangarrgoowany *coverb+SAY/DO_REFL.* make self mad. Wangarrgoowanya yarremiyanya. *We make ourselves mad.*

wangarroony, wangarrool, wangarroom; wangarrwoony, wangarrwool, wangarrwoom REDUP: **wanga-wangarrwoom** *adjective.* looking different, unrecogisable. • Daambi wangarroom. *The country looks different.*

wanga-wanga *coverb+SAY/DO.* miss someone. • Ngayin-ga Jandaloowoon-nga wanga-wanga ngenarn-nooggoowa. *I am Jandaloo (sending this message), I miss you (I feel lonely because you are gone).* SEE: **barndawarlawarla, wang-wang, wanganga**.

wangawoony, wangawool *noun.* baby. SEE: **nyimbelawoony, wililji**.

Wangga, Wanggal *noun feminine.* song and dance style. [NOTE: originated from north of Port Keats, men play didjeridoo and clapsticks, men and women dance, used by Gija in public before young men go away with men only and at funerals with smoking ceremonies; referred to as 'Wangga' in Kriol, becomes a feminine noun *Wanggal* when occurring in a full Gija sentence]

wanggarl *coverb+SAY/DO.* be tired, be lazy. • Ngoowan wanggarl nimbirn, miyale benewam-yayi! *Don't be lazy! Go and get some meat for us.* • Wanggarl ngenarn. *I'm tired.* • Wanggarl boorroorn-joo. *The two of them are tired.* • Garninya? Wanggarl-ma nerne? *Now? Are you tired?*

wanggarlge *coverb+FALL/GO_DOWN.* become tired. • Boorroordboo-ngarri ngoorroo-ngoorroo-biny, baagoo boorroordboo googan wanggarlgenga berroowoonbe,' ngenani. *'They come from all over the place, they go to sleep just because they get tired,' I said.*

wanggarlge *coverb+PUT.* make someone tired. • Wanggarlgoowoo ngenilinji wanyageny. *The little boy is making me tired.* [NOTE: *-ge* becomes *-goo* if followed by the continuous suffix to coverbs *-woo*]

wanggarlge *coverb+GET.* make someone tired. • Wanggarlge yinamennha. *You are making me tired.*

wanggarlwoony, wanggarlwool, wanggarlwoom *adjective.* lazy.

Wanggarnaban *noun.* place near Mendoowoorrji on Bedford Downs. LIT: 'place having crows'.

wanggarnal *noun feminine.* crow. *Corvus orru*. [NOTE: Naangari skin; one of the dreamings for the Warrmarn area together with *warrarnany* the wedge-tailed eagle; at Christmas time Wanggarnal brings presents for the children at the Ngalangangpum School instead of Santa Claus]

wanggooloo *coverb+GO_ALONG.* be sick of something, be tired of waiting. • Deg-gayan ngelamande:::, wanggooloo ngelanyge, marrrana nginbiyan bagoo-girrim. *I have been waiting all day, I'm sick of it and I am going home to sleep.*

Wanggoon *noun.* Roses Yard, place on

-wanggoony, -wanggool, -wanggoom

Springvale that is a source of white pipe clay.

-wanggoony, -wanggool, -wanggoom *suffix.* person belonging to a particular place or country. • Rijarrwanggool. *Woman belonging to the place called Rijarr (Turner River).*
• Darrajayin-wanggoon-nga. *I am a person from Darrajayin.* [NOTE: affixed to place names or locative demonstratives, must agree in gender with the person described]

wang-wang *coverb+SAY/DO.* be lonely.
• Wang-wang nyerne. *She is lonely.* SEE: **barndawarlawarla, wanga-wanga**.

wang-wang *coverb+SAY/DO_M.* be lonely.
• Wang-wang woomanyande. *She was lonely.* SEE: **barndawarlawarla, wanga-wanga**.

wani *particle.* like that.

wanimiyanya *verb.* she was DOING together with something. • . . . girli wanimiyanya nganyjoowarrji-ni . . . *she was walking along with the snake (wrapped around her).* [NOTE: -mi- inserted before the verb stem refers to the snake]

wanimiyanyji *verb.* he was DOING together with someone/something.

waningerreg *adverb.* this many. SEE: **wayiningerreg**.

waniya *verb.* he/she/it PLACED.

waniyanya *verb.* she/it (feminine) PLACED.

waniyanyji *verb.* he/it (masculine) PLACED.

waniyid *verb.* she/he/it BECAME.

waniyidja *verb.* she/it (feminine) BECAME.

waniyidjende *verb.* he/it (masculine) used to BECOME. • Yirraniyinde-noongoo manbe-ngarri waniyidjende, galyegbe. *We used to wait for it (fruit of sandpaper fig) to get black and soft.*

waniyidji *verb.* he/it (masculine) BECAME.

wan'gil *noun.* rifle. SEE: **derlbawoogajil, doorlgajim**.

wan'gim *noun.* smoke. [NOTE: Southern dialect] SEE: **goongooloo**.

wan'goony REDUP: wan'goo-wan'goom. *noun.* older teenage boy. • Wan'goo-wan'goo-woorrarrem. *All the teenage boys.* • Ngoowan garij nyimberrimbe joogoorrool, ngoowan. Googbel-birri lamba-lambarnbe dam, wan'goo-wan'goom. *They cannot say the name of the bush orange. It is forbidden to young men and teenage boys.* SEE: **lambarnji**. [NOTE: wan'goony is older than *lambarnji*]

wanooward *verb.* he/she/it WENT DOWN.

-wany *coverb suffix.* continuous suffix to coverbs. SEE: **-bany**.

wanyagarrany, wanyagarral *noun.* child. [NOTE: Southern dialect] SEE: **wanyagewarrany**.

wanyagel, wanyanggel *noun.* little girl.
• Wanyagel gedba nyanidja nyengen joomoorloonha-ngarri Nyawanal. *The little girl, Nyawana your daughter whom you look after, found it.*

wanyagen *temporal.* when small, when young.
• Ngayin wanyagen ngenaniyinde-ngarri, garlmi yirramande. *When I was small, we used to fish by pushing a wall of spinifex through the water.*

wanyageny, wanyanggeny *noun.* little boy.

wanyageny, wanyagel, wanyagem *adjective.* little. • 'Nga! Ngoorroona lalanggarrany gedba yirrayidji,' woomberrama. 'Wanyageny,' berrani. 'Ngoowan wanyageny,' nyanini Nyawanal, 'nawarrany, nawarrany lalanggarrany.' *'Hey! We saw a crocodile over there,' they said. 'A little one,' they said. 'Not a little one,' said Nyawana, 'a big one, a big crocodile.'* [NOTE: most common use of the word is with the meaning 'child', the reduplicated form *wanyanyagem* means 'children'; people from southwest areas often say *wanyangge-*, some say *winyangke*]

wanyagewarrany, wanyagewarral *noun.* child. SEE: **wanyageny**.

wanyagibawa *coverb+BECOME.* get to have little ones/babies. • Ger-ngarri boorroorn wanyagibawa waniyid warrarnanyi. *When the wind blows the eagle has little ones.*

wanyagem, wanyanggem *adjective.* a bit of something. • Berrembiya jalij ginini wanyanggem. *It rained here a little bit.*

wanyanggeny, wanyanggel, wanyanggem *adjective.* little. SEE: **wanyageny**.

wanyanggewarrany, wanyanggewarral *noun.* child. SEE: **wanyagewarrany**.

wanyanyagem, wanyanyanggem *adjective.* little ones. • Wanyanyage-moowam yirramanyi binyjiwinyji-moowam. *We only caught little ones, little catfish.*
• Wanyanyanggem moorrgoom doowab berrayi. *Lots of little tiny grasshoppers fly around.*

wanyanyagem, wanyanyanggem *noun.* children. • Wanyanyagem yirramoorloowardji bardooyan, ngaalooyan daayan. *We looked after the children right back in the shade at the camp.* • Berrayin-gili gendang wanyanyagem gedba nyimberrayid-gili. *The children came down from up there and found it.* [NOTE: different forms are dialect variants]

wanyarriny *noun.* bauhinia. *Lysiphyllum cunninghamii.* [NOTE: ash used with chewing tobacco and for detoxifying *garnawoony*] SEE: **goonjiny**.

wanyerrwany *coverb+SAY/DO.* flog. • Goowoolem benema-noo wanyerrwany nginini. *He got a stick for him and belted him.* SEE: **wanyoorr**.

wanyja *particle.* maybe. SEE: **wanyji**. [NOTE: *wanyja* follows vowels, elided to *-anyja* following consonants]

wanyjag *coverb+SAY/DO.* become skinny. • Wanyjag berrani-yoo. *The two of them became skinny.*

wanyjany, wanyjal, wanyjam *adjective.* skinny.

wanyji *particle.* maybe. [NOTE: sometimes appears as an independent word and sometimes as a suffix]

-wanyji *suffix.* maybe. SEE: **-anyji**. [NOTE: *-anyji* follows consonants, *-wanyji* follows vowels]

wanyoorr *coverb+SAY/DO_M.* flog, hit with strap, whip or steel rope. • Dayemab bemberramangbende, goowoolen wanyoorr woomberramande-boorroo. *They used to tie them up to a tree and flog them.*

wany-wany *coverb+SAY/DO.* swim, paddle along. • Wany-wany nginini-noongoo. *He swam to him.*

wany-wany *coverb+GO_ALONG.* swim, paddle along. • Wany-wany wiyinji. *He is swimming along.*

war *coverb+SAY/DO.* run down (water fall). • Jadany goorloony war-ngarri ngerne. *The rain ran down as a waterfall.*

wara *interjection.* alright.

waraga REDUP: **waraga-waraga**. *coverb+DO_REFL.* make each other weak. • Waraga-waraga berramiyinbende-yoo. *The two of them kept on making each other weak (wearing themselves out by belting each other).* • Waraga berramiyinbende deyena. *They really wore each other out there.*

waramboorr, waramboorrji *noun.* snake vine. *Tinospora smilacina.* [NOTE: bound around a nulla-nulla and then scorched to make design]

waramil *noun feminine.* first section of a corroborree sung while people are painting up and then repeated in between the different sections, chorus. SEE: **waranggil**.

warangan, warangan-warangan *coverb+HIT.* spin something like a fishing line to throw out, swing something around and around. • Ngerlam warangan benijtha ngerr beniyinnha yilag goorloom wirli-wirli-ngarriya. *Spin the line around and throw it down in the water from up high.* • Waranganbe bemberrayidbende dam lamba-lambarnbe. *It (big wind) was swinging the young men around and around then.*

waranggan REDUP: **wara-waranggan**. *adverb.* fast, quick.

waranggan REDUP: **wara-waranggan**. *interjection.* hurry up, do it fast, quickly.

waranggi *coverb+GO_ALONG.* fly around and around and up and up (bird). • Waranggi wananyjende gerloorroogoo. *He (owl) was flying around and around up there.* [NOTE: original translation given was 'be dizzy']

waranggil *noun feminine.* first section of a corroborree sung while people are painting up and then repeated in between the different sections, chorus. SEE: **waramil**.

warany, waranya, waranyjawa *interjection.* alright.

warda *coverb+HIT.* love, like, want. • Warda-ma jooniyinha. *Do you love it?* • Warda niyinnha-ngoo. *I love you. / I like you.* • Men'gawoony, warda niyin'ge. *He is good, I like him.* • Yilgoowoorroony, warda-girriwoorroon-nga, yilwarraya. *He is bad, I really don't like him.*

warda *interjection.* goodness.

wardal *noun feminine.* star.

wardawoo *interjection.* oh goodness, ouch.

wardayi *interjection.* exclamation (indicates tiredness or pain).

wardim *noun.* collarbone.

wardoo *noun.* brother-in-law, sister-in-law (when spoken to). SEE: **ngawooji**.

wardool *noun feminine.* sister-in-law. SEE: **ngawooji**.

wardoony *noun masculine.* brother-in-law. SEE: **ngawooji**.

Waren-waren *noun.* Calico Springs.

warernji *noun masculine.* coolibah tree. *Eucalyptus tectifica, E. microtheca, E. limitaris, E. tephrodes.* [NOTE: *bin'gany*, sugar leaf (lerp)

species found on *warernji*; inner bark used to make *bijam* used for straining honey]

wari *coverb+BE/STAY.* become angry with someone.
• Yangel dal boora-boorab nyerne-ngiyi, ngeleli-wayi wari nyimbinya-ngiyi dawarr-warriny-ayi, nyimiyinya. *Some girl comes out to the other one and this other going to get wild with her and hit her herself like that.*

wari-bawoorroony, wari-bawoorrool, wari-bawoorroom *adjective.* quiet, not aggressive.
• Ngoowany wari-bawoorroony. *Not him, he is not cheeky.*

warij *coverb+SAY/DO.* beat spinifex to extract resin.
• Gerre-gerrewoon gaaljiwa warij nginbirn. *I will beat the spinifex for the resin at Stoney Creek.*

warim *noun.* fight. • Mendoowoon warim nawarram ngoorrooma yilag. *There was a big fight down there at the creek at night.*

Waringararra *noun.* name of the western-most country estate in Gija lands.

waringarrim, waringarriny, waringarril, waringarrem *adjective.* many, plentiful.
• Daloony ngenengga nginji waringarriny. *Green plum is plentiful here.*

waringarrim *noun.* big group. • Waringarrim berraniyinde ngenenggayana. *Lots of people used to stay here.* [NOTE: sometimes used to refer to people coming from the desert south of Gija country] SEE: **melagawoom**

waringarriya *adjective.* all, the whole lot.
• Yirrinji-ngarri ngenengga waringarriya jarrag yirriyande Gijamoowam. *When we sit here, we all speak only Gija.* SEE: **melagawiya**.

wariny *coverb+SAY/DO.* be angry.
• Yagengerrambi wariny berrani-ni. *The others were angry with him.*

wariny *coverb+GET.* be angry. • Nyamanil wariny nyanemanyji. *The old woman was angry.*
• Wariny ngenamanyji. *I'm angry.* • Nyamanil wariny nyanemanyji-ni marloogany. *The old woman was angry with the old man.* [NOTE: person who is angry is the direct object, a kind of passive 'he/she/I were made angry'. In the example *Wariny nyanemanyji-ni* 'She was angry with him', the old man is cross-referenced by the indirect object, the woman is the direct object.]

wariny *coverb+SAY/DO_M.* be angry. • Nginyi gooroorroonggoony wariny wanemanyji-birri, ngoolnga-gany. *This nail-tailed wallaby,*

his brother-in-law, was angry with them.

waringye *coverb+GET.* make angry. • Waringye ngenamanyji. *He made me angry.*

waringye REDUP: **waringye-waringye**. *coverb+DO_REFL.* make each other angry, get angry with each other. • Waringye berramiyin-joo. *They got wild with each other. They made each other angry.* • Waringye-waringye berramiyin. *They all got angry with one another.*

warirrinji *noun masculine.* dodder laurel. *Cassytha filiformis.* [NOTE: type of parasitic vine that sprawls over trees and shrubs; stems are soaked in water that is then used as a washing medicine]

wari-wari *coverb +SAY/DO.* argue for something.
• Wari-wari woomenyande-boorroo daam dam. *She keeps arguing for that country.*

wari-wari *coverb+DO_REFL.* argue. • Wari-wari nyaliny berramiyanbe-gili. *They had another argument.* • Ngoowan wari-wari narrimijtha-yoo. *Don't you two fight.* SEE: **wari**.

wari-wari *coverb+GET.* scold. • Wari-wari nginimanyji. *He scolded him.*

wariwoony, wariwool, wariwoom *adjective.* aggressive, likely to bite, fight or attack (Kriol: 'cheeky').

warl *coverb+GET.* pull out (sinew). • Warl benamanyji. *He pulled out the sinew (from the kangaroo tail).*

warl *coverb+HIT.* wrap fresh sinew on spear shaft.
• Dangembi jirlwa warl boomberrayidbende garloomboo-yoorroong, warl-ngarri barndeg bemberrayang-bende barnden garloomboom-boorroo. *Then they used to wrap the fresh sinews on a spear shaft then put them to dry out in the sun to be used for making spears.*

warlagarriny *noun masculine.* supplejack. *Ventilago viminalis.* [NOTE: used to make boomerangs, fighting sticks and shields; bark used to make medicine for washing sores]

warlaginy, warlagil *noun.* puppy, physical child of mother. SEE: **warlarlayim**.

warlalarre *noun.* placenta.

warlanganbe, warlangeb *coverb+HIT.* wind swing people and trees from side to side.
• Warlanganbe bemberrayidbe. *The wind blew them from side to side.* • Warlangeb yinayidji-yarre. *The wind blew us from side to side.*

warlanginy, warlangem *noun.* big wind,

cyclone, first rainstorm, storm that comes very fast.

warlangooboo *coverb.* wind/cyclone chase someone. • *Doomboo-garri yirrani, wel warlangooboowa yinaroonji-yarre.* When we went through the gap a big wind (cyclone) came after us.

warlarla *coverb+GO_ALONG.* go along moving from side to side, move along in a waving line. • *Birrkoolany warlarla wiyinji.* The centipede is moving along with its body going from side to side. • *Dawool warlarlayi wiyinya.* The black-headed python is going along moving from side to side.

warlarlayim *noun.* puppies, baby animals or birds. SEE: **warlaginy**.

warlarriny *noun masculine.* white gum, ghost gum. *Corymbia bella.* [NOTE: good ashes for chewing tobacco]

warlawarr *coverb+DO_REFL.* paint something white on self. • *Warlawarr-gala ngendemij.* I will paint something white on myself.

warlawarre *noun.* white paint on something. • *Garloomboombiya berrembi warlawarr-bam.* These spears here are painted white.

warlawarra *coverb+HIT.* leave behind. • *Warlawarra noonayid ngarrgalemga.* I left my money behind. SEE: **gad**

Warlawoon *noun.* country between Tableland and Bedford.

warlawoorroowoorroo *noun.* tall flowering stems on spinifex.

warlayi *coverb+SAY/DO.* be happy for country. • *Warlayi ngenarn jaam ngagenybe-boorroo daam.* I am happy for my country.

warlbawoony *noun masculine.* agile wallaby, river wallaby. *Macropus agilis.*

warlboorroo *noun.* pubic cover made from spun hair or fur, worn by men before the arrival of Europeans (Kriol: 'naga', 'cock-rag'). **janigim, jarnim, nyagoom.**

warlele *noun.* meat juice, meat stock, soup. SEE: **wooroom**.

warlenggenany *noun masculine.* water snake, water python. *Liasis fuscus.*

warliberawoony, warliny *noun masculine.* grey goshawk. *Accipiter novaehollandiae.*

warlimarrgool *noun feminine.* butterfly, moth. Lepidoptera. [NOTE: young men are not supposed to say this word as it is used as a euphemism for women's genitals]

warlambany *noun.* plains kangaroo, antilopine wallaby. *Macropus antilopinus.* SEE: **jarlangarnany** (male), **gawoorrngarndil** (female).

Warloo *noun.* place in Rusty Peters' country on Springvale. SEE: **Thalinyman**. [NOTE: Rusty Peters says that Warloo is the *gardiya* name for the place]

warloom *noun.* body hair, fur.

Warloongarrim *noun.* song and dance style associated with ceremonies for young men.

warloowoodboojjel, warloowidboojgel *noun feminine.* marsupial mouse, stripe-faced dunnart. *Sminthopsis macroura.* [NOTE: makes mist like smoke on the hills in the wet time] SEE: **jaranel, nyilimbiny, yiroowoonji**.

warl-warl *coverb+BE/STAY.* be water running down. • *Goorloonyi danyi warl-warla nginji.* That water is running down now. SEE: **war**.

warnajarr *coverb+SAY/DO.* run away. • *Jawarlaliny warnajarr nginini yoorloo.* The tata lizard ran downstream.

warnajarr *coverb+SAY/DO_M.* run down, run away. • *Warnajarr woomberrama-yoo bangarinyga.* The two of them ran down.

Warnambany *noun.* Glass Hill. [NOTE: In the dreamtime Warnambany was a man who spoke Miriwoong; stands near Rawooliliny (Mt Buchanan), a man who spoke Gija]

warnamberrel *noun feminine.* wattle species. *Acacia* ssp. [NOTE: wood can be used to make *jiwiny*, the hard wooden part of a spear shaft; Nambin skin]

warnarrany, warnarral, warnarram REDUP: **warna-warnarram**. *adjective.* old, from long ago.

warnarram REDUP: **warna-warnarram**. *temporal.* long ago. • *Warna-warnarramga majany ngenaniyinde booleman ngelgang-ngooyoo.* I've been running stock camps for a long time.

warnarran, warnarrayan *adverb.* for a long time. *temporal.* long ago.

warndaj SEE: **wandaj**.

warndalij *coverb+BE/STAY.* be long stretch of water ahead. • *Goorloony nawarragawoony warndalij boorroonboo, ngenengga gerlirrang.* The river water stretches a long way ahead here coming from the west.

warndiwal *noun.* type of kapok bush.

warn'gan

Cochlospermum fraseri v. *heteronemum*. [NOTE: has similar flowers to *goonjal* but has hairy leaves and different growth pattern; roots are edible but taste 'gummy'; eaten after cooking and combined with cooked pounded mature boab seeds] SEE: **malanyjarrji, ngalwany.**

warn'gan *temporal.* cold time.

warn'gany, warn'gal, warn'gam *adjective.* cold.

warn'gany *coverb+FALL/GO_DOWN.* become cold.
- **Warn'gany berraard-yarri.** *It got cold on us.*

warn'ganybe *coverb+HIT.* make cold.
- **Warn'ganybe nginiyinji.** *I am getting cold. It is making me cold.*

warn'ganybe *coverb+BECOME.* become cold.
- **Warn'ganybe wiyinji.** *It is getting cold.*

warn'ganyboo *coverb+BE/STAY.* be cold.
- **Warn'gam, warn'gam! Woontha gaboo warn'gayam! Warn'ganyboo boorroowoonboo-yarri, ngooloo-ngooloon therijboo-ngarri nyoowoonya, malalali warn'ganyboo.** *It's cold, it's cold. Indeed what a very cold day. The cold time is here and when the sun goes down in the afternoon it is cold.*

warn'ganyge *coverb+HIT.* be made cold.
- **Mendoowoon-ga ger-ngarri boorroorn warn'ganyge nginiyinji.** *In the night when the wind blows, it makes me cold.*

warn'gil, warn'gim SEE: **wan'gil, wan'gim.**

Warnmarnjooloogoon *noun.* lagoon near Greenvale. [NOTE: Lena Nyadbi was born at this place]

warnngemaj *coverb+GET.* pick up someone and take away.
- **Warnngemaj ninemangge.** *I picked him up and took him away.*

warnngemaj *coverb+HIT.* take someone away.
- **Warnngemajga ngoorrayidbe-ngiyi wanyagewarrany ngoorroon-gili goowoole.** *They took that little boy of hers away there to school.*
- **Warnngemaj goorrayid nginyjiny, Turkey Creek-biny.** *They called this man up from Turkey Creek.*

warnngemaj *coverb+FALL/GO_DOWN.* go and get someone.
- **Warnngemaj-bijal nginiwardji.** *He wanted to go and get him.*

Warooban *noun.* place where the bat speared the crocodile in dreamtime.

waroogoobiny *locative.* on the left side.
- **Waroogoobiny ngerr nginini.** *He threw from the left. He threw it with his left hand.*

waroogoony, waroogool, waroogoom *adjective.* left-handed.
- **Waroogoony yanggi-gela nheraj nalijam-boorroo.** *I'll ask Left Hand if he wants tea.* SEE: **waroogoobiny.**

waroorroony *noun masculine.* Milky Way.

waroowool *coverb+BECOME.* become quiet in a strange or worrying way.
- **Waroowool woomberrayid daam, ganarram ngoowan gere-gere ngij woomberrayid.** *The country became quiet like something bad would happen, leaves did not blow in wind, the country got dark.*

warr REDUP: **warr-warr.** *coverb+SAY/DO_M.* put up shelter (e.g. a tent); spin a web; make a net, twist around (vine around trees).
- **Baarnji warr wanema.** *The spider made a web.*
- **Warr-warr wanema baarnji ngoorroo-ngoorrooma, goowoole-yirrin.** *The spider made a web everywhere in all the trees.*

warr *coverb+GET.* put up shelter (e.g. a tent); spin a web; make a net.
- **Warr benama.** *He/she made a shelter.*

warra *coverb+HIT.* watch, look around standing upright.
- **Warra beniyinji.** *He is watching them.*
- **Warra ngiyinya ngiliwool.** *His wife is watching.*
- **Warra wanyji yininyji-yoowoo ngoomool-baya.** *He must have come looking for us on a cloud.*
- **Thoowoo warra jooniyinnha?** *What are you watching?*
- **Ngoorroom warra nooniyin'ge melagawoom joorroob-garri woomberriyinbe.** *I am watching that big mob over there walking in a line.* SEE: **warra-warra.**

warrag Redup: **warrag-warrag.** *coverb+GO_ALONG.* walk.
- **Warrag wiyinji.** *He is walking.*
- **Ngoorroola warrag-warrag wiyinya.** *She keeps walking non-stop.* SEE: **girli.**

warrajbagowool *coverb+SAY/DO.* all move arms in the special way women do when dancing Wangga style dance (plural subject).
- **Warrajbagoowool boorroorn melagawoom ngali-ngalim.** *All the women are dancing moving their arms in the way called* warrajbe.

warrajbe, warrajbany *coverb+SAY/DO.* move arms in the special way women do when dancing Wangga style dance.
- **Warrajbe-gala yarra.** *Let's do* warrajpe *movements.*

warralaj *coverb+SAY/DO.* scratch in sand (e.g. to get soak water or a goanna making a hole).
- **Woobooj-garri dany goorloony dam-ningi warralaj nimbirn belag joowimnha. Men'gawoony.** *When digging that soak*

Figure 85. *Warrambany: Warrambany loorlg-garri nginiyi yilag.*

water you will scratch in the sand and clean it, good. • **Warralaj gala beniyi-nga, joordoo-joordoobam, belalg gala benem-nga goorloom.** *Scratch in the sand for me, it has dirt, clean that (soak) water for me.* [NOTE: Kriol comment from Mabel Juli: 'we do em got a finger you know *warralaj*, even kangaroo when they got no water']

warralaj *coverb+BECOME.* become covered up (goanna in hole), make a hole and be in it (goanna). • **Ngoorroomga, Gilban na, doorib-garri nginji bardoo-biny, warralaj-garri waniyid gilbany dany, ngarranggarnin.** *That there is the place called Gilban, place of the rasp-tailed goanna where that rasp-tailed goanna was covered up in dreamtime.*

warralaj *coverb+DO_REFL.* cover self (goanna in hole). • **Danya garndoowoolany warralaj nginimiyinji.** *That goanna covered himself in the hole.* [NOTE: goannas bury themselves underground in the cold time]

warramale *noun.* eyelash.

warrambany *noun masculine.* floodwater.

warraminab REDUP: **warra-warraminab.** *coverb+GO/COME.* floodwater come and spread. • **Jalij berrani, goorrngambi, warra-warraminab berrayin.** *It rained and the water spread everywhere.*

warraminany *noun masculine.* running floodwater.

warranyja *coverb+GO_ALONG.* go along tipping out. • **Warranyja wananyjende danyi gardiyany.** *It all spilled out on that white man as he went along.*

warranyja *coverb+SAY/DO.* waste something, tip something out. • **Warranyja boorroorn.** *They waste them (e.g. little catfish).* SEE: **woombool.**

warranyjag *coverb.* make tip out, make spill, waste. • **Warranyjagoowayi-ngarri nyimberramiyidbende dal weginel, belawambi dam boonoo-wayiya berrangirriyin mawoondem-birri.** *When they made the wagon tip out with everything, they used the flour to paint themselves like with white clay.*

warrarnany *noun masculine.* wedge-tailed eagle (Kriol: 'eaglehawk'). *Aquila audax.* SEE: **garnbarrany, garnbidany, girliwirringiny, wirli-wirlingarnany.**

warraroony, warreroony *noun.* bendee, tree species with edible gum. *Terminalia bursarina.* SEE: **yirriyarriny.** [NOTE: grows in river beds,

Warraroony

Figure 86. *Warrg: Martin Joogoord, Ray Patrick, Peter Bray: Warna-warnarram warrg berrani warrg-galembi.* (Photo Bill Genat.)

e.g. Bow River crossing]
Warraroony *noun.* Ord River crossing area south of Spring Creek.
warra-warra *coverb+SAY/DO_M.* watch, look around. • *Warra-warra yarramande garra-garraroon. We used to look around every afternoon.*
warra-warra *coverb+GO_ALONG.* go along looking around. • *Banane ngenayin-ngarri ngoorr-ngoorr-baya warra-warra-ngarri ngelanyge, jadany jalij wananyjende dan daan nawiyangen-noongoo. When I was going along the road by car and I was looking around, the rain was raining on his country.*
warrayany, warrayiny *noun.* type of sugar leaf (edible lerp) species found on river red gum, *bilirn, Eucalyptus camaldulensis*; river country sugar leaf.
warrayelji, warrayele *noun.* sand, sugar • *Warrayele yindiyinha. Give me sugar.* SEE: **ngayawarle**.
warrern *coverb+FALL/GO_DOWN.* get sick. • *Warrern nginiward. He got sick.* • *Warrern-ngarri nimboowoonha gaboowa nimbirn? If you get sick what will you do?*
warrern *coverb+SAY/DO.* be sick. • *Warrern berrani-yoo. They two were sick.*
warrernbeny, warrernbel, warrernbem *adjective.* sick (person).
warrernji *noun masculine.* praying mantis. [NOTE: called *warrernji* because it makes people sick]
warrern'ge *coverb+GET.* make sick. • *Warrern'ge yinema-yarri. He made us sick.*
warrern-warrern-nhawoony, warrern-warrern-nhawool, warrern-warrern-nhawoom *adjective.* sickly, one who gets sick.
warrg REDUP: **warrg-warrg**. *coverb+SAY/DO.* dance. • *Ngarranggarnin joonbam warrg berrani binyjirrminy, warrarnany, manggerregerreny. In the dreamtime the bat, the eagle and the tata lizard were dancing Joonba.* • *Warrg-warrg barroo-gili. You all dance around!* • *Mendoowoon warrg yirrirn Joonbam. We will dance Joonba at night.*
warrg *coverb+SAY/DO_M.* dance. • *Warrg wanemayinde-yarri goorlada-bany. He was dancing around us with a big wooden spear.*
warrg *coverb+GO_ALONG.* dance. • *Wayiniya warrgji woomberranybende. Then they danced like that.* • *Joowarrim-birri banji-ngarri nyimberramangbe, warrgaa wananyande dali ngalil. The spirits made her find it (the*

corroboree) and then that woman danced. • **Warrg-galen-ngoongoo.** *You are a good dancer.* • **Warrg giliyin'ge, ngalany ngiliyin'ge.** *I dance and I sing.*

warrgam *noun.* work. • **Warrgam yirramande mayaroon-ga.** *We used to work on the station.* [NOTE: from English 'work']

warrgam-bawoorroony, warrgam-bawoorrool, warrgam-bawoorroom *adjective.* lazy, person who won't work. [NOTE: from English 'work']

warrgamge *coverb+GET.* make someone work. • **Warrgamge ngoorramangbe-gili.** *They made him work.* [NOTE: from English 'work']

warri REDUP: **warri-warri.** *coverb+SAY/DO.* cry for relation. • **Warri-warri berrani ngoorriyana.** *They were all crying over there.* • **Dinil biyaya wananya-noo, bawoo wanemanyande-noo, warri nyanini-noo.** *The woodswallow woman was looking for him, she was calling him and crying for him.*

warrij-warrij *coverb+SAY/DO.* walk along quickly moving arms back and forth. • **Ngoorroonya warrij-warrij ngerne.** *He is walking over there.*

warrimiril *noun feminine.* small straight woomera used with short fighting spear.

-warriny *suffix.* two, together. [NOTE: attached to nouns and pronouns]

warri-warri *interjection.* word said when someone else is heard to swear (father or mother, uncle, aunt) or the name of someone who has died is heard; euphemism said instead of something that cannot be said by the speaker because it is indecent. SEE: **yigelany, ngagoony.**

warri-warri
coverb+GO_ALONG_TOGETHER. cry for relation. • **Warri-warri woomberramiyanyboo-noo nyaganyji-ni, thamanybaya barlegboo ngoorramingaboordboo jiyilem.** *They were all crying for their uncle and grandfather who were killed by those men.*

warriwoo *coverb+GET.* cry for a relation when seeing them again. • **Warriwoo-wayi benamanyji-yoo.** *He pretended to cry for the two of them like that.* • **Warriwoo benamanya-yoo.** *She cried for the two of them.*

warrmaj *coverb+BRING/TAKE.* hit. • **Ngoowan warrmaj joowida.** *Don't hit her.*

Warrmalam *noun.* non-Gija people from the desert south of Gija country.

Warrmarn *noun.* Warmun, Turkey Creek.

warrmayi *coverb+SAY/DO.* not sharing something, being greedy for something. • **Warrmayi boorroorn-boorroo merndam.** *They get greedy for money, they don't share.*

warrmayi *coverb+SAY/DO_M.* not sharing something, being greedy for something. • **Warrmayi jemenande-yirri.** *You don't share with us.*

warr-warr *coverb+GO_ALONG.* put up shelter (e.g. a tent); spin a web, make a net, make a nest. • **Googanda warr-warr ngilin'gende.** *I do nothing but make webs (spider).* • **Nginyga laarne, warr-warr-ngarri wananyji-yarre.** *This one (the eagle) up there where our dreaming makes a nest.*

warr-warr *coverb+SAY/DO.* put up shelter (e.g. a tent); spin a web; make a net. • **Warr-warr nginini berrema daam-noongoo.** *He put his tent up here.* SEE: **woorr-woorr.**

wawalji *noun masculine.* small water yam, water plant with edible tubers/yams. *Cycnogeton dubium.* [NOTE: edible part grows in bunches on stringy roots rather like peanuts, similar in growth to *jawooloo-wooloony.*] SEE: **yamoony.**

wawalji, wawalel, wawale *noun.* green ant. *Oecophylla smaragdina.* SEE: **minyal, waawalji.** [NOTE: crushed juice from green ants used to improve voice of singers]

wawanggoony, wawanggoom *noun.* white inside part of boab nut when dry.

wawarrel *noun.* green ant nest. SEE: **minyal, waawalji.**

wawirriny *noun masculine.* big red kangaroo. *Macropus rufus.*

wawoo *interjection.* a call (made to ward off danger). • **Wawoo, marra biyarr, yoowoorlngbiyan-ngoo.** *Hey, go away, you keep talking same time when we are talking.*

wawoog *coverb+SAY/DO_M.* cook on coals. • **Wawoog woomberramande.** *They used to cook it.*

wawoog *coverb+HIT.* cook on coals. • **Wawoog benayidji.** *He cooked it (non-singular).* • **Wawoog nginiyid jiyirriny.** *He cooked the kangaroo.* • **Mirlim welerren wawoog benij.** *Cook the liver on the charcoal.*

wawoog REDUP: **wawawoog.** *coverb+SAY/DO.* cook on coals. • **Wawoog-garri nginini . . .** *When he was cooking . . .*

wawooleny *noun masculine.* frillneck lizard,

Wawoonboolooloom

(Kriol: 'blanket lizard'). *Chlamydosaurus kingii*. SEE: **gerdanji**.

Wawoonboolooloom noun. Bedford Downs. SEE: **Barangen**.

wawoonggany, wawoonggal, wawoonggam REDUP: **wawawoonggam**. *adjective*. outsider, minding own business, having no relations, alone to fend for oneself, one who is not involved in a particular event or situation.

wawoordjil noun feminine. barramundi. *Lates calcarifer*. [NOTE: *wawoordjil* refers to the way the tail swings from side to side when barramundi are swimming] SEE: **balgal, dayiwool, dawoogjil, nyilibal**.

Wawoorrjan noun. place near Goongewayin.

wawoorrmarndiny noun masculine. freshwater crocodile. SEE: **lalanggarrany**.

wawoorroon adverb. do something by mistake. • Thed goorrawoonbe wawoorroon. *They killed him by mistake.* Wawoorroon nanida-ngoo, gaageny. *I hit you by mistake poor thing.*

wawoo-wawoog coverb+SAY/DO. cook something on coals. • Wawoo-wawoog nginini dany warrarnany. *That eagle was cooking (his rock wallabies).*

wawoo-wawoog coverb+SAY/DO_M. cook something on coals. • Wawoo-wawoog woomberramaande-yarre. *They used to cook them for us.*

-wayi, -ayi suffix. in this/that way, like that

wayi particle. like this/that. SEE: **-wayi/-ayi** suffix.

Wayilangen noun. Two Mile Creek.

wayina REDUP: **wayi-wayina**. particle. like this/that. SEE: **wayi, -wayi/-ayi** suffix, **wayini**.

wayinawoo adverb. like that then.

wayingge coverb+HIT. cause someone to be the same way, give someone something (e.g. sickness). • Mawiyaban-nga. Ngoowan maj yinbimnha, wayingge ninbijge-ninggi. *I have poison. Don't touch me, I might give it to you.*

wayini, wayiniwany adverb, particle. like that, thus. • Nginya nawarragawoony nginji, wayini gendoowa balmendeg ginini. *This is the river, it goes up like that to form a junction with the other.*

wayinigana adverb. because of this, that is how, that is the reason why.

wayinigelaj adverb. like that.

wayinijarrany, wayinijarral, wayinijarram adjective. that kind, like that.

wayiningerreg adverb. that many.

wayininji particle. while, at the same time. • Mayim jang yirrani wayininji wandaj benayanyji joowegbi Magany, marrarna nginiyin. *We were having our dinner when Makany rolled his swag and set off.*

wayininy, wayinil, wayinim adjective. that kind of one. • Wayinili barra jilbama nyooloojge. *Do you think I'm scared of that kind of a woman? I'm not scared of that kind.* • Wayininyi barra jilbama noowoojge. *Do you think I'm scared of that kind of man?*

wayiniwoojoo interjection. don't do that.

wayiniya particle. until, like that. • Dangembi ngoowana wari-wari yarramiyinyande wayiniya biri nginiward Queensland-yoorroong. *From that day on we didn't have any more arguments till he had to go back to Queensland.*

wayiniyana REDUP: **wayi-wayiniyana**. adverb. like at this time, while.

wayirran locative. along the side of the hill.

wayiwoorrool noun feminine. turtle. SEE: **darndal, bilidbal, balarnel**. [NOTE: Southern dialect, except for *darndal* which is Northern]

wedaga, wedagaya coverb+BE/STAY. be reconciled, make up after a quarrel. • Wedagaya yarrenya. *Let's be friends now.*

weg REDUP: **weg-weg**. coverb+SAY/DO. frog croak. • Wek ngerne. *He croaks (frog).* • Wek-wek boorroorn. *They are croaking.*

wegerlel noun feminine. big tick. *Rhipicephalus sanguineus*. SEE: **birlinyil**.

wegerr coverb+GO_ALONG. be hardly able to walk. • Dany gendalooganly wegerr wiyinji. *That short fat man can hardly walk.*

wela interjection. hey, hey you, you there. [NOTE: often in joking context]

welang coverb+HIT. put in front, go in front/ahead of someone. • Welang yinayid. *You go ahead of me (in front)!*

welangen, welengen, woolangen locative. in front, ahead (in space). • Welangen biyarra! *You go ahead (in front)!*

welangen, woolangen temporal. before (in time), first. • Gaboowa yarrirn woolangen? *What do we do first?*

welayi, weleyi interjection. you there. SEE: **wela**.

weleberr coverb+GO_ALONG. wriggle sideways. • Ngoowan! Wayinigan'ga weleberr wimbirrigbe ganjimbi dam. *No, the bullet* *might wriggle sideways!*

weloowoomoorany *noun masculine.* long-necked turtle. *Chelodina rugosa.* SEE: **lawarrbal, wirriwoonany, woorlemerewal.** [NOTE: unusual gender, turtles are nearly always feminine]

welerrem SEE: **werlerrem.**

weleweny, weloowoony *noun masculine.* tall grass species. *Arundinella nepalensis.* [NOTE: grows near water, young boys used to use it to make little toy spears]

welrayiny *noun masculine.* quinine tree, 'emu tucker'. *Petalostigma pubescens.*

welyerr-welyerrji, welyerr-welyerrel, welyerr-welyerre *adjective.* wrinkled, having wrinkles. • *Welyerr-welyerre-ngoo.* You have wrinkles.

Wengenban, Woongenban *noun.* a place on Alice Downs.

wengenji, woongenji *noun masculine.* tea-tree. *Leptospermum madidum; Melaleuca bracteata.* [NOTE: flowers smell like custard, according to Hector Jandany]

wenggarrem *noun.* nape of neck.

wenthawoolenji *noun masculine.* Kalumburu gum. *Eucalyptus herbertiana.*

werd *coverb+HIT.* bite. • *Ngagenyil gooral ngamarram werd jimberrayidbewa.* My mother was bitten by a snake.
• *Minyjoowoo-giny dany joolany werd ginbiji.* That dog with big teeth might bite me.
• *Boornool werd ngenayid.* A fly bit me (hence I have bung-eye).

werdag *coverb+BECOME.* go across/meet.
• *Werdag waniyidji-boorroo berrema na.* He met them here then.

werd-bawoorroony, werd-bawoorrool, werd-bawoorroom *adjective.* one who does not bite. • *Jirrayany dany men'gawoony werd-bawoorroony.* That good one is alright, he won't bite.

werd-nhawoony, werd-nhawool, werd-nhawoom *adjective.* biter, one that bites.
• *Thengawiny werd-nhawoony.* The type of ant called thengawiny bites.

weren *coverb+GET.* wrap around. • *Weren nyanema.* He (snake) wrapped himself around her (woman). • *Weren nginimanyji.* He wrapped it around him/it (masculine).

weren *coverb+BE/STAY.* be wrapped around.
• *Weren nginji.* It is wrapped around / twined

around (e.g. vine around tree).

were-were *coverb+HIT.* throw spears at someone.
• *Were-werewa benayidji garloomboom na.* They threw spears at him then.

were-were *coverb+GO/COME.* throw spears.
• *Were-were nginiyi danyi garloomboony.* He threw that spear.

were-were *coverb+SAY/DO_M.* throw spears.
• *Were-were woomberramande garloomboom gendoowagoo.* They were throwing spears up (at him).

werlalji *noun.* kurrajong. *Brachychiton diversifolius.* [NOTE: has edible seeds, frayed sticks are used for honey spoons]

werlarlambalji *noun masculine.* roots of *malawany, mangoonyji*, the freshwater mangrove. *Barringtonia acutangula.* SEE: **malawany, mangoonyji.** [NOTE: used as fish poison]

werlemen, werlemenel REDUP: **werlerlemen; werlerlemenbe; werle-werlemen.** *noun.* young woman at puberty, teenage girl.

werlemenboo *coverb+GO/COME.* keep on growing into a young woman. • *Nawarrawoo nyidja, werlemenel. Goornawool werlemenboo nyidja.* She is getting big. The little girl is becoming a young woman.

werlerlewoony, werlerlewool, werlerlewoom *adjective.* poor thing. SEE: **gaageny, goorlanggeny, merelegbeny.**

werlerreg *coverb+BURN/BITE.* burn to charcoal.
• *Nyinjiny noonayid, wayinigana werlerreg benawoorran.* I forgot about it, so it burned to charcoal.

werlerreg *coverb+FALL/GO_DOWN.* become charcoal, die down (fire). • *Jigili, werlerreg nginiward.* Yuck, it (damper left in the fire too long) has burned to charcoal.

werlerrem, werlerreny *noun.* charcoal.

werlge-werlge *coverb.* be stuck.
• *Werlge-werlge woomberramandi-yoo bajalarrin.* They two were stuck in the bucket (two turtles).

werlmerrem, wirlmerrem *noun.* kidney.

werlwe *coverb+SAY/DO_REFL.* make self part of the country in dreamtime. • *Dana belegan, derd janoowardja, marrgewa werlwe nyanengirriyin.* There in the middle she got stuck, and she is still there, she made herself part of the country, becoming a dreaming place.

werlwe, werlweny *coverb+GET.* become part of

werlweny, werlwel, werlwem

country in dreamtime. • **Ngarranggarninji, ngarranggarninji werlwe-ngarri nyanemanyji-birri.** *From dreamtime, from dreamtime, when she (barramundi woman) became part of the country on them (the women who were trying to catch her who also turned to stone) (example from the Dayiwool Moonga-moonga song).* • **Werlwenya nginimanyji.** *He became a dreaming rock then.* [NOTE: transitive verb – what is the subject, the person (e.g. frillneck lizard who was a man) who became stone the subject or the forces of nature and the dreamtime, ngarranggarnin, that made him turn to stone?]

werlweny, werlwel, werlwem *noun.* place where an ancestral being has become part of the country, dreaming place for that entity.

werl-werl *coverb+SAY/DO.* swim, to move along in water (fish). • **Goorndarrim werl-werl boorroorn.** *The fish are swimming.*

werl-werl *coverb+GO_ALONG.* swim, to move along in water (fish). • **Dala moornmoordel werl-werl wiyinya goorloon.** *The golden spotted perch is swimming in the water.*
• **Goorndarrim werl-werl woomberriyinbe.** *The fish are swimming along.*

werna-werna *coverb+HIT.* take dogs hunting.
• **Joolam boorroordboo ngenengga werna-werna yirriyinji.** *The dogs go here, we take them hunting.*

werndelg *coverb+GO/COME.* fall/come off.
• **Werndelg ngoowiyayin-ngirri.** *It is going to come off on me (injured toenail).*

werndelgbany *coverb.* pull quickly and throw down.

werndelg *coverb+BRING/TAKE.* dog grab someone. • **Joolama-birri loorroob-garri ngoorranybende wernderlg-garri ngoorranybe, waliga nginiyin thoondooloom.** *When they chased him with the dogs and they (dogs) grabbed hold of him, he went inside a hollow log.*

werndij *coverb+SAY/DO.* throw spear.
• **Wayiniganji binyjirrminy garloomboom benamanyji, werndij nginini-ni, nginingaboordji.** *Then the bat picked up his spears, threw one at him and speared him.*

werndij *coverb+SAY/DO_REFL.* throw spears at each other. • **Werndij berrangirriyinbende garloomboo-moowam-birri.** *They only used to fight by throwing spears at each other (not shooting).*]

werndij *coverb+GO_ALONG.* go along throwing spears. • **Yinanyjende-nga-yirri, werndij-garri wananyjende, jiyirrem-anyji, yilag-garnam-anyji, darndam-anyji thoowoo-thoowoom.** *He used to take us then when he went throwing them, maybe at kangaroos, maybe crocodiles, maybe turtles, all kind of things.*

werndij REDUP: **werndi-werndij, werndij-werndij.** *coverb+PUT.* throw spear. • **Werndij-gala nheraj.** *I'll try throwing it.*

werndij *coverb+SAY/DO_M.* throw spear. • **Thalg nginema, werndij wanema, nginingaboord jiyirriny.** *He hooked up his spear in his woomera, he threw it, he speared the kangaroo.*

wernebe *coverb+BE/STAY.* be warm. • **Wernebe nginji.** *He sitting in a warm place.* • **Wawooleny ngarag benamany marnem, wernebe ngininiyinde warn'gan.** *The frillneck lizard made a fire and used to stay in the warm place in the cold weather time.*

werne-werneb *coverb+SAY/DO.* warm.
• **Werne-werneb nyerne marnen nyamanil.** *The old woman is warming herself by the fire.*

wern'galge *coverb+EAT.* eat only the one thing, eat something bad. • **Goorloo-moowam wern'galge noonoongoon'gende.** *I live on water only (dragonfly speaking).*
• **Goorlanggeny joolany ngagenyji wern'galge benangoon, thoowoorranyji.** *My poor dog ate something no good, I don't know what.*

werreralji, werreralel, werrerale *noun.* blowfly. • **Werrerali doo boornoom jang ngenarn.** *I (willie wagtail) eat blowflies and flies.*

werrerre *coverb+BRING/TAKE.* rock to comfort someone (e.g. a parent rocking a crying child). • **Men'gawoony ngaaloony werrerre ngenayinji. Yirdarrge ngenayidji.** *The good shade was rocking me and made me go to sleep (Rusty Peters talking about a tree he slept under when he had the flu).*

werrerre-werrerre *coverb+HIT.* rock someone to comfort them. • **Werrerre-werrerre nginiyidja goorndoogany.** *She rocked the little boy.*

werrg *coverb+FALL/GO_DOWN.* fall down (group).
• **Werrg berrawardbe.** *They all fell down.*
• **Danya minyjaarrany werrg nginiward balawan.** *That black plum (entity), fell down on the ground.* SEE: **wirrg, woorrg**.

werrgalen *temporal.* hot time when green leaves

appear before the rain. SEE: **barnden**.

werrgalji, werrgalel, werrgale REDUP: **werrga-werrgale**. *adjective*. green. • **Ngayin-ga werrgal-ban-nga berndoowalemga.** *I have a green headband.* • **Yarren-ga-gili werrgal-ban-yarre berndoowalemga.** *We all have green headbands.*

werrgalji, werrgalel, werrgale *noun*. green plant, vegetable, green grass. • **Werrgale mayim.** *Green vegetables.*

werrgal; werrgalwany *coverb+BECOME*. become green. • **Girinyil dal ngarra-ngarrawoo benamenya warn'gam, gerrij-garri wiyinji dany jadany werrgalwany-ngarri woomberriyinbe mangoonyji.** *That katydid grasshopper lets people know about the cold, when the rain stops and the grass is green (like the green sections in the painting).* • **Miyale werrgal woomberrayidboo, yilgoowoorroom ngard boorroorn nhoowoole.** *The meat has become green, it smells bad, stinking.*

werrgeb *coverb+SAY/DO_M*. throw down. • **Nawarrarrany werrgeb wanemanyande, ngenengga balawan yilag.** *She used to throw lots of them down here on the flat ground.* SEE: **wirrg, woorrg**.

werrgereb *coverb+FALL/GO_DOWN*. fall down (e.g. seeds). • **Werrgereb berraward** *They all fell down (seeds).*

werrgereb; werrgereg *coverb+SAY/DO*. throw. • **Gendoowa-yoorroong werrgereb ginini wanyanyagem.** *He threw all the little ones (fish) upstream.*

werrweny, werrwel, werrwem *adjective*. one who talks a long time. • **Werrwen-ngoo, jarrag jemenande.** *You have been talking for a long time.*

Wethan *noun*. place on Springvale Station near the birthplace of Rusty Peters.

wethed *coverb+FALL/GO_DOWN*. fall to ground. • **Wethed janoowardja nyamanil dal.** *The old woman fell to the ground.*

wethed *coverb+HIT/CUT*. throw down. • **Wethed benawoonji doorlgajim.** *He threw down the rifle.*

wethed *coverb+HIT*. throw away, throw down. • **Wethed niniyidge.** *I thew it down.* • **Wethedbebe ngoorrayidbende-yoo.** *The two of them really threw them down.*

widirr *coverb+BECOME*. wobble along (e.g. drunk or weak). • **Widirr wiyinji.** *He is going wobbling along.*

wigamany *noun*. water goanna, Merten's water monitor. *Varanus mertensi, V. mitchelli*. SEE: **janawany**.

wigil *noun feminine*. daughter.

wiginy *noun masculine*. son.

-wija; woojal; -bija; -bijal *coverb suffix*. want to.

wijerraj *coverb+SAY/DO_REFL*. make marks on self. • **Wijerraj nginingirriyinjende nganoonggoon.** *He used to make marks on his arm.* [NOTE: can be permanent, e.g. with a hot wire, or temporary by scratching the skin lightly to make a mark]

wijgel *noun feminine*. yellow whip snake. SEE: **wandawandal**. [NOTE: Naminyji skin]

wijginy *adjective*. scraped (swearing). • **Manam wijginy.** *He's got a tight arse, been scraped (swearing).* • **Ngoorrinya wijginy, yangoorra-anyji wij goorrama.** *That one is tight arsed, someone scraped him.* [NOTE: old people's word]

wiji *coverb+SAY/DO*. to run (one, two or three people or things). • **Nginya gerliwirring wiji ngerne, goorloony.** *This water (waterfall seen in the painting) runs down from up there.* SEE: **yoowoorr**.

wiji *coverb+GO/COME*. to run (one, two or three people or things). • **Wiji berrayi.** *They ran.* SEE: **yoowoorr**.

wiji *coverb+FALL/GO_DOWN_WITH*. run away with something. • **Wiji nyanoomoowardja joolooj janoomoowardjande-ni warlagarriny goodoorriny-berra goodoorriny.** *She ran away carrying that supplejack tree used to make fighting sticks.*

wiji REDUP: **wiji-wiji**. *coverb+LEAVE*. run away and leave someone. • **Baremanbemga wiji-wiji joonoowoorroonha.** *You are running away from the doctors.*

wiji *coverb+BRING/TAKE*. run away taking something. • **Joowarriny wiji yinanyji-yarri-yoo nawan-yoorroong.** *A ghost took us two to his cave.*

wiji *coverb+SAY/DO_M*. to run (one, two or three people). • **Wiji yirramande-noo.** *We used to run to him.* SEE: **yoowoorr**.

wijige *coverb+GET*. make someone run, frighten. • **Wijige nyanema.** *It made her run.*

wijigoowany REDUP: **wiji-wijigoowany**. *coverb+GET*. make someone go running. • **Wijigoowany ngoorrama.** *They made him*

wijinga

go running.

wijinga *coverb+GO_ALONG.* run. • *Nyanagawoony wijinga wanany, Yooloomboo-biny.* The river runs down from Tableland. • *Yagenginy nyanagawoony wijinga wanany ngelmang. Dawson Downs-yoorroong wijinga wanany.* Another river runs down from the east. It runs down to Dawson Downs. [NOTE: Southern dialect]

wijinga *coverb+SAY/DO.* to run.
• *Thoowoorranyji-boorroo wijinga ngerne.* He is running for something. [NOTE: Southern dialect]

wijiwany *coverb+BE/STAY.* go running. • *Wijiwany ngenaniyin ngaginyil-ngiyi gawangen.* I was running to my aunt.

wij-wij *coverb+GET.* scrape off bark from sticks to use for dancing or to make the hard wooden part of spears. • *Wij-wij gala benem dam goowoolem warrg-girrem.* Clean off those little sticks for dancing. [NOTE: movement of the hand is away from the person doing it]

wilawoony, wilawool, wilawoom *adjective.* tasty, sweet. SEE: **wilyawoony, menherrgayiny.**

wili *coverb+FALL/GO_DOWN.* try to hit someone/something, hunt something. • *Wili berraardbende.* They kept trying to hit him.

wilili *coverb+SAY/DO.* round up animals.
• *Ngoowan wilili nimbirn dan-ga.* Don't go rounding them up there.

wililib *coverb+PUT.* hunt, try to hit, round up.
• *Wililib nginiyanyji nginya joomooloony, ngenengga yilag waniyidji dalyalya.* It (lightning) was trying to hit this boab tree but struck the ground. • *Wanyanyagem berrayin wayini dali nyamanil wililib benaya.* All the kids were going like that and that old woman went and chased them, trying to hit them. • *Wililib yinanyji-yarre.* He is trying to hit us.

wililib *coverb+HIT.* • *Danya wililib beniyinji waringarrim.* He is rushing up to throw things at everybody.

wililji, wililel *noun.* baby. • *Wililban-nga.* I have a baby. SEE: **nyimbelawoony, wangawoony.**

wilinggeny; wilyinggeny REDUP: **wiling-wilinggembi.** *noun.* young man.

wilinyji, wilinyel, wilinybe *noun.* caustic bush. *Grevillea pyramidalis.* [NOTE: black ash used to blacken hair or body for corroboree; caustic sap used to tattoo body]

wiliwirrel, wiliwirrirrel, wiliwoorrool *noun feminine.* cabbage ghost gum. *Corymbia flavescens.*

wiliwirrin *noun.* hunting ground.

wilmoorroo; wilymoorre *noun.* wire, telephone, telegram.

wil-wil *coverb+SAY/DO.* do jumping dance movement (women's dance movement).
• *Wil-wil berrani.* They (women) were all dancing doing wil-wil.

wil-wil *coverb+SAY/DO_M.* jumping dance movement done by women. • *Wil-wil woomberrama nyamani.* The old women all danced doing wil-wil.

wilyawoony, wilyawool, wilyawoom *adjective.* tasty, sweet. SEE: **wilawoony, menherrgayiny.**

wimarnmard *coverb+SAY/DO.* sprinkle.
• *Wimarnmard boorroorn.* They are sprinkling (water on the grass).

wimbija *verb.* she/it (feminine) will BECOME.

wimbiji *verb.* he/it (masculine) will BECOME.

wimbimji *verb.* he/it (masculine) will SAY/DO.

wimbirrigbe *verb.* they will GO ALONG.

wimbirrijbe *verb.* they will BECOME.

wimbirriyinbe *verb.* they are BECOMING.

Wimeroorroon *noun.* Rail Yard.

Wimirriny *noun.* Caroline Pool. SEE: **Wimngayirriny.**

wimiyinji *verb.* he DOES HIMSELF.

wimiyinyande *verb.* she keeps on DOING HERSELF.

Wimngayirriny *noun.* Caroline Pool. SEE: **Wimirriny.**

winbarniny *noun masculine.* wattle species. *Acacia umbellata.* [NOTE: has edible gum]

Winberrji *noun.* Police Rock Hole, place on Bedford Downs.

wingalawoog *coverb+BRING/TAKE.* make sound echo loudly all around. • *'Dana wingalawoog benanyji, ngalany nginini,' berrani.* 'He was making a loud echoing sound all around there as he sang,' they said. • *Menkawoog benamanyji daam wingalawoog-garri nginini, ngalany-galeny.* The good singer made the country good when he made the sound echo all around.

wingenoowoony, wingenoowool, wingenoowoom *adjective.* drunk, wobbling not walking straight.

winggernanggoo *interjection.* goodness me, strewth. [NOTE: considered swearing by some people]

wingini *coverb+GO_ALONG.* go around and around while dizzy.
wingini *coverb+SAY/DO.* be dizzy, be drunk.
• Goonggooloo wingini ngenarn. *I'm dizzy (my head is spinning).* • Wingini-merrarrem ngoorloorloog-garri berrani. *They are all dizzy from drinking,*
winginig *coverb+HIT.* make someone dizzy.
• Winginig-garri ngoorrayid, gerloorroogoo doowab-garri nginiyin, wingini wananyjende, jag giniyin, nginyi ngoomoolji. *When they made him dizzy and he flew up into the sky, he went round and around and one cloud came out.*
winginig *coverb+PUT.* get drunk, get dizzy. • Ngoorroon galma-galmang babjin winginig-garri ngoorriyangbe goorloonyga wariwoony. Marrarna yamboorroowoorroobja ngoorroona goorndarri-ban. *Over there in the pub to the east they will all be getting drunk. Let's leave them all and go to that fishing place.*
winginigoowool *coverb+SAY/DO.* be dizzy, be drunk (plural subject). • Winginigoowool boorroorn. *They are all dizzy drinking.*
wininibal *noun feminine.* emu with chicks.
wininim *noun.* emu chicks.
winyanyanggem *noun.* children. [NOTE: uncommon dialectal variation] SEE: **wanyanyagem.**
winyji-ngarnany, winyji-ngarnal, winyji-ngarnam *adjective.* spring country dweller, belonging to the spring country. • Nginyji winyji-ngarnany goowooloony. *This is a spring country tree.*
winyjiny, winyjim *noun.* spring, spring water.
winyjirrab *coverb+HIT.* make someone sick by magic. • Ngoowan narriyannha-birri bagoo boorroonboo. Winyjirrab nambirrijtha-boorroo. *Don't go to them there, they are sleeping. They will make you sick.*
winyjirram *noun.* spirit. SEE: **birlirre, yoongoom.**
winymany, winymal, winymam *adjective.* skinny. SEE: **wanyjany.**
wirabal *noun feminine.* big bony bream, bony bream. *Nematalosa erebi.* [NOTE: has *wirany* 'little string' from dreamtime, *ngarranggarnin*] SEE: **lilinyil.**
wirany *noun.* little string or whisker as on a bony bream.
wiram *noun.* whip.

wiram *noun.* frayed stick or bark for getting honey. [NOTE: made from *goonjal, warndiwal,* 'kapok bush' or *warernji,* 'coolibah']
wirangbawarrany, wirangbawarral, wirangbawarram *adjective.* having slack feet, feet that flap about when walking.
• Thambarlam wirangbawarran-nga. *My feet are slack.*
Wirdim *noun.* Red Butt. SEE: **Doogoorrenyinem.**
wird-wird *coverb+SAY/DO.* wag tail (e.g. dog, horse). • Ngoorroonya wird-wird ngerne joolany, bilij-anyji benayid jarrambayim-anyji. *The dog is wagging its tail, maybe it has found a goanna.*
wiriny REDUP: **wiriny-wiriny.** *coverb+SAY/DO.* whistle. • Wiriny ngerne. *He is whistling.*
• Melagawoom wiriny-wiriny boorroorn. *They are all whistling.*
wirlarrji *noun.* millet, native grass with edible seeds, johnnycake grass. *Panicum decompositum, Sporobolus australasicus, Eragrostis tenellula.* [NOTE: Paddy Williams remembered it growing everywhere when he was young; seed was gathered, ground and made into damper; made very rare by the introduction of cattle]
wirlgil, wirlginy. *noun.* number 7 boomerang.
wirlinyin *locative.* on the hill top.
wirlibja REDUP: **wirli-wirlibja.** *locative.* higher up (on tree or stick). • Wirlibja ngerd beniyinha ngoowan yilag, wirli-wirliyan. *Cut it (stick or bamboo) a bit higher up, not down there, higher up.* • Wirli-wirlibja barraj beniyinha. *Cut it higher up.*
wirlij REDUP: **wirlij-wirlij.** *coverb+PUT.* cover, put on top. • Banjalgboo wirlij benajtha-noo wanyageny bagoo-girrim. *Put a blanket over it for the little boy for sleeping (so that he can sleep).* • Manbiny dany wirlij biyajtha lawagbiny-ni. *Put that black one on the white one.* • Wanyaginy dany ngarrgaleny wirlij biyajtha-ni nawarrany. *Put that little one on the big one.*
wirlij-wirlij *coverb+DO_REFL.* get on top of each other, have sex. • Bagoo-ngarri berraniyindi-yoo, wirlij-wirlij-garri berrangirriyinbende-yoo. *The place where they two (the moon and girl in dreamtime) were lying down getting on top of each other having sex.* SEE: **moorniny, tharriny.**
wirli-wirligajil *noun feminine.* aeroplane. • Wirli-

wirli-wirlim

wirligajil ngelela wirli-wirlin nyidja-ngarri. *This is an aeroplane that goes high above.* LIT: 'on top for using'. SEE: **wirli-wirlingarnal**.

wirli-wirlim *noun.* fishing line.
• . . . wirli-wirlim-boorroo . . . *for fishing*

wirli-wirlimilim *noun.* things from on top of something. • Dam wirli-wirlimilim lerlg benemnha gaardaya. *That thing from the top (bark of tree or hide of bullock), peel it off carefully/slowly.* • Ngenengga gajim jinbimoorloonha-ngarri, dam wirli-wirlimilim berrem ngaandem jinbimoorloonnha-ngarri gaardaya wayina lerlg jinbimnha. *Here where you have a sore (with a Band-aid), that thing you have on top of the flesh here, peel it off slowly like that.*

wirli-wirlin; wirlin *locative.* on top of the hills, high on top, over, up high in the sky, on the high part of something (e.g. a tree).
• Ngelela tharriyarrel, thad nyinya wirli-wirlin. *This is the ranbow standing up high in the sky.* • Nawarrany, nawarrany, googan wirlin gadem woomberramande-ni danyga gamanggarrji. *Lots and lots of it, they just used to cut that bamboo up on top there.* • Wirliyan gadem benem. *Cut it right up high (i.e. not down at the bottom but higher up).* [NOTE: reduplicated form *wirli-wirlin* much more frequently heard than *wirlin*]

wirli-wirlingarnal *noun feminine.* aeroplane. LIT: 'on-top dweller'. SEE: **wirli-wirligajil**.

wirli-wirlingarnany *noun masculine.* wedge-tailed eagle (Kriol: 'eaglehawk'). *Aquila audax.* LIT: 'on-top dweller'. SEE: **warrarnany, garnbarrany, garnbidany, girliwirringiny**.

wirnan *noun.* traditional trade, exchange of goods.

wirnbaj *coverb+GO_ALONG.* swing tail (dog).
• Wirnbaj wiyinji joolany. *The dog is swinging his tail.*

wirnbel *noun feminine.* pandanus. *Pandanus aquaticus, P. spiralis.* • Nginyjinya wigamany bagoo nginji laarne wirnbel-ngiyi. *Here is a water goanna sleeping on top of the pandanus.*

wirndoowool *noun feminine.* curlew. *Burhinus magnirostris.*

wirniny *noun.* spring pandanus. *Pandanus spiralis.* SEE: **wirnbel**. [NOTE: most Gija people are not familiar with this word but use *wirnbel* for any kind of pandanus]

wirnmirnmaj *coverb+SAY/DO.* make sparks.
• Moorloo-boorroo wirnmirnmaj-garri birrirn jarrg-garri birriwoon-ngirri. *For eyes when it (welder) is making sparks that might get in my eyes (i.e. googles).* SEE: **nhil, ninirl**.

wirraj *coverb+HIT.* make ripples. • Wirraj benayid goorloom ngarrgalinyga waj-garri janiyid. *It made the water ripple when you threw the stone.*

wirrarraj *coverb+SAY/DO.* be ripples on water.
• Wirrarraj boorroorn goorrngam. *There are ripples on the water.*

wirrg *coverb+GO/COME.* become thin, shed weight.
• Wirrg naniyi, ngaande-bawoorroon-jaya-ngoo. *You have got thin, you are like someone with no flesh.*

wirrg *coverb+BECOME.* shed leaves (tree), lose leaves. • Ngoorroonya goowooleny wirrg waniyid, ganarra-bawoorroony. *That tree has lost its leaves.*

wirridim, wirridiny *noun.* plains, open place. water from tree in dry place. • Ngoorloorloog berrani-yoo goorloony dany wirridiny, goowoolewanggoony, goowooloon nginji-ngarri, wirridiny. *They two were drinking that water living in the trees in the dry place.* [NOTE: refers to open plain country near Turner River; also one of the songs in Buttercup Mung Mung's Woorra-woorral (mermaid) Moonga-moonga is about that place]

wirrijga *coverb+GO_ALONG.* go along alone, walk along by oneself. • Marrarn girlirli wananyji wirrijga wananyji, berrtha-bawoorroony. *He went walking away by himself with no friends.*

wirrilijgel *noun feminine.* rainbow lorikeet, 'blue mountain'. *Trichoglossus haematodus.* [NOTE: word not supposed to be said by young men who say *thirrilngarnal* instead]

wirrilij-wirrilij *coverb+GO_ALONG.* go along calling 'wirrilij-wirrilij' (northern rosella, rainbow lorikeet). • Bawoo-wawoo-ngarri nyerne, wirrilij-wirrilij wiyinya. *When she calls, she goes along saying 'wirrilij-wirrilij'.*

-wirrin *suffix.* place where something takes place habitually. [NOTE: can be attached to nouns or coverbs, e.g. *goorndarriwirrin* 'usual fishing place', *joogboowirrin* 'usual hunting place'; most common use *daawirrin* 'traditional camping place.]

wirrindiny *noun masculine.* pied butcherbird. *Cracticus nigrogularis.*

Wirrindiny-bawoo-ngarri-wanema *noun.* place name. LIT: 'the place where the butcherbird called out'.

wirringgoonel *noun feminine.* cockatiel, weero. *Nymphicus hollandicus.*

wirrirrel; wirrirril *noun feminine.* little lorikeet, green lorikeet, varied lorikeet. *Psitteuteles versicolor.*

wirrirrij *coverb+SAY/DO.* scoop out dirty water when making a soak. • **Wirrirrij nyerne dama goorrngam joordoobam.** *She is cleaning out that dirty water.* [NOTE: Southern dialect] SEE: **warralaj.**

wirriwoonany *noun masculine.* long-necked turtle. *Chelodina rugosa.* SEE: **lawarrbal, woorlemerewal, weloowoomoorany.** [NOTE: unusual gender, turtles are nearly always feminine]

wirriya *coverb+SAY/DO.* feel happy. • **Wirriya ngenarn jaam.** *I feel happy.* • **Wirriya ngenarn-noo ngagenyji wiginy.** *I am happy for my son.*

wirrmagany *noun masculine.* initiated boy.

wirrwirril, wirrwirrji *noun.* white dragon tree, corkwood. *Sesbania formosa.* [NOTE: can be used to make woomeras if *garndiwalel* is not available; charcoal made from the bark used to be rubbed on the heads of new babies]

Wirwirji *noun.* place in Paddy Bedford's mother's country. [NOTE: deep waterhole called Tea Hole, Donkey Hole or Police Hole in different accounts]

wiwayi *coverb+HIT.* wave something to get rid of flies. • **Boornoom dam wiwayi bamberrji-gili.** *Chase (by waving something back and forth) all those flies.*

wiwayi-wiwayi *coverb+SAY/DO.* wave something to get rid of flies. • **Boornoombi wiwayi-wiwayiya barrern-gili.** *All wave little branches to get rid of the flies.*

wiyarre *coverb+GO_ALONG.* swim along (duck). • **Jibilyoowoo-warriny wiyarre woomberriyinbe-yoo goorloon.** *The two ducks are going swimming along in the water.*

wiyarrel *noun.* emu. *Dromaius novaehollandiae.* SEE: **garnanganyjel, ngarabarral.** [NOTE: word from Mabel Downs and Texas side]

wiyawoog *coverb+SAY/DO_M.* speak/sing to ward off danger, speak causing a permanent change in the landscape, speak to send something away. • **Wiyawoog woomberrama, wiyawoog ngoorrooma.** *They spoke to hunt away the danger.* [NOTE: different from *goorara* 'talk to country to make something good, to increase something']

wiyawoog *coverb+HIT.* speak/sing to ward off danger. • **Wiyawoog-garri nyimberriyinbe dal.** *They say the words to protect themselves from her (old women getting ground sugarbag from the place where a* yarralali *'spirit woman' lives).*

wiyawoog *coverb+SAY/DO.* speak causing a permanent change in the landscape. • **Wiyawoog ginini-noongoo, 'Ngoowan narriyannha ngenengga, ngoowan, mangoony-bawoorroon.'** *He spoke about it (the heron talking about the freshwater mangrove), 'Don't come here, no, this place will be without freshwater mangrove plants.'*

wiyilam *noun.* armband worn by men who are mourning a deceased relation. • **Wiyilam binbimoorliya ngenengga nganoonggoon.** *He will wear a mourning armband here on the arm.* SEE: **doonggooloo.**

wiyinjende *verb.* he/it (masculine) keeps on GOING ALONG. • **Therrendang wiyinjende gangganyi.** *Grandson keeps going along facing this way.*

wiyinji *verb.* 1. he/it (masculine) is BECOMING. • **Berrjil-ngarri wiyinji dama jirrgawoorra ngerne ganjimbi dam.** *When it becomes dry the seeds fall down.* 2. he/it (masculine) is GOING ALONG. • **Jadany jalij wiyinji.** *The rain is raining.*

wiyinya *verb.* 1. she/it (feminine) is BECOMING. • **Gerewoolba-ngarri wiyinya lelerd boomberriyinbe.** *When it has eggs (becomes egg having) they bust it open.* 2. she/it (feminine) is GOING ALONG. • **Deg wiyinya ngarem-boorroo.** *She goes along looking for sugarbag (bush honey).*

wiyinyande; winyande *verb.* she/it (feminine) keeps GOING ALONG. • **Lagarr wiyinyande ngarembi.** *She keeps on going cutting sugarbag.*

wiyird *coverb+SAY/DO_M.* spin hair, fur or fibres to make string. • **Wiyird woomberramande goorlgoon-gili warlboorroom, laj-girrim-boorroo.** *They used to spin (fur) to make string for those things to wear, the hair belts that they could hang things from.*

wiyooloonya *verb.* it (feminine) PUTS itself, is PLACED. • **Garrwaroon berr-ngarri wiyooloonya.** *When it gets bright in the afternoon (sun going down).*

-woo; -boo *coverb suffix.* sequential suffix to

wooboo

Figure 87. *Woobooj: Birrmarriya Shirley Purdie: Naangarila woobooj nyerne goonjal.*

coverbs, 'and then'. SEE: **-boo**.
wooboo *coverb+HIT.* cook on coals. • *Wooboo benayidji mayim men'gawoom. He cooked the good food on the coals.* SEE: **wawoog**.
wooboo *coverb+SAY/DO.* cook, cook something on the coals. • *Mambarre, wooboo yarroorn mayim. Wait, we are cooking food.*
wooboo *coverb+SAY/DO_M.* cook, cook something on the coals. • *Wooboo wanemanyande-boorroo mayim. She (station cook) used to cook food for them.*
woobooj REDUP: **woobooj-woobooj; wooboobooj**. *coverb+SAY/DO_M.* dig. • *Woobooj-gala ngelem-noo. Let me dig for it.*
woobooj REDUP: **woobooj-woobooj**. *coverb+SAY/DO.* dig. • *Ngarranggarninji, ngarranggarninji woobooj-garri nerne-ngiyi dala. From the dreamtime, from the dreamtime, when you dig up the place belonging to that woman.* • *Woobooj boorroorn. They are digging.*
woobooj *coverb+GET.* dig. • *Berrema dagoorlam woobooj benamanyji-boorroo. Here are the deep holes he dug for them (to put fish in).*
woobooj *coverb+GO_ALONG.* go digging. • *Ngaboony woobooj wananyjende gananybe-birri mawoondoomga. Father used to go and dig up that white clay with a wooden crowbar.*
wooboongeny, wooboongel, wooboongem *adjective.* cooked on the coals.
woodiji *noun.* song to make someone love the singer. SEE: **yirrbinji**.
woogoony; wegeny *noun masculine.* brown frog. *Neobatrachus aquilonius*.
woog-woog *coverb+SAY/DO.* say 'woog-woog' (frog).
Woojaninin *noun.* spring at foot of Mount King.
woolangen; welangen *locative.* in front, ahead (in space). • *Welangen biyarra! You go ahead (in front)!*
woolangen; welangen *temporal.* before (in time), first. • *Gaboowa yarrirn woolangen? What do we do first?*
woolanggoorral *noun feminine.* female freshwater crocodile. *Crocodylus johnstonii*.
Woolanggoorrwarriny *noun.* place northeast of Bungles.

Woolarrngayan *noun.* Stoney Creek, place on west side of Bedford Downs Station.
woolngal *noun.* bean species. *Canavalia papuana*. SEE: **digoorlool**.
Wooloony; Wooloowooloowany *noun.* place near Balan'gerr on Texas Downs Station.
wooloorr *coverb+GET.* like.
woolthoob *coverb+PUT.* throw down.
• Woolthoob-gala noondaj marnen. *Let me throw it on the fire*
woomal *noun.* stone axe. SEE: **manyjangal, ngajiral**. [NOTE: *woomal* is not supposed to be said by young men; they have to say *mayinggal*. Gija words for axe are euphemisms for clitoris, particularly *woomal*.]
woombardgoony *noun.* rock wallaby. SEE: **woombarnoongoony, doowanggoonyji, woonyjoorroony**.
Woombarlan *noun.* place in Purnululu National Park with 'dangerous' water.
woombarnoongoony *noun.* rock wallaby. SEE: **woombardgoony, doowanggoonyji, woonyjoorroony**.
woomberrama *verb.* they SAID/DID.
woomberramande *verb.* they used to SAY/DO, they were SAYING/DOING.
woomberramangbe; woomberramangboo *verb.* they SAID/DID.
woomberramangbende; woomberramanbende *verb.* they used to SAY/DO.
woomberranybe; woomberranyboo *verb.* they were GOING ALONG.
woomberranybende *verb.* they used to GO ALONG.
woomberrayangbe *verb.* they were PLACING, it (non-singular) was TAKING UP A PLACE.
woomberrayi *verb.* let them SAY/DO.
• Boorral-gala woomberrayi-yoo yiwiny. *Let them have a feed of louse.*
woomberrayid *verb.* they BECAME.
woomberrayidbe *verb.* they BECAME.
woomberrayidbende *verb.* they USED TO BECOME.
woomberremenbe *verb.* they SAY/DO.
woomberremenbende *verb.* they keep on SAYING/DOING.
woomberrigbe *verb.* they will be GOING ALONG.
woomberriyanbe *verb.* they were PLACING.
woomberriyilinbe *verb.* they are PLACING.
woomberriyin *verb.* **1.** they GO ALONG. **2.** they become.
woomberriyinbe *verb.* **1.** they are GOING ALONG. **2.** they are becoming.
woomberriyinbende *verb.* they keep on GOING ALONG.
woombijende *verb.* he/it (masculine) will be BECOMING.
woombiyanyande *verb.* she will keep on SAYING/DOING
woombiyidji *verb.* he/it (masculine) wanted to BECOME.
woombool *coverb+HIT.* pour out (water), tip something out. • Woombool barrij-gili dany warrayany. *You all tip out that sugar leaf.*
• Woombool noonayidge. *I poured out the water.*
woombool *coverb+FALL/GO_DOWN.* spill, pour down (water). • Woombool berradboo goorrngam. *The water spilled.*
woomboolngem *noun.* something that has been poured out, someone who poured it out.
woomenjende *verb.* he is SAYING/DOING.
woomenji *verb.* he/it (masculine) is SAYING/DOING.
woomenya *verb.* she/it (feminine) is SAYING/DOING.
woomenyande *verb.* she keeps on SAYING/DOING.
woomiyinya *verb.* she is DOING.
woonawoorroony *noun.* young man with forehead band.
woonboorr *coverb+HIT.* knock down.
• Mayaroom-anyji woonboorr binbiji. *He might be going to knock down that house.* SEE: **woor**.
woonboorr *coverb+WOUND.* dig and knock down. • Ngarranggarninji, ngarranggarninji woonboorr-ngarri janewan-ngiyiwa. *From dreamtime, from dreamtime, when you dug and knocked down her place.* SEE: **woor**.
woonboorr *coverb+GO_ALONG.* go along knocking down. • Woonboorr wananyande ngoorrooma Nanal-ngooyoo yilangoogoo ngoorroom. *She (the rainbow snake that made the flood) went knocking down Shirley Purdie's place there and going down over there.*
woonboorr *coverb+SAY/DO_M.* knock down.
• Woonboorr woomberrama-gili. *They all knocked them down (mud nests covering cave paintings).*
woongamenji *verb.* he/it (masculine)

woongamenya

GOES THROUGH.

woongamenya *verb.* she/it (feminine) GOES THROUGH.

Woongenban; Wengenban *noun.* place on Alice Downs.

woongenji; wengenji *noun masculine.* tea-tree. *Leptospermum madidum; Melaleuca bracteata.* [NOTE: flowers smell like custard, according to Hector Jandany]

woonggariny; woonggareny REDUP: **woongga-woonggarem.** *noun.* kangaroo joey. [NOTE: should not be touched by young people]

woonoongoony *noun masculine.* waterlily type.

woontha, wentha *interjection.* well then, yes then.

woonthool, woonthoony *noun.* **1.** earth worm. Annelida, Oligochaeta. **2.** blind snake. *Anilios* spp.

woonyjoorroony *noun masculine.* rock wallaby. SEE: **woombardgoony, doowanggoonyji, woombarnoongoony.**

woor *coverb+HIT.* knock down. • *Jalawoonany woor benayidji mayaroom.* The willy-willy knocked down the house. SEE: **derinyberr.**

wooraj *coverb+GO/COME.* come closer, move closer, come forward, come this way.
• *Nyengen wooraj biyany.* You (one) come here!
• *Nenggerren-gili wooraj barriyany-gili.* All of you come over here! • *Wooraj-anyji ngidji degboo woomenji-noonggoorroo.* He might be coming close looking at all of you.

wooraybiny *directional.* this way.

woorayibe *directional.* coming this way.

woorayibenginy, woorayibengel, woorayibengim *adjective.* one who is coming this way.

woorayigoo; woorayigoo-yoorroong *directional.* this way, towards this way.

woordij *coverb+HIT.* throw spear. • *Marrarn woordij benayid-birri.* He already threw spears at them. • *Danya wariwoony thalg benama woordij-girriny-anyji.* That aggressive man hooked up spears in his woomera, maybe to throw.

woordoorr *coverb+FALL/GO_DOWN.* seeds/fruit on tree finish/all fall down. • *Woordoorr-ngarri berrewoonbe.* When the seeds/fruit finish (e.g. on snappy gum tree, black plum), when the seeds/fruit all fall down. SEE: **werrg, jirrgawoorr.**

woordoorr-woordoorrji *noun masculine.* nail-tailed wallaby. *Onychogalea unguifera.* SEE: **gooroorroonggoony, goon'goodoogoodoony, woorrood-woorroodji.** [NOTE: left handed from the dreamtime, *ngarranggarnin*; Janama skin, brother-in-law of the moon]

wooriny-wooriny *coverb+SAY/DO_M.* call out (bird). • *Gayiyanyji wooriny-wooriny woomenji.* It (bird) is calling out somewhere.

woorlagany, woorlagal, woorlagam *adjective.* promiscuous, being a whore, sleeps around. • *Ngelelga woorlagajirral.* This is a promiscuous woman.

Woorlalwan *noun.* Bullock Hole, place on the Upper Panton downstream from Garn'gin where the moon knelt in dreamtime.

woorlboorr *coverb+SAY/DO.* river come rushing over. • *Woorlboorr nginini.* The river came rushing over (during big rain).

woorlem; werlem; woorloom *noun.* neck, throat.

woorlemerewal *noun feminine.* long-necked turtle. *Chelodina rugosa.* SEE: **lawarrbal, wirriwoonany, weloowoomoorany.**

woorlengerriny; werlngerreny *noun masculine.* eel-tailed catfish (large species), Rendhal's catfish. *Porochilus rendahli.* SEE: **girlinyiny.**

woorlmooj-woorlmooj *coverb+SAY/DO.* feel tingling in body part giving a sign about relations. • *Berrem, goonggooloom woorlmooj-woorlmooj-garri boorroorn, ganggam-boorroo.* Here (shows head), when it tingles (jump-jump), it is for relations we call *ganggayi* (maternal grandmother's generation or woman's daughters children). SEE: **jarrawoorl, jirreg.**

woorlngooroony *noun.* sandalwood. *Santalum lanceolatum.*

woorloorrmarlinji *noun masculine.* red-eyed mullet. *Liza* spp.

woorl-woorl *coverb+BECOME.* be slow, take one's time. • *Ngoorroonya woorl-woorl wiyinji bardoon.* That bloke is coming along slowly behind. • *Woorl-woorljiya jiyinha.* You are really slow.

wooroom *noun.* juice, meat stock, soup. SEE: **warlele.**

Woorranggan *noun.* place in Rusty Peters' country, to the west of Thalinyman.

woorranggool *noun feminine.* artefact made

Worla

from sticks and wool (formerly painted string) carried or worn around the head or shoulders in dance performances; paintings carried on the shoulders in the Goorirr-goorirr found by Rover Thomas and frequently performed at Warrmarn. • *Wandaj ngerne woorranggool Goorirr-goorirrel. He is carrying the painted board for the Goorirr-goorirr song and dance performance.*

-woorrarrem REDUP: **-woorrarrerrarrem.** *suffix.* all kinds. • *Melagawoom deg yirramanyi warlbawoo-woorrarrem. We saw lots, agile wallabies and all kinds.*

woorra-woorral *noun feminine.* mermaid, water dwelling spirit woman. [NOTE: Buttercup Mung Mung found a Moonga-moonga style Joonba about the *woorra-woorral* at Warrmarn]

Woorrayan *noun.* Fig Tree Rock Hole.

Woorreralbam *noun.* an alternate name for Frog Hollow.

Woorreranginy *noun.* Frog Hollow.

woorrg REDUP: **woorrg-woorrg.** *coverb+HIT.* throw down. • *Danyi gerndi-werndiny woorrg nginiyidji-ningi jalariny. That one (eagle) threw the male ones (rock wallabies) down to the egret (white crane).* • *Jaroom thenbel manam woorrg bemberrayidbende. They pull out the guts and shit and throw it away.*

woorrg *coverb+BE/STAY.* sit down. • *Marnen woorrg yirraniyinde. We all used to sit down at the fireplace.*

woorrg *coverb+FALL/GO_DOWN.* fall down. • *Dangembi woorrg-garri boorroowoonbe gooyarrg boorroorn. Then when they all (big grasshoppers) fall down they gather them up.*

woorrgaj *coverb+PUT.* pull out a big rock (e.g. when digging ground sugarbag). • *Ngarrgale-bany-anyji woorrgaj-gala noondaj. If there is a big rock I'll have to pull it out.*

woorrgerne *coverb+SAY/DO_M.* be halfway to somewhere, be almost at a destination. • *Mayaroo woorrgerne wanemanyji. He was already halfway to the station house.*

woorrg-woorrgbany *coverb.* go falling down.

woorrij *coverb+BRING/TAKE.* take someone away making them leave. • *Woorrij ngenanyji. It (country) took me away, making me leave (made me forget everything and leave).*

woorrij *coverb+GO/COME.* leave behind, be already gone. • *Ngoowana, marrarn woorrij nginiyin. He had already gone and left them behind.* • *Woorrij nyaniyinya. She had already gone.*

woorrjib *coverb+BE/STAY.* sitting (plural). • *Woorrjib boorroonboo-ngirri. They are all sitting down with me.* • *Woorrjib narroonnha. You are all sitting.* SEE: **roorrjib**.

woorrjininy *noun.* sandy ground.

woorrngoord *coverb+GO/COME.* be aching, be in pain. • *Woorrngoord ngenayi. I'm aching. / I have a pain.*

woorrngoord *coverb+SAY/DO.* ache, have a pain, be hurting. • *Woorrngoord ngenarn. I'm aching. / I have a pain.* • *Gaya woorrngoord nerne? Where do you hurt?*

-woorroo- *suffix.* not having, without, not being. [NOTE: affixed to nouns and adjectives, followed by appropriate gender markers]

woorrood-woorroodji *noun.* nail-tailed wallaby. *Onychogalea unguifera.* SEE: **gooroorroonggoony, goon'goodoogoodoony, woordoorr-woordoorrji.** [NOTE: left-handed from the dreamtime, *ngarranggarnin*; Janama skin, brother-in-law of the moon]

woorrwal *coverb.* be mortally wounded. • *woorrwal-girrem* for kill them • *Woorrwal woomemiyinji garloomboo-baya jiyirriny. The kangaroo has been wounded and is running away with a spear in him.*

woorr-woorr *coverb+SAY/DO.* make web. • *Baarnji woorr-woorr ngirni daam. The spider made his web home.* SEE: **warr-warr**.

Worla *noun.* language spoken west of Gija.

Yy

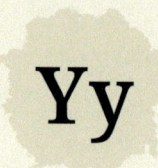

yaalji, yaale *noun.* mist, dew.
yab *coverb+FALL/GO_DOWN.* hide in grass. • **Yab nginiward.** *He hid in the grass*
yabirlil *noun.* large shell, baler shell. • **Yalawoog nyilayangge yabirlil.** *I got lots of baler shell.* • **Melagawoom yabirlim boorroonboo yiligin nawane.** *There are lots of baler shells in the cave.* [NOTE: young people are not supposed to say this word]
yad *coverb+SAY/DO.* be looking for a fight. • **Nginyjinyji jiyiliny yad ngerne warim-boorroo.** *This man is looking for a fight.*
yad *coverb+SAY/DO_M.* be looking for a fight. • **Ngoorrinya yad woomenjende.** *This man is looking for a fight.*
yad *coverb+SAY/DO_REFL.* go looking for a fight with each other. • **Boorrooben jiyile-warriny yad-yad berrengirriyan-joo.** *Those two men are looking for a fight with each other.*
yade *verb.* let us (you (one) and me) BE/STAY. SEE: yadiya.
yadin *verb.* we should BE/BE STAYING.
yadiya *verb.* let us (you (one) and me) BE/STAY. SEE: yade.
yage REDUP: **yage-yage**. *particle.* other, on the other hand.
yagebawarinyiny, yagebawarinyil, yagebawarinyim *adjective.* looking different. • **Yagebawarinyin-jaya-ngoongoo.** *You look different altogether.*
yagebawirri *adverb.* each in their own place.
yagebayoorroong *locative.* to one side.
yagengeny, yagengel, yagengem *noun.* another, different one. • **Nginyji yagenge yoorloo nginji.** *This other one (river shown in painting) is downstream.* • **Yagengel-ngirri barnale.** *I have another one (tick) on my shoulder.*
yagengerrany, yagengerral, yagengerram *adjective.* other.
yagewalany, yagewalal, yagewalam; yagoowalany *adjective.* different, no good. SEE: yagengeny.
yagewany, yagewal, yagewam *adjective.* looking different.
yagewarinyji, yagewarinyel, yagewarinybe *adjective.* being a different way.

yagoorn *coverb+PUT.* tell someone a lie. • **Yagoornanyji nhiyan.** *You must be lying.* • **Yagoorn yinayanha.** *You lied to me.* [NOTE: person lied to is the direct object]
yagoorn *coverb+SAY/DO_M.* be lying. • **Yagoorn wanemayinde.** *He was lying.*
yagoorn *coverb+SAY/DO.* tell a lie, pretend. • **Yagoorn nginini dany jalariny.** *That egret (white crane) told a lie.*
yagoornbeny, yagoornbel, yagoornbem *adjective.* liar.
yag-yag *coverb+PUT.* line up (transitive), put in line. • **Yag-yag benayanyji.** *He put them in a line.*
yajany *adverb.* together separate from others. • **Yajanydawa dayi boomberrembe jarragbi-ngerroowa Jandaloowoon-nga.** *They can learn to talk from me, Jandany.*
yajany *coverb+BE/STAY.* being the same kind. • **Ngoowan yajany boorroonboo-yoo, nawarrabebem ganarramga-ni jirrindinya.** *The two of them are not the same, the leaves of the Hakea arostra are a bit bigger.*
yajany *coverb+HAVE.* having the same. • **Thawalambi miyi yajany benemoorloonji wayiniya gooma dany gernembowoorroony.** *It (birrinydilinyji, an Acacia) has the same kinds of flowers as the plant called gernembowoorriny (also an Acacia).*
yalamarriny, yalamarrim *noun masculine.* edible tuber species, type of bush potato. *Ipomoea costata.* SEE: berlayiny, bigoordany, dawoonyil, larrwany.
yalamboorrmany *noun masculine.* saltwater crocodile. *Crocodylus porosus.* [NOTE: does not live in Gija country]
Yalan *noun.* place near the river on the eastern side of the highway from Gilban.
yalarrngarnany *noun masculine.* jabiru. *Ephippiorhynchus asiaticus.*
yalawoog *coverb+HIT, coverb+PUT.* gather a lot of something. • **Yalawoog bemberrayidbe / yalawoog goorrayangbe.** *They got a big mob. They got a lot.*
yalawoog *coverb+GET.* gather a lot of something. • **Melagawoom garndinyga nginyji yalawoog**

yarrimnya daa-yoorroong. *We will get the biggest mob of* garndiny *yams together in our camp.*

yalginybeny, yalginybel, yalginybem *adjective.* bony, skinny.

yalg-yalg *coverb+BE/STAY.* have arms hanging down loosely. • *Yalg-yalg nginji nganoonggoom. He has his arms hanging down (wallaby in photo).*

yalg-yalg; yal-yalg *coverb+BE/STAY.* be hanging down. • *Yalg-yalgji nyinya gamoombi-ngiyi. Her breasts are hanging down now.*
• *Nyingiyana yal-yalg ninnha. You have loose skin hanging under the chin.*

yalg-yalgbany; yal-yalgbany; yalg-yalgwany *coverb.* put arm down hanging loosely. • *Yalg-yalgbany biyarra. You go with your arms hanging down.* • *Yalg-yalgwany barriyinnha. You all go with your arms hanging down.*

yalij *coverb.* be worn out, be tired. • *'Yalij-ma nerne?' 'Ngiyi yalij ngenan'ge.' 'Are you worn out?' 'Yes I am worn out.'* SEE: **wanggarl.**

yalijge *coverb+GET.* make someone tired. • *Yalijge yinamenha. You are making me tired.*

yalirrwany *coverb+FALL/GO_DOWN.* become middle-aged. • *Yalirrwany-ngarri yarrewoonya. When we get middle-aged.*

yamayarram *noun.* short fighting stick carried by women together with the longer stick called *goordooroony.* SEE: **wabagoorreny.**

yambarn *coverb+DO_REFL.* tie up hair. • *Gerdanji yambarn-ngarri nginimiyin. (The place where) the frillneck lizard tied up his hair (in dreamtime).*

yambarram *noun.* hair (of head).

yamberraj *verb.* let's all PUT them/it (non-singular).

yamberraja *verb.* let's all PUT them/it (non-singular).

yamberrama *verb.* 1. we SAID/DID. 2. we GOT them/it (non-singular).

yamberramanya *verb.* we GOT them/it (non-singular).

yamberramenya *verb.* we are all GETTING them/it (non-singular).

yamberramoorliya *verb.* we will HAVE/KEEP/LOOK AFTER them/it (non-singular).

yamberramoorloon *verb.* we HAVE/HOLD/KEEP them/it (non-singular). [NOTE: unusual for present tense; would expect *yamberramoorloonyan*]

yamberramoorloowardja *verb.* we HAD them/it (non-singular).

yamberrangoonya *verb.* we EAT them/it (non-singular).

yamberranya *verb.* we TOOK them/it (non-singular).

yamberrawoorroob *verb.* we will LEAVE them/it (non-singular).

yamberregbany *verb.* let's all BRING them/it (non-singular).

yamberrem *verb.* let's GET them/it (non-singular).

yamberremenyande *verb.* we keep GETTING them/it (non-singular).

yamberrija *verb.* let's all HIT them/it (non-singular).

yamberrim *verb.* we will GET them/it (non-singular).

yamberrimnya *verb.* we will be GETTING them/it (non-singular).

yamberrimoorliya *verb.* we will HAVE/HOLD/KEEP them/it (non-singular).

yamberriyaja *verb.* we will PUT them/it (non-singular).

yamberriyilinya *verb.* we are PUTTING them.

yamberriyinya *verb.* we are HITTING them.

yambil *coverb+BECOME.* be slow. • *Ngoowan yambil nyaliny waniyidji. He was not lazy again.*
• *Thoowoo-boorrooo yambil jiyinnha? Why are you going slow?*

yambil *coverb+PUT.* make someone slow, delay someone. • *Yambil yinilinji-yoowoo jarragboo-boorroo marrge. He is holding us back/making us wait here for (more) language, wait.*

yambilji, yambilel, yambilbe *adjective.* slow. SEE: **yambilwoony.**

yambilwoony, yambilwool, yambilwoom *adjective.* very slow. • *Yambilwoonjaya-ngoo. You are very slow.* SEE: **yambilji.**

yambirraja *verb.* we will be PUTTING them/it (non-singular). [NOTE: Southern dialect] SEE: **yambirriyaja.**

yambirrija *verb.* we will be HITTING them/it (non-singular).

yambirrimnya; yamberremnya *verb.* we will GET them/it (non-singular).

yambirriwoorroobja *verb.* we will LEAVE them/it (non-singular).

yambirriyaja *verb.* we will be PUTTING them/it (non-singular).

yamboorroowoorroobja

Figure 88. *Yarajbe: Dirrji Wandarrany Rusty Peters: Yarajbe ngiyilinji gamanggarrji marabam-birri.*

yamboorroowoorroobja *verb.* let's all leave them/it (non-singular).

yamoony *noun.* small water yam. *Cycnogeton dubium.* SEE: **wawalji**.

yan *coverb+BRING/TAKE.* wash away (flood). • Yan ngenanyji. *The flood took me away.* • Yan benanyji. *It washed it/them away.*

yanemanya *verb.* you (one) and I GOT him/her/it.

yang *coverb+HIT.* bet with someone. • Yang nginiyidji. *He made a bet with him.*

yangajalil *noun.* cabbage palm. *Livistona victoriae.* SEE: **yingajalil, danarrel, ngamalil**.

yangel, yangal *interrogative.* who (feminine)? • Yangeli dali? *Who is that (feminine one)?*

yangelanyji *interrogative.* someone (feminine). • Yangel-anyji binarri-woorroon-nga. Nyengen-anyji binarri-ngoo. *She is someone I don't know. You might know her.*

yanggi *coverb+PUT.* ask. • Yanggi ngenayanyji. *He asked me.* • Biyarr-gala-noowa! Yanggi-gala biyil ngoonyjoom-boorroo. *Go after him! Ask him for tobacco!* • Yinginybe-ngiyi berrem yangelanyji. Yanggi-gala nyilaj. *I don't know her name. I must ask her.*

yanggiji *coverb+GET.* ask. • Yayiben yanggiji yirremenyi-noonggoorroo-yoo. *We are asking you two.* • Miyi yanggiji nyilemen'ge ngaginyel gawangel, 'Thoowoorra-boorroo roord dinnha? Warrern-ma nerne?' *I ask my aunt too, 'Why are you sitting there? Are you sick?'* • Barle-girrim yanggiji nginimanyji. *He asked to ride it.* • Yanggijiwa joonboomanha-yoo damboomga merrerreb-garri wananyjende-berrab-doo gibi-yibin. *You should ask those two where he hid with them all over the bush.*

yangirnanyji *interrogative.* someone (masculine).

yangirni; yangirna *interrogative.* who (masculine)? • Yangirni danyi? *Who is that man?*

yangoorra *interrogative.* who (plural)? • Yangoorra dambi? *Who are they?*

yangoorranyji *interrogative.* someone (plural).

yangoowoo *interrogative.* who? • Goowoomji nginini, 'Yarra-gela-ni Stan Jonesji yangoowoo berrani yijiyamga.' *Paddy said to Rod, 'We'll go and see Stan and see which one of you is telling the truth.'* • Yangoowoo-nhangoo? *Who are you?*

yaniya *verb.* you (one) and I CAME/WENT.

yaniyin *verb.* you (one) and I were GOING.

yan'gag *coverb+GET.* hook up fish through the gills on a stick. • Yan'gag benamanyji goorndarrim. *He hooked up the fish.*

yan'gam *noun.* stick used to hook up fish.

yara *verb.* let us (you (one) and I) GO.

yaraj *verb.* let us (you (one) and I) PUT him/her/it.

yarajbe *coverb+PUT.* press to straighten.
• Yarajbe ngiyilinji marabam-birri. *He is straightening it (spear) by pressing it on the hot dirt.*

Yarangga *noun.* Chinamans Garden.

yara-yaraj *coverb+PUT.* press to straighten.
• Garloomboony yara-yaraj ngiyilinji. *He is straightening the spear.* • 'Yara-yaraj-gala nharajgoo,' nyanini-ni. *'Let me press her to help her to straighten out,' she said to him.*

yara-yaraj *coverb+SAY/DO_M.* straighten.
• Yara-yaraj woomberramande. *They used to straighten them.*

yarayinde *verb.* you (one) and I kept on GOING.

yardeg *coverb+BE/STAY.* understand. • Nginyjiny Miriwoom-birri jarrag ginini, nginyjinyi yardeg boorroonboo-ni. *This one spoke Miriwoong to them and they understand him.*

yardem *noun.* ears. • Ngelela Joomenal yardenanyji beniyinya. *This person, Eileen, maybe remembers that (information) (lit. 'carries it (the thing being spoken about) in her ears maybe').*

yardemerewany *noun masculine.* donkey. *Equus asinus.* LIT: 'long ears'.

yardewoorriny, yardewoorrool, yardewoorroom *adjective.* deaf. LIT: 'having no ears'. SEE: **birn'goolji**.

yard-yard *coverb+SAY/DO.* shake. • Ngalany ngoorramangboo marrarna yard-yard ginini dijbela nginiwardji. *They 'sung' him and he started shaking and died.* SEE: **mirr-mirr**.

yaremij *verb.* let us (you (one) and I) DO TO EACH OTHER.

yarengerrij *verb.* let us (you (one) and I) SAY/DO TO EACH OTHER.

yarija *verb.* you (one) and I will HIT him/her/it.

Yarin *noun.* White Water, place on Springvale Station near Newman Hole.

yaringirrij *verb.* you (one) and I will SAY/DO TO EACH OTHER.

yarlarliny *noun masculine.* yellow-coloured head louse. *Pediculus humanus.* SEE: **yiwiny**.

yarlgal, yarlgany, yarlgam *noun.* spearhead made from white stone, white stone used to make spearheads, white chert.

Yarliyil *noun.* Halls Creek.

yarliyilji *noun masculine.* wattle species common in the Halls Creek area. *Acacia* sp. aff. *lysiphloia.* SEE: **diwinji**.

yarlooloo *coverb+GET.* break leg of something.
• Yarlooloo nginimanyji. *He broke its leg.*
• Yarlooloo boomberramangbende. *They used to break the legs (of the kangaroos before cooking).*

yarnderre *noun.* fingernail, toenail, claw.
• Yarnderre-giny-jaya-nga. *I've got a long fingernail.* • Jalinggiril yarnderre. *It has sharp claws* (nyoorroongool).

yarn'gal *noun.* woomera, hook. SEE: **ngawalel**.

yarr *coverb+GO/COME.* put hand in hole, reach for something. • Yarr-gala barriyin-noongoo nginyjiny gayirriny. *You try and feel inside this hole for some ground sugarbag.* • Yarr ngenayin-ngooyoo. *I put my hand in for her (hole where 'porcupine' had been shot).*

yarra *verb.* let us all GO.

yarra REDUP: **yarra-yarra**. *coverb+GET.* take someone away (spirits or people conducting ceremony). • Deyena joowarrimbi yarra boomberramangboo damgawoo thamanyji-ngarrem. *It was there that the spirits took away those people with my grandfather (and taught them).* • Yarra-yarra boomberramangbende, ngenengga-wayi ninjirrim boomberrayangbende nyoomboorroo, ngelga warrg-garri woomberramande. *They used to take them away when they were putting sticks in their noses to make the hole and they were dancing this* Joonba.

yarraj *verb.* let us all PUT ourselves.

Yarralaliban *noun.* place in George Mung Mung's country.

yarralalil *noun.* spirit woman living in caves who takes men away.

yarramanya *verb.* we were all GETTING him/her/it.

yarramiyinyande *verb.* we used to DO TO OURSELVES/EACH OTHER.

yarramoorloowardji *verb.* we (exclusive) HAD him/her/it.

yarrang

yarrang *verb.* we will EAT him/her/it.
yarrangirriyin *verb.* we DID TO OURSELVES/EACH OTHER.
yarrani *verb.* we (inclusive) SAID/DID.
yarraniyin *verb.* we WERE/WERE STAYING.
yarranya *verb.* we were GOING ALONG.
yarrarra *coverb+SAY/DO.* be strong (in sinews).
- Men'gawoog nimbimji-ni jirloowam yiligin, yarrarra nimbirn jirloowam. *It will make your sinews good inside, make your sinews strong.*

yarrarrage *coverb+GET.* make strong (in sinews).
- Mooroonggoorroon-ngoo yarrarrage yinama jirlwam. *You (a doctor) are clever, you make me feel good in the sinews.*

Yarrawaren *noun.* place in Ngarrgooroon Country.
yarraware *coverb+HIT.* be aching, have a funny feeling in the sinews. • Yarraware-ngarri yiniyinji-yoowoo, goonthoorroo-boorroo dany wawanggoony, men'gawoony jang-girriny. *When we are aching, when we have a cold that dry boab pith is good to eat.*
- Yarraware ngeninyinji jirlwan. *I feel funny in the sinews.* (Kriol: '*I feel funny la string.*') [NOTE: impersonal construction, person with the feeling is the direct object]

yarrawoorroob; yarroowoorroob *verb.* we will LEAVE him/her/it.
yarrayaja *verb.* we will PUT him/her/it.
- Gawayin, mengerr yarrayaja. *Never mind, we will have to push it (bogged car).* SEE: **yarriyaja**.

yarrayilin *verb.* we PUT ourselves.
yarrayilinnya *verb.* we were PUTTING ourselves.
yarrayi; yarrayin; yarraya *verb.* we went.
yarrayinde *verb.* we kept on GOING.
yarreben *pronoun.* we/us two (exclusive). [NOTE: also recorded with extra dual suffix, *yarreben-doo* and *yarreben-joo*]
yarrreg *verb.* let's TAKE it.
yarregbany *verb.* let's BRING it.
yarrem *verb.* let's GET him/her/it.
yarrema; yarrama *verb.* 1. we all GOT him/her/it. 2. we all SAID/DID.
yarremande; yarramande *verb.* we all used to SAY/DO.
yarremengerrij *verb.* let's SAY/DO TO OURSELVES/EACH OTHER.
yarremenya *verb.* we are all GETTING him/her/it.
yarremenyande *verb.* we keep on GETTING him/her/it.
yarremija *verb.* we will be DOING TO OURSELVES/EACH OTHER.
yarremnya *verb.* let's keep GETTING him/her/it.
yarren; yarroon *pronoun.* we/us (exclusive).
yarrengaboord *verb.* we SPEARED him/her/it.
yarrengerrij *verb.* let all of us SAY/DO TO EACH OTHER.
yarrenya *verb.* we ARE/STAY (inclusive). SEE: **yarroonya**.
yarrern *verb.* we all SAY/DO.
yarrewa *verb.* let's WOUND ourselves.
yarrewany *pronoun.* we/us (exclusive) ourselves, our turn.
yarreward; yarrooward *verb.* we all FELL/WENT DOWN.
yarrewarriny *pronoun.* we/us (exclusive) by ourselves.
yarrewoo *verb.* let's FALL/GO DOWN.
yarrewoonya *verb.* we FALL/GO DOWN.
yarrgalal, yarrgalany *noun.* hairy water yam. *Aponogeton vanbruggenii.*
yarridja *verb.* we HIT him/her/it.
yarrija *verb.* 1. we all will HIT him/her/it. 2. we all will BECOME.
yarrimij; yarremij *verb.* we will DO TO OURSELVES/EACH OTHER.
yarrimnya *verb.* we (inclusive) will GET him/her/it.
yarrimnyande *verb.* we (inclusive) will keep on GETTING him/her/it.
yarrimoorliyan *verb.* we will HAVE/BE HOLDING/KEEPING him/her/it.
yarringirridja *verb.* we HIT each other.
yarrinya *verb.* we will BE/STAY.
yarrinyande *verb.* we will BE/BE STAYING.
yarrirn *verb.* we all will SAY/DO.
yarriwiriny *noun masculine.* poisonous snake species, ringed brown snake, 'emu killer'. *Pseudonaja modesta.* [NOTE: 'tiger snake' found in black soil country; said to jump up and bite emus] SEE: **jarloongoorroobarndegji**.
yarriwiya *verb.* we will all FALL/GO DOWN. SEE: **yarriwoon**.
yarriwoon *verb.* we will all FALL/GO DOWN. SEE: **yarriwiya**.
yarriya *verb.* we all will GO.
yarriyaja *verb.* we will PUT him/her/it.
- Miyalji-yoowoorroo men'gawoony gerd yarriyaja. *This is our good meat to cook.* SEE: **yarrayaja**.

yarriyan *verb.* we all will be GOING.
yarriyande *verb.* we will keep on GOING.

Figure 89. *Yawardal: Yawardal warlagibal jang nyerne minybernem.*

yarriyangeny, yarriyangel, yarriyangem *possessive pronoun.* ours (exclusive). • *Berrema yarriyangem-yarre, nenggerriyangembi yagebaya.* This is ours, the other one belongs to all of you.
yarriyi *verb.* we should GO.
yarriyilija *verb.* we will SAY to each other?
yarriyilinya *verb.* we are PUTTING him/her/it.
yarriyin *verb.* we were GOING/COMING.
yarriyinde *verb.* we used to be GOING/COMING.
yarriyinya *verb.* 1. we are HITTING him/her/it. 2. we are GOING ALONG.
yarroodja *verb.* we all are GOING/COMING. SEE: yarroordja.
yarrooj *verb.* will we all HIT him/her/it? • *Gayi nyawanyi daj yarrooj?* Where will we smash up this tail?
yarroomayande *verb.* we all would have kept on SAYING/DOING.
yarroomayinde; yarremayinde *verb.* we all used to SAY/DO.
yarroomenyande *verb.* we keep on SAYING/DOING.
yarrooni *verb.* we (inclusive) would have SAID/DID.
yarrooniyinde *verb.* we might have all kept on BEING/STAYING.
yarroonya *verb.* we all BE/STAY.
yarroonyande *verb.* we all keep on BEING/STAYING.
yarroordja *verb.* we all are GOING/COMING.
yarroorn *verb.* we (inclusive) are SAYING/DOING.
yarrooward; yarreward *verb.* we all FELL/WENT DOWN.
yarroowardjande *verb.* we all kept on FALLING/GOING DOWN.
yarroowoo *verb.* let's GO DOWN.
yarroowoonya *verb.* we are all GOING DOWN.
yawa *coverb+PUT.* cut into small pieces; divide up. • *Yawa niniyangge mooloonggoom, ngaandem, therlam-ni dama.* I divided up the fat, the flesh and the back part there.
yawa *coverb+BE/STAY.* be spread out everywhere. • *Yawa boorroonboo jinybam.* Boomerangs are spread out everywhere.
yaward *coverb+GO/COME.* go away and look for something. • *Yaward ngidjende-boorroo-yoo ngaginyil-ngiyi ngoorr-ngoorrool.* He has gone looking for those two with my motor car.
yawardal *noun feminine.* mare. *Equus caballus.*

yawardany

SEE: **dimanal**.
yawardany noun masculine. horse. *Equus caballus*. SEE: **dimanany**.
yawilam noun. valley, hollow.
yawoog coverb+GO/COME. fly away, take off.
• Jiregema yawoog berrayi. *All the birds took off.*
yawoog coverb+LEAVE. all take off and leave someone. • Gaboowa berrembi ngayi, yawoog yimberrawoorrood-yoowoorroo wela! *What these that have all taken off and left us, goodness!*
yawool-yawooloo noun. boggy ground. [NOTE: type of soil that cars and horses can quickly and easily sink into after some rain] SEE: **darradbem**.
yawoonyji; yawinyji noun. deep coolamon.
yawoorroogboo coverb+GO/COME. being a person who lost a brother or sister. • Ngenengga yawoorroogboo-ngarri-ya nirda gendang Jambabjen Mabel-Down jambab. *Here where you are a person with no brother, coming down from Mabel Down Jump-Up (i.e. your brother who died coming down the Mabel Downs Jump-Up; said to identify a person being spoken about in a conversation).*
yawoorrool noun. woman who has had a sibling die.
yawoorroom noun. lower leg. [NOTE: if someone feels tingling, 'jump-jump', in this part a brother or sister is coming]
yawoorroony noun. man who has had a sibling die.
yawoo-yawoo coverb+SAY_DO_REFL. chase something together. • Warrarnany yawoo-yawoo-wayi berramengirriyin-doo woombarnoongoonyga. *The wedge-tailed eagle (eaglehawk) was hunting (with the egret, white crane), chasing rock wallabies and shouting at them.* [NOTE: only one of the hunters is named in this sentence; the reciprocal/reflexive form of the verb is used to show that the action is for their mutual benefit and the 'object' noun takes emphatic *-ga* and is singular]
yayi interjection. a noisy call.
yayi coverb+SAY/DO. feel itchy. • Yayi ngenarn nyoomboorroo yiligin-ngirri. *I feel itchy inside my nose.*
yayi coverb+HIT. be itchy. • Yayi ngiyinji. *He is itchy.*

yayiben pronoun. you (one) and me. SEE: **yayin**.
yayig coverb+SAY/DO. call out making a noise.
• Ngoowan yayig darrirn-boorroo. *Don't make a noise about it (when they pierce your nose).*
yayiggoolg coverb+SAY/DO_REFL. be all laughing and talking making a noise together.
• Yayiggoolg berrangirriyinbe. *They were all laughing and talking, making a noise together.*
yayin pronoun. you (one) and me. SEE: **yayiben**.
yayiyangeny, yayiyangel, yayiyangem possessive pronoun. belonging to you (one) and me. • Damgawa yayiyangem. *That belongs to you and me.*
yayi-yayi coverb+SAY/DO. make a noise talking/calling out. • Rangga barrenha-boorroo-yoo yayi-yayi-ngarri birrirn. *You two listen to the noise of them talking.*
yerderr coverb+FALL/GO_DOWN. kneel down.
• Ngarranggarnin-ga, jalarinyga yerderr nginiwardji. *The egret knelt down in dreamtime.* SEE: **balmarr, nadiling**.
yerderrwany coverb+HAVE. keep something while kneeling down. • Yerderrwany barremoorloo. *You all hold it while kneeling.*
yerderrwanybeny, yerderrwanybel, yerderrwanybem adjective. someone who is kneeling down.
yi interjection. what a ghost said when coming to abduct two boys.
yib coverb+FALL/GO_DOWN. duck down. • Yib nginiwardji. *He ducked down.*
yidja verb. you (one) and I are GOING/COMING.
yidjande verb. you (one) and I keep GOING/COMING.
yigarrwoony, yigarrwool, yigarrwoom adjective. itchy, sexy, horny. • Ngalilga miyi yigarrwool. *That woman is itchy too.*
yigelany interjection. said when brother, sister or grandparent (*thamany, ganggayi, gelagi, ngawooji*) swears SEE: **warri-warri, ngagoony**.
yigily-yigily coverb+SAY/DO. swing hips from side to side. • Yigily-yigily barroo-gili moon'goom dam. *All swing your hips from side to side.* SEE: **loomayi**.
yijim, yijiyam adjective. true. • Berrembi jarragbe yijiyam. *These are true words. This is a true story.*
yijiyan adverb. truthfully. • Yijiyan jarrag ngenarn-ninggi. *I am speaking to you truthfully.*
yil REDUP: **yil-yil**. coverb+GET. break off. • Yil benamanyji. *He broke it (branch) off.* [NOTE:

reduplicated form is swearing (Rusty Peters)]

yilag *directional.* downhill, down to water, down at the river. • Berdi-berdij nginini lalanggarrany, yilag wiji nginini goorloo-yoorroong. *The crocodile got up and ran down into the water.* • Nginya gerliwirring wiji ngerne, goorloony, jamboorn ngiyilinji dan yilag gidji, jamboorn ngenengga. *This is the water running down from on top filling it up, down there it goes, filling it up here (talking about waterfall in painting).*

yilaggarnany REDUP: *yili-yilaggarnam. noun.* crocodile. LIT: 'one who lives on the bottom'. SEE: lalanggarrany, wawoorrmarndiny.

yilang; yilangbiny *directional.* from down there.

yilangoogoo *directional.* downwards, going down.

yilberrwany *coverb+FALL/GO_DOWN.* fall off (e.g. leaves). • Danya joomooloony ganarrambi dam yilberrwany berrooward. *The leaves have fallen off that boab tree. / That boab tree has lost its leaves.*

yilewarrge *coverb+GET.* make someone feel bad. • Yilewarrge yimberremenbe-yoowoo jarrag-garri boorroorn-yarri. *They make us feel bad when they are talking to us.* • Yilewarrge ngemberremenbe jirlwam. *They hurt my feelings. They make me feel nervous.*

yilgiya *adverb.* good shot, well done. • Yilgiya boonganynha! *You spear it with a good shot!* • Men'gawiya linga-linga barrern-gili dam miyale-boorroo gawilig-girrim, yilgiya theb bamberrajtha. *It's a good idea to make sure the fridge door is always properly closed.*

yilgoorriya *coverb+BECOME.* become bad. • Dala yilgoorriya waniyid-yarri. *That one has become bad (about to give birth) on us.*

yilgoorroony, yilgoorrool, yilgoorroom *adjective.* bad, old, unwell. [NOTE: Southern dialect]

yilgoowoorroony, yilgoowoorrool, yilgoowoorroom REDUP: *yilgi-yilgoorroom, yilgoo-yilgoowoorroom. adjective.* bad, old, unwell. LIT: 'good-not having'. • Moorloo yilgoowoorroon-nga. *I have a bad eye.* • Ngoowan, yilgoorrool-doo. *No, the two women were both no good (ill).* [NOTE: sometimes heard as *yilgoowoorriny*]

yilgoowoorroog *coverb+GET.* make bad, make sick. LIT: 'good-not having-causative'. • Yilgoowoorroog benamanyji-yoo dany-gany. *That creature had made the two of them sick (lit. 'made them bad').*

yilib; yileb *coverb+GO/COME.* get up early. • Ngoowa yilib nirda. *You don't get up early.*

yiligibiny *locative.* along the bottom, underneath.

yiligin *locative.* inside, underneath.

yilingarriny, yilingarril, yilingarrim *adjective.* lazy, person who is always loafing about waiting for someone else to get meat. • Yilingarrayan-ngoo. *You are really lazy.*

yiliwarrge *coverb+GET.* wake someone up. • Yiliwarrge yimberramangbende-yarre mendoowoon-ga. *They were waking us up all night (crying children in the children's hospital where Peggy Patrick was staying as a carer for her grandson).*

yiloowoogda; yilawoogda *adverb.* ready. • Marnem jardgi nginbirn yiloowoogda. *I will set the fire ready (for when you come back with the meat).* • Boonoo-boonoo gala yarremij yilawoogda Joonbal-ngooyoo. *Let's paint ourselves ready for the song and dance event.*

yilwarrag *coverb+GO/COME.* do something completely, do something that is forever. • Jimerrawoona yilwarrag nyaniyinya. *She is going right away for good.*

yilwarrany, yilwarral, yilwarram *adjective.* completely, forever. • Yilwarral marrarn nyimbiyanya. *She is going away for good.*

yilwarraya *adverb.* completely, forever. • Marrarn nyimbiyanya yilwarraya. *She is going away for good.*

yilyiwany *coverb+SAY/DO.* sneak away, go sneaking away. • Yilyiwanya ngoonbirn goorndarri-geny. *I should sneak away to go fishing.*

yilyiwoo *coverb+GO/COME.* sneak away. • Yilyiwoo nginiyin danyi jalariny derrmerle-gili. *That white crane got up and sneaked away to a narrow rocky place.*

yimarlji *noun.* sandpaper fig. *Ficus aculeata* var. *aculeata*, *F. aculeata* var. *indecora*. SEE: yingarrjiny.

yimberramangbe *verb.* they were GETTING us.
yimberramangbende *verb.* they used to GET us.
yimberramangbende-yarre *verb.* they used to GET us.
yimberramangbende-yoowoo *verb.* they used to GET us all.
yimberramanha, yimberramannha *verb.* you all GOT me.

yimberrama-yoowoo

yimberrama-yoowoo *verb.* they GOT all of us.
yimberramenbe *verb.* they GET us.
yimberramenbe-yoowoo; yimberremenbe-yoowoo *verb.* they are GETTING us.
yimberramoorda *verb.* you all will SWEAR at me.
yimberramoorloowardbe *verb.* they HAD us, they were KEEPING us.
yimberranganynha *verb.* you will all SPEAR me.
yimberrannha-gili *verb.* you all are BRINGING/TAKING me.
yimberranybe *verb.* they were BRINGING/TAKING us.
yimberranybende *verb.* they used to BRING/TAKE us.
yimberranybe-ngarri-yarre *verb.* when they were BRINGING/TAKING us.
yimberranybi-yarre; yimberranybe-yarre *verb.* they were BRINGING/TAKING us.
yimberrany-gili *verb.* you all BROUGHT/TOOK me.
yimberranynha-gili *verb.* you all were BRINGING/TAKING me.
yimberrawoodayi *verb.* they two LEFT me.
yimberrawoorroodbi-yoowoo *verb.* they LEFT us all.
yimberrawoorrood-yarre; yimberramoorrood-yarre *verb.* you LEFT us all.
yimberrawoorrood-yoowoorroo *verb.* they LEFT us all.
yimberrayangbende-yarre *verb.* they used to PUT us.
yimberrayangbe-yarre *verb.* they were PUTTING us.
yimberrayid *verb.* they HIT me.
yimberrayidbende-yarre *verb.* they used to HIT us.
yimberrayidbe-yarre; yimberrayidboo-yarre *verb.* they were HITTING us.
yimberrayidjende *verb.* they used to HIT me.
yimberrayid-yoowoo *verb.* they HIT us all.
yimberrayinnha *verb.* you all were GIVING me. • Ngoowan yimberrayinnha-gili werlerlemenbe jamberramoorloowarda. *You wouldn't give me any of those young women you kept.*
yimberrayin-yarre *verb.* they are GIVING us.
yimberreg *verb.* you all should TAKE me.
yimberrigbany *verb.* you all should TAKE me along.
yimberrigtha *verb.* you all should TAKE me.
yimberrem *verb.* you all should GET me.
yimberremenbende-yoowoo *verb.* they keep on GETTING us.
yimberremenbe-yarre *verb.* they are GETTING us (exclusive).
yimberremenbi-yoo *verb.* they are GETTING us two.
yimberremnha *verb.* you all should GET me.
yimberremnha-yarri *verb.* you all should GET us.
yimberrennha *verb.* you all are BRINGING/TAKING me.
yimberrij *verb.* they will HIT me.
yimberrijbe-yoowoorroo *verb.* they will HIT us all.
yimberrijbi-yoowoo *verb.* they will be HITTING us all.
yimberriwoonnha *verb.* you all are WOUNDING me.
yimberriyajtha-yerri *verb.* you all will PUT us.
yimberriyi *verb.* you all GIVE me.
• Barriyanyma-ngirri-yoo ngabayi-warriny, boorrale yimberriyi-yoo. *Won't you come here to me, my two sons, and give me food.*
yimberriyilinha *verb.* you all are PUTTING me.
yimberriyinbe *verb.* they are HITTING me.
yimbimnha *verb.* you (one) should GET me.
yimbirrigbende-yoowoorroo *verb.* they will keep on TAKING us (inclusive).
yimbirrigbe-yoowoo *verb.* they will be TAKING us (inclusive).
yimbirrimbi-yarre *verb.* they will be GETTING us.
yimbirrimbi-yarri-yoo *verb.* they will be GETTING us two.
yimbirrimnha *verb.* you all will be GETTING me.
yimbirrimnha-yarre *verb.* you all will be GETTING us.
yimbirrinha *verb.* you all are BRINGING/TAKING me.
yimbirriyin *verb.* they will GIVE me.
yimbirriyin-yarre *verb.* they will GIVE us.
yimbirriyin-yarri-yoo *verb.* they will GIVE us two.
yimele *coverb+GET.* steal. • Yimele nharem-ngoongoo! *I'm going to steal you!* • Mayi-bawoorroon-ngage. Wanyagoowarrany yimele ngenamanyji mayim. *I have no food. A little boy stole it. / A little boy robbed me of the food.*
• Yimele-ngarri joonemenha-ngage

merndam. *Because you stole my money.*
• Girrganyji, wawooleny-noongoo yimele benamanyji. *The brown falcon came and stole from the frillneck lizard.* [NOTE: in the first example the person addressed is the object and the 'thing' stolen; in the second example the person who was robbed is the object, but in the last two examples the things stolen are cross-referenced as the object]

yimele *coverb+SAY/DO.* steal. • Yimele nginini girrganyji dany. *That brown falcon stole.*

yinama *verb.* you GOT me.

yinamanha; yinemanha *verb.* you were GETTING me.

yinamannhande *verb.* you used to GET me.

yinamannha-yarre *verb.* you were GETTING us (exclusive).

yinamannha-yoowoo *verb.* you were GETTING us (inclusive).

yinamanyjende-yarre *verb.* he used to GET us (exclusive).

yinamanyjende-yoowoo *verb.* he used to GET us (inclusive).

yinamanyji *verb.* he was GETTING me.

yinamanyji-yarre *verb.* he was GETTING us.

yinamanyji-yarri-yoo *verb.* he was GETTING us two.

yinamenji *verb.* he is GETTING me.

yinamenji-yarre *verb.* he is GETTING us.

yinamenji-yayi *verb.* he is GETTING us two (you (one) and me).

yinamenji-yoowoo; yinamenji-yoowoorroo *verb.* he is GETTING us all.

yinamena; yinamennha; yinemena; yinemennha *verb.* you (one) are GETTING me.

yinameny *noun masculine.* hare wallaby, possum, quoll. [NOTE: word used by different people to mean various small mammals that have not been seen in Gija country for a long time. Jack Britten gave this word in 1987 on seeing the hare wallaby picture in Ride (1970), *Lagorchestes conspicillatus*. The cognate word '*yinamang*' was given in the 1970s for the same picture in Miriwoong (SEE: **moorloogoorndoorlgoorndoolji**). Winnie Badbarriya used this word meaning 'possum', *Petropseudes dahli, Trichosurus vulpecula.* SEE: **garndoorroony, nanggoony**. It is also used meaning 'quoll', *Dasyurus hallucatus*, in Purdie et al. (2018). SEE: **bawoogoony**.

yinamenya *verb.* she is GETTING me.

yinamenya-yarre *verb.* she is GETTING us (exclusive).

yinamenya-yoowoo *verb.* she is GETTING us (inclusive).

yinamoorlardja *verb.* she used to HAVE/HOLD/KEEP me.

yinamoorlardji *verb.* he used to HAVE/HOLD/KEEP me.

yinamoorloonha *verb.* you (one) will HAVE/KEEP me.

yinamoorloowardjende-yarre *verb.* he used to HAVE/KEEP us.

yinang *coverb+HIT.* look around carefully for something. • Yinang beniyinji thoowoorranyji-boorroo. *He is looking around carefully for something.*

yinangabennha *verb.* you are SPEARING me.

yinangaboorda *verb.* you SPEARED/POKED me.

yinangambenji-yoowoo *verb.* he is SPEARING/POKING us.

yinanyande-yarre *verb.* she used to BRING/TAKE us.

yinanya-yarre *verb.* she BROUGHT/TOOK us.

yinanyjende-yarre *verb.* he used to BRING/TAKE us.

yinanyji-yarre *verb.* he BROUGHT/TOOK us.

yinanyji-yarri-yoo *verb.* he BROUGHT/TOOK us two.

yinara *noun.* opposite generational moiety.
• Yinara-noonggoorroo-yoo-ngageny. *You two are in the other generational group from me. You two are yinara to me.* ('We play against you fellas.' Woman of Nyawoorroo skin talking to Nambin and Nangari.) [NOTE: see Figure 9 Gija skin names, page 12]. SEE: **jarlinybaroom, jarlinyjaroom**.

yinawoon *verb.* you WOUNDED me.

yinawoorrood *verb.* you LEFT me.

yinawoorroodji-yarre *verb.* he LEFT us (exclusive).

yinawoorrood-yarre *verb.* you LEFT us.

yinawoorroona *verb.* you are LEAVING me.

yinayanha *verb.* you are PUTTING me.

yinayanya-yarre *verb.* she PUT us.

yinayanyjende-yarre *verb.* he used to PUT us.

yinayanyji-yarre *verb.* he PUT us.

yinayid *verb.* he/she/it HIT me.

yinayidja-yarre *verb.* she/it (feminine) HIT us.

yinayidjande-yarre *verb.* she used to HIT us.

yinayidjende-yarre *verb.* he used to HIT us.

yinayidji-yarre *verb.* he/it (masculine) HIT us.

yinayid-yarre

yinayid-yarre *verb.* he/she/it HIT us.
yinayinnha *verb.* you GAVE (it to) me.
yinayitha *verb.* you were HITTING me.
yinbengany *verb.* you will SPEAR me.
yinbidande *verb.* you keep on BRINGING/TAKING me.
yinbiji-yoowoo *verb.* he/it (masculine) will HIT us.
yinbimji-yoowoo *verb.* he/it (masculine) will GET us.
yinbimnha *verb.* you (one) will GET me.
yinbinganynha *verb.* you will SPEAR/POKE me.
yinboowoorroob *verb.* you will LEAVE me.
yinboowoorroobja-yoowoo *verb.* she will LEAVE us all.
yinboowoorroobji-yarre *verb.* he will LEAVE us.
yindaj *verb.* PUT me!
yindegbany *verb.* BRING me!
yindegbany-yarre *verb.* BRING all of us!
yindegbany-yarri-yoo *verb.* BRING us two!
yindemnha *verb.* you GET me!
yindemnha-yarre *verb.* you GET all of us!
yindemnha-yarri-yoo *verb.* you GET us two!
yindeda *verb.* you TAKE me! SEE: **yindegbany**.
yindij *verb.* HIT me!
yindiyi *verb.* you GIVE (it to) me! [NOTE: recipient is cross-referenced as the direct object in the prefix]
yindiyinnha *verb.* you should/must GIVE (it to) me!
yindoowoorroob *verb.* you (one) LEAVE me, you move away from me. • *Wayini-gala yindoowoorroob! Give me room! You should move away from me like that!*
yinema-yarri *verb.* he/it (masculine) GOT us (exclusive).
yinemenji-yoowoo, yinemenji-yoowoorroo he/it (masculine) is GETTING us (inclusive). SEE: **yinamenji-yoowoorroo**.
yinemenya-yarr *verb.* she/it (feminine) is GETTING us (exclusive).
yingajalil *noun feminine.* cabbage palm. *Livistona victoriae.* SEE: **yangajalil, danarrel, ngamalil**.
yingal-yingalji *noun.* part under chin.
Yingandaliny; Yingandalel; Yingandale *noun.* Maud Creek. [NOTE: also the name of an old man buried there that Peggy Patrick called *thamanyji*]
Yingarringenden *noun.* place near Osmond River.
Yingarrjiny *noun.* place on Bedford Downs west of Mount King. LIT: 'place of the sandpaper fig'.
yingarrjiny *noun.* sandpaper fig. *Ficus aculeata* var. *aculeata, F. aculeata* var. *indecora*. SEE: **yimarlji**.
yingerriwoony; yingerroony *noun masculine.* rainbow snake. SEE: **garlooroony, goorlabal**. [NOTE: used by Peggy Patrick to mean 'rainbow snake'; Eileen Bray suggests that this may be a particular place belonging to the *garlooroony*]
yinggerd *coverb+GO_ALONG.* be something moving in the distance that can only just be seen. • *Yinggerd-garri woomberranybende, joorroob-garri berrayinde mernmerdgalem, thambarlam bare-warij berrani-noo. When the police were moving in the distance, coming along in a line, they were tracking his footprints.*
yinginybe; yinginybi *noun.* name. • *Yinginybe-ngirri babinyin-nga. My name is 'The Fighter.'* • *Nawarram-ngirri yinginybe. I am famous (lit. 'My name is big').*
yininyji-yoowoo *verb.* he is HITTING all of us.
yiniyanyji *verb.* he was PUTTING me.
yiniyanyji-yarre *verb.* he was PUTTING us.
yiniyilinji *verb.* he/it (masculine) is PUTTING me. SEE: **yiniyooloonji**.
yiniyilinji-yarre *verb.* he/it (masculine) is PUTTING us all.
yiniyilinnha-yarre *verb.* you (one) are PUTTING us.
yiniyinha *verb.* you (one) are HITTING me.
yiniyinji *verb.* he/it (masculine) is HITTING me.
yiniyinji-yarre *verb.* he/it (masculine) is HITTING us all.
yiniyinji-yoowoo *verb.* he/it (masculine) is HITTING us all.
yiniyinnha *verb.* you (one) are HITTING me.
yiniyooloonya *verb.* she is PUTTING me.
yiniyooloonji *verb.* he is PUTTING me. SEE: **yiniyilinji**.
yinyeg *coverb+SAY/DO.* suck. • *Birriyan-ngarri ngenengga, yinyeg birrirn-birri goongoorloom, gamaliwam. If strangers come here they (bats) will suck their blood.*
yinyeg REDUP: **yinyeg-yinyeg**. *coverb+SAY/DO_M.* suck up juice/liquid. • *Yinyeg woomenyande. She keeps on sucking (juice).* • *Yinyeg-yinyeg woomberramande dalga thawalal, dal goonji-ngarnal. They used to suck (honey) from the flowers of the bauhinia.*
yinyjoong *coverb+GO/COME.* disperse. • *Yinyjoong nginiyi jadanyga, birriny-moowam*

boorroonboo. *The rain has gone now, the sky is clear.* • Yinyjoong berrayin dambi waringarrimbe ngelamoogoo, boowoorroogoo, nyoowooloogoo. *That big crowd of people dispersed and went east, north and south.*

yirdarr *coverb+DO_REFL.* go to sleep. • Yidarr yirramiyin-joo. *We two went to sleep.*

yirdardarr *coverb+FALL/GO_DOWN.* go to sleep. • Mendoowoomga boorroordboo:::, yirdardarr yarroowoonya, yoowoorroon-ga. *Night came and we all went to sleep.*

yirdarrge *coverb+HIT.* make someone go to sleep (e.g. by rocking as a baby). • Yirdarrge ngenayidji. *It (good shade) made me go to sleep.*

yireg-yireg *coverb+SAY/DO_M.* straighten spears. • Yireg-yireg woomberramande garloomboom. *They were straightening spears.*

yiroowoonji, yiroowoonbe *noun masculine.* marsupial mouse. *Pseudomys nanus, P. desertor.* • Ngalanygaleny. *A good singer (in dreamtime).* [NOTE: mate of *bawoodany*, 'painted lizard' and *boonoonggoony*, 'hill country goanna'; makes mist like smoke on the hills in the wet time, the origin of smoking ceremonies; was a '*ngalanygaleny*', good singer in dreamtime] SEE: **jaranel, nyilimbil, nyilimbiny.**

yirr *coverb+BRING/TAKE.* wait for someone, give time to someone. • Yirr nginanyji. *He waited for him.*

yirr *coverb+PUT.* wait for someone. • Yirr-ngarri yamberriliyinya. *When we were waiting for them.*

yirr *coverb+HIT.* wait for someone. • Yirr niyin'ge. *I am waiting for him.*

yirraardjende *verb.* we kept FALLING/GOING DOWN. [NOTE: Southern dialect]

yirradjende; yirrardjende *verb.* we (exclusive) keep on GOING/COMING.

yirradji; yirrardji *verb.* we (exclusive) are GOING/COMING.

Yirralalam *noun.* Packsaddle Plain area near Kununurra. [NOTE: Miriwoong estate name]

yirrama *verb.* **1.** we (exclusive) SAID/DID. **2.** we (exclusive) GOT him/her/it.

yirramande *verb.* we (exclusive) were SAYING/DOING.

yirramanya *verb.* **1.** we (inclusive) were SAYING/DOING. *verb.* **2.** we (inclusive) were GETTING him/her/it.

yirramanyende; yirramangjende *verb.* we (exclusive) used to GET him/her/it.

yirramanyji; yirramanyi *verb* we (exclusive) GOT him/her/it.

yirramenjende *verb.* we (exclusive) keep on GETTING him/her/it.

yirramenji; yirremenji *verb.* we (exclusive) are GETTING him/her/it.

yirramimanyja *verb.* we FOLLOWED him/her/it.

yirramimanyjende *verb.* we used to FOLLOW him/her/it.

yirramiyinde *verb.* we used TO DO TO OURSELVES/EACH OTHER.

yirramiyinji-yoo *verb.* we two DID TO OURSELVES/EACH OTHER.

yirramiyiny-joo *verb.* we two DID TO OURSELVES/EACH OTHER.

yirramoorloowardji *verb.* we (exclusive) HAVE him/her/it.

yirrangirriyin *verb.* we all DID TO OURSELVES/EACH OTHER.

yirrangirriyinjende *verb.* we used to SAY/DO TO OURSELVES/EACH OTHER.

yirrangoon *verb.* we (exclusive) ATE him/her/it.

yirrani *verb.* we (exclusive) SAID/DID.

yirraniyin *verb.* we (exclusive) WERE, we WERE STAYING.

yirraniyinde *verb.* we (exclusive) used to BE/STAY.

yirranji; yirranyi *verb.* we ARE, we are all STAYING. [NOTE: *yirranyi* also recorded as meaning 'we went along'] SEE: **yirranyji.**

yirranya *verb.* we WENT ALONG. Girlirli yirranya gibinji. *We walked along in the bush.*

yirranybe; yirranybany *coverb+BECOME.* become hard to see, become dull (e.g. stars). • Wardamga dam yirranybe woomberrayidbe. *The stars were becoming dull (hard to see).*

yirranybeny, yirranybel, yirranybem *adjective.* having to squint eyes to see. • Moorloo yirranyben-nga. *I'm squinty eyed.*

yirranyjende *verb.* **1.** we (exclusive) used to BRING/TAKE him/her/it. **2.** we (exclusive) used to GO ALONG.

yirranyji *verb.* **1.** we (exclusive) BROUGHT/TOOK him/her/it. **2.** we (exclusive) went along.

yirrardjende; yirradjende *verb.* we (exclusive) keep on GOING/COMING.

yirrardji; yirradji *verb.* we (exclusive) are GOING/COMING.

yirrarn

yirrarn *verb.* we (exclusive) SAY/DO.
yirraward *verb.* we FELL/WENT DOWN.
yirrawardji *verb.* we FELL/WENT DOWN.
yirrawoorremiyinji-yoo *verb.* we LEFT EACH OTHER.
yirrawoorrood *verb.* we (exclusive) LEFT him/her/it.
yirrawoorroodjende *verb.* we (exclusive) were LEAVING him/her/it.
yirrawoorroodji *verb.* we (exclusive) LEFT him/her/it.
yirrayanyjende *verb.* we (exclusive) used to PUT him/her/it.
yirrayanyji *verb.* we (exclusive) PUT him/her/it.
yirrayanyjinde *verb.* we (exclusive) used to PUT him/her/it.
yirraya-yoo *verb.* we two (exclusive) PUT him/her/it.
yirrayi *verb.* we (exclusive) WENT/CAME.
yirrayidjende *verb.* we (exclusive) used to HIT him/her/it.
yirrayidji *verb.* **1.** we (exclusive) HIT him/her/it. **2.** we (exclusive) BECAME.
yirrayidji-yoo *verb.* **1.** we two HIT him. **2.** we two BECAME.
yirrayin *verb.* we (exclusive) were GOING/COMING.
yirrayinde *verb.* we (exclusive) used to GO/COME.
yirrayinjende *verb.* we (exclusive) used to keep GOING/COMING.
yirrayinji *verb.* we (exclusive) were GOING/COMING.
yirrberda *coverb+FALL/GO_DOWN.* run and hide.
• Googanda thoowiyanyji birriyan-ngarri, yirrberda nginboowoon gerlernen. *If something comes, I run and hide in the tall spinifex.*
yirrbinji *noun.* song to make someone love the singer. SEE: **woodiji**.
yirregbany-noonggoo *verb.* we will TAKE you all.
yirremiji *verb.* we will DO TO OURSELVES/EACH OTHER.
yirremiyinji *verb.* we are DOING TO OURSELVES/EACH OTHER.
yirremoorloonji *verb.* we HAVE him/her/it.
yirremoorloon-yoo *verb.* we two HAVE him/her/it.
yirremoorloowoonde-ngoongoo *verb.* we should have KEPT you.
yirremoowoonji *verb.* we are GETTING AND HITTING it.
yirrengambenji *verb.* we SPEAR him/her/it.
yirrengamenji *verb.* we will have to SPEAR him/her/it.
yirrerij *coverb+GO/COME.* be dead tired/exhausted.
• Yirrerij ngenayin. *I was exhausted.*
yirrewoonji *verb.* we are FALLING/GOING DOWN.
yirrgawa *coverb+SAY/DO_REFL.* disagree, not like one another. • Yirrgawa berrangirriyin na. *They did not like each other then.*
yirrgawoo *coverb+PUT.* talk badly about someone, run someone down when talking about them, refuse something because you want something else. • Yirrgawoo naniyanyji-ni lalanggarrany-gany. *The crocodile was talking about you.*
yirrgawoo *coverb+SAY/DO.* refuse something because you want something else.
• Gangal-ngooyoo gangal, yirrgawoo nerne? *Which one do you want, you are refusing this one (said to moon when they were asking which woman he wanted to marry but he was hanging out for the woman of his mother-in-law skin)?*
yirrgawoo *coverb+SAY/DO_M.* refuse something because you want something else. • Yirrgawoo wanemayinde-ngooyoo thoowernde-manbel, thamboorroogala. *He was refusing on account of the black-headed snake, who was his mother-in-law skin.*
yirrijende *verb.* **1.** we will keep HITTING him/her/it. **2.** we will keep BECOMING.
yirriji *verb.* we will HIT him/her/it.
yirrilinji *verb.* we PUT him/her/it.
yirriliyanyji *verb.* we were PUTTING ourselves.
yirril-yirrilji; yirrel-yirrelji *noun masculine.* red-backed fairy wren. *Malurus melanocephalus.*
yirrim *verb.* we will GET him/her/it.
yirrimnyi; yirrimji; yirremnyi *verb.* we will GET him/her/it.
Yirrine *noun.* place with flat ground and sharp pointed hills east of Warrmarn.
yirringaragjil *noun feminine.* black-faced cuckoo shrike. *Coracina novaehollandiae.* [NOTE: word also recorded as 'white-bellied cuckoo-shrike' *C. papuensis*] SEE: **miliwoorrangel**.
yirringirriyan; yirrengirriyan *verb.* we all DO TO OURSELVES/EACH OTHER.
yirrinjende *verb.* we will BE/BE STAYING.
yirrinji *verb.* **1.** we will BE/STAY. **2.** we are GOING ALONG.
yirrinyi *verb.* we ARE/ARE STAYING.

yirrinyngoorlg *coverb.* inhale aroma, smell a perfume. SEE: **ngawoombij**.

yirrirn *verb.* we will SAY/DO.

yirriwan *verb.* we will CUT ourselves.

yirriwoorroobji *verb.* we will LEAVE him/her/it.

yirriyaji *verb.* we will PUT him/her/it.

yirriyan *verb.* we (exclusive) will be GOING/COMING.

yirriyande *verb.* we (exclusive) will keep on GOING/COMING.

yirriyanyji *verb.* we (exclusive) PUT him/her/it.

yirriyanyji-ngoongoo *verb.* we (exclusive) PUT you (one).

yirriyarriny *noun.* yellow jacket, tree with edible gum. *Terminalia canescens.* SEE: **berewereny**. [NOTE: resembles *warraroony* but grows on ground away from the river]

yirriyin *verb.* we HIT him/her/it. [NOTE: homophonous with GIVE]

yirriyin *verb.* we GIVE him/her/it.

yirriyi-ngoongoo *verb.* we will GIVE you. [NOTE: possibly *yirriyin-ngoongoo* with the 'n' elided; recipient is the object – the gift is not cross-referenced] • *Ngoowan yirriyin-ngoongoo. We cannot give her to you (mother-in-law skin woman to moon as wife).*

yirriyinji *verb.* we are HITTING him/her/it.

yirriyinji-ngoongoo *verb.* we are HITTING you (one).

yirri-yirri *coverb+SAY/DO_M.* keep DOING something. • *Giyale dan yirri-yirri woomberramande. They always kept going back to the same place.*

yirrjib *coverb+PUT.* do properly, do truly. • *Yirrjib ngoorrayangbende. They did it properly. / They put it on properly.* SEE: **joodoog**.

yirroowidji *verb.* we might HIT him/her/it.

yiwijge *coverb.* become scrubby, become overgrown with plants. • *Yiwijge woomberrayid ngagenybe daam. My place has become scrubby (overgrown with bamboo).*

yiwiny, yiwim *noun.* louse, head lice. *Pediculus humanus.* SEE: **yarlarliny**.

yiwiny *noun.* lice grass. *Cyperus javanicus.*

yiwinybeb *coverb+GO/COME.* take off. • *Gaboo-wanyji berrani-ni yiwinybeb nginiyi. They did something to him and he took off (i.e. he left).*

yiwirlib *coverb+HIT.* wipe out tracks, cover something over. • *Yiwirlib beniyinnha dam thambarlam, deg bimberrimbe. You wipe out those tracks somebody might see.*

yiwirn, yiwirnji *noun.* wet season, set-in rain in the wet season.

yiwirn; yiwirn'gen *temporal.* wet season time, time of set-in rain in the wet season. SEE: **jadagen**.

yiwirrirrim *adjective.* many. • *Garrayil-ngarri wimbija, binbimnya-wanyji wanyanyagem yiwirrirrim. When she grows up she might have lots of children.* • *Warlarlayimbi yiwirrirrim-ngiyi jirrawoogool joondaleli. The one pet dog has lots of puppies.*

yiwiya *verb.* we two (you and me) will go. SEE: **yoowiya**.

yiwooltheleny, yiwoolthelel, yiwoolthelem *adjective.* wooly one (like a sheep). • *'Ngoowananyji jarrinyinji dany, yage ngarnelanyji, yiwoolthelel,' nginini-ngooyoo jiyigjel. 'Maybe not that devil dog, but maybe that other one, the wooly one,' he said about that sheep.*

yiyi *interjection.* yes. SEE: **ngiyi**.

yiyig-yiyig *coverb+HIT.* (birds) say 'yiyig-yiyig' at someone. • *Berrema yiyig-yiyig yimberriyinbe-yoowoo. They (birds) are saying 'yiyig-yiyig' at us.*

yoo *conjunctive particle.* and. SEE: **joo, doo**. [NOTE: joins nouns]

-yoo *suffix.* dual suffix to verbs. SEE: **-doo, -joo**.

yoob *coverb+HIT.* cover earth oven. • *Yoob benayidji. He covered the earth oven.*

yoob-yoobgajil *noun feminine.* camel. *Camelus dromedaries.* [NOTE: the Gija name, *yoob-yoobgajil*, refers to the way that camels bob their heads up and down when they walk; many camels were brought to Gija country in the early twentieth century to carry heavy loads; feral camels are still seen occasionally in the southern part of Gija country] SEE: **gamoolel**.

yoodooboorr *coverb+SAY/DO_M.* duck out of the way when someone tries to hit. • *Garda-gardan yoodooboorr woomberrama-yoo, dambi goorabe-warriny. Those two old men ducked out of the way as fast as possible.*

yoodoong *coverb+BE/STAY.* put head down for a short time. • *Yoodoong nginji. He has his head down.*

yooj *coverb+FALL/GO_DOWN.* bend down. • *Yooj nginiwardji. He bent down.*

yooloojge *coverb+BURN/BITE.* become really cooked. • *Yooloojge-ngarri ngiwiwarriyi*

Yooloomboo

Figure 90. *Yoonggoony: Joordjoordel Topsy Springvale: Joordjoordel deg nyerne thambarlamningi yoonggoony yilag ngarrgalen.*

boog yarrimnya. *When it gets really cooked we pull it out of the oven.*
Yooloomboo noun. Tableland Station.
yooloony REDUP: **yooloo-yooloony; yooloony-yooloony**. coverb+PUT. put something (e.g. paperbark) under one's arm to use for carrying things. • Merndam benamanya, yooloony benayanyande. *She got some paperpark and put it under her arm (to carry something).* SEE: **joolooj**.
yool-yool coverb. carry (kangaroo).
yoombany noun. grass yam, type of edible root. *Ipomoea* sp. aff. *graminea*. SEE: **nyoombany**.
yoomooj REDUP: **yoomooj-yoomooj**. coverb+SAY/DO. close eyes.
• Yoomooj-yoomooj-gala barroo-gili. *All close your eyes.*
Yoona noun. type of song and dance that used to be performed at Larrelarren. [NOTE: Miriwoong say this was used as the public song and dance with all the women sitting there before the young men were taken away]
yoonbanyji-yarre verb. he/it (masculine) wanted to BRING/TAKE us. • **Loorlg-anyji**

yoonbanyji-yarre yilag. *It might have washed us all downstream.*
yoonbida verb. you should/might TAKE me.
yoonbiji-yarre verb. he wanted to HIT us.
• Yilaganyji nyirreg yoonbiji-yarre. *Maybe it wanted to drown us.*
yoonbij-yarri verb. he/she wanted to HIT us.
• Theda yoonbij-yarre. *He/she wanted to hit us.*
yoonbiyidjende-yoowoo verb. he would have kept on HITTING us.
yoonggoony noun. big-foot ghost, (Kriol 'hairy man ghost'. [NOTE: sounds rather like a relation of the Yeti]
yoongoom noun. spirit. SEE: **birlirre**. [NOTE: used by Catholics to mean 'holy spirit']
Yoonoorr noun. Kilfoyle's Yard, estate east of Ngarrgooroon.
yoorayi coverb+SAY/DO_M. dig a soak. • Dal yoorayi woomberramande-ngiyi, binarriya nyimberramoorlaardbende goorloom benemoorloonya yilag. *They would dig a soak near it (bullrushes) because they knew that it held water underneath in the ground.* [NOTE: digging gently in damp ground makes water

accumulate in the depression; this is known as 'digging a soak']

yoorayimem *noun.* soak.

yoorl *coverb.* go different way.

yoorlag *coverb+HIT.* vomit something out. • Yoorlag beniyinji wirrirril doo lagarnel. *He (rainbow snake) vomits out the little green lorikeets and the witchetty grubs.*

yoorlag *coverb+SAY/DO.* vomit. • Yoorlag nginini. *He vomited.* • Ngoowan dam jang nimbirn, yoorlag dimbirn. *Don't eat that, you will vomit.* • Thoowoorranyji bemberrangoonbe, yoorlag boorroorn. *They ate something, they are vomiting.* • Yoorlag-merrarriny boorroorn, thoowoorranyji mayim yilgoowoorroom jang berrani. *The whole lot of them are vomiting, they must have eaten something bad.*

Yoorlgooban *noun.* hilly country on Texas with lots of kangaroos.

yoorloo *directional.* downstream. • Nginya nawarragawoony nginji. Wayini gendoowa balmendeg ginini, yoorloo ngidji, dagoorlan, jamboorn ngoowoonji goorloony. *This is the river. It goes up like that to form a junction and runs down to fill the deep waterhole with water (talking about a painting).*

yoorloongoogoo; yoorlangoogoo *directional.* going downstream.

yoorloongoojarriny, yoorloojarriny *directional.* further downstream.

yoorn'goorr *coverb+PUT.* cook in the ground, cook in earth oven. • Jard-gela noondaj-gooyoo gernanyjel yoorn'goorra nyilij ngaalooyan ngenenggayana mawoorriyan. *Let me make a fire to roast the echidna right here, right in the shade close to the bloodwood tree.* SEE: **yoorn'goorr-yoorn'goorr**.

yoorn'goorr REDUP: **yoorn'goorr-yoorn'goorr**. *coverb+SAY/DO.* cook in the ground, cook in earth oven. • Yoorn'goorr yirrani-boorroo. *We cooked it in the ground for them.* • . . . mayi-galiny yoorn'goorr-yoorn'goorr-ngarri ngerne . . . *where the cook was cooking something in the ground.*

yoorn'goorr-yoorn'goorr *coverb+GO_ALONG.* cook in the ground, cook in earth oven. • Yoorn'goorr-yoorn'goorr ngiliyande. *I will be cooking (something in the ground).*

yooroorroom; yooroowoorroom *noun.* scrub country.

Figure 91. *Yoorayimem: Goobooji Rosie Malgil: Nyawoorrool wirrirrij nyerne dam goorrngam joordoobam yoorayimem-boorroo.*

yoorr

yoorr REDUP: **yoorr-yoorr**. *coverb+HIT*. rub with paint. • **Yoorr ngiyinya nawooloony mawoondoom-birri.** *She is rubbing paint on the fighting stick.*

yoorr *coverb+DO_REFL*. paint self/each other. • **Yoorr berramiyin-gili.** *They are all painting each other.*

yoorrg *coverb+HIT*. rub with paint or ash. • **Yoorrg yarridja.** *We rub ashes on it.* • **Yoorrg beneda-gili.** *You paint all of them.*

yoorriyangeny, yoorriyangel, yoorriyangem *possessive pronoun*. ours (inclusive). [NOTE: Southern dialect] SEE: **yoowoorriyangeny.**

yoorroo *interjection*. look out. [NOTE: Southern dialect]

yoorroondoorroom *noun*. dancing style. [NOTE: 'like rock and roll'] • **Warrg berrani yoorroondooroom, garnanyjel madi-madi nyimberriyinbe dala ngarabarral.** *They were dancing in the rock and roll style, copying that emu.*

-yoorroong *suffix*. towards, into, onto. SEE: **-gili.**

yoorroon; yoowoorroon *pronoun*. we (inclusive). [NOTE: form *yoorroon* used by people from Southern part of Gija country; some people alternate between *yoowoorroon* and *yoorroon*]

yoorrooniyin *verb*. we (inclusive) would have BEEN/BEEN STAYING.

yoorrwab REDUP: **yoorrwa-yoorrwab**. *coverb+GET*. rub with sweat from armpit. • **Yoorrwa-yoorrwab jimberramangbe ganarram-birri.** *They rubbed their sweat on her with leaves.* SEE: **yoorrwam.**

yoorrwam; yoorram *noun*. armpit hair. • **Dala ngalil yoorrwa-gel.** *That woman has long hair in her armpit.* • **Yoorrwam minyarr-minyarre.** *Smelly armpit hair.* • **Yoorrwam minyarr-minyarrel dali ngalil.** *That woman has smelly armpit hair.*

yoowalany, yoowalam *noun*. black soil yam, vine with edible roots. *Ipomoea aquatica*. SEE: **garndiny.**

yoowan *verb*. you (one) and I will be GOING.

Yoowangeny *noun*. Mud Springs on Bedford Downs, in Paddy Bedford's mother's country.

yoowarrge *coverb+GET*. flirt with someone. • **Yoowarrge nemenji-ni.** *He is flirting with you.*

yoowarrnhawoony, yoowarrnhawool, yoowarrnhawoom *noun*. sexy one, raunchy one.

yoowarroony, yoowarrool, yoowarroom, yoowarrwoony *adjective*. sexy, horny (Kriol: 'tickly'). SEE: **gayawoony, yigarrwoony.**

yoowimija *verb*. you (one) and I will DO TO EACH OTHER.

yoowiya *verb*. we two (inclusive) will GO/COME. SEE: **yiwiya.**

yoowiyan *verb*. we two (inclusive) will be GOING/COMING.

yoowoo *interjection*. yes. SEE: **ngiyi.**

yoowoomnya; yoowimnya *verb*. you (one) and I will GET him/her/it.

yoowoonybeb *coverb+GO/COME*. go in somewhere, disappear. • **Yoowoonybeb berrayi-yoo darnda-warriny walig berraard-joo mangoonyen.** *The two turtles disappeared and went into the grass.*

yoowoorl *coverb+SAY/DO_M*. speak loudly. • **Yoowoorl woomenya, nyoowoole ngoorriyana.** *She is speaking loudly right over there to the south.*

yoowoorlbeny, yoowoorlbel, yoowoorlbem *adjective*. person who speaks loudly.

yoowoorlngbe *coverb+WOUND_REFL*. tell each other off. • **Yoowoorlngbe berrewanboo-yoo.** *Those two are 'tongue banging' each other.*

yoowoorlngbe *coverb+PUT*. make noise and disturb someone. • **Yoowoorlngbe yiniyilinnha-yarre, marrarn biyarra.** *You are making too much noise near us, go away (said about big noisy machine).*

yoowoorlngbiyany, yoowoorlngbiyal, yoowoorlngbiyam *adjective*. person who speaks loudly cutting across others who are trying to talk. • **Dala ngalil yoowoorlngbiyal.** *That woman is speaking loudly across us.*

yoowoorlngboo *coverb+HIT*. make big noise at someone. • **Lowenmowiny yoowoorlngboo yiniyinji-yoowoo yardem.** *The lawn mower is making a big noise in our ears.*

yoowoorr *coverb+SAY/DO*. run (group). • **Waringarrim yoowoorr boorroorn daa-yoorroong.** *They are all running back to camp.* [NOTE: plural only (more than three)]. SEE: **wiji.**

yoowoorr *coverb+SAY/DO_M*. run (group). • **Yoowoorr woomberrama.** *They ran.* [NOTE: plural only (more than three). SEE: **wiji** 'run' referring to one, two or three runners.]

yoowoorr; yewerr *coverb+LEAVE*. run and leave

(group). • Yoowoorr-gela yarroowoorroob. *We will run away and leave him.* [NOTE: plural only (more than three); SEE: **wiji** 'run' referring to one, two or three runners.]

yoowoorr *coverb+GO/COME.* run (group).
• Yoowoorr yirrayin na goorloorr. *We all ran up there then.* [NOTE: plural only (more than three)]. SEE: **wiji**.

yoowoorrge REDUP: **yoowoorr-yoowoorrge**. *coverb+GET.* make run (group). • Yoowoorr-yoowoorrge benamanyji gerlirrin, goorlanggam. *It (flood) made them all run in the west, poor things.* • Yoowoorrge benamanyji girlirre-milimbi. *It (flood) made all the people from the west run.* [NOTE: plural only (more than three)]

yoowoorriyangeny, yoowoorriyangel, yoowoorriyangem *possessive pronoun.* ours (inclusive).

yoowoorroon; yoorroon *pronoun.* we (inclusive). [NOTE: form *yoorroon* used by people from Southern part of Gija country; some people alternate between *yoowoorroon* and *yoorroon*]

yoowoorroowarriny *pronoun.* we/us (inclusive) by ourselves.

yoowoorrwany *pronoun.* we/us (inclusive) ourselves, our turn.

yoowoorr-yoowoorr; yewerr-yewerr *coverb+SAY/DO.* run (group).
• Woombarnoongoombi yewerr-yewerr berrani nawane walilig. *All the rock wallabies ran into the cave.* [NOTE: plural only (more than three)]

7 English to Gija word finder

Aa

Aboriginal man............*noun masculine* **jiyiliny**
Aboriginal people........*noun* **jiyilem**
Aboriginal woman........*noun feminine* **ngalil**;
  noun feminine **langgoornool**;
  langgoornel;
  noun feminine **jiyilil**
Aboriginal way, in the..*adjective* **jiyilengem**
Acacia SEE tree species: **wattle**
aching, be....................*coverb+GO/COME* **woorrngoord**;
  coverb+SAY/DO **woorrngoord**;
  coverb+HIT **yarraware**
adder, death.................*noun masculine* **damberrji**;
  noun masculine **ngadarrji**
adolescent boy.............*noun masculine* **lambarnji**;
  noun masculine **waarrany**
adult..............................*adjective* **garrayilji, garrayilel, garrayile**
  adult man.....................*noun masculine* **garrayilji**
  adult woman................*noun feminine* **garrayilel**
  adults...........................*noun* **garrayile**
  become adult ....*coverb+GO/COME* **garrayilgbe**
aeroplane......................*noun feminine* **wirli-wirligajil**;
  noun feminine **wirli-wirlingarnal**
afraid, be......................*coverb+SAY/DO* **jilba**;
  coverb+SAY/DO_M **jilba**
  make afraid ....*coverb+GET* **jilbage**
  be afraid of someone/
  something ....*coverb+HIT* **jilba**
after...............................*adverb* **bardoobiny**
  person or thing
  that comes after ....*noun* **bardoongeny, bardoongel, bardoongem**
after that......................*temporal* **boorroongenji**
afternoon ....*temporal* **garraroon, garrwaroon**;
  temporal **ngooloo-ngooloon**
  be afternoon ....*coverb+GO_DOWN_M* **garrwaroon**
  be becoming
  afternoon ....*coverb+FALL/GO_DOWN* **garraroony, garraroonyboo**
  go in the afternoon ......*coverb+GO/COME* **garrwaroowany**
  late afternoon...............*temporal* **ngooloo-ngooliyan**
afterwards....................*locative* **bardoon**
again..............................*adverb* **ngoorlan'gayiny**;
  adverb **ngoorlanyaliny**;
  particle **nyaliny**

age mate ....*noun* **jimarriny, jimarril, jimarrim**
  age mate (spoken to) ....*noun* **jimarri**
aggressive ....*adjective* **wariwoony, wariwool, wariwoom**
  aggressive person........*adjective* **babinyiny, babinyil, babinyem**;
  adjective **boorlgarrijbeny, boorlgarrijbel, boorlgarrijbem**
agile wallaby ....*noun masculine* **warlbawoony**
ah! ....*interjection* **aa**;
  interjection **nga**
ahead............................*locative* **welangen**
air compressor.............*noun* **boomi-girrem**
Alice Downs..................*noun* **Binoowoo, Binoowoon**
alive ....*adjective* **mooliny, moolil, moolim**
  be alive ....*coverb+BE/STAY* **milin**
all ....*adjective* **melagawiya**;
  adjective **melagawoom**;
  adjective **melaya**;
  adjective **waringarriya**;
  adjective **waringarrim**
all over the bush..........*locative* **gibi-yibin**
all over the place ....*locative* **ngoorroo-ngoorroon**
almost/already ....*adverb* **ngarriyan**
alone, go along.............*coverb+GO_ALONG* **wirrijga**
alone, stay ....*coverb+BE/STAY* **doomooge**
along the bottom ....*locative* **yiligibiny**
along the side of the hill...............................*locative* **wayirran**
a lot, have.....................*coverb+EAT* **noongoo**
already..........................*adverb* **marra**;
  adverb **marrarn**
  already/almost ....*adverb* **ngarriyan**
alright............................*adjective* **jirrayany, jirrayal, jirrayam, jirram**;
  adjective **nyoonggayany, nyoonggayal, nyoonggayam**;
  interjection **jirrayam**;
  interjection **nyoonggayam**;
  interjection **wara**;
  interjection **warany**
  alright then..................*interjection* **waranya**;
  interjection **waranyjawa**
also.................................*particle* **miyi**;
  particle **nyaliny**
always............................*adverb* **jimerrawoon**

amass	*coverb+GET* **yalawoog**; *coverb+HIT* **yalawoog**
ambush	*coverb+BE/STAY* **joog**; *coverb+FALL/GO_DOWN* **joog**
ancestral being's place	*noun* **werlweny, werlwel, werlwem**
and	*conjunctive particle* **doo**; *conjunctive particle* **joo**; *conjunctive particle* **yoo**
angel	*noun* **nyaarrji, nyaarrel**
angry	*adjective* **ganggerrweny, ganggerrwel, ganggerrwem**
be angry	*coverb+GET* **wariny**; *coverb+GO/COME* **ganggerr**; *coverb+SAY/DO* **wariny**; *coverb+SAY/DO_M* **wariny**
be always angry	*coverb* **ganggerr-ganggerrgayan**
become angry	*coverb+FALL/GO_DOWN* **ngoony**
get angry	*coverb+GO/COME* **ngarr**
make each other angry	*coverb+DO_REFL* **warinyge**
make someone angry	*coverb+GET* **ganggerrge**; *coverb+GET* **warinyge**
angry with	
be angry with each other	*coverb+SAY/DO_REFL* **ganggerr**
be angry with someone	*coverb+SPEAR* **ganggerr-ganggerr**
become angry with someone	*coverb+BE/STAY* **wari**; *COVERB+FALL/GO_DOWN* **boorlooj**
animal	*noun* **miyalji, miyalel, miyale**
ankle	*noun* **boodoom**; *noun* **lenggale**
annoy	*coverb* **nyinge-nyingeg**
another one	*noun* **yagengeny, yagengel, yagengem**
ant (generic)	*noun* **raginy, ragil, ragim**
ant species	*noun masculine* **binyinyiny**
black ant species	*noun masculine* **miginy**
black biting ant species	*noun masculine* **thengawiny**
black smelly ant species	*noun masculine* **binginy**
bull ant	*noun masculine* **goorn'gany**
green ant	*noun feminine* **minyal**; *noun* **waawalji, waawalel, waawale, wawalji, wawalel, wawale**
red ant	*noun masculine* **jangalangaliny**
stink ant	*noun masculine* **goonyoorrji**
white ant (termines)	*noun feminine* **gooroorrooroorrool**; *noun* **moonggoorl**
antbed	*noun feminine* **jamerndel**
antbed larvae	*noun feminine* **ngawagool**
ant hill SEE antbed	
antilopine wallaby	*noun masculine* **jarlangarnany**; *noun masculine* **warlambany**
antilopine wallaby, female	*noun feminine* **gawoorrngarndil**
anus	*noun* **manam**; *noun* **thoomboonyboo**
anything	*noun* **dini-dininy**
anytime, sometime	*temporal* **garawanyji**; *temporal* **geragwaloon**
appear	*coverb+BE/STAY* **boorab**; *coverb+FALL/GO_DOWN* **boorab**; *coverb+GO/COME* **boon'gaj**; *coverb+GO/COME* **boorab**
appear in sky	*coverb+GO/COME* **jag**
appear suddenly	*coverb+GO/COME* **ngag**
make appear	*coverb+BRING/TAKE* **boorab**
archer fish	*noun feminine* **loowarrel**
argue	*coverb+DO_REFL* **wari-wari**
arm	*noun* **nganoonggoom**
arm, upper	*noun* **goordangalam**
put arm down loosely	*coverb* **yalg-yalgbany**
stretch arm out to one side	*coverb+SAY/DO* **mira**
arms	
have arms hanging down loosely	*coverb+BE/STAY* **yalg-yalg**
hold in arms	*coverb+HAVE* **ngamanang**
pose with arms folded	*coverb+BE/STAY* **ngarajbe**
put arms around self	*coverb+DO_REFL* **lawoorr**
put arms around someone	*coverb+GET* **lawoorr**
stand with arms out and chest straight	*coverb+BE/STAY* **tharrboolirr**
stretch arms out	*coverb+SAY/DO* **goorl**
armband	*noun* **gooloong-gooloong**
armpit	*noun* **garrwim**
armpit hair	*noun* **yoorrwam, yoorram**

aroma, give off

aroma, give off	*coverb+GO/COME* **ngawoombij**; *coverb+SAY/DO* **ngabibij**; *coverb+SAY/DO* **ngawoombij**
aroma, inhale	*coverb* **yirrinyngoorlg**
around	
fly around and around up and up (bird)	*coverb+GO_ALONG* **waranggi**
go around a bend	*coverb+GO/COME* **wambalayiny**, **wambelayig**
go around something	*coverb+FALL/GO_DOWN* **ged**
make someone go around and around something	*coverb+GET* **ged-gedgoowany**
spin (something) around and around	*coverb+HIT* **warangan**, **warangan-warangan**
arrive	*coverb+GO/COME* **ngarij**
arrive to someone suddenly	*coverb+GO/COME* **ngag**
ash	*noun* **gawoornbe**
spread out hot ashes to cook something	*coverb+PUT* **garayarr**
ashamed, be	*coverb+SAY/DO* **ganybel**
Ashburton Range	*noun* **Jin'gaweny**
aside, put	*coverb+PUT* **gemag**
ask	*coverb+GET* **yanggiji**; *coverb+PUT* **yanggi**
ask dreaming place for help	*coverb+PUT* **goorara**
ask for	*coverb+SAY/DO* **banya**
ask on behalf of someone	*coverb* **gamalg**
be asking for something (e.g. food)	*coverb+GO_ALONG* **banya-banya**
keep on asking questions	*coverb+SAY/DO_M* **wagirr**
keep on asking without stopping	*coverb+GET* **beringye**; *coverb+GET* **nyirle-nyirleg**
at fault, be	*coverb+HIT* **gooj**
at sunrise	*temporal* **rarrgalen**
at sunset	*temporal* **garraroon**, **garrwaroon**
at the same time	*particle* **wayininji**
attach self close to tree so as to not be seen	*coverb+SAY/DO* **laberd-laberd**
attack/menace	*coverb+SAY/DO_M* **walaji**;
attack/menace someone	*coverb+HIT* **walaji**; *coverb+WOUND* **walaji**
attempt	*coverb+PUT* **gool**
aunt	*noun feminine* **gawangel**
aunt (spoken to)	*noun feminine* **gawayi**
avoidance relationship, people in	*noun* **nyingginy, nyinggil, nyinggim**
awake	*adjective* **mooliny, moolil, moolim**
away, fly	*coverb+GO/COME* **yawoog**; *coverb+LEAVE* **doowab**
fly away into sky	*coverb+BE/STAY* **thoowoog**
away from action	*locative* **geman**
put away from action	*coverb+PUT* **gemag**
axe	*noun feminine* **manyjangal**; *noun feminine* **ngajiral**
axe (said by young men who are not allowed to say the other words)	*noun feminine* **mayinggal**
stone axe	*noun feminine* **thalerrel**; *noun feminine* **woomal**

Bb

baby	*noun* **wangawoony, wangawool**; *noun* **wililji, wililel**; *noun* **nyimbelawoony, nyimbelawool**
crawling baby	*noun* **joongoorleny, joongoorlel, joongoorlem**
cute/fat baby	*adjective* **baam-baamboony, baam-baambool, baam-baamboom**
new-born baby	*noun* **marlirnbany**; *noun* **nyarlimbiny, nyarlimbel, nyarlimbim**
baby animals or birds	*noun* **warlarlayim**
baby kangaroo (joey)	*noun* **woonggariny**
back	*noun* **therlam**
backbone	*noun* **therlam**
back of shoulders	*noun* **barnale**
base of back	*noun* **loorndoomooroom**; *noun* **moon'goom**
be with back to someone/action	*coverb+BE/STAY* **thelngoorroob**
have backache	*coverb+SAY/DO* **nhij**
backside	*noun* **manam**
backstop, group of people acting as	*noun* **gerlalbam**
backwards, go	*coverb+GO/COME* **rerreg**

bad	*adjective* yilgoowoorroony, yilgoowoorrool, yilgoowoorroom
become bad	*coverb+BECOME* yilgoorriya
feel bad	*coverb+SAY/DO* boothal
make bad	*coverb+GET* yilgoowoorroog
bad smelling	*adjective* nhoowoolji, nhoowoolel, nhoowoole
go/become bad smelling	*coverb+GET* nhoowooljiny; *coverb+GO/COME* nhoowoolgbany
bag	*noun* garraginy; *noun* wananginy
bail someone up and harrass them	*coverb+HIT/CUT* joorraj
bald	*adjective* ngererrnginy, ngererrngil, ngererrngim
baler shell	*noun feminine* yabirlil
ball	*noun* boorljany, boorljam; *noun* goordoony
balloon	*noun feminine* booboogarral
bamboo	*noun* gamanggarrji, gamanggarre
bamboo, large type	*noun* milinyin
banana, bush	*noun feminine* goolibil
bandicoot	*noun masculine* goojinji; *noun masculine* jinberrji
golden bandicoot	*noun feminine* nyarlgool
band worn on the arm, armband	*noun* gooloong-gooloong
banging, make noise by	*coverb+SAY/DO_M* dal-dal
bank of creek	*noun* banderre; *locative* garlirrin
roots or hole in bank	*noun* nan'goon
steep bank	*noun* gawarre, gawarriny
banyan	*noun* barlngel
bark	*noun* bernngam
bark (dog)	*coverb+SAY/DO* roong, roong-roong; *coverb+SAY/DO_M* roong-roong
bark at someone (dog)	*coverb+HIT* roong-roong
bark from tree, hit	*coverb+HIT* doog
barramundi	*noun feminine* balgal; *noun feminine* dawoogjil; *noun feminine* dayiwool; *noun feminine* nyilibal; *noun feminine* wawoordjil
base of back	*noun* loorndoomooroom; *noun* moon'goom

beef

basin, deep dish, rubbish bin	*noun* jaboogoom, jaboogoony, jaboogool
basket	*noun* dagoorlam; *noun* rarribany
bat, fruit	*noun feminine* walimalil
bat species, insect-eating	*noun masculine* barn'galji; *noun masculine* binyjirrminy; *noun masculine* boorroombiny
bat's wing coral tree, *Erythrina vespertilio*	*noun feminine* garndiwarlel
bathe	*coverb+FALL/GO_DOWN* nyirreg
make bathe	*coverb+HIT* nyirreg
battery	*noun* ngerren'gajim
car battery	*noun phrase* ngerren'gajim ngoorrngoorrool-ngooyoo
Battery Creek	*noun* Joogoorreyirrin
bauhinia	*noun masculine* goonjiny; *noun masculine* wanyarriny
bauhinia seed-pods	*noun* gerlalim
bean, wild jack	*noun feminine* digoorlool; *noun feminine* woolngal
beard	*noun* thawoorem
beat spinifex to extract resin	*coverb+SAY/DO* warij
beaten coolibah fibres	*noun* bijam
beating heart, have	*coverb+SAY/DO* berreg-berreg
beautiful, be	*coverb+SAY/DO* doordoog
because of this	*adverb* wayinigana
Bedford Downs	*noun* Wawoonboolooloom
Bedford Downs Station	*noun* Barangen
bee, native sugarbag	*noun* moowany, moowal; *noun feminine* ngawooral
ground-living sugarbag bee species	*noun masculine* gayirriny; *noun masculine* boorrwoorrji
tree-living sugarbag bee species	*noun feminine* beranggool; *noun masculine* gerrayiny; *noun masculine* nhawiny
beehive, native pollen sacs in	*noun* lanany; *noun* lernjim
wax lid in	*noun* darlam
beeswax	*noun* ganggarrji, ganggarre; *noun* joornoogji, joornoogbi
'beef' (Kriol word for any meat)	*noun* miyale, miyalji, miyalel

beetle

beetle	*noun masculine* **landiny**
before	*temporal* **welangen, woolangen**
beg	*coverb+SAY/DO* **mern**
behind	*adverb* **bardoobiny**; *locative* **bardoon**
be behind something	*coverb+BE/STAY* **laberd**
get behind something	*coverb+FALL/GO_DOWN* **waman**
hide behind	*coverb+FALL/GO_DOWN* **dern**
person or thing that comes behind/after	*noun* **bardoongeny, bardoongel, bardoongem**
stay behind	*coverb+PLACE* **ngadi**; *coverb+SAY/DO* **ngadidi**
believe	*coverb+GET* **dawoong**; *coverb+GET* **ngoongoo**
belly button	*noun* **dinyjile**
belonging to/living in the bush	*adjective* **gibi-ngarnany, gibi-ngarnal, gibi-ngarnam**
belt each other with sticks	*coverb+SAY/DO_REFL* **ngooyood**
belt someone with a stick	*coverb+SAY/DO_M* **darroorl**; *coverb+HIT* **darroorl**
belt, hair	*noun* **goodam**
bend	
bend down	*coverb+BE/STAY* **nhoony**; *coverb+FALL/GO_DOWN* **yooj**
bend down, bend and put head down	*coverb+SAY/DO* **jooloog**
bend legs up	*coverb+BE/STAY* **narloog**
bend over	*coverb+BE/STAY* **jooloorrooj**
bend something	*coverb+PUT* **dinygoorlg**
bent, be	*coverb+BE/STAY* **dinygoorlg**
be bent around	*coverb+BE/STAY* **doon**
bent down, having head down	*adjective* **jooloogbayiny, jooloogbayil, jooloogbayim**
have one leg bent up	*coverb+BE/STAY* **dandawa**
best you can	*adverb* **garda-gardawoo**
bet with someone	*coverb+HIT* **yang**
between	*locative* **belegan**
big	*adjective* **nawarrany, nawarral, nawarram**
become big	*coverb+GO/COME* **nawarrawoo**; *coverb+GO/COME* **nawarra**
very big	*adjective* **namboorroongoony, namboorroongool, namboorroongoom**
big semen (swear word)	*interjection* **ngarndaginy, ngarndagel**
bilby	*noun feminine* **lilgoonel**
billy can	*noun masculine* **bajalarriny**; *noun* **dibam**; *noun* **gardag, gardagboo**
Billy Mac Spring	*noun* **Jawigin**
Binays Pocket	*noun* **Jengoowoon**; *noun* **Marle**
bindi-eye	*noun masculine* **bagany, bagam**; *noun masculine* **boorndalji**; *noun* **marlagal**
bird (generic)	*noun feminine* **jiregel**
bar-shouldered dove	*noun feminine* **gelaroogool, goolaroogool**; *noun feminine* **marrawayil**
black cormorant	*noun masculine* **doowoodji**
black-faced cuckoo shrike	*noun feminine* **miliwoorrangel**; *noun feminine* **yirringaragjil**
brolga	*noun feminine* **goorrarndal**
brown falcon	*noun masculine* **girrganyji**
bronzewing pigeon	*noun feminine* **loowoo-loowoorrel**
budgerigar	*noun feminine* **goolyoolyool**
buff-banded rail	*noun feminine* **goolijil**
bush turkey, bustard	*noun feminine* **birn'girrbal**; *noun feminine* **galamoordal**
butcher bird	*noun masculine* **wirrindiny**
channel-billed cuckoo	*noun feminine* **goorra-goorral**
cockatiel	*noun feminine* **wirringgoonel**
coot	*noun feminine* **goolijil**
crested pigeon	*noun feminine* **balarayil**
curlew	*noun feminine* **wirndoowool**
dangerous night bird	*noun* **joowany, joowal**
diver jack	*noun masculine* **boorrijiny**; *noun masculine* **garrang-garranginy**; *noun masculine* **mawoorooriny**
dollar bird	*noun masculine* **dimberralgarlgarlji**
dotterel	*noun feminine* **bilinyirrinyirril**
duck	*noun* **jibilyoowool, jibilyiwoony**
egret	*noun masculine* **jalariny**
emu	*noun feminine* **garnanganyjel**; *noun feminine* **ngarabarral**; *noun feminine* **wiyarrel**
emu chicks	*noun* **wininim**

bite

emu chicks, half grown	*noun* **doorrja-doorrjam**
fairy martin	*noun feminine* **jirrinyngalil**
fork-tailed kite	*noun masculine* **ganjalji**
galah	*noun feminine* **gerliny-gerlinyil**
greater bower-bird	*noun masculine* **joowijgarneny**
green pigmy goose	*noun feminine* **nyiman'gool**
grey-crowned babbler	*noun feminine* **ganggangel**
grey goshawk	*noun masculine* **warliberawoony, warliny**
hawk/kite type	*noun masculine* **gardagarrji**
ibis	*noun feminine* **joodoojgajil**
jabiru	*noun masculine* **yalarrngarnany**
kingfisher	*noun feminine* **jigerrel**
kite/hawk type	*noun masculine* **gardagarrji**
koel	*noun* **doowageny**
koel, female	*noun* **girlgoowal**
kookaburra	*noun* **jawoorroony, jawoorrool**
little corella	*noun* **labany, labal**
little friar bird	*noun masculine* **jinggerawoogoony**
little green lorikeet	*noun feminine* **wirrirrel**
little woodswallow	*noun feminine* **dinil**
magpie	*noun masculine* **gemerlawoorroony**; *noun masculine* **gerreranggoolji**
magpie goose	*noun* **ngarlagangarril, ngarlagangarriny**
mistletoe bird	*noun masculine* **jirlmirndiny**; *noun masculine* **jiwirnbenji**
nankeen kestrel	*noun masculine* **gardagarrji**; *noun femininine* **marl-marlel**; *noun feminine* **marrg-marrgjil**; *noun masculine* **waaliny**
nankeen night heron	*noun feminine* **jawoombal**
nightjar	*noun masculine* **barnanggany**
northern rosella	*noun feminine* **gooldany-gooldanyel**
olive-backed oriole	*noun feminine* **binbinajgel**
owl	*noun masculine* **doomboony**
owlet nightjar	*noun masculine* **thirringgenji**
pardalote species	*noun feminine* **joonjoonoonoojgel**
peaceful dove	*noun feminine* **goorloordoogjil, goorloordoordoogjil**
peewee, magpie lark	*noun feminine* **birlrrijgel**; *noun* **goorliyirrel**
pelican	*noun masculine* **dabaroony**
pheasant coucal	*noun masculine* **thoolthoolji**
quail	*noun feminine* **jibigel**
rainbow bird	*noun feminine* **birrid-birridel**
rainbow lorikeet	*noun feminine* **wirrilijgel**
rainbow lorikeet, red-winged parrot (word used by young men instead of *wirrilijgel* or *ginyginyel*)	*noun feminine* **thirrilngarnal**
red-backed wren	*noun masculine* **yirril-yirrilji**
red-winged parrot	*noun feminine* **ginyginyel**
restless flycatcher	*noun feminine* **goorlawoorlal**
Richard's pipit	*noun masculine* **balalayingarnany**
rock pigeon	*noun feminine* **manboorlool**
rufous songlark	*noun* **binyjirrmiyanma**; *noun* **gawarnngarnany**
rufous whistler	*noun feminine* **jiyig-jiyiggil, jiyig-jiyigjel**
scissors grinder	*noun feminine* **goorlawoorlal**
silver-crowned friar bird	*noun masculine* **gagoowany**
spinifex pigeon	*noun feminine* **galawarrjil**
spoonbill	*noun masculine* **galba-galbany**
spotted pardalote	*noun feminine* **binbininidgel**
sulphur-crested cockatoo	*noun masculine* **ngamarriny**; *noun masculine* **ngayirr-ngayirrji**
tawny frogmouth	*noun feminine* **goorrgoorrjil**
wedge-tailed eagle	*noun masculine* **warrarnany**; *noun masculine* **garnbidany**; *noun masculine* **wirli-wirlingarnany**; *noun masculine* **girliwirringiny**
whistling kite	*noun feminine* **booloogool**
white-bellied cuckoo shrike	*noun feminine* **yirringaragjil**
white-breasted woodswallow	*noun* **jinba-jinbalji, jinba-jinbalel**
white-faced heron	*noun masculine* **ginyany**
white-necked heron	*noun masculine* **binggoo-binggoony**
willie wagtail	*noun masculine* **jigirridji, jigirrid-jigirridji**; *noun masculine* **jindiwirrij**
yellow-faced miner	*noun feminine* **biyig-biyiggel**
zebra finch	*noun feminine* **nyinyil, niyinyil**
bird, become a	*coverb+BECOME_REFL* **jirege**
bird nest	*noun* **boolmim**
bite	*coverb+HIT* **werd**
bite lip	*coverb+DO_REFL* **niny**

bitter melon, small

bite on something
(e.g. boab seed) .... *coverb+BURN/BITE* **noord**;
coverb+SAY/DO **noord**;
coverb+GO_ALONG **noonoord**
jump and bite .... *coverb+FALL/GO_DOWN* **jarrbird**
one who does not bite .. *adjective* **werd-bawoorroony, werd-bawoorrool, werd-bawoorroom**
one that bites .... *adjective* **werd-nhawoony, werd-nhawool**
bitter melon, small .... *noun feminine* **gagoolanyil**; *noun feminine* **gilyalal**
black .... *adjective* **manbeny, manbel, manbem**
be black .... *coverb+BE/STAY* **manbe-manbe**
become black .... *coverb+BECOME* **manbe**
become black in fire ...... *coverb+BURN/BITE* **manbeg**
make black .... *coverb+BRING/TAKE* **manbeg**; *coverb+GET* **manbeg**
blackened by smoke ..... *adjective* **manbooloo-wooloo**
black ant species .... *noun masculine* **miginy**
black biting ant species .... *noun masculine* **thengawiny**
black smelly ant species .... *noun masculine* **binginy**
black bream .... *noun* **garriyil, garriyiny**; *noun masculine* **jambinbaroony**
black cockatoo .... *noun feminine* **derranel, derranil**; *noun feminine* **mardangarril**
black-faced cuckoo shrike .... *noun feminine* **miliwoorrangel**; *noun feminine* **yirringaragjil**
black-headed python ... *noun feminine* **dawool**; *noun feminine* **thoowerndemanbel**
blackmast (kind of very small fish) .... *noun masculine* **jirrgilji**
black plum .... *noun masculine* **minyjaarrany, minyjiwarrany**
big cake made of ground black plum .... *noun masculine* **nanggeriny**
dry fallen black plum fruit .... *noun* **binbarrji**
Euphorbia species used to put on coals when cooking black plum .... *noun masculine* **minyanyany**
first fruit of black plum .. *noun* **jawoorlji**
black soil .... *noun* **gawarnbe**
bladder .... *noun* **jarnangarre**
blame someone .... *coverb+HIT* **gooj**

blanket .... *noun* **banjal**; *noun feminine* **banjalgjel**; *noun* **bool-boole**
bleed, make self .... *coverb+DO_REFL* **giyawoolge**
bless .... *coverb+GET* **ngambarl**; *coverb+GET* **ngamal**
blind .... *adjective* **jarlboorrji, jarlboorrel, jarlboorroo**
become blind .... *coverb+FALL/GO_DOWN* **jarlboorr**
blind snake .... *noun* **woonthool, woonthoony**
blink .... *coverb+SAY/DO_M* **minilg, mirnilg**
block blows with nulla-nulla .... *coverb+PUT* **goowarri**
blocking blows with nulla-nulla, woman who is good at .... *noun feminine* **goowarrigalel**
block hole .... *coverb+PUT* **bindid**
block holes .... *coverb+SAY/DO* **bindid-bindid**
block off .... *coverb+PLACE_M* **theb**
block off something ...... *coverb+BRING/TAKE* **jarrga**; *coverb+SAY/DO_M* **jarrga-jarrga**
block off with grass wall .... *coverb+PUT* **jarrga**; *coverb+PUT* **jarrgab**
blocked, be .... *coverb+SAY/DO* **thoolg**
blocked ears, have .... *coverb+SAY/DO* **theb**; *coverb+SAY/DO* **thoolg**
blonde-haired .... *adjective* **giwinarlany, giwinarlal, giwinarlam**
blood .... *noun* **giyawoole**; *noun* **goongoorloom**
bloodwood .... *noun masculine* **mawoorroony**
bloodwood flowers .... *noun feminine* **jirliwoorril**
bloodwood gum .... *noun masculine* **galiwoony**
bloodwood, mountain .. *noun masculine* **thaliwarn, thaliwarnji**
bloodwood, scraggy ..... *noun masculine* **marlambeny**
blowfly .... *noun* **werreralji, werreralel, werrerale**
blow nose .... *coverb+SAY/DO* **nyiny**
blow out fire .... *coverb+HIT* **thooloob**
blow something .... *coverb+PUT* **boomi**
wind blow something ... *coverb+GET* **gerge**
blow up, make fire .... *coverb+GET* **ngerroowoogoo**
blow wind .... *coverb+HIT* **waj**; *coverb+SAY/DO* **ger**
wind blowing .... *coverb+GO/COME* **gere-gere**
bludge .... *coverb+HIT* **mern**
blue crane .... *noun masculine* **ginyany**

Blue Dress (place name)	noun	Gerlinggengayin
blue-tongue lizard	noun feminine	loomoogool
blue/green	adjective	girliny-girlinyji, girliny-girlinyel, girliny-girlinybe
go blue/green (meat)	coverb+BECOME	girliny-girliny
bluebell, rough	noun feminine	giwinboorrel
blue-winged kookaburra	noun	jawoorrool, jawoorroony
call made by blue-winged kookaburra	coverb+SAY/DO	goorrarrg, jawoorrg-jawoorrg
blunt	adjective	nhoonmoony, nhoonmool, nhoonmoom
blurry eyed, become	coverb	wanganyge
boab tree	noun masculine	joomooloony
boab nuts (whole)	noun	joomooloom; noun larrgardim
boab seeds	noun	jililiny, jililem
white inside part of boab nuts when dry	noun masculine	wawanggoony
boat	noun feminine	larndoorrool; noun feminine dimal
body, dead	noun	garajbe; noun goonyingarre
body hair	noun	warloom
body part throbbing	coverb+SAY/DO	jarrawoorl
body part twitching because of a relation	coverb+GO/COME	jarrarrawoorl
body, side of body	noun	thambem
boggy ground	noun	yawool-yawooloo
boggy place	noun	darradbem
boil	noun feminine	merrjil
boiling, be	coverb+BURN/BITE	boonany-boonany
bone	noun	goojim; noun mayiwarndem
backbone	noun	therlam
collarbone	noun	wardim
jaw bone	noun	ngawalem
little bone in leg, fibula	noun	ninjirri
rib bone	noun	jilemberre; noun walamboom
tail bone, coccyx	noun	nyidim
thigh bone	noun	gerlalbam
bones, be made dry white	coverb+GET	langany-langany
bones fall to pieces	coverb+BE/STAY	lalinybarr
bones lying around	coverb+BE/STAY	lalalinybalg
bony	adjective	jandanbeny; adjective yalginybeny, yalginybel, yalginybem
bony bream	noun feminine	lilinyil
bony bream, big	noun feminine	wirabal
book	noun	mirli-mirlim, merle-merlem
bookkeeper	noun	merndagaleny, merndagalel, merndagalem
boomerang	noun feminine	baljarranggool; noun feminine gamanyjel; noun feminine garrabiril; noun goorroobardool, goorroobardoony; noun feminine jinybal
clap with boomerangs	coverb+SAY/DO	birr-birr
number 7 boomerang	noun	wirlgil, wirlginy
throw a boomerang	coverb+SAY/DO_M	garrara
boot	noun masculine	jandamaji
born, be	coverb+FALL/GO_DOWN	balngarnag (Southern dialect); coverb+SAY/DO bedalg
boss	noun	majany, majal
bossy	adjective	nyirli-nyirliwoom
bottom, along the	locative	yiligibiny
bottom, go along wriggling (your)	coverb+GO_ALONG	moongooli-moongooli
bottom stuck out, having (your)	adjective	nanybayiny, nanybayil, nanybayim
bough shed	noun	boolmim
boulder	noun masculine	joowoorlinyji
bower-bird	noun masculine	joowijgarneny
bower-bird's bower	noun	boolmim
Bow River Station	noun	Joowoorlinyji, Joowoorlinybany
boy (one having a spear), male	noun masculine	garloomboo-bany
boy, adolescent	noun masculine	lambarnji; noun masculine waarrany
boy, little	noun masculine	goorndoogany; noun masculine jangadany (Southern dialect); noun masculine wanyageny
braggart	adjective	thawoolarrji, thawoolarrel, thawoolarrem
brain	noun	goonggooloom
branches	noun	barndale

Gija Dictionary

brand cattle

branches, leafy .... *noun* **ganarram**
brand cattle .... *coverb+SAY/DO* **jily-jily**
brave .... *adjective* **girriyiny, girriyil, giyirrim**
bread/non-meat food ... *noun* **mayim, mayiny, mayil**
break .... *coverb+FALL/GO_DOWN* **deberr;**
coverb+GET **deberr**
  break glass .... *coverb+HIT* **therl**
  break leg of something .... *coverb+GET* **yarlooloo**
  break stick and make noise .... *coverb+SAY/DO* **dijarr**
  break up .... *coverb+GET* **goojoog**
  fall and break .... *coverb+FALL/GO_DOWN* **bijaj;**
coverb+FALL/GO_DOWN **deberr**
  spear and break .... *coverb+SPEAR* **deberr**
break away .... *noun* **jarlanggam**
break off .... *coverb+GET* **deberr, deberrg;**
coverb+SAY/DO_M **debereberr;**
coverb+GET **denggij;**
coverb+GET **yil**
  break/cut off .... *coverb+GET* **degerd;**
coverb+HIT **degerd**
bream
  black bream .... *noun* **garriyil, garriyiny;**
noun masculine **jambinbaroony**
  bony bream .... *noun feminine* **lilinyil**
  bony bream, big .... *noun feminine* **wirabal**
breast .... *noun* **gamoom**
breath
  breath, be out of .... *coverb+SAY/DO_M* **gerndeng**
  breath, be short of .... *coverb+GO/COME* **giningoob;**
coverb+GO/COME **reminy**
  breath, gasp for .... *coverb+BRING/TAKE* **reminy**
breathe .... *coverb+SAY/DO* **ngayirr**
breathing in fright,
  stop .... *coverb+BRING/TAKE* **gengereb**
breeze, in the .... *locative, temporal* **gerawalen**
bright, become .... *coverb+PLACE* **berr;**
coverb+SAY/DO_M **dirr**
bright-coloured as at sunrise or sunset .... *adjective* **galayimarrji, galayimarrel, galayimarre**
bright-coloured, look ... *coverb+GO/COME* **berr**
bright light, in .... *noun* **diyilijilin**
brightness at sunrise or sunset, in .... *locative noun* **galayimarran**
bring
  bring a big lot .... *coverb+BRING/TAKE* **nawaraya**
  bring back .... *coverb+GET_HIT* **biri**

  bring/take back .... *coverb+BRING/TAKE* **biri;**
coverb+BRING/TAKE **biriwoorrg**
  bring/take closer .... *coverb+BRING/TAKE* **ngirribag**
  bring down .... *coverb+FALL/GO_DOWN_WITH*
thoodboo
  bring out .... *coverb+BRING/TAKE* **boorab**
  bring young man out after initiation .... *coverb+BRING/TAKE* **joolooloong**
broken .... *adjective* **deberrngeny, deberrngel, deberrngem**
brolga .... *noun feminine* **goorrarndal**
brother .... *noun masculine* **ngajiny**
  brother (spoken to) .... *noun* **ngaji**
  brother (woman speaking) .... *noun masculine* **garloomboo-bany**
  brother's child .... *noun* **barnalnginy, barnalngel**
  older brother .... *noun masculine* **booloongoony;**
noun masculine **goorabeny**
  younger brother .... *noun masculine* **bariyiny**
brother-in-law .... *noun* **ngoolngany;**
noun **mandirriny;**
noun **wardoony**
  brother-in-law (spoken to) .... *noun* **ngoolnga;**
noun **mandirri;**
noun **wardoo**
  brother-in-law of woman (spoken to) .... *noun masculine* **ngawooji**
brown falcon .... *noun masculine* **girrganyji**
brown grasshopper species .... *noun* **girndilji**
brown snake, western .. *noun masculine* **jadiwiriny**
bubbling up .... *coverb+SAY/DO* **boonany**
bucket .... *noun* **bajalarriny, balayarriny**
budgerigar .... *noun feminine* **goolyoolyool**
buffalo .... *noun feminine* **bardarramalbal;**
noun masculine **barndalebany**
buff-banded rail .... *noun feminine* **goolijil**
building .... *noun* **mayaroony, mayaroom**
bull .... *noun masculine* **boolngayirriny;**
noun masculine **booloomanji;**
noun masculine **boorroonany**
bull ant .... *noun masculine* **goorn'gany**
bull bar .... *noun* **lernngej-girrem**
Bull Hole .... *noun* **Geminymiyan**
bullet/seed .... *noun* **ganjiny, ganjim**
bullock .... *noun feminine* **booloomanel**
  part of bullock guts ...... *noun* **boorrooloo**
bullrushes .... *noun feminine* **beremerrel**

bush salt

bump into................*coverb+HIT* **lernngej**;
         coverb+HIT **linggood**
  bump into each other...*coverb+CUT_REFL* **linggood**
bumpy, lumpy...............*adjective* **jambooggany, jambooggal, jambooggam**
bundle of things for ceremony or later use................*noun* **balem, baalem**; *noun* **balwam**; *noun* **boolbam**
bundle, roll into paperbark...................*coverb* **gerndab**
bung-eyed.....................*adjective* **nheng-nhegany, nheng-nhegal, nheng-nhegam**
Bungle Bungles, Purnululu National Park............................*noun* **Boornoolooloo**
Bungle Bungle Outcamp...................*noun* **Gawarre**
burial place, cemetery..*noun* **doorroom, doorroom-boorroo goonyingarre**; *noun* **dooyoorroon**
  burial place, put in cave as.........................*coverb+PUT* **doorrman**; *coverb+PUT* **doorroon**
burial platform ....*noun* **bernderre**
buried, be......................*coverb+BE/STAY* **thereg**
burn
  be all burned up ....*coverb+BURN/BITE* **gererreb**
  be burnt up and fall ......*coverb+FALL/GO_DOWN* **thaloorrg**
  be burning far away......*coverb+BE/STAY* **mala-malab**
  burn hair ....*coverb+GET* **gerijaleb**
  burn someone with end of stick..................*coverb+PUT* **jilyiwoog**; *coverb+SAY/DO* **jily-jily**
  burn something............*coverb+BURN/BITE* **booj, boodooj**; *coverb+PUT* **babij**; *coverb+PUT* **booj-booj**
  get burned in fire..........*coverb+BURN/BITE* **jililib**
  get burnt ....*coverb+BURN/BITE* **bab**; *coverb+BURN/BITE* **babij**; *coverb+BURN/BITE* **neg**; *coverb+BURN/BITE_REFL* **booj, boodooj**
burning hot...................*adjective* **marnebam**
burp ....*coverb+SAY/DO_M* **thoowoorrag**
Burton's legless lizard ..*noun feminine* **baljawoorrool**
bury.................................*coverb+PUT* **thereg**
  bury self ....*coverb+DO_REFL* **thereg**; *coverb+SAY/PLACE_REFL* **thereg**

bush
  in the bush ....*locative* **gibin**
  belonging to/living in the bush ....*adjective* **gibi-ngarnany, gibi-ngarnal, gibi-ngarnam**
  floodwater spread over the bush ....*coverb+GO/COME* **gibiwoonab** *coverb+GO/COME* **warraminab**
  right in the/all over the bush ....*locative* **gibi-yibin**
bush banana ....*noun feminine* **goolibil**
bush coconut ....*noun* **barlabil**
bush cucumber, Cucumis melo................*noun feminine* **jilinybel**
  big bush cucumber, *Cucumis picrocarpus*.......*noun feminine* **garerlel**
bush food, white currant ....*noun masculine* **berenggarrji**; *noun masculine* **goowarroolji**; *noun masculine* **ngoorrwany**; *noun masculine* **roonggoony**
bush grape ....*noun* **jimirlbel**
bush honey....................*noun* **ngarem, ngariny, ngarel**
bush lemongrass ....*noun masculine* **ngarrngarrji**
bush onion, Cyperus bulbosus.........*noun* **joorndany, joorndam**
bush orange ....*noun feminine* **joogoorrool**
bush pawpaw................*noun masculine* **bambilyiny**; *noun feminine* **marranyil**
bush peanut (nutwood) ....*noun* **bardiginy, bardigel**
bush peanut (cowpea yam) ....*noun masculine* **wanarrji**
bush peanut (red-flowered kurrajong)...*noun masculine* **dayimbalji**
bush potato, *Brachystelma glabriflorum*.................*noun masculine* **banariny**
  bush potato, desert yam, *Ipomoea costata* ....*noun masculine* **berlayiny**; *noun masculine* **bigoordany**; *noun feminine* **dawoonyil**; *noun masculine* **larrwany**; *noun masculine* **yalamarriny**
  SEE ALSO **root species, elible; tuber species, edible; yam**
bush salt ....*noun* **garragoonbe**

bush tea

bush tea.........................*noun masculine* **barnabeliny;**
　　　　　　　　　　　　noun masculine
　　　　　　　　　　　　lamba-lambarrji,
　　　　　　　　　　　　lambarr-lambarrji;
　　　　　　　　　　　　noun masculine **manyanyiny**
bush tobacco.................*noun* **binggoonyel,**
　　　　　　　　　　　　binggoonyji
bush tomato...................*noun feminine* **girlil**
bush turkey ....*noun feminine* **birn'girrbal;**
　　　　　　　　　　　　noun feminine **galamoordal**
bush Vicks, strong-
　smelling herb
　species ....*noun masculine* **gooroongoony**
bushfire ....*noun* **mawarrji**
　light bushfire ....*coverb+PLACE_M* **mawarr**
bust ....*coverb+BECOME* **doorlboog**
　bust making a
　　loud noise.....................*coverb+SAY/DO_M* **doorlboog**
　bust something open ...*coverb+HIT* **lerlerd**
bustard ....*noun feminine* **birn'girrbal;**
　　　　　　　　　　　　noun feminine **galamoordal**
but....................................*particle* **goo, goowoo**
butcher bird ....*noun masculine* **wirrindiny**
butterfly, moth
　(can be swearing) ......*noun feminine* **warlimarrgool**
buzz................................*coverb+GO_ALONG* **ngoorr**
　have buzzing in ears .....*coverb+SAY/DO* **ngoorr**
　make buzzing noise ....*coverb+SAY/DO* **thengenge**
by myself ....*pronoun* **ngayiwany;**
　　　　　　　　　　　　pronoun **ngayiwarriny**

Cc

cabbage gum ....*noun masculine* **boonbany**
　cabbage gum, silver .....*noun masculine* **linyjilji**
calf muscle ....*noun* **boolyam;**
　　　　　　　　　　　　noun **dimboom,**
　　　　　　　　　　　　dimboowoom
calf with horns..............*noun feminine* **bardarramalbal**
Calico Springs ....*noun* **Waren-waren**
call, a noisy call.............*interjection* **yayi**
call made by blue-
　winged kookaburra ...*coverb+SAY/DO* **goorrarrg;**
　　　　　　　　　　　　coverb+SAY/DO
　　　　　　　　　　　　jawoorrg-jawoorrg
call made by crow.........*interjection* **waag-waag**
call of *girrganyji*,
　brown falcon ....*interjection* **girr-girr**
call out............................*coverb+SAY/DO* **bawoo;**
　　　　　　　　　　　　coverb+SAY/DO_M **bawoo**

be calling out
　(dogs, cattle).................*coverb+SAY/DO* **moowoolooloob**
　call out making a noise..*coverb+SAY/DO* **yayig;**
　　　　　　　　　　　　coverb+SAY/DO **yayi-yayi**
camel ....*noun feminine* **gamoolel;**
　　　　　　　　　　　　noun feminine **yoob-yoobgajil**
camel bush, rough
　bluebell, *Trichodesma*
　zeylanicum ....*noun feminine* **giwinboorrel**
Camel Gap ....*noun* **Gernawarliyan**
camera (thing for when
　you get shadows).......*phrase* **ngaaloom-boorroo**
　　　　　　　　　　　　joonbimnha-ngarri
camp/home/country....*noun* **daam**
　camping place ....*noun* **daawirrin**
camp
　be camping ....*coverb+BE/STAY* **derreb;**
　　　　　　　　　　　　coverb+SAY/DO **derreb**
　camp alone...................*coverb+SAY/DO_M* **therema**
　camp habitually ....*coverb+SAY/DO* **daa-daa**
　go camping out ....*coverb+GO/COME* **derrerreb**
　look after/keep
　　someone in camp.........*coverb+HAVE* **derreb**
　make camp ....*coverb+FALL/GO_DOWN* **derreb;**
　　　　　　　　　　　　coverb+GO/COME **derreb;**
　　　　　　　　　　　　coverb+SAY/DO **derrerreb;**
　　　　　　　　　　　　coverb+BECOME **joondooj;**
　　　　　　　　　　　　coverb+SAY/DO_M **joondoo;**
　　　　　　　　　　　　coverb+SAY/DO_M
　　　　　　　　　　　　joondoo-joondoo
cane grass ....*noun masculine* **marliny**
can't be caught up
　with ....*adjective* **jalbaga-woorroony,**
　　　　　　　　　　　　jalbaga-woorrool,
　　　　　　　　　　　　jalbaga-woorroom
can't listen, keep
　doing that thing
　all the way ....*adjective* **nyerlginy, nyerlgel,**
　　　　　　　　　　　　nyerlgem
car ....*noun feminine*
　　　　　　　　　　　　ngoorr-ngoorrgalil
　car/truck......................*noun feminine*
　　　　　　　　　　　　ngoorr-ngoorrool
　car/truck/motor-bike ....*noun feminine*
　　　　　　　　　　　　ngoorr-ngoorrgajil
　car jack, thing for
　　lifting..............................*noun* **jarrward-girrem**
　car key ....*noun phrase* **nyarlarlam**
　　　　　　　　　　　　ngoorrngoorrool-ngooyoo;
　　　　　　　　　　　　noun **ngoorrngoorrge-girrem**

car radiator	*noun phrase* **goorrnga-girrem dam bemberrooloonboo-ngarri-ngiyi**	catch up with, someone/thing that nobody can	*adjective* **jalbaga-woorroony, jalbaga-woorrool, jalbaga-woorroom**
old noisy car	*noun* **garrang-garranginy**		

Carola Gully/
Growler Gully ....*noun* **Joogoomoorndin**
Caroline Pool ....*noun* **Wimirriny;**
   noun **Wimngayirriny**
carry
   carry on arms ....*coverb+GET* **ngamanang**
   carry under arm ....*coverb+BRING/TAKE* **joolooj;**
      coverb+SAY/DO **joolooj;**
      coverb+SAY/DO_M **joolooj;**
      coverb+PUT **yooloony**
   put under arm to carry..*coverb+PUT* **joolooj**
   carry back....................*coverb+BRING/TAKE* **biri**
   carry in hair belt ....*coverb+BRING/TAKE* **goorlgoon**
   carry with hands down..*coverb+HIT* **goorrooj**
   carry in the mouth........*coverb+BRING/TAKE* **gered**
   carry (kangaroo)............*coverb* **yool-yool**
   carry something
   hanging.......................*coverb+HIT* **rarriny;**
      coverb+BRING/TAKE **rarrwayi**
   carry something
   hidden ....*coverb+BRING/TAKE* **booroo**
   carry on shoulder ....*coverb+BRING/TAKE* **wandaj;**
      coverb+PUT **wandaj;**
      coverb+SAY/DO **wandaj**
   be carrying on
   shoulder.......................*coverb+GET* **wandajboo**
   carry along on
   shoulders ....*coverb+BRING/TAKE* **barle**
   carry on shoulders ....*coverb+GO/COME* **barle;**
      coverb+SAY/DO **wanda-wandaj;**
      coverb+SAY/DO_M **wanda-wandaj**
   carry someone on
   shoulders ....*coverb+HIT* **barle**
   go along carrying
   something on
   shoulder ....*coverb+GO_ALONG* **wandandaj**
carved groove ....*noun* **boonarram**
cat ....*noun masculine* **dijarrji;**
      noun masculine **goordoony;**
      noun masculine **ngirrngiliny;**
      noun masculine **ngirrngiliwoony**
catch in fingers ....*coverb+GET* **labag**
catch in hand ....*coverb+GET* **dambang**
catch up with
   someone ....*coverb+GET* **jalba**

caterpillar......................*noun feminine* **booboogarral;**
   noun **joombayiny, joombayil**
caterpillar, hairy............*noun masculine* **nyingginy**
catfish
   catfish species,
   eel-tailed ....*noun masculine* **jirrgoolji**
   catfish species, small
   eel tailed......................*noun masculine* **ngirndany**
   catfish species, large
   eel-tailed; Rendhal's
   catfish..........................*noun masculine* **woorlengerriny**
   catfish, large
   fork-tailed.....................*noun masculine* **dalinyji**
   catfish, small
   fork-tailed.....................*noun masculine* **binyjiwinyjiny, binyjiwoonyjiny**
cause to sleep ....*coverb+HIT* **yirdarrge**
caustic bush, *Grevillea*
   pyramidalis ....*noun* **wilinyji, wilinyel, wilinybe**
caustic vine,
   Cynanchum viminale....*noun masculine* **ganyjewoony, garnjiwoony**
cave..................................*noun* **nawan, nawanji**
cemetery ....*noun* **doorroom, doorroom-boorroo goonyingarre**
centipede ....*noun masculine* **birrgoolany**
ceremony, finish ....*coverb+SAY/DO* **mar-maroora**
chains ....*noun* **jangal-jangal, janga-jangal**
Chamberlain Gorge ....*noun* **Gooroorrbin**
chameleon dragon,
   lizard species ....*noun* **bawoodany**
champion ....*adjective* **gawoothany**
change............................*coverb+FALL/GO_DOWN* **goornag;**
   coverb+GIVE **goornag;**
   coverb+PUT **goorag**
channel-billed cuckoo..*noun feminine* **goorra-goorral**
charcoal..........................*noun* **werlerrem, werlerreny**
   become charcoal ....*coverb+FALL/GO_DOWN* **werlerreg**
   burn to charcoal ....*coverb+BURN/BITE* **werlerreg**
chase...............................*coverb+BRING/TAKE* **joorra;**
   coverb+GET **loorroob;**
   coverb+GET_HIT **loorroob;**
   coverb+HIT **loorroob;**
   coverb+SAY/DO **loorroob**

chat

chase after	*coverb+FOLLOW* **loorroob**
chase game, muster	*coverb+PUT* **joorra**
chase together	*coverb+SAY/DO_REFL* **yawoo-yawoo**
go chasing	*coverb+HIT* **loorroobbany**
chat	*coverb+SAY/DO* **bal**;
	coverb+BE/STAY **bal**;
	coverb+SAY/DO_M **bal**
chat to each other	*coverb+SAY/DO_REFL* **bal**
cheek	*noun* **limimim**;
	noun **ngan'gerre**
'cheeky'	*adjective* **wariwoony, wariwool, wariwoom**
'cheeky' yam	*noun masculine* **garnawoony**
cheque	*noun* **ganarram**
cherabin, freshwater prawn	*noun feminine* **jalijgel**
chest	*noun* **doomoorroo**;
	noun **manggam**
shake chest	*coverb+SAY/DO_M* **mel-mel**
stand with chest straight and arms out	*coverb+BE/STAY* **tharrboolirr**
chew tobacco	*coverb+PUT* **ngoorinyja**
child	*noun masculine* **goorndoogany**;
	noun feminine **goorndoogal**;
	noun **jangadany, jangadal, jangadam**;
	noun **wanyagarrany, wanyagarral**;
	noun **wanyagewarrany, wanyagewarral**
child of aunt (man's sister)	*noun* **ngaboony, ngabool**
child of father (spoken to)	*noun* **ngabayi**
female child of father	*noun feminine* **ngabool**
male child of father	*noun masculine* **ngaboony**
child of mother	*noun* **ngalangangeny, ngalangangel, ngalangangem**
physical child of mother	*noun* **warlaginy, warlagil**
child of mother (spoken to)	*noun* **ngalanga**
child of uncle (mother's brother)	*noun* **garliny, garlil**
child of uncle (spoken to)	*noun* **garli**
children	*noun* **goorndoorndoogam**;
	noun **wanyanyagem, wanyanyanggem, winyanyanggem**
children's python	*noun* **binbinginy**
chin	*noun* **nanggooroo**
part under chin	*noun* **yingal-yingalji**
Chinamans Garden	*noun* **Yarangga**
chip off wood	*coverb+HIT* **jem-jem**
choke	*coverb+SAY/DO* **gang**
choke someone	*coverb+GET* **gim**
choose to stay somewhere	*coverb* **dangoorayi**
chop	*coverb+HIT* **gaj**
chop something	*coverb+HIT* **gadij**;
	coverb+SAY/DO **gardij**
chop sugarbag/cut off roots	*coverb+SAY/DO* **lawoog**
chop tree	*coverb+HIT* **lagarr**
be chopping sugarbag	*coverb+BE/STAY* **lawoog**
go chopping sugarbag	*coverb+GO_ALONG* **lawoog**
go chopping	*coverb+GO/COME* **lawoogbany**
cicada	*noun feminine* **lirrinil**
cicatrice	*noun* **gemerre**
cigarette	*noun* **thoolngoonyji, thoolngoonybe**
smoke cigarettes	*coverb+SAY/DO* **thoolngoony**
claim someone	*coverb+GET* **goondoony**
clamp self onto something	*coverb+FALL/GO_DOWN* **labij**
clap	*coverb+SAY/DO* **boorrg-boorrg**
clap boomerangs	*coverb+SAY/DO* **birr-birr**
clap clapsticks once	*coverb* **gil**
clap knees together	*coverb+SAY/DO_M* **ngim-ngim**
clap on thighs loudly	*coverb+SAY/DO* **derlawoog-derlawoog**
clapsticks	*noun* **garnbag, garbagbe**;
	noun **gil-gile**
play clapsticks	*coverb+SAY/DO_M* **gil-gil**
milkwood tree, *Wrightia saligna*, used to make clapsticks	*noun* **garnbagji**;
	noun **gil-gilji**
claw	*noun* **yarnderre**
clean	*coverb+HIT* **berarr**
clean ground	*coverb+SAY/DO_M* **belag**
make self clean	*coverb+SAY/DO_REFL* **men'gawoog**
clean out soak water	*coverb+SAY/DO* **wirrirrij**
clean something (remove covering)	*coverb+HIT* **belag**
clear, become	*coverb+BECOME* **baralala**

clear/open, be	*coverb+BE/STAY* **denggelalab**
clear up (rain)	*coverb+GO/COME* **yinyjoong**
clear way through	*locative noun* **banbinan**
make a clear way through	*coverb+GET* **banbinag**
clench fists tightly	*coverb+SAY/DO_REFL* **moorr**
clever	*adjective* **nyarlany, nyarlal, nyarlam**
clever at doing things, tricky	*adjective* **boorloo-boorloony, boorloo-boorlool, boorloo-boorliny**
clever at learning language quickly	*coverb+GET* **tharimbirij**
make clever	*coverb+GET* **baremanbege**
think self clever (show off)	*coverb+SAY/DO* **garn'garr**
clever man, clever person	*noun* **baremanbeny, baremanbel**; *noun* **baroomanbeny, baroomanbel**; *noun masculine* **mooroonggoorroony**; *noun* **mabarn**; *noun* **nyangoobany, nyangoobal**
cliff	*noun* **gawarre, gawarriny**
Clifton Hole	*noun* **Larreniny**
climb	*coverb+GO/COME* **berdij**; *coverb+SAY/DO* **berdij**; *coverb+SAY/DO_M* **berdij**
climb (plural)	*coverb+GO/COME* **baard**; *coverb+GO/COME* **baward**
climb and leave (plural)	*coverb+LEAVE* **baward**
climb to top	*coverb+SAY/DO_M* **gij**
climb to/reach top	*coverb+GO/COME* **gij**
make climb	*coverb+HIT* **berdijge**
climbing	*coverb+GO_ALONG* **berde-werdij**
go along climbing	*coverb+GO_ALONG* **berdi-werdij**
take climbing	*coverb+BRING/TAKE* **berdij**
clingy, be (wanting to be looked after)	*coverb+SAY/DO_M* **ngamarr**
clitoris	*noun* **jinderre, jindirrji**
close	*locative* **marragoowoorroon**; *adjective* **ngirribany, ngirribal, ngirribam**; *adverb* **ngirriban**
bring/take closer	*coverb+BRING/TAKE* **ngirribag**
come close	*coverb+FALL/GO_DOWN* **ngirribagboo**
come/go close	*coverb+GO/COME* **ngirribag**
go down close	*coverb+FALL/GO_DOWN* **ngirribag**
come closer	*coverb+GO/COME* **ngirribag, ngirrirribag, ngirribagboo**; *coverb+GO/COME* **wooraj**
move closer	*coverb+SAY/DO_M* **ngirribagboo**
close, standing all around	*coverb+BE/STAY* **jarrngarengaj**
close to tree, attach self so as to not be seen	*coverb+SAY/DO* **laberd-laberd**
close	*coverb+PUT* **theb**; *coverb+PUT* **berreb**
close eyes	*coverb+SAY/DO* **yoomooj**
close selves up	*coverb+SAY/PLACE_REFL* **theb**
close in	*coverb+GO/COME* **nyimboo**
close in on someone	*coverb+PUT* **berrgen**
close in on someone, country	*coverb+GO/COME* **nyimbe**
clothes	*noun* **mayaroom, mayaroony**
put on clothes	*coverb+PUT* **dim**; *coverb+PUT* **laj**
wear clothes	*coverb+BRING/TAKE* **laj**
cloud	*noun* **ngoomoolji, ngoomooloo**
cloud build up in hot time	*coverb+FALL/GO_DOWN* **jadag-jadag**
clouds build up before rain	*coverb+SAY/DO_M* **jawoorl-jawoorl**
clouds come out	*coverb* **boonggarr-boonggarr**
coals, cook on	*coverb+HIT* **gerd**; *coverb+PUT* **gerd**; *coverb+SAY/DO_M* **gerd**
coals, cooking on	*coverb+SAY/DO* **gerd-gerd**
coals, fire die down to	*coverb+BURN/BITE* **moonoorroony**
coccyx, tail bone	*noun* **nyidim**
cockatiel	*noun feminine* **wirringgoonel**
cockatoo call	*coverb* **ngayirrg-ngayirrg**
cockatoo, sulphur-crested	*noun masculine* **ngamarriny**; *noun masculine* **ngayirr-ngayirrji**
cockatoo, white (little corella)	*noun* **labany, labal**; *noun* **ngayilanji, ngayilanil**
'cock rag' (Kriol for pubic covering)	*noun* **jarnim**; *noun* **warlboorroo**

cockroach

cockroach	*noun* goomboolangil, goomboolanginy; *noun* jarnangarre
coiled up, be	*coverb+BE/STAY* nyamooloong, nyamoolyoo
coins	*noun* merlgam
cold	*adjective* gawiliny, gawilil, gawilim; *adjective* warn'gany, warn'gal, warn'gam
be cold	*coverb+BE/STAY* warn'ganyboo
become cold	*coverb+BECOME* warn'ganybe; *coverb+BURN/BITE* gawilig; *coverb+FALL/GO_DOWN* gawilge
make cold	*coverb+HIT* warn'ganyge *coverb+PUT* gawilig
cold (illness)	*noun* goonthoorrji, goonthoorroo
cold-season rain	*noun* goorloowanginy, goorloowabany
cold season, cold time	*temporal* warn'gan
collarbone	*noun* wardim
collect	*coverb+GET* gooyarrg; *coverb+SAY/DO* gooyarrg
collect stuff ready together	*coverb+GET* ngooloongooloomenbe
go collecting	*coverb+GO_ALONG* gooyarrg
collide with	*coverb+HIT* linggood
comb	*noun* jiyigajim
comb self	*coverb+DO_REFL* jiyi
come across plenty of something	*coverb+GO/COME* darreg
come behind	*coverb+FOLLOW* jalyberrnga
come behind and block	*coverb+BECOME* lenggeb; *coverb+GO/COME* lenggeb; *coverb+SAY/DO_M* lenggeb
come behind and take over	*coverb+HIT* lenggeb
come down	*coverb+SAY/DO_M* thoorr
come in and out (bees)	*coverb+SAY/DO* tharroorroo
come into the open	*coverb+FALL/GO_DOWN* balngarnag
come off (e.g. clothing, something wrapped around)	*coverb+GO/COME* belalg
come off (e.g. axe head off handle)	*coverb+GO/COME* doonggoony
come off (e.g. fingernail, shell)	*coverb+GO/COME* lerlbag; *coverb+GO/COME* lerlg
come off (fall off)	*coverb+GO/COME* werndelg
come on	*interjection* ma; *interjection* marra
come out	*coverb+FALL/GO_DOWN* boorab; *coverb+GO/COME* boorab; *coverb+GO/COME* boon'gaj; *coverb+GO/COME* thenbelbany; *coverb+SAY/DO* boorab; *coverb+SAY/DO* boorarrgarr
be coming out	*coverb+SAY/DO_M* doorloorloog
come out (plural)	*coverb+SAY/DO* boon'gararr; *coverb_SAY/DO* boon'garr-boon'garr
come out (flowers)	*coverb+HIT* doorloorloog
come out of ground (new plants), grow	*coverb+GET* bedawalge
come out, place where someone is about to/when ready to	*locative, temporal* berabwalen, berabwaloon, berabwaloojen
come out to top	*coverb+SAY/DO* bedal
come together, family	*coverb+GO/COME* daboorlg
come towards	*coverb+GO/COME* wooraj
come upon someone and harrass them	*coverb+HIT/CUT* joorraj
come upon someone suddenly	*coverb+GO/COME* ngag
come upon something and get shock	*coverb+PLACE* jarda
come without proper speech to grieving people	*coverb+GO_ALONG* booliyi
coming down to a point (hill)	*coverb+BE/STAY* nyoorrnga
coming from south	*coverb* ngiri-ngirigbe
coming this way	*directional* woorayibe
one who is coming this way	*adjective* woorayibenginy, woorayibengel, woorayibengim
completely	*adjective* yilwarrany, yilwarral; *adverb* yilwarraya
contemporary	*noun* jimarriny, jimarril, jimarrim
contractions, have (for childbirth)	*coverb+SAY/DO* lerrij

Always read the full information for each word in its main entry.

cook	*coverb+SAY/DO_M* **wawoog**;
	noun **mayigaleny, mayigalel**
cook in ground	*coverb+GET* **goonggoon**;
	coverb+GO_ALONG **yoorn'goorr-yoorn'goorr**;
	coverb+HIT **goonggoon**;
	coverb+PUT **goonggoon**;
	coverb+PUT **yoorn'goorr**;
	coverb+SAY/DO **yoorn'goorr**
cook on coals	*coverb+HIT* **gerd**;
	coverb+HIT **wawoog**;
	coverb+SAY/DO **wooboo**;
	coverb+HIT **wooboo**;
	coverb+PUT **gerd**;
	coverb+SAY/DO **wawoog**;
	coverb+SAY/DO **wawoo-wawoog**;
	coverb+SAY/DO_M **gerd**;
	coverb+SAY/DO_M **wawoo-wawoog**
cooking on coals	*coverb+SAY/DO* **gerd-gerd**
cooked	*adjective* **babijgeny, babijgel, babijgem**;
	adjective **gerdgem**
be cooked/ripe	*coverb+BURN/BITE* **babij**
become really cooked	*coverb+BURN/BITE* **yooloojge**
cooked in ground	*adjective* **goonggoonngem**
get cooked	*coverb+BURN/BITE* **ngawoorr**
cool	*adjective* **ngarliyiny, ngarliyil, ngarliyim**
be made cool	*coverb+FALL/GO_DOWN* **ngarliyig**
cool down	*coverb+FALL/GO_DOWN* **ngarli**;
	coverb+SAY/DO **ngarli**;
	coverb+BURN/BITE **ngarliyig**
cool someone/ something down	*coverb+HIT* **ngarliyig**
make cool	*coverb+GET* **ngarliyig**
coolamon	*noun masculine* **goowirriny**;
	noun masculine **larndoorrji**
big coolamon for carrying babies	*noun masculine* **walanarriny**
deep coolamon	*noun masculine* **yawoonyji, yawinyji**
coolibah tree	*noun masculine* **warernji**
coot, Eurasian	*noun feminine* **goolijil**
copulate	*coverb* **moorniny**;
	coverb+SAY/DO **tharriny**
copy	*coverb+SAY/DO* **madi**
copy someone	*coverb+HIT* **madi**
someone who is good at copying	*noun* **madiwoony, madiwool**

corella	*noun* **labany, labal**;
	noun **ngayilanji, ngayilanil**
call of corella	*coverb+SAY/DO* **ngayarrg**
little corella	*noun* **labany, labal**
corkwood	
Sesbania formosa	*noun* **wirrwirril, wirrwirrji**
Hakea lorea	*noun masculine* **jawoolyiny**
cormorant, black	*noun masculine* **doowoodji**
corpse	*noun* **garajbe**;
	noun **goonyingarre**
correct	*adjective* **joodoony, joodool, joodoom**
Corymbia	
Corymbia abbreviata, scraggy bloodwood	*noun masculine* **marlambeny**
Corymbia aspera	*noun masculine* **booniny**
Corymbia bella, ghost gum, white gum	*noun masculine* **warlarriny**;
	noun masculine **lawoorany**
Corymbia collina, mountain/Kimberley/ silver-leaved bloodwood	*noun masculine* **thaliwarn**
Corymbia confertiflora, *C. grandifolia*, cabbage gum	*noun masculine* **boonbany**
Corymbia dichromophloia, *C. terminalis*, *C. polycarpa*, bloodwood	*noun masculine* **mawoorroony**
Corymbia flavescens, cabbage ghost gum	*noun* **wiliwirrel, wiliwirrirrel, wiliwoorrool**
Corymbia ptychocarpa	*noun masculine* **booniny**
SEE ALSO: Eucalyptus	
cough	*coverb+SAY/DO* **goonthoorr, goothoorr**;
	noun **goonggoorr**
be coughing	*coverb+SAY/DO_M* **goonthoorrg**
country	*noun* **daam**
become country	*coverb+GET* **ngarranggarniny**;
	coverb+GET **werlweny**
countryman	*noun* **ninggoowoony, ninggoowool, ninggoowoom**
mother's father's country	*noun* **gamerrem**
country owner	*noun* **daawany, daawal, daawam**;
	noun **daawayalam**

couple of years ahead

talk to spirits in
country..........................*coverb+SAY/DO* **goorara**;
 coverb+PUT **goorara**
couple of years ahead,
 after a long time........*temporal* **ngarriwarloojen**
cousins from one
 family..........................*noun* **doomoorr-ngarnany,**
 doomoorr-ngarnal,
 doomoorr-ngarnam
cover..............................*coverb+HIT* **bool**;
 coverb+PUT **wirlij**
 be covered..................*coverb+BE/STAY* **bool-bool**
 be covered up..............*coverb+BE/STAY* **thereg**
 cover earth oven..........*coverb+HIT* **yoob**
 cover over....................*coverb+HIT* **yiwirleb**
 cover self....................*coverb+DO_REFL* **bool-bool**;
 coverb+SAY/PLACE_REFL **bool**;
 coverb+SAY/PLACE_REFL **bool-bool**
 cover self in ground
 (e.g. goanna)................*coverb+SAY/PLACE_REFL* **therramij**
 cover with dirt.............*coverb+PUT* **thereg**
crab................................*noun feminine* **moorlgoorrool**
 crab-like species, small.*noun feminine* **nyoorroorn-**
 nyoorroornel
crack...............................*noun* **lagim**
 become cracked...........*coverb+FALL/GO_DOWN* **lerd**;
 coverb+GO/COME **lerlerd**
 crack something open..*coverb+HIT* **lerlerd**
 crack skin off seed........*coverb+SAY/DO_M* **thil-thil**
cramp, get/have............*coverb+GET* **garn'giny**
 have a cramp................*coverb+SAY/DO* **garn'ginybe**
 have cramp in neck.......*coverb+SAY/DO* **wag**
crane, blue
 (white-faced heron)...*noun masculine* **ginyany**
crane, white (egret)......*noun masculine* **jalariny**
cranky............................*adjective* **jirninybiny,**
 jirninybel, jirninybim
 be cranky.....................*coverb+GO_ALONG* **jirniny-jirniny**
 be cranky with each
 other............................*coverb+HIT_REFL* **jirniny**;
 coverb+SAY/DO_REFL **jirniny**
 be cranky with
 someone......................*coverb+SPEAR* **jirniny**
 get cranky....................*coverb+SAY/DO_M* **jirniny**
crawl..............................*coverb+SAY/DO* **gerarr**
 crawl on stomach.........*coverb* **bardib**
 crawling baby...............*noun* **joongoorleny,**
 joongoorlel
crazy...............................*adjective* **merlarnji, merlarnel,**
 merlarnbe
 be crazy........................*coverb+SAY/DO* **merlarn**

go crazy........................*coverb+SAY/DO_M* **merlarn**
create, cause to exist...*coverb+GET* **banji**;
 coverb GO_ALONG **banji**
creek..............................*noun* **jarlanggam**
crested pigeon..............*noun feminine* **balarayil**
cricket............................*noun feminine* **birrid-birridel**;
 noun feminine
 binggoo-binggool
crippled.........................*adjective* **nyarliwiny, nyarliwil,**
 nyarliwim
 be crippled...................*coverb+SAY/DO* **mayajarrg**;
 coverb+FALL/GO_DOWN **bilg**
 become crippled...........*coverb+SAY/DO_M* **nyarli**;
 coverb+GO/COME **bilg**
croaking (frogs)............*coverb+SAY/DO* **weg-weg**
crocodile
 freshwater crocodile.....*noun masculine* **lalanggarrany**;
 noun masculine
 wawoorrmarndiny;
 noun masculine **yilaggarnany**
 female freshwater
 crocodile.......................*noun feminine* **woolanggoorral**
 juvenile freshwater
 crocodile.......................*noun masculine* **ngambarnji**
 saltwater crocodile.......*noun masculine*
 yalamboorrmany
Crocodile Hole...............*noun* **Roogoon**
crooked..........................*adjective* **dinygoorleny,**
 dinygoorlel, dinygoorle
cross-eyed......................*adjective* **ligirriny, ligirril,**
 ligirrim
cross-legged, sit............*coverb+BE/STAY* **balbirrin**
cross over with
 someone......................*coverb+GO/BECOME* **jarrg**
crouching, be................*coverb+BE/STAY* **jarranang**
crow...............................*noun feminine* **malgirrambal**;
 noun feminine **waag-waagjil**;
 noun feminine **wanggarnal**
crowd in........................*coverb+FALL/GO_DOWN* **leb**
crowd together.............*coverb+DO_REFL* **leb-leb**
crustacean with a long
 thin tail, small............*noun feminine* **birinyboorrool**
cry..................................*coverb+SAY/DO* **ngardawoo**
 be made to cry..............*coverb+GO/COME* **ngardawooge**
 cry at someone............*coverb+SPEAR*
 ngarda-ngardawoo
 cry for relation..............*coverb* **warri-warri**;
 coverb+SAY/DO **warri**
 cry on seeing relation...*coverb+GET* **warriwoo**
 make cry......................*coverb+GET* **ngardawooge**;
 coverb+HIT **ngardawooge**

cuckoo, channel-billed..*noun feminine* **goorra-goorral**
cuckoo shrike,
  black-faced ....*noun feminine* **miliwoorrangel;**
                              noun feminine **yirringaragjil**
cuckoo shrike,
  white-bellied ....*noun feminine* **yirringaragjil**
cucumber, bush,
  Cucumis melo...............*noun feminine* **jilinybel**
cucumber, big bush,
  Cucumis picrocarpus....*noun feminine* **garerlel**
cumbungi ....*noun feminine* **beremerrel**
cup ....*noun* **gardag, gardagboo**
cured, be........................*coverb+SAY/DO_M* **men'gawoog**
curled around (snake),
  be................................*coverb+SAY/DO* **nyaloonggooj**
curlew ....*noun feminine* **wirndoowool**
current ....*noun* **thoolooloorrji**
cut ....*coverb+SAY/DO* **gardij**
  cut hair off ....*coverb+CUT_REFL* **bilijig**
  cut meat, cut off meat...*coverb+HIT* **begerr**
  cut tree..........................*coverb+GO_ALONG* **doowoo**
  cut down tree ....*coverb+SAY/DO_M* **thel;**
                              coverb+HIT **thel**
  cut self..........................*coverb+BURN/BITE_REFL* **barraj;**
                              coverb+BURN/BITE_REFL **gadij;**
                                coverb+DO_REFL **gerrbij-gerrbij**
  fall and cut self ....*coverb+FALL/GO_DOWN* **gadij**
  cut something ....*coverb+HIT* **barraj;**
                                coverb+HIT **gaj;**
                                coverb+HIT **gadij**
  cut stick for spear, etc...*coverb* **ngerd**
  cut sugarbag ....*coverb+HIT* **jarn**
  cut umbilical cord ....*coverb+PUT* **darr**
  cut off at base...............*coverb+HIT* **thel**
  cut up ....*coverb* **therrbag;**
                                coverb+HIT **gerrbij**
  cut up meat ....*coverb+GET* **bag;**
                                coverb+HIT **bag;**
                                coverb+SAY/DO_M **thelberr**
  be cutting something
  up...................................*coverb+SAY/DO* **bag-bag**
  go along cutting/
  splitting ....*coverb+GO_ALONG* **lagarr**
  go and cut ....*coverb+GO/COME* **gethed**
cute (baby) ....*adjective* **baam-baamboony,**
                                baam-baambool, baam-
                                baamboom
cycad..............................*noun masculine* **nganthanji**
cyclone...........................*noun* **warlanginy, warlangem**
  cyclone chase
  someone ....*coverb* **warlangooboo**

cypress pine ....*noun masculine* **gooweriny**

Dd

dad (spoken about) ......*noun* **ngaboony**
dad (spoken to) ....*noun* **ngabayi**
dance ....*coverb+GO_ALONG* **warrg;**
                                coverb+SAY/DO **warrg;**
                                coverb+SAY/DO_M **warrg**
  dance artefact ....*noun feminine* **woorranggool**
  dance moving knees
  in and out ....*coverb+SAY/DO* **ngim-ngim**
  dancing style like
  'rock and roll' ....*noun* **yoorroondoorroom**
  turning while dancing...*coverb+GO_ALONG* **doorl-doorl**
  SEE ALSO: **song and dance**
dance movement in
  Wangga and Lirrga,
  women's......................*coverb+SAY/DO* **warrajbe**
dance movement,
  women's jumping ......*coverb+SAY/DO* **wil-wil;**
                                coverb+SAY/DO_M **wil-wil**
dance and song style
  with clap sticks ....*noun* **Balga, Balgal;**
                                noun **Joonba, Joonbal**
  with didjeridoo and
  clap sticks.....................*noun* **Lirrga, Lirrgal**
                                noun **Wangga, Wanggal**
  SEE ALSO: **song and dance**
dangerous night bird ...*noun* **joowany, joowal**
dangerous person ....*noun* **mawoongarriny,**
                                mawoongarril
dangerous place,
  spiritually...................*noun* **doomoorriny,**
                                doomoorrinyji,
                                doomoorrinyil,
                                doomoorrinybe;
                                noun **joomboorrirriny;**
                                noun **joomoorririny,**
                                joomoorrirrim
dangerous place, be.....*coverb* **joomboorrirrig**
dark................................*adjective* **mandegerreny**
  become dark ....*coverb+FALL/GO_DOWN* **manbe**

darkness, in

be getting dark.............*coverb+FALL/GO_DOWN* **garraroony, garrwaroony;** *coverb+FALL/GO_DOWN* **man-manbe;** *coverb+FALL/GO_DOWN* **mawoorrboonybe;** *coverb+FALL/GO_DOWN* **merdbenybe, merdbe-merdbe**
get dark.....................*coverb+FALL/GO_DOWN* **man;** *coverb+FALL/GO_DOWN* **merdbe-merdbe;** *coverb+FALL/GO_DOWN* **ngij;** *coverb+FALL/GO_DOWN* **nyiganybe;** *coverb+FALL/GO_DOWN M* **mendoowoonyboo;** *coverb+GO DOWN M* **man**
go while it is getting dark.......................*coverb+GO/COME* **garrwaroowany**
darkness, in..................*temporal* **mendoowoon**
daughter of man..........*noun feminine* **ngabool**
  daughter of man (spoken to).....................*noun* **ngabayi**
daughter of man or woman......................*noun feminine* **wigil**
daughter of woman.....*noun feminine* **ngalangangel**
  daughter of woman (spoken to)....................*noun* **ngalanga**
daughter-in-law of man..........................*noun* **lambarram**
daughter-in-law of woman......................*noun feminine* **goorrijil**
dawn...............................*noun* **rangarrwam**
  dawn, at dawn..............*temporal* **rangarrwan**
  dawn (be dawn)............*coverb* **rangarrg;** *coverb+FALL/GO_DOWN* **rangarrg**
  dawn (just at dawn, right at dawn)...............*temporal* **rangarrwayan**
day breaking.................*coverb+GO/COME* **merala**
  daybreak come.............*coverb+GO/COME* **melng**
daytime, in the..............*temporal* **dirranden, derranden**
dazzled...........................*coverb+GO_ALONG* **damana;** *coverb+SAY/DO* **damana**
dead, be all...................*coverb+BE/STAY* **gererreb**
dead body.....................*noun* **garajbe;** *noun* **goonyingarre**
dead meat....................*adjective* **gern'gany, gern'gal, gern'gam**
dead person.................*noun* **joowarriny, joowarril**

deaf................................*adjective* **birn'goolji, birn'goolool, birn'gooloo;** *adjective* **yardewoorriny, yardewoorrool, yardewoorroom**
  be deaf........................*coverb+SAY/DO* **theb;** *coverb+BE/STAY* **thebbany**
  make deaf...................*coverb+HIT* **nyin'ge**
death adder.................*noun masculine* **damberrji;** *noun masculine* **ngadarrji**
deep dish.....................*noun* **jaboogoom, jaboogoony, jaboogool**
deep hole.....................*noun* **dagoorlany, dagoorlan**
  fill deep hole (water running).............*coverb+SAY/PLACE_REFL* **jamboorn**
  make deep hole...........*coverb+GET* **dagoorlagbe**
  put in deep hole ....*coverb+HIT* **dagoorlaj**
defecate........................*coverb+HIT* **therraj;** *coverb+HIT* **therrilaj**
delay someone ....*coverb+PUT* **yambil**
delicious ....*adjective* **joornanygarreny, joornanygarrel, joornanygarrem**
demand with menaces......................*coverb+SAY/DO_M* **walaji**
desert people................*noun* **warrmalam**
desert woomera ....*noun feminine* **bigirrel**
devil ....*noun* **joowarriny, joowarril**
devil dog.......................*noun masculine* **jarrinyin;** *noun masculine* **mooloogoorrji**
  name of a devil dog ......*noun* **Jilinyangarriny**
dew ....*noun* **yaalji, yaale**
diamond-patterned......*adjective* **mernderr-mernderr**
diarrhoea......................*noun* **galyoolyoom**
Dick Yard ....*noun* **Ngayewoorre**
Dicky Spring on Bedford Downs...........*noun* **Jimbirlan**
didjeridoo.....................*noun feminine* **gooloomboong, gooloomboongnyel;** *noun feminine* **jooboony, jooboonyel**
die ....*coverb+FALL/GO_DOWN* **gern'gag;** *coverb+FALL/GO_DOWN* **goonyingarrg;** *coverb+FALL/GO_DOWN* **nang;** *coverb+FALL/GO_DOWN* **themerr**
  all die...........................*coverb+FALL/GO_DOWN* **gooroorroony**
  cause to die ....*coverb+GET* **nanggegboo**
  die (plural).................*coverb+GO/COME* **nanggayig**
  die suddenly in group...*coverb+FALL/GO_DOWN* **goord**

die with others in
group .... *coverb+GO_BECOME* **goord**
go away and die .... *coverb+FALL/GO_DOWN* **marrarn**
diesel .... *noun phrase* **yagengem bijid-bijidbe mooloonggoojam**
different .... *adjective* **yagewany, yagewal, yagewam**
different (not good) ...... *adjective* **yagewalal, yagewalany, yagewalam**
different one .... *noun* **yagengeny, yagengel, yagengem**
different-looking .... *adjective* **yagebawarinyiny, yagebawarinyil, yagebawarinyim**
go different way .... *coverb* **yoorl**
something going a
different way .... *adjective* **yagewarinyji, yagewarinyil, yagewarinybe**
dig .... *coverb+GET* **woobooj**;
coverb+GO_ALONG **woobooj**;
coverb+GO/COME **jarrij**;
coverb+SAY/DO **jarrij**;
coverb+SAY/DO **woobooj**;
coverb+SAY/DO_M **woobooj**
dig around around
for something .... *coverb+SAY/DO* **joorndaj**;
coverb+SAY/DO **joorndajgoowool**
dig out .... *coverb+PUT* **thoorrboord**;
coverb+SAY/DO **thoorrboord**
dig out and put aside .... *coverb+GET* **looward**
dig up .... *coverb+GET* **jarrij**;
coverb+GET_HIT **jarrij**;
coverb+GET **rebej**
be digging .... *coverb+SAY/DO* **jarrij-jarrij**
go digging .... *coverb+GO/COME* **jarrijbany**
digging stick .... *noun masculine* **ganany, gananyji**
dingo .... *noun masculine* **marranyji**
dip .... *coverb+PUT* **jaj**
dirt, hot .... *noun* **gernjile**;
noun **maram**
dirty .... *adjective* **joordoobany, joordoobal, joordoobam**
disagree .... *coverb+SAY/DO_REFL* **yirrgawa**
disappear .... *coverb+FALL/GO_DOWN* **darag**;
coverb+GO/COME **darag**;
coverb+GO/COME **yoowoonybeb**
disappear leaving
someone .... *coverb+LEAVE* **darag**
disbelieve / ignore .... *coverb+HIT* **bany**

dish, deep .... *noun* **jaboogoom, jaboogoony, jaboogool**
wooden dish
(coolamon) .... *noun masculine* **goowirriny**;
noun masculine **larndoorrji**;
noun masculine **walanarriny**;
noun masculine **yawoonyji, yawinyji**
dislike .... *coverb+GET* **boothalwoo**;
coverb+PUT **daying**
dislike and tell off .... *coverb+HIT* **girriyag**
dislike each other .... *coverb+SAY/DO_REFL* **yirrgawa**;
coverb+WOUND_REFL **ganggerre**
dislike someone .... *coverb+BURN/BITE* **ganggerre**;
coverb+PUT **jigi-jigili**
disperse .... *coverb+GO/COME* **yinyjoong**
dive .... *coverb+FALL/GO_DOWN* **jijberrg**;
coverb+FALL/GO_DOWN **jijbi-jijberrg**
dive and grab .... *coverb* **barrad**
dive in .... *coverb+FALL/GO_DOWN* **jilyboorrg**;
coverb+FALL/GO_DOWN **nyimoog, nyimoog-nyimoog**;
coverb+SAY/DO **nyimooga**;
coverb+FALL/GO_DOWN **nyirreg**;
coverb+FALL/GO_DOWN **thoorrboong**
diver jack (bird) .... *noun masculine* **boorrijiny**;
noun masculine **garrang-garranginy**
call of diver jack .... *coverb+SAY/DO* **garrang-garrang**
divide .... *coverb+PUT* **yawa**
dizzy, be .... *coverb+SAY/DO* **wingini**
be dizzy (plural) .... *coverb+SAY/DO* **winginigoowool**
go around and around
while dizzy .... *coverb+GO_ALONG* **wingini**
make dizzy .... *coverb+HIT* **winginig**
do all night until dawn .. *coverb* **rangarrwanyge**
dodder laurel,
Cassytha filiformis .... *noun masculine* **warirrinji**
do properly .... *coverb+PUT* **joodoog**;
coverb+PUT **yirrjib**
do something
completely .... *coverb+GO/COME* **yilwarrag**
do something that is
forever .... *coverb+GO/COME* **yilwarrag**
do to the east .... *coverb+SAY/DO* **ngelamoogoog**
dob someone in .... *coverb+BRING/TAKE* **berag**

doctor

doctor .... *noun* **baremanbeny, baremanbel;**
noun **baroomanbeny, baroomanbel;**
noun masculine **mooroonggoorroony;**
noun **mabarn;**
noun **nyangoobany; nyangoobal**
  doctor (Southern dialect) .... *noun* **melngarribany, melngarribal**
dodge .... *coverb+SAY/DO_M* **min'giri**
dog .... *noun masculine* **joolany;**
noun masculine **ngarriyanyji**
  devil/ghost dog .... *noun masculine* **jarrinyin;**
noun masculine **mooloogoorrji**
  dog grab someone .... *coverb* **wernderlg**
  female dog .... *noun feminine* **joolal**
  pet dog .... *noun* **joondalji, joondalel**
  take dogs hunting .... *coverb* **werna-werna**
dollar bird .... *noun masculine* **dimberralgarlgarlji**
Dolly Hole .... *noun* **Janderrji**
donkey .... *noun masculine* **yardemerewany**
don't do it .... *interjection* **rega**
dots, be painted with ... *adjective* **dilg-dilgbawool, dilg-dilgbawoom, dilg-dilgbawoony**
  paint dots on self for dancing .... *coverb+SAY/DO_REFL* **dab-dab, dag-dag;**
coverb+BURN/BITE_REFL **dilg-dilg**
  paint dots on something .... *coverb+SAY/DO* **dag-dag;**
coverb+PUT **dilg-dilg**
dotterel .... *noun feminine* **bilinyirrinyirril**
dove, bar-shouldered ... *noun feminine* **gelaroogool, goolaroogool;**
noun feminine **marrawayil**
dove, peaceful .... *noun feminine* **goorloordoogjil, goorloordoordoogjil**
down .... *directional* **yilag**
  be going down .... *coverb+FALL/GO_DOWN* **thoodboo;**
coverb+SAY/DO_M **thoothood**
  bring down .... *coverb+GET_HIT* **thoodboo**
  down from top .... *directional* **gerliwirring**
  down to water .... *directional* **yilag**
  from down there .... *directional* **yilang, yilangbiny**
  go down .... *coverb+FALL/GO_DOWN* **thood;**
coverb+GO/COME **thoodboo**
  go down across .... *directional* **loonggiyengen**
downwards / going down .... *directional* **yilangoogoo**
downstream .... *directional* **yoorloo**
  going downstream .... *directional* **yoorloongoogoo**
  from downstream .... *directional* **loonggoong**
  further downstream ..... *directional* **yoorloongoojarriny**
  downstream there .... *directional* **loowoongoo**
drag concealed spear with toes .... *coverb+BRING/TAKE* **bililib**
dragonfly .... *noun masculine* **birrinyoowoorlji**
draw in sand .... *coverb+SAY/DO* **gerniny-gerniny**
draw someone in sorcery .... *coverb+PUT* **jigerl**
dream .... *coverb+GET* **gooni;**
noun **gooniny, goonil, goonim**
  be dreaming .... *coverb+GO/COME* **goonijib**
dreaming
  dreaming, dreamtime thing .... *noun* **gooningarriny, gooningarril, gooningarrim**
  become part of the dreamtime .... *coverb+GET* **ngarranggarniny**
  belonging to the dreamtime .... *adjective* **ngarranggarniny, ngarranggarnil, ngarrangarnim**
  in dreamtime .... *temporal* **ngarranggarnin**
  dreaming place .... *noun* **werlweny, werlwel, werlwem**
  ask dreaming place for help .... *coverb+PUT* **goorara**
  personal dreaming .... *noun* **gooniny, goonil, goonim**
dress .... *noun* **jina-jinam**
driftwood .... *noun* **miyingenbe**
drink .... *coverb+FALL/GO_DOWN* **ngoorloog;**
coverb+SAY/DO **ngoorloog;**
coverb+SAY/DO_M **ngoorloog**
  be drinking .... *coverb+SAY/DO* **ngoorloorloog;**
coverb+SAY/DO_M **ngoorloorloog**
  go alone drinking .... *coverb+GO_ALONG* **ngoorloorloog**
  give someone a drink ... *coverb+HIT* **ngoorloorloog**
  go down to drink .... *coverb+FALL/GO_DOWN* **ngoorloog**
drip .... *coverb+SAY/DO* **larroorroo**
  drip rain .... *coverb+SAY/DO* **tharroorroo**
  drip sweat .... *coverb+GO_ALONG* **larroorroo**

drive	*coverb+BRING/TAKE* **joorra**;
	coverb+SAY/DO **joorra**
drive into water	*coverb+HIT* **jawoorr**
drop	*coverb+HIT* **jid**;
	coverb+HIT **jood**
drop off	*coverb+FALL/GO_DOWN* **jid**
drop out	*coverb+SAY/DO* **jirrgawoorr**
make drop out	*coverb+HIT* **jirrgawoorrg**
drown	*coverb+SAY/DO* **ngamoonayi**;
	coverb+WOUND_REFL **nyimeniny**
drown someone	*coverb+BRING/TAKE* **derawoog**;
	coverb+HIT **nyirreg**;
	coverb+HIT **nyoomoog**
drown something/someone	*coverb+HIT* **nyimeniny**;
	coverb+HIT **nyimoog**
make water run and drown someone	*coverb+HIT* **thoorroorroog**
try to drown someone	*coverb+BRING/TAKE* **thoorroogboo**
drum	*noun* **barndawoom**
drunk, be	*coverb+SAY/DO* **wingini**
be drunk (plural)	*coverb+SAY/DO* **winginigoowool**
get drunk	*coverb+PUT* **winginig**
drunk wobbling	*adjective* **wingenoowoony**, **wingenoowool**
drunkards	*noun* **ngoorloog-bayilim**
dry	*adjective* **berrjele, berrjelji, berrjelel**;
	adjective **dilboony, dilboom**
dry bark	*noun* **lirn'girre**
dry bark/empty pod/fish scale	*noun* **lirlmim**
be made dry white bones	*coverb+GET* **langany-langany**
dry camp without water	*noun* **barradan**
dry grass	*noun* **minybernem**
dry out	*coverb+SAY/DO_M* **mard**
dry up (waterhole)	*coverb+GO/COME* **lintharrg**
duck	*noun* **jibilyoowool, jibilyiwoony**
duck down	*coverb+FALL/GO_DOWN* **yib**
duck out of way	*coverb+SAY/DO_M* **yoodooboorr**
dust	*noun* **joordoom**
dust rising	*coverb+BE/STAY* **dooloomayib**
dusty	*adjective* **joordoobany, joordoobal, joordoobam**
dynamite	*noun feminine* **marnel**

Ee

each in their own place	*adverb* **yagebawirri**
each other	
hit each other	*coverb+SAY/DO_REFL* **dawarrji**
hold each other	*coverb+DO_REFL* **gerneg**
hug each other	*coverb+SAY/DO_REFL* **boorroongoo**
kill each other	*coverb+SAY_REFL* **mawoo-mawoonde**;
	coverb+SAY/DO_REFL **thedji**
kill each other (many)	*coverb+WOUND_REFL* **goord**
kiss each other	*coverb+SAY/DO_REFL* **boony-boony**
know each other	*coverb+DO_REFL* **ngarra**
laugh at each other	*coverb+SAY/DO_REFL* **garl-garl**
nudge each other	*coverb+SAY/DO_REFL* **nhoorrngoog**;
	coverb+SAY/DO_REFL **nhoorr-nhoorr**
pick out each other	*coverb+SAY/DO_REFL* **gooraj**
poke each other/self	*coverb+SPEAR_REFL* **jagij**
shove each other	*coverb+SAY/DO_REFL* **jarl-jarl**
talk to each other	*coverb+SAY/DO_REFL* **bal**
tickle each other	*coverb+DO_REFL* **gejig**;
	coverb+DO_REFL **jigij-jigij**
eagle, wedge-tailed	*noun masculine* **garnbarrany**;
	noun masculine **garnbidany**;
	noun masculine **girliwirringiny**;
	noun masculine **warrarnany**;
	noun masculine **wirli-wirlingarnany**
Eagle Hawk Bottle Tree	*noun* **Goonyoorrban, Goonyirribany**
early morning	*temporal* **nyigamirribda**;
	temporal **nyiga-nyigawa**
ears	*noun* **yardem**
ear wax	*noun* **garrarram**
earth oven, pull out of	*coverb+GET* **doorrbood**
earth, the	*noun* **gamerrem**
earwig	*noun feminine* **gibigel**
east	
from the east	*directional* **ngelmang**;
	directional **ngelmibiny**
in the east	*directional* **ngelmin, ngilmin**
to the east	*directional* **ngela**;
	directional **ngelamoogoo**
to the east, moving around from south to north or north to south (e.g. rain)	*directional* **galmang**

eat

eat	coverb+BURN/BITE **jang**;
	coverb+GO_ALONG **joord**;
	coverb+SAY/DO **jang**;
	coverb+SAY/DO **jang-jang**;
	coverb+SAY/DO **joord**;
	coverb+SAY/DO_M **jang**;
	coverb+SAY/DO_M **jang-jang**
eat by handful	coverb+GO/COME **ngambooroony**
eat by handful, gobble	coverb+SAY/DO_M **mangoony**
eat leftover bits	coverb+SAY/DO **garrid-garrid**
eat old ones with no beef/scavenge (e.g. crow)	coverb+SAY/DO_M **nyoornayi**
eat one thing only	coverb+EAT **wern'galge**
eat something until full	coverb+EAT **boorral**
eat so that one's anus sticks out (swearing)	coverb+EAT **thoomboonygoo**; coverb+HIT **thoomboonygoo**
eat something bad	coverb+EAT **wern'galge**
eat too much and sleep	coverb+LEAVE **ngarloogoo**
eat until can't eat anymore	coverb+EAT **nanggeg**
eat until full	coverb+EAT **lerreg**; coverb+GO_ALONG **boorroo-boorral**; coverb+EAT **boorral**; coverb+EAT **gig**
eat/drink all of something	coverb+EAT **gerrejbe**
when eaten	adverb **janggan**
eating, all	coverb+EAT **nawiri-wirib**
eating all around (kangaroos)	coverb+SAY/DO **nawooririb**
eating, finish	coverb+EAT MID **gerrij**
echidna	noun feminine **bagabal**; noun feminine **gernanyjel**
edge of something	locative **thayin**
edge of creek	noun **banderre**
roots at edge of water	noun **nan'goon**
shallow edge of water	noun **garlirriny**
walk along the edge of something	coverb+GO_ALONG **bardib**; coverb+GO_ALONG **thayinbe**
egg	noun feminine **gerewoolel**; noun **goomboonyel, goomboonyji**
lay eggs	coverb+SAY/DO **joorrooji**
egret (white crane)	noun masculine **jalariny**
elbow	noun **joonggoom**

Elbow Hole	noun **Thawoon'goorroo**
elder	noun **manambarrany, manambarral, manambarram**
male elder	noun masculine **gooroogoorany**; noun masculine **marloogany**
electricity	noun **ngerrenbe-boorroo**
Elgee Cliffs	noun **Garlmanderre**; noun **Gelawarliny**
embarrass someone	coverb+GET **ganybelgbe**; coverb+GET **moojoonggoolg**
embarrassed, be	coverb+SAY/DO **ganybel**
emerge	coverb+BECOME **doorloog**; coverb+BECOME **doorloorloog**; coverb+GO_ALONG **doorloorloog**
be emerging	coverb+SAY/DO_M **doorloorloog**
just emerging	coverb+BECOME **doolgboo**
empty pod/dry bark/fish scale	noun **lirlmim**
empty something	coverb+HIT **larroo**
emu	noun feminine **garnanganyjel**; noun feminine **ngarabarral**; noun feminine **wiyarrel**
emu chicks	noun **wininim**
emu chicks, half grown	noun **doorrja-doorrjam**
emu feathers	noun **ngoojabal, ngoojam**
emu with chicks	noun feminine **wininibal**
emu apple, fish poison tree	noun masculine **nyarerrji**
'emu killer' (northern shovel-nosed snake)	noun masculine **goodawoodany**
'emu killer' (northern snake lizard)	noun masculine **joowarribarndegji**
'emu killer' (ringed brown snake)	noun masculine **jarloongoorrobarndegji**; noun masculine **yarriwirriny**
'emu tucker' (quinine tree)	noun masculine **welrayiny**
end of spear	noun **nyilenggam**
enemy	noun **ginyirriny, ginyirril**
engine	noun **ngoorr-ngoorroo**
enjoy sweet taste	coverb+GO/COME **menherrgarr**
enter	coverb+FALL/GO_DOWN **walig**
entrance of native beehive	noun **moorloo**
erect shelter	coverb+GET **warr**
erection (swearing)	noun **doolmoorroony**

fall

Eucalyptus SEE ALSO *Corymbia*
Eucalyptus brevifolia,
E. confluens, snappy gum ..*noun* **thalngarrji**
Eucalyptus camaldulensis,
river red gum................*noun* **bilirnji, bilirnbe;**
................................*noun masculine* **dimalan;**
................................*noun masculine* **garranggany**
Eucalyptus cupularis,
Halls Creek white gum ..*noun masculine* **theliny-thelinyji**
Eucalyptus herbertiana,
Kalumburu gum ....*noun masculine* **wenthawoolenji**
Eucalyptus jensenii,
Corymbia dichromophloia,
C. terminalis, C. polycarpa,
bloodwood ....*noun masculine* **mawoorroony**
Eucalyptus limitaris,
E. microtheca, E. obconica,
E. tephrodes,
coolibah tree ....*noun masculine* **warernji**
Eucalyptus miniata,
Corymbia aspera,
C. ptychocarpa (different
trees with same name)..*noun masculine* **booniny**
Eucalyptus pruinosa,
silver box, smoky
cabbage gum ....*noun masculine* **linyjilji**
euphemism, word
used as ....*interjection* **warri-warri**
Euphorbia species
used when cooking
minyjaarrany ....*noun* **minyanyany**
evening, early ....*temporal* **ngarlngarlban**
every night ....*temporal* **mendoowoomoowan**
everybody......................*noun* **gamingoorroom**
everyone........................*adjective* **melagawiya;**
................................*adjective* **waringarriya**
everything....................*noun* **dini-dininy;**
................................*noun* **thoowoo-thoowoom**
everywhere ....*locative* **ngoorroo-ngoorroon**
exchange of goods ....*noun* **wirnan**
exclamation (of pain) ...*interjection* **wardayi**
exclamation (on
seeing cute baby) ....*interjection* **anyany**
exhausted, be ....*coverb+DO_REFL* **naman;**
................................*coverb+GO/COME* **yirrerij**
explain............................*coverb+GET* **lirrgarn**
eye..................................*noun* **moorloo**
close eyes ....*coverb+SAY/DO* **yoomooj**
open eyes.....................*coverb+GET* **berl**
hit in eye........................*coverb+HIT* **darlg**
poke in eye ....*coverb+GET* **darlg**
having eyes stuck
together partly closed ..*adjective* **nhegbayiny, nhegbayil, nhegbayim;**
................................*adjective* **nheng-nhegany, nheng-nhegal, nheng-nhegam**
having squinting eyes...*adjective* **yirranybeny, yirranybel, yirranybem**
eyebrow..........................*noun* **biwoorre**
eyelash ....*noun* **warramale**
eye on someone, have..*coverb+GET* **derlmenyji**

Ff

face ....*noun* **mirrngem**
hide face with hand ......*coverb+SAY/PLACE_REFL* **booroo**
facing someone, be ......*coverb+BE/STAY* **therrendang**
facing someone, put
something to be ....*coverb+PUT* **therrendang**
faeces.............................*noun* **manam**
fairy martin ....*noun feminine* **jirrinyngalil**
falcon, brown................*noun masculine* **girrganyji**
falcon, peregrine..........*noun masculine* **minymijginy, minymirdginy**
fall ....*coverb+FALL/GO_DOWN* **boodbaj**
fall (plural) ....*coverb+FALL/GO_DOWN* **werrg**
fall/come off ....*coverb+GO/COME* **werndelg**
fall and be burnt up ......*coverb+FALL/GO_DOWN* **thaloorrg**
fall and break................*coverb+FALL/GO_DOWN* **bijaj;**
................................*coverb+FALL/GO_DOWN* **deberr**
fall down.......................*coverb+FALL/GO_DOWN* **bard;**
................................*coverb+FALL/GO_DOWN* **bardal;**
................................*coverb+FALL/GO_DOWN* **barljarr;**
................................*coverb+FALL/GO_DOWN* **barljarrwany;**
................................*coverb+FALL/GO_DOWN* **wethed;**
................................*coverb+FALL/GO_DOWN* **woorrg;**
................................*coverb+GO_ALONG* **barndalgaa;**
................................*coverb+SAY/DO* **barljarr**
fall and hurt self ....*coverb+FALL/GO_DOWN* **geberd;**
................................*coverb+FALL/GO_DOWN* **mirl-mirlge;**
................................*coverb+FALL/GO_DOWN* **thalijbel**
fall flat on stomach ....*coverb+FALL/GO_DOWN* **ngarloogoo**
fall off (e.g. leaves) ....*coverb+FALL/GO_DOWN* **yilberrwany**
fall from top..................*coverb+FALL/GO_DOWN* **bang**

falls, open so that someone

fall with wind	*coverb+FALL/GO_DOWN* **ngarloogoo**	short and fat	*adjective* **gendaloogany, gendaloogal, gendaloogam**
falls, open so that someone	*coverb+HIT* **bang**	father	*noun masculine* **ngaboony**
family come together	*coverb+GO/COME* **daboorlg**	father/child of father (spoken to)	*noun* **ngabayi**
famous, I am	*noun phrase* **nawarram-ngirri yinginybe**	father's father	*noun masculine* **gelaginy**
fan fire to get started	*coverb+SAY/DO_M* **wawood**	father's sister	*noun feminine* **gawangel**
far	*adjective* **meraangarriny, meraangarril, meraangarrim**; *adjective* **merewany, merewal, merewam**; *adjective* **merewagawoony, merewagawool, merewagawoom**; *adjective* **merewangarriny, merewangarril, merewangarrim**; *adverb* **marra**	father-in-law	*noun masculine* **lambarrany**
		favourite place	*noun* **giyale**
		feast	*noun* **mingayoorroom, mingayoorriny**
		feather	*noun* **birn'girre**; *noun* **ganalam**
		emu feathers	*noun* **ngoojabal, ngoojam**
		feathers used for dancing headdress	*noun* **darrgam**
		feed, a good	*noun* **boorrale**
		feed baby from mouth	*coverb+GIVE* **thab**
		feeding, be	*coverb+SAY/DO* **ngereb-ngereb**
		feel bad	*coverb+SAY/DO* **boothal**
go very far	*adverb* **gamberarra-gamberarra**	feel glad	*coverb* **nger**; *coverb* **werlge-werlge**; *coverb* **thamalarrg**
far away	*adverb* **ngirribawoorroon**		
not far away	*locative* **marragoowoorroon**	feel hot	*coverb+SAY/DO* **boorn**
send far away	*coverb+HIT* **marrangag**	feel itchy	*coverb+SAY/DO* **yayi**
take far away	*coverb+HIT* **dawadag**	feel like not eating	*coverb+SAY/DO* **ngarloo**; *coverb+SAY/DO_M* **ngarloo**
very far away	*adverb* **gayirra-goolaniyid**		
far out, sticking	*adjective* **marrajgany, marrajgal, marrajgam**	feel proud	*coverb+SAY/DO* **gerlmarr**
farewell	*coverb+GET* **mathe**; *coverb+SAY/DO_REFL* **mathe-mathe**	feel sad inside	*coverb+BE/STAY* **moolooloongboo**
		feel sick	*coverb+FALL/GO_DOWN* **ngarl**
fart, to	*coverb* **thiny**; *coverb* **thirriny**	feel someone's heart	*coverb+GET* **mam**
		feel sorry	*coverb+SAY/DO* **mooloorroo**
fast	*adverb* **waranggan**	feel sorry for each other	*coverb+SAY/DO_REFL* **mooloorroo**
make go fast	*coverb+HIT* **thoony**	make someone feel sorry	*coverb* **mereleg**
take off fast	*adverb* **garda-gardan**		
fat	*noun* **mooloonggoom**	feel for lice	*coverb+SAY/DO_REFL* **doogoo-doogoo**
fat (of animal), meat	*adjective* **mooloonggoo-galeny, mooloonggoo-galel, mooloonggoo-galem**; *adjective* **marlawoorrgoony, marlawoorrgool, marlawoorrgoom**	feel with hand/try out	*coverb+GO_ALONG* **manmaj**
		feelings, nerves, sinew	*noun* **jirlwam**; *noun* **nganyjoom**
		feel nerve jump	*coverb+BECOME* **jirreg**
		feeling in guts	*noun* **liyanbe**
fat baby	*adjective* **baam-baamboony, baam-baambool, baam-baamboom**	get a fright/ funny feeling	*coverb+GO/COME* **berrngerl**
		have a bad feeling	*coverb+GO/COME* **berrngerl**
fat person	*adjective* **jaroogoony, jaroogool, jaroogoom**	feel strange	*coverb+SAY/DO* **jiwoore**
fat female wallaby	*noun feminine* **marliwal**		

fire

feel tingling in
  body part......................*coverb+SAY/DO*
  woorlmooj-woorlmooj
feet, having slack ....*adjective* **wirangbawarrany,**
  wirangbawarral,
  wirangbawarram
  SEE ALSO **foot**
female child of father ..*noun feminine* **ngabool**
female dog ....*noun feminine* **joolal**
female goanna...............*noun feminine* **thoogool**
female koel ....*noun feminine* **girlgoowal**
fence..............................*noun* **ngerlam**
few ....*adjective* **jirra-jirrawoom**
fibula..............................*noun* **ninjirri**
fig species
  cluster fig......................*noun masculine* **goonangginy;**
    noun masculine **jawoonany;**
    noun masculine **ngalalabany**
  river fig........................*noun masculine* **ganambiny;**
    noun masculine **jabayiny**
  rock fig ....*noun masculine* **banggoonji,**
    banggoornji
  sandpaper fig...............*noun masculine* **yimarlji;**
    noun masculine **yingarrjiny**
Fig Tree Hole ....*noun* **Jamelayigoon**
fight ....*noun* **warim**
  fight for something
    (e.g. country) ....*coverb+HIT* **bagarr**
fight, looking for a ....*coverb+GO_ALONG* **baja-baja;**
    coverb+DO_REFL **berag**
  go looking for a fight ....*coverb+SAY/DO* **yad;**
    coverb+SAY/DO_M **yad**
  go looking for a fight
    with each other............*coverb+SAY/DO_REFL* **yad**
  someone looking for
    a fight ....*adjective* **boontherranybiny,**
    boontherranybel,
    boontherranybem;
    adjective **babinyiny, babinyil,**
    babinyem;
    adjective **boorlgarrijbeny,**
    boorlgarrijbel,
    boorlgarrijbem
fighter.............................*adjective* **babinyiny, babinyil**
fighting spear, short ....*noun masculine* **malmoorrji;**
    noun masculine **ngoorniny**
fighting stick.................*noun masculine* **goordooroom;**
    noun masculine **nawooloony**
  small fighting stick........*noun masculine* **wabagoorreny,**
    waboogoorroony;
    noun **yamayarram**

fighting, stop
  someone ....*coverb+SAY/DO* **jawa-jawayi**
file something to make
  it sharp or shine ....*coverb+PUT* **boorr-boorr**
fill ....*coverb+SAY/DO* **tharrgi;**
    coverb+SAY/DO_M **tharrgi**
  fill up ....*coverb+PUT* **jamboorn;**
    coverb+PUT **tharr**
  fill deep hole
    (water running)............*coverb+SAY/PLACE_REFL* **jamboorn**
  fill self with food ....*coverb+EAT* **lerreg**
finches in general ....*noun feminine* **nyinyil, niyinyil**
finch, zebra ....*noun feminine* **nyinyil, niyinyil**
find..................................*coverb+GO_ALONG* **biji;**
    coverb+GO/COME **ngarayi;**
    coverb+HIT **bilij;**
    coverb+HIT **gedba;**
    coverb+HIT **ngarayi;**
    coverb+HIT/CUT **ngarayi;**
    coverb+PUT **ngarayi;**
    coverb+SAY/DO **biji**
  cause someone to
    find song ....*coverb+GET* **banji**
  find place
    (conception spirit).........*coverb+BURN/BITE* **bilij**
finding meat, good at ..*adjective*
    moonthoorroogaleny,
    moonthoorroogalel,
    moonthoorroogalem
fine..................................*adjective* **booloorroo**
fingernail.......................*noun* **yarnderre**
fingers/hand ....*noun* **marlam**
fingers, pick up small
  objects one by one
  with ....*coverb+SAY/DO* **barniny**
fingers, sqeeze
  together with ....*coverb+SAY/DO_M* **goolmaj**
finish..............................*coverb+BECOME* **gerrij;**
    coverb+FALL/GO_DOWN **gerrij;**
    coverb+GO/COME **gerrij;**
    particle **gerrij**
  finish by burning............*coverb+BURN/BITE* **gerrij**
  finish by eating ....*coverb+EAT* **gerrij**
  finish ceremony ....*coverb+SAY/DO* **mar-maroora**
  finish eating...................*coverb+EAT MID* **gerrij**
  finish (seeds on tree) ....*coverb+FALL/GO_DOWN* **woordoorr**
  finish something............*coverb+GET* **gerrij**
  finish something up......*coverb+HIT* **gerrij**
  finish/all die ....*coverb+SAY/DO* **gerrij**
fire...................................*noun* **marnem, marneny;**
    noun **thoonbam**

firefly

fire die down to coals....*coverb+BURN/BITE* **moonoorroony**
fan fire to get started....*coverb+SAY/DO_M* **wawood**
fire go out....................*coverb+FALL/GO_DOWN* **thoomooj**
light fire........................*coverb+PUT* **girrem**
make a fire..................*coverb+PUT* **jardgi**;
    coverb+SAY/DO **jardgi**;
    coverb+SAY/DO_M **jardgi**
make fire flare up
with big flames ....*coverb+PUT* **gawara**
make fire light up..........*coverb+PUT* **ngerren**
make fire with fire
drill..............................*coverb+HIT* **biyird-biyird**;
    coverb+SAY/DO **biyird-biyird**
pull from fire.................*coverb+GET* **boog**
put on fire to heat..........*coverb+PUT* **jaa**
put out fire....................*coverb+PUT* **thoomooj**
set fire to something ....*coverb+PUT* **boodooj**;
    coverb+PUT **booj**;
    coverb+SAY/DO **booj-booj**;
    coverb+PLACE **booj**
throw something
on fire ....*coverb+HIT* **thaloorrg**
firefly ....*noun feminine* **ngoorrwangarnal**
firestick..........................*noun* **goonggalam**, **goonggalany**
firewood ....*noun* **marnem**, **marneny**; *noun* **thoonbam**
heap up firewood ....*coverb+PUT* **jaleng**
firm, become................*coverb+BECOME* **bagarrji**
first fruit of black plum
(*minyjiwarrany*) ....*noun* **jawoorlji**
first rain.........................*noun* **warlanginy**, **warlangem**
first time, the ....*adverb* **gelengiyana**
fish (catch)
collect fish, after
poisoning with grass
and other plants...........*coverb+GET* **rawalgbany**
fishing line...................*noun* **ngerlam**; *noun* **wirli-wirlim**
hook up fish.................*coverb+GET* **yan'gag**
push spinifex/grass
through water to
catch fish ....*coverb+SAY/DO* **garlmi**;
    coverb+SAY/DO_M **garlmi**;
    coverb+GO_ALONG **gerlgayi**;
    coverb+SAY/DO **gerlgayi**;
    coverb+GO/COME **gerlgayi**
stick used to
hook up fish.................*noun* **yan'gam**

fish poison tree, freshwater
mangrove ....*noun masculine* **malawany**; *noun masculine* **mangoonyji**
fish (generic).................*noun feminine* **goorndarril**
fish scale......................*noun* **lirlmim**; *noun* **lirn'girre**; *noun* **nyilim**
make dried fish into
powder........................*coverb* **mily**
fish species
barramundi ....*noun feminine* **balgal**; *noun feminine* **dawoogjil**; *noun feminine* **dayiwool**; *noun feminine* **nyilibal**; *noun feminine* **wawoordjil**
barramundi's mother
(has three sharp
spikes on back)............*noun feminine* **bawoogool**
barred grunter
(little striped fish) ....*noun feminine* **goodabal**
barred grunter,
Amniataba percoides ......*noun feminine* **ngenderr-ngenderrel** *noun feminine* **goodabal**
black bream.................*noun* **garriyil**, **garriyiny**; *noun* **jambinbaroony**
blackmast.....................*noun masculine* **jirrgilji**
bony bream ....*noun* **lilinyil**, **lilinybe**
bony bream, large ....*noun feminine* **wirabal**
eel-tailed catfish, large ..*noun masculine* **woorlengerriny**
eel-tailed catfish, small..*noun masculine* **ngirndany**
fork-tailed catfish,
large.............................*noun masculine* **dalinyji**
fork-tailed catfish,
small (same species
as *dalinyji*) ....*noun masculine* **binyjiwinyjiny**, **binyjiwoonyjiny**
long tom,
freshwater garfish ....*noun masculine* **bayirrany**; *noun masculine* **jalgirri-girriny**
red-eyed mullet...........*noun masculine* **woorloorrmarlinji**
rifle fish ....*noun feminine* **loowarrel**
rock cod.......................*noun masculine* **nyagoornany**
small striped fish
species ....*noun feminine* **dinbirril**; *noun feminine* **rerregjel**

food, look for

spangled perch	*noun feminine* **moornmoordel, moornmoordool, moornmoordbe;** *noun feminine* **moowalangel**
tiny fish species	*noun feminine* **gawil**
flame	*noun* **ngawoorroorroom, ngawoorroo-woorroom**
flap wings	*coverb+GO_ALONG* **marl-marl**
flap wings (bird)	*coverb+GO_ALONG* **barl**
flare up	*coverb+SAY/DO* **ngerren**
flash (lightning)	*coverb+SAY/DO* **menan**
flashing lightning	*coverb+GO_ALONG* **merrngag;** *coverb+SAY/DO* **merrngag**
be flashing (lightning)	*coverb+SAY/DO_M* **menan**
flat arsed (swearing)	*adjective* **barndiny, barndil, barndim**
flat country	*noun* **marralan**
flat ground	*noun* **balawam;** *noun* **balgam**
flat rock	*noun* **barlalim;** *noun* **barlwany;** *noun* **barloom**
Flat Rock (place on Mabel Downs)	*noun* **Ngiwoowan**
Flat Rock (place near Billy Mac Spring)	*noun* **Barlngen**
flat, tyre go	*coverb+FALL/GO_DOWN* **danyja;** *coverb+SAY/DO_M* **danyjag**
flesh	*noun* **ngaandem**
Fletcher Creek	*noun* **Gerregerrewoon**
flicker (e.g. stars)	*coverb+SAY/DO* **menan;** *coverb+SAY/DO* **minilg-minilg, mirnilg-mirnilg**
flickering light, be	*coverb+SAY/DO* **miny-miny**
flirt	*coverb+GET* **goonyjiri;** *coverb+GET* **yoowarrge**
flirting person	*adjective* **goonyjiriwoony, goonyjiriwool, goonyjirriwoom**
float	*coverb+GO/COME* **boowoob**
flog	*coverb+SAY/DO* **wanyerrwany;** *coverb+SAY/DO_M* **wanyoorr**
flood	*coverb+GO/COME* **loorlg**
flood come and block access	*coverb+GO/COME* **lenggeb;** *coverb+SAY/DO_M* **lenggeb**
flood take away	*coverb+BRING/TAKE* **loorlg**
flood wash away	*coverb+BRING/TAKE* **yan**
flood debris, heap up	*coverb+PUT* **derlg**
floodwater	*noun masculine* **warrambany**
floodwater coming/ rising	*coverb+GO/COME* **barlanbe**
floodwater spread over bush	*coverb+GO/COME* **gibiwoonab;** *coverb+GO/COME* **warraminab**
running floodwater	*noun masculine* **warraminany**
flotsam	*noun* **miyingenbe**
flower	*noun* **thawalam**
flowers of bloodwood	*noun feminine* **jirliwoorril**
flowers of snappy gum	*noun* **goorramindiny, goorramindil**
flu, get	*coverb+GET* **goonthoorri**
fluid in movement, watery	*adjective* **goorloowoorloony, goorloowoorlool, goorloowoorloom**
fly	*noun feminine* **boornool, boornoom;** *noun masculine* **boornoongiliwoony**
blowfly	*noun* **werreralji, werreralel, werrerrale**
firefly	*noun feminine* **ngoorrwangarnal**
march fly (small black biting species)	*noun masculine* **goorrjalji**
fly	*coverb+GO/COME* **doowab**
fly around and around up and up (bird)	*coverb+GO_ALONG* **waranggi**
fly away	*coverb+GO/COME* **yawoog;** *coverb+LEAVE* **doowab**
fly away into sky	*coverb+BE/STAY* **thoowoog**
flycatcher, restless	*noun feminine* **goorlawoorlal**
flying-fox	*noun* **walimalil, walimaliny**
follow	*coverb+GET* **belayig;** *coverb+GO/COME* **thewerr;** *coverb+SAY/DO_M* **belayig;** *coverb+SAY/DO_REFL* **belayig**
follow someone	*coverb+BRING/TAKE* **jirrgaj**
follow track	*coverb+BRING/TAKE* **barij**
follow and watch	*coverb+FOLLOW* **deg**
follow watching	*coverb +FOLLOW* **degbe**
fontanelle	*noun* **ngingim**
food, full of	*adjective* **gigbawoony, gigbawool, gigbawoom**
be full of food	*coverb+SAY/DO* **gig**
fill self with food	*coverb+EAT* **lerreg**
food in someone's mouth, put	*coverb+GIVE* **thab**
food, look for	*coverb+SAY/DO* **joorndaj**
look for food (plural)	*coverb+SAY/DO* **joorndajgoowool**

food, meat

food, meat .... *noun* miyalji, miyalel, miyale
food, non-meat .... *noun* mayiny, mayil, mayim
food, plant that bears
  lots of .... *noun* mayigaleny, mayigalel
food, share .... *coverb+GO/COME*
                    ngajarrg-ngajarrg
foot .... *noun* thambarlam;
                    noun thengam
  put foot on .... *coverb+SAY/DO_M* bad
  put foot on something.. *coverb+GET* bad
foot of tree .... *noun* loorndoony
football .... *noun* boorljany, boorljam
footprint .... *noun* thambarlam
for a long time .... *temporal* warna-warnarram;
                    adverb warnarrayan
for good .... *adverb* jimerrawoon
for no particular
reason .... *particle* googan
forbidden .... *adjective* googbeny, googbel,
                    googbem;
                    adjective goornboony,
                    goornbool, goornboom
  forbidden to do
  something .... *coverb+SAY/DO_REFL* goog
forehead .... *noun* moowooloom
  forehead band .... *noun* berndoowalem
foreskin .... *noun* bijam
  having foreskin
  (swearing) .... *interjection* bijabany
forever .... *adjective* yilwarrany, yilwarral,
                    yilwarram;
                    adverb yilwarraya;
                    adverb jimerrawoon
forget .... *coverb+BE/STAY* nyin;
                    coverb+GET nyin;
                    coverb+GET wangarrg;
                    coverb+SAY/DO nyin;
                    coverb+SAY/DO wangarr;
                    coverb+SAY/DO_M wangala
  forget and leave .... *coverb+LEAVE* nyin
  make forget .... *coverb+GET* wangarrge
  start forgetting .... *coverb+GET* nyinjinybany
forgetful .... *adjective*
                    wangarrgbanynhawoony,
                    wangarrgbanynhawool,
                    wangarrgbanynhawoom
forked .... *adjective* balmendoowoobany,
                    balmendoowoobal,
                    balmendoowoobam
  forked branch/root .... *noun* barndalebany
  form a fork in river .... *coverb+SAY/DO* balmendeg

frayed stick/bark for
  honey .... *noun* wiram
fresh .... *adjective* gelengawoony,
                    gelengawool,
                    gelengawoom;
                    adjective gelengeny, gelengel,
                    gelengem
freshwater mussel .... *noun feminine* gerrewool
friar bird, little .... *noun masculine*
                    jinggerawoogoony
friar bird,
  silver-crowned .... *noun masculine* gagoowany
friend .... *noun* jarlijiny, jarlijil, jarlijim
  friend (spoken to) .... *noun* jarlayi
  friends .... *noun* betham, berrtham
  have friends .... *coverb+BECOME* bethaba
  having no friends/
  relations .... *adjective* liwaya-bawoorroony,
                    liwaya-bawoorrool,
                    liwaya-bawoorroom;
                    adjective wawoonggany,
                    wawoonggal, wawoonggam
fright, get a .... *coverb+SAY/DO* ngirlarr
fright, give a .... *coverb+GET* boorrngoordge;
                    coverb+GET nganggerrge;
                    coverb+GET ngelyarrge
fright, make someone
  shake with .... *coverb+GET* mirr-mirrge
fright,
  stop breathing in .... *coverb+BRING/TAKE* gengereb
frighten .... *coverb+GET* jilbage
  be frightened .... *coverb+SAY/DO* jilba;
                    coverb+SAY/DO_M jilba
  frighten animal .... *coverb+GET* bela;
                    coverb+HIT bela
frightening .... *adjective* jilbawoony,
                    jilbawool, jilbawoom
frillneck lizard .... *noun masculine* gerdanji;
                    noun masculine wawooleny
  frillneck lizard putting
  up frill .... *coverb* belan
frog
  brown frog .... *noun masculine* woogoony,
                    wegeny
  green tree frog .... *noun masculine* laarn-ngarnany
  sand frog, large .... *noun masculine* balngawoon,
                    balngawoonji
  sand frog, small .... *noun feminine*
                    nangala-nangalal

full of food

small frog species,
rocket frog,
sharp-nosed frog .... *noun masculine* **jirraginy**
frog croak .... *coverb+SAY/DO* **weg, weg-weg, woog-woog**
Frog Hollow .... *noun* **Woorreralbam**; *noun* **Woorreranginy**
from
  from downhill .... *directional* **yilang**
  from downstream .... *directional* **loonggoong**
  from upstream .... *directional* **gendang**
  from every place .... *adverb* **ngoorroo-ngoorroo-biny**
  from here .... *demonstrative* **berre-biny**
  from the east .... *directional* **ngelmang**; *directional* **ngelmibiny**
  from the higher side ..... *directional* **gendayingibiny**
  from the north .... *directional* **biyoorroong**; *directional* **biyirribiny**
  from the south .... *directional* **ngerig**; *directional* **ngerijibiny**
  from the west .... *directional* **gerlirrang**; *directional* **gerlirrangbiny**
  person from the west ... *adjective* **girlirremiliny, girlirremilil, girlirremilim**
front, in .... *locative* **welangen, woolangen**
  put in front .... *coverb+HIT* **welang**
front lower body .... *noun* **ngaroom**
fruit species
  Buchanania obovata,
    green plum .... *noun masculine* **daaloony, daloony**
  Capparis lasiantha,
    bush pawpaw .... *noun masculine* **bambilyiny**; *noun feminine* **marranyil**
  Capparis umbonata,
    bush orange .... *noun feminine* **joogoorrool**
  Carissa lanceolata,
    konkerberry .... *noun masculine* **biriyalji**
  Cucumis melo,
    bush cucumber .... *noun feminine* **jilinybel**
  Erythroxylum ellipticum,
    kerosene wood .... *noun feminine* **mindi-mindil**; *noun feminine* **binyji-binyjil**
  Ficus aculeata var. *aculeata*, *F. aculeata* var. *indecora*,
    sandpaper fig .... *noun masculine* **yingarrjiny, yimarlji**

  Ficus coronulata,
    river fig .... *noun masculine* **ganambiny, jabayiny**
  Ficus racemosa,
    cluster fig .... *noun masculine* **goonangginy**; *noun* **jawoonany**; *noun* **ngalalabany**
  Ficus platypoda, *F. atricha*, *F. brachypoda*,
    rock fig .... *noun masculine* **banggoonji, banggoornji**; *noun masculine* **jimirlbiny**
  Ficus virens, banyan .... *noun* **barlngel**
  Flueggea virosa,
    white currant .... *noun masculine* **berenggarrji**; *noun masculine* **goowarroolji**; *noun masculine* **ngoorrwany**; *noun* **roonggoony**
  Grewia species .... *noun masculine* **garrawiny**; *noun* **gawoorroony**; *noun* **ngoojal**; *noun* **ngoowardiny**
  Marsdenia viridiflora,
    bush banana .... *noun feminine* **goolibil**
  melon (edible, inedible and exotic) .... *noun* **ngayalel**
  Persoonia falcata,
    geebung .... *noun masculine* **gantheliny**
  Sersalisia sericea,
    wild prune .... *noun* **binyjirliny**
  Solanum echinatum,
    bush tomato .... *noun feminine* **girlil**
  Vitex glabrata,
    black plum .... *noun* **minyjaarrany, minyjiwarrany**
  Zizyphus quadriloculans,
    brown plum .... *noun masculine* **madarrgoony**
fuck .... *coverb* **moorniny**; *coverb+SAY/DO* **tharriny**
full (e.g. bucket, waterhole), be .... *coverb+BE/STAY* **jamboorn**; *coverb+HAVE* **jamboorn**
full, eat until .... *coverb+EAT* **boorral**; *coverb+EAT* **gig**
  make oneself full by eating something .... *coverb+EAT* **jarrayilge**
full (swearing), make ... *coverb* **merlngard**
full of food .... *adjective* **gigbawoony, gigbawool, gigbawoom**
  be full of food .... *coverb+SAY/DO* **gig**; *coverb+SAY/DO_M* **gig**

fun, have

fun, have .... *coverb+DO_REFL* **mool-moolji**
  have fun together .... *coverb+SAY/DO_REFL* **ngoolya-ngoolya**
  all have fun together .... *coverb+SAY/DO_REFL* **barlijgoowool**
fun, make together .... *coverb+DO_REFL* **jawirij**
fun of each other,
  make .... *coverb+PUT* **birriman**; *coverb+PUT SELF* **birriman**
funny .... *adjective* **barlijbeny, barlijbel, barlijbem**
funeral .... *noun* **jilam**
fungus species .... *noun feminine* **binoowoonggool**; *noun* **moorrji**
fur .... *noun* **warloom**
  singe off fur .... *coverb+HIT* **gawal**
furry-leaved kapok
  bush .... *noun masculine* **malanyjarrji**; *noun masculine* **ngalwany**; *noun feminine* **warndiwal**
furry (like leaves of furry-leaved kapok bush) .... *adjective* **nyinggiwoony, nyinggiwool, nyinggiwoom**
further .... *adverb* **merewan**
  further downstream ..... *directional* **yoorloongoojarriny**
  further upstream .... *directional* **gendoowajarriny**
  further to the east .... *directional* **ngelagoorloorr**
  further to the north ...... *directional* **boowoorrgoorloorr, boorrgoorloorr**
  further to the south ...... *directional* **nyoowoolgoorloorr**
  further to the west .... *directional* **gerliyirrgoorloorr**

Gg

galah .... *noun feminine* **gerliny-gerlinyil**
gang up on,
  'double bank' .... *coverb+FALL/GO_DOWN* **joog**
gap .... *noun* **doomboom**
  be a gap through hills ... *coverb+SAY/DO* **doomboomab**
  go through gap .... *coverb+FALL/GO_DOWN* **doomboo**; *coverb+GO/COME* **doomboo**
gardenia, native .... *noun masculine* **mardany**
garfish, freshwater
  (long tom) .... *noun masculine* **bayirrany**; *noun masculine* **jalgirri-girriny**
gasp for breath .... *coverb+BRING/TAKE* **reminy**; *coverb+GO_ALONG* **ngayirr**

gather a lot of
  something .... *coverb+GET* **yalawoog**; *coverb+HIT* **yalawoog**
gather and fill up .... *coverb+GET* **jamboorn**
gather together .... *coverb+DO_REFL* **nambarr**
  gather together for Joonba song and dance .... *coverb+BE/STAY* **joonbamirrib**
  gather together in large group .... *coverb+GO/COME* **nyawoorn**
  gather together on something .... *coverb+BRING/TAKE* **nyawoorroo-woorroo**; *coverb+GET* **nyawoorroorroo**
gecko .... *noun masculine* **mendoowoony, moondoowoony**; *noun masculine* **nyigany**
  barking gecko .... *noun feminine* **bedarrel**
  knob-tailed gecko .... *noun feminine* **booyooj-booyoojgel, booyooj-booyoojjel, booyij-booyijgel**; *noun feminine* **booyoord-booyoordjil**
geebung
  (*Persoonia falcata*) ...... *noun masculine* **gantheliny**
generation, new .... *noun* **bardoongeny, bardoongel, bardoongem**
generational moiety ... *noun* **jarlinyjaroom, jarlinybaroom**
generator/electricity ... *noun* **ngerrenbe-boorroo**
generous .... *adjective* **jangarrgany, jangarrgal, jangarrgam**
get
  get angry .... *coverb+GO/COME* **ngarr**
  get astride .... *coverb+FALL/GO_DOWN* **barle**
  get big mob of something .... *coverb+GET* **gooroomboorrg**
  get burnt .... *coverb+BURN/BITE* **baberr**
  get close .... *coverb+FALL/GO_DOWN* **leb**
  get cooked .... *coverb+BURN/BITE* **baberr**
  get drunk .... *coverb+PUT* **winginig**
  get fish with grass and other plants .... *coverb+GET* **rawalgbany**
  get grey hair .... *coverb+GET* **boolganybany**
  get hot .... *coverb+SAY/DO_M* **boord**; *coverb+BURN/BITE* **loordboog**
  get married .... *coverb+BECOME* **ngaliba**
  get a fright .... *coverb+HIT* **lare**; *coverb+SAY/DO* **ngirlarr**
  get a fright/bad feeling . *coverb+GO/COME* **berrngerl**
  get in and go .... *coverb+GO/COME* **dagoorr**

go and get someone

get into something	*coverb+FALL/GO_DOWN* **dagoorr**
get into water	*coverb+FALL/GO_DOWN* **nyirreg**
get lost	*coverb+FALL/GO_DOWN* **wangarrag**
get lumps out of something (e.g. ash, ochre)	*coverb+SAY/DO* **darda-darda**
get on lap	*coverb+FALL/GO_DOWN* **jamoorrg**
get on shoulders	*coverb+FALL/GO_DOWN* **barle**
get really soft (meat)	*coverb+BURN/BITE* **nyangoolyoo-ngoolyoog**
get rubbish out of something, e.g. ash, ochre, ground up food	*coverb+GET* **therra-therra**
get stuck	*coverb+FALL/GO_DOWN* **larr**
get stuck in mind	*coverb+FALL/GO_DOWN* **darrngig**
get stuck up high	*coverb+BURN/BITE_REFL* **dard**
get stuck / tangled up	*coverb+GO/COME* **dardbany**
get things ready for an event	*coverb+SAY/DO* **jama**; *coverb+GET* **ngooloongooloomenbe**
get together	*coverb+WOUND_REFL* **narloob**
get up	*coverb+BE/STAY* **berdij**; *coverb+SAY/DO* **berdi-berdij**; *coverb+SAY/DO* **berdij**
get up early	*coverb+GO/COME* **yilib**
get up/be reborn	*coverb+SAY/DO* **baward**
getting dark	*coverb+FALL/GO_DOWN* **mawoorrboonybe**
ghost	*noun* **joowarriny, joowarril**; *noun* **nyaarrji, nyaarrel**
ghost, big-foot	*noun masculine* **yoonggoony**
ghost dog	*noun* **jarrinyin, jarrinyinji**; *noun* **mooloogoorrji**
ghost gum tree, white gum	*noun masculine* **warlarriny**
giant gudgeon, rock cod	*noun masculine* **nyagoornany**
gift	*noun* **boolbam**
Gija person	*noun* **Gijabany, Gijabal, Gijabam**
girl, little	*noun feminine* **goorndoogal**; *noun feminine* **jangadal** (Southern dialect); *noun feminine* **wanyagel**
little girl before puberty	*noun feminine* **goornawool**
girl with nice legs	*noun feminine* **dimboogalel**
give	*coverb+HIT* **waj**; *coverb+SAY/DO* **waj**; *coverb+SAY/DO_M* **waj**
give a drink	*coverb+HIT* **ngoorloorloog**
give a fright	*coverb+GET* **ngelyarr**
give a meal to someone	*coverb+GIVE M* **boorral**
give a shove	*coverb+PUT* **jarl**
give back	*coverb+GIVE* **biri**; *coverb+GIVE* **biriwoorrg**
give each other	*coverb+SAY/DO_REFL* **waj**
give up hope	*coverb+SAY/PLACE_REFL* **nyoorl**
glad, feel	*coverb+SAY/DO_M* **nger**
glad inside, be	*coverb* **thamalarrg**
glance sideways at someone	*coverb+SPEAR* **ngirril**
glands in groin	*noun* **baljawoorroo**
glass	*noun* **mooloogoonbe**
Glass Hill	*noun* **Warnambany**
glasses, spectacles	*noun* **mooloogoon deg-girrem**
glow	*coverb+BE/STAY* **marrarab**; *noun* **marraram**
go across/meet	*coverb+BECOME* **werdag**
go along	
go along being greedy	*coverb+GO_ALONG* **marr-marr**
go along cutting	*coverb+GO_ALONG* **lagarrwany**
go along cutting/splitting	*coverb+GO_ALONG* **lagarr**
go along digging	*coverb+GO_ALONG* **jarrij**
go along drinking	*coverb+GO_ALONG* **ngoorloorloog**
go along eating	*coverb+GO_ALONG* **jang**
go along hanging on	*coverb+GO/COME* **rarrinybe**
go along hiding	*coverb+GO_ALONG* **merrerreb**
go along hitting	*coverb+HIT* **doojoodbany**
go along in waving line	*coverb+GO_ALONG* **warlarla**
go along listening	*coverb+GO_ALONG* **rangga-rangga**
go along looking	*coverb+GO_ALONG* **deg**
go along looking back	*coverb+GO/COME* **wadboo-wadboo**
go along staring	*coverb+GO/COME* **lang**
go along throwing spears	*coverb+GO_ALONG* **werndij**
go along tipping out	*coverb+GO_ALONG* **warranyja**
go along waving	*coverb+GO_ALONG* **mangan-mangan**
go and cut	*coverb+GO/COME* **getherd**
go and get someone	*coverb+FALL/GO_DOWN* **warnngemaj**

go and leave

go and leave
  (plural subject) .... *coverb+GO/COME* **berrawoog**
go and leave someone
  (plural subject) .... *coverb+LEAVE* **berrawoog**
go and stay for a
  long time .... *coverb+GO/COME* **nyenberrg**
go around .... *coverb+FALL/GO_DOWN* **ged**
  go around and around
    being dizzy .... *coverb+GO_ALONG* **wingini**
go away .... *coverb+GO/COME* **marra**;
                              coverb+GO/COME **marrarn**
  go away for a
    long time .... *coverb+GO/COME* **nyirl**
  go away and leave .... *coverb+LEAVE* **marrarn**
                              coverb+LEAVE **barlberr**
  go away and leave
    someone .... *coverb+LEAVE* **marra**
  go away turning back
    on someone/action ...... *coverb+GO/COME* **thoolngoorroo**
go backwards .... *coverb+GO/COME* **rerreg**
go bad .... *coverb+GET* **nhoowooljiny**;
                              coverb+GO/COME **nhoowoolgbany**
go behind tree .... *coverb+FALL/GO_DOWN* **geren**;
                              coverb+FALL/GO_DOWN **laberd**
go blue/green (meat) ...... *coverb+BECOME* **girliny-girliny**
go calling out .... *coverb+GO_ALONG* **bawoo**
go camping out .... *coverb+BECOME* **derrerreb**;
                              coverb+GO_ALONG **derrerreb**;
                              coverb+GO/COME **derrerrebany**;
                              coverb+SAY/DO_M **derrerreb**
go different way .... *coverb* **yoorl**
  go different ways,
    split up .... *coverb+DO_REFL* **barlberr**
go down .... *coverb+FALL/GO_DOWN* **thood**
  go down (sun) .... *coverb+FALL/GO_DOWN* **therrij, therrijboo**
  go down and fill .... *coverb+FALL/GO_DOWN* **jamboorn**
go far .... *coverb+GO/COME* **woorrij**
go get them .... *interjection* **boorlbawoog**
go grey .... *coverb+GET* **langgenybany**
go hunting .... *coverb+HIT* **bardgi**
                              coverb+GO/COME **bardgiwany**;
                              coverb+GO/COME **nyalalawany**;
                              coverb+SAY/DO_M **barda-wardaj**;
                              coverb+GO/COME **joogboo**;
                              coverb+GO/COME **joogbany**

go in .... *coverb+FALL/GO_DOWN* **walig**;
                              coverb+GO_BECOME **walig**;
                              coverb+GO/COME **walig**;
                              coverb+GO/COME **walilig**;
                              coverb+SAY/DO_M **walilig**
  go in crowd .... *coverb+GO/COME* **leb-leb**
  go in line .... *coverb+GO/COME* **doorib**
  go into hole
    (e.g. goanna) .... *coverb+DO_REFL* **nhiny**;
                              coverb+SAY/PLACE_REFL **therramij**
  make someone go in .... *coverb+HIT* **walige**
go looking for .... *coverb+GO/COME* **biya**;
                              coverb+GO/COME **biyawany**
go miles and miles .... *adverb* **gamberarra-gamberarra**
go naked .... *coverb+GO/COME* **loonggaya**
go north .... *coverb+FALL/GO_DOWN* **boowoorroogoob**
go off in a huff .... *coverb+GO/COME* **ngarr**
go out, fire .... *coverb+FALL/GO_DOWN* **thoomooj**
go out together in
  back of truck .... *coverb+GO/COME* **janbaroorrg**
go past .... *coverb+GO/COME* **beraj**;
                              coverb+HIT **marraj**
  go past something .... *coverb+HIT* **beraj**
go right away .... *coverb+GO/COME* **birraroob**
go around and around,
  make .... *coverb+GET* **ged-gedgoowany**
go around corner .... *coverb+FALL/GO_DOWN* **waman**
go running .... *coverb+BE/STAY* **wijiwany**
go saying
  'gelyeg-gelyeg' .... *coverb+GO_ALONG* **gelyeg-gelyeg**
go sneaking around ...... *coverb+GO_ALONG* **mari-mari**
go somewhere .... *coverb+GO/COME* **garnawarrab**
go swimming .... *coverb+FALL/GO_DOWN* **nyirreg**
go through .... *coverb+GO/COME* **thoorrbool**
  be unable to go
    through .... *coverb+SAY/DO* **thoolg**
  go through gap
    between hills .... *coverb+SAY/DO* **doomboo-doomboo**
  go through gaps in
    the hills .... *coverb+SAY/DO_M* **doomboo-roombool**
go together in
  one line .... *coverb+SAY/DO* **joorroob**;
                              coverb+SAY/DO_M **joorroob**
go up and down,
  many .... *coverb+SAY/DO* **goongarr**

go up and down the same track every day	*coverb+SAY/DO* **thoowool, thoowool-thoowool**
go up high	*coverb+GO/COME* **gawarab**
go up to the end of the river, go right to the top of the hill or tree	*coverb+GO/COME* **jabig**
go very far	*adverb* **gamberarra-gamberarra**
go while it is getting dark	*coverb+GO/COME* **garrwaroowany**
go with head one side	*coverb+GO/COME* **lig**
goanna	*noun masculine* **ganyarrany**; *noun masculine* **garndoowoolany**; *noun masculine* **jarrambayiny**
a goanna species	*noun masculine* **gariyaliny**
female goanna	*noun feminine* **thoogool**
hill country goanna	*noun masculine* **boonoonggoony**
rasp-tailed goanna	*noun masculine* **gilbany**
spotted tree goanna	*noun feminine* **bardil**; *noun feminine* **bijil**
water goanna	*noun masculine* **wigamany**
water goanna species (mother of *wigamany*)	*noun feminine* **goorlawoorlal**
small species of goanna	*noun masculine* **goordiny**; *noun masculine* **nganyjalany**
very small species of goanna	*noun masculine* **jangalangalany**; *noun masculine* **lirri-lirriny**
goanna tail, tip of	*noun* **nyiwirle**
goat	*noun feminine* **miyinggajil**
gobble	*coverb+SAY/DO_M* **mangoony**
going in (plural)	*coverb+FALL/GO_DOWN* **waliligboo**
going along, knock down	*coverb+HIT* **derinyberrwany**
gold, alluvial	*noun feminine* **ngarrgalel**
gone, be	*coverb+SAY/DO_M* **ngoowag**
good	*adjective* **men'gawoony, men'gawool, men'gawoom**
be good	*coverb+BE/STAY* **men'gawiya**
be made good	*coverb+SAY/DO_M* **men'gawoog**
become good	*coverb+BECOME* **men'gawoo**; *coverb+SAY/DO* **men'gawoo**
make good	*coverb+GET* **men'gawoog**; *coverb+HIT* **men'gawoog**
make self good	*coverb+SAY/DO_REFL* **men'gawoog**
good at something	*adjective* **ngelgany, ngelgal**; *adjective* **nyarlany, nyarlal**
good at finding meat	*adjective* **moonthoorroogaleny, moonthoorroogalel, moonthoorroogalem**
good at getting bush honey, woman who is	*noun feminine* **ngaregalel**
good at making sound by clapping thighs	*adjective* **derlawoog-galem**
woman who is good at blocking blows with nulla-nulla	*noun feminine* **goowarrigalel**
good cook	*noun* **mayigalel, mayigaleny, mayigalem**
good-looking	*adjective* **doordoogany, doordoogal**; *adjective* **jarloongoorroony, jarloongoorrool, jarloongoorroom**; *adjective* **joornanygarreny, joornanygarrel, joornanygarrem**
make good-looking	*coverb+DO_REFL* **joornanygarreg**; *coverb+SAY/DO* **doordoog**
good shot	*adverb* **yilgiya**
good singer	*noun* **ngalanygaleny, ngalanygalel, ngalanygalem**
good size	*coverb+BE/STAY* **ngarrjan**
goodbye, be saying	*coverb+SAY/DO_M* **mathe-mathe**
goodness	*interjection* **marri**; *interjection* **warda**
goodness me	*interjection* **winggernanggoo**
goose, green pigmy	*noun feminine* **nyiman'gool**
goose, magpie	*noun* **ngarlagangarril, ngarlagangarriny**
goosebumps, have	*coverb+SAY/DO* **rawoorl**
goosebumps, give someone	*coverb+HIT* **goon'gany-goon'gany**; *coverb+GET* **rawoorlgoowany**
gorge	*noun* **derrgerne**; *noun* **tharreyimerle**
goshawk, grey	*noun masculine* **warliberawoony, warliny**
grab	*coverb+GET* **gamboord**; *coverb+PUT* **gamboord**
grab from each other	*coverb+DO_REFL* **marlalji**; *coverb+SAY/DO_REFL* **thoorroobji**
grab from two sides	*coverb+BRING/TAKE* **nyirrng**

granddaughter (man's daughter's daughter)

granddaughter (man's daughter's daughter)..*noun feminine* **thamanyel, thamanybe**

granddaughter (man's son's daughter)..........*noun feminine* **gelaagil, gelaagim**

granddaughter (woman's daughter's daughter)....................*noun feminine* **ganggal, ganggam**

granddaughter (woman's daughter's son)..........*noun feminnine* **ngawoojil**

grandfather (father's father)..........*noun masculine* **gelaaginy, gelaagim**

grandfather (mother's father)........*noun masculine* **thamanyji, thamanybe**

grandfather's sister (father's father's sister).........................*noun feminine* **gelaagil, gelaagim**

grandfather's sister (mother's father's sister).........................*noun feminine* **thamanyel, thamanybe**

grandmother (father's mother)........*noun feminine* **ngawoojil, ngawoojim**

grandmother (father's mother; spoken to).......*noun feminine* **ngawooji**

grandmother (mother's mother).....*noun feminine* **ganggal, ganggam**

grandmother's brother (father's mother's brother)......................*noun masculine* **ngawoojiny, ngawoojim**

grandmother's brother (mother's mother's brother)......................*noun masculine* **ganggany, ganggam**

grandson (man's daughter's son)..........*noun masculine* **thamanyji, thamanybe**

grandson (man's son's son)...................*noun masculine* **gelaginy, gelagim; gelaaginy, gelaagim**

grandson (woman's daughter's son)..........*noun masculine* **ganggany, ganggam**

grandson (woman's son's son)....................*noun masculine* **ngawoojiny, ngawoojim**

granny..........................*noun* **ganggany, ganggal, ganggam**

granny (spoken to).......*noun* **ganggayi**

grass..............................*noun* **roorrany, roorram**

dry grass ....*noun* **minybernem**

grass with edible seeds, millet ....*noun* **wirlarrji**

green grass ....*noun* **majalji, majale;** *noun* **werrgalji, werrgale**

grass species that has sticks used for painting dots ....*noun masculine* **jarn'girriny**

itchy grass ....*noun masculine* **jardiny, jardinyji**

johnnycake grass..........*noun masculine* **wirlarrji**

long sugar grass...........*noun masculine* **gilemberrji**

tall grass species found near water, *Arundinella nepalensis*......................*noun masculine* **weleweny, weloowoony**

grass, get tangled up or trip over in ....*coverb+GO/COME* **rardbany**

grass, hide in.................*coverb+FALL/GO_DOWN* **yab**

grass, pull up ....*coverb+GET* **ngoojoorr-ngoojoorr;** *coverb+SAY/DO* **ral**

grass yam ....*noun masculine* **nyoombany;** *noun masculine* **yoombany**

grass-leaf yam ....*noun masculine* **jawooloo-wooloony**

grasshopper..................*noun feminine* **birlbirljil** *noun* **girndilji**

grasshopper species with green and yellow stripes down its long body ....*noun feminine* **goorrandal, goorrarndal**

grasshopper species like *moorrgoony* but bigger ....*noun masculine* **janyoowoony**

green katydid grasshopper.................*noun feminine* **girinyil**

large grasshopper species seen in August..*noun masculine* **gelambawoony**

gum, edible

very large grasshopper species	*noun masculine* **malnginyji**
very small pretty grasshopper species	*noun masculine* **moorrgoony**
graveyard	*noun* **doorroom, doorroom-boorroo goonyingarre**
greedy	*adjective* **gerreleny, gerrelel**; *adjective* **gerreleginy**; *adjective* **gerrijbendeny, gerrijbendel, gerrijbendem**
be greedy	*coverb+SAY/DO* **ngala-ngala**; *coverb+SAY/DO_M* **ngala-ngala**; *coverb+SAY/DO* **warrmayi**; *coverb+SAY/DO_M* **warrmayi**
go along being greedy	*coverb+GO_ALONG* **marr-marr**
greedy wanting everything	*coverb+SAY/DO* **marr-marr**
green	*adjective* **werrgalji, werrgalel, werrgale**
become green	*coverb+BECOME* **werrgalwany**
green ant	*noun feminine* **minyal**; *noun* **waawal, wawalji, wawalel, wawale**
green ant nest	*noun* **wawarrel**
green grass	*noun* **majalji, majale**; *noun* **werrgalji, werrgale**
green pigmy goose	*noun feminine* **nyiman'gool**
green plant/vegetable	*noun* **werrgalji, werrgalel, werrgale**
green plum	*noun masculine* **daaloony**
green tree frog	*noun masculine* **laarn-ngarnany**
greenhide	*noun* **moogoonybe**
Greenvale	*noun* **Diringin**
grevillea, silver, *Grevillea refracta*	*noun masculine* **garndarndarrji**; *noun feminine* **tharriyarril**
Grewia species	*noun* **garrawiny**; *noun* **gawoorroony**; *noun* **ngoojal**; *noun* **ngoowardiny**
grey-crowned babbler	*noun feminine* **ganggangel**
grey hair	*noun* **boolgam**
get grey hair	*coverb+GET* **boolganybany**
go grey	*coverb+GET* **langgenybany**
grind	*coverb+GO_ALONG* **goodoo**; *coverb+PUT* **goodoo**; *coverb+SAY/DO_M* **goodoo-goodoo**
grind teeth	*coverb+SAY/DO* **dadigirrij**
grinder (workshop tool)	*noun* **boorr-boorrgirrem**
make grinding noise	*coverb+SAY/DO* **loorlgoodaj**
grindstone	*noun masculine* **goodoo-goodoogirriny**
grit teeth	*coverb+DO_REFL* **niny**
groin, glands in	*noun* **baljawoorroo**
groove, carved	*noun* **boonarram**
ground	*noun* **jilam**
boggy ground	*noun* **yawool-yawooloo**
flat ground	*noun* **balawam**; *noun* **balgam**
sandy ground	*noun* **woorrjininy**
ground black plum, big cake made of	*noun masculine* **nanggeriny**
ground, hit the	*coverb+BECOME* **dalyalya**
ground, hunting	*noun* **wiliwirrin**
ground, stab the	*coverb+GO_THROUGH* **jida-jida**; *coverb+SAY/DO* **jida**; *coverb+SAY/DO_M* **jida**
ground sugarbag	*noun masculine* **gayirriny**; *noun masculine* **boorrwoorrji**
ground-up	*adjective* **goodoongeny, goodoongel, goodoongem**
group, run/move around in a	*coverb+GO/COME* **rarrawoolib**
group stay together	*coverb+BE/STAY* **daminemenag**
grow	*coverb+BECOME* **doorloog**; *coverb+BECOME* **doorloorloog**; *coverb+GET* **bedawalge**; *coverb+GO/COME* **bedawalg**; *coverb+SAY/DO* **bedalg**; *coverb+SAY/DO* **nawarra**; *coverb+SAY/DO_M* **bed, bood**; *coverb+SAY/DO_M* **bedada, boodada**
grow flat (e.g. bush tobacco plant)	*coverb+FALL/GO_DOWN* **balg**
grow thickly	*coverb+SAY/DO_M* **berlgerren**
grow together	*coverb* **berr**
growl	*coverb+GO_ALONG* **ngoorr**; *coverb+SAY/DO* **ngoorr-ngoorr**
Growler Gully	*noun* **Garliwoorrangen**
grown up	*adjective* **garrayilji, garrayilel, garrayile**
grub, itchy	*noun masculine* **nyingginy**
grub, witchetty	*noun feminine* **lagarnel, lagarnbe**; *noun feminine* **lajel**
grumpy	*adjective* **jirninybiny, jirninybel, jirninybim**
gully/creek	*noun* **jarlanggam**
gum, edible	*noun* **nyaarndem**

gum from bloodwood

gum from bloodwood,
  tree species with
  edible gum .... *noun* **nyaarndiny;**
                                  noun **nyambarrginy;**
                                  noun **thaleginy;**
                                  noun masculine **warraroony**
gum from bloodwood,
  red .... *noun masculine* **galiwoony**
gum tree, cabbage,
  Corymbia species .... *noun masculine* **boonbany**
gum tree, river red,
  Eucalyptus
  camaldulensis .... *noun* **bilirnji, bilirnbe;**
                                  noun **garranggany**
gum tree, silver
  cabbage, *Eucalyptus*
  pruinosa .... *noun masculine* **linyjilji**
gum tree, snappy,
  Eucalyptus species ...... *noun masculine* **thalngarrji**
gush out (water) .... *coverb+SAY/DO* **nherraj**
gut something .... *coverb+HIT* **thenbel;**
                                  coverb+SAY/DO **thelbij;**
                                  coverb+SAY/DO_M **thelberr**
guts
  'big' guts .... *noun* **jaramberle**
  'inside' guts, large
    intestine .... *noun* **jaroom**
  'little round' guts .... *noun* **jangga-jangga**
  'long intestine', guts ..... *noun* **liyirrim**
  part of guts where food
    is minced up in bullock .. *noun* **boorrooloo**
'guts'
  (Kriol for stomach) ..... *noun* **jaam**
guts, feeling in .... *noun* **liyanbe**
guts, pull out .... *coverb+HIT* **thenbel;**
                                  coverb+SAY/DO **thelbij**

Hh

Hadler Spring .... *noun* **Jadibany**
hailstones .... *noun* **gerawarrel;**
                                  noun **gooroowarrbany**
hair .... *noun* **yambarram**
  armpit hair .... *noun* **yoorrwam, yoorram**
  blonde hair .... *adjective* **giwinarlany,**
                                  giwinarlal
  hair, grey hair .... *noun* **boolgam**
  pubic hair .... *noun* **ngoorroornbe**
hair standing on end .... *coverb+GO/COME* **joorarrg**
hair, comb own .... *coverb+DO_REFL* **jiyi**
hair, cut off own .... *coverb+CUT_REFL* **birlijig**
hair, cut off someone's . *coverb+HIT* **birlijig**
hair, pull out .... *coverb+GET* **ngooj;**
                                  coverb+GET
                                  ngoojoorr-ngoojoorr;
                                  coverb+SAY/DO_M **ngoojoorr**
hair, tie up .... *coverb+DO_REFL* **yambarn**
hair belt .... *noun* **goodam**
  carry something in
    hair belt .... *coverb+BRING/TAKE* **goorlgoon**
  put something in
    hair belt .... *coverb+PUT* **goorlgoon**
hair style,
  old fashioned .... *noun* **moordoorram**
hairy caterpillar .... *noun masculine* **nyingginy**
hairy
  (like an itchy grub) ..... *adjective* **nyinggiwoony,**
                                  nyinggiwool, nyinggiwoom
hairy man, big-foot ...... *noun masculine* **yoonggoony**
hairy water yam .... *noun* **yarrgalal, yarrgalany**
Haley's Comet .... *noun* **jiwibal, jiwibany**
half raw .... *adjective* **waltherre**
halfway from/to
  somewhere, get .... *coverb+HIT* **jalayi**
halfway, be .... *coverb+SAY/DO_M* **woorrgerne**
Halls Creek .... *noun* **Yarliyil**
hand .... *noun* **marlam**
  feel with hands .... *coverb+GET* **manymaj**
  hide face with hand ...... *coverb+SAY/PLACE_REFL* **booroo**
  scoop up with hand ...... *coverb+GET* **goorooj**
  put hands on someone . *coverb+GET* **mam**
  put hands on self to
    feel for something .... *coverb+SAY/DO_REFL* **manymaj**
handle .... *noun* **rarrim**
handsome .... *adjective* **doordoogany,**
                                  doordoogal;
                                  coverb+SAY/DO **doordoog**
hang on .... *coverb+SAY/DO_M* **rarrwayi**
hang up .... *coverb+PUT* **dard**
  hang something up ...... *coverb+PUT* **rarrwayi**
hanging .... *coverb+HIT* **rarriny**
  be hanging .... *coverb+BE/STAY* **rarriny;**
                                  coverb+BE/STAY **rarrwayi;**
                                  coverb+SAY/DO **rarre-rarriny;**
                                  coverb+SAY/DO **rarrinyboo**
  carry something
    hanging .... *coverb+BRING/TAKE* **rarrwayi;**
                                  coverb+SAY/DO **rarrwayi**
  hanging on side .... *coverb+BE/STAY* **lambood**
  hanging up .... *coverb+BE/STAY* **dard**
  have something
    hanging .... *coverb+GO AFTER* **rarrwayi**
hanging down, be .... *coverb+BE/STAY* **yalg-yalg**

hanging down loosely, arms	*coverb+BE/STAY* **yalg-yalg**
hanging down, hold something that is	*coverb+HAVE* **rarriny**
hanging on, go along	*coverb+GO/COME* **rarrinybe**
hangover, have a	*coverb+GO/COME* **joomboowoo**
Hann Spring	*noun* **Thawooloon**
happen upon someone/something suddenly	*coverb+GO/COME* **ngag**
happy	*adjective* **gooloo-gooloowoony, gooloo-gooloowool, gooloo-gooloowoom**
be happy	*coverb+SAY/DO* **gooloo-gooloo**; *coverb+SAY/DO_M* **gooloo, gooloo-gooloo**
be happy together	*coverb+SAY_REFL* **gooloowala**
make happy	*coverb+GET* **gooloogoo**
make each other happy	*coverb+DO_REFL* **mool-moolji**
happy, new, young	*adjective* **gooloongarriny, gooloongarril, gooloongarrim**
hard	*adverb* **garda-gardawoo**
become hard	*coverb+BECOME* **bagarrji**
hard, strong	*adjective* **bagarrjiny, bagarrjil, bagarrjim**
hard with someone, be	*coverb+HIT* **bagarrji**
hare wallaby	*noun masculine* **yinameny**
hat	*noun feminine* **magardal**
hatch	*coverb+BE/STAY* **lerlg**
have a lot	*coverb+EAT* **noongoog**
have body part twitching because of a relation	*coverb+GO/COME* **jarrarrawoorl**
have buzzing in ears	*coverb+SAY/DO* **ngoorr**
have eye on someone	*coverb+GET* **derlmenyji**
have friends	*coverb+BECOME* **bethaban**
have funny feeling in ears	*coverb+SAY/DO* **nyin**
have goosebumps	*coverb+SAY/DO* **rawoorl**
have hangover	*coverb+GO/COME* **joomboowoo**
have headache	*coverb+SAY/DO* **lardbe**; *coverb+GO/COME* **lard**; *coverb+SAY/DO* **ngen**
have something in the mouth	*coverb+HAVE* **gered**
have stomach ache	*coverb+SAY/DO* **ngarr**
having sores	*adjective* **gajibany, gaji-gajibany**; *adjective* **gerrmabany**
having a foreskin (swearing)	*interjection* **bijabany**
having a shaved head	*adjective* **ngererrnginy, ngererrngil, ngererrngim**
having no friends or relations	*adjective* **liwaya-bawoorroony, liwaya-bawoorrool, liwaya-bawoorroom**
having no good legs	*adjective* **goomoorroony, goomoorrool, goomoorroom**
having no husband	*coverb* **ngoolngawoogbeliny**
having squinting eyes	*adjective* **yirranybeny, yirranybel, yirranybem**
having/knowing nothing	*adjective* **ngoowangarnany, ngoowangarnal, ngoowangarnam**
hawk/kite, type of	*noun masculine* **gardagarrji**
he/him	*pronoun* **nhawoon, nawoon**
he himself	*pronoun* **nhawoowarriny, nawoowarriny**
he himself, he in turn	*pronoun* **nhawany, nawany, nhawoowany, nawoowany**
he's the one	*demonstrative* **deyenya**
head	*noun* **doomoom**; *noun* **goonggooloom**
having shaved/ bald head	*adjective* **ngererrnginy**
hit each other over head	*coverb+WOUND_REFL* **nanbardi**
hit lightly on head	*coverb+HIT* **ding**
put head down	*coverb+PUT* **dareng**
head down	*coverb+BE/STAY* **joonbooroong**
shake head from side to side	*coverb+SAY/DO* **ngen-ngen**
head lice	*noun* **yiwiny, yiwim**
yellow-coloured head lice	*noun masculine* **yarlarliny**
head sideways	*coverb+BE/STAY* **lig**
head to one side	*adjective* **ligbayiny, ligbayil, ligbayim**
headache, have	*coverb+SAY/DO* **lardbe**; *coverb+GO/COME* **lard**; *coverb+SAY/DO* **ngen**
headband	*noun* **berndoowalem**
woman's headband	*noun* **jingirri-ngirrim**

headdress, paperbark

headdress, paperbark..*noun* **goomoonoongam**;
　　　　　　　　　　noun **goorlgoordoogoordoo**
heal ....*coverb+BECOME* **jarr**;
　　　　　　　　　　coverb+SAY/DO **jarr**
heap flood debris ....*coverb+PUT* **derlg**
heap up..........................*coverb+PUT* **jamboorn**;
　　　　　　　　　　coverb+PUT **joon'goo**;
　　　　　　　　　　coverb+SAY/DO_M
　　　　　　　　　　joon'goo-joon'goo
　big mob heap up ....*coverb+GO/COME* **daboorlg**
　heap up firewood ....*coverb+PUT* **jaleng**
　heap up in one place ....*coverb+PUT* **moondoorr**
heaped up ....*coverb+BE/STAY* **moondoorr**
　be heaped up ....*coverb+BE/STAY* **joon'goo**
hear................................*coverb+BRING/TAKE* **rangga**;
　　　　　　　　　　coverb+GET **rangga**;
　　　　　　　　　　coverb+SAY/DO **rangga**
　hear each other ....*coverb+SAY/DO_REFL* **rangga**
heart ....*noun* **doolboom**;
　　　　　　　　　　noun **dooloom**;
　　　　　　　　　　noun **giningim**
　have heart beating ....*coverb+SAY/DO* **berreg-berreg**
　heart throbbing.............*coverb* **dig-dig**;
　　　　　　　　　　coverb **doob-doob**
heat something ....*coverb+BURN/BITE* **jaa**
　put on fire to heat.........*coverb+PUT* **jaa**
heavy ....*adjective* **joomboony**,
　　　　　　　　　　joombool, joomboom
　be heavy.......................*coverb+BRING/TAKE* **joomboo**
heavy object, place.......*coverb+PLACE* **moord**
helicopter ....*noun feminine*
　　　　　　　　　　birrinyoowoorlel;
　　　　　　　　　　noun feminine **galayigajil**
help ....*coverb+PUT* **marlam**;
　　　　　　　　　　coverb+HIT **marlam**
　ask dreaming place
　for help........................*coverb+PUT* **goorara**
her
　all the things from her ..*pronoun* **ngalemelewam**
　her/she.........................*pronoun* **ngalen**
　her turn ....*pronoun* **ngalewany**
　hers...............................*possessive pronoun*
　　　　　　　　　　ngaliyangeny, ngaliyangel,
　　　　　　　　　　ngaliyangem
　herself..........................*pronoun* **ngalewarriny**;
　　　　　　　　　　pronoun **ngalewany**
　for her ....*benefactive enclitic pronoun*
　　　　　　　　　　-ngooyoo
　from/after/because
　of her............................*ablative enclitic pronoun* **-ngiyiwa**

　to her............................*indirect object enclitic pronoun*
　　　　　　　　　　-ngiyi
　with her ....*commitative enclitic pronoun*
　　　　　　　　　　-ngiyab
herb species,
　strong-smelling..........*noun masculine* **gooroongoony**
here................................*demonstrative* **berrem,**
　　　　　　　　　　berrewam;
　　　　　　　　　　demonstrative **birriyam**;
　　　　　　　　　　demonstrative **gayana**;
　　　　　　　　　　demonstrative **ngenengga,**
　　　　　　　　　　ngenega
heron, white-faced.......*noun masculine* **ginyany**
heron, white-necked ....*noun masculine* **binggoo-**
　　　　　　　　　　binggoony
hey ....*interjection* **marri**;
　　　　　　　　　　interjection **ngayi**;
　　　　　　　　　　interjection **wa**;
　　　　　　　　　　interjection **wela**
hiccups, have ....*coverb+SAY/DO* **lengag**
hiccups, get...................*coverb+EAT* **lengagge**
hide ....*coverb+BE/STAY* **merreb**;
　　　　　　　　　　coverb+FALL/GO_DOWN **merreb**;
　　　　　　　　　　coverb+FALL/GO_DOWN
　　　　　　　　　　moorndoog;
　　　　　　　　　　coverb+SAY/DO_M **merre-merreb**;
　　　　　　　　　　noun **wangarrem**
　carry something
　hidden ....*coverb+BRING/TAKE* **booroo**
　hide behind ....*coverb+FALL/GO_DOWN* **dern**
　hide face with hand ......*coverb+SAY/PLACE_REFL* **booroo**
　hide in grass ....*coverb+FALL/GO_DOWN* **yab**
　hide self.......................*coverb+PUT SELF* **merrerrebbe**
　hide something ....*coverb+PUT* **booroo**;
　　　　　　　　　　coverb+PUT **doorroon**;
　　　　　　　　　　coverb+PUT **merreb**;
　　　　　　　　　　coverb+PUT **moorndoog**
　run and hide ....*coverb+FALL/GO_DOWN* **yirrberda**
hiding, be ....*coverb+BE/STAY* **merrerreb**;
　　　　　　　　　　coverb+SAY/DO_M **merrerreb**
hiding, go along ....*coverb+GO_ALONG* **merrerreb**
high as possible in
　a tree, go....................*coverb+GO/COME* **jabijbe**
high on top....................*locative* **wirli-wirlin**
high place, in a.............*locative* **gawarrangbiny**
high, go up ....*coverb+GO/COME* **gawarab**
high, up ....*locative* **laarne**
higher side, from the ...*directional* **gendayingibiny**
higher side, on the ....*directional* **gendayingen**
higher up (on tree
　or stick) ....*locative* **wirlibja**

hitting something, make sound by

hill .... noun **ngaarriny**;
                                     noun **ngarrgaleny, ngarrgalem**
   small round hill .... noun **goowaleny**
hill, along the side
   of .... *locative* **wayirran**
   go along side of hill ...... *coverb+GO/COME* **lambag, lamba-biny**
hill, side of .... *locative* **gawalalanygarre**;
                                    locative **lamban**
hill top
   be on top of a hill .... *coverb+BE/STAY* **garinybe**
   on top of the hills .... *locative* **wirli-wirlin**;
                                      locative **wirlinyin**
hill coming down to
   a point .... *coverb+BE/STAY* **nyoorrnga**
hill stretching out,
   be a .... *coverb+BE/STAY* **moorndood**
hill kangaroo, female ... *noun feminine* **barawool**
hill kangaroo,
   little male .... *noun masculine* **baloobanggoony**
hill kangaroo, male ...... *noun masculine* **jirrgany**;
                                    noun masculine **moordany**
him
   him/he .... *pronoun* **nhawoon**
   him only .... *pronoun* **nhawoomoowam**
   himself .... *pronoun* **nawiyan, nhawiyan**
   for him .... *benefactive enclitic pronoun* **-noong, noongoo**
   from/after/because
     of him .... *ablative enclitic pronoun* **-noowa**
   to him .... *indirect object enclitic pronoun* **-ni, -ningi**
   with him .... *commitative enclitic pronoun* **-niyab**
hip .... *noun* **merandam**
his .... *possessive pronoun* **nhawiyangeny, nhawiyangel, nhawiyangem**
   his turn .... *pronoun* **nhawoowany**;
                                  pronoun **nhawoowarriny**

hit .... *coverb+BRING/TAKE* **warrmaj**;
                                     coverb+GET **doojood**;
                                     coverb+HIT **dawarr**;
                                     coverb+HIT **doog**;
                                     coverb+HIT **doojood**;
                                     coverb+HIT **men'gerr**;
                                     coverb+HIT **thawoorr**;
                                     coverb+HIT **thedbany**;
                                     coverb+SAY/DO_M **dagidji**;
                                     coverb+SAY/DO_M **dawarr**;
                                     coverb+SAY/DO_M **thedji**
   be about to hit .... *coverb+GET* **mad**
   hit in eye .... *coverb+HIT* **darlg**
   hit lightly on head .... *coverb+HIT* **ding**
   hit on head .... *coverb+HIT* **dalooj**
   hit self .... *coverb+DO_REFL* **dawarr**
   hit someone/
     something .... *coverb+HIT* **therlad**
   hit stick on stick .... *coverb+HIT* **garn**
   hit the ground .... *coverb+BECOME* **dalyalya**
hit and kill .... *coverb+BECOME* **thed**;
                                     coverb+GO/COME **thed**;
                                     coverb+HIT **thed**;
                                     coverb+SAY/DO **thedji**;
                                     coverb+SAY/DO_M **thed**;
                                     coverb+WOUND **thed**
hit and killed .... *adjective* **thedgil, thedginy, thedgem**
hit each other .... *coverb+SAY/DO_REFL* **dawarr, dawarrji**
   hit each other
     over head .... *coverb+WOUND_REFL* **nanbardi**
hit by something, get ... *coverb+FALL/GO_DOWN* **therlad**
   get hit with something
     small like a stone .... *coverb+FALL/GO_DOWN* **nyirerrege**
hit with something .... *coverb+HIT* **tharn**
   hit someone with
     a stick .... *coverb+SAY/DO_M* **darroorl**;
                                     coverb+HIT **darroorl**
   hit tree with axe/rock .... *coverb+HIT* **doowoo**
   hit with something
     small like a stone .... *coverb+HIT* **nyirerrege**
hitting against
   something, kill by ...... *coverb+GET* **bareng**
hitting one stick down
   on the other, be .... *coverb+SAY/DO* **garn-garn**
hitting something,
   make sound by .... *coverb* **doowoog**
   good at making drum
   sound by hitting space
   between crossed legs ... *adjective* **barndawooggalim**

hitting, go along

hitting, go along	*coverb+HIT* **doojoodbany**
hoarse voice, having a	*adjective* **garengbeny, garengbel, garengbem**
hoarse voice, speak with a	*coverb+SAY/DO_M* **gareng**
hold in arms	*coverb+HAVE* **ngamanang**
hold on to someone/ something	*coverb+GET* **gerneg**
hold something	*coverb+HAVE* **gerneg**; *coverb+GET* **roo**
hold each other	*coverb+DO_REFL* **gerneg**
hold self	*coverb+DO_REFL* **roo**
hold something that is hanging down	*coverb+HAVE* **rarriny**
hole	*noun* **nawan, nawanji**; *noun* **thoorlngem**
deep hole	*noun* **dagoorlany, dagoorlan**
hole in bank	*noun* **nan'goon**
hole in ground used for cooking	*noun* **goorrgoom**
hole through a rock, be an opening like a window or a	*coverb+BE/STAY* **denggelalab**
hole through, make	*coverb+GO_THROUGH* **thoorl**
hole, fall in deep (e.g. car)	*coverb+FALL/GO_DOWN* **dagoorlaj**
hole, go into (e.g. goanna)	*coverb+DO_REFL* **nhiny**
hole, make deep	*coverb+GET* **dagoorlagbe**
hole, put in deep	*coverb+HIT* **dagoorlaj**
holes in something, make	*coverb+GET* **doongooroog**
hollow, valley	*noun* **yawilam**
hollow ground	*noun* **dagoorlam**
hollow log	*noun* **thaloorroony**; *noun* **thoondooloom**
hollow sound, make	*coverb+SAY/DO* **loorrloorrjaya**
home/camp/country	*noun* **daam**
honey	*noun* **girrangem**
bush honey	*noun* **ngarem, ngariny, ngarel**
woman who is good at getting bush honey	*noun feminine* **ngaregalel**
honey, suck	*coverb+PUT* **mengelarr**
suck off honey	*coverb+GET* **janaj**; *coverb+PUT* **janaj**
hook	*noun* **nyarlanam**; *noun* **yarn'gal**
hook on woomera	*noun masculine* **mirlirdiny**
hook spear	*noun* **tharrimin**
hook something up	*coverb+PUT* **garayil**
hook up fish	*coverb+GET* **yan'gag**
stick used to hook up fish	*noun* **yan'gam**
hook up spear in woomera	*coverb+GET* **thalg**
hooked stick	*noun* **nyanggernam**
hornet species	*noun masculine* **boorrngoornji, boorrngoornngoornji, boorrngoorrngooroony**
horny, sexy	*adjective* **yigarrwoony, yigarrwool, yigarrwoom**; *adjective* **yoowarroony, yoowarrool, yoowarroom**
horrible	*adjective* **jigiliny, jigilil, jigilim**
horse	*noun masculine* **dimanany**; *noun masculine* **yawardany**
trot along on horse	*coverb+GO/COME* **joog-joog**
hot	*adjective* **loordbeny, loordbel, loordbem**; *adjective* **marnebam**
become hot	*coverb+BECOME* **loordbe**; *coverb+BECOME* **barndiny**
feel hot	*coverb+SAY/DO* **boorn**
get hot	*coverb+BURN/BITE* **loordboog**
hot time	*temporal* **boornmarrwoon**
be hot time of day	*coverb+FALL/GO_DOWN* **nyare**
hot season	*temporal* **barnden**; *temporal* **malwalan**
hot time (when people depend on 'living' water)	*temporal* **barranggan**
hot ashes spread out to cook something	*coverb+PUT* **garayarr**
hot dirt	*noun* **gernjile**; *noun* **maram**
hot dirt/sand	*noun* **maram**
hot stones	*noun* **garanybe**
hot, very	*adjective* **dooboorrngbeny, dooboorrngbel, dooboorrngbem**
house	*noun* **mayaroony, mayaroom**
how?	*interrogative* **gaboojana**
how many?, how much?	*interrogative* **gaboongerreg**
howl	*coverb+SAY/DO* **moowoog**
hug each other	*coverb+SAY/DO_REFL* **boorroongoo**
humbugged (pushed) to do something, be	*coverb+SAY/DO* **nyirli-nyirli**
humbug someone	*coverb+GET* **berinyge**; *coverb+GET* **nyirle-nyirleg**

inspect species

humbug (push) someone to do something, people who ....*adjective* **nyirli-nyirliwoom**
humourless ....*adjective* **barlij-bawoorroony, barlij-bawoorrool**
hungry ....*adjective* **goorninyany, goorninyal, goorninyam**
  be hungry ....*coverb+SAY/DO* **goorninya**
  make hungry ....*coverb+GET* **goorninyag**
  make self hungry ......*coverb+FALL/GO_DOWN* **goorninyag**
hunt at night ....*coverb+GO_ALONG* **jana**
hunt/hit something, try to ....*coverb+FALL/GO_DOWN* **wili**
hunt/try to hit/ round up ....*coverb+PUT* **wililib**
hunting, go ....*coverb+SAY/DO_M* **barda-wardaj;**
                     coverb+GO/COME **bardgiwany;**
                     coverb+GO/COME **joogboo, joogbany;**
                     coverb+GO/COME **nyalalawany**
  take dogs hunting ......*coverb* **werna-werna**
hunting ground ....*noun* **wiliwirrin**
hurry ....*coverb+SAY/DO* **magoo-magoo**
  be in a hurry ....*coverb+BE/STAY* **garrany**
  hurry after ....*coverb+GO/COME* **thewerr**
hurt self ....*coverb+FALL/GO_DOWN* **geberd**
  fall and hurt self ....*coverb+FALL/GO_DOWN* **mirl-mirlge;**
                     coverb+FALL/GO_DOWN **thalijbel**
hurting, be ....*coverb+SAY/DO* **majarr;**
                     coverb+SAY/DO **mirl-mirl;**
                     coverb+SAY/DO **woorrngoord**
husband ....*noun masculine* **ngoolngany**
husband stealer ....*noun feminine* **ginyirril**

I i

I/me SEE me/I
I'm the one ....*pronoun* **ngayana**
I see! ....*interjection* **nga**
ibis ....*noun masculine* **jandiyandiny;**
                     noun feminine **joodoojgajil**
idea ....*noun* **rinyiny**
ignore, disbelieve ....*coverb+HIT* **bany**
ignore requests, someone who does ....*adjective* **garlabawoorroony, garlabawoorrool, garlabawoorroom**
imitate ....*coverb+HIT* **madi;**
                     coverb+SAY/DO **madi**

immediately ....*adverb* **joodiya**
imperative ....*suffix* **-gala, -gela**
important ....*adjective* **nawarrany, nawarral, nawarram**
  be important ....*coverb+BE/STAY* **nawarra**
  important person ....*noun* **manambarrany, manambarral, manambarram**
in the east ....*directional* **ngelmin**
in the north ....*directional* **biyirrin**
in the south ....*directional* **ngerijin**
in the west ....*directional* **gerlirrin**
inhale aroma ....*coverb* **yirrinyngoorlg**
injection ....*noun* **goorloorrgirrem**
insect bite, swell from ..*coverb+GO/COME* **loob-loob**
insect species
  beetle ....*noun masculine* **landiny**
  blowfly ....*noun masculine* **werreralji, werreralel, werrerrale**
  butterfly, moth (can be swearing) ....*noun feminine* **warlimarrgool**
  caterpillar ....*noun feminine* **booboogarral;**
                 noun **joombayiny, joombayil**
  centipede ....*noun masculine* **birrgoolany**
  cicada ....*noun feminine* **lirrinil**
  dragonfly ....*noun masculine* **birrinyoowoorlji**
  earwig ....*noun feminine* **gibigel**
  firefly ....*noun feminine* **ngoorrwangarnal**
  fly ....*coverb+GO/COME* **doowab;**
                 noun feminine **boornool, boornoom;**
                 noun masculine **boornoongiliwoony**
  gall insect ....*noun* **barlabil;**
                 noun **gerdadal**
  grasshopper ....*noun feminine* **birlbirljil;**
                 noun **girndilji**
  grasshopper, green katydid ....*noun feminine* **girinyil**
  grasshopper species with green and yellow stripes down its long body ....*noun feminine* **goorrandal, goorrarndal**
  grasshopper species like *moorrgoony* but bigger ....*noun masculine* **janyoowoony**
  grasshopper species seen in August, large ....*noun masculine* **gelambawoony**

inside

grasshopper species, very large	*noun masculine* **malnginyji**
grasshopper species, very small pretty	*noun masculine* **moorrgoony**
green ant	*noun feminine* **minyal**; *noun* **waawal, wawalji, wawalel, wawale**
ground-living sugarbag bee species	*noun masculine* **gayirriny**; *noun masculine* **boorrwoorrji**
head lice	*noun* **yiwiny, yiwim**
head lice, yellow-coloured	*noun masculine* **yarlarliny**
hairy caterpillar	*noun masculine* **nyingginy**
hornet species	*noun masculine* **boorrngoornji, boorrngoornngoornji, boorrngoorrngooroony**
kangaroo tick	*noun* **loorrma-loorrma**
katydid grasshopper	*noun feminine* **girinyil**
lerp species (sugar leaf)	*noun* **bin'gany**; *noun* **daliyany**; *noun masculine* **wanamarriny**; *noun* **warrayany, warrayiny**
maggots	*noun* **waanyim**
march fly (small black biting species)	*noun masculine* **goorrjalji**
moth, butterfly (can be swearing)	*noun feminine* **warlimarrgool**
native sugarbag bee	*noun* **moowany, moowal**
paper wasp, large	*noun feminine* **merrembernel**
sand wasp	*noun feminine* **ngirrngirril**
scorpion	*noun masculine* **galarrwoorany**
stick insect	*noun masculine* **boornarrany**
tick, small	*noun feminine* **birlinyil**
tick, big brown	*noun feminine* **wegerlel**
tick, big kangaroo	*noun* **loorrma-loorrma**; *noun feminine* **ngawooral**
tree-living sugarbag bee species	*noun feminine* **beranggool**; *noun masculine* **gerrayiny**; *noun masculine* **nhawiny**
wasp species	*noun masculine* **birrinyoorlji**
inside	*locative* **yiligin**
intestines, large	*noun* **jaroom**
intestines, long	*noun* **liyirrim**
introduce someone safely (e.g. to country)	*coverb+PUT* **mantha**
introduced safely, be (e.g. to country)	*coverb+FALL/GO_DOWN* **mantha**
iron spearhead	*noun* **jabirriny, jabirrim**
ironwood tree (only northern part of Gija country)	*noun* **berawooroony**
island, flat ground in river bed	*noun* **balawam**
Island Yard	*noun* **Mende-menden**
itchy, horny, sexy	*adjective* **yigarrwoony, yigarrwool, yigarrwoom**; *adjective* **yoowarroony, yoowarrool, yoowarroom**
itchy, be	*coverb+HIT* **yayi**
feel itchy	*coverb+SAY/DO* **yayi**

Jj

jabbing at	*coverb+GO_ALONG* **jagirr**
jabiru	*noun masculine* **yalarrngarnany**
jack, thing for lifting car	*noun* **jarrward-girrem**
Jack Yard	*noun* **Thamoorrmoorr**
Jack Flood (place)	*noun* **Garnkoorlbany**
jaw	*noun* **ngan'gerre**
jaw bone	*noun* **ngawalem**
jealous	*adjective* **gemerrem-nhawoony, gemerrem-nhawool, gemerrem-nhawoom**; *coverb+GET* **marroo**
be jealous	*coverb+SAY/DO* **dem-dem**; *coverb+SAY/DO_REFL* **derlaj**; *coverb* **marroo-marroo**; *coverb+SAY/DO* **marroo-marroo**; *coverb+SAY/DO_M* **moongoorr**
jealously attack	*coverb+HIT* **walaji**
jealously refuse to share	*coverb+GET* **moongoorr**
jealous way, speak behind someone's back in a	*coverb+PUT* **ngoon**
jealous talk about people behind their back	*noun* **ngoonbe**
Jeffrey Well	*noun* **Roorrany, Roorraroorrany**
jerry can	*noun phrase* **bajalarrim bijid-bijidbe-boorroo**
joey	*noun* **woonggariny**
jog along	*coverb+GO_ALONG* **garr-garr**
johnnycake grass	*noun masculine* **wirlarrji**

join spearhead to spear	coverb+GET **thoord**; coverb+SAY/DO_M **thoord-thoord**
join strips of something to make long	coverb+PUT **jererd**
join together (rivers)	coverb+WOUND_REFL **nalooga**
join/meet	coverb+HIT **jidi**
joke, one who does not/cannot	adjective **barlij-bawoorroony, barlij-bawoorrool**
jokes, make	coverb+GO_ALONG **barlij-barlij**
all make jokes together	coverb+SAY/DO_REFL **barlijgoowool**
make jokes together	coverb+SAY/DO_REFL **birriman**
joking	adjective **barlijbeny, barlijbel, barlijbem**
be joking together	coverb+SAY/DO_REFL **barlij**
joking words	noun **barlijbem**
juice/liquid, suck up	coverb+SAY/DO_M **yinyeg**
juice of meat	noun **wooroom**; coverb+SAY/DO **yinyeg**
jump	coverb+BE/STAY **jarrg**
be jumping (plural)	coverb+SAY/DO **jarrgooroog**
jump about	coverb+SAY/DO **bard-bard**
jump and bite	coverb+FALL/GO_DOWN **jarrbird**
jump down	coverb+SAY/DO **jarrg**
jump in water	coverb+FALL/GO_DOWN **jirlbeg**
jump/get down/cross over	coverb+FALL/GO_DOWN **jarrg**
junction	noun **balmendoowoom**
form junction with another river	coverb+SAY/DO **balmendeg**
just	conjunctive particle **gooma**; particle **googan**; particle **goo, goowoo**; particle **miya**
just as	conjunctive particle **gooma**
just emerging	coverb+BECOME **doolgboo**

Kk

kangaroo (generic)	noun **jiyirriny, jiyirrel, jiyirrem**
baby kangaroo (joey)	noun **woonggariny**
big red kangaroo	noun masculine **wawirriny**
female hill kangaroo	noun feminine **barawool**
female plains kangaroo	noun feminine **gawoorrngarndil**
little male hill kangaroo	noun masculine **baloobanggoony**
male hill kangaroo	noun masculine **jirrgany**; noun masculine **moordany**
plains kangaroo	noun masculine **jarlangarnany**; noun masculine **warlambany**
kangaroo pouch	noun **ngaroom**
kangaroo tail sausage	noun **goorlany**
kangaroo tick	noun **loorrma-loorrma**
kangaroo, top half of	noun masculine **dawoorrji**
kapok bush	noun feminine **goonjal**
kapok bush, furry-leaved	noun masculine **malanyjarrji**; noun masculine **ngalwany**; noun feminine **warndiwal**
kapok bush, round fluffy seed pods of	noun **booboogarral**
katydid grasshopper	noun feminine **girinyil**
keep doing something	coverb+SAY/DO_M **yirri-yirri**
keep for oneself	coverb+GET **marroo**; coverb+SAY/DO **dangoori**
keep in mind	coverb **dalberr**
keep looking at someone	coverb+GO/COME **lerrma**
keep something while kneeling down	coverb+HAVE **yerderrwany**
keep still	coverb+GO/COME **gerrji**
keep talking loudly	coverb+SAY/DO_M **delanggerr**
keep up with	adverb **jooliya**
kerosene wood tree, *Erythroxylum ellipticum*	noun feminine **mindi-mindil**
kestrel, nankeen	noun masculine **gardagarrji**; noun femininine **marl-marlel**; noun feminine **marrg-marrgjil**; noun masculine **waaliny**
key	noun **nyarlarlam**
car key	noun **nyarlarlam ngoorrngoorrool-ngooyoo**; noun **ngoorrngoorrge-girrem**
kick someone/something	coverb+HIT **berd**
kick something accidentally	coverb+FALL/GO_DOWN **berd**; coverb+FALL/GO_DOWN **nyalg**
kidney	noun **werlmerrem, wirlmerrem**
Kilfoyle's Yard	noun **Yoonoorr**
kill	coverb **goonyingarrg**; coverb+GET **nanggegboo**; coverb+GET **thedji**; coverb+GO_ALONG **thedji**; coverb+HIT **nanggeg**

kill, knock down

kill many	*coverb+WOUND* **goord**
kill many at once	*coverb+GET* **goord**;
	coverb+HIT **goord**
kill parent and child together	*coverb* **barlegboo**
kill self	*coverb+CUT_SELF* **thed**
kill with one blow	*coverb+SAY/DO_M* **jin'gerdi**
kill by hitting against something	*coverb+GET* **bareng**
kill by spearing	*coverb+SPEAR* **nang**
race up and kill someone	*coverb+HIT* **galaleb**
kill, knock down	*coverb+HIT* **nanggeg**
kill each other	*coverb+SAY_REFL* **mawoo-mawoonde**;
	coverb+SAY/DO_REFL **thedji**
kill each other, many	*coverb+WOUND_REFL* **goord**
killed, hit and	*adjective* **thedgil, thedginy, thedgem**
killer	*noun* **tharranggal**
kindling	*noun* **marloorloom**
king brown snake	*noun masculine* **lan'gerrji**;
	noun masculine **loonboorroony**
kingfisher	*noun feminine* **jigerrel**
kino, bloodwood gum	*noun masculine* **galiwoony**
kiss each other	*coverb+SAY/DO_REFL* **boony-boony**
kiss someone	*coverb+PUT* **boony**;
	coverb+HIT **thoong**
kite, fork-tailed	*noun masculine* **ganjalji**
kite, whistling	*noun* **booloogool**
knead	*coverb+SAY/DO_M* **goodaj**
	coverb+GET **goodaj-goodaj**
knee	*noun* **manyjoorroo**
be no good in the knee	*coverb+BECOME* **bilgbayi**
having a bad knee	*adjective* **bilgbayiny, bilgbayil, bilgbayim**
knee-cap	*noun* **bilim**
kneel down	*coverb+FALL/GO_DOWN* **nadiling**;
	coverb+FALL/GO_DOWN **yerderr**
kneeling down, keep something while	*coverb+HAVE* **yerderrwany**
kneeling down, someone who is	*adjective* **yerderrwanybeny, yerderrwanybel, yerderrwanybem**
kneeling down, be	*coverb+BE/STAY* **balmarr**;
	coverb+BE/STAY **nadiling**
knife	*noun masculine* **barrajgajiny**;
	noun masculine **begerrgajiny**;
	noun masculine **gerrbijgajiny**
knock back, reject	*coverb+SAY/DO* **garn'garr**
knock down	*coverb+GET* **doombaj**;
	coverb+HIT **nanggeg**;
	coverb+HIT **woonboorr**;
	coverb+HIT **woor**;
	coverb+SAY/DO_M **woonboorr**
knock down going along	*coverb+HIT* **derinyberrwany**
knock down, kill	*coverb+HIT* **nanggeg**
knock someone into water	*coverb+HIT* **nyoomoog**
knock something (e.g. flying fox) and cut off head	*coverb* **goorrjib**
knocked down, be	*coverb+FALL/GO_DOWN* **derinyberrwany**
knocking down, go along	*coverb+GO_ALONG* **woonboorr**
know	*coverb+GET* **ngoongoo**;
	coverb+SAY/DO_M **ngarra**
not know	*coverb+HIT* **ganginy**
know each other	*coverb+DO_REFL* **ngarra**
know someone/something	*coverb+GET* **ngarra**
knowing	*adjective* **binarriny, binarril, binarrim**
not knowing	*adjective* **binarri-woorroony, binarri-woorrool, binarri-woorroom**
knowing nothing	*adjective* **birawoo**;
	adjective **ngoowangarnany, ngoowangarnal, ngoowangarnam**
koel	*noun* **doowageny**
female koel	*noun* **girlgoowal**
konkerberry	*noun masculine* **biriyalji**
kookaburra	*noun* **jawoorroony, jawoorrool**
kurrajong species	
Brachychiton diversifolius	*noun masculine* **werlalji**
Brachychiton fitzgeraldianus	*noun masculine* **banjaroony**
red-flowered, Brachychiton viscidulus	*noun masculine* **dayimbalji**
	noun masculine **therranggelji**

LI

labia (swearing)	*noun feminine* **ngooboongool**
ladder, magic	*noun masculine* **barrgoorany**
land	*coverb+FALL/GO_DOWN* **barr**

Leichhardt tree

landing, be	*coverb+SAY/DO* **barre-warre**
land snail	*noun* **barlilmal**
language	*noun* **jarragbe, jarragboo**
speak language	*coverb+GO_ALONG* **jarrag**
language name	*noun* **Gija**;
	noun **Goowoorrinyji**;
	noun **Jaru, Jaroo**;
	noun **Malngin**;
	noun **Miriwoong**;
	noun **Worla**
Lansdowne	*noun* **Garragin**
lap	*noun* **birrmale**;
	noun **jamoorr**
get on lap	*coverb+FALL/GO_DOWN* **jamoorrg**
put on lap (e.g. child)	*coverb+PUT* **jamoorrg**
large eel-tailed catfish	*noun masculine* **woorlengerriny**
large fork-tailed catfish	*noun masculine* **dalinyji**
larvae, antbed	*noun feminine* **ngawagool**
last one	*noun* **jiroo-girrim**
late	*adverb* **bardoo-bardoo**
late afternoon	*temporal* **ngoolooo-ngooliyan**
later	*adverb* **gara**;
	temporal **gerag**;
	temporal **ngarriwarloon**
laugh	*coverb+SAY/DO* **garl-garl**
laugh and make noise together	*coverb+SAY/DO_REFL* **yayiggoolg**
laugh at each other	*coverb+SAY/DO_REFL* **garl-garl**
make someone laugh	*coverb+GET* **garl-garlge**
one who doesn't laugh	*adjective* **garl-garl-bawoorroony**
law man or woman	*noun* **manambarrany, manambarral, manambarram**
lay eggs	*coverb+SAY/DO* **joorrooji**
lazy	*adjective* **ngamarrwoony, ngamarrwool**;
	coverb+SAY/DO_M **ngamarr**;
	adjective **wanggarlwoony, wanggarlwool, wanggarlwoom**;
	adjective **warrgam-bawoorroony, warrgam-bawoorrool, warrgam-bawoorroom**;
	adjective **yilingarriny, yilingarril, yilingarrim**;
	coverb+SAY/DO **wanggarl**
leader	*noun* **manambarrany, manambarral, manambarram**
leafy branches	*noun* **ganarram**
leaking, be	*coverb+GO_ALONG* **jindag-jindag**
lean	*coverb+FALL/GO_DOWN* **ngirndirring**
be leaning	*coverb+BE/STAY* **ngirndirring**
lean back looking up	*coverb+BE/STAY* **ngawarrang**
lean something	*coverb+PUT* **ngirndirring**
learn	*coverb+GO/COME* **bina**;
	coverb+BE/STAY **binarrig**;
	coverb+GET **dayi**;
	coverb+GO_ALONG **binarriwoo**
learn something	*coverb+BRING/TAKE* **binarri**
learning language quickly, clever at	*coverb+GET* **tharimbirij**
leather	*noun* **wangarrem**
leave behind	*coverb+HIT* **wala**;
	coverb+HIT **warlawarra**;
	coverb+GO/COME **woorrij**
leave each other	*coverb+LEAVE_REFL* **gad**
leave for later	*coverb+BECOME* **marndi**;
	coverb+HIT **marndi**
leave someone, fly away and	*coverb+LEAVE* **doowab**
leave someone/something	*coverb+LEAVE* **gad**
leave, take off and	*coverb+LEAVE* **yawoog**
leaves	*noun* **ganarram**
shed leaves	*coverb+BECOME* **wirrg**
leech, water	*noun feminine* **jirlanyel, jirlanybe**
left side, on the	*locative* **waroogoobiny**
left-handed	*adjective* **waroogoony, waroogool, waroogoom**
leg	*noun* **gerlalbam**
lower leg	*noun* **yawoorroom**
leg bent up, have one	*coverb+BE/STAY* **dandawa**
legs, become old and have no-good	*coverb+GO_ALONG* **goomoorroowoo**
legs, having nice	*adjectives* **dimboogaleny, dimboogalel, dimboogalem**
legs, no-good	*adjective* **goomoorroony, goomoorrool, goomoorroom**
legs, open	*coverb+BE/STAY* **larl**
Leichhardt tree	*noun* **marroorool**;
	noun **ngimilil, ngimirlil**

lemongrass, bush

lemongrass, bush .... *noun* **malmalji**;
    noun masculine **ngarrngarrji**
lemonwood .... *noun* **lawoony**
lend a hand .... *coverb+PUT* **marlam**;
    coverb+HIT **marlam**
lerp species,
  sugar leaf .... *noun* **bin'gany**;
    noun **daliyany**;
    noun masculine **wanamarriny**;
    noun **warrayany, warrayiny**
lever out .... *coverb+PUT* **thera**;
    coverb+SAY/DO_M **thera**;
    coverb+GET **looward**
  lever out/rip off .... *coverb+BE/STAY* **lerawoog**
  levering out .... *coverb+GO/COME* **thera**
liar .... *adjective* **ngamibany, ngamibal**;
    adjective **ngarlibany, ngarlipal**;
    adjective **yagoornbeny, yagoornbel, yagoornbem**
lice grass,
  Cyperus javanicus .... *noun* **yiwiny, yiwim**
lice, feel for .... *coverb+SAY/DO_REFL* **doogoo-doogoo**
lice, head .... *noun* **yiwiny, yiwim**
lick .... *coverb+SAY/DO_REFL* **menhang**
lie down .... *coverb+FALL/GO_DOWN* **bagoo**;
    coverb+GO_ALONG **bagoo**
  lie down on stomach .... *coverb+BE/STAY* **moondoorroong**
  lie flat on stomach .... *coverb+BE/STAY* **loomboord**;
    coverb+BE/STAY **moog**
  lie stomach-down .... *coverb+BE/STAY* **moord**
  lie self down .... *coverb+DO_REFL* **bagoo**
  lie in sun .... *coverb+BE/STAY* **barndeg**
lie to someone .... *coverb+PUT* **ngoorlooba**;
    coverb+PUT **yagoorn**
lift .... *coverb+GET* **jarrward**
light .... *noun* **diyile**;
    noun **marayam**
light, in bright .... *noun* **diyilijilin**
light bushfire .... *coverb+PLACE M* **mawarr**
light fire .... *coverb+PUT* **girrem**;
    coverb+PUT **thaleng**
  unable to light fire .... *coverb+SAY/DO* **jilyirr**
light (weight) .... *adjective* **rambe-rambem**;
    adjective **rarangem**
  make something light
  (weight) .... *coverb+GET* **rarangeg**
light/give sign .... *coverb+PUT* **dilg**
lightning .... *noun masculine* **malngirriny**

lightning, be flashing .... *coverb+GO_ALONG* **merrngag**;
    coverb+SAY/DO **merrngag**
Lightning Creek .... *noun* **Lerndijwanema**
lightning flash .... *coverb+SAY/DO* **menan**
lightning, go along
  flashing .... *coverb+GO_ALONG* **menan**
like/love/want .... *coverb+GET* **dawoong**;
    coverb+GET **maja**;
    coverb **marrga**;
    coverb+HIT **malirri, marrirri**;
    coverb+GET **marroo-marroo**;
    coverb+SAY/DO **marroo-marroo**;
    coverb+HIT **warda**;
    coverb+GET **wooloorr**
like me .... *pronoun* **ngayijan**
like that .... *adjective* **wayinijarrany, wayinijarral, wayinijarram**;
    adverb **wayinigelaj**;
    adverb **wayiniya**;
    particle **wani**;
    particle **wayini**
like that, make .... *coverb+HIT* **wayingge**
like that then .... *adverb* **wayinawoo**
like this/that .... *particle* **wayi**;
    particle **wayina**
lily species,
  Crinum angustifolium .. *noun masculine* **baljanggarrji**;
    noun **lanboodany**;
    noun masculine **ngoorloongginy**
limestone .... *noun masculine* **minyjiwoorrji**
line, be in (hills) .... *coverb+BE/STAY* **doorib**
line, be in one .... *coverb+BE/STAY* **wana-wana**
line, be stretched
  across in straight .... *coverb+BE/STAY* **wanan**;
    coverb+BE/STAY **wandarra**
line, go in .... *coverb+GO/COME* **doori-doorib**
line, go together
  in one .... *coverb+SAY/DO* **joorroob**;
    coverb+SAY/DO_M **joorroob**
line of spikes on
  crocodile's tail .... *noun* **bawardjangoorroom**
line up .... *coverb+PUT* **yag-yag**
lips .... *noun* **marloowoorroo**
Lissadell Station .... *noun* **Thildoowan**
listen .... *coverb+BE/STAY* **ranggab**;
    coverb+BRING/TAKE **rangga**;
    coverb+GET **rangga**;
    coverb+GO/COME **ranggab**;
    coverb+SAY/DO **rangga**
  listen to each other .... *coverb+SAY/DO_REFL* **rangga**

long tom, freshwater garfish

one who can't listen......*adjective* **garlabawoorroony, garlabawoorrool, garlabawoorroom**
little..............................*adjective* **wanyageny, wanyagel, wanyagem;** *noun* **wanyageny;** *noun* **wanyagel, wanyanggel**
little boy ....*noun masculine* **goorndoogany;** *noun masculine* **jangadany** (Southern dialect); *noun masculine* **wanyageny**
little friar bird ....*noun masculine* **jinggerawoogoony**
little green lorikeet ....*noun feminine* **wirrirrel**
little ones......................*adjective* **wanyanyagem;** *adjective* **wanyanyanggem**
little bit, do a little bit of something..............*coverb* **wanyanggeb**
little ones, get to have ..*coverb+BECOME* **wanyagibawa**
liver..............................*noun* **mirlim**
Livistona palm ....*noun feminine* **danarrel;** *noun feminine* **ngamalil;** *noun feminine* **yangajalil, yingajalil**
lizard species
  barking gecko...............*noun* **bedarrel**
  blue-tongue lizard ....*noun feminine* **loomoogool**
  Burton's legless lizard ..*noun feminine* **baljawoorrool**
  chameleon dragon ....*noun* **bawoodany**
  frillneck lizard ....*noun masculine* **gerdanji;** *noun masculine* **wawooleny**
  gecko............................*noun masculine* **mendoowoony, moondoowoony;** *noun masculine* **nyigany**
  knob-tailed gecko.........*noun feminine* **booyooj-booyoojgel, booyooj-booyoojjel, booyij-booyijgel;** *noun feminine* **booyoord-booyoordjil**
  lizard species like a blue-tongue ....*noun feminine* **barndel**
  northern snake lizard, 'emu killer' ....*noun masculine* **joowarribarndegji**
  other lizard species ......*noun* **barloongarnany;** *noun* **ngarlalmanginy**
  slender skink ....*noun feminine* **gamool**
  slippery lizard ....*noun feminine* **bararril;** *noun* **jamboorral**
  spotted tree goanna.....*noun feminine* **bardil;** *noun feminine* **bijil**

tata lizard ....*noun masculine* **jawarlaliny;** *noun masculine* **jawariny;** *noun masculine* **manggerregerreny**
very small skink, slender snake-eyed skink ....*noun* **mili-milil**
SEE ALSO **goanna**
loaded with fruit/flowers (tree or plant), be.......*coverb+GO_ALONG* **dijboord**
loafs about waiting for others to get meat.....*adjective* **yilingarriny, yilingarril, yilingarrim**
locked up, be.................*coverb+SAY/DO* **moogoogoob**
log, hollow....................*noun* **thaloorroony;** *noun* **thoondooloom**
lonely, be ....*coverb+BE/STAY* **barndawarlawarla;** *coverb+SAY/DO_M* **menyawenya;** *coverb+SAY/DO* **wang-wang;** *coverb+SAY/DO_M* **wang-wang**
long...............................*adjective* **meraangarriny, meraangarril, meraangarrim;** *adjective* **merewany, merewal, merewam;** *adjective* **merewagawoony, merewagawool, merewagawoom;** *adjective* **merewangarriny, merewangarril, merewangarrim**
long ago ....*temporal* **ngarranggarnin;** *temporal* **ngamoo-ngamoongoon;** *temporal* **ngamoongoon;** *temporal* **warnarram;** *temporal* **warna-warnarram**
  from long ago...............*adjective* **ngamoo-ngamoom;** *adjective* **warnarrany, warnarral, warnarram**
  not too long ago...........*temporal* **gelengeben**
long (make long action).....*coverb+GET* **merewagboo**
long time, after a..........*temporal* **ngarriwarloojen**
long time, for a ....*adverb* **warnarrayan**
long time, go away for a..............*coverb+GO/COME* **nyirl**
long tom, freshwater garfish ...*noun masculine* **bayirrany;** *noun masculine* **jalgirri-girriny**

look

look .... *coverb+SAY/DO* **deg**;
　　　　　　　　　　　　coverb+SAY/DO_M **deg**
look after someone .... *coverb* **maroorr**;
　　　　　　　　　　　　coverb+GET **moorroo**
　look after someone/
　something .... *coverb* **maroolooya**
look around .... *coverb+SAY/DO* **biya**;
　　　　　　　　　　　　coverb+SAY/DO **gaman**;
　　　　　　　　　　　　coverb+SAY/DO_M **gaman**
　look around for
　something .... *coverb+HIT* **yinang**
look at from side .... *coverb+GET* **lirring**
look at something .... *coverb+GET* **deg**
　look at self/each other .. *coverb+DO_REFL* **deg**
look back .... *coverb+SAY/DO* **wad**
　look back, keep on
　making someone .... *coverb+GET* **wad-wadgewany**
look for .... *coverb+GET* **biya**;
　　　　　　　　　　　　coverb+GO_ALONG **biya**;
　　　　　　　　　　　　coverb+GO_ALONG **biyanga**;
　　　　　　　　　　　　coverb+HIT/CUT **biya**;
　　　　　　　　　　　　coverb+HIT2 **biya**;
　　　　　　　　　　　　coverb+SAY/DO **biya-wiya**;
　　　　　　　　　　　　coverb+SAY/DO **derde-yerdeg**;
　　　　　　　　　　　　coverb+SAY/DO_M **degbe**
　look for food .... *coverb+SAY/DO* **joorndaj**
　look for food
　(plural subject) .... *coverb+SAY/DO* **joorndajgoowool**
　look for (something)
　on self .... *coverb* **biya**
look out!
　(Southern dialect) .... *interjection* **yoorroo**
look properly .... *coverb+GET* **degijiya**
look sideways .... *coverb+SAY/DO* **lirring**
looking .... *coverb+GO_ALONG* **biya-wiya**
looking after,
　wanting .... *coverb+SAY/DO_M* **ngamarr**;
　　　　　　　　　　　　adjective **ngamarrwoony**,
　　　　　　　　　　　　ngamarrwool
looking at someone,
　keep .... *coverb+GO/COME* **lerrma**
looking back, be .... *coverb+BE/STAY* **wad**
looking straight ahead,
　sitting down .... *coverb+BE/STAY* **jarranang**
looking for fight .... *adjective* **boontherrany-biny**;
　　　　　　　　　　　　coverb+GO_ALONG **baja-baja**
　be looking for a fight .... *coverb+SAY/DO* **yad**;
　　　　　　　　　　　　coverb+SAY/DO_M **yad**
　go looking for a fight
　with each other .... *coverb+SAY/DO_REFL* **yad**

looking for, go .... *coverb+GO/COME* **biya**;
　　　　　　　　　　　　coverb+GO/COME **biyawany**
looking for scraps, be ... *coverb+SAY/DO* **garrid-garrid**
looking, go along .... *coverb+GO_ALONG* **deg**
looking up, lean back ... *coverb+BE/STAY* **ngawarrang**
loose tooth, be .... *adjective* **lamany**
lorikeet, little green ..... *noun feminine* **wirrirrel**
lorikeet, rainbow .... *noun feminine* **wirrilijgel**
lose .... *coverb+HIT* **wangarrg**
lose weight .... *coverb+GO/COME* **wirrg**
lost, get .... *coverb+FALL/GO_DOWN* **wangarrag**
loud .... *adverb* **garda-gardawoo**
　person who speaks
　loudly .... *adjective* **yoowoorlbeny**,
　　　　　　　　　　　　yoowoorlbel, **yoowoorlbem**
　speak loudly .... *coverb+SAY/DO* **lerra**;
　　　　　　　　　　　　coverb+SAY/DO_M **yoowoorl**
love .... *coverb+GET* **dawoong**;
　　　　　　　　　　　　coverb+GET **ngoongoo**;
　　　　　　　　　　　　coverb+HIT **warda**
　be in love .... *coverb+BE/STAY* **dawoong**
　love/want someone ...... *coverb+GET* **goondoony**
　make love .... *coverb+SAY/DO_REFL*
　　　　　　　　　　　　ngoolnga-ngoolnga
　make love to someone .. *coverb+PUT* **ngoolnga**
love/like .... *coverb+HIT* **marrirri**
　love/want/like .... *coverb+GET* **dawoong**;
　　　　　　　　　　　　coverb+GET **maja**;
　　　　　　　　　　　　coverb **marrga**;
　　　　　　　　　　　　coverb+HIT **malirri**, **marrirri**;
　　　　　　　　　　　　coverb+GET **marroo-marroo**;
　　　　　　　　　　　　coverb+SAY/DO **marroo-marroo**;
　　　　　　　　　　　　coverb+HIT **warda**;
　　　　　　　　　　　　coverb+GET **wooloorr**
love song .... *noun* **woodiji**;
　　　　　　　　　　　　noun **yirrbinji**
lover, take away
　leading by arm .... *coverb+GET* **binggoo**;
　　　　　　　　　　　　coverb+SAY/DO_M
　　　　　　　　　　　　binggoo-binggoo
low .... *adjective* **maroongoony**,
　　　　　　　　　　　　maroongool, **maroongoom**
lower back .... *noun* **moon'goo**
lumps and sores
　sticking out, have ...... *coverb* **gerrmabany**
lump on tree, burl .... *noun* **joorl-joorloo**
lumps, come out in ...... *coverb+GO/COME* **loob-loob**;
　　　　　　　　　　　　coverb+SAY/DO **loob-loob**;
　　　　　　　　　　　　coverb+SAY/DO **loomoorrmoorr**

lumps, one that causes	*adjective* loomoorrmoorr-nhawoony, loomoorrmoorr-nhawool, loomoorrmorr-nhawoom
lumpy	*adjective* boolngarrbany, boolngarrbal, boolngarrbam; *adjective* jambooggany, jambooggal, jambooggam
lungs	*noun* gawoom; *noun* ranggoo
lying, be (telling lies)	*coverb+SAY/DO_M* ngoorlooba; *coverb+SAY/DO_M* yagoorn
lying down, be	*coverb+BE/STAY* bagoo
lying in the sun, be	*coverb+BE/STAY* barndeg

Mm

Mabel Downs	*noun* Gilban
mad	*adjective* merlarnji, merlarnel, merlarnbe; *adjective* wangalany, wangalal, wangalam
be mad	*coverb+SAY/DO* merlarn
become mad	*coverb+BECOME* wangalawoo
go mad	*coverb+SAY/DO_M* merlarn
go/get mad	*coverb+BECOME* wangala
made mad	*coverb+GET* wangalag
made mad by spirits	*coverb+SAY/DO_M* thedji
mad person	*noun* ganarra-ngarnany, ganarra-ngarnal; *noun* walganji walganel
Mad Gap	*noun* Gooweriny
made, be	*coverb+BECOME* ngarag
made pregnant	*coverb+SPEAR* jaawag
maggots	*noun* waanyim
magic ladder	*noun masculine* barrgoorany
magic man	*noun* mabarn; *noun* baremanbeny, baroomanbeny
magic power	*noun* mayam
magic stone	*noun* mabarn
magpie	*noun masculine* gemerlawoorroony; *noun masculine* goorrooranggoolji
magpie goose	*noun* ngarlagangarril, ngarlagangarriny
magpie lark	*noun feminine* birlirrijgel; *noun* goorliyirrel

make	*coverb+GET* ngarag; *coverb+HIT* ngarag; *coverb+SAY/DO_M* ngarag
make appear	*coverb+BRING/TAKE* boorab
make bad	*coverb+GET* yilgoowoorroog
make black	*coverb+BRING/TAKE* manbeg; *coverb+GET* manbeg
make camp	*coverb+BECOME* joondooj; *coverb+SAY/DO_M* joondoo; *coverb+SAY/DO_M* joondoo-joondoo
make clever	*coverb+GET* baremanbege
make climb	*coverb+HIT* berdijge
make cry	*coverb+GET* ngardawooge
make deaf	*coverb+HIT* nyin'ge
make dizzy	*coverb+HIT* winginig
make drop out	*coverb+HIT* jirrgawoorrg
make each other happy	*coverb+DO_REFL* mool-moolji
make fire	*coverb+PUT* jardgi; *coverb+SAY/DO* jardgi; *coverb+SAY/DO_M* jardgi
make fire flare up with big flames	*coverb+PUT* gawara
make fire with fire drill	*coverb+HIT* biyird-biyird; *coverb+SAY/DO* biyird-biyird
make forget	*coverb+GET* wangarrge
make full	*coverb* merlngard
make fun of each other	*coverb+PUT* birriman; *coverb+PUT SELF* birriman
make fun together	*coverb+DO_REFL* jawirij
make go and leave	*coverb+BRING/TAKE* woorrij
make go fast	*coverb+HIT* thoony
make good	*coverb+GET* men'gawoog; *coverb+HIT* men'gawoog
make good-looking	*coverb+DO_REFL* joornanygarreg
make happy	*coverb+GET* gooloogoo
make hole through	*coverb+GO_THROUGH* thoorl
make holes in	*coverb+GET* doongooroog
make hungry	*coverb+GET* goorninyag
make laugh	*coverb+GET* garl-garlge
make like that	*coverb+HIT* wayingge
make love	*coverb+SAY/DO_REFL* ngoolnga-ngoolnga
make love to someone	*coverb+PUT* ngoolnga
man who likes to make love to women	*noun* ngoolnga-ngoolnga-nhawoony
make mad	*coverb+SAY/DO_M* thedji
make marks on self	*coverb+SAY/DO_REFL* wijerraj

make mistake

make mistake .... *coverb+HIT* **beroowal**
make nest .... *coverb+GO_ALONG* **warr-warr**
make noise/sound
  go making rustling
  noise through grass ..... *coverb+GO/COME* **rawoolilib**
  laugh and make noise
  calling out together ...... *coverb+SAY/DO_REFL* **yayiggoolg**
  make big noise at
  someone .... *coverb+HIT* **yoowoorlngboo**
  make buzzing noise ...... *coverb+SAY/DO* **thengenge**
  make grinding noise ..... *coverb+SAY/DO* **loorlgoodaj**
  make hollow sound .... *coverb+SAY/DO* **loorrloorrjaya**
  make noise by banging . *coverb+SAY/DO_M* **dal-dal**;
                              coverb+HIT **daly**
  make noise calling out .. *coverb+SAY/DO* **yayig, yayi-yayi**
  make ringing sound
  (e.g. bell) .... *coverb+HIT* **lerlerl**
  make sound echo
  loudly all around .... *coverb+BRING/TAKE* **wingalawoog**
  SEE ALSO **noise**; **sound**
make oneself really
  full by eating
  something .... *coverb+EAT* **jarrayilge**
make pretty .... *coverb+DO_REFL* **joornanygarreg**
make rude sign .... *coverb+GET* **rany**
make run .... *coverb+GET* **wijige**;
                              coverb+GET **wijigoowany**
  make run away fast .... *coverb+HIT/CUT* **thoonyga**
make sad .... *coverb+GET* **mooloorroog**
make safe .... *coverb+PUT* **mantha**
make self good .... *coverb+SAY/DO_REFL* **men'gawoog**
make self hungry .... *coverb+FALL/GO_DOWN*
                              goorninyag
make sharp .... *coverb+PUT* **boorr-boorr**
make sick .... *coverb+GET* **yilgoowoorroog**
make sleep .... *coverb+HIT* **yirdarrge**
make smoke .... *coverb+PLACE* **dooloo**;
                              coverb+PUT **dooloo**
make smooth .... *coverb+GET* **banheng**
make soft .... *coverb* **galyegbeg**
make someone have
  goosebumps .... *coverb+GET* **goon'gany-
                              goon'gany**;
                              coverb+GET **rawoorlgoowany**
make someone shake
  and stagger .... *coverb+GET* **benjilgoowany**
make someone sick
  by magic .... *coverb+HIT* **winyjirrab**
make sore .... *coverb+GET* **gajig**

make sparks .... *coverb+SAY/DO* **nhil, nhil-nhil**;
                              coverb+SAY/DO **ninirl**;
                              coverb+SAY/DO **wirnmirnmaj**
make sticky .... *coverb+GET* **bendereg**
make strong .... *coverb+GET* **bagarrjig**
make tired .... *coverb+GET* **wanggarlge**;
                              coverb+PUT **wanggarlge**;
                              coverb+GET **yalijge**
make tongue feel funny
  by eating something
  bitter .... *coverb+EAT* **dagalge**
make tracks .... *coverb+SAY/DO_M* **barn'ga**
make trouble for self ... *coverb+SAY/PLACE_REFL* **gooj**
make trouble for
  someone .... *coverb+PUT* **gooj**
make walk .... *coverb+GET* **girligewa**
make water run and
  drown someone .... *coverb+HIT* **thoorroorroog**
make web .... *coverb+GO_ALONG* **warr-warr**;
                              coverb+SAY/DO **warr-warr**
make web/twist
  around .... *coverb+SAY/DO_M* **warr**
make wet .... *coverb+GET* **jirlanyjag**;
                              coverb+HIT **jirlanyjag**
make windbreak .... *coverb+SAY/DO_M* **jarrga-jarrga**
make young men .... *coverb+GO_ALONG* **goodaj-goodaj**
making, be .... *coverb+SAY/DO* **ngarag**;
                              coverb+SAY/DO **ngara-ngarag**
making, go along .... *coverb+GO_ALONG* **ngarag**
making self up
  (e.g. clouds), be .... *coverb+DO_REFL* **ngarag**
making sound by
  clapping thighs,
  good at .... *adjective* **derlawoog-galem**
male .... *adjective* **gerndiny,
                              gerndi-werndiny**
man .... *noun masculine* **jiyiliny**
  adult man .... *noun masculine* **garrayilji**
  old man .... *noun masculine*
                              gooroogoorany;
                              noun **marloogany**
  man who cannot do
  without a woman .... *noun masculine*
                              ngalingoonybiny
  man who doesn't
  know/like women .... *noun* **malirrany**
  man who has been
  through all law .... *noun masculine* **wanemany**
  man whose brother or
  sister has died .... *noun masculine* **yawoorroony**

man whose child has died	*noun masculine* **thalebany**
man whose parent, uncle or aunt has died	*noun masculine* **ngamanyiny**
man whose wife has died	*noun masculine* **thoombawoony**
young man	*noun masculine* **jambalngarriny**
young man with headband	*noun masculine* **lambarnji**
man's sister's child	*noun* **garliny, garlil**
man's sister's daughter's child	*noun* **ganggany, ganggal, ganggam**
man's sister's daughter's husband	*noun masculine* **baliyany**
mangrove, river	*noun* **jinggoolji**
many	*adjective* **garawirrim**; *adjective* **melagawoom, melagawoony, melagawool**; *adjective* **nawarrany, nawarral, nawarram**; *adjective* **waringarrim, waringarriny, waringarril**; *noun* **nawarragam**; *noun* **nawarrangim**; *adjective* **yiwirrirrim**
marble	*noun masculine* **goordoony**
march fly, small black biting species	*noun masculine* **goorrjalji**
mare	*noun feminine* **dimanal**; *noun feminine* **yawardal**
marks on self, make	*coverb+SAY/DO_REFL* **wijerraj**
married, get	*coverb+BECOME* **ngaliba**
marsupial mouse	*noun feminine* **jaranel**; *noun* **nyilimbil, nyilimbiny**; *noun masculine* **yiroowoonji**
massacre site	*noun* **Goordbelayin**
masturbate	*coverb+DO_REFL* **nheleb**
matches	*noun* **girremgajim**
strike a match	*coverb+PUT* **girrem**
maternal grandfather	*noun masculine* **thamanyji**; *noun masculine* **jawoojiny**
maternal grandfather's sister	*noun feminine* **thamanyel**
Maud Creek	*noun* **Yingandaliny, Yingandalel, Yingandale**
maybe	*particle* **wanyji**
McKenna Spring	*noun* **Nganyjarriwoony**
McPhee Hole	*noun* **Jawoorraban**
me/I	*pronoun* **ngayin**
for me	*benefactive enclitic pronoun* **-nga, -ngage, -ngageny**
from/after/because of me	*ablative enclitic pronoun* **-ngerroowa**; *ablative enclitic pronoun* **-ngerra** (Southern dialect)
like me	*pronoun* **ngayijan**
to me	*indirect object enclitic pronoun* **-ngirri**
with me	*commitative enclitic pronoun* **-ngerrab**
me and you (one)	*pronoun* **yayiben, yayin**
belonging to me and you (one)	*possessive pronoun* **yayiyangeny, yayiyangel, yayiyangem**
meal, a filling	*noun* **boorrale**
meal, give someone a	*coverb+GIVE M* **boorral**
meat	*noun* **miyale, miyalji, miyalel**
be without meat	*coverb+BE/STAY* **miyaloob**
cut up meat	*coverb+HIT* **begerr**; *coverb+GET* **bag**; *coverb+HIT* **bag**; *coverb+SAY/DO_M* **thelberr**
good at finding meat	*adjective* **moonthoorroogaleny, moonthoorroogalel, moonthoorroogalem**
meat juice	*noun* **warlele**; *noun* **wooroom**
pull meat from fire	*coverb+PUT* **thoorrboord**
rotten meat	*noun* **goonarre**
Medicine Pocket	*noun* **Mendoowoorrji**
meet	*coverb+BURN/BITE_REFL* **jidi**; *coverb+GO/COME* **manthan**; *coverb+GO/COME* **ngarij**; *coverb+HIT* **manthan**; *coverb+PUT* **manthan**
meet someone	*coverb+GET* **ngarij**
melaleuca species	*noun masculine* **moonggoolji**
melon, small bitter bush	*noun feminine* **gagoolanyil**; *noun feminine* **gilyalal**
watermelon	*noun feminine* **ngayalel**
menace/attack	*coverb+HIT* **walaji**; *coverb+SAY/DO_M* **walaji**; *coverb+WOUND* **walaji**
menace/attack someone	*coverb+WOUND* **walaji**
mermaid	*noun feminine* **woorra-woorral**

midday

midday	*temporal* nyarewarloon
middle	*locative* belegan; *locative* belegawirrin
middle-aged, become	*coverb+FALL/GO_DOWN* yalirrwany
middle, go into	*coverb+FALL/GO_DOWN* belegag
middle, in the	*adjective* belegany, belegal, belegam
middle of the night	*temporal* mendoowiyan
middle-sized	*adjective* belegany, belegal, belegam
midnight	*temporal* belegawirrin
miles and miles, go	*adverb* gamberarra-gamberarra
milk	*noun* gamoom
Milky Way	*noun* waroorroony
millet grass	*noun* wirlarrji
mimic	*noun* madiwoony, madiwool
mince	*coverb+GET* moojooroog
mince up	*coverb+GET* doongooroog
mind/look after	*coverb+GET* moorroo
mind, keep in	*coverb* dalberr
mind, stick in	*coverb+FALL/GO_DOWN* larrngib
minding own business	*adjective* wawoonggany, wawoonggal, wawoonggam
mine	*possessive pronoun* ngagenyji, ngagenyil, ngagenybe
miner, yellow-faced	*noun feminine* biyig-biyiggel
miss (when trying to hit or spear)	*coverb+GET* berleb; *coverb+HIT* beroowal
miss (e.g. spear slipped past side of body)	*coverb+GO/COME* beraj
miss someone	*coverb+SAY/DO* mooloorroo; *coverb+SAY/DO* wanga-wanga; *coverb+SAY/DO* gaman
mist	*noun* yaalji, yaale
mist/heat haze	*noun* jooroomoorroo
mistake	*coverb+FALL/GO_DOWN* ngaj
mistake, do by	*adverb* wawoorroon
mistake, make (miss)	*coverb+HIT* beroowal
mistletoe	*noun masculine* manthoornji
small mistletoe	*noun feminine* janil, janim
mistletoe bird	*noun masculine* jirlmirndiny; *noun masculine* jiwirnbenji
moiety, generational	*noun* jarlinyjaroom, jarlinybaroom
moiety, opposite generational; what the two generational moieties call each other	*noun* yinara
money	*noun* ngarrgaleny, ngarrgalem
paper money	*noun* ganarram; *noun* merlgam; *noun* merndany, merndam
month	*noun* garn'gim
Moola Bulla	*noun* Ngarraarnji, Ngarrawarnji
moon	*noun masculine* garn'giny; *noun masculine* jawoorranyji
be new moon	*coverb+HIT* janggarr
moon grub	*noun masculine* garn'giny
moonlight, sitting in	*locative/temporal* garn'girrayijirran
morning	*temporal* dirrandem, derrandem
morning star	*noun* jiwibal, jiwibany
mosquito	*noun masculine* nyiwiny, nyiwinyji
mosquito net	*noun* gernalim
moth, butterfly (can be swearing)	*noun feminine* warlimarrgool
mother, mother's sister	*noun feminine* gooral
mother (spoken to)	*noun* goorayi
mother, uncle, father or aunt	*noun* manaroony, manarool
mother-in-law of man	*noun feminine* thamboorrool
mother-in-law/ daughter-in-law of woman	*noun feminine* goorrijil
mother-in-law's brother, woman's	*noun masculine* goorrijiny
mother-in-law/ son-in-law (spoken to)	*noun* bajoog
mother's brother (uncle)	*noun masculine* nyaganyji
mother's brother (uncle) (spoken to)	*noun* nyagayi
mother's father	*noun masculine* jawoojiny; *noun masculine* thamanyji
mother's father (spoken to)	*noun* jawooji; *noun* thamany
mother's father's country	*noun* gamerrem
mother's father's sister	*noun feminine* thamanyel
mother's father's sister (spoken to)	*noun* thamany

mother's mother .... *noun feminine* **ganggal**
  mother's mother
  (spoken to).................... *noun* **ganggayi**
mother's mother's
  sister............................. *noun feminine* **ganggal**
  mother's mother's
  sister (spoken to) .... *noun* **ganggayi**
mother's mother's
  brother........................ *noun masculine* **ganggany**
  mother's mother's
  brother (spoken to)....... *noun* **ganggayi**
mother's sister............... *noun feminine* **gamelanyel**;
                                         noun feminine **gooral**
Motor Car Yard.............. *noun* **Barlooban**
mould, puffball fungus .*noun masculine* **langany**
mouldy............................. *adjective* **langabany**
Mount Amherst .... *noun* **Garlgarran**
Mount Buchanan.......... *noun* **Rawooliliny**
Mount Evelyn .... *noun* **Goodoogoodoo**
Mount King .... *noun* **Garnanganyjen**
mourning necklace
  made of hair or
  string............................ *noun* **doonggoolji,**
                                          doonggooloo
  person who is wearing
  a mourning necklace ....*noun* **doonggoolbany,**
                                          doonggoolbal
mouse .... *noun feminine* **jaranel**;
                                   noun **nyilimbil, nyilimbiny**;
                                   noun masculine **yiroowoonji**
moustache .... *noun* **ngoonjoo-ngoonjoom**;
                                      noun **thawoorem**
mouth .... *noun* **thoowerndem**
  carry in the mouth........*coverb+BRING/TAKE* **gered**
  have in the mouth.........*coverb+HAVE* **gered**
  have mouth open .... *coverb+BE/STAY* **ngam**
  pick up with the mouth..*coverb+GET* **gered**
  put hand over mouth....*coverb+DO_REFL* **moom**;
                                      coverb+GET **moom**
move around in a
  group........................... *coverb+GO/COME* **rarrawoolib**
move away .... *coverb+SAY/PLACE_REFL* **ngoon'goo**
move backwards........... *coverb+GO_ALONG* **rerreg**
move behind
  someone .... *coverb+SAY/DO* **jagard**
move closer................... *coverb+GO/COME* **ngirribag,**
                                    ngirribagboo, ngirrirribag
move over...................... *coverb+GO_ALONG* **rerreg**
move something............ *coverb+GET* **rerreg**
moving, be .... *coverb+SAY/DO* **nyoongoon**
moving in the distance,
  be just seen .... *coverb+GO_ALONG* **yinggerd**
mud................................. *noun* **nhoonbam**
  white mud .... *noun* **balarrji, balarre**
  feel around in mud and
  pull something up .... *coverb+SAY/DO_M* **loogaj**
Mud Springs................... *noun* **Yoowangeny**
mullet, red-eyed .... *noun masculine*
                                      woorloorrmarlinji
murder............................*coverb+SAY/DO* **marrngen**
murderer .... *noun* **gerrijbendiny**;
                                      noun **joowarrigaliny**;
                                      noun **mawoondoongarnayin**;
                                      noun **mawoongarriny,**
                                      mawoongarril
mushroom species .... *noun* **binoowoonggool**;
                                      noun **moorrji**
mussel, freshwater....... *noun feminine* **gerrewool**
muster .... *coverb+PUT* **joorra**;
                                      coverb+GO_ALONG **majoorroom**;
                                      coverb+SAY/DO **majoorroom**
myself .... *pronoun* **ngayiwany**;
                                      pronoun **ngayiwarrin**

Nn

'naga', Kriol word for
  pubic covering............. *noun* **jarnim**;
                                      noun **warlboorroo**
nail, fingernail/toenail..*noun* **yarnderre**
nail-tailed wallaby .... *noun masculine*
                                      goon'goodoogoodoony;
                                      noun masculine
                                      gooroorroonggoony;
                                      noun masculine
                                      woorrood-woorroodji;
                                      noun masculine
                                      woordoorr-woordoorrji
naked, be....................... *coverb+BE/STAY* **loonggaya**
naked, go....................... *coverb+GO/COME* **loonggaya**
name............................... *noun* **yinginybe, yinginybi**
  be saying a name.......... *coverb+GO/COME* **garijib**
  person with same
  name .... *noun* **narroogoo**
  say a name .... *coverb+GET* **garij**
                                      coverb+SAY/DO_M **garij**
  say each other's name ..*coverb+DO_REFL* **garij**
nankeen night heron ...*noun feminine* **jawoombal**
narrow place .... *noun* **derrmerle**
native bee...................... *noun* **moowany, moowal**;
                                      noun feminine **ngawooral**

navel

navel	*noun* **dinyjile**
neck	*noun* **wenggarrem**;
	noun **werlem, woorlem, woorloom**
get/have twisted neck	*coverb+BE/STAY* **wag**
twist someone's neck	*coverb+GET* **wag**
necklace made of hair or string, mourning	*noun* **doonggoolji, doonggooloo**
nerve jump, feel	*coverb+BECOME* **jirreg**
nerves, sinew	*noun* **jirlwam**; *noun* **nganyjoom**
nest, bird	*noun* **boolmim**
make nest	*coverb+GO/COME* **bool**; *coverb+GO_ALONG* **warr-warr**
net	*noun* **gernalil, gernalim**
never mind	*particle* **gawayin, gawayinde**; *particle* **miya**
new	*adjective* **gelengawoony, gelengawool, gelengawoom**; *adjective* **gelengeny, gelengel, gelengem**
new/not ready	*adjective* **gelengoowoony, gelengoowool, gelengoowoom**
new fruit growing on tree, be	*coverb+SAY/DO_M* **jawoorl-jawoorl**
new generation	*noun* **bardoongeny, bardoongel, bardoongem**
new moon, be	*coverb+HIT* **janggarr**
next day	*temporal* **magarne**; *temporal* **nyigawa**
next morning	*temporal* **jaroongem**
nice looking	*adjective* **berlengbeny, berlengbel, berlengbem**
night	
be nightfall	*coverb+FALL/GO_DOWN* **mendoowoony**; *coverb+FALL/GO_DOWN* **mendoowoonybe**
become night-time	*coverb+FALL/GO_DOWN M* **mendoowoonyboo**
every night	*temporal* **mendoowoomoowan**
night-time	*temporal* **merdben**; *temporal* **nyigan**
night, at	*temporal* **mendoowoon**
hunt at night	*coverb+GO_ALONG* **jana**
only at night	*temporal* **mendoowoomoowan**
middle of the night	*temporal* **mendoowiyan**
walk around/hunt at night	*coverb+GO_ALONG* **jana**
go walking all night	*coverb+SAY/DO_M* **nyalngawoog**
night bird, dangerous	*noun* **joowany, joowal**
night dwellers, dark spirits	*noun* **mendoowoongarnam**
nightjar	*noun masculine* **barnanggany**
nightjar, owlet	*noun masculine* **thirringgenji**
no	*interjection* **ngoowan**
nod head	*coverb+SAY/DO* **noonaj**
no-good legs, having	*adjective* **goomoorroony, goomoorrool, goomoorroom**
noise, make	*coverb+SAY/DO* **ngarl-ngarl**
go making rustling noise through grass	*coverb+GO/COME* **rawoolilib**
laugh and make noise calling out together	*coverb+SAY/DO_REFL* **yayiggoolg**
make big noise at someone	*coverb+HIT* **yoowoorlngboo**
make buzzing noise	*coverb+SAY/DO* **thengenge**
make grinding noise	*coverb+SAY/DO* **loorlgoodaj**
make noise by banging	*coverb+SAY/DO_M* **dal-dal**; *coverb+HIT* **daly**
make noise behind someone	*coverb+SAY/DO* **jabarr**
make noise calling ou	*coverb+SAY/DO* **yayig, yayi-yayi**
make noise and disturb someone	*coverb+PUT* **yoowoorlngbe**
SEE ALSO sound	
non-meat food	*noun* **mayim, mayiny, mayil**
north	
from the north	*directional* **biyoorroong**; *directional* **biyirri-biny**
further north	*directional* **boorrgoorloorr, boowoorrgoorloorr**
go north	*coverb+FALL/GO_DOWN* **boowoorroogoob**
in the north	*directional* **biyirrin**
to the north	*directional* **boowoorr, boowoorroogoo**
northern rosella	*noun feminine* **gooldany-gooldanyel**
nose	*noun* **marnale**; *noun* **nyoomboorroo**
nose, blow	*coverb+SAY/DO* **nyiny, nyoony**

nose peg	*noun* nanyjoorroo; *noun* ninjirri
not	*particle* ngoowan
not answer	*coverb+BECOME* linggara-gara
not at all	*interjection* ngoowangarnan
not eating, feel like	*coverb+SAY/DO* ngarloo; *coverb+SAY/DO_M* ngarloo
not far away	*locative* marragoowoorroon
not knowing	*adjective* binarri-woorroony, binarri-woorrool, binarri-woorroom
not recognise	*coverb+FALL/GO_DOWN* ngaj
not recognise/know someone	*coverb+HIT* ganginy
not share	*coverb+GET* daboo
not sharing	*coverb* warrmayi; *coverb* warrmayi
not there, be	*coverb+SAY/DO_M* ngoowag
not wanting to talk to anyone	*adjective* boothalwoony, boothalwool, boothalwoom
nothing	*adjective* ngoowany, ngoowal; *interjection* ngoowangarnan
be nothing	*coverb+SAY/DO_M* ngoowag
be nothing there	*coverb+BE/STAY* ngawaying
notes (money)	*noun* ganarram; *noun* merlgam; *noun* merndany, merndam
now	*temporal* gelengen; *temporal* gilingin
nude, be	*coverb+BE/STAY* loonggaya
nude, go	*coverb+GO/COME* loonggaya
nudge	*coverb+HIT* nhoorr; *coverb+HIT* nhoorrngoog; *coverb+PUT* nhoorr
nudge each other	*coverb+SAY/DO_REFL* nhoorrngoog; *coverb+SAY/DO_REFL* nhoorr-nhoorr
nulla-nulla	*noun* goordooroom; *noun* nawooloony
tree used for making nulla-nulla	*noun masculine* goonanderoony
woman who is good at blocking blows with nulla-nulla	*noun feminine* goowarrigalel
nutwood	*noun masculine* bardiginy; *noun feminine* bardigel; *noun* baregel

Oo

ochre	*noun feminine* jilangarnal
red ochre	*noun feminine* badel, badem; *noun feminine* danggal, danggam
reddish yellow ochre	*noun* boorrngooroony, boorrngoorroom
white ochre	*noun feminine* galadil; *noun feminine* mawoondool
yellow ochre	*noun* boorrngooroony, boorrngoorroom; *adjective* goorndoorlji, goorndoorloo
O'Donnell Range	*noun* Jimbirlan
offended, be	*coverb+HIT* roog
oh dear!	*interjection* marri
oh goodness!	*interjection* wardawoo
oh no!	*interjection* ngaga
okay	*adjective* jirrayany, jirrayal, jirrayam, jirram; *adjective* nyoonggayany, nyoonggayal, nyoonggayam; *interjection* jirrayam; *interjection* nyoonggayam; *interjection* wara; *interjection* warany
old	*adjective* gelengoowoorroony, gelengoowoorrool, gelengoowoorroom; *adjective* warnarrany, warnarral, warnarram
become old and have no-good legs	*coverb+GO_ALONG* goomoorroowoo
old man	*noun masculine* gooroogoorany; *noun* marloogany
old people	*noun* garrenbawoorroom
old woman	*noun feminine* nyamanil, nyamanel
become an old woman	*coverb+BECOME* nyamani
older brother	*noun masculine* goorabeny; *noun masculine* booloongoony
older sister	*noun feminine* goorabel; *noun feminine* booloongool
on the higher side	*directional* gendayingen
on the other hand	*particle* yage
on the right side	*locative* joodoobiny
on the side	*locative* limbalbiny

on this side

on this side .... *demonstrative* **berrebiny**
on top, high .... *locative* **wirli-wirlin**
on top of a hill, be .... *coverb+BE/STAY* **garinybe**
on top of the hills .... *locative* **wirli-wirlin**
once .... *adverb* **jirrawoo-moowam**
one .... *adjective* **jirrawoony, jirrawool, jirrawoom;** *adjective* **jirrawoogeny, jirrawoogel;** *adjective* **jirrawoonginy, jirrawoongil, jirrawoongim**
   for one day .... *temporal* **jirrawoogen barnden**
one who asks questions all the time .... *adjective* **wagirrwoony, wagirrwool, wagirrwoom**
one who can't joke .... *adjective* **barlij-bawoorroony, barlij-bawoorrool, barlij-bawoorroom**
one who chases .... *adjective* **loorroob-nhawoony, loorroob-nhawool, loorroob-nhawoom**
one who gets thirsty .... *adjective* **reme-remeny-nhawoony, reme-remeny-nhawool, reme-remeny-nhawoom**
one who likes loving up to women .... *adjective* **ngoolnga-ngoolnga-nhawoony**
one who pours out .... *noun* **woomboolngem**
one who swears .... *adjective* **roowaj-nhawoony, roowaj-nhawool, roowaj-nhawoom**
one who talks a long time .... *adjective* **werrweny, werrwel, werrwem**
onion, bush .... *noun* **joorndany, joorndam**
open .... *coverb+DO_REFL* **berl;** *coverb+GO/COME* **berl**
open bank of river or creek so that someone falls .... *coverb+HIT* **bang**
open country .... *noun* **balngarnam**
open eyes .... *coverb+GET* **berl**
open legs .... *coverb+BE/STAY* **larl**
open out .... *coverb+SAY/DO_M* **jalag**
open place .... *noun* **barawoorroom;** *noun* **balawam;** *noun* **balgam;** *noun* **wirridim**

open something to look around .... *coverb+PUT* **rembarrg**
open stomach .... *coverb+GET* **thelberr;** *coverb+HIT* **thelberr**
opening through, be an .... *coverb+BE/STAY* **doomboolalib**
orange, bush .... *noun feminine* **joogoorrool**
orchid, *Cymbidium canaliculatum* .... *noun masculine* **ganyjalarrji;** *noun masculine* **garloonggoony**
Ord River crossing area south of Spring Creek .... *noun* **Warraroony**
oriole, olive-backed ...... *noun feminine* **binbinajgel**
Osmond Valley .... *noun* **Loomoogoon**
other .... *adjective* **yagengerrany, yagengerral, yagengerram**
   other one .... *noun* **yagengeny, yagengel, yagengem**
   on the other hand .... *particle* **yage**
ouch! .... *interjection* **wardawoo**
ours (dual inclusive) .... *possessive pronoun* **yayiyangeny, yayiyangel, yayiyangem**
ours (exclusive) .... *possessive pronoun* **yarriyangeny, yarriyangel, yarriyangem**
ours (inclusive) .... *possessive pronoun* **yoowoorriyangeny, yoowoorriyangel, yoowoorriyangem**
outside .... *locative* **geman**
   put outside .... *coverb+PUT* **gemag**
outsider .... *adjective* **wawoonggany, wawoonggal, wawoonggam**
overgrown with plants, become .... *coverb* **yiwijge**
overflow .... *coverb+GO/COME* **gibiwoonab**
owl .... *noun masculine* **doomboony**
owlet nightjar .... *noun masculine* **thirringgenji**
owner of country .... *noun* **daawany, daawal, daawam**
own thing, one who does their own thing, not interfering .... *adjective* **berawoony, berawool, berawoom**

Pp

paddy melon	*noun feminine* **gagoolanyil**
pain, be in	*coverb+SAY/DO* **majarr**;
	coverb+SAY/DO **mirl-mirl**;
	coverb +GO/COME **woorrngoord**
pain, cause to shake with	*coverb+GET* **therrngarn'ge**
pain, childbirth	*coverb+SAY/DO* **lerrij**
pain, have a	*coverb+SAY/DO* **woorrngoord**
paint	*coverb+HIT* **boonoo**;
	coverb+HIT **yoorrg**;
	coverb+SAY/DO **boonoo-boonoo**;
	coverb+SAY/DO_M **boonoo**;
	coverb+SAY/DO **nyoon-nyoon**;
	coverb+GET **nyoon**;
	coverb+BRING/TAKE **boonoo**
paint dots	*coverb+SAY/DO* **dag-dag**
paint dots on self	*coverb+DO_REFL* **dab-dab**
paint face white	*coverb+BURN/BITE_REFL* **nanggalag**
paint self	*coverb+SAY/DO_REFL* **boonoo**;
	coverb+CUT_SELF **barrg**;
	coverb+DO_REFL **barrg**
paint self/each other	*coverb+DO_REFL* **yoorr**
paint someone/something	*coverb* **barrg**;
	coverb+GO_ALONG **barrg-barrg**
paint, white	*noun* **galadil**
paint, yellow	*noun* **goombarriyil**
painted	*adjective* **boonoomawoony, boonoomawool, boonoomawoom**
painted marks used as decoration	*noun* **boowarraj**
painted with white paint, having face	*adjective* **nanggalagmawoony, nanggalagmawool, nanggalagmawoom**
painting, put dots on	*coverb+PUT* **dilg-dilg**
painting, stick used for	*noun* **jarn'girriny**
palm, cycad	*noun masculine* **nganthanji**
palm, cabbage, *Livistona victoriae*	*noun feminine* **danarrel**;
	noun feminine **yangajalil**;
	noun feminine **yingajalil**
Palm Spring (out from Halls Creek)	*noun* **Lingga**
pancreas	*noun* **garliyarlim**;
	noun **gerlalim**
pandanus	*noun feminine* **wirnbel**
pandanus, spring, *Pandanus spiralis*	*noun* **wirniny**
pannikin	*noun* **gardag, gardagboo**
panting	*coverb+GO_ALONG* **ngayirr**
be panting	*coverb+SAY/DO_M* **roonggerr**
paper	*noun* **merndany, merndam**
paper money	*noun* **ganarram**;
	noun **merlgam**;
	noun **merndany, merndam**
paper wasp, large	*noun feminine* **merrembernel**
paperbark	*noun* **merndany, merndam**
paperbark headdress	*noun* **goomoonoongam**;
	noun **goorlgoordoogoordoo**
paperbark species, small, *Melaleuca acacioides*	*noun masculine* **jinjilji**
Melaleuca nervosa	*noun feminine* **banderanil**
paperbark, tear off pieces of	*coverb+SAY/DO_M* **laroog**
paperbark bundle, roll into	*coverb+PUT* **gerndab**
paperbark tree, get sheets from	*coverb+GET* **dooroog**;
	coverb+SAY/DO_M **dooroog**
pardalote	*noun feminine* **joonjoonoonoojgel**
parent, parents' siblings	*noun* **manaroony, manarool**
parent and child together, kill	*coverb* **barlegboo**
parent, uncle or aunt has died, person whose	*noun* **ngamanyiny, ngamanyil**
parrot, red-winged	*noun feminine* **ginyginyel**
part of cattle stomach	*noun* **boorrooloo**;
	noun **marralam**
pass through	*coverb+BE/STAY* **beraj**
pass wind, to	*coverb* **thiny**;
	coverb **thirriny**
past something, go	*coverb+HIT* **beraj**
path	*noun* **bananbe**
pay	*coverb+GET* **waj**
peaceful dove	*noun feminine* **goorloordoogjil, goorloordoordoogjil**
peanut, bush	
cowpea yam	*noun masculine* **wanarrji**
nutwood	*noun* **bardiginy, bardigel**
red-flowered kurrajong	*noun masculine* **dayimbalji**

pearl shell

pearl shell......................*noun feminine* **jagoorlil, jagoorlim**
  large pearl-shell
    pendant......................*noun feminine* **galoowalel**
peel..............................*coverb+GET* **belag;**
                              coverb+SAY/DO **lerlb**
peep..............................*coverb+SAY/DO* **riyi**
peep over....................*coverb+GO/COME* **bed**
  be peeping over..........*coverb+BE/STAY* **bed**
  peep over at someone..*coverb+SPEAR* **bed**
peeping........................*coverb+BE/STAY* **riyi**
peewee, magpie lark....*noun feminine* **birlirrijgel;**
                              noun **goorliyirrel**
pelican.........................*noun masculine* **dabaroony**
Pelican Hole.................*noun* **Baljarran'ga**
pencil...........................*noun masculine* **mangadany**
pencil yam....................*noun masculine* **ngawoonyji**
pendant, pearl-shell.....*noun* **galoowalel**
penis............................*noun masculine* **gerlenggeny**
people from the west...*noun* **girli-girlirrangem**
people, old...................*noun* **garrenbawoorroom**
people who humbug
  (push) someone to
  do something.............*adjective* **nyirli-nyirliwoom**
peregrine falcon...........*noun masculine* **minymijginy, minymirdginy**
permanent ('living')
  water...........................*noun* **barranggany**
persistent....................*adjective* **nyirlginy, nyirlgil, nyirlgim**
person, Aboriginal........*noun* **jiyiliny, jiyilel, jiyilem**
person of mixed
  descent......................*adjective* **ngelyagbeny, ngelyagbel, ngelyagbem**
person one is sorry for.*noun* **gaageny, gaagel, gaagembi;**
                           noun **goorlanggeny, goorlanggel, goorlanggem;**
                           adjective **merelegbeny, merelegbel, merelegbem**
person, senior...............*noun* **manambarrany, manambarral, manambarram**
person, white................*noun* **gardiyany, gardiyal;**
                           adjective **ngelyagbeny, ngelyagbel, ngelyagbem;**
                           noun **wajbaloony, wajbalool**
person who leads lover
  away by the wrist.......*noun* **binggoom**

person whose brother
  or sister has died........*noun* **yawoorroony, yawoorrool**
  being a person whose
  brother or sister
  has died........................*coverb+GO/COME* **yawoorroogboo**
person whose child
  has died........................*noun* **thalebany, thalebal**
  being a person whose
  child has died...............*coverb+GO/COME* **thalebagboo**
person whose husband
  or wife has died,
  widow/widower..........*noun* **thoombawoony, thoombawool**
  being a person whose
  husband or wife
  has died........................*coverb+GO/COME* **thoombawoogboo**
person whose parent,
  uncle or aunt has
  died..............................*noun* **ngamanyiny, ngamanyil**
  being a person whose
  parent, uncle or aunt
  has died........................*coverb+GO/COME* **ngamanyigboo**
pet dog..........................*noun* **joondalji, joondalel**
petrol............................*noun* **bijid-bijidbe**
pheasant coucal...........*noun masculine* **thoolthoolji**
phlegm..........................*noun* **goonthoorrji, goonthoorroo**
photograph...................*noun* **ngaaloom**
physical child of
  mother........................*noun* **warlaginy, warlagil**
pick out........................*coverb+SAY/DO* **gooraj-gooraj**
  pick each other out........*coverb+SAY/DO_REFL* **gooraj**
pick out seeds or stuff
  from teeth with a
  little stick.....................*coverb+SAY/DO* **thirrilimbi**
pick up..........................*coverb+GET* **bib;**
                           coverb+GET **gooyarrg;**
                           coverb+SAY/DO **gooyarrg;**
                           coverb+SAY/DO **ngooyarr**
  pick up and take............*coverb+BRING/TAKE* **bib**
  pick up small objects
  one by one with
  fingers..........................*coverb+SAY/DO* **barniny**
  pick up someone and
  take away.....................*coverb+GET* **warnngemaj**
  pick up with the mouth..*coverb+GET* **gered**
picking up, go...............*coverb+GO_ALONG* **gooyarrg**
pierce............................*coverb+SAY/DO_M* **tharrboord**

Police Rock Hole

pierce and make water
  spurt out .... *coverb+SPEAR* **derlbawoo**
pig .... *noun feminine* **bigi-bigil**;
                               noun feminine
                                 ngoorrg-ngoorrgjil
pigeon species
  bronzewing pigeon....... *noun feminine*
                                 loowoo-loowoorrel
  crested pigeon .... *noun feminine* **balarayil**
  rock pigeon .... *noun feminine* **manboorlool**
  spinifex pigeon............. *noun feminine* **galawarrjil**
pillow .... *noun* **dirdim**
  make pillow for self....... *coverb+DO_REFL* **dirdi**
pinch someone .... *coverb+GO_ALONG* **gooyarrg**
pipit, Richard's .... *noun masculine*
                                 balalayingarnany
place of ancestral
  being .... *noun* **werlweny, werlwel,**
                                 werlwem
place, dreaming............ *noun* **werlweny, werlwel,**
                                 werlwem
place, open.................... *noun* **balgam**;
                                 noun **barawoorroom**;
                                 noun **baroowoorroom**
place, same .... *noun* **ginyane**;
                                 noun **giyale**
place where many
  killed/massacre site... *noun* **Goordbelayin**
place where one
  comes out .... *locative* **berabwalen**
place/heap up
  together...................... *coverb+PUT* **moondoorr**
place/put heavy
  object .... *coverb+PLACE* **moord**
place/put in an
  upright position .... *coverb+PUT* **thad**
place/stand upright ..... *coverb+GO_THROUGH* **jad**;
                                 coverb+PUT **jad**
placed/put, be .... *coverb+BE/STAY* **doorroon**
placenta........................ *noun* **warlawarre**
plain country,
  flat open country .... *noun* **balngarnam**
plains .... *noun* **wirridim**
plains kangaroo............ *noun masculine* **jarlangarnany**;
                                 noun masculine **warlambany**
  female plains
    kangaroo...................... *noun feminine* **gawoorrngarndil**
plane.............................. *noun feminine* **wirli-wirligajil**;
                                 noun feminine
                                 wirli-wirlingarnal

plant.............................. *noun* **goowooleny,**
                                 goowoolem
plant bearing lots of
  food .... *noun* **mayigalel, mayigaleny**
platypus........................ *noun feminine* **daboonggool**;
                                 noun feminine **nyoorroongool**
play .... *coverb+GO/COME* **boorooj**;
                                 coverb+SAY/DO **boorooj**;
                                 coverb+SAY/DO **boorij**;
                                 coverb+SAY/DO **thoorroojga**;
                                 coverb+SAY/DO_M **boorooj**
  go playing about .... *coverb+GO/COME* **booroojbany**
  play with something/
    someone .... *coverb+HIT* **boorooj**;
                                 coverb+SAY/DO_M **boorooj**
play around................... *coverb+SAY/DO_M* **manana**
play clapsticks............... *coverb+SAY/DO_M* **gil-gil**
playground.................... *noun* **booroojwirrin**
plot against someone .. *coverb+PUT* **ngoorriri**
pluck .... *coverb+GET*
                                 ngoojoorr-ngoojoorr;
                                 coverb+SAY/DO_M **ngoojoorr**
  pluck feathers............... *coverb+GET* **ngooj**
plum, black.................... *noun masculine* **minyjiwarrany**;
                                 noun masculine **minyjaarrany**
plum, brown.................. *noun masculine* **madarrgoony**
plum, green .... *noun masculine* **daaloony,**
                                 daloony
point at/show .... *coverb+PUT* **jirri**
point,
  hardwood spear......... *noun masculine* **jiwiny**
pointed .... *adjective* **jarroomboony,**
                                 jarroombool, jarroomboom
poison............................ *noun* **mawiyam**
  poison fish (to catch)..... *coverb+GET* **jaloowib**;
                                 coverb+HIT **jaliwoob**
  poison self..................... *coverb+CUT_REFL* **mawiyab**
  poison someone............ *coverb+SAY/DO_M* **mawiyab**
poke............................... *coverb+GET* **tharrboord**;
                                 coverb+HIT **thard**;
                                 coverb+PUT **nhen**
  poke in eye .... *coverb+GET* **darlg**
  poke self/each other..... *coverb+SPEAR_REFL* **jagij**
  poke stick into hole....... *coverb+SAY/DO_M* **nhen-nhen**
  poke with stick.............. *coverb+PUT*
                                 goorloorr-goorloorr
poke/stab something... *coverb+SAY/DO* **jagij**
Police Hole .... *noun* **Ngarrmaliny**
Police Rock Hole .... *noun* **Winberrji**

policeman

policeman ... *noun masculine* **mernmerdgaleny**; *noun masculine* **ngerlabany**
pollen sacs in native beehive ... *noun* **lanany**; *noun* **lernjim**
poo, defecate ... *coverb+HIT* **therraj**; *coverb+HIT* **therrilaj**
poor thing ... *noun* **gaageny, gaagel, gaagembi**; *noun* **goorlanggeny, goorlanggel, goorlanggem**; *adjective* **merelegbeny, merelegbel, merelegbem**; *adjective* **werlerlewoony, werlerlewool, werlerlewoom**
'porcupine' (Kriol for echidna) ... *noun feminine* **bagabal**; *noun feminine* **gernanyjel**
pose with arms folded ... *coverb+BE/STAY* **ngarajbe**
possibly ... *particle* **gardawoorroom, gardawoorroon**
possum species ... *noun masculine* **yinameny**
  brushtail possum, *Trichosurus vulpecula* ... *noun masculine* **nanggoony**
  rock ringtail possum, *Petropseudes dahli* ... *noun masculine* **garndoorroony**
potato: SEE bush potato; root species, edible; tuber species, edible; yam
pouch, kangaroo ... *noun* **ngaroom**
pound ... *coverb+HIT* **nyeg**; *coverb+SAY/DO_M* **daj**
pour ... *coverb+FALL/GO_DOWN* **thoorroorroo**
  pour out ... *coverb+HIT* **woombool**
  pour something ... *coverb+PUT* **tharroo**
  pour water on someone ... *coverb+HIT* **mamag**
power/magic ... *noun* **mayam**
praise someone ... *coverb+GET* **marrga**
'praise-em up' (sometimes considered swearing) ... *adjective* **ngoorloony, ngoorlool**
prawn, freshwater ... *noun feminine* **jalijgel**
praying mantis ... *noun masculine* **warrernji**
pregnant, become ... *coverb+BECOME* **jaawany, jaawawany**
pregnant, be made ... *coverb+SPEAR* **jaawag**

prepare things for an event ... *coverb+SAY/DO* **jama**; *coverb+GET* **ngooloongooloomenbe**
presents ... *noun* **balem, baalem**; *noun* **balwam**; *noun* **boolbam**
press on something ... *coverb+HIT* **moord**; *coverb+PUT* **moord**
press to straighten ... *coverb+PUT* **yarajbe**; *coverb+PUT* **yara-yaraj**
pressure-flake stone ... *coverb+GO/COME* **lendij, lendej**; *coverb+PUT* **lendej**; *coverb+SAY/DO_M* **lendij, lendej**
pretend ... *coverb+SAY/DO* **yagoorn**
pretend to hit ... *coverb+GET* **mad**
pretty ... *adjective* **doordoogany, doordoogal**; *adjective* **jambirrany, jambirral, jambirram**; *adjective* **joornanygarreny, joornanygarrel, joornanygarrem**
  make pretty ... *coverb+DO_REFL* **joornanygarreg**
previous ... *adjective* **ngamoo-ngamoom**
  previously ... *temporal* **ngamoongoon, ngamoo-ngamoongoon**
prickle ... *noun masculine* **bagany, bagam**; *noun masculine* **boorndalji, boorndale**; *noun* **marlagal**
prickly ... *adjective* **boornda-boorndabany, boornda-boorndabal, boornda-boorndabam**
  become prickly ... *coverb+BECOME* **bagaba**; *coverb+BECOME* **boorndalba**
prickle bush, *Dichrostachys spicata* ... *noun* **gooloomarram**
prickly wattle, *Acacia farnesiana* ... *noun masculine* **baga-wagany**; *noun masculine* **moorrooloomboony**
promiscuous ... *adjective* **woorlagany, woorlagal**
promise ... *noun* **boontham**
promise daughter to man ... *coverb+PUT* **roord**
promised husband ... *noun masculine* **boonthany**
promised wife ... *noun feminine* **boonthal**

put on lap

properly, do	*coverb+PUT* joodoog;
	coverb+PUT yirrjib
protruding	*adjective* jambalgem;
	coverb+BE/STAY thirringangab
proud, feel	*coverb+SAY/DO* gerlmarr
pubic cover	*noun* jarnim;
	noun warlboorroo
pubic hair	*noun* ngoorroornbe
pubic tassell	*noun* nyagoom
puffball fungus, mould	*noun masculine* langany
pull	*coverb+GET* rerr;
	coverb+SAY/DO rerr;
	coverb+SAY/DO rerreb;
	coverb+SAY/DO_M rerr
pull along	*coverb+BRING/TAKE* rerr
pull back hard	*coverb+GO/COME* therrmawiya
pull from fire	*coverb+GET* boog
pull off (e.g. fruit off tree, ticks off dog)	*coverb+GET* denggij
pull out	*coverb* thoorrooleb;
	coverb+GET beralg;
	coverb+GET randany;
	coverb+GET rarrirrij, rererrij;
	coverb+GET goorrg;
	coverb+SAY/DO_M goorrg
pull out grass	*coverb+SAY/DO* ral
pull out guts	*coverb+HIT* thenbel;
	coverb+SAY/DO thelbij
pull out hair	*coverb+GET* ngooj;
	coverb+GET ngoojoorr-ngoojoorr;
	coverb+SAY/DO_M ngoojoorr
pull out rock	*coverb+PUT* woorrgaj
pull out sinew	*coverb+GET* warl
pull out of earth oven	*coverb+GET* boog;
	coverb+GET doorrbood
pull quickly and throw	*coverb* werndelgbany
pull something like a fishing line	*coverb+GET* rendany
pull up	*coverb+GET* rerroob, roorroob
feel in mud and pull up	*coverb+SAY/DO_M* loogaj
pull up grass	*coverb+GET* ngoojoorr-ngoojoorr;
	coverb+SAY/DO_M ngoojoorr
pull up spinifex	*coverb+HIT* therdboo
pull something up	*coverb+GO_ALONG* rarr
pupa of *joombayil*	*noun* boomboongel
puppy	*noun* warlaginy, warlagil
puppies	*noun* warlarlayim
Purnululu National Park, Bungle Bungles	*noun* Boornoolooloo
pus	*noun* gambirn
push	*coverb+PUT* ben
push quickly	*coverb+PUT* jarl
push self back	*coverb+GO/COME* mengerr
push/hit with end of stick	*coverb+SAY/DO_M* dag
pushed (humbugged) to do something, be	*coverb+SAY/DO* nyirli-nyirli
pushy	*adjective* nyirli-nyirliwoom
put arms around self	*coverb+DO_REFL* lawoorr
put arms around someone	*coverb+GET* lawoorr
put arm down loosely	*coverb* yalg-yalgbany
put away	*coverb+PUT* doorroon
put away from action	*coverb+PUT* gemag
put back	*coverb+PUT* ngadi
put dots on painting	*coverb+PUT* dilg-dilg
put down	*coverb+HIT* roord;
	coverb+HIT jood;
	coverb+PUT joorroo;
	coverb+PUT roord;
	coverb+SAY/DO joorrooji
put facing up	*coverb+PUT* gerloorroogeb
put fire out	*coverb+PUT* thoomooj
put food in someone's mouth	*coverb+GIVE* thab
put foot on/step on	*coverb+SAY/DO_M* bad
put hand in hole	*coverb+GO/COME* yarr
put hands on	*coverb+GET* mam;
	coverb+GET manymaj
put hands on self	*coverb+SAY/DO_REFL* manymaj
put head down	*coverb+BE/STAY* yoodoong;
	coverb+PUT dareng
put in	*coverb+HIT* walig;
	coverb+PUT dagoorr;
	coverb+PUT walig
put in front	*coverb+HIT* welang
put in hair belt	*coverb+PUT* goorlgoon
put in hole	*coverb+HIT* dagoorlaj
put in mouth	*coverb+PUT* tharrmoong
put in straight line	*coverb+PUT* wandarra
put in sun	*coverb+PUT* barndeg
put in water to soak	*coverb+PUT* jawoorr
put off	*coverb+HIT* marndi
put on a forehead band	*coverb+SAY/DO_REFL* berndoowaleb
put on clothes	*coverb+PUT* laj
put on lap (e.g. child)	*coverb+PUT* jamoorrg

put on shoulders to carry

put on shoulders to carry	*coverb+PUT* **barle**; *coverb+PUT* **wandaj, wanda-wandaj**; *coverb+BRING/TAKE* **wandaj, wanda-wandaj**
put on top	*coverb+PUT* **wirlij**
put on fire to heat	*coverb+PUT* **jaa**
put out fire	*coverb+PUT* **thoomooj**
put outside	*coverb+PUT* **gemag**
put self at side	*coverb+DO_REFL* **doorroon**
put someone off	*coverb+GET* **boothalge**
put something in water	*coverb+HIT* **nyimoog**
put something on top of someone/something	*coverb+SAY/DO* **thoorroo-thoorroo**
put something on top of something	*coverb+PUT* **limboord**
put sticking up	*coverb+PUT* **rang**
put with stomach pointing up	*coverb+PUT* **gerloorroogeb**
put together	*coverb+PUT* **moondoorr**
put things together	*coverb+SAY/DO* **jama**
put together in large group	*coverb+PUT* **nyawoorn**
put under arm	*coverb+PUT* **yooloony**
put upside down	*coverb+PUT* **dareng**
put weight on something	*coverb+HIT* **moord**; *coverb+PUT* **moord**; *coverb+PUT* **nambalg**
put wood in place for fire	*coverb+PUT* **jard**
python, black-headed	*noun feminine* **dawool**; *noun feminine* **thoowerndemanbel**
python, children's	*noun* **binbinginy**
python, olive	*noun masculine* **dooloodbinyji**
python, water	*noun masculine* **warlenggenany**

Qq

quail	*noun feminine* **jibigel**
quartz	*noun* **manjalji, manjale**
quick/fast	*adverb* **waranggan**
quickly in a good way	*adverb* **lirlij**
quickly pull and throw	*coverb* **werndelgbany**
quickly push	*coverb+PUT* **jarl**
quickly take off	*adverb* **garda-gardan**
quickly, walk	*coverb+SAY/DO* **warrij-warrij**
quiet (not aggressive)	*adjective* **wari-bawoorroony, wari-bawoorrool**
quiet, be	*coverb+GO/COME* **nag**; *coverb+GO/COME* **nagarr**; *coverb+SAY/DO* **nyireg**
become quiet	*coverb+BECOME* **nag**
quiet, stay	*coverb+GO/COME* **girrji**
stay very quiet	*coverb+GO/COME* **gerrji**
quietly, talk (group)	*coverb+SAY/DO* **ngoorn-ngoorn**
quinine tree	*noun masculine* **welrayiny**
quoll	*noun masculine* **bawoogoony**

Rr

race up and kill someone	*coverb+HIT* **galaleb**
radiating, be	*coverb+SAY/DO* **ngoowoob**
radiator, car	*noun phrase* **goorrnga-girrem dam bemberrooloonboo-ngarri-ngiyi**
radio	*noun* **jarraggajim, jarraggajiny**
rag used to tie something	*noun* **ngerlam**
Rail Yard	*noun* **Wimeroorroon**
rain	*noun* **jadany**
be raining	*coverb+BECOME* **jalij**; *coverb+FALL/GO_DOWN* **jalij**; *coverb+SAY/DO_M* **jada-jadawany**; *coverb+SAY/DO_M* **jalij**; *coverb+SAY/DO* **jalij**
be spitting/sprinkling rain	*coverb+SAY/DO_M* **jimbi-jimbij**
cold-season rain	*noun masculine* **goorloowanginy, goorloowabany**
drip rain	*coverb+SAY/DO* **tharroorroo**
first rain-storm	*noun* **warlangem**
heavy rain	*noun* **lalawoorroony, lalawoorroom**
make rain	*coverb+PUT* **nyood**
rain big drops	*coverb+SAY/DO* **larrg-larrg**
rain clear up/disperse	*coverb+GO/COME* **yinyjoong**
rain falling down	*coverb* **boorliyirr**

rain from the south	*noun* **jabananggany**
season of set-in rain	*temporal* **yiwirn'gen**
set-in rain	*noun* **yiwirn**
start to rain	*coverb+DO_REFL* **boorliyirrg**; *coverb+DO_REFL* **boorli-boorlirrg**; *coverb+GO_ALONG* **boorlirrg-boorlirrg**
stop (rain)	*coverb+GO/COME* **nanggerrg**
time of set-in rain	*temporal* **yiwirn'gen**
rainbow	*noun feminine* **tharriyarril**
rainbow bird	*noun feminine* **birrid-birridel**
rainbow lorikeet	*noun feminine* **wirrilijgel**
rainbow lorikeet (said by young men)	*noun feminine* **thirrilngarnal**
rainbow snake	*noun masculine* **garlooroony**; *noun feminine* **goorlabal**; *noun masculine* **yingerriwoony**
rainbow snake scales	*noun* **manyawoorlale**
range of steep hills	*noun* **gawarre, gawarriny**
rash, come out in	*coverb+SAY/DO* **loomoorrmoorr**
rash, one that causes a	*adjective* **loomoorrmoorr-nhawoony, loomoorrmoorr-nhawool, loomoorrmorr-nhawoom**
rasp-tailed goanna	*noun masculine* **gilbany**
rat/mouse	*noun feminine* **jaranel**; *noun* **nyilimbil, nyilimbiny**; *noun masculine* **yiroowoonji**
rat, water	*noun feminine* **nyoorroongool**
rattling, go along	*coverb+GO_ALONG* **larra-larraj**
raw	*adjective* **gern'gany, gern'gal, gern'gam**
reach destination	*coverb+FALL/GO_DOWN* **dawoolan**
reach for something	*coverb+GO/COME* **yarr**
reach halfway to destination	*coverb+HIT* **jalayi**
reach top	*coverb+SAY/DO_M* **gij**
read	*coverb+SAY/DO_M* **lendij, lendej**
ready	*adverb* **yiloowoogtha**; *particle* **jamoonin**
get ready	*coverb+SAY/DO* **jama**; *coverb+GET* **ngooloongooloomenbe**
realise one is about to die	*coverb+SAY/PLACE_REFL* **nyoorl**
reborn, reincarnated	*adjective* **jarrinybany, jarrinybal**
spirit of person that is reborn after death	*noun* **jarrinybe**
reborn (jumped up) from something/ someone that previously existed	*adjective* **bawardngoorriny**
recognise	*coverb+GET* **ngarra**
not recognise	*coverb+HIT* **ganginy**; *coverb+HIT* **ngany**
reconciled, be	*coverb+BE/STAY* **wedag**
recover, get better	*coverb+PUT* **jarr**; *coverb+SAY/DO_M* **ngere**
rectum	*noun* **gerrelem**
red	*adjective* **galimbirrji, galimbirril, galimbirre**
red ant	*noun masculine* **gangalangaliny**
red ochre	*noun feminine* **badel, badem**; *noun feminine* **danggal, danggam**
red water	*noun* **jirlewoorrji, jirlewoorre**
red-coloured soil	*noun* **jirlewoorrji, jirlewoorre**
red (some say a bit swearing)	*adjective* **ngenhengbeny, ngenhengbel, ngenhengbem**
Red Butt	*noun* **Wirdim**
Red Butt, place near	*noun* **Doogoorrenyinem**
Red Hill, near Halls Creek	*noun* **Thalngarrngarrem**
red kangaroo, big	*noun masculine* **wawirriny**
Red Pocket	*noun* **Jirljin**
red river gum	SEE **river red gum**
red-backed wren	*noun masculine* **yirril-yirrilji**
red-flowered kurrajong	*noun* **dayimbalji**
red-winged parrot	*noun feminine* **ginyginyel**
reeds, bullrush, *Typha domingensis*	*noun* **beremerrel**
reeds, water sedge, *Cyperus vaginatus*	*noun* **thelinjany**; *noun* **theltheny**
refuse something because you want something else	*coverb+SAY/DO* **yirrgawoo**; *coverb+SAY/DO_M* **yirrgawoo**
refuse to answer	*coverb+SPEAR* **linggara-gara**
refuse to listen to advice	*coverb+HIT* **bagarrji**
refuse to move, sit and	*coverb+GO/COME* **balg**
refuse to share with someone	*coverb+HIT* **dangoori**

reincarnated

reincarnated .... *adjective* **jarrinybany, jarrinybal**
reject .... *coverb+SAY/DO* **garn'garr**
remember .... *coverb+FALL/GO_DOWN* **linga**
remind .... *coverb+GET* **lingage**;
                                   coverb+PUT **linga**
Rendhal's catfish .... *noun masculine* **woorlengerriny**
repairing something,
  be .... *coverb+SAY/DO* **ngarag**
resin type .... *noun* **binyinyiny**
  spinifex resin .... *noun* **gaalji, gaale**
'respect language',
  talk about
  mother-in-law using .. *coverb+SAY/DO* **melera**
responsible person ...... *adjective* **garrayilji, garrayilel, garrayile**
rest .... *coverb+FALL/GO_DOWN* **ngarrirrij**;
                             coverb+SAY/DO **ngarrij**
  be resting .... *coverb+BE/STAY* **ngarrirrij**
  have a rest .... *coverb+BE/STAY* **ngarrij**
return .... *coverb+FALL/GO_DOWN* **biri**;
                             coverb+GO/COME **biri**;
                             coverb+SAY/DO_M **biri**
  return (plural) .... *coverb+GO/COME* **biriwoorrg**
rib bone .... *noun* **jilemberre**;
                             noun **walamboom**
ride .... *coverb+GO/COME* **barle**
  be riding .... *coverb+FALL/GO_DOWN* **barle-warle**
  ride (e.g. horses) .... *coverb+SAY/DO* **barle-warle**
  ride something .... *coverb+GET* **barle**;
                             coverb+HIT **barle**
rifle .... *noun feminine* **derlbawoogajil**;
                             noun **doorlgajim**;
                             noun feminine **warn'gil**
rifle fish .... *noun feminine* **loowarrel**
right, be .... *coverb+SAY/DO_M* **ngarra**
right here .... *locative* **ngenenggayana**
right side .... *locative* **joodoobiny**
ring place .... *noun* **barawoorroom**
ringing sound,
  make (e.g. bell) .... *coverb+HIT* **lerlerl**
ringworm .... *noun* **gerrmam**
rip off .... *coverb+BE/STAY* **lerawoog**
ripe .... *adjective* **babijgeny, babijgel, babijgem**
  ripen .... *coverb+BURN/BITE* **ngawoorr**
ripping up, go along ..... *coverb+GO_ALONG* **denggerr**
ripple .... *coverb+SAY/DO* **ngarla-ngarla**
  be ripples on water ...... *coverb+SAY/DO* **wirrarraj**
  make ripples .... *coverb+HIT* **wirraj**

river .... *noun* **nawarragawoony**;
                             noun **nyanagawoony**
  river come over bank .... *coverb+SAY/DO* **woorlboorr**
river fig .... *noun* **goonangginy**;
                             noun masculine **jawoonany**
river red gum .... *noun* **bilirnji**;
                             noun **dimalan**;
                             noun **garranggany**
river wallaby .... *noun masculine* **warlbawoony**
road .... *noun* **bananbe**
  on the road .... *locative* **banane**
roasted .... *adjective* **goonggoonngem**
rock .... *noun* **ngarrgaleny, ngarrgalem**;
                             noun **ngaarriny**
  flat rock .... *noun* **barlalim**;
                             noun **barlawany**
  pull out rock .... *coverb+PUT* **woorrgaj**
  rock used to make
    something smooth .... *adjective* **booloorroo**
  rocks under burial
    platform .... *noun* **janderre**
  throw rock in water ...... *coverb+SAY/DO* **darloo**
rock cod .... *noun* **nyagoornany**
rock fig .... *noun* **banggoonji, banggoornji**;
                             noun **jimirlbiny**
rock goanna,
  hill country goanna ... *noun masculine* **boonoonggoony**
rockhole .... *noun* **dagoorlany, dagoorlan**
rock wallaby .... *noun masculine* **doowanggoonyji**;
                             noun masculine **woombardgoony**;
                             noun masculine **woombarnoongoony**;
                             noun masculine **woonyjoorroony**
  fat female rock wallaby .. *noun feminine* **marliwal**;
                             noun feminine **thoorrmal**
rock (movement)
  rock to comfort .... *coverb+BRING/TAKE* **werrerre**;
                             coverb+HIT **werrerre, werrerre-werrerre**
  rock from side to side ... *coverb+SAY/DO* **ngen**
  rock up and down,
    move from side to side .. *coverb+GO_ALONG* **loomayi**
rocky/holey country
  in gorge .... *noun* **thamoonmoorroo**

rush out (water)

roll into paperbark
   bundle .... *coverb+PUT* **gerndab**
roll over .... *coverb+FALL/GO_DOWN*
   rembelenga
roll something .... *coverb* **gerr-gerr**
roly-poly (plant) .... *noun* **moolirrji**
root, butt of tree .... *noun* **garndiny, garndim**
root species, edible
   black-soil yam, *Ipomoea*
   abrupta, *I. aquatica* .... *noun* **garndiny**
   bush potato,
   Brachystelma
   glabriflorum .... *noun masculine* **banariny**
   kapok bush root,
   Cochlospermum
   fraseri var. *fraseri* .... *noun feminine* **goonjal**
   furry-leaved kapok
   bush root,
   Cochlospermum fraseri
   var. *heteronemum* .... *noun masculine* **malanyjarrji**;
   noun masculine **ngalwany**;
   noun feminine **warndiwal**
   SEE ALSO bush potato; tuber species, edible; yam
roots .... *noun* **lenggale, lenggam**
   roots at side of water ....*noun* **nan'goon**
rosella, northern .... *noun feminine*
   gooldany-gooldanyel
rosella yam,
   Abelmoschus
   ficulneus .... *noun feminine* **goornoogal**
rosewood .... *noun* **malaliny, marlarriny**
rotten meat .... *noun* **goonarre**
rough .... *adjective* **boolngarrbany**;
   adjective **booloorrji**,
   booloorrel, booloorroo
rough bluebell, camel
   bush, *Trichodesma*
   zeylanicum .... *noun feminine* **giwinboorrel**
rough surface,
   having a .... *adjective* **joomoorr-joomoorre**
round fluffy seed pods
   of kapok bush .... *noun* **booboogarral**
round hill, small .... *noun* **goowaleny**
round thing .... *noun* **goordoony**
   little round things .... *noun* **joorlgoorlgoom**
round up animals .... *coverb+SAY/DO* **wilili**
   round up/hunt/
   try to hit .... *coverb+PUT* **wililib**
rub between hands to
   clean skin off
   bush onions .... *coverb+HIT* **boorlirri**
rub hands down stick
   to get something off ..*coverb+PUT* **biyirr-biyirrbe**
rub hands down stick
   to get fruit off .... *coverb+GET* **biyirr**
rub on .... *coverb+BRING/TAKE* **nyoon**;
   coverb+HIT **yoorrg**;
   SAY/DO **nyoon-nyoon**
rub to increase game ...*coverb+GET* **gelng**
rub with paint .... *coverb+HIT* **yoorr**
rub with sweat from
   armpit .... *coverb+GET* **yoorrwab**
rubbish bin, basin,
   deep dish .... *noun* **jaboogoom,
   jaboogoony, jaboogool**
rude sign, make .... *coverb+GET* **rany**
rufous whistler .... *noun feminine* **jiyig-jiyigel**
rumbling stomach
   from hunger, have .....*coverb+SAY/DO* **goorlirlij**
run .... *coverb+GO_ALONG* **wijinga**;
   coverb+GO/COME **wiji**;
   coverb+SAY/DO **wiji**;
   coverb+SAY/DO **wijinga**;
   coverb+SAY/DO_M **wiji**
   go running .... *coverb+BE/STAY* **wijiwany**
   run (group) .... *coverb+GO/COME* **yoowoorr**;
   coverb+SAY/DO **yoowoorr**;
   coverb+SAY/DO
   yoowoorr-yoowoorr;
   coverb+SAY/DO_M **yoowoorr**
   run and hide .... *coverb+FALL/GO_DOWN* **yirrberda**
   run and leave .... *coverb+LEAVE* **wiji**
   run and leave (group) ...*coverb+LEAVE* **yoowoorr**
run around in a group ..*coverb+GO/COME* **rarrawoolib**
run away fast .... *coverb+GO/COME* **thoony**
   make run away fast .... *coverb+HIT/CUT* **thoony**
   run away carrying
   something .... *coverb+BRING/TAKE* **wiji**
run down .... *coverb+SAY/DO_M* **warnajarr**
run down, tears .... *coverb+GO/COME*
   mooroorl-mooroorl
run down, water .... *coverb+SAY/DO* **jalawoorr**
run flat out .... *coverb* **men-men**
run, make .... *coverb+GET* **wijige**;
   coverb+GET **wijigoowany**
run, make lots .... *coverb+GET* **yoowoorrge**
run taking something ..*coverb+BRING/TAKE* **wiji**
run with something ..... *coverb+GO_BECOME* **wiji**
run without looking
   back .... *coverb+GO/COME* **thern**
rush .... *coverb+SAY/DO* **loorr**
rush out (water) .... *coverb+SAY/DO* **nherraj**

Ss

rustling noise through
   grass, go making a......coverb+GO/COME **rawoolilib**

sacred place,
   important ....noun **doomoorriny,
                                  doomoorrinyji,
                                  doomoorrinyil,
                                  doomoorrinybe;**
                                  noun **joomoorririny,
                                  joomoorrirrim**
sacred/secret things
   (dangerous word).........noun **daroogoo**
sad................................coverb+SAY/DO **mooloorroo**
   become sad..................coverb+BECOME **mooloorroo**
   feel sad inside..............coverb+SAY/DO **jirr-jirr;**
                                  coverb+BE/STAY
                                  moolooloongboo
   make sad ....coverb+GET **jirr-jirrge;**
                                  coverb+GET **mooloorroog**
saddle ....noun **bernngam**
Saddler's Jump-Up..........noun **Thalngarrwany**
safely introduce............coverb+PUT **mantha**
saliva...............................noun **ganggoom**
salt ....noun **garam;**
                                  noun **gilyam;**
                                  noun **girlarlam;**
   bush salt......................noun **garragoonbe**
saltwater crocodile.......noun masculine
                                  yalamboorrmany
same, being the............coverb+BE/STAY **yajany**
same, having the..........coverb+HAVE **yajany**
same name,
   person with ....noun **narroogoo**
same place ....noun **ginyane;**
                                  noun **giyale**
sand ....noun **ngayawarlji,
                                  ngayawarle;**
                                  noun **warrayelji, warrayele**
   spread sand..................coverb+PUT **thoorroo**
sand frog, large ....noun masculine **balngawoon,
                                  balngawoonji**
sand frog, small...........noun feminine
                                  nangala-nangalal
sand wasp ....noun feminine **ngirrngirril**
sand, wet......................noun **giyim**
sandalwood...................noun masculine
                                  woorlngooroony
sandpaper fig................noun masculine **yimarlji;**
                                  noun masculine **yingarrjiny**

sandstone......................noun **booloorrji, booloorroo**
sandy ground................noun **woorrjininy**
sap from bloodwood....noun **galiwoony**
sausage,
   kangaroo tail ....noun **goorlany**
save................................coverb+GET **jariyi**
sawfish, freshwater......noun masculine **bayirrany;**
                                  noun feminine **garlwanyil**
say 'eh?' ....coverb+SAY/DO **ngoord**
say 'gaag',
   make someone...........coverb+GET **gaagge**
say goodbye ....coverb+GET **mathe;**
                                  coverb+SAY/DO_REFL
                                  mathe-mathe
say name ....coverb+GET **garij;**
                                  coverb+SAY/DO_M **garij**
   be saying name ....coverb+GO/COME **garijib**
   say each other's name ..coverb+DO_REFL **garij**
say 'woog-woog' (frog)..coverb+SAY/DO **woog-woog**
saying 'gaag-gaag',
   go along ....coverb+GO_ALONG **gaag-gaag**
saying 'no',
   shake head ....coverb+SAY/DO **ngen-ngen**
scabies ....noun masculine **nyingginy**
scale, fish.....................noun **lirlmim;**
                                  noun **lirn'girre;**
                                  noun **nyilim**
scales of rainbow
   snake...........................noun **manyawoorlale**
scar from sore...............noun **garlge**
scar, tribal ....noun **gemerre**
scared, be ....coverb+SAY/DO **jilba;**
                                  coverb+SAY/DO_M **jilba**
scary ....adjective **jilbawoony,
                                  jilbawool, jilbawoom**
scavenge ....coverb+SAY/DO **garrid-garrid;**
                                  coverb+SAY/DO_M **nyoornayi**
school teacher ....noun **lendijgaleny,
                                  lendijgalel, lendijgalem;**
                                  noun **merndagaleny,
                                  merndagalel, merndagalem**
scissors grinder,
   restless flycatcher,
   Myiagra inquieta ....noun feminine **goorlawoorlal**
scold...............................coverb+GET **wari-wari;**
                                  coverb+SAY/DO **ngalerr**
scoop up ....coverb+GET **rebej**
   scoop up water............coverb+GET **jerreb**
   scoop up with hand ......coverb+GET **goorooj**
scorpion.........................noun masculine **galarrwoorany**
   water scorpion.............noun feminine **bindirijgel**

shake

scrape . . . . *coverb+GET* **therr-therr**;
	coverb+SAY/DO **therr-therrb**
  scrape and make
	smooth . . . . *coverb* **jaloorl-jaloorl**
  scrape off bark
	from sticks . . . . *coverb+GET* **wij-wij**
scratch self . . . . *coverb+DO_REFL* **girr, girr-girr**
scratch self, dog . . . . *coverb+DO_REFL* **therr, therr-therr**;
	coverb+SAY/DO_REFL **therr**
scratch someone/
	something . . . . *coverb+GET* **girr-girr**
scratches, one that . . . . *adjective* **girranynhawoony, girranynhawool, girranynhawoom**
scratches on self,
	make long . . . . *coverb+DO_REFL* **jirawoorr**
scratches on someone,
	make long . . . . *coverb+GET* **jirawoorr**
scrub country . . . . *noun* **yooroorroom, yooroowoorroom**
  become scrubby
	(country) . . . . *coverb* **yiwijge**
season, cold . . . . *temporal* **warn'gan**
season, hot . . . . *temporal* **barnden**;
	temporal **malwalan**
season, wet . . . . *temporal* **jadagen, jadagin**
sea water . . . . *noun* **ngabarl-ngabarl**
secret sign, give . . . . *coverb+HIT* **nhoorr**
secretly, come . . . . *coverb+GO/COME* **reganyda, reganyja**
see . . . . *coverb+HIT* **gedba**;
	coverb+SAY/DO **deg**
  see something . . . . *coverb+GET* **deg**
seed/seed pod/bullet . . . *noun* **ganjiny, ganjim**
seed pods, bauhinia . . . . . *noun* **gerlalim**
seeds, boab . . . . *noun* **jililiny, jililem**
seeds on tree finish/
	fall . . . . *coverb+FALL/GO_DOWN* **woordoorr**
seen moving in the
	distance, be just . . . . *coverb+GO_ALONG* **yinggerd**
self, hurt . . . . *coverb+FALL/GO_DOWN* **geberd**
  fall and hurt self . . . . *coverb+FALL/GO_DOWN* **mirl-mirlge**
semen . . . . *noun* **ngarndam**
  big semen
	(swear word) . . . . *interjection* **ngarndaginy, ngarndagel**
send . . . . *coverb+HIT* **berra, berra-werra**
  send far away . . . . *coverb+HIT* **marrangag**

senior person . . . . *noun* **manambarrany, manambarral, manambarram**
  senior person: mother,
	uncle, father or aunt . . . . . *noun* **manaroony, manarool**
separate . . . . *coverb+DO_REFL* **barlberr**;
	coverb+GO/COME **barlberr**;
	coverb+LEAVE **barlberr**;
	coverb+LEAVE_REFL **gad**
separate from others . . . *adverb* **yajany**
separate rubbish
	from something
	(e.g. ash, ochre) . . . . *coverb+HIT* **darda-darda**
sesbania species with
	tall stems used as
	spear shafts . . . . *noun masculine* **gilin'goowoony**
set fire to something
	(e.g. bush or grass) . . . . *coverb+PUT* **boodooj**;
	coverb+PUT **booj**;
	coverb+SAY/DO **booj-booj**
set-in rain . . . . *noun* **yiwirn**
  time of set-in rain . . . . *temporal* **yiwirn'gen**
set off . . . . *coverb+GO/COME* **marra**
set on fire . . . . *coverb+PLACE* **booj**
settle down . . . . *coverb+FALL/GO_DOWN* **ngarli**;
	coverb+SAY/DO **ngarli**
sexy . . . . *adjective* **gayawoony, gayawool, gayawoom**;
	adjective **yigarrwoony, yigarrwool, yigarrwoom**;
	adjective **yoowarroony, yoowarrool, yoowarroom**
  sexy one, raunchy one . . *noun* **yoowarrnhawoony, yoowarrnhawool, yoowarrnhawoom**
shade . . . . *noun* **manggoom**;
	noun **ngaaloom**
  be big shade . . . . *coverb+BECOME* **doonggood**
shade eyes from sun
	when looking . . . . *coverb+PUT* **galayi**
shadow . . . . *noun* **ngaaloom**
shake . . . . *coverb+SAY/DO* **mirr**;
	coverb+SAY/DO **therrngarn**;
	coverb+SAY/DO **yard-yard**
  be shaking . . . . *coverb+SAY/DO* **jerr-jerr**;
	coverb+SAY/DO **nyoongoon**
  shake chest . . . . *coverb+SAY/DO_M* **mel-mel**
  shake head from
	side to side . . . . *coverb+SAY/DO* **ngen-ngen**
  shake water off self . . . . . . *coverb+SAY/DO* **doowerrberr**

shake with fright, make someone

shake with fright,
  make someone............coverb+GET **mirr-mirrge**
shake with pain,
  cause to......................coverb+GET **therrngarn'ge**
shaky paw lizard............noun masculine **jawarlaliny**;
  noun masculine **manggerregerreny**
shallow edge of creek..locative **garlirrin**
shallow water................noun **gajam**;
  noun **garlirriny**
shame, having no..........adjective **ganybelbawoorroony, ganybelbawoorrool, ganybelbawoorroom**
shame,
  make someone feel....coverb+GET **ganybelgbe**;
  coverb+GET **ganybelge**
shamed..........................coverb+GO/COME **ganybelgbe**
  make shamed...............coverb+GET **moojoonggoolg**
share food......................coverb+GO/COME **ngajarrg-ngajarrg**
share out.......................coverb+SAY/DO_REFL2 **jayi**
  not sharing....................coverb+SAY/DO **warrmayi**;
  coverb+SAY/DO_M **warrmayi**
share, person who
  refuses to.....................adjective **dangoorinhawoony, dangoorinhawool, dangoorinhawoom**
share with someone,
  refuse to.......................coverb+GET **daboo**
  coverb+HIT **dangoori**
sharp..............................adjective **jalinggiriny, jalinggiril, jalinggirim**
  sharp spine..................noun **bagam**
  small sharp stick used
  to make spearheads.....noun **mangadany**
sharpen.........................coverb+GET **jalinggirig**;
  coverb+PUT **boorr-boorr**;
  coverb+PUT **geraj-geraj**;
  coverb+PUT **jalinggirig**;
  coverb+SAY/DO **geraj-geraj**
sharpened.....................adjective **jarroomboony, jarroombool, jarroomboom**
shave hair off head......coverb+HIT **ngererr**
  having shaved head......adjective **ngererrnginy**
she..................................pronoun **ngalen**
  she's the one................demonstrative **deyela, diyala**;
  demonstrative **ngaliyana**
shed leaves...................coverb+BECOME **wirrg**
shed skin.......................coverb **nyarlool**

sheep............................noun feminine **googoonjal**;
  noun feminine **jiyigjel**
shell...............................noun **lirn'girre**
  large baler shell............noun feminine **yabirlil**
  pearl shell.....................noun feminine **jagoorlil**
  pearl-shell pendant......noun **galoowalel**
shells carried by clever
  men, small white........noun **binyjawinyjal, binyjawinyjam**
shield.............................noun feminine **mirdal**
shine..............................coverb+SAY/DO **minin-minin**
shining, be....................coverb+SAY/DO **belany-belany**;
  coverb+SAY/DO **merli-merliliny**;
  coverb+SAY/DO **merliny-merliny**;
  coverb+SAY/DO **miliny-miliny**
shiny..............................adjective **berleng-berlengeny, berleng-berlengel, berleng-berlengem**;
  adjective **mililinybem**;
  adjective **mililinygany, mililinygal, mililinygam**
shit/faeces....................noun **manam**
shit/defecate................coverb+HIT **therraj**;
  coverb+HIT **therrilaj**
shitwood.......................noun masculine **jarlaloony**
shiver............................coverb+HIT **lerle**;
  coverb+SAY/DO **lerle**;
  coverb+SAY/DO **mirr-mirr**
shock, get a..................coverb+SAY/DO **ngirlarr**
  suddenly come and
  get a shock..................coverb+GO/COME **jarda**
shock, give a................coverb+GET **ngelyarr**
shoot..............................coverb+HIT **derlbawoo**
short..............................adjective **goothoongoony, goothoongool, goothoongoom**;
  adjective **goothoongoowarrany, goothoongoowarral, goothoongoowarram**
  short and fat................adjective **gendaloogany, gendaloogal, gendaloogoom**
short-sighted...............adjective **nyamiginy, nyamigil, nyamigim**
short spear...................noun **goombam**
shoulders......................noun **bambalam**
  back of shoulders........noun **barnale**
  shoulder blade............noun **lawardem**
shout at someone........coverb+SAY/DO **ngalerr**
shove each other.........coverb+SAY/DO_REFL **jarl-jarl**

show	*coverb+BRING/TAKE* **jirri**;
	coverb+GET **jirri**;
	coverb+HIT **jirri**;
	coverb+PUT **giwaj**;
	coverb+PUT **jirri**;
	coverb+BRING/TAKE **bina**
show off	*coverb+SAY/DO* **garn'garr**;
	coverb+SAY/DO **gerlmarr**
shrivelled	*adjective* **tharleny, tharlel, tharlem**
shy	*adjective* **ligbayiny, ligbayil, ligbayim**;
	adjective **moojoongbeny, moojoongbel, moojoongbem**
be shy	*coverb+SAY/DO* **ganybel**;
	coverb+SAY/DO **moojoong**
be shy (plural)	*coverb+SAY/DO* **moojoonggoowool**
sibling	*noun* **ngajiny, ngajil, ngajim**
older sibling	*noun* **goorabeny, goorabel, goorabem**;
	noun **booloongoony, booloongool, booloongoom**
younger sibling	*noun* **bariyiny, bariyil, bariyim**;
	noun **gooloongarriny, gooloongarril, gooloongarrim**
sibling (spoken to)	*noun* **ngaji**
sibling, be the next	*coverb+BE/STAY* **wad**
sick	*adjective* **warrernbeny, warrernbel, warrernbem**
be sick	*coverb+SAY/DO* **warrern**
feel sick	*coverb+FALL/GO_DOWN* **ngarl**
get sick	*coverb+FALL/GO_DOWN* **warrern**
make sick	*coverb+GET* **warrern'ge**
sick of something, be	*coverb+GO_ALONG* **wanggooloo**
sickly	*adjective* **warrern-warrern-nhawoony, warrern-warrern-nhawool, warrern-warrern-nhawoom**
side, along the	*locative* **limbalbiny**
side of body	*noun* **thambem**
side of hill	*locative* **gawalalanygarre**;
	locative **lamban**
along side of hill	*locative* **wayirran**
go along side of hill	*coverb+GO/COME* **lambag, lamba-biny**
side/edge of something	*locative* **thayin**
side of woomera	*noun* **walamboom**
side to side, swing hips	*coverb+SAY/DO* **yigily-yigily**
sideways	*locative* **lirring**
glance sideways	*coverb+SPEAR* **lirring**
have head sideways	*coverb+BE/STAY* **lig**
lie down sideways	*coverb+BE/STAY* **ngirndirring**
look at someone sideways	*coverb+GET* **lirring**
	coverb+SPEAR **ngirril**
look sideways	*coverb+SAY/DO* **lirring**
wriggle sideways	*coverb+GO_ALONG* **weleberr**
'sideways', talk about mother-in-law	*coverb+SAY/DO* **melera**
sight, go out of	*coverb+FALL/GO_DOWN* **darag**;
	coverb+GO/COME **darag**
go out of sight leaving someone	*coverb+LEAVE* **darag**
sign, give	*coverb+PUT* **liya**
sign, give secret	*coverb+HIT* **nhoorr**
sign, make rude	*coverb+GET* **rany**
silhouetted in a gap, be	*locative* **ngarayiwarran**
silver-crowned friar bird	*noun masculine* **gagoowany**
sinew, 'string'	*noun* **jirlwam**;
	noun **nganyjoom**
pull out sinew	*coverb+GET* **warl**
wrap sinew on spear shaft	*coverb+HIT* **warl**
sinews, be strong in	*coverb+SAY/DO* **yarrara**
sinews, make strong in	*coverb+GET* **yarrarage**
sing	*coverb+GO_ALONG* **ngalany**;
	coverb+SAY/DO **ngalany**;
	coverb+SAY/DO_M **ngalany**
sing self	*coverb+DO_REFL* **ngalany**
sing someone	*coverb+GET* **ngalany**;
	coverb+WOUND **ngalany**
singer, good	*noun* **ngalanygaleny, ngalanygalel, ngalanygalem**
sing/pronounce song words	*coverb+GET* **garij**
sing/speak to ward off danger	*coverb+HIT* **wiyawoog**;
	coverb+SAY/DO_M **wiyawoog**
singe	*coverb+GET* **gerijaleb**
singe fur/skin off	*coverb+HIT* **gawal**
sinking, be	*coverb+FALL/GO_DOWN* **nyimininybe**
sister	*noun feminine* **ngajil**

sister-in-law

mother's sister	*noun feminine* **gamelanyel**
older sister	*noun feminine* **goorabel**;
	noun feminine **booloongool**
sister (man speaking)	*noun feminine* **garloomboo-bawoorrool**
sister (spoken to)	*noun* **ngaji**
younger sister	*noun feminine* **bariyil**
sister-in-law	*noun feminine* **ngoolngal**;
	noun feminine **wardool**
sister-in-law (spoken to)	*noun* **ngoolnga**;
	noun **wardoo**
sister-in-law of man	*noun feminine* **ngawoojil**
sister-in-law of man (spoken to)	*noun* **ngawooji**
sit	*coverb+BE/STAY* **roord**
be sitting	*coverb+BE/STAY* **roord**
sit (plural)	*coverb+BE/STAY* **roorrjib**
sit and refuse to move	*coverb+GO/COME* **balg**
sit and look after someone	*coverb+HAVE* **roord**
sit down	*coverb* **looloo**;
	coverb+BE/STAY **woorrg**;
	coverb+FALL/GO_DOWN **roord**
sitting (plural)	*coverb+BE/STAY* **woorrjib**
sit cross-legged	*coverb+BE/STAY* **balbirrin**
sit holding	*coverb+HAVE* **roord**
sit with back to someone	*coverb+BE/STAY* **thoolngoorroob**
sit with back to someone (plural)	*coverb+BE/STAY* **thoolngoo-yoolngoorroob**
sitting down with knees up, be	*coverb+BE/STAY* **jarranang**
Six Mile	*noun* **Goowoorljin**
skin (people or animal)	*noun* **manyjangalam**;
	noun **moogoonybe**;
	noun **wajawoorroo**;
	noun **wangarrem**
shed skin (goanna, cicada)	*coverb* **nyarlool**
skin (e.g. of onion)	*noun* **lirn'girre**
skin hanging down like a flying fox, have	*adjective* **wanboorrbany, wanboorrbal, wanboorrbam**
skin names (when spoken about)	*noun masculine* **Jaangariny**;
	noun masculine **Jagarrany**;
	noun masculine **Jambinji, Jambirnji**;
	noun masculine **Jangalany**;
	noun masculine **Jawalyiny**;
	noun masculine **Jawanji, Janamany**;
	noun masculine **Joongoorrany**;
	noun masculine **Joowoorroony, Joolamany**;
	noun feminine **Naangaril, Nangaril**;
	noun feminine **Nagarral**;
	noun feminine **Nambinil, Nambirnil**;
	noun feminine **Naminyjili**;
	noun feminine **Nangalal**;
	noun feminine **Nyaajarril, Nyawajarril**;
	noun feminine **Nyawanal**;
	noun feminine **Nyawoorrool**
skin names (when spoken to)	*noun* **Jaangari**;
	noun **Jagarra**;
	noun **Jambin, Jambirn**;
	noun **Jangala**;
	noun **Jawalyi**;
	noun **Jawan, Janama**;
	noun **Joongoorra**;
	noun **Joowoorroo, Joolama**;
	noun **Naangari, Nangari**;
	noun **Nagarra**;
	noun **Nambin, Nambirn**;
	noun **Naminyji**;
	noun **Nangala**;
	noun **Nyaajarri, Nyawajarri**;
	noun **Nyawana**;
	noun **Nyawoorroo**
skinny	*adjective* **wanyjany, wanyjal, wanyjam**;
	adjective **winymany, winymal, winymam**;
	adjective **yalginybeny, yalginybel, yalginybem**
become skinny	*coverb+SAY/DO* **mawij**;
	coverb+SAY/DO **wanyjag**
skirt	*noun* **barndi-warndim**

skiting/bragging one	*adjective* **thawoolarrji, thawoolarrel, thawoolarrem**
sky	*noun* **birrinyji, birrinybe**
sky, appear in	*coverb+GO/COME* **jag**
slack feet, having	*adjective* **wirangbawarrany, wirangbawarral, wirangbawarram**
slap	*coverb+HIT* **benyeg**; *coverb+HIT* **booboorrg**
sleep	*coverb+DO_REFL* **bagoo**; *noun* **mooyoony, mooyoom**
be sleeping	*coverb+BE/STAY* **bagoo**
be sleeping (plural)	*coverb+BE/STAY* **bawagoo**
go and sleep (plural)	*coverb+GO/COME* **baagoo**
go to sleep	*coverb+FALL/GO_DOWN* **bagoo**; *coverb+DO_REFL* **yirdarr**; *coverb+FALL/GO_DOWN* **yirdardarr**
go to sleep (plural)	*coverb+FALL/GO_DOWN* **bawagoo**
slice something	*coverb+HIT* **barraj**; *coverb* **bilyoog-bilyoog**
slip past	*coverb+GO/COME* **beraj**
slip past someone	*coverb+HIT* **beraj-beraj**
slippery	*adjective* **berlengbeny, berlengbel, berlengbem**
make slippery	*coverb+GET* **berlengbeg**
slippery lizard	*noun feminine* **bararril**
slow	*adjective* **bedagbeny, bedagbel, bedagbem**; *adjective* **bedawoony, bedawool bedawoom**; *adjective* **bithawoony, bithawool, bithawoom**; *adjective* **yambilji, yambilel, yambilbe**; *adjective* **yambilwoony, yambilwool, yambilwoom**
be slow	*coverb+BECOME* **woorl-woorl**; *coverb+BECOME* **yambil**
make someone slow	*coverb+PUT* **yambil**
slowly	*adverb* **gaardaya**
go along slowly	*coverb+GO_ALONG* **gathathag**
slurp up (e.g. juice, fat, soup)	*coverb+BE/STAY* **liwij**; *coverb+SAY/DO* **ngathoogooj**
slurred speech, have	*coverb+FALL/GO_DOWN* **waly**
smack water, make noise	*coverb+BE/STAY* **derlawoog**
small/little	*adjective* **wanyageny, wanyagel, wanyagem**; *noun* **wanyageny**; *noun* **wanyagel, wanyanggel**
little boy	*noun* **wanyageny**
little girl	*noun* **wanyagel, wanyanggel**
small round hill	*noun* **goowaleny**
smart	*adjective* **ngelgany, ngelgal**; *adjective* **nyarlany, nyarlal**
smart fantastic one	*adjective* **bangganangoony**
smash	*coverb+HIT* **daj**; *coverb+HIT* **dalbarr**; *coverb+HIT* **goolboorr**; *coverb+HIT* **jalmoorrg**; *coverb+SAY/DO_M* **daj**; *coverb+SAY/DO_M* **dooljoog**
smash into	*coverb+FALL/GO_DOWN* **ban'gerr**
smash something	*coverb+HIT* **naj**
smash up as with a mortar and pestle	*coverb+SAY/DO* **naj**
smell	*coverb+GET* **ngard**; *coverb+GO/COME* **ngard**; *coverb+GO/COME* **ngardboo**; *coverb+SAY/DO* **ngabibij**; *coverb+SAY/DO* **ngard**; *coverb+SAY/DO_M* **ngard**
smell (intransitive)	*coverb+GO/COME* **ngawoombij**
smell a perfume	*coverb* **yirrinyngoorlg**; *coverb+SAY/DO* **ngawoombij**
smelling bad	*adjective* **nhoowoolji, nhoowoolel, nhoowoole**
smelly	*adjective* **minyarr-minyarreny, minyarr-minyarrel, minyarr-minyarre**; *adjective* **ngardbiny, ngardbel, ngardbim**
be smelly	*coverb+BE/STAY* **nangoolooloob**
be really smelly	*coverb+BECOME* **themberrbe**
smile	*coverb+SAY/DO_M* **melele**
smoke	*noun* **goongooloo**; *noun* **warn'gim**
make smoke	*coverb+PLACE* **dooloo**; *coverb+PUT* **dooloo**
smoke someone (ceremony)	*coverb+PUT* **dooloo**
smoke (cigarettes/ganja), to	*coverb+SAY/DO* **thoolngoony**
smoking (fire), be a	*coverb+BE/STAY* **dooloomab**; *coverb+SAY/DO* **dooloo**; *coverb+SAY/DO_M* **dooloo**; *coverb+SAY/DO* **doolloorayi**
smoking (fire) a long way off, be a	*coverb+SAY/DO* **looj**
smooth	*adjective* **booloorroo**

smooth, slippery

make smooth	*coverb+GET* **banheng**; *coverb+GET* **berlengbeg**
scrape and make smooth	*coverb* **jaloorl-jaloorl**
smooth, slippery	*adjective* **berlengbeny, berlengbel, berlengbem**
snail, land	*noun* **barlilmal**
snake bird	*noun masculine* **boorrijiny**; *noun masculine* **garrang-garranginy**; *noun masculine* **mawoorooriny**
snake (generic)	*noun masculine* **ngamarrany**; *noun masculine* **nganyjoowarrji**
black-headed python	*noun feminine* **dawool**; *noun feminine* **thoowerndemanbel**
blind snake	*noun* **woonthool, woonthoony**
children's python	*noun masculine* **bimbinginy**
curl snake, little spotted snake	*noun masculine* **jilinggoowiny**
death adder	*noun masculine* **damberrji**; *noun masculine* **ngadarrji**
king brown	*noun masculine* **lan'gerrji**; *noun masculine* **loonboorroony**
northern shovel-nosed snake ('emu killer')	*noun masculine* **goodawoodany**
olive python	*noun masculine* **dooloodbinyji**
rainbow snake	*noun masculine* **garlooroony**; *noun feminine* **goorlabal**
ringed brown snake ('emu killer')	*noun masculine* **jarloongoorroobarndegji**; *noun masculine* **yarriwiriny**
small snake species	*noun masculine* **jilyiwoony**
tree snake	*noun feminine* **wandawandal**
very big snake species	*noun feminine* **gawingel**
water python, water snake	*noun masculine* **warlenggenany**
western brown	*noun* **jadiwiriny**
whip snake	*noun feminine* **wandawandal**; *noun feminine* **wijgel**
snake be curled around	*coverb+SAY/DO* **nyaloonggooj**
snake tail, tip of	*noun* **nyiwirle**
snake vine	*noun* **waramboorr, waramboorrji**
snappy gum	*noun masculine* **thalngarrji**
snappy gum flowers	*noun* **goorramindiny, goorramindil**
snatch	*coverb+GET* **thoorroob**
sneak away	*coverb+GO/COME* **yilyiwoo**; *coverb+SAY/DO* **yilyiwany**
sneak up without letting anyone know	*coverb+GO/COME* **reganyda, reganyja**
sneak up on someone	*coverb+BRING/TAKE* **bandaj**; *coverb+GO_ALONG* **bandaj**; *coverb+GET* **jara**; *coverb+BRING/TAKE* **mari-mari**; *coverb+HIT* **mari, mari-mari, mariwoo**
sneeze	*coverb+SAY/DO* **dinyjirr**; *coverb+SAY/DO_M* **dinyjirr**
sniff	*coverb+SAY/DO* **ngard-ngard**
snore	*coverb+BE/STAY* **nyoorrg**; *coverb+BE/STAY* **nyoorrmirlib**
snot	*noun* **nyinggelarre**
soak, a	*noun* **yoorayimem**
dig a soak	*coverb+SAY/DO_M* **yoorayi**
soak something	*coverb+GET* **jaloob**
soak in water	*coverb+BE/STAY* **jawoorr**; *coverb+PUT* **jawoorr**
soap	*noun* **nyoomarlim**
sob	*coverb+SAY/DO* **ngang**; *coverb+SAY/DO* **ring-ring**
soft	*adjective* **galyegbeny, galyegbel, galyegbem**
make soft	*coverb* **galyegbeg**
soft (swearing)	*adjective* **gajoowoony, gajoowool, gajoowoom**
soil, black	*noun* **gawarnbe**
soil type, light coloured	*noun* **boolngan-boolngan**
soil type, red coloured	*noun* **jirlewoorrji, jirlewoorre**
someone	*interrogative* **yangoorranyji**
someone (feminine)	*interrogative* **yangelanyji**
someone (masculine)	*interrogative* **yangirnanyji**
someone who doesn't do something	*adjective* **ngoowany, ngoowal**
someone who takes no notice of requests	*adjective* **garlabawoorroony, garlabawoorrool, garlabawoorroom**
someone work, make	*coverb+GET* **warrgamge**
something	*interrogative* **thoorranyji**; *interrogative* **thoowiyanyji**; *interrogative* **thoowoorranyji**
something happening	*interrogative* **gaboowanyji, gabaanyi**
something poured out	*noun* **woomboolngem**
sometime unknown	*interrogative* **gayigananyji**

sometime, anytime ...... *temporal* **garawanyji**;
temporal **geragwaloon**
somewhere, at .... *interrogative* **gayanyji**;
interrogative **gayiyanyji**
somewhere, go .... *coverb+GO/COME* **garnawarrab**
somewhere, to .... *interrogative* **gabiyanyji**
son of man .... *noun masculine* **ngaboony**
  son of man (spoken to) .. *noun* **ngabayi**
son of man or woman .. *noun masculine* **wiginy**
son of woman .... *noun masculine* **ngalangangeny**
  son of woman
  (spoken to) .... *noun* **ngalanga**
son-in-law of man .... *noun masculine* **lambarrany**
son-in-law of woman ... *noun masculine* **thamboorroony**
song .... *noun* **ngalanybe**
  love song .... *noun* **woodiji**;
  noun **yirrbinji**
  song chorus .... *noun* **waramil**
song and dance cycle
  name .... *noun* **Dawarloowarlool**;
  noun **Goorirr-goorirr**;
  noun **Warloongarrim**
  'dangerous' song and
  dance cycle .... *noun* **Jooloorroo**
  type of women's song
  and dance cycle .... *noun* **Bandirrim**
song and dance style ... *noun* **Balga**;
  noun **Joonbal, Joonbam**;
  noun **Moonga-moonga**
  song and dance style
  with didjeridoo and
  clapsticks .... *noun* **Lirrgal**;
  noun **Wangga, Wanggal**
song, cause someone
  to find .... *coverb+GET* **banji**
songlark, rufous .... *noun* **binyjirrmiyanma**;
  noun **gawarnngarnany**
sool up a dog .... *coverb+SAY/DO* **boobayi**
soon .... *particle* **jamoonin**
sooty .... *adjective* **manbooloo-wooloo**
Sophie Downs,
  hill near .... *noun* **Boolooriny**
sorcerer .... *noun* **mabarn**
sore, sores .... *noun* **gajim**;
  noun **gerrmam**
sore, feel .... *coverb+SAY/DO* **mirl-mirl**
sore, make .... *coverb+GET* **gajig**
sore, scar from .... *noun* **garlge**
sores, having .... *adjective* **gajibany, gajibal,**
  gajibam, gaji-gajibany
  have little sores .... *coverb+HAVE* **moorl-moorl**
  having sores and
  lumps sticking out .... *adjective* **gerrmabany,**
  gerrmabal, gerrmabam
  say someone has sores . *coverb+SAY/DO* **gerrma-gerrma**
sorghum, wild .... *noun masculine* **marliny**
sorry, be .... *coverb+BECOME* **dooboo-yooboo**
sorry, feel .... *coverb+SAY/DO* **mooloorroo**
  feel sorry for each
  other .... *coverb+SAY/DO_REFL* **mooloorroo**
  make someone feel
  sorry .... *coverb* **mereleg**
sorry
  (words used to say) .... *phrase* **gaboo ngenani** (I am),
  gaboo yarrani (we are)
sound
  good at making drum
  sound by hitting space
  between crossed legs ... *adjective* **barndawooggalim**
  make hollow sound .... *coverb+SAY/DO* **loorrloorrjaya**
  make ringing sound
  (e.g. bell) .... *coverb+HIT* **lerlerl**
  make sound echo
  loudly all around .... *coverb+BRING/TAKE* **wingalawoog**
  sound of hitting
  something .... *interjection* **doowoo**
  SEE ALSO **noise**
soup .... *noun* **wooroom**
south
  around from the south . *directional* **ngerijingarriya**
  from south .... *directional* **ngerig**;
  directional **ngeriji-biny**
  further to the south ...... *directional* **nyoowoolgoorloorr**
  going south .... *adjective* **nyoowooloogbal,**
  nyoowooloogbany,
  nyoowooloogbam
  in the south .... *directional* **ngerijen**
  to the south .... *directional* **nyoowool,**
  nyoowooloogoo
sparkle (stars) .... *coverb+SAY/DO* **menan**
  be sparkling (stars) .... *coverb+SAY/DO_M* **menan**
spark, make fire .... *coverb+SAY/DO* **nhil, nhil-nhil**
sparks, make .... *coverb+SAY/DO* **ninirl**;
  coverb+SAY/DO **wirnmirnmaj**
speak .... *coverb+BE/STAY* **jarrag**
  person who speaks
  loudly .... *adjective* **yoowoorlbeny,**
  yoowoorlbel, yoowoorlbem
  speak causing a
  permanent change
  in the landscape .... *coverb+SAY/DO* **wiyawoog**;
  coverb+SAY/DO_M **wiyawoog**

spear

speak language .... *coverb+GO_ALONG* **jarrag**
speak loudly .... *coverb+SAY/DO_M* **yoowoorl**
speak with power to change state/country ... *coverb+HIT* **gooyoorrgboo**
speak to country .... *coverb+SAY/DO_M* **barrayi**
speak/sing to ward off danger .... *coverb+HIT* **wiyawoog**; *coverb+SAY/DO_M* **wiyawoog**
spear .... *coverb+GET* **tharrbood**; *coverb+HIT* **loonyoorr**; *coverb+SPEAR* **tharrbood, tharrboord**; *noun masculine* **garloomboony**
  kill by spearing .... *coverb+SPEAR* **nang**
  spear and break............ *coverb+SPEAR* **deberr**
  spear in heart .... *coverb+SPEAR* **thoorlboog**
  spear properly............... *coverb+SAY/DO_M* **jin'gerdi**
  spear right through ...... *coverb+SPEAR* **nyindoorrg**
  throw spear .... *coverb+PUT* **werndij**; *coverb+SAY/DO* **werndij**; *coverb+SAY/DO_M* **werndij**
  throw spear to hunt game .... *coverb+GET* **werndij**
spear with toes, drag ... *coverb+BRING/TAKE* **bililib**
spear (type)
  hook spear .... *noun* **tharrimin**
  large wooden spear....... *noun masculine* **goorladany**
  part of spear made of bamboo .... *noun* **nyilenggam**
  short spear .... *noun* **goombam**
  short fighting spear....... *noun masculine* **malmoorrji**; *noun masculine* **ngoorniny**
spear end .... *noun* **nyilenggam**
spear, hook up in woomera..................... *coverb+GET* **thalg**
spear, straighten .... *coverb+SAY/DO_M* **yireg-yireg**
spear, tie together parts of........................ *coverb* **bereg-bereg**
spearhead used for revenge killing, small............................ *noun feminine* **nhayirril**
spearhead, iron .... *noun* **jabirriny, jabirrim**
spearhead, stone.......... *noun* **gooroowal**; *noun* **jimbirlany, jimbirlal, jimbirlam**
  hard stick used for making stone spearheads.................. *noun* **mangadany**
  white stone spearhead..................... *noun* **yarlgal, yarlgany, yarlgam**

spears, throw .... *coverb+GO/COME* **were-were**
  throw spears at each other .... *coverb+SAY/DO_REFL* **werndij**
  throw spears at someone .... *coverb+HIT* **were-were**; *coverb+SAY/DO_M* **were-were**
spears, tie up with sinew .... *coverb+HIT* **bereg**
speech, have slurred .... *coverb+FALL/GO_DOWN* **waly**
speech sound, make .... *coverb* **nhared**
spider............................. *noun masculine* **baarnji**
spider web, make .... *coverb+SAY/DO* **woorr-woorr**
spill................................ *coverb+FALL/GO_DOWN* **woombool**
spin hair or wool to make string .... *coverb+SAY/DO_M* **wiyird**
spin something like a fishing line around and around .... *coverb+HIT* **warangan, warangan-warangan**
spindle........................... *noun* **bardim**
spine, sharp .... *noun* **bagam**
spinifex........................... *noun masculine* **nyiyirriny**
  pull spinifex up .... *coverb+HIT* **therdboo**
  spinifex resin .... *noun* **gaalji, gaale**
spinifex pigeon .... *noun feminine* **galawarrjil**
spinifex species, large hard .... *noun masculine* **garral-garralji**; *noun masculine* **jirriny-jirrinyji**
spinifex species, flower stems on .... *noun* **warlawoorroowoorroo**
spinifex species used to make resin .... *noun masculine* **gerlerneny**; *noun masculine* **miloowoony**
spirit................................ *noun* **joowarriny, joowarril**; *noun* **nyaarrji, nyaarrel**
spirit man, little .... *noun masculine* **rayiny**
spirit man with big feet .... *noun masculine* **yoonggoony**
spirit of person .... *noun* **birlirre**; *noun* **winyjirram**; *noun* **yoongoom**
spirit of person that is reborn after death........ *noun* **jarrinybe**
spirit woman living in caves .... *noun feminine* **yarralalil**
spirit woman, name of a..................... *noun* **Ganggamel**
spirits looking after someone's place......... *noun* **waloom**
spirits, night................. *noun* **mendoowoongarnam**

star

English	Gija
spiritually dangerous place	*noun* doomoorriny, doomoorrinyji, doomoorrinyil, doomoorrinybe; *noun* joomboorrirriny; *noun* joomoorririny, joomoorrirrim
spit	*coverb+SAY/DO* gooyoorrg; *coverb+GO/COME* thoobag; *coverb+SAY/DO_M* thebag
spit, spittle	*noun* ganggoom
splashing feet when walking in water	*coverb+GO_ALONG* jaboorr
split (intransitive)	*coverb+GO/COME* lag
split (transitive)	*coverb+HIT* lag
split open	*coverb+SAY/DO* lagarr
spoonbill	*noun masculine* galba-galbany
spotted	*adjective* dilg-dilgbawool, dilg-dilgbawoom, dilg-dilgbawoony
spotted pardalote	*noun feminine* binbininidgel
spouse	*noun* ngoolngany, ngoolngal
spouse (spoken to)	*noun* ngoolnga
spouse of someone a person calls 'granny' or 'ganggayi'	*noun* ben'galiny, ben'galil
spouse of someone a person calls 'granny' or 'ganggayi' (spoken to)	*noun* ben'gali
spread across	*coverb+FALL/GO_DOWN* wananbany
spread out	*coverb+BE/STAY* yawa
spread out hot ashes to cook something	*coverb+PUT* garayarr
spread pieces	*coverb+PUT* yawa
spread out, something that is	*noun* banjal; *noun feminine* banjalgjel
spread something out	*coverb+PUT* banjalg
spread sand	*coverb+PUT* thoorroo
spring, spring water	*noun* winyjiny, winyjim
Spring Creek Station	*noun* Mayimboorroon
spring dweller	*adjective* winyji-ngarnany, winyji-ngarnal, winyji-ngarnam
Springvale Station	*noun* Balinyin
long hill on Springvale Station	*noun* Darrajayin
place on Springvale Station	*noun* Nganirrin
sprinkle	*coverb+SAY/DO* wimarnmard
sprinkle water on someone	*coverb+HIT* mamag; *coverb+BRING/TAKE* mamag
spurt out	*coverb+SAY/DO_M* doorlboog
make spurt out	*coverb+GET* doorlboog; *coverb+HIT* doorlboog
squash	*coverb+HIT* jilarrg
squashed	*adjective* jilarrgeny, jilarrgel, jilarrgem
squat	*coverb+BE/STAY* ngaram
be squatting	*coverb+BE/STAY* jarrboolab
be squatting (plural)	*coverb+BE/STAY* jarrboo-yarrboolab
squeeze	*coverb+GET* jany; *coverb+SAY/DO_M* jany; *coverb+SAY/DO_M* janynga
squeeze together with fingers	*coverb+SAY/DO_M* goolmaj
squinting eyes, having	*adjective* yirranybeny, yirranybel, yirranybem
stab ground	*coverb+GO_THROUGH* jida-jida; *coverb+SAY/DO* jida; *coverb+SAY/DO_M* jida
go along stabbing ground	*coverb+GO_ALONG* jida
stab/poke something	*coverb+SAY/DO* jagij
stand	*coverb+BE/STAY* thad
be standing	*coverb+BE/STAY* thadboo
stand (plural)	*coverb+BE/STAY* thaarr; *coverb+BE/STAY* tharreb; *coverb+BE/STAY* thayarr
stand holding	*coverb+HAVE* thad
stand something up	*coverb+PUT* thad
stand, stop and (non-singular)	*coverb+FALL/GO_DOWN* thayarr
stand straight and tall	*coverb+BE/STAY* tharrbelil; *coverb+BE/STAY* tharrboolirr
stand up	*coverb+FALL/GO_DOWN* jad; *coverb+FALL/GO_DOWN* thad
stand up agressively	*coverb+SAY/DO_M* ganberaj
standing up all around	*coverb+BE/STAY* jaringindij
standing close all around	*coverb+BE/STAY* jarrngarengaj
standing together, be all	*coverb+BE/STAY* janbaroorrg
standing upright, be	*coverb+BE/STAY* jad
star	*noun feminine* wardal
morning star	*noun* jiwibal, jiwibany

stare

stars sparkle	*coverb+SAY/DO* **menan**
stars twinkling	*coverb+GO/COME* **jalgoorrg**
stare	*coverb+BE/STAY* **lang**; *coverb+GO/COME* **lerrma**
be staring with wide eyes	*coverb+BECOME* **lirrij**
go along staring	*coverb+GO/COME* **lang**
start forgetting	*coverb+GET* **nyinjinybany**
Station Creek on Texas Downs	*noun* **Gamanggerrngarrin**
stay alone	*coverb+BE/STAY* **doomooge**
stay behind	*coverb+PLACE* **ngadi**; *coverb+SAY/DO* **ngadidi**
stay for good	*coverb+FALL/GO_DOWN* **mawoorrg**
stay in big group	*coverb+BE/STAY* **damarramarra**
stay in one place	*coverb+BE/STAY* **balg**: *coverb+SAY/DO_M* **nyad**
stay somewhere, choose to	*coverb* **dangoorayi**
stay with someone	*coverb+GET* **thad**
stay quiet	*coverb+GO/COME* **girrji**
steal	*coverb+GET* **yimele**; *coverb+SAY/DO* **yimele**
'stealing bird', greater bower-bird	*noun* **joowijgarneny**
steaming	*coverb+SAY/DO* **ngoowoob**
steep bank	*noun* **gawarre, gawarriny**
stem of waterlily flower	*noun* **danggarriny**
step on something	*coverb+SAY/DO_M* **bad**; *coverb+GET* **bad**
stick	*noun* **goonyjany, goonyjal, goonyjam**; *noun* **goowooleny, goowoolem**
digging stick	*noun* **ganany, gananyji**
fighting stick	*noun* **goordooroom**; *noun masculine* **nawooloony**
frayed stick for mopping honey	*noun* **wiram**
small fighting stick	*noun masculine* **wabagoorreny**; *noun* **yamayarram**
small sticks (kindling)	*noun* **marloorloom**
small very hard stick used to make stone spearheads	*noun masculine* **mangadany**
stick used for painting	*noun* **jarn'girriny**
stick used to hook up fish	*noun* **yan'gam**
stick with hook	*noun* **nyanggernam**
stick, break off	*coverb+GET* **dijgawoorr**
stick, cut for spear, etc.	*coverb+SAY/DO* **ngerd**
stick, be hitting one down on another	*coverb+SAY/DO* **garn-garn**
stick/attach spearhead to spear	*coverb+GET* **thoord**; *coverb+SAY/DO_M* **thoord-thoord**
stick in mind	*coverb+FALL/GO_DOWN* **larrngib**
stick insect	*noun masculine* **boornarrany**
stick on	*coverb+GET* **nyad**; *coverb+PUT* **limboog**; *coverb+PUT* **loobag-loobag**; *coverb+PUT* **nyanmaj**
stick on/together	*coverb+GET* **nhem**
stick on stick, hit	*coverb+HIT* **garn**
stick, poke with	*coverb+PUT* **goorloorr-goorloorr**
stick, push/hit with end of	*coverb+SAY/DO_M* **dag**
stick something on	*coverb+PUT* **lembood**; *coverb+SAY/DO_M* **lemboo-lembood**
stick tight	*coverb+HIT* **bagarr**
stick, throw	*coverb+SAY/DO_M* **goorroorroo**
sticking out	*adjective* **jambalgeny, jambalgel, jambalgem**
sticking out, be	*coverb+BE/STAY* **thamboong**; *coverb+BE/STAY* **thirringangab**
sticking far out	*adjective* **marrajgany, marrajgal, marrajgam**
sticking up	*adjective* **bedajbayim, bedajbayil, bedajbayim**
stiff, become	*coverb+BECOME* **nanoojboo**
still	*adverb* **miyawanya**; *particle* **marrge**
still, keep	*coverb+GO/COME* **gerrji**
sting	*coverb+HIT* **nyirerrege**
stink ants	*noun masculine* **goonyoorrji**
stinky	*adjective* **nhoowoolji, nhoowoolel, nhoowoole**
become stinking	*coverb+GO/COME* **nhoowoolgbany**
stock from meat	*noun* **wooroom**
stomach	*noun* **jaam**
part of cattle stomach	*noun* **boorrooloo**; *noun* **marralam**
stomach (internal part)	*noun* **jaroom**
stomach ache, have	*coverb+SAY/DO* **ngarr**
stomach cavity, put rocks and leaves in (e.g. kangaroo)	*noun* **girringilyim**

400 Always read the full information for each word in its main entry.

stomach-down, lie	*coverb+BE/STAY* moog;
	coverb+BE/STAY moord;
	coverb+BE/STAY loomboord;
	coverb+BE/STAY moondoorroong
stomach, feel sick in	*coverb+FALL/GO_DOWN* ngarl
stomach, having big stomach	*adjective* jaroogoony, jaroogool, jaroogoom
stomach, open	*coverb+GET* thelberr;
	coverb+HIT thelberr
stomach pointing up, put	*coverb+PUT* gerloorroogeb
stomach rumbling from hunger, have	*coverb+SAY/DO* goorlirlij
stone	*noun* ngaarriny;
	noun ngarrgaleny, ngarrgalem
stone axe	*noun feminine* woomal
stone spearhead	*noun* jimbirlany, jimbirlal, jimbirlam
stone used to make something smooth	*adjective* booloorroo
stones, country with lots of little	*noun* gerdgardbe
stones, hot	*noun* garanybe
Stoney Creek (on Bedford Downs)	*noun* Woolarrngayan
stop	*coverb+FALL/GO_DOWN* nag;
	coverb+GO/COME naleg;
	interjection rega
be stopped	*coverb+GO/COME* nangag
stop and stand (plural)	*coverb+FALL/GO_DOWN* thayarr
stop fighting	*coverb+SAY/DO* jawa-jaway
stop someone doing	*coverb+GET* ngarrarlji;
	coverb+PUT ngarrarlg
stop someone, kind of people who	*adjective* ngarrarlg-ngarrarlggem
stop something coming	*coverb+BRING/TAKE* jarrga
storm bird	
channel-billed cuckoo	*noun feminine* goorra-goorral
koel	*noun masculine* doowageny
female koel	*noun feminine* girlgoowal
story	*noun* jarragbe, jarragboo;
	noun manoom
story, joking	*noun* barlijbem
straight	*adjective* joodoony, joodool, joodoom;
	adjective joodoombarrany, joodoombarral, joodoobarram
straight and nice looking	*adjective* jalabgany, jalabgal, jalabgam
straight ahead	*adverb* joodiya
straight and tall, stand	*coverb+BE/STAY* tharrbelil
straight away	*adverb* joodiya
straight down	*directional* dega
straight line, be stretched across in	*coverb+BE/STAY* wandarra
straight there	*directional* dega
straighten	*coverb+PUT* joodoog;
	coverb+SAY/DO_M yara-yaraj
straighten by pressing	*coverb+PUT* yarajbe;
	coverb+PUT yara-yaraj
straighten one's back	*coverb+BE/STAY* nany
straighten self	*coverb+DO_REFL* joodoog
straighten spears	*coverb+SAY/DO_M* yireg-yireg
strange, feel	*coverb+SAY/DO* jiwoore
stranger	*noun* gamaliwany, gamaliwal, gamaliwam;
	noun jemenngarram;
	noun ngayanboo;
	noun ngoolmoorroony, ngoolmoorrool, ngoolmoorroo, ngoolmoowoorroo
strength, magic	*noun* mayam
strenuously	*adverb* garda-gardawoo
stretch arm out to one side	*coverb+SAY/DO* mira
stretch arms out	*coverb+SAY/DO* goorl
stretch out by shooting, cause to	*coverb+HIT* barndarn'ge
stretched across in straight line, be	*coverb+BE/STAY* wanan;
	coverb+BE/STAY wandarra
strewth!	*interjection* winggernanggoo
strike a match	*coverb+PUT* girrem
string	*noun* ngerlam
string/sinew	*noun* jirlwam
string handle	*noun* rarrim

striped

striped	*adjective* **mernderr-mernderr**; *adjective* **ngende-ngenderrmawoom, ngende-ngenderrmawoony, ngende-ngenderrmawool**; *adjective* **jarri-jarrirrijmawoom**; *coverb* **jarri-jarrirrij**
striped fish species	*noun feminine* **goodabal**
striped snake species	*noun masculine* **goodawoodany**
stroke, have a	*coverb+SAY/DO* **thoorroorooroo**
strong	*adjective* **bagarrjiny, bagarrjil, bagarrjim**
become strong	*coverb+BECOME* **bagarrji**
make strong	*coverb+GET* **bagarrjig**
strong in sinews, be	*coverb+SAY/DO* **yarrarra**
make strong in sinews	*coverb+GET* **yarrarrage**
strong at singing	*adjective* **dedarleny, dedarlel, dedarlem**
strong-smelling herb species	*noun masculine* **gooroongoony**
structure made of sticks placed high	*noun* **bernderre**
struggle in water	*coverb+SAY/DO* **ngamoonayi**
stuck, be	*coverb+BE/STAY* **nhembad**
stuck, become	*coverb+BECOME* **bagarrji**
stuck, get	*coverb+FALL/GO_DOWN* **derd**; *coverb+FALL/GO_DOWN* **larr**; *coverb+FALL/GO_DOWN* **nhembad**; *coverb+FALL/GO_DOWN* **nhembadbe**; *coverb+FALL/GO_DOWN* **therrbeg**
stuffed with food, become	*coverb+BECOME* **berlgerren**
stung, get	*coverb+FALL/GO_DOWN* **nyirerrege**
subincision (swearing)	*noun* **jaboolany**; *noun* **jagoola**
successful	*adjective* **ngoorloony, ngoorlool**
suck	*coverb+BE/STAY* **liwij**; *coverb+BURN/BITE* **biny**; *coverb+BURN/BITE_REFL* **thoong**; *coverb+SAY/DO* **biny**; *coverb+SAY/DO* **joong-joong**; *coverb+SAY/DO* **joony-joony**; *coverb+SAY/DO* **yinyeg**; *coverb+SAY/DO_M* **liwij**; *coverb+SAY/DO_REFL* **thoong-thoong**
suck honey	*coverb+PUT* **mengelarr**
suck honey off	*coverb+GET* **janaj**; *coverb+PUT* **janaj**
suck up	*coverb+GO/COME* **loowoontherr-loowoontherr**; *coverb+SAY/DO* **ngathoogooj**
suck up juice	*coverb+SAY/DO_M* **yinyeg**
suck up juice/liquid	*coverb+SAY/DO* **yinyeg**
suckle	*coverb+SAY/DO* **thoong**
suddenly	*adverb* **man'garraya**
suddenly come	*coverb+GO/COME* **ngag**
suddenly come and get a shock	*coverb+GO/COME* **jarda**
sugar	*noun* **jilam**; *noun* **gerdgardbe**; *noun* **roongalga**; *noun* **warrayiny**; *noun* **warrayele**
sugarbag bee	*noun* **moowany, moowal**; *noun* **ngawooral**
ground-living sugarbag species	*noun masculine* **gayirriny**; *noun masculine* **boorrwoorrji**
sugarbag wax	*noun* **ganggarrji, ganggarre**; *noun* **joornoogji, joornoogbi**
tree-living sugarbag species	*noun feminine* **beranggool**; *noun masculine* **gerrayiny**; *noun masculine* **nhawiny**
sugarbag, cut	*coverb+HIT* **jarn**
sugarbag, go chopping	*coverb+GO_ALONG* **lawoog**
sugar grass	*noun masculine* **gilemberrji**
sugar leaf (lerp species)	*noun masculine* **bin'gany**; *noun masculine* **daliyany**; *noun masculine* **wanamarriny**; *noun masculine* **warrayany, warrayiny**
sulk	*coverb+GO/COME* **roog**; *coverb+HIT* **roog**
sulphur-crested cockatoo	*noun masculine* **ngamarriny**; *noun masculine* **ngayirr-ngayirrji**
sun	*noun feminine* **barndel**; *noun feminine* **malalal**; *noun feminine* **malwalal**
sunglasses	*noun* **yirranybebeny mooloogoonji**
sun go down	*coverb+FALL/GO_DOWN* **therrijboo**
sun, lie in; sunbathe	*coverb+BE/STAY* **barndeg**

take off (leave)

sun, put in .... *coverb+PUT* **barndeg**
sunrise .... *noun* **rarrgalil**
  at sunrise .... *temporal* **rarrgalen**
sunset, at .... *temporal* **garraroon,
    garrwaroon**
sunset, be .... *coverb+SAY/DO* **mawoorroo**
sunset, go at .... *coverb+GO/COME*
    garrwaroowany
supplejack tree .... *noun masculine* **warlagarriny**
swag .... *noun phrase* **bool-boolgajim
    bagoo-girrem gibin**
swagger .... *coverb+GO_ALONG* **loomayi**
swallow SEE woodswallow
swear .... *coverb+SAY/DO_M* **roorrij;**
    coverb+SAY/DO **roowaj**
  swear at each other ...... *coverb+DO_REFL* **roorrij**
  swear at someone .... *coverb+GET* **roorraj**
swearing .... *noun* **roorrijbe**
  response when brother,
  sister or grandparent
  swears .... *interjection* **yigelany**
  response if
  mother-in-law or
  son-in-law is sworn ...... *coverb+SAY/DO* **biny-biny**
  response if speaker's
  brother-in-law or
  sister-in-law is sworn .... *interjection* **ngagoony**
  response when
  swearing or name of
  a dead person is heard .. *interjection* **warri-warri**
sweat .... *coverb+GET* **jirriliny;**
    coverb+PUT **jirriliny;**
    noun **boodoonggili,
    boodoonggooloo;**
    noun **malngoonybe**
sweat, drip .... *coverb+GO_ALONG* **larroorroo**
sweat, smell of .... *noun* **malngoonybe**
sweet .... *adjective* **menherrgayiny,
    menherrgayil,
    menherrgayim;**
    adjective **wilyawoony,
    wilyawool, wilyawoom;**
    adjective **wilawoony, wilawool,
    wilawoom**
sweet taste, enjoy .... *coverb+GO/COME* **menherrgarr**
sweep/clean .... *coverb+HIT* **berarr**
swell and become
  unable to walk .... *coverb+GO/COME* **bilg**
swell from insect bite ... *coverb+GO/COME* **loob-loob;**
    coverb+SAY/DO **loob-loob**
swell up .... *coverb+GO/COME* **bembere**

swim .... *coverb+GO_ALONG* **barl-warl;**
    coverb+GO_ALONG **wany-wany;**
    coverb+SAY/DO **wany-wany;**
    coverb+SAY/DO **werl-werl**
  be swimming .... *coverb+BE/STAY* **nyirreg;**
    coverb+SAY/DO **nyirrega;**
    coverb+SAY/DO_M **nyirrega**
  swim along .... *coverb+GO_ALONG* **werl-werl**
  swim along (duck) .... *coverb+GO_ALONG* **wiyarre**
  swim like a turtle
  (breast stroke) .... *coverb+GO_ALONG* **barl**
swing hips from side
  to side .... *coverb+SAY/DO* **yigily-yigily**
swing something
  around and around .... *coverb+HIT* **warangan,
    warangan-warangan**
swing tail .... *coverb+GO_ALONG* **wirnbaj**

Tt

table .... *noun phrase* **barlalijam jang-
    girrem**
Tableland Station .... *noun* **Yooloomboo**
tablets .... *noun* **joorlgoorlgoom**
tadpoles .... *noun* **giljerrengginy**
tail .... *noun* **nyawam**
  tip of tail (goanna or
  snake) .... *noun* **nyiwirle**
tail, swing .... *coverb+GO_ALONG* **wirnbaj**
tail, wag .... *coverb+SAY/DO* **wird-wird**
take away .... *coverb+BRING/TAKE* **marra;**
    coverb+BRING/TAKE **marrarn;**
    coverb+HIT **marrarn**
  take away carrying
  under arm .... *coverb+GO_BECOME* **joolooj**
  take far away .... *coverb+HIT* **dawadag**
  take someone away ...... *coverb+GET* **yarra;**
    coverb+HIT **warnngemaj**
  take someone away
  (e.g. cyclone) .... *coverb+BRING/TAKE* **therroowoog**
take back .... *coverb+BRING/TAKE* **biri**
take to a different
  place .... *coverb+BRING/TAKE* **dawadag**
take dogs hunting .... *coverb* **werna-werna**
take down .... *coverb+BRING/TAKE* **jarrg**
take in .... *coverb+BRING/TAKE* **walig;**
    coverb+GET_HIT **waligboo**
take something off ...... *coverb+GET* **beralg**
take off (i.e. leave) .... *coverb+GO/COME* **yawoog;**
    coverb+LEAVE **yawoog;**
    coverb+GO/COME **yiwinybeb**

take off quickly

take off quickly .... *adverb* **garda-gardan**
take out teeth .... *coverb+GET* **loowoo**
take someone down ..... *coverb+HIT* **nyiremoorl**
take someone's place ... *coverb+BRING/TAKE* **rooloo**
take through .... *coverb+BRING/TAKE* **thoorrbool**
take (transport) .... *coverb+BRING/TAKE* **moorrga**
take turns .... *coverb+SAY/DO_REFL* **goornag**
take lover away
  leading by arm .... *coverb+GET* **binggoo**;
                coverb+SAY/DO_M
                binggoo-binggoo
take/bring back .... *coverb+BRING/TAKE* **biri**;
                coverb+BRING/TAKE **biriwoorrg**
take/bring closer .... *coverb+BRING/TAKE* **ngirribag**
take one's time .... *coverb+BECOME* **woorl-woorl**
taking something, run ... *coverb+BRING/TAKE* **wiji**
talk .... *coverb+BE/STAY* **bal**;
                coverb+GO/COME **jarrag-jarrag**;
                coverb+SAY/DO **bal**;
                coverb+SAY/DO **jarrag**;
                coverb+SAY/DO_M **bal**;
                coverb+SAY/DO_M **jarrag**
  keep talking loudly .... *coverb+SAY/DO_M* **delanggerr**
  talk (group) .... *coverb+SAY/DO* **wig-wig**
  talk loudly (plural) .... *coverb+BE/STAY* **jarranyngoorlg**
  talk (plural) .... *coverb+SAY/DO* **jarroo-jarroo**
talk about someone ..... *coverb+PUT* **yirrgawoo**
talk behind
  someone's back .... *coverb+PUT* **ngoorrri**
  talk behind someone's
  back in a jealous way .... *coverb+PUT* **ngoorn**
talk together (plural) ... *coverb+SAY/DO_REFL* **jawool**
talk quietly
  (in a group) .... *coverb+SAY/DO* **ngoorn-ngoorn**
talk sideways about
  mother-in-law .... *coverb+SAY/DO* **melera**
talk to country .... *coverb+SAY/DO_M* **barrayi**
talk to each other .... *coverb+SAY/DO_REFL* **bal**
talk to people who have
  had a death in the
  family as if nothing
  had happened .... *coverb+GO_ALONG* **booliyi**
talk to self/each other .. *coverb+SAY/DO_REFL* **jarrag**
talk to spirits in
  country .... *coverb+SAY/DO* **goorara**;
                coverb+PUT **goorara**
talk to anyone,
  not wanting to .... *adjective* **boothalwoony,
                boothalwool, boothalwoom**

talk together with
  family after someone
  has died to sort out
  what happened .... *coverb+SAY/DO_REFL* **manarr-manarr**
talk, jealous .... *noun* **ngoornbe**
tall .... *adjective* **meraangarriny,
                meraangarril,
                meraangarrim**;
                adjective **merewany, merewal, merewam**
  tall and thin .... *adjective* **garrwarla-warlany,
                garrwarla-warlal,
                garrwarla-warlam**
tangled up or stuck,
  get .... *coverb+GO/COME* **dardbany**
tangled up and trip
  over, get .... *coverb+GO/COME* **rardbany**
taro, *Colocasia
  esculenta* .... *noun masculine* **jimarniny, jemaniny**
tasteless .... *adjective* **thalenggeny, thalenggel, thalenggem**
tasty .... *adjective* **menherrgayiny, menherrgayil, menherrgayim**;
                adjective **wilyawoony, wilyawool, wilyawoom**;
                adjective **wilawoony, wilawool, wilawoom**
tata lizard .... *noun masculine* **jawarlaliny**;
                noun masculine **manggerregerreny**
tawny frogmouth .... *noun feminine* **goorrgoorrjil**
tea .... *noun* **nalijam**
tea, bush tea,
  *Apowollastonia
  verbesinoides* .... *noun* **lamba-lambarrji, lambarr-lambarrji**
tea-tree, *Leptospermum
madidum; Melaleuca
bracteata* .... *noun masculine* **wengenji, woongenji**
teach .... *coverb+BRING/TAKE* **bina**;
                coverb+GET **binarrig**;
                coverb+GIVE **binarrig**;
                coverb+PUT **jidi**;
                coverb+GET **lirrgarn**
  teach properly .... *coverb+BURN/BITE* **joodoob**

thin, become

teacher, school	*noun* lendijgaleny, lendijgalel, lendijgalem; *noun* merndagaleny, merndagalel, merndagalem
tear off pieces of paperbark	*coverb+SAY/DO_M* laroog
tears	*noun* mooroorloo
have tears running	*coverb+SAY/DO* mooroorl-mooroorl
tears run down	*coverb+GO/COME* mooroorl-mooroorl
teary eyed	*adjective* mooroorlbany, mooroorlbal, mooroorlbam
tease	*coverb+GET* birrga-wirrga; *coverb+GET* goonyjiri; *coverb+GET* jing; *coverb+SPEAR* birrga-wirrga; *coverb+SPEAR* goonyjiri
teenage boy	*noun masculine* lambarnji; *noun masculine* waarrany
teenage girl	*noun feminine* werlemen, werlemenel
teeth	*noun* minyjoowoom; *noun* ngirrimem, ngirriminy
clean teeth using grass	*coverb* therrilimbi
grind teeth	*coverb+SAY/DO* dadigirrij
have teeth on edge	*coverb+SAY/DO* ngar
take out teeth	*coverb+GET* loowoo
teeth, having no	*adjective* leg-legginy, leg-leggil, leg-leggim; *adjective* loowoo-loowoonginy, loowoo-loowoongil, loowoo-loowoongim
telegram	*noun* wilmoorroo, wilymoorre
telephone	*noun* wilmoorroo, wilymoorre
tell	*coverb+SAY/DO* bal; *coverb+BE/STAY* bal; *coverb+SAY/DO_M* bal
tell each other	*coverb+SAY/DO_REFL* bal
tell someone	*coverb+GET* jarrag
tell each other off	*coverb+WOUND_REFL* yoowoorlngbe
tell lies	*coverb+SAY/DO* yagoorn
tell lies (a bit swearing)	*coverb+SAY/DO* ngoolooba, ngoorlooba
tell on someone	*coverb+BRING/TAKE* berag
tell someone off about something disliked	*coverb+HIT* girriyag
tent	*noun* bandarram
termites	*noun* gooroorrooroorrool; *noun* moonggoorl
termite mound	*noun feminine* jamerndel
termite larvae	*noun feminine* ngawagool
testicles	*noun* goolyany, goolyam; *noun* ngalyarre
Texas Downs, long hill on the way to	*noun* Balan'gerr
Texas Downs Station	*noun* Gawoornben, Gawoornboon
Texas Downs Station house, hill near	*noun* Joowarlgerrji
Texas Fish Hole	*noun* Tharemariny
that	*demonstrative* dany, dal, dam
that there	*demonstrative* ngoorroony, ngoorrool, ngoorroom
that kind	*adjective* wayininy, wayinil; *adjective* wayinijarrany, wayinijarral, wayinijarram
that many	*adverb* wayiningerreg
that thing I can't think of	*noun* ngarnji, ngarnel, ngarnbe; *locative* ngarne; *coverb* ngarn
that time when	*temporal particle* ginyanbe
that's right	*interjection* ngiyi
that's the thing and then	*interjection* e-e
theirs	*possessive pronoun* boorriyangeny, boorriyangel, boorriyangem
then	*adverb* dangembi
then like that	*adverb* wayiniyana
there	*demonstrative* dan
over there	*demonstrative* ngoorroon
right there	*demonstrative* deyena, diyana
right over there	*demonstrative* ngoorriyana
these	*demonstrative* berrem, berrewam; *demonstrative* birriyam
these two	*demonstrative* berrebaarriny; *demonstrative* berrebem; *demonstrative* berre-warriny
they, them	*pronoun* boorroon
they themselves	*pronoun* boorroowany
they/them two	*pronoun* boorrooben
thigh	*noun* baliyarram; *noun* gerlalbam
thigh bone	*noun* gerlalbam
thin, become	*coverb+GO/COME* wirrg

thin, tall and

thin, tall and	*adjective* **garrwarla-warlany, garrwarla-warlal, garrwarla-warlam**
thin waist, having a	*adjective* **garrgbayiny, garrgbayil**
think about	*coverb+GET* **linga-linga**
think about someone/something	*coverb+GET* **linga**; *coverb+SAY/DO_M* **liwarag**; *coverb+GET* **miyi-miyi**; *coverb+SAY/DO* **miyi-miyi**
think, make	*coverb+PUT* **linga**
make think about someone/something	*coverb+GET* **merrwardge**
think someone can't do something	*coverb+GET* **wadoo-wadoo**
thinking	*coverb+SAY/DO* **linga**
be thinking	*coverb+BE/STAY* **linga**
thirsty, be	*coverb+GO/COME* **reminy**; *coverb+GO/COME* **raj**
thirsty, make	*coverb+PUT* **reminyge**
make self thirsty	*coverb+EAT* **reminyge**
thirsty, one who gets	*adjective* **reme-remeny-nhawoony, reme-remeny-nhawool**
this, these here	*demonstrative* **berrem**
this (feminine)	*demonstrative* **ngel, ngelel**
this (masculine)	*demonstrative* **nginy, nginyjiny**
this many	*adverb* **waningerreg**
this way	*demonstrative* **berrebiny**; *directional* **woorayibiny**; *directional* **woorayigoo-yoorroong**
come this way	*coverb+GO/COME* **wooraj**
coming this way	*directional* **woorayibe**
those	*demonstrative* **deyema**
those/that (non-singular)	*demonstrative* **dam**
thoughts	*noun* **lingam**
three	*adjective* **merrgernbe, merrgernbem**
throat	*noun* **werlem, woorlem, woorloom**
throbbing, be (body part from exercise)	*coverb+HIT* **merrgeb**
throbbing heart (from feeling for someone or exercise)	*coverb+SAY/DO* **dig-dig**; *coverb+SAY/DO* **doob-doob**
through, break/bring	*coverb+GO_THROUGH* **thoorrbool**
through, go	*coverb+GO/COME* **thoorrbool**
throw	*coverb+BRING/TAKE* **ngerr**; *coverb+HIT* **ngerr**; *coverb+HIT* **waj**; *coverb+SAY/DO* **ngerr**; *coverb+SAY/DO* **werrgereb**; *coverb+SAY/DO_M* **ngerr**
be throwing	*coverb+HIT* **wajbe**
throw a boomerang	*coverb+SAY/DO_M* **garrara**
throw down	*coverb+PUT* **woolthoob**; *coverb+HIT* **bardal**; *coverb+HIT* **barljarr**; *coverb+HIT* **werrgereb**; *coverb+HIT* **wethed**; *coverb+HIT/CUT* **wethed**; *coverb+SAY/DO_M* **werrgeb**; *coverb+HIT* **woorrg, woorrg-woorrg**
throw down/away	*coverb+HIT/CUT* **wethed**
throw into water	*coverb+HIT* **jijberrg**
throw rock in water	*coverb+SAY/DO* **darloo**
throw something on fire	*coverb+HIT* **thaloorrg**
throw spear	*coverb+HIT* **woordij**; *coverb+PUT* **werndij**; *coverb+SAY/DO* **werndij**; *coverb+SAY/DO_M* **werndij**
throw spear to hunt game	*coverb+GET* **werndij**
throw spears	*coverb+GO/COME* **were-were**
throw spears at each other	*coverb+SAY/DO_REFL* **werndij**
throw spears at someone	*coverb+HIT* **were-were**; *coverb+SAY/DO_M* **were-were**
throw stick	*coverb+SAY/DO_M* **goorroorroo**
throw things at someone	*coverb+PUT* **ngerr-ngerrji**
throw to each other	*coverb+SAY/DO_REFL2* **ngerr-ngerrji**
thunder	*coverb+FALL/GO_DOWN* **doorig-doorig**
thundering, be	*coverb+GO_ALONG* **doori, dooriyi**; *coverb+GO/COME* **doori-doorib**
thus	*particle* **wayini**
tick, small	*noun feminine* **birlinyil**
tick, big brown	*noun feminine* **wegerlel**
tick, big kangaroo	*noun* **loorrma-loorrma**
tickle	*coverb+GET* **jigij**; *coverb+GET* **jigij-jigij**
tickle each other	*coverb+DO_REFL* **gejig**; *coverb+DO_REFL* **jigij-jigij**

toothpick, use a

tickle someone	*coverb+GET* **gejig**
tie on self	*coverb+DO_REFL* **merd**
tie spear parts together	*coverb* **bereg-bereg**
tie up	*coverb+GET* **merd**;
	coverb+SAY/DO **mernmerd**;
	coverb+SAY/DO_M **mernmerd**
tie up hair	*coverb+DO_REFL* **yambarn**
tie up spears with sinew	*coverb+HIT* **bereg**
tighten	*coverb+GET* **bagarrjig**
time, for a long	*adverb* **warnarrayan**
time of day	*noun* **barndel, barndem**
time of set-in rain	*noun* **yiwirn'gen**
tingling in body part, feel	*coverb+SAY/DO* **woorlmooj-woorlmooj**
tip of goanna or snake tail	*noun* **nyiwirle**
tip out	*coverb+FALL/GO_DOWN* **woombool**
go along tipping out	*coverb+GO_ALONG* **warranyja**
make tip out	*coverb* **warranyjag**
tip something out	*coverb+SAY/DO* **warranyja**
tired, be	*coverb+SAY/DO* **wanggarl**;
	adjective **ligbayiny, ligbayil, ligbayim**
become tired	*coverb+FALL/GO_DOWN* **wanggarlge**
be dead tired	*coverb+GO/COME* **yirrerij**
make someone tired	*coverb+GET* **wanggarlge, wanggarlgoo**;
	coverb+PUT **wanggarlge, wanggarlgoo**;
	coverb+GET **yalijge**
tired of waiting, be	*coverb+GO_ALONG* **wanggooloo**
to one side	*locative* **yagebayoorroong**
to the east	*directional* **ngela**;
	directional **ngelamoogoo**
further to the east	*directional* **ngelagoorloorr**
to the north	*directional* **boowoorr**;
	directional **boowoorroogoo**
further to the north	*directional* **boorrgoorloorr, boowoorrgoorloorr**
to the south	*directional* **nyoowool, nyoowooloogoo**
further to the south	*directional* **nyoowoolgoorloorr**
to the west	*directional* **gerliyirr, gerlirroogoo**
further to the west	*directional* **gerliyirrgoorloorr**
tobacco	*noun* **ngoonyjoom**
bush tobacco	*noun* **binggoonyel, binggoonyji**
tobacco, chew	*coverb+PUT* **ngoorinyja**
tobacco/ganja, smoke	*coverb+SAY/DO* **thoolngoony**
today	*temporal* **gelengen**;
	temporal **gilingin, gilyingin**
toddler, fat (Southern dialect)	*noun* **joorlgoony, joorlgool**
toe-cutter, water scorpion	*noun feminine* **bindirijgel**
toenail	*noun* **yarnderre**
toes (same as words for foot)	*noun* **thambarlam**;
	noun **thengam**
toes, drag spear with	*coverb+BRING/TAKE* **bililib**
together	*adverb* **yajany**
be together	*adjective* **daminam**;
	coverb+BE/STAY **barleg-barleg**
together in line, come	*coverb+SAY/DO_M* **joorroob**
toilet (polite), go to the	(*verb GO/COME*) **jaam-boorroo**;
	coverb **jimbi-jimbij**
toilet (defecate), go to the	*coverb+HIT* **therraj**;
	coverb+HIT **therrilaj**
toilet (urinate), go to the	*coverb+SAY/DO* **goomboo**;
	coverb+GO/COME **goomboowany**;
	coverb+GO/COME **jarnangarr**
tomato, bush, *Solanum echinatum*	*noun feminine* **girlil**
tomato, type of bush, *Solanum chippendalei*	*noun feminine* **nganyjarlil**
tomorrow	*temporal* **magarne**;
	temporal **nyigan**;
	temporal **nyigawa**
tongue	*noun* **thalalam**
flick tongue in and out	*coverb+SAY/DO* **minyoolang-minyoolang**
make tongue feel funny by eating something bitter	*coverb+EAT* **dagalge**
too	*particle* **miyi**
tooth fall out	*coverb+GO/COM* **leg**
tooth, loose	*adjective* **lamany**
toothpick, use a	*coverb+SAY/DO* **thirrilimbi**

Gija Dictionary

toothless

toothless................*adjective* **leg-legginy, leg-leggil, leg-leggim;** *adjective* **loowoo-loowoonginy, loowoo-loowoongil, loowoo-loowoongim**
top, climb to/reach.......*coverb+GO/COME* **gij**
top, down from...........*directional* **gerliwirring**
top, hill......................*locative* **wirli;** *locative* **wirlinyin**
  be on top of a hill.........*coverb+BE/STAY* **garinybe**
  on top of the hills..........*locative* **wirli-wirlin**
top, on......................*locative* **laarne**
  put something on top...*coverb+HIT* **thoorroo;** *coverb+SAY/DI* **thoorroo-thoorroo**
top, up on...................*locative* **gawarabaran**
torch........................*noun* **diligajim**
torn, something that is torn..................*adjective, noun* **thenggerrb-ngem, thenggerrngem**
touch......................*coverb+GET* **maj**
towards, come..............*coverb+GO/COME* **wooraj**
track, road..................*noun* **bananbe**
track someone..............*coverb+GET* **barij-barij**
  follow a track...............*coverb+BRING/TAKE* **barij**
  make tracks..................*coverb+SAY/DO_M* **barn'ga**
tracks, wipe out..........*coverb* **yiwirlib**
trade.......................*noun* **wirnan**
traditional owner of country.....................*noun* **daawany, daawal, daawam**
translate...................*coverb+GIVE* **goornag**
transport..................*coverb+BRING/TAKE* **moorrga;** *coverb+PUT* **moorrga**
trap fish....................*coverb+PUT* **moongerri**
tread on something.....*coverb+GET* **bad**
tree..........................*noun* **goonyjany, goonyjal, goonyjam;** *noun* **goowooleny, goowoolem**
tree butt....................*noun* **garndiny, garndim**
tree, cut....................*coverb+GO_ALONG* **doowoo**
tree, something that has been cut down, e.g...........................*adjective* **thelngim**
tree, cut down.............*coverb+HIT* **thel**
tree, foot of................*noun* **loorndoony**
tree, go behind............*coverb+FALL/GO_DOWN* **geren**
tree, go high as possible in...................*coverb+GO/COME* **jabijbe**
tree, hit with axe/rock..*coverb+HIT* **doowoo**
tree, lump/burl on........*noun* **joorl-joorloo**
tree snake.....................*noun feminine* **wandawandal**
tree species
  Acacia coriacea, nulla-nulla tree.............*noun masculine* **goonanderoony, goornandooroony**
  Acacia colei, silver wattle..................*noun masculine* **garndawarranginy**
  Acacia hemignosta, club-leaf wattle.............*noun masculine* **boorroornji, boorrooroo**
  Acacia holosericea, wattle species with curly seed pods............*noun masculine* **garn'goorlji;** *noun masculine* **garndawarranginy**
  Acacia lysiphloia, turpentine wattle..........*noun masculine* **baalinyji, balinyji**
  Acacia sp. aff. lysiphloia, wattle species common in Halls Creek area........*noun masculine* **diwinji;** *noun masculine* **yarliyilji**
  Acacia sp., unidentified wattle species...............*noun feminine* **wanamberrel**
  Acacia platycarpa, wattle species with curly seed pods............*noun masculine* **garn'goorlji**
  Acacia plectocarpa, skinny-leaf wattle.........*noun masculine* **birrindilinyji**
  Acacia tumida, wattle species with curly seed pods....................*noun masculine* **garn'goorlji**
  Acacia umbellata............*noun masculine* **winbarniny**
  Atalaya hemiglauca, white wood..................*noun masculine* **jiwerd-jiwerdji;** *noun masculine* **loowarriny**
  Barringtonia acutangula, freshwater mangrove...*noun masculine* **malawany;** *noun masculine* **mangoonyji**
  Callitris intratropica, cypress pine.................*noun masculine* **gooweriny**
  Capparis umbonata, bush orange (young men not allowed to say).........................*noun feminine* **joogoorrool**

tree species

Capparis umbonata,
bush orange (word
said by young men) ......*noun feminine* **goordirdal**
Celtis strychnoides ....*noun masculine*
thoowoonggeny
Corymbia abbreviata,
scraggy bloodwood......*noun masculine* **marlambeny**
Corymbia aspera,
hill bloodwood..............*noun masculine* **booniny**
Corymbia bella, ghost
gum, white gum ....*noun masculine* **warlarriny**;
noun masculine **lawoorany**
Corymbia collina,
mountain/Kimberley/
silver-leaved
bloodwood....................*noun masculine* **thaliwarn**
Corymbia confertiflora,
cabbage gum ....*noun masculine* **boonbany**
Corymbia dichromophloia,
bloodwood....................*noun masculine* **mawoorroony**
Corymbia flavescens,
cabbage ghost gum .....*noun* **wiliwirrel, wiliwirrirrel,**
wiliwoorrool
Corymbia grandifolia
cabbage gum ....*noun masculine* **boonbany**
Corymbia polycarpa,
bloodwood....................*noun masculine* **mawoorroony**
Corymbia ptychocarpa ....*noun masculine* **booniny**
Corymbia terminalis,
bloodwood....................*noun masculine* **mawoorroony**
Erythrina vespertilio,
bat's wing coral tree .....*noun feminine* **garndiwarlel**
Erythroxylum ellipticum,
kerosene wood ....*noun feminine* **mindi-mindil**;
noun feminine **binyji-binyjil**
Eucalyptus brevifolia,
snappy gum...................*noun* **thalngarrji**
Eucalyptus camaldulensis,
river red gum.................*noun* **bilirnji, bilirnbe**;
noun masculine **dimalan**;
noun masculine **garranggany**
Eucalyptus confluens,
snappy gum...................*noun* **thalngarrji**
Eucalyptus cupularis,
Halls Creek white gum ..*noun masculine* **theliny-thelinyji**
Eucalyptus herbertiana,
Kalumburu gum ....*noun masculine*
wenthawoolenji
Eucalyptus jensenii,
bloodwood....................*noun masculine* **mawoorroony**

Eucalyptus limitaris,
coolibah tree ....*noun masculine* **warernji**
Eucalyptus miniata ....*noun masculine* **booniny**
Eucalyptus microtheca,
coolibah tree ....*noun masculine* **warernji**
Eucalyptus obconica,
black box coolibah tree..*noun masculine* **jaroowenyji**
Eucalyptus pruinosa,
silver box, smoky
cabbage gum ....*noun masculine* **linyjilji**
Eucalyptus tephrodes,
coolibah tree ....*noun masculine* **warernji**
Ficus aculeata var.
aculeata, sandpaper fig..*noun masculine* **yimarlji**;
noun masculine **yingarrjiny**
Ficus aculeata var.
indecora, sandpaper fig..*noun masculine* **yimarlji**;
noun masculine **yingarrjiny**
Ficus atricha, rock fig .....*noun masculine* **banggoornji**
Ficus brachypoda,
rock fig ....*noun masculine* **banggoornji**
Ficus coronulata,
river fig.........................*noun masculine* **ganambiny**;
noun masculine **jabayiny**
Ficus platypoda,
rock fig ....*noun masculine* **banggoornji**
Ficus racemosa,
cluster fig......................*noun masculine* **goonangginy**;
noun masculine **jawoonany**;
noun masculine **ngalalabany**
Gardenia megasperma,
G. dacryoides,
native gardenia.............*noun masculine* **mardany**
Gyrocarpus americana,
shitwood,
helicopter tree..............*noun masculine* **jarlaloony**
Hakea arborescens,
boomerang tree ....*noun masculine* **jirrindiny**
Hakea macrocarpa,
nulla-nulla tree ....*noun masculine*
goonanderoony,
goornandooroony
Lophostemon grandifloras,
river mangrove.............*noun masculine* **jinggoolji**
Lysiphyllum cunninghamii,
bauhinia ....*noun masculine* **goonjiny**;
noun masculine **wanyarriny**
Mallotus nesophilus,
yellow ball tree ....*noun feminine* **goorndoorlbal**

Gija Dictionary 409

tricky

Nauclea orientalis,
Leichardt tree .... *noun feminine* **marroorool**;
                              noun feminine **ngimirlil**
Pandanus aquaticus,
P. spiralis, pandanus ...... *noun feminine* **wirnbel**
Persoonia falcata,
geebung .... *noun masculine* **gantheliny**
Phyllanthus reticulatus .... *noun masculine* **nyirndiwarliny**
Sersalisia sericea,
wild prune .... *noun* **binyjirliny**
Terminalia arostrata,
nutwood .... *noun* **bardiginy, bardigel**
Terminalia bursarina,
bendee .... *noun masculine* **warraroony**
Terminalia canescens,
yellow jacket .... *noun masculine* **berewereny**;
                              noun masculine **yirriyarriny**
Terminalia platyphylla,
river gum .... *noun masculine* **nyaarndiny**;
                              noun masculine **nyambarrginy**;
                              noun masculine **nyarlany**;
                              noun masculine **thaleginy**
Terminalia platyptera,
winged terminalia .... *noun masculine* **gooroorrji**
Terminalia volucris,
rosewood .... *noun masculine* **malaliny, marlarriny**
Vachellia valida,
woomera tree .... *noun feminine* **joornjoornel**
Ventilago viminalis,
supplejack .... *noun masculine* **warlagarriny**
Wrightia saligna,
milkwood .... *noun masculine* **garnbagji**;
                              noun masculine **gilgilji**
tricky .... *adjective* **boorloo-boorloony, boorloo-boorlool, boorloo-boorliny**
trip over .... *coverb+FALL/GO_DOWN* **nyaj**;
                              coverb+FALL/GO_DOWN **rard, rardbany**
  trip over while going
    along .... *coverb+GO/COME* **rardbany**
trot along on horse ...... *coverb+GO/COME* **joog-joog**
trouble for self, make .. *coverb+SAY/PLACE_REFL* **gooj**
trouble for someone,
  make .... *coverb+PUT* **gooj**
trouble, look for .... *coverb+HIT* **walaji**
trousers .... *noun* **joorrooloonggoom**
truck .... *noun feminine* **larndoorrool**
true .... *adjective* **yijim, yijiyam**
truthfully .... *adverb* **yijiyan**

try .... *coverb+PUT* **gool**
try to hit/hunt
  something .... *coverb+FALL/GO_DOWN* **wili**
try out, test
  something .... *coverb+GET* **manmad**
try self at something .... *coverb+SAY/PLACE_REFL* **gool**
try to drown someone .. *coverb+BRING/TAKE* **thoorroogboo**
tuber species, edible
  *Brachystelma
  glabriflorum* .... *noun masculine* **banariny**
  Ipomoea costata .... *noun* **berlayiny**;
                              noun **bigoordany**;
                              noun **larrwany**;
                              noun **yalamarriny**
  SEE ALSO bush potato; root species, edible; yam
Tunganary .... *noun* **Thoowoonggoonarrin**
turkey bush (small
  shrub) *Calytrix brownii,
  C. exstipulata* .... *noun masculine* **mangadany**
turkey, bush;
  bustard (bird) .... *noun feminine* **birn'girrbal**
                              noun feminine **galamoordal**
Turkey Creek .... *noun* **Warrmarn**
turn around .... *coverb+FALL/GO_DOWN* **doowoorrng**
turn back on
  someone/action .... *coverb+FALL/GO_DOWN* **thelngoorroob**
turn, her .... *pronoun* **ngalewany**
turn, his .... *pronoun* **nawoowany**
turn off, to .... *coverb+GO/COME* **dinygoorlg**
turn something over .... *coverb+PUT* **doowoorrng**
turn to face someone ... *coverb+BE/STAY* **therrendang**
turning while dancing .. *coverb+GO_ALONG* **doorl-doorl**
Turner River .... *noun* **Rijarr**
turpentine wattle .... *noun masculine* **balinyji**;
                              noun masculine **baalinyji**
turtle .... *noun feminine* **balarnel**;
                              noun feminine **darndal**;
                              noun feminine **wayiwoorrool**
  long-necked turtle .... *noun* **lawarrbal, lawarrbany**;
                              noun masculine **wirriwoonany**
                              noun masculine **weloowoomoorany**;
                              noun feminine **woorlemerewal**
Twenty Mile,
  on Bedford Downs ..... *noun* **Girlingmanji**
twinkling, stars .... *coverb+GO/COME* **jalgoorrg**
twist someone's neck ... *coverb+GET* **wag**

twisted neck,
  get/have .... *coverb+BE/STAY* **wag**
twitch .... *coverb+SAY/DO* **therrngarn**
  feel a twitch .... *coverb+BECOME* **jirreg**
two .... *adjective* **bangariny,**
                                  bangariny-warriny
tyre go flat .... *coverb+FALL/GO_DOWN* **danyja;**
                                  coverb+SAY/DO_M **danyjag**

Uu

ugly .... *adjective* **jigiliny, jigilil, jigilim**
umbilical cord .... *noun* **dinyjile**
  cut umbilical cord .... *coverb+PUT* **darr**
unable to do
  something, be .... *coverb+SAY/DO*
                                  ngoowa-ngoowag
unable to light
  (e.g. fire) .... *coverb+SAY/DO* **jilyirr**
uncle .... *noun masculine* **nyaganyji**
  uncle (when
  spoken to) .... *noun* **nyagayi**
uncooked meat .... *adjective* **gern'gany, gern'gal,**
                                  gern'gam
underneath .... *locative* **yiligin;**
                                  locative **yiligibiny**
underside of
  woomera .... *noun* **therlam**
understand .... *coverb+BE/STAY* **yardeg;**
                                  coverb+BRING/TAKE **rangga;**
                                  coverb+SAY/DO **rangga**
undress .... *coverb+DO_REFL* **beralg**
uninterested/
  not interfering .... *adjective* **berawoony,**
                                  berawool, berawoom
unrecognisable .... *adjective* **wangarroony,**
                                  wangarrool, wangarroom,
                                  wangarrwoony,
                                  wangarrwool,
                                  wangarrwoom
unripe (fruit) .... *adjective* **gelengoowoony,**
                                  gelengoowool,
                                  gelengoowoom
unripe/raw .... *adjective* **gern'gany, gern'gal,**
                                  gern'gam
unsuccessful, be .... *coverb+SAY/DO*
                                  ngoowa-ngoowag
until .... *adverb* **wayiniya**
unwrap .... *coverb+GO/COME* **belalg**

us, to (dual inclusive)

up .... *directional* **gerloorroogoo;**
                                  directional **gerloowirrgoo;**
                                  directional **gerloowoorr;**
                                  directional **goorloorroogoo**
up high .... *locative* **laarne**
up hill .... *directional* **gendewa**
up into .... *directional* **gendewa**
up on top .... *locative* **gawarabaran**
up that way .... *directional* **gerlirrijarriny**
up there .... *directional* **gaande**
  from up there .... *directional* **gerloowoorrng**
upright, place
  something .... *coverb+GO_THROUGH* **jad;**
                                  coverb+PUT **jad**
upright position,
  place in .... *coverb+PUT* **thad**
upright, be standing .... *coverb+BE/STAY* **jad**
upset, feel .... *coverb+SAY/DO* **jirr-jirr**
upset, make someone .. *coverb+GET* **jirr-jirrge**
upside down, put
  something .... *coverb+PUT* **dareng**
upstream .... *directional* **gaande**
upstream, going .... *directional* **gendewa,**
                                  gendewagoo
  from upstream .... *directional* **gendang**
urine .... *noun* **goomboo;**
                                  noun **jarnangarre**
  urinate .... *coverb+SAY/DO* **goomboo;**
  go urinating
  (not polite) .... *coverb+GO/COME*
                                  goomboowany;
                                  coverb+GO/COME **jarnangarr**
us, for (dual inclusive) .. *benefactive enclitic pronoun*
                                  -yoowoo
us, for (exclusive) .... *benefactive enclitic pronoun* **-yarre**
us, for (inclusive) .... *benefactive enclitic pronoun*
                                  -yoowoorr, -yoowoorroo
us three, for
  (inclusive) .... *benefactive enclitic pronoun*
                                  -yoorroo-yoo
us, from/after/because
  of (dual inclusive) .... *ablative enclitic pronoun* **-yoowa**
us, from/after/because
  of (exclusive) .... *ablative enclitic pronoun* **-yirrewa,**
                                  -yirroowa
us, from/after/because
  of (inclusive) .... *ablative enclitic pronoun*
                                  -yoowoorrowa, -yoorroowa,
                                  -yoorra, -yarrewa
us, to (dual inclusive) .. *indirect object enclitic pronoun*
                                  -yayi

us, to (exclusive)

us, to (exclusive)............*indirect object enclitic pronoun* **-yirri**
us, to (inclusive)............*indirect object enclitic pronoun* **-yarri**
us two, to (exclusive)....*indirect object enclitic pronoun* **-yirri-yoo**
us three, to (inclusive)..*indirect object enclitic pronoun* **-yarri-yoo**
us, with (exclusive).......*commitative enclitic pronoun* **-yirrab**
us, with (inclusive) ....*commitative enclitic pronoun* **-yarrab**
us/we (dual inclusive)..*pronoun* **yayin, yayiben**
us/we (exclusive)..........*pronoun* **yarren**
us/we (inclusive)...........*pronoun* **yoowoorroon**
us/we (inclusive)
  (Southern dialect).........*pronoun* **yoorroon**
us/we (exclusive)
  by ourselves................*pronoun* **yarrewarriny**
us/we (exclusive)
  ourselves, our turn ....*pronoun* **yarrewany**
us/we (inclusive)
  by ourselves................*pronoun* **yoowoorroowarriny**
us/we (inclusive)
  ourselves, our turn ....*pronoun* **yoowoorrwany**
us/we two (exclusive) ..*pronoun* **yarreben**

Vv

vagina............................*noun* **boonthoorroo**;
                             noun **garlam**;
                             noun **milam**
valley.............................*noun* **tharreyimele**;
                             noun **yawilam**
vegetable food.............*noun* **mayim, mayiny, mayil**
Venus............................*noun* **jiwibal, jiwibany**
very hot ....*adjective* **dooboorrngbeny, dooboorrngbel, dooboorrngbem**
Violet Valley ....*noun* **Baloowa**
voice, having a hoarse..*adjective* **garengbeny, garengbel, garengbem**
voice, speak with a
  hoarse ....*coverb+SAY/DO_M* **gareng**
vomit............................*coverb+SAY/DO* **yoorlag**
vomit something out ...*coverb+HIT* **yoorlag**

Ww

wag tail (dog)...............*coverb+SAY/DO* **wird-wird**
waist ....*noun* **goorlgoom**
having a thin waist........*adjective* **garrgbayiny, garrgbayil**
wait ....*interjection* **mamberre**;
                             interjection **marrge**
wait for someone ....*coverb+BE/STAY* **liga**;
                             coverb+BRING/TAKE **yirr**
waiting, be tired of.......*coverb+GO_ALONG* **wanggooloo**
wake someone up ....*coverb+GET* **yiliwarrge**;
                             coverb+PUT **berdij**
walk ....*coverb+GO_ALONG* **warrag**;
                             coverb+GO/COME **girlib**;
                             coverb+SAY/DO **girli**;
                             coverb+SAY/DO_M **girlirli**
be unable to walk ....*coverb+SAY/DO* **mayajarrg**;
                             coverb+FALL/GO_DOWN **bilg**
be hardly able to walk...*coverb+GO_ALONG* **wegerr**
become unable
  to walk ....*coverb+GO/COME* **bilg**
being unable to walk ....*adjective* **nyarliwiny, nyarliwil, nyarliwim**
make walk.....................*coverb+GET* **girligewa**
walk along ....*coverb+GO_ALONG* **girli**;
                             coverb+GO_ALONG **girliwany**;
                             coverb+SAY/DO **girlirlib**
walk along edge
  of something ....*coverb+GO_ALONG* **bardib**
walk at night ....*coverb+GO_ALONG* **jana**
walk away leaving
  someone ....*coverb+LEAVE* **girlib**
walk in water
  splashing feet ....*coverb+GO_ALONG* **jaboorr**
walk quickly ....*coverb+SAY/DO* **warrij-warrij**
walking..........................*coverb+SAY/DO* **girlirli**
be walking ....*coverb+GO_ALONG* **girlirli**
go walking about
  slowly ....*coverb+GO_ALONG* **nyalala**
go walking all night.......*coverb+SAY/DO_M* **nyalngawoog**
start walking (toddler)
  (Southern dialect).........*coverb+GO_ALONG* **bardawoog**
walking stick.................*noun* **jidali-girrem**
wall ....*noun* **jarrgam**
wallaby species
  agile wallaby.................*noun masculine* **warlbawoony**
  antilopine wallaby
  (plains kangaroo)..........*noun masculine* **jarlangarnany**;
                           noun masculine **warlambany**
  female antilopine wallaby
  (plains kangaroo)..........*noun feminine* **gawoorrngarndil**
  fat female rock wallaby..*noun feminine* **marliwal**;
                           noun feminine **thoorrmal**

water weeds like grass

hare wallaby	*noun masculine* **moorloogoorn-doorlgoorndoolji;**
	noun masculine **yinameny**
nail-tailed wallaby	*noun masculine* **goon'goodoogoodoony;**
	noun masculine **gooroorroonggoony;**
	noun masculine **woorrood-woorroodji**
	noun masculine **woordoorr-woordoorrji**
river wallaby	*noun masculine* **warlbawoony**
rock wallaby	*noun masculine* **doowanggoonyji;**
	noun masculine **woombardgoony;**
	noun masculine **woombarnoongoony;**
	noun masculine **woonyjoorroony**
wallaroo, common (female), (hill kangaroo)	*noun feminine* **barawool**
wallaroo, common (little male), (hill kangaroo)	*noun masculine* **baloobanggoony**
wallaroo, common (male), (hill kangaroo)	*noun masculine* **jirrgany;**
	noun masculine **moordany**
wander about (many)	*coverb+SAY/DO* **goongarr**
want everything, greedy	*coverb+SAY/DO* **marr-marr**
want someone to do something everywhere	*coverb+GET* **nyirli-nyirligboo**
want/like/love	*coverb+GET* **dawoong;**
	coverb+GET **maja;**
	coverb **marrga;**
	coverb+HIT **malirri, marrirri;**
	coverb+GET **marroo-marroo;**
	coverb+SAY/DO **marroo-marroo;**
	coverb+HIT **warda;**
	coverb+GET **wooloorr**
wanting to be carried or looked after all the time	*adjective* **ngamarrwoony, ngamarrwool;**
	coverb+SAY/DO_M **ngamarr**
wanting looking after	*coverb+SAY/DO_M* **ngamarr**
want looking after	*adjective* **ngamarrwoony, ngamarrwool**
want/love someone	*coverb+GET* **goondoony**
warm	*coverb+SAY/DO* **werne-werneb**
be warm	*coverb+BE/STAY* **wernebe**
warm something	*coverb+PUT* **jaa, jaa-jaa**
Warmun	*noun* **Warrmarn**
wash	*coverb+GET* **loogoorr**
wash self	*coverb+DO_REFL* **loogoorr**
wash away (flood)	*coverb+GET* **loorlg;**
	coverb+GET **thoorl;**
	coverb+BRING/TAKE **yan**
wasp species	*noun masculine* **birrinyoorlji**
large paper wasp, wasp species	*noun feminine* **merrembernel**
sand wasp	*noun feminine* **ngirrngirril**
waste something, tip something out	*coverb+SAY/DO* **warranyja**
watch	*coverb+BRING/TAKE* **deg;**
	coverb+HIT **warra;**
	coverb+SAY/DO_M **deg**
watch and follow	*coverb+FOLLOW* **deg**
watching, following	*coverb +FOLLOW* **degbe**
water	*noun* **goorloom;**
	noun **goorrngam, goorrngany**
permanent water	*noun masculine* **barranggany**
red water	*noun* **jirliwoorrji**
sea water	*noun* **ngabarl-ngabarl**
shallow water	*noun* **gajam;**
	noun **garlirriny**
shallow edge of water	*noun* **garlirriny**
water dweller	*adjective* **goorloongarnany, goorloongarnal, goorloongarnam**
water goanna	*noun masculine* **wigamany**
water goanna species (mother of *wigamany*)	*noun feminine* **goorlawoorlal**
waterhole, deep	*noun* **garlooroony**
water plant with edible tubers/yams	*noun* **wawalji**
water rat	*noun feminine* **nyoorroongool**
water-scorpion, toe-cutter	*noun feminine* **bindirijgel**
water sedge	*noun* **thelinjany;**
	noun **theltheny**
water snake	*noun masculine* **warlenggenany**
water weed	*noun* **marlirn**
water weeds like grass	*noun* **mangoonyji**

Gija Dictionary 413

water yam, hairy, *Aponogeton vanbruggenii*

water yam, hairy,
*Aponogeton
vanbruggenii* .... *noun* **yarrgalal, yarrgalany**
water yam, red hairy,
*Aponogeton
euryspermus* .... *noun feminine* **ngelinggel**
water yam, small,
Cycnogeton dubium ..... *noun masculine* **wawalji**;
noun masculine **yamoony**
water, be a long
stretch of, ahead .... *coverb+BE/STAY* **warndalij**
water, dive into .... *coverb+FALL/GO_DOWN* **nyirreg**
water, down to .... *directional* **yilag**
water, drive into .... *coverb+HIT* **jawoorr**
water, drying up in
dry season .... *coverb+GO/COME* **lintharrg**
water, get into .... *coverb+FALL/GO_DOWN* **jawoorr**;
coverb+SAY/DO **jawoorr**;
coverb+FALL/GO_DOWN
nyimoog-nyimoog;
coverb+SAY/DO **nyimoog,
nyimooga**
all get into water .... *coverb+SAY/DO_M* **jawoorrinyalg**;
coverb+SAY/DO_M **jawoorroorr**
water, 'living'
(permanent) .... *noun* **barranggany**
water, pour .... *coverb+PUT* **tharroo**
pour water on
someone/something ..... *coverb+BRING/TAKE* **mamag**;
coverb+HIT **mamag**
water run down .... *coverb+SAY/DO* **jalawoorr**;
coverb+SAY/DO **tharroorroo**;
coverb+SAY/DO **war**
be water running
down .... *coverb+BE/STAY* **warl-warl**
make water run and
drown someone .... *coverb+HIT* **thoorroorroog**
water running .... *coverb+SAY/DO* **thoorroorroo**
noun **thoolooloorrji,
thoolooloorroo**
water, scoop up .... *coverb+GET* **jerreb**
water, shake off self ..... *coverb+SAY/DO* **doowerrberr**
water, smack to make
noise .... *coverb+BE/STAY* **derlawoog**
water, throw into .... *coverb+HIT* **jawoorroorr**;
coverb+HIT **jijberrg**
waterfall .... *noun* **jadany**;
noun **thoolooloorrji,
thoolooloorroo**
Waterfall Creek .... *noun* **Ngirndirriman'gen**
waterlily .... *noun masculine* **garrjany**

waterlily flower stem ..... *noun masculine* **danggarriny**
waterlily root .... *noun masculine* **gelewoorrji**
type of waterlily .... *noun masculine* **woonoongoony**
water, stab ground
and hit .... *coverb+HIT* **dalala**
watering, be .... *coverb+SAY/DO* **mamag**
watery .... *adjective* **goorloowoorloony,
goorloowoorlool,
goorloowoorloom**
watery-eyed .... *adjective* **mooroorlbany,
mooroorlbal, mooroorlbam**
wattle
club-leaf wattle,
Acacia hemignosta .... *noun masculine* **berewereny**;
noun masculine **boorroornji,
boorrooroo**
salt wattle,
Acacia ampliceps .... *noun masculine* **merenyji,
mirinji**
skinny-leaf wattle,
Acacia plectocarpa .... *noun masculine* **birrindilinyji**
silky wattle,
Acacia acradenia .... *noun masculine* **tharn'geny**
turpentine wattle,
Acacia lysiphloia .... *noun masculine* **balinyji**;
noun masculine **baalinyji**
wattle species,
Acacia umbellata .... *noun* **winbarniny**
wattle species, prickly,
Vachellia farnesiana .... *noun masculine* **bagawagany**;
noun masculine
moorrooloomboony
wattle species common
in Halls Creek area,
Acacia sp. aff. lysiphloia ... *noun masculine* **diwinji**;
noun masculine **yarliyilji**
wattle species used to
make *jiwiny*, small .... *noun masculine* **mindalngarriny**
wattle species with
curly seed pods, *Acacia
tumida, A. holosericea,
A. platycarpa* .... *noun masculine* **garn'goorlji**
wattle species,
other unidentified .... *noun* **warnamberrel**
wave .... *coverb+SAY/DO* **mangan**;
coverb+SAY/DO_M **mingany-
mingany**
wave branches .... *coverb+DO_REFL*
mingany-mingany

what thing (masculine)?

wave something to
  get rid of flies ....*coverb+HIT* **wiwayi**;
                    coverb+SAY/DO **wiwayi-wiwayi**
waves..........................*noun* **ngabarl-ngabarl**
  be waves...................*coverb+SAY/DO* **ngabarl-ngabarl**
waving line,
  go along in.................*coverb+GO_ALONG* **warlarla**
wax, bees
  (sugarbag wax) ....*noun* **ganggarrji, ganggarre**;
                    noun **joornoogji, joornoogbi**
wax lid in beehive.........*noun* **darlam**
we (dual inclusive)
  are the ones................*pronoun* **yayana**
we (exclusive) are
  the ones ....*pronoun* **yarriyana**
we (inclusive) are
  the ones ....*pronoun* **yoorriyana, yoowoorriyana**
we/us (dual inclusive)..*pronoun* **yayin, yayiben**
we/us (exclusive)..........*pronoun* **yarren**
we/us (inclusive)...........*pronoun* **yoowoorroon**
we/us (inclusive)
  (Southern dialect).........*pronoun* **yoorroon**
we/us (inclusive)
  ourselves....................*pronoun* **yoowoorroowarriny**
we/us (inclusive)
  ourselves, our turn ....*pronoun* **yoowoorrwany**
we/us (exclusive)
  by ourselves...............*pronoun* **yarrewarriny**
we/us (exclusive)
  ourselves....................*pronoun* **yarrewany**
we/us two (exclusive) ..*pronoun* **yarreben**
weak, make
  each other ....*coverb+DO_REFL* **waraga**
wear clothes..................*coverb+BRING/TAKE* **laj**
weather, hot...................*temporal* **barranggan**
web, make (spider).......*coverb+SAY/DO* **woorr-woorr**
webbed............................*adjective* **wanboorrbany, wanboorrbal, wanboorrbam**
wedge-tailed eagle.......*noun masculine* **garnbarrany**;
                    noun masculine **garnbidany**;
                      noun masculine **girliwirringiny**;
                      noun masculine **warrarnany**;
                      noun masculine **wirli-wirlingarnany**
weero...............................*noun feminine* **wirringgoonel**
weight on something,
  put................................*coverb+PLACE* **moord**;
                      coverb+PUT **moord**
welded/joined
  together (e.g. hills) ....*coverb+BE/STAY* **lab**

well done.......................*adverb* **yilgiya**
well then.......................*interjection* **wentha, woontha**
Wesley Spring ....*noun* **Nhanban**
west
  from the west ....*directional* **gerlirrang**
  further west................*directional* **gerlirrijarriny**
  in the west ....*directional* **gerlirrin, girlirrin**
  in the west moving
  between north
  and south ....*directional* **gerlirringarri**
  people from the west ...*noun* **girli-girlirrangem**
  person from the west ...*adjective* **girlirremiliny, girlirremilil, girlirremilim**
  to the west ....*directional* **gerlirroogoo**;
                    directional **gerliyirr**
western brown snake ..*noun* **jadiwiriny**
wet ....*adjective* **dilboowoorroony, dilboowoorrool, dilboowoorroom**;
                    adjective **giyiny, giyil, giyim**;
                    adjective **jirlanyjany, jirlanyjal, jirlanyjam**
  become wet..................*coverb+BECOME* **jirlanyjag**
  make wet.....................*coverb+GET* **jirlanyjag**;
                    coverb+HIT **jirlanyjag**
wet sand ....*noun* **giyim**
wet season ....*temporal* **jadagen, jadagin**
what action?..................*interrogative* **gaboo, gaboowa**
  what action?
  (Southern dialect)..........*interrogative* **gaba**
what are you? ....*interrogative* **thoowoonhangoo**
  what are you (plural)? ...*interrogative* **thoowoonhanoonggerroo**
what? because of..........*interrogative* **thoowoo-berra, thoo-berra**
what did you say?.........*interjection* **ayi**
what for? ....*interrogative* **thoowoorra-boorroo, thoowoo-boorroo**
what? for doing ....*interrogative* **thoowoo-girriny**
what is happening?......*interrogative* **gaboowa**
what kind are you?.......*interrogative* **thiwingen-nha-ngoo**
what now?.....................*interrogative* **garninya**
what thing
  (feminine)?..................*interrogative* **thengela**
what thing
  (masculine)? ....*interrogative* **thini, thiniwa**

Gija Dictionary 415

what thing (non-singular)?

what thing (non-singular)?, (general question when the gender or number of a noun is unknown) ...*interrogative* **thoowoo, thoowi, thoowoorra**

what's wrong? (Southern dialect) ....*interrogative* **gabagirrem, gabagirriny, gabagirrel**

when? ....*interrogative* **gayigan, gayigana**

when? (Southern dialect) ....*interrogative* **gaboogana**

when small ....*temporal* **wanyagen**

when the wind is blowing ....*locative, temporal* **gerawalen**

where? ....*interrogative* **gawoo, gayi, gayiwa**

where are they/it (non-singular)? ....*interrogative* **gawoorra**

where? belonging/living ....*interrogative* **gayi-ngarnany, gayi-ngarnal, gayi-ngarnam**

where? coming from ....*interrogative* **gayi-miliny, gayi-milil, gayi-milim**

where from? ....*interrogative* **gayi-biny**

where is he/it (masculine)? ....*interrogative* **garniwa**

where is he/it (masculine)? (Southern dialect) ....*interrogative* **garnang**

where is she/it (feminine)? ....*interrogative* **gangel, gangela**

where to? ....*interrogative* **gabinga**; *interrogative* **gabiyi**

where to? (Southern dialect) ....*interrogative* **gabinga**

where to go, be unable to see ....*coverb+GO_ALONG* **gamaama**

where/what? ....*interrogative* **garni**

whether or not ....*particle* **galama**

which one (feminine)? ..*interrogative* **gangel**

which one (feminine) was it now? ....*interrogative* **gangalgarnangga**

which one (masculine) was it now? ....*interrogative* **gaboonigarnangga**

while ....*particle* **wayininji**

whimper ....*coverb+SAY/DO* **nyoorlg-nyoorlg**

whine ....*coverb+SAY/DO* **moowoog**

whip snake ....*noun feminine* **wandawandal**; *noun* **wijgel**

whisper ....*coverb+SAY/DO* **nyam**

whisper to someone .....*coverb+PUT* **nyam**

whistle ....*coverb+SAY/DO* **wiriny**

whistling in ears, have ..*coverb* **noorroo**; *coverb+SAY/DO* **ngoorr**

whistling kite ....*noun feminine* **booloogool**

white ....*adjective* **gawarangbeny, gawarangbel, gawarangbem**; *adjective* **lawagbeny, lawagbel, lawagbem**; *adjective* **waagoom, wagoony, wagool, wagoom**

be white ....*coverb+BE/STAY* **jawoogbe**; *coverb+BE/STAY* **lawag**

white ants ....*noun feminine* **gooroorrooroorrool**

white bones, be made dry ....*coverb+GET* **langany-langany**

white bones, cause to become ....*coverb+HIT* **lawoony-lawoony**

white clay ....*noun feminine* **galadil**; *noun feminine* **mawoondool, mawoondoom**

white crane (egret) ....*noun masculine* **jalariny**

white currant ....*noun masculine* **berenggarrji**; *noun masculine* **goowarroolji**; *noun masculine* **ngoorrwany**; *noun masculine* **roonggoony**

white-faced heron ....*noun masculine* **ginyany**

white gum tree, ghost gum ....*noun masculine* **warlarriny**

white inside part of boab nut when dry ....*noun* **wawanggoony**

white mud ....*noun masculine* **balarrji, balarre**

white-necked heron .....*noun masculine* **binggoo-binggoony**

white ochre, white paint ....*noun feminine* **galadil**; *noun feminine* **mawoondool, mawoondoom**

white paint on something ....*noun* **warlawarre**

white person ....*noun* **gardiyany**; *noun* **wajbaloony**

white person's way ....*adjective* **gardiyangem**

white woman ....*noun feminine* **lawagjil**; *noun feminine* **nyamanil, nyamanel**

white stone .... *noun* manjalji, manjale
  white stone spearhead .. *noun* yarlgal, yarlgany, yarlgam
white substance used for love magic .... *noun* jirril
White Water .... *noun* Yarin
whitewood tree .... *noun masculine* jiwerd-jiwerdji; *noun masculine* loowarriny
who (feminine)? .... *interrogative* yangela
who (masculine)? .... *interrogative* yangirni
who (plural, unknown gender)? .... *interrogative* yangoorra
who are you (one)? .... *interrogative* yangoowoo-nha-ngoo
who are you (plural)? ... *interrogative* yangoowoo-nha-noonggerroo?
why? .... *interrogative* thoowoo-berra, thoo-berra
wide-eyed .... *adjective* lirrijbayiny, lirrijbayil, lirrijbayim; *adjective* lirrijgeny, lirrijgel, lirrijgem
widow .... *noun feminine* thoombawool
widower .... *noun masculine* thoombawoony
wife .... *noun feminine* langgoornool; *noun feminine* ngoolngal
wife stealer .... *noun masculine* ginyirriny
wild grape .... *noun feminine* jimirlbel
wild prune .... *noun* binyjirliny
wild tea .... *noun masculine* barnabeliny; *noun masculine* lamba-lambarrji, lambarr-lambarrji; *noun masculine* manyanyiny
willie wagtail .... *noun masculine* jigirridji, jigirrid-jigirridji; *noun masculine* jindiwirrij
willy-willy .... *noun* jalawoonany; *noun* mayawanji
wind .... *noun* gern'galeny; *noun* waloorrji, waloorroo
  big wind .... *noun* warlanginy, warlangem
  wind blow .... *coverb+SAY/DO* ger
  wind blow something ... *coverb+GET* gerge
  wind blowing .... *coverb+GO/COME* ger-ger
  wind/cyclone chase someone .... *coverb* warlangooboo
  wind swing people and trees from side to side .. *coverb+HIT* warlanganbe; *coverb+HIT* warlangeb
windbreak .... *noun* jarrgam
  make a windbreak .... *coverb+BRING/TAKE* jarrga; *coverb+SAY/DO_M* jarrga-jarrga
window, be an opening like a .... *coverb+BE/STAY* denggelalab
windpipe .... *noun* garndarr-garndarre
wing .... *noun* barndam
winnow .... *coverb+SAY/DO* therra-therra
wipe out tracks .... *coverb+HIT* yiwirlib
wire .... *noun* ngerlam; *noun* wilmoorroo, wilymoorre
witchetty grub .... *noun feminine* barlganyel; *noun* lagarnel, lagarnbe; *noun* lajel
wobble along .... *coverb+BECOME* widirr
  wobbling, drunk .... *adjective* wingenoowoony, wingenoowool, wingenoowoom
woman .... *noun feminine* ngalil, ngalim, ngali-ngalim; *noun feminine* langgoornool, langoornbe
  adult woman .... *noun feminine* garrayilel
  become an old woman .... *coverb+BECOME* nyamani
  old woman .... *noun feminine* nyamanil, nyamanel
  white woman .... *noun feminine* lawagjil
  woman who cannot do without a man .... *noun feminine* jiyilengoonybel
  woman whose brother or sister has died .... *noun feminine* yawoorrool
  woman whose child has died .... *noun feminine* thalebal
  woman whose husband has died .... *noun feminine* thoombawool
  woman whose parent, uncle or aunt has died .. *noun feminine* ngamanyil
woman's daughter's child .... *noun* ganggany, ganggal, ganggam
woman's mother-in-law .... *noun feminine* goorrijil
woman's mother-in-law's brother .... *noun masculine* goorrijiny
woman's son-in-law ..... *noun masculine* thamboorroony
woman's son-in-law's sister .... *noun feminine* thamboorrool
woman's son's child (spoken to) .... *noun* ngawooji
woman's son's daughter .... *noun feminine* ngawoojil

woman's son's son

woman's son's son........noun masculine **ngawoojiny**
women's dance movement in Wangga and Lirrga....coverb+SAY/DO **warrajbe**
women's jumping dance movement..........coverb+SAY/DO **wil-wil**;
coverb+SAY/DO_M **wil-wil**
wooden dish (coolamon)..................noun masculine **goowirriny**;
noun masculine **larndoorrji**;
noun masculine **walanarriny**;
noun masculine **yawoonyji, yawinyji**
wooden spear, large.....noun masculine **goorladany**
wood used for spear points..........................noun masculine **jiwiny**
woodswallow, little......noun feminine **dinil**
woodswallow, white-breasted..........noun **jinba-jinbalel, jinba-jinbalji**
wooly (like a sheep)......adjective **yiwooltheleny, yiwoolthelel, yiwoolthelem**
woomera......................noun feminine **ngawalel**;
noun feminine **yarn'gal**
desert woomera...........noun feminine **bigirrel**
middle section of woomera......................noun **doomoorroo**
side of woomera...........noun **walamboom**
small straight woomera used with short fighting spear......noun feminine **warrimiril**
underside of woomera..noun **therlam**
woomera handle..........noun **lenggale**
woomera hook............noun **mirlirdi**
Wooneba (Winipe, Wirneba) Spring........noun **Wanbin**
word..............................noun **jarragbe**;
noun **manoom**
words, joking................noun **barlijbem**
word said to cause important effect.........interjection **shaa**
work..............................noun **warrgam**
make someone work....coverb+GET **warrgamge**
world, the......................noun **gamerrem**
worms/maggots...........noun **waanyim**
earth worm..................noun **woonthool, woonthoony**
wrap around.................coverb+GET **weren**
wrapped around...........coverb+BE/STAY **weren**
wrap fresh sinew on spear shaft.................coverb+HIT **warl**

wren, red-backed.........noun masculine **yirril-yirrilji**
wriggle..........................coverb+SAY/DO_REFL **doowerrberr**
wriggle sideways..........coverb+GO_ALONG **weleberr**
wriggling big bottom, go along......................coverb+GO_ALONG **moongooli-moongooli**
wrinkled........................adjective **tharleny, tharlel, tharlem**;
adjective **welyerr-welyerrji, welyerr-welyerrel, welyerr-welyerre**
wrist...............................noun **garrayile**;
noun **mooyooloo**
write..............................coverb+GO/COME **lendij, lendej**;
coverb+PUT **lendej**
writhe in agony, cause to......................coverb+GET **therrngarn'ge**
Wyndham....................noun **Darrarroo**

#

yam
black soil yam, *Ipomoea abrupta, I. aquatica*........noun **garndiny**;
noun **yoowalany, yoowalam**
bush peanut, *Vigna vexillata*................noun masculine **wanarrji**
bush yam, *Cayratia trifolia*..............noun **bigininy**
'cheeky' yam, *Dioscorea bulbifera*.........noun **garnawoony**
cowpea yam, *Vigna vexillata*................noun masculine **wanarrji**
desert yam, *Ipomoea costata*............noun masculine **berlayiny**;
noun masculine **bigoordany**;
noun feminine **dawoonyil**;
noun masculine **larrwany**;
noun masculine **yalamarriny**
grass yam, *Ipomoea sp. aff. graminea*............noun masculine **nyoombany**;
noun **yoombany**
grass-leaf yam, *Curculigo ensifolia*..........noun masculine **jawooloo-wooloony**
hairy water yam, *Aponogeton vanbruggenii*.................noun **yarrgalal, yarrgalany**
long yam, *Dioscorea transversa*......noun masculine **jilirr-jilirrji**

your turn (plural)

pencil yam, *Vigna lanceolata* var. *latifolia*....*noun masculine* **ngawoonyji**
red hairy water yam, *Aponogeton euryspermus*.................*noun feminine* **ngelinggel**
rosella yam, *Abelmoschus ficulneus*....*noun feminine* **goornoogal**
rubber yam, *Typhonium liliifolium*........*noun masculine* **gayilarriny**
small water yam, *Cycnogeton dubium*........*noun masculine* **wawalji**; *noun masculine* **yamoony**
sweet round yam, *Brachystelma glabriflorum*..................*noun masculine* **banariny**
yam species similar to sweet round yam..........*noun feminine* **mambanel**
yam species similar to pencil yam ....*noun* **jirn'gawool**
SEE ALSO **bush potato**; **root species, edible**; **tuber species, edible**
yawn ....*coverb+SAY/DO* **ngaboorayi**
yellow ....*adjective* **goorndoo-goorndoorlji**, **goorndoo-goorndoorlel**, **goorndoo-goorndoorloo**; *adjective* **goorndoorlji**, **goorndoorlool**, **goorndoorloo**
yellow ball tree, *Mallotus nesophilus*.....*noun feminine* **goorndoorlbal**
yellow-faced miner......*noun feminine* **biyig-biyiggel**
yellow ochre.................*noun* **boorrngooroo**, **boorrngooroom** *noun* **goorndoorlji**, **goorndoorloo**
yes..................................*interjection* **nga**; *interjection* **ngiyi**; *interjection* **yiyi**; *interjection* **yoowoo**
yes then.......................*interjection* **wentha, woontha**
yesterday......................*temporal* **jaroongem**; *temporal* **ngooloo-ngooloon**; *temporal* **ngooloo-ngooliyan**
yet/still ....*particle* **marrge**
you all ....*pronoun* **nenggerren**, **nenggerren-gili**
after/because of you all..........................*ablative enclitic pronoun* **-narroowa**

for you all......................*benefactive enclitic pronoun* **-nooggoo, -nooggoorroo**
to you all........................*indirect object enclitic pronoun* **-narri**
with you all ....*commitative enclitic pronoun* **-narrab**
you all are the ones ......*pronoun* **nenggerriyana**
you (all) yourselves........*pronoun* **nenggerrewarriny**
you (all) yourselves, your turn ....*pronoun* **nenggerrewany**
you (one) ....*pronoun* **nyengen**
after/because of you (one) ....*ablative enclitic pronoun* **-nenggoowa**
for you (one) ....*benefactive enclitic pronoun* **-ngoo, -ngoongoo**
to you (one)....................*indirect object enclitic pronoun* **-ninggi**
with you (one)...............*commitative enclitic pronoun* **-nenggab**
you (one) and me..........*pronoun* **yayin, yayiben**
you (one) are the one....*pronoun* **nyingiyana**
you (one) in turn ....*pronoun* **nyengoowany, nyingoowany**
you (one) yourself.........*pronoun* **nyengewarriny, nyingoowarriny**
you (one) yourself, your turn ....*pronoun* **nyengoowany, nyingoowany**
you (plural) are the ones..............................*pronoun* **nenggerriyana**
you there ....*interjection* **welayi**
you two..........................*pronoun* **nenggerreben**
you yourselves..............*pronoun* **nenggerrewarriny**
you yourselves, your turn (all).......................*pronoun* **nenggerrewany**
young man.....................*noun masculine* **lambarnji**; *noun masculine* **waarrany**; *noun masculine* **wilinggeny**
young man with forehead band...............*noun masculine* **woonawoorroony**
young men, make..........*coverb+GO_ALONG* **goodaj-goodaj**
young woman................*noun* **werlemen, werlemenel**
youngest child ....*noun* **bardoongeny**, **bardoongel, bardoongem**
your turn (one) ....*pronoun* **nyengoowany, nyingoowany**
your turn (plural)..........*pronoun* **nenggerrewany**

yours (one) and mine

yours (one) and mine ....*possessive pronoun* **yayiyangeny, yayiyangel, yayiyangem**

yours (plural) ....*possessive pronoun* **nenggerriyangeny, nenggerriyangel, nenggerriyangem;** *possessive pronoun* **ninggerriyany, ninggerriyal, ninggerriyam**

yours (singular) ....*possessive pronoun* **nyingiyangeny, nyingiyangel, nyingiyangem**

youth ....*noun masculine* **lambarnji;** *noun masculine* **wilinggeny**

yuk! ....*interjection* **jigili**

yukky ....*adjective* **jigiliny, jigilil, jigilim**

Zz

zebra finch ....*noun feminine* **nyinyil, niyinyil**